CHALIAPIN

Fedor Chaliapin, 1899. Courtesy of EMI MUSIC.

CHALIAPIN

A CRITICAL BIOGRAPHY

BY
Victor Borovsky

ALFRED A. KNOPF · 1988 · NEW YORK

First published in Great Britain 1988 by Hamish Hamilton Ltd
Copyright © 1988 by Victor Borovsky
Discography copyright © 1972 by Alan Kelly.
This revised and expanded discography copyright © 1988
by Alan Kelly and Vladimir Gurvich

Library of Congress Cataloging-in-Publication Data

Borovsky, Victor, 1939–
Chaliapin: a critical biography.
Bibliography: p.
Discography: p.
Includes index.
1. Chaliapin, Fyodor Ivanovich, 1873–1938.
2. Singers—Soviet Union—Biography. I. Title.
ML420.S53B67 1988   782.1'092'4 [B]   87–46005
ISBN 0-394-56096-5

Printed and bound in Great Britain
by Butler & Tanner Ltd, Frome and London

TO JUDITH AND HARRY BAUM

'He alone is dead who has been forgotten.'

I read these words once in a cemetery somewhere. If they are true, Chaliapin will never die; for with his fabulous talent this marvellous artist can never be forgotten. . . .

To future generations Chaliapin will become a legend.

Sergei Rachmaninov

CONTENTS

AUTHOR'S NOTE

A PREFACE IS USUALLY a veiled apology or an explanation, and has always seemed superfluous to me: if the author cannot convince his reader through the main body of his work, what will be the use of a brief foreword? But circumstances proved stronger than personal opinion; the book I was now writing – about one of the greatest names of Russian culture – was intended for a Western public. In the Soviet Union it is impossible to find someone who has never heard of Chaliapin. Here, however, as I have had many occasions to verify, his memory is on the whole limited to a narrow circle of specialists and record collectors. At first I had difficulty in believing this and stubbornly blamed myself; it is after all well known that names often sound very different in a foreign language. But careful pronunciation was no guarantee of success. 'Charlie who? Oh yes, it rings a bell. My old uncle used to talk about him. He rather liked him, you know.'

The British Library catalogues showed that my fears were well-founded. Chaliapin was the subject of a short book pub-lished in France some eighteen years ago,* but in neither English nor German nor Italian is there a single work which might give present-day opera-lovers an idea of what he did for twentieth-century theatre, nor explain why his achievement cannot be allowed to disappear together with the grandparents who once upon a time used to rave about his performances. Thus it was that the desire to write an artistic biography arose.

The path between dreams and their realisation is a difficult one, and I would never have reached its end without the support of a great many people. In the long list of those who have helped me (it is unfortunately impossible to name them all), I should like to thank the General Director of the Royal Opera House,

* Goury, Jean: *Fédor Chaliapine*, Société de Diffusion d'Art Lyrique, Paris 1969.

Covent Garden, Sir John Tooley; the Organising Secretary of the Friends of Covent Garden, the Honourable Kensington Davison; and the Head of the Archive, Francesca Franchi, for their generous assistance in the early stages. I should also like to thank Alexander Schouvaloff, Curator of the Theatre Museum in London; John Roberts, Director of the Great Britain–USSR Association; Nina Froud; Isabella Wallich; Isolde Lochhead; Caroline Blakiston; Ruth Harrison; Judith Barber; Aage Haugland; John Smith; Stephen Jolly; Keith Hardwick; Nikita Lobanov; Robert Tuggle, Director of Archives of the Metropolitan Opera, New York, and his colleague Thom Carlson; Ian Lyon; Syd Grey; and Seva Novgorodsev.

I owe a special debt of gratitude to Michael Allen, Director of Finance and Administration, EMI Music; Doris Lessing; Michael Savage; and Vladimir Gurvich. I am greatly obliged to Sir John and Lady Sainsbury for their encouragement. Further thanks to Janette Field for her patience and indefatigable typing.

To give the full account of my indebtedness, I must also mention here those who in their time have taught me to understand the theatre, and in particular one of its highest peaks – the art of Chaliapin. They are Dr. Vladimir Drankov, Professors Moisei Yankovsky and Abram Gozenpud, and Chaliapin's singing partner the baritone Sergei Levik. I learnt a great deal both in conversations with them and from their writings.

And then there is a little story which I heard as a child, at an age when I had no real idea of who Fedor Chaliapin was. It concerns a certain schoolboy living in Petrograd at the time of the First World War. Like many of his companions, he dreamed of seeing Chaliapin perform. His parents were not rich and could only send him just enough for his keep and his school fees. So he decided to try to make his wish come true without help. One evening, mingling with the crowd, he managed to slip into the auditorium, but there he was stopped. 'Let's see your ticket.' 'I don't know where it is. I must have lost it somewhere. . . .' 'No admittance without ticket,' said the usher sternly, elbowing the boy towards the exit. 'How dare you?' the youth suddenly blurted out, to his own amazement. 'Chaliapin himself invited me and said I should go and see him after the performance.' 'Why wait so long then?' retorted the attendant with a malicious smile. 'Let's go right now.' Chaliapin, already made up and in costume (for *Don Quichotte*), was sitting in his dressing-room talking with somebody. Stopping in mid-sentence, he looked in surprise at the anxious red face of the boy and at the usher holding him by the scruff of the neck. 'What's the matter?' 'Well, you see . . .' the man started to say, but the boy cut him short. 'Fedor Ivanovich, I keep telling him that I know you but he won't believe me.' The few seconds of the ensuing pause seemed like an eternity. 'But what is this?' Chaliapin said suddenly, smiling broadly. 'Of course he knows me – and very well too, I can assure you. Give him the best seat you can.' That schoolboy was my father. . . .

V.B.
London, 1987

Unless otherwise stated, the translations from the Russian and the transliterations of Russian proper names are the author's own.

The author and the publishers owe an additional debt of gratitude to EMI Music for generous help with illustrations.

Before the Curtain Rises

'Chaliapin stands at the summit, set apart from the others.'

Konstantin Stanislavsky

THIS book is about the life and art of a genius, the incomparable Russian singer Fedor Ivanovich Chaliapin (1873–1938), a name that quickly springs to mind in any attempt at analysing the inexplicable and magical quality of talent. Educated Russians regard him as part of their cultural heritage: Chekhov referred to him as 'the great Chaliapin'[1] and Gorky voiced the feelings of a whole nation when he said: 'In Russian art, Chaliapin, like Pushkin, is an epoch.'[2]

Holding a unique position in the history of the theatre, he is deservedly known as a reformer of twentieth-century opera. Despite the passage of time, the rapture and the wild enthusiasm he evoked in his public still seem fully justified. Memoirs, recordings and photographs of him in different roles – photographs which bear little resemblance to the real Chaliapin but which are astonishingly convincing as likenesses of the characters he portrayed – enable us to share the delight of those lucky enough to see and hear him in person. Their number is fast dwindling, but Chaliapin's impact on the roles he sang and his importance in the evolution of contemporary theatre remain undiminished; the art he created has a timeless quality, retaining much that is fresh and exciting.

Chaliapin transcended the usual limits of his profession: his name is linked with those of countless writers, composers and directors. He set a standard of perfection, an example of enduring value, as this excerpt from an article by a Soviet actor illustrates: 'Nikolai Cherkasov was asked by Sergei Eisenstein to take the leading role in the film *Ivan the Terrible*. During his early youth he had been employed at the Mariinsky Theatre in Petersburg as a supernumerary and had had many opportunities of seeing Chaliapin's performances. Cherkasov showed Eisenstein how Chaliapin walked, the look in his eyes, which sceptre he carried, what make-up he used and thus "assisted" spent several hours going through some of the scenes, after which Eisenstein exclaimed: "That's it! Play it just like that!"[3]

The revitalising effect of Chaliapin on various other aspects of artistic creativity was universally acknowledged, both in the West and in Russia, during his own lifetime. Stanislavsky wrote: 'Synthesis has rarely been achieved by anyone in the arts, particularly in the theatre. Chaliapin is the only case I can think of,'[4] and he was often heard to say: 'My system is taken straight from Chaliapin ... '.[5] 'You are to music what Tolstoy is to literature,'[6] said Gorky in a letter to the singer, a view echoed by Rachmaninov: 'It is impossible to describe how he sang. He sang as Tolstoy wrote.'[7] Glazunov once told Chaliapin: 'What a pity it is that Tchaikovsky did not hear you. He would certainly have composed something for you.'[8] Leonid Andreev, a prominent Russian author of the early twentieth century whose tragic view of the world was expressed in a mixture of bitter irony and fatalistic despair, wrote in one of his essays: 'I walk and I think − I walk and I think − and I think of Fedor Chaliapin. It is night now; the town has quietened down and sleeps. The dark street is silent − the room is silent − the doors are open to light shadows, to vague, odd dreams conjured up by the great artist and singer. I walk and I think of Chaliapin. I remember his singing, his strong and well-proportioned body, his surprisingly mobile face, his typical Russian look − and a strange transformation takes place before my eyes. Behind the soft outline of the genial countenance of a simple moujik, Mephistopheles himself is looking at me, with his angular features and his satanic intelligence, his diabolic malice and enigmatic aloofness. Mephistopheles himself, I tell you ... a real devil breathing ill-will. Then in a fittingly mysterious manner, Mephistopheles turns back into Chaliapin − the soft outline of that clever peasant's face returns for an instant, and Tsar Boris* slowly enters, at once doleful and majestic, his step perfectly even, something no amount of acting, only long years in power can achieve. It is the handsome visage of a tyrant consumed by passion, of a criminal, a hero seeking to consolidate his throne

* Boris Godunov − *Boris Godunov* by Modest Mussorgsky.

Chaliapin, in the late 1890s.

by spilling sacred blood, a powerful intellect and a firm will, but a vulnerable human being. And behind Boris – Tsar Ivan* hissing with spite, cunning, wise, vicious and unhappy; and a little further, the austere beauty of barbarous Holofernes;† harmless Farlaf‡ in the full panoply of his cowardly stupidity, good nature and impulsive roguishness; and finally, the most recent of them – Eryomka.§ This amazing collection of characters is portrayed by just one face; this extraordinary variety of human souls, minds and feelings, is gathered within one single soul and mind – those of the humble peasant Fedor Chaliapin, who is now, by virtue of his talent, a European celebrity. With what insight and originality must a man be endowed in order to overcome space, time and circumstance, to penetrate to its innermost depth the soul of another being who is totally different from him in age, nationality and historical outlook; and manage to comprehend all of its most subtle complexities?'9

One might think that such pronouncements are to be found only in Russia, where Chaliapin was a prominent public figure. However, personal recollections of eyewitnesses and a great number of newspaper and magazine articles written over the years in different languages record for us the effect Chaliapin produced on Western audiences. Some impressions were noted down immediately after a performance, others were distant memories, but all of them are agreed on one thing: the encounter with Chaliapin was an unforgettable experience – it was unique. 'During my twenty-five years in opera,' wrote the Italian soprano Toti dal Monte, 'I sang under the baton of the great Arturo Toscanini, I had the best singers in the world for partners, but meeting Chaliapin remains the most vivid and thrilling memory of all.'10 'Of superb physique, he had an uncanny gift for cosmetic metamorphosis, and adding to dramatic gifts a magnificent voice that rolled out like melodious thunder, it was easy for him to equal the triumphs of even Caruso those days!' recalled Geraldine Farrar.11 'He was

* Ivan the Terrible – *The Maid of Pskov* by Nikolai Rimsky-Korsakov.
† Holofernes – *Judith* by Alexander Serov.
‡ Farlaf – *Ruslan and Ludmilla* by Mikhail Glinka.
§ Eryomka – *The Power of Evil* by Alexander Serov.

unrivalled as a singing actor, in his age or any subsequent one,' affirmed Rosa Ponselle.[12] After attending Chaliapin's first Covent Garden performance (1926) Dame Nellie Melba declared to the correspondent of the *Evening Standard*: 'It is a long time since I have listened through an evening with more intense pleasure. Chaliapin proved himself one of the masters both of stage and opera. His acting was just as good as his operatic performance and that says a good deal.'[13]

The list of tributes is endless. Tito Gobbi, for instance, considered him to stand, together with Enrico Caruso, and Titta Ruffo, 'beyond human limitations, bordering on myth, illuminating forever the operatic firmament',[14] while Titta Ruffo himself, when asked about the 'greatest artists' with whom he had sung, exclaimed: 'Greatest artists? I know famous artists, but there is only one greatest artist: Chaliapin. He is the greatest, unique, glowing talent. A genius! Chaliapin, only him.'[15] 'He and Patti are phenomena which appear once in centuries,' said Saint-Saëns.[16]

Gordon Craig, in his book on Henry Irving, remarked: 'Speaking of Chaliapin, you'd never find yourselves saying that he was "interesting" or "able" or "intelligent". You would go much further than that. I think you would call him "immense", "magnetic".'[17] John Barrymore was once discussing a pro-spective role which he eventually decided not to accept. The producer suggested offering it to Chaliapin instead: 'You and he are the only ones who can do justice to this part.' 'Listen,' answered Barrymore seriously, 'when you say the name of Chaliapin, pause for a minute – because I'm not fit to be mentioned in the same breath with him.'[18]

Chaliapin has certainly given rise to more thought-provoking comments than any other singer at any time. These refer mainly to his technique in preparing for a role and to the fundamental problems faced by the singing actor, as opposed to the acting singer. Herein lies the difference in style between Chaliapin and many other artists. Only his approach will produce the type of operatic performance he was striving for, in which singers no longer stand in costume and make-up with their arms either pressed to their chest or flung wide open, addressing to the audience what they should really be telling their stage companions, but instead participate in a clearly conceived performance of musical drama. Only on the rare occasions when this difficult objective is achieved does opera become a true alliance of music and theatre.

Chaliapin did not arrive at this method immediately, but once convinced that he had found the right one, he defended it relentlessly and without compromise.

His views, however, are not shared by everyone, as Tito Schipa demonstrates in his 'Memories of Chaliapin': 'I must admit that I do not attach a great deal of importance to where I stand on stage. The main thing, from my point of view, is the singing, the sound, the vocal expressiveness.'[19] This attitude still has many advocates amongst both performers and public. It is one of the reasons why Chaliapin's role in the development of the theatre does not simply belong to history, and why he continues to influence the work of operatic artists. In the opinion of Gianandrea Gavazzeni, conductor at La Scala, 'Chaliapin's powers of invention have had a deep effect on Italian theatre. Chaliapin had the ability to create a unified whole out of a variety of cultures from every corner of the world, and the art of this great Russian singer left profound and indelible marks, not only on the performance of Russian operas by Italian singers, but also in a wider sense on their entire style of vocal and dramatic interpretation, particularly where the music of Verdi and the Verists is concerned. Thus his influence can be felt to this day in the treatment of such roles as King Philip in *Don Carlos* or Fiesco in *Simon Boccanegra*.'[20] Interesting to note, Gavazzeni emphasized the legacy of innovations left by Chaliapin even in roles which he never sang, such as Fiesco.

The German singer Hans Hotter paid him still greater tribute in a BBC radio interview at the end of 1983: 'The strongest impression I had came from Chaliapin, whom I unfortunately did not meet personally, but heard on stage and in concert,'[21] and he added in a letter to the writer of this book: ' ... in fact, my whole career as a singer would be unthinkable without the imprints this unique artist has left on my artistic mind. It seems hard to describe exactly the character of such an influence, but in my belief expressions like magic or even daemonic would not be exaggerated.'[22] Hotter is closely identified with Wagnerian roles which Chaliapin never performed.

This observation introduces the notion of a broader understanding of 'Chaliapin's tradition' – a tradition which has developed as a complex process, for which there is no straightforward explanation. Setting up a chart, passing from name to name, from decade to decade, does not bring the answer nearer. In order to trace its progress, one has first to realise that it consists of several stages, and continues to evolve intermittently. Only then is it possible to speak of a tradition, of the fundamental ideas Chaliapin brought into the interpretation of operatic roles. Moreover, Chaliapin's system grew side by side with Stanislavsky's and deserves to be studied with the same attention and thoroughness. Stanislavsky himself acknowledged this early in the 1920s when considering the possibility of opening an opera workshop to train young singers: 'We cannot create a Chaliapin, but we must create a Chaliapin school. . . . The only correct approach to opera is Chaliapin's approach, which proceeds not from the external reality of the character being portrayed, but from its inner reality, its psychological depth.'[23]

Time and again Chaliapin, engaged initially simply as a bass singer, would end up in full partnership with the author of the opera's original plot and with its composer. In the minds of contemporary readers and spectators, the name of Chaliapin is inseparable from the characters of Boris Godunov, Don Basilio, King Philip, Mephistopheles and Don Quixote. Pushkin and Mussorgsky, Beaumarchais and Rossini, Cervantes and Massenet, Goethe with Gounod and Boïto, all had in Chaliapin a true interpreter. His performances were in total harmony with the composer's intention, and their artistic validity can never be questioned. Boïto, after hearing Chaliapin's Mephistopheles, joyously exclaimed: 'At last I see my own conception of the role! At last I have found my devil.'[24]

But what is then left to those who never saw Chaliapin on the stage? Is there really anything to say about an actor whose art is to a great extent lost to us? Chaliapin seems to have fared a little better than other performers of his day. He made a great number of recordings and even a sound film. But this is not a completely satisfactory answer. 'He is among all singers', wrote a critic in the *Manchester Guardian* in 1926, 'the one most in need of being seen in order to be properly heard. Those who could only know his art from gramophone records can have but a faint idea of his power of swaying and subduing the audience.'[25] A similar opinion is held by Herbert von Karajan ('I fear that the records could not give us today the real picture of this unique artist')[26] and by Sir Neville Cardus ('You can get no more idea of Chaliapin from a gramophone record than you get of a pterodactyl by looking at a skeleton preserved in a museum – because he was such an enormous, abounding personality on the stage').[27]

Is it possible to put into words the impressions of the spectator? The greater the actor, the more difficult the task, and most of Chaliapin's eminent contemporaries, even those gifted with sensitivity and a literary turn of mind, shrank from the attempt. 'Chaliapin's ability to enthral the audience by his mere presence on stage through some sort of direct power, and to hold thousands of people spellbound, was unbelievable,'[28] Alexandre Benois was to recall many years later, while another Russian painter, Ilya Repin, wrote shortly after attending a performance: 'I saw Chaliapin as Holofernes. It was the acme of genius. . . . How he reclined on the sofa! The Eastern despot, the conqueror in a foul mood. The whole theatre held its breath – so deep and murderously potent was the despair of the absolute ruler.'[29] 'No, no words, no picture can give even a vague idea of it. Yes, this is genius.'[30]

It might at first glance seem easier to talk of Chaliapin the man. Both he and the numerous memoirs fixing (sometimes even in great detail) various moments of his life are helpful in this. However, beneath the mass of reports and the veil of legend one cannot always see clearly the wise, lively, mischievous and sad countenance of Chaliapin: although this famous artist lived in the glare of publicity, his true nature is screened by a mist. Only a few knew what he was really like. The circumstances in which he grew up engendered in him mistrust and fear of people, made it necessary to wear a mask which was only very seldom

Chaliapin, 1903.

lifted. 'In real life as in the theatre,' wrote a Parisian acquaint-ance who was familiar with Chaliapin in the 1930s, when he was no longer young, 'this superhuman personage could take thousands of different aspects: hence the incomplete or ten-dentious character of so many judgements passed on him by insufficiently informed witnesses.'[31]

Biography is the reconstruction of a vanished past. The facts which are preserved will have to be connected by the bridge of imagination; a leap over the unknown will have to be made with the help of guesswork, a search for genuine links between events and dates, between the great and the small, the artistic side and the human side, which were once so intimately bonded in that gigantic Russian phenomenon – Fedor Chaliapin.

What then remains for the historian of the theatre to do? How can he best capture the essence of this colossal talent in order to render it accessible to the reader? There seems to be only one way: by selecting what is most significant from countless reviews, interviews and books, from Chaliapin's corre-spondence, as well as from recollections of eyewitnesses, rela-tives, friends and foes. A detailed description of his main roles must of course be included and an account given of the impressions left by Chaliapin's performances. When, in addition, we have delved into his creative method and defined some of the principles of his professional approach, the object of the present work will have been attained. . . .

Fedor Chaliapin himself has recounted the story of his life in two books. His style is colourful and expressive; he does not restrict himself to plain facts, to a list of incidents he observed or took part in. What he gives us is the intimate diary of a man's soul, a kind of introspective self-portrait. The integral text (integral at least according to E. Grosheva, who edited, revised and annotated it) of his first work – *Stranitsy iz moei zhizni* (Pages from My Life) – was not printed in the USSR until 1957.*

The reason for doubting the complete authenticity of these memoirs will become apparent a little further on.

---

* Fedor Ivanovich Chaliapin. Literary works. Letters. I. Chaliapina: *Memories of my father. Iskusstvo*, vol. 1, Moscow 1957.

A different edition, or more accurately a different version, had appeared in New York thirty years earlier.* The Soviet publication, covering his childhood, his youth and the beginning of his career, takes the reader as far as the First World War. The American volume contains not only the same chapters (with certain alterations, some of them important), but also two new, long ones where Chaliapin continues his narrative up to 1927, describing five years under the Soviet regime and his impressions of life in the West, particularly in England and America.

His second book, *Maska i dusha*,† is known in English as *Man and Mask*, but the literal translation of the Russian title is 'Mask and Soul', and this raises a point of general interest which seems to deserve a digression. For Russians, the word 'dusha' has far wider and deeper implications than the English word 'soul'. The term is common in literature from Pushkin to Pasternak, from Dostoevsky to Chekhov, in Stanislavsky's theoretical works and in the practical training of actors, in ordinary conversation between ordinary people, in Russian thinking and in Russian usage; it assumes dozens of subtle shades and can convey a state of mind or explain actions and their motives. It is at least as important as mental powers, if not more so. This concept is indispensable when talking of Chaliapin the quintessential Russian and Chaliapin the true artistic prodigy.

Expressions like 'inner world' and 'innermost feelings' have to be used for want of something better, and the onus of dealing with the inadequacy of the word 'soul' is left to the reader. He has to rely for a large part on his imagination and his sensitivity to try to understand another culture, another psychological make-up.

Chaliapin attached great significance to the Russian title of the book: mask and soul are closely related, as in life, where the exterior is a reflection of the interior; but on stage, if any

---

* Fedor Ivanovich Chaliapin. *Pages from My Life: an autobiography.* (Authorised translation by H.M. Buck.) Harper & Brothers, New York 1927.

† Chaliapin, F.I. *Mask and Soul – My forty years in the theatre.* Contemporary notes. Paris 1932.

attempt to follow Chaliapin's precepts is to be made, this relationship must appear clear and plausible. Chaliapin's books will be quoted here many times, and not just because of the importance of a man's own testimony in the study of his life. Anyone even remotely connected with the theatre, or who has a general interest in the arts, would find them worth reading. They reveal an extraordinarily rich and fulfilled personality in which, as in a real masterpiece, nothing is superfluous, nothing disturbs the development of the main theme, every incidental detail somehow enhances the effect of the whole.

Chaliapin knew great poverty and long periods of adversity to which he could easily have succumbed a hundred times, sinking forever into the morass of Russia's grim reality, as did so many others, perhaps no less able than he. Yet he managed not only to survive, but even to shape his own destiny, never losing contact with the inner voice of his talent or the true instinct of his inspiration, always faithful to his greatest joy and his greatest torment – THE THEATRE. 'If I amounted to anything in life, it was as an actor and a singer,' wrote Chaliapin towards the end of his days. 'I was totally committed to my vocation. I had no other ruling passion whatever, no particular taste for anything other than the stage.'[32]

These words are undoubtedly true, but clearly do him less than justice. Chaliapin had been blessed with an abundance of gifts. As Rachmaninov remarked, he showed 'a boundless and phenomenal talent in whatever he turned his hand to.'[33]

His curiosity and his natural aptitudes extended to many spheres; his drawings and his clay-modelling showed talent; he moved with natural ease and grace, was an expert fencer, loved sport in general and everything which had to do with clowning skills. Foreign languages, particularly in their phonetic aspect, presented little difficulty to him. His two books, his articles, letters and poetry are clear evidence of an outstanding literary ability. Chaliapin was also very fortunate in his personal appearance, which was admirably suited to the theatre. His large, mobile face, free from any sharply distinctive features, could easily be made up to portray kings or drunken peasants, noblemen or commoners.

Tall, broad-shouldered, of athletic build, Chaliapin compared favourably with dancers in the flexibility and sculptural
expressiveness of his body. 'Some of the movements of his
Varlaam during the inn scene of *Boris Godunov* created a
stronger impression of dance than certain entire ballets,' said
the choreographer Mikhail Fokine.[34]

But Chaliapin's greatest gift of all was perhaps an innate love
of art. He knew everything about the actor's profession, both
in theory and in practice, since he had himself 'tried' all its
forms and facets and once told a BBC broadcaster that 'he had
appeared in variety, in vaudeville, in comedy, in light opera, in
grand opera, in every form of entertainment except the circus
and he didn't give up hope of appearing in that before he died.'[35]

Interest in the mysterious and miraculous transformation of
a boy from the poorer classes of Russian society into a singer
of unprecedented fame grew more or less side by side with
interest in his work. Triumphant guest appearances abroad
further intensified public attention. Books,* stories and articles
on the life and career of Chaliapin soon began to appear.
Leading Russian newspapers announced once that the Italian
house of Ricordi intended to publish his memoirs under the title
of *My Life*, and even printed excerpts from them. Not for the
first time, Chaliapin was obliged to caution readers against any
publication about his life,† and disclaimed at a press conference

---

* Georgevich, N. (Shebuev, N.) *Life of F. I. Chaliapin and his artistic significance.*
Odessa 1903.

   M. K. *The Life and Art of Fedor Ivanovich Chaliapin.* Moscow 1903.

   Penyaef, L. *Chaliapin's first steps in the artistic world.* Moscow 1903.

   Sivkov, P. M. *F. I. Chaliapin: life and artistic significance.* St. Petersburg 1908.

   Lipaev, I. *Chaliapin – singer and artist.* St. Petersburg 1914.

   Stark, E. ('Siegfried'). *Chaliapin.* Petrograd 1915. *Fedor Ivanovich Chaliapin*
(Biography & stage creations). Moscow 1915.

   † A letter from Chaliapin was printed in the newspaper *Russkoe Slovo* (Russian
Word) of November 21st, 1912: 'On my arrival in Moscow on the 18th of this
month, I discovered to my great surprise that the newspaper *Vechernie Izvestiya*
(Evening News) had for some time been printing articles entitled "My life, extracts
from F. I. Chaliapin's Memoirs", and that these articles, on several occasions, bore
my signature "Fedor Chaliapin". I have reacted with indifference to all the rumours
about my memoirs, etc ... etc ... but when these rumours take the shape of articles,
and when my name even appears at the bottom, I am forced to declare that I have
never written, nor am I writing, any memoirs whatever their title, and that all that
is printed in the newspaper *Vechernie Izvestiya* is a complete and utter lie, produced

any connection with these so-called 'memoirs', the manuscript of which had allegedly been stolen from him.[36] He added that he had long intended to write an autobiography.

However, professional engagements at home and abroad repeatedly forced him to postpone the project. The extent of his real commitment to the idea is difficult to gauge now. His closest friend Gorky did not hear about it from the singer but from their mutual acquaintance Konstantin Petrovich Pyatnitsky, who visited the writer in Capri. Gorky sent Chaliapin an anxious letter from the island in September 1909, urging him to apply himself earnestly to the book and offering his help. 'Come and stay with me for a month or so, you can dictate your life to me and I'll write it down, or else I can join you anywhere you like abroad and we will work together on this, three or four hours a day. I shall of course not hinder you in any way, I will only point out what needs to be emphasised and what should remain in the shadow. If you want I will supply the language, if not, you make whatever alterations you like. Believe me, I have no thought of self-advancement with this, absolutely not. It must be you, speaking about yourself' (underlined by Gorky). 'Ask Konstantin Petrovich, how dear and important to me is this wonderful idea of yours, he will tell you.'[37] There is no record of Chaliapin's answer to this letter, but the plan did not materialise until several years later. Chaliapin wrote to his daughter Irina in April 1916: 'I will be in Peter [Petrograd] until May 16th and then I may go with Maxim to the Crimea. He feels dreadful as far as his health is concerned and it is imperative that he should spend some time warming himself in the sun ... and so I decided to resort to cunning by proposing the following: I would, I said, write my memoirs, and he could edit what I had written. They will be printed in his magazine called *Letopis* [Annals]. The idea greatly appealed to him and he decided to go to the Crimea with me.'[38] Gorky

by the fertile imagination of the editorial staff, evidently using my name to speculate. The impertinent liberty taken by the newspaper compels me to make them legally answerable, which is what I am going to do. – Fedor Chaliapin.'

Quoted from *Chronicle of the life and career of F.I. Chaliapin*, vol. 2, Leningrad 1985, pp. 43–44.

arrived in Foros* accompanied by a secretary. He and Chaliapin met every morning, and their work together would sometimes continue throughout the day. Chaliapin talked; Gorky took notes and asked questions. Everything Chaliapin said was taken down in shorthand, then transcribed and finally edited. The first draft of the 'Autobiography' took about a month to complete, after which Gorky returned to Petrograd. He wrote to a friend: 'I only yesterday came back from the Crimea where I was Chaliapin's guest while I helped him with his autobiography.'[39]

Later, in the autumn, they both re-read the work done in the summer, making additions and corrections. It was typed in duplicate: one copy was lodged with the publisher, the other remained with Chaliapin. In October 1916 advertisements inviting subscriptions to *Letopis* started to appear, announcing the serialisation in the magazine of 'F. Chaliapin – An Autobiography. Edited by M. Gorky.' Publication of the memoirs finally began in 1917, but was halted before completion in December of that year when the magazine closed.

Five years elapsed. In the summer of 1922 Chaliapin went abroad on tour, never to return. Gorky's fate followed a different course: he settled down in the Soviet Union, growing increasingly dependent on its system and at times ranting against the West. The tone of his letters to Chaliapin changed entirely. Let us abandon for the moment any further discussion of the relationship between Chaliapin and Gorky (which will be treated at some length in the Epilogue) and continue the tale of the vicissitudes suffered by the autobiography. In 1926 it came out in book form in Leningrad and was re-issued a year later. When Chaliapin found out about this he was annoyed, since it threatened to ruin his own plans for an American edition which was by then already in preparation. 'It grieves me for two reasons,' he wrote to Gorky, 'firstly because I had been waiting for the right moment to sell to a publisher and secondly, because there are some things in it which I wanted to alter before it went into print. Last winter I was so pleased to have been

---

* Foros – small settlement in the Crimea.

Maxim Gorky and Fedor Chaliapin.

offered a suitable price in New York, as I told you at our last meeting in Naples. I was pleased because this sale would have brought enough money and, in your precarious position with its various literary squabbles and difficulties, would have given you some temporary material help, since I myself did not want to take any money and, to be honest, did not feel I had any right to. I have been upset by this unpleasant affair most of all on your account ... but ... what can one do? Hard Luck!'[40]

Chaliapin's cordial and sincere letter could not prevent the situation from becoming heated. Someone reported to Gorky that Chaliapin was spreading rumours accusing him of behaving improperly and of having sold the manuscript to Priboi.*

Gorky was not slow to react: 'Dear friend, As I already wrote to you, Priboi only published the part of your "Memoirs" which had been printed in *Letopis*. Printing of the "Memoirs" ceased before the end because the censorship closed *Letopis*. I do not know who is working at Priboi and have no connection whatsoever with this publisher. You should write to Priboi to send you the royalties on the book or to give them to someone specified by you. I don't want to have anything to do with this or the "Memoirs" in general, and I am not accepting the American money which you set aside as my share.'[41] The singer was in correspondence with the Soviet publisher, who not only offered to pay him, but also gave assurances that the text used in the book they had brought out was exactly the same as in *Letopis* and that the still unpublished remainder would not be printed without his permission.

Chaliapin did not accept the proposal, sent Gorky half of the five thousand dollars he had earned from the American sale and wrote to him: 'I well remember how much was printed in *Letopis*, and from the book brought out by Priboi and the write-up in it, I have definitely established the fact that they printed more than in *Letopis*. I was hurt by the tone of your letter. If I have bothered with the material side of this book and worried about it, it was only so that you could receive a few thousand dollars which, I presumed, would not be unwelcome to you.'[42]

---

* Priboi (Surf): name of Leningrad publishing house.

Chaliapin's disquiet was not unjustified. In 1926 Gorky had written to him: 'Dear Fedor Ivanovich, Maria Valentinovna* is not quite right: I did have the original manuscript of the "Memoirs", but I burnt it before going abroad, together with some others.'[43]

Let us now compare these words with the note written by E. Grosheva, who, as mentioned earlier, prepared the publication of the 'complete' Russian edition of *Pages from My Life*: 'The first half of the autobiography is printed as in the periodical *Letopis* of 1917 (Nos. 1–12) with the reinstatement of censored gaps in the original. The concluding part of the autobiography comes from A. M. Gorky's manuscript, kept in A. M. Gorky's archive at the Institute of World Literature named after A. M. Gorky.'[44] Then the words of the Devil in Mikhail Bulgakov's novel *The Master and Margarita* must really be true: 'Manuscripts do not burn!'

By refusing not only money but the rights to the book, Chaliapin was playing into the hands of his enemies. When a few years later in Paris he sued the Soviet authorities, this was used against him. Chaliapin lost the case; the verdict was also influenced by Gorky's evidence, although it did not correspond at all to what he had previously said. He now claimed: 'Fedor was incapable of writing because he was lazy,' and added that their collaboration on the book had been a matter of just a few sessions. 'Chaliapin did not devote more than ten hours to it. I put his chaotic stories in order and re-wrote them, adding everything Chaliapin had told me on earlier occasions.'[45] Gorky also stated that the idea of writing the memoirs was exclusively his, and declared in a letter to Chaliapin: 'Three quarters of your memoirs are my work.'[46] This was not enough: after all, if you are going to demonstrate your loyalty, you can't do it by halves. Gorky wrote to the Soviet Ambassador in Paris and sent an open letter to the two main Soviet newspapers, *Pravda* and *Izvestia*, reiterating the same theme: 'I tried unsuccessfully for several years to persuade Chaliapin to write his autobiography. For a time Chaliapin spent one hour a day nar-

* Maria Valentinovna Petzold – Chaliapin's second wife.

rating his life to me, and I polished and edited the typewritten text.... '[47]

This then is how Gorky came to be regarded as the real author of Chaliapin's memoirs. Without wishing to belittle the importance of Gorky's editorial work, and leaving aside the question of whether the editor of a book can have any claim to be its author, one nevertheless cannot, when comparing *Mask and Soul* (even though this, too, was edited) with opinions expressed by Chaliapin in his letters and interviews, avoid reaching the conclusion that only Chaliapin could have written them. The clear, vivid and profoundly original language is unmistakably *his*, as is the manner of constructing a sentence or emphasising a word. Curiously enough, this very individual use of language is still quite perceptible and has not been lost in the re-telling by people who had heard the story from Chaliapin himself.

Attempts to attribute the authorship to Gorky can go to absurd lengths. For instance, all Soviet scholars who have studied the life and career of Chaliapin omit any reference to the American edition of his book. It is only cursorily mentioned in the three-tome collection of material, letters and documents (Moscow 1976, 1977 and 1979) and altogether missing in the many biographies, articles and memoirs which have been written about him. We should not be too harsh in our criticism: this conduct is no doubt dictated by force rather than by choice, and anyway, the American edition is not available in the Soviet Union.

To conform with ideological demands, Gorky was represented – even in his own lifetime – as a great and wise proletarian writer, whose origins gave him a clear-sighted grasp of the 'necessary reforms' which revolution had brought to the people. Chaliapin on the other hand was cast in the role of the artistic genius who was, however, politically naive and incapable of making correct judgements under the difficult conditions which accompanied the building of a 'new, happy life'. The indifference and the contempt with which he treated Gorky's wise counsel led him to commit an incalculable amount of mistakes, and in particular the worst one of all – emigration.

One can understand why in the USSR similar clichés return in study after study of Chaliapin. Soviet scholars cannot say anything else, even if they wanted to – but what is incomprehensible is that they should be repeated in Western publications such as 'Chaliapin – an autobiography as told to Maxim Gorky, translated from the original Russian by Nina Froud and James Hanley', printed in London in 1968 by Macdonald. At the very beginning of her translator's notes, Mrs. Froud goes even further than Soviet musicologists and refers to 'a manuscript about the singer written by Maxim Gorky ... ' which 'had been serialised in the Russian journal *Letopis* in 1917' (p.7). Claiming to have made original discoveries after lengthy research in Soviet archives, she continues: 'The resulting twelve years have been spent by James Hanley and myself, unravelling further mysteries, putting pieces together and finding even greater treasures, diaries, letters and contemporary newspaper reports, out of which grew the pattern and volume of the present book.' In actual fact, as Edward Crankshaw remarked: 'All the matter in the book has long been available in Russian and needed only to be translated.'[*48] The prefacing articles together with the careful selection of material and the contents of the bibliography – all appear to indicate a desire to avoid questioning the official Soviet viewpoint.

According to Mrs. Froud, Chaliapin's memoirs having in the American edition 'lost the touch of Gorky's hand', a 'fascinating story had been rendered unreadable'.

One may share her views on the translation – it is certainly clumsy and stiff – but this does not in any way diminish the value of the work. Taking into consideration the evidence already known, one must conclude that this is indeed Fedor Chaliapin's authentic autobiography. Furthermore, whenever Mrs. Froud refers to Chaliapin's second book, *Mask and Soul*, whose complete Russian or English editions could easily be studied without fear of unpleasant consequences, she clearly used the considerably abbreviated text published in the USSR,† amputated of three whole chapters – 'Kanuny' (On the Eve),

---

* See footnote on page 13.

† See bibliography in *Chaliapin: an autobiography as told to Maxim Gorky*, p. 308.

'Pod bolshevikami' (Under the Bolsheviks) and 'Gorky', some one hundred and sixty pages – and of all the remarks against the regime with which Chaliapin had generously peppered his book.

Had the compilers consulted the complete version, they could have saved themselves a lot of time and 'discovered' a number of well-known facts: Gorky did not always loudly proclaim his love and worship of Soviet power, and Chaliapin was not a mere dupe who fed upon the wits and opinions of his friend. At one time, their outlooks were, as Chaliapin acknowledges, very similar: 'Gorky and I shared the same belief.'[49] 'The practice of Bolshevism proved even more dreadful than its theories,' declared Chaliapin in Paris ten years after his departure from Russia in 1922, 'and perhaps the most terrible aspect of the regime was that Bolshevism had become completely saturated with that awful intolerance and bigotry, that obtuse smugness which is Russian philistinism. And it is not with philistinism alone but generally speaking with all the negative aspect of the Russian mentality that Bolshevism has become imbued. It seemed to be like a parade of all the characters ... in Russian satirical literature, from Fonvizin to Zoshchenko. They all came to offer their best to Vladimir Ilich Lenin.... '[50]

In the years 1917–1918, Gorky wrote: 'The working class cannot fail to see that Lenin is only doing some experimenting with their living tissues, with their blood. The working class must know that miracles don't exist, that they are going to face hunger, the complete disruption of industry, chaos in transport, a long term of bloody anarchy followed by a no less bloody and dismal reaction. Aren't all those who disagree seized and dragged off to jail under the Lenin regime just as they were under the Romanovs?'[51] 'The reformers from the Smol'ny* don't care about Russia, they sacrifice her in cold blood to their chimeric dream of world or European revolution. And while I can, I will not cease repeating to the Russian proletariat: "You are being led to your ruin, you are being used for an inhuman experiment, in the eyes of your leaders you are not human

* Smol'ny – formerly a convent, it became the headquarters of the Bolsheviks during the Revolution.

beings".'[52] 'Our revolution has given free range to every evil and bestial instinct. We see that the ranks of the Soviet power's servants provide a regular catch of bribe-takers, profiteers and swindlers, while good and honest people, in order not to starve to death, sell newspapers on the streets and undertake heavy manual work.... This is a nightmare, it is pure Russian nonsense, and there is nothing wrong in saying that this is idiocy!'[53]

'I remember my mother saying,' recalled Chaliapin's youngest daughter, Dasya, 'that it was Gorky, seeing what post-revolutionary Russia was turning into, who advised us to leave. "This is no place for you," he said, especially for Fedya. "You must go abroad...." '[54]

Let us, however, return to the Russian version of *Pages from My Life*. Before publication of the first chapters, Chaliapin had wanted to add a short introduction. Written in Gorky's hand as dicated by Chaliapin, this introduction remains in the Soviet archives and has never been printed. Chaliapin states in its opening sentence that this autobiography was prompted by the desire to arouse feelings of interest in and respect for the common man. He ends with these words: 'I would ask the reader to believe that I have no need to pretend, to hide my shortcomings, to try to justify myself or, generally speaking, to make myself out to be better than I am.'[55]

Fifteen years later, he repeated the essence of his remark in the final words of the introduction to *Mask and Soul*. 'I would like to point out that in my book I strove, above all, to be entirely truthful. I appear before the reader without make-up ... '[56] Chaliapin knew very well that 'the man who never has to justify himself in his own eyes does not exist.'[57] Is this perhaps why he tries so hard to show himself 'as he is', why he always seems to feel the need to account for his actions or defend himself? But against whom – who is attacking him? On the contrary, 'wherever he showed himself, everybody knew and recognised him, everyone who passed him smiled and looked back at him,'[58] and he invariably made a powerful and unforgettable first impression. 'Even without realising that this was a famous artist, I could not fail to notice him if only for his physical appearance: he was clearly a type of Northern Slav one rarely meets, fair-haired, tall, broad-shouldered and expressing himself in the language of the common people so rich in well-chosen terms and laced with Russian humour – he was just like a country lad. His conversation was full of casual witticisms, unconsciously interspersed with profound observations. His mind seemed to hold a ready store of colourful imagery. He was brimming over with cheerful bonhomie, taking pleasure in life and in the society of other people. His wit was without bitterness or malice. It was lighthearted laughter and suffused his whole being with a kind of inner radiance of strong, limpid sunshine, as if he belonged to another world like the firebird shining in the dark,'[59] recalls the writer Stepan Skitalets.

'Chaliapin would stop by a table,' writes Jacques Feschotte in his book *Ce Géant – Féodor Chaliapine*, 'the men would stand up to greet him, the women smiled at him. What did he say to them? It was now my turn not to hear. But what I can guarantee is that after a few moments the face of those he was talking to underwent a transformation: the men's expressions seemed more lively and as if illuminated; the women looked more beautiful. Fedor's magnetic power visibly asserted itself and when he moved on, after taking his leave, to the next table, one witnessed the same phenomenon in reverse. All those he had as it were raised up to himself then seemed simply to return to their own selves, having come down again to their ordinary level after those instants of high-soaring.... This kind of taking over ... was one of the incontrovertible elements of his power.'[60]

Others, however, saw him in a different light. And indeed he was not always like that. According to his daughter Lydia, 'his charm was irresistible ... but not everyone felt at ease with him; his presence could make people tremble despite themselves. His personality was overwhelming, provoking admiration mingled with fear – at any moment he was liable to lose his temper and fly into a rage; there was no way of anticipating his reactions. He often became angry – really angry, not just cross – over trifles, but a trifle could also put him in the happiest frame of mind. When he was in a temper his whole face would turn white. Even his eyes turned "white" at such moments. Normally light green, they became transparent and colourless; his eyebrows too somehow faded, and his whole face became so haggard and alarming that people preferred to get out of his sight. His gaze would pierce right through you. It seemed he knew in advance what you might think, what you were going to do ... '[61]

Chaliapin was quite aware of his lack of restraint in expressing his feelings. Trying to describe a typical Russian, he seems to be speaking about himself: 'The Russian temperament does not appear to know half measures. It is by disposition inclined to extremes of mood and sensitivity. Such is our strange Russian nature that its good and its bad sides know no moderation.'[62]

Singers, even the most famous ones, did not as a rule question his supremacy in artistic matters. They would wait uncomplainingly for hours on end if he was late for rehearsal. He was capable of outrageous behaviour: he might beat the time with his foot for the 'benefit' of his partners during a performance, or go up to the footlights to show the conductor how to conduct the orchestra. He could, following a slight mistake in a *morceau d'ensemble*, 'lose control of himself and shout across the auditorium: "It's impossible to sing with you, you have no rhythm!" '[63] During a performance of *Boris Godunov* at Covent Garden 'he walked off the stage in the middle of the scene while Prince Shuisky was addressing an impassioned appeal to him. It was said afterwards that he went into the wings to make some very emphatic remarks to the electrician, who resented them.'[64] Yet if for some reason Chaliapin was in low spirits and declined to go on with a performance, the audience would not go home, even when everybody knew that he had already removed his make-up and left the theatre. (Just suppose someone managed to persuade him to come back – after all, it did sometimes happen!)

He dictated the terms of his contracts to theatre managers and personally selected the conductors for his performances. Evidence of this is to be found in letters to the Director of the Imperial Theatres, Vladimir Telyakovsky, on whose desk Chaliapin was in the habit of depositing 'memoranda' after regular clashes with his colleagues. The bone of contention on one occasion was the tempo adopted by the conductor of the Bolshoi Theatre, Ulrich Avranek, in Dargomyzhsky's *Rusalka*, which was not to Chaliapin's taste. Without going into further details, here is the text of Chaliapin's missive in full:

'CONDITIONS UNDER WHICH I, CHALIAPIN, AM PREPARED TO WORK AT THE IMPERIAL THEATRES:

1. All operas in which I appear will be conducted by either Coates or Cooper.

2. While I am on stage, i.e. during rehearsals or during performances, a fully authorised member of the managerial staff must be present at all times, so that I may at any moment address to him any requests of an artistic nature so that he may deal with any shortcomings in connection with on-stage arrangements.

3. An administrative director to be appointed (abolish the term 'principal director' as basically inaccurate).

4. Official notification to all persons taking part in performances or rehearsals in which I sing, to all other artists and the chorus (if necessary) that they are to give serious consideration to whatever remarks I may make pertaining to stage business and to submit to my professional demands as if I were principal director or stage manager.

5. The authority of the so-called principal director to be transferred to me.

6. Application for improvements in the stage lighting of the Bolshoi Theatre must be submitted without delay.

7. I draw the management's attention to the fact that the presence of Avranek in the theatre as *conductor* [Chaliapin's italics] is not only of no use and no interest to anyone, but is even pernicious since it affects all the artists, even though they may not be aware of it. It is corrupting in musical terms, and therefore his complete removal from the conductor's stand is advisable.

Fedor Chaliapin.'[65]

Fred Gaisberg, who for decades worked with countless great musicians and artists from the earliest days of the gramophone era, writes in his article 'Recording Chaliapin in Moscow': 'Firstly, he selects that hour of the twenty-four in which the voice reaches its best, be it two in the afternoon or midnight. When that time arrives Chaliapin appears in the Gramophone laboratory. Perhaps the Band and Staff have been waiting five or six hours. It does not matter. It is peculiar of the man that where and in what he enters he takes command. Once the writer was arranging for a Chaliapin session and consulted him, asking if such and such a director would be agreeable. "Yes, yes," he replied, "anyone will do, for it is I who will direct." '[66]

Gaisberg also remembers how Chaliapin, driving him in a sleigh around the Bolshoi Theatre square in 1910, proudly showed him 'the long line of people who queued up to buy tickets for a performance of *Boris* and . . . pointed to the cavalry patrolling to keep the line in order.'[67]

But while the adulation of the crowds might be gratifying and even desirable, Chaliapin secretly despised it. He did not trust their love. He often said that the artist is 'the plaything of the public, nothing more. If the voice fails, the man is finished, forgotten by all, abandoned, like some wooden soldier, once a child's favourite toy, now a tiresome object.'[68] Admirers of Chaliapin's art did not merely consist of anonymous crowds, but also of such monumental figures as the elderly, grey-haired Tolstoy, an outwardly severe personage, furtively wiping away a tear lest somebody notice his emotion as he heard Chaliapin sing and afterwards sending him his complete works with a touching dedication.

The Russian opera singer Alexander Davydov quotes Adelina Patti's enthusiastic words: 'Chaliapin won my heart once and for all. He is a supreme vocalist and a supreme artist. I even made his personal acquaintance. I found him totally bewitching.'[69]

Yet a note of insecurity, of painful vulnerability still manifested itself from time to time, in letters, or in unusually frank conversations with close friends. In moments of weariness he would say in despair: 'I am alone . . . I am alone . . . ' writes the singer's daughter Irina.[70] The louder the shouts of delight, it seemed, the stronger the sensation of isolation and anxiety. There were times during the happy and harmonious periods of his life when Chaliapin's artistic self-expression and what he called his 'commitment' seemed to be effortless. At other times, when this equilibrium was somehow disturbed, he was liable to withdraw into himself, or else resort to scandalous scenes, provocation and insult.

The story of Chaliapin's life, and particularly that of his childhood and youth, goes a long way towards explaining his complex, difficult and seemingly paradoxical personality. His character was undoubtedly affected by the exceptionally high demands he made on himself and others. He was unable to tolerate laziness, sloppiness and ineptitude at work – and when he encountered mediocrity in any form would fly into an uncontrollable rage. Chaliapin devoted much time to reflecting on his relationship with art and with the public to whom it was addressed. Many years later, when he wanted to express thoughts which were obviously of cardinal importance to him, he wrote: 'At the heart of my efforts to refine my work was a struggle against shallow brilliance, which takes the place of inner illumination, a struggle against artificial complexity, which destroys splendid simplicity, and against the pursuit of stilted effects, which disfigure majestic beauty.'[71]

This is how he summed up his contribution to THE THEATRE, how he formulated his artistic credo – a little pompously perhaps, but with complete sincerity. It would take almost a lifetime for Chaliapin to be able to utter such words....

CHAPTER 1

The Road to the Stage

'When God created Chaliapin, he must
have been in a particularly good mood and
created him to bring joy to all.'

Vladimir Nemirovich-Danchenko

FEDOR IVANOVICH CHALIAPIN was born on February 1st (13th Old Style), 1873 in Kazan, the son of a clerk in the district town council. His father, Ivan Yakovlevich (1838–1901), was a peasant who as a young man had left his native village for the city in search of higher wages. There he had to take whatever work he could find, until the local sacristan taught him to read and write and he obtained a position as transcriber of documents. Chaliapin's mother, Avdotia Mikhailovna (1845–1891), was a quiet, gentle and unobtrusive woman, with light brown hair and a pleasant face. She remained illiterate all her life. After her marriage, her time was spent doing housework, sewing and washing for her family and generally making ends meet. 'Thanks to my mother's hard work,' recalled Chaliapin, 'we always had a clean and tidy home, a lamp burned permanently in front of the ikon, and I often caught the look of sorrow and resignation in my mother's grey eyes when she gazed at the ikon lit by a flickering flame.'[1]

Long after Chaliapin had become world-famous, his passport still continued to bear the entry 'Origin: peasant'. In Tsarist Russia, this restricted education and career prospects, as a letter from Rachmaninov to the Director of the Moscow Seminary on behalf of Chaliapin illustrates: 'The artist Chaliapin wishes to send to your seminary his fourteen-year-old brother who, I must tell you, does not know his notes or his alphabet too well, but in my opinion has an exceptional ear for music and is very gifted. The reasons prompting Chaliapin to seek a place for his brother at your establishment are: first, the boy is insufficiently prepared for a special music school; secondly, since this boy is rather difficult, he needs a private boarding school where he will be under constant supervision. However, other private boarding schools, such as a Military Academy, are out of the question, since the Chaliapins are peasants.'[2]

Before going to school, Fedor Chaliapin had been taught reading and writing by an older boy who lived in the same house as he. 'I was quite clever, I had no difficulty in learning, and this made me careless and lazy in my studies ... I kept losing my textbooks, I sometimes sold them to buy sweets, and as a result I practically never knew my lessons....'[3] A report from one of his tutors describes the boy as 'a good pupil, displaying a quick and inquisitive mind.'[4]

All around him, from childhood onwards, he saw nothing but poverty, misfortune, coarseness and gruelling hard work, alternating with bouts of drunkenness and fighting. 'On the whole, I did not particularly resent being beaten, I took it as the normal run of things. I knew that ... everyone got beaten; you always got beaten, morning, noon and night. Beatings were an established part of life, inescapable.'[5]

This gives an idea of Russian life in general, but the word 'beating' recurs like a leitmotif in Chaliapin's childhood memories.

'I was beaten mercilessly. I'm surprised they didn't cripple me as a little boy. I think that this wasn't for want of trying on their part, but rather due to the solidity of my bones....'[6] He is referring to the treatment he received in the cobbler's workshop where he was apprenticed. His father had placed him there after he flatly refused to go back to school. ('Cut me in half if you like, I won't go to that school, I won't!') The teacher was also in the habit of dispensing beatings and 'very painful ones' at that. The cobbler was his godfather, and this might be why 'there was no beating on the first day'. He soon left and went to another cobbler, then to a turner; but all attempts to master a trade came to nothing. The work bored him; his thoughts already ran in a different direction. An article in the American newspaper *The Sun*, published after Chaliapin's death in April 1938, quotes him as saying: 'I could not do the work because I could not keep my mind on the task. I would hit my thumb oftener that I would hit the pegs I was driving into the soles of the boots. I would hear the birds outside and try to imitate them. My ragged clothing would be transmuted into the finery of princes as I stepped before imaginary audiences to sing songs

The room (in Kazan) where Chaliapin was born on February 1st, 1873.

The house in the Sukonnaya settlement (outside Kazan) where Chaliapin spent his early years.

that had never been written. I would hear the applause of the crowd and then I would notice that I had hit my thumb with the hammer.'[7]

All the same, he must have acquired some skills; when he was preparing for his debut at La Scala in 1901, he explained to the astonished theatrical shoemaker exactly what kind of sandals he wanted and how to make them.[8]

Before long he was in trouble with the turner too. 'My master provided vile food. The work was too hard for me physically. My master often took me with him to market where he bought long birch poles which I had to carry home. I repeat, I was skinny. My bones stuck out everywhere, and I was only ten years old. One day, I was carrying the wood home and, having reached breaking point, I dropped the poles, huddled against a fence and started to cry. A gentleman came up to me, asked me why I was crying, and when I told him what it was all about, he picked up the wood and went along with me. When we arrived at the workshop, I was amazed to hear him give my master a good dressing down. "I'll take you to court," he shouted. My master listened to him in silence, but after this kind man had gone he gave me a sound thrashing, yelling "How dare you complain? How dare you?" But I had not complained, I had only said that I could not carry the wood and was afraid of being late for work. When he had finished beating me my master threatened to give me the sack if I ever gave him this sort of trouble again. I shrank away from him.'[9] The boy was then sent to the town of Arsk, which his father had selected because it had a trade school but neither theatre nor any other form of entertainment to distract him.

Chaliapin wanted at first to learn joinery but quickly changed his mind: 'The instructor beat the apprentices, and me more often than most, with any handy instrument or pieces of timber, he did it with set squares and with planks, poked you in the stomach with a plane, hit you on the head with a chisel. I asked to be transferred to bookbinding; the instruments there were not so heavy, and it was less painful to be hit on the head with books than with boards five centimetres thick.'[10]

One of his classmates remembers the Chaliapin of these years: 'An able student, not a bad singer, a good gymnast, a loyal comrade and for a boy of his age quite mature. He soon became the life and soul of our group.'[11] Chaliapin's training was interrupted by his mother's serious illness ('I was sure she was dying'), and he had to return home.

Kazan, situated on the Volga, was already at that time a large provincial town peopled mainly by Russians and Tartars* and renowned in the whole country for its university. It was a thriving business centre with a lively cultural and social life, visited regularly by touring companies giving performances of plays and opera. The Chaliapins had made their home in the Sukonnaya Settlement, then on the outskirts of Kazan. Small, dreary wooden houses, mostly dilapidated, lined narrow, unlit tracks. Visitors rarely came from the town and the inhabitants

---

* Kazan is now the capital of the Tartar Soviet Autonomous Republic.

Kazan at the turn of the century

of the suburbs had no reason to go there. Their way of life was rural and patriarchal, far removed from the bustle of the big city.

Chaliapin's early childhood memories are not associated with Kazan itself – he does not even mention it. The circle of his companions was limited to other boys living in the same poor district. He had few opportunities to come into contact with secondary school pupils or with university students; class distinction separated him from both groups.

The knowledge he managed to acquire was erratic and superficial; to all intents and purposes Chaliapin received no education at all. Despairing of teaching his son any kind of trade, his father decided to find him work where he was himself employed. Chaliapin fortunately wrote a fair hand, and so the thirteen-year-old youth became a clerk. 'We copied voluminous reports with a mass of figures and often stayed late into the night, sleeping on the desks in our office.'[12] Alas, things went wrong again; he was absent-minded and mixed up papers, or even lost them altogether, and on some days he simply did not bother to turn up for work. Finally dismissed from the offices of the local law courts, he roamed the streets, afraid to go home. The Chaliapin family had to bear an additional misfortune: Ivan Chaliapin was a confirmed alcoholic and squandered Fedor's low and irregular wages, as well as his own, on drink. His father's payday – on the twentieth of each month – was a date forever etched in Chaliapin's mind. This was the only day when his mother prepared *pel 'meni* (a kind of dumpling with various fillings). It was a festive occasion all the children* looked forward to, but it also meant that their father would come home drunk and life, which was uneasy enough at the best of times, would turn into a veritable nightmare. 'At first the day would pass without quarrelling, my mother just crying quietly in some corner, but then my father got rougher and rougher with her, until he finally beat her before my very eyes. . . . He once beat her unconscious and I was convinced that he had killed her; she was lying on a trunk, her dress torn, motionless, not breathing and her eyes shut. I burst out crying in despair, and she, regaining consciousness, looked around frantically and then comforted me: "Don't cry, it's all right." After the row, life would return to normal. Father duly resumed his duties at the office. Mother spun, sewed, cleaned and washed. She always sang as she worked, her voice having a peculiarly sad and thoughtful quality. . . .'[13]

The dull and cheerless existence of the Russian people has produced a type of song which is indeed sad and thoughtful. An attentive ear will discern in it many features of the Russian character and way of life. 'From coachmen to leading poet, we all sing mournfully. The Russian song is a doleful dirge,' says Pushkin in his poem 'The Little House in Kolomna'. The manner in which the songs are performed is very distinctive; in

---

*In addition to Fedor (the oldest) there were another two sons and a daughter: Nikolai, Vassili and Eudokia. The second son and the daughter died in infancy, but the youngest, Vassili, who after the parents' death was looked after by Chaliapin, became a medical attendant and died during the typhus epidemic of 1915. We know that he had a fine tenor voice but that he was an alcoholic like his father.

folksong tradition the sound is a means, not an end. Listening to his mother probably provided the only moments of joy Chaliapin knew in early childhood, and many of her melodies later figured in his recitals and recordings. Singing afforded a glimpse into the charms of life, so rare as to be almost unattainable and thus all the more desirable. Chaliapin looked back many years later at the little boy quietly seeking refuge in a dark corner of the *izba*: 'The sad words of the song led me to gentle day-dreaming: I flew over the earth on a fiery steed, raced across the fields through downy snow, I imagined God opening the golden cage of the fire-red sunbird each morning to let him out into the vast blue expanse of the sky.'[14] As far back as Chaliapin's memories went, he always sang.

What else did he remember from his childhood, first in the village, then in Kazan? Not much. He could, like Chekhov, say: 'There was no childhood in my childhood.' Nearby Lake Kaban was his favourite haunt and he spent many happy hours there: in the summer he loved to climb a tree and sit in its branches 'till dawn, like a night bird, thinking about something or other while gazing far out into the lake. The peace and tranquillity put order in my thoughts, took my mind off the awfulness into which life was slowly and lazily drifting.'[15] In the winter there were often scuffles on the frozen lake between Tartars and Russians: first among young children, then older ones, until finally grown-ups joined in. The brawls sometimes degenerated into street fighting with the arrival of new groups of people. The fire brigade once had to come to the rescue and douse the combatants in water. Chaliapin was a regular and eager participant in these battles and the 'experience' was not wasted. He never forgot anything he learnt from life or from other people: he knew that the best form of protection was to let no one come too close, and to hit out first, quickly and efficiently, so that nobody would try again. He also knew that the best form of defence is attack.

In 1913, during a guest performance of *Boris Godunov* at Drury Lane in the presence of the Royal Family, an argument flared up between Diaghilev and the Russian chorus about the payment of their salary. As he was preparing to make his entrance Chaliapin discovered that the chorus was not on the stage. After a brief but stormy exchange, he struck one of its members. Sir Thomas Beecham gives a vivid account of what followed: 'Like a pack of wolves the rest of the chorus flung themselves upon him [Chaliapin], brandishing the tall staves they were to use in the next scene; the small English group rushed to his assistance and the stage-door keeper telephoned for aid to the police station.... Very soon something like order was re-established and Chaliapin departed for his dressing-room, passing through a human corridor of protection in the shape of the British constabulary.' The rest of the performance continued normally, the chorus going 'through the great revolution scene with more than usual fire and enthusiasm'. Chaliapin 'at first declined to emerge from his room, but on being assured that he would be well guarded, finally came out with a loaded revolver in either pocket'.[16] He later commented on the incident: 'My life has not been so sheltered that I don't know how to cope in such circumstances. All this is nothing new, I have been beaten and I have beaten others. In Russia you obviously can't live without fighting.'[17]

The painter Konstantin Korovin, a close friend of his, witnessed another incident. One day, Chaliapin was sitting in his dressing-room at the Bolshoi Theatre, saying anxiously: 'We'd better wait for a while. Let's leave by the stage door. I don't like meeting fans after singing.' 'We went out into the street through one of the side doors used by stagehands and members of the chorus, but nevertheless, in spite of the blinding snow, when we reached our carriage a crowd surged around us. Somebody shouted "Let's toss Chaliapin." [This is a Russian way of showing admiration, the 'victim' being repeatedly thrown into the air.] Two men tried to seize him by the waist and by the legs. Chaliapin ducked, grabbed a third fellow standing nearby, and lifting him up threw him into the crowd. The man hit the pavement and gave out a croaking sound. The crowd dispersed. Chaliapin and I quickly got into the carriage and left. I was amazed at Chaliapin's strength – how easily he had lifted the man and thrown him into the crowd.'[18]

Life in the Chaliapin family grew steadily more wretched and miserable as the years passed. His father found it increasingly difficult to manage the long walks to and from work; his mother had to take menial jobs wherever she could. The children were regularly left to themselves, shut up in a room the whole day. Fedor used to remove the window frame so they could all climb out onto the street and return home in good time before their parents.

One winter, tired out after playing with a makeshift skate-board, Chaliapin wandered into a church to get warm and noticed that some boys of his own age were singing there. In their hands they were holding some strange paper covered with lines. This was his first encounter with choral singing, and he liked it very much. A precentor, who was a neighbour of the Chaliapins, tested his voice and pitch, wrote down some notes and, with a few words of explanation, told him to go and study. 'What a deep pleasure it was to know that there were such things as notes in this world, and that these notes were written in special symbols, unknown to me till then. And I had mastered them! And by looking at this magically ruled paper, I could produce a succession of pleasant sounds.'[19]

He sang in the choir for almost six years, and learnt a great deal in the process. Indeed, this period became the foundation of his vocal and musical education. With one year of singing lessons in Tiflis from September 1892 to September 1893, it represents the sum total of Chaliapin's 'musical universities'.

The church choir, however, was not his only passion; another had grown with him from childhood: the theatre. Chaliapin recalled undergoing his 'first searing exposure to the theatre' when he was eight years old at the local fairground, where he saw a clown called Yashka, famous at the time in the Volga region. His daring tricks, and the knack he had of producing gales of Homeric laughter from vast crowds of spectators, all entranced Chaliapin to the point of leaving him utterly drained. He stood for hours in the bitter cold, unable to tear his eyes away from the show.

Chaliapin, as a rule, never missed anything out of the ordinary; he had a real craving for it. What more telling example of this could there be than his own admission: 'Also I loved fires. They always had a special life of their own and were especially exciting and dramatic occasions. It was already interesting that people were gathering for a fire and not, like the common inhabitants of our Sukonnaya settlement, to decide on such matters as which tavern to go to or whom to beat up – this in itself was enough to make a fire a special treat'?[20]

Naturally his admiration for Yashka led him to think: 'What a man! If only I could be like that!' But what made the strongest impression on the young Chaliapin, what literally transformed his world, was the action taking place on the stage, the playing itself: 'Wouldn't it be wonderful *not to be oneself* [Chaliapin's italics] for a while! And so when at school the teacher asked me something I didn't know, I pulled a silly face. . . . I was aping Yashka and for a moment I had a feeling of "I not being me". And it was delicious.'[21] And when at the age of twelve he happened to find himself in a theatre, his fate was sealed. Nothing could stop Chaliapin, neither his father's beatings nor the gibes of his friends. A casual visit determined the course of his life. 'The curtain came down but I still stayed there, under the spell of a kind of dream such as I had never had before, but had always longed for; I long for it even today. People were shouting, pushing, coming and going but I was still standing there. When the performance was over and they started to put out the lights, I was overcome by sadness. I had pins and needles in my arms and legs. I remember being unsteady on my feet when I went out into the street.'[22]

The theatre 'drove him out of his mind'. Everything around now had to look just as it would on the stage. He did not want to know or take notice of anything else. 'The theatre has always been sacred to me; it was the influence that gave life a meaning, an ambition. . . . What did I find so wonderful there?' wrote Chaliapin in the *Chicago Herald and Examiner* in 1923. 'First, I heard actors speaking with an articulation that was wholly superior to the kind of talk I heard in my daily environment. Second, I heard a new language, a polished form of expression that made me realise there was a value in words, in the way to speak and to express oneself. Third, I saw the actors were better dressed than the people I met in my daily life. I saw that there was a meaning to good clothes, a grace that made one look and feel better. The combined beauty of all this told me that there was a new life.'[23]

Deep down, Chaliapin had decided that this was the right faith for him to embrace. 'On my way home along deserted streets, as if in a dream I saw the streetlamps, few and far between, winking at each other. Stopping repeatedly as I walked along the pavement, I went over the actors' magnificent speeches in my memory and declaimed them aloud, imitating every gesture and facial expression.'[24]

A short time later he saw his first opera, and it made an even stronger impression on him than the theatre. These two experiences can be said to mark a turning point in his artistic growth, and from then on the twin aspects of his talent – singing and acting – ceased to develop along parallel lines and started to converge. He saw that what people said, thought and felt in real life could be expressed in song. 'I was astonished to find that there was a form of life in which people sang about everything instead of speaking as they usually do in the streets and houses of Kazan. I could not help being stunned by this kind of life conducted entirely in song. . . . Good Lord, I thought, what if it was like that everywhere, what if everybody sang – in the streets, at the baths and at work?!'[25]

Young Chaliapin devised a curious game for himself, combining song and vivid, emotionally evocative speech. 'Dreaming of such a fascinating existence, I naturally started to turn my humdrum life into an opera. My father would say to me: Fedka, bring the *kvass* [a very popular drink made from fermented rye bread]. I'd answer in a high treble: I'll brii-iing it right awa-aaay! He'd say: What are you yelling for? Or I would sing: Dad, get up and come and have some tee-eea! He'd glare at me and say to my mother: You see? That's what these "theatres" do to you.'[26] His father may have taken a dim view of this constant speech-and-song playacting, but the unique psychological perception of Chaliapin's modulations as a singer stemmed directly from it.

It is remarkable that even after his son had become an international celebrity, Chaliapin's father could still not come to terms with 'these damn theatres'. In autobiographical articles published by the London *Evening News* in 1931, Chaliapin said: 'I remember bringing my father to the theatre in Moscow when I was playing a big opera and had roles which kept me almost permanently on stage. He came to town and I took him to the theatre, put him in a fine box from which he could see everything and feel utterly at home. I played my best naturally, to show my father what a great man I had become. I was interested to know what the effect upon him would be, as he was seeing grand opera in all its glory for the first time in his simple life. When I went round to see him afterwards I was amazed. He shook his head sadly at me and said: Come now, give it up, my boy! He put his strong hand on my shoulder as I stood before him in my fine robes – imagining myself a resplendent figure. "This is not work, honest work. This is nonsense!" he exclaimed.'[27]

Chaliapin had reached the point where he was no longer satisfied to be just a spectator. He wanted to get behind the scenes, to understand 'where they could get a moon from, where people disappeared to, how a town could be built so quickly, how the costumes were made and where all this bright life vanished to after the performance.'[28]

Why was the attraction so strong? Was it due to the inherent demands of his own talent or to a desire to lose himself in another life, unlike his own? Chaliapin explains his taste for the theatre in this way, but there was an additional factor – it lies in the very nature of the theatre and in the unique opportunities open to the actor. Not just the pleasure, as Chaliapin so precisely put it, of 'not being oneself', the thrilling sensation of 'I not being me'. Of course, each role brings new faces and new surroundings and thus gives good reason for a succession of metamorphoses, but acting on stage is not only a question of entering into someone else's life, someone else's personality. It is not only the fascinating process of exploring the labyrinth of another person's inner world. When an actor assumes a role, he endeavours to free himself from everything which circumscribes his own personality. Acting on stage is a transition, a sally, albeit shortlived, into the realm of freedom. The mere fact that the actor makes this transition from the lowly position allocated to him in real life to a part in the play being enacted on stage is in itself an act of tremendous liberation, but in Russia this process had always been very strictly controlled.

(Long before the Revolution, the question of who would play whom on the stage was not dependent on artistic considerations, and in contemporary Russia this is still the case. Tsar Nicholas I ruled that functionaries would not be allowed to act in a theatre without having first been stripped of their ranks and titles. On the other hand, by appearing as princes, tsars, generals and other high-ranking personages serfs might even gain their freedom. Actors were of no importance at all: only the social masks portrayed on the stage mattered. A famous Soviet actor was once forbidden to take the part of Nicholas II in a film because he had previously been seen in the role of Lenin.)

Young Chaliapin, aspiring to the stage, saw the theatre as a challenge to the bitter but established order of things. It created a genuine brotherhood, a spiritual democracy. Theatrical illusion gave a foretaste of liberty. For him, there was nowhere else to go.

Chaliapin started his career in Kazan (1884–1885 season). Dressed up as a Negro, he was one of a crowd of extras in Meyerbeer's *L'Africaine* shouting loud 'hurrahs' in honour of a certain Vasco da Gama, of whom he had never heard.* His situation gradually improved and he appeared fairly regularly as part of the faceless multitude. Things sometimes got out of hand, as on the day when stage fighting turned into real fighting. 'Chaliapin had the sense to drench the combatants with the fire-hose standing by the front of the curtain ready for use. Victors and vanquished rushed to their dressing-rooms to put on dry clothes. And so peace was restored,' recalled the producer.[29]

While continuing to work as a clerk and earning a little extra money in the church choir, Chaliapin made straight for the theatre whenever he had a free moment. His zeal was eventually

---

* This is what Chaliapin says in his memoirs, but there is also a newspaper interview in which he names Glinka's *A Life for the Tsar* instead of *L'Africaine*. See Yu. Kotlyarov and V. Garmash: *Chronicle of the life and career of F.I. Chaliapin*, Leningrad 1984, vol. 1, p. 23.

rewarded with an offer of the part of a gendarme in a French melodrama. All went well during rehearsals, but at the actual performance he was overcome by stagefright. 'I cannot say how I felt that evening. All I can remember is a series of agonisingly unpleasant sensations. I felt as if my heart was being plucked out, falling away from me, I felt a stab, a sharp pain. I remember that someone opened a door and pushed me onto the stage. My feet seemed to have taken root in the floorboards, my arms were glued to my sides, my tongue had swollen to fill my whole mouth, I had turned into wood. I could not utter a word, I could not move a finger. Everything was swimming before me ... the stage was swaying. I felt I was vanishing, dying. The curtain came down, and I still stood there motionless, just like a stone, until the tall, thin producer, white with rage, began to beat me, tearing my gendarme's costume off me.'[30]

Tortured by shame, Chaliapin hid for two days in a derelict barn and went without food. 'It seemed to me that everybody, the whole town, and even the women hanging out the washing – everybody knew how I had made a fool of myself and been beaten.'[31] He never forgot the incident. Many years later he confided to Tamara Karsavina in Monte Carlo: 'But that was nothing to compare with the good shaking my impresario* gave me after – bang on one ear, bang on the other.'[32] When Chaliapin presented himself for work three days later, he was told that he had been dismissed. As his voice had broken, he could no longer earn anything in the choir. The theatre was closed for the summer and, in any case, Chaliapin could not even think of showing his face there. His father now got drunk almost every day, and his mother, whose strength was rapidly declining, tried to provide for the family.

The spirits of the Chaliapins were very low – nothing went right for them in Kazan, which seemed to be under a curse. They decided to try their luck somewhere else, sold some belongings and set off for Astrakhan, further down the Volga; fate might be kinder there and offer brighter opportunities.

The departure from Kazan signalled a new phase in Chal-

---

*Karsavina mistakenly uses the word 'impresario'. It was in fact the producer.

47

iapin's life. He left behind childhood and adolescence – his most difficult but also in some ways his happiest years. Only one bright prospect relieved the gloom of the future: his artistic aspirations.

Life in Astrakhan proved even harder than in Kazan: there was no work for anyone. After quarrelling with his father, who categorically opposed any of his attempts to find employment in the theatre, and once even tore the score of *Carmen* to shreds, Chaliapin resolved to go to the Fair of Nizhni-Novgorod.* He left his family for the first time at the age of seventeen and embarked on an unsettled period of constant travel. This was the start of a new, independent life, during which he would have to face testing times unaided, resist manifold temptations and try to avoid making too many mistakes – all this with only instinct to guide him.

He earned his living on the way by loading and unloading steamships. When evening came his whole body ached. The ships sometimes carried watermelons. If he bought some bread to go with the fruit, it was possible to hold hunger at bay for a while. In this way, Chaliapin managed to get back to Kazan, where he had a reunion with his friends lasting all night. In the morning, the ship steamed away, leaving Chaliapin behind, asleep. Once more, he had to try and find work and again copy documents for a pittance. In the evenings, if at all possible, he went to the theatre. The producer Nikolai Bogolyubov, who was in charge of hiring the extras for dramatic performances, saw him there: 'This seemingly awkward boy, looking like an ungainly young colt, was genuinely in love with the theatre, or rather was born for it. Whether Fedor appeared as a silent executioner in a maudlin melodrama, a stern *oprichnik*† in the retinue of Ivan the Terrible, or a footman with long sidewhiskers handing a letter to a woman whose lover has just committed suicide because of her unfaithfulness – everything this silent extra did conveyed the art of the theatre at its best.'[33]

And so the winter passed. Early in the summer, an acquaint-

---

* Now Gorky.

† *Oprichnik* – member of the 'Oprichnina', a special force of bodyguards also used for punitive expeditions, under the direct control of Ivan the Terrible.

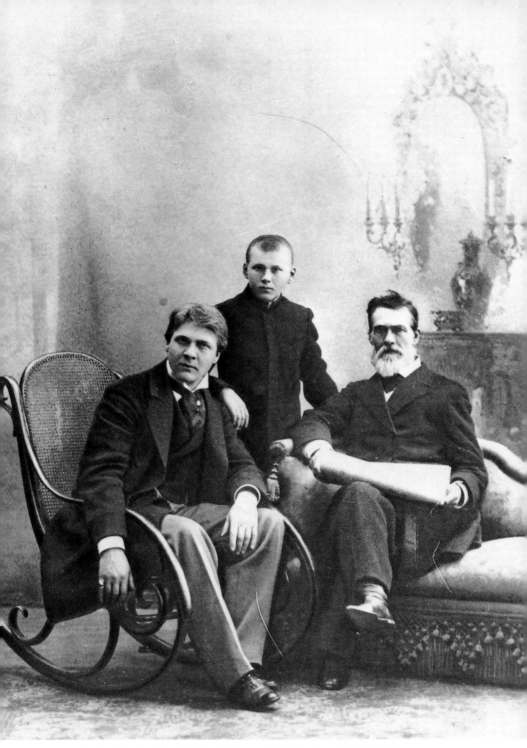

Fedor Chaliapin with his father and his brother Vasili, 1898.

ance told him that the well-known provincial baritone S. Semyonov-Samarsky was recruiting a chorus to perform in Ufa. At Semyonov-Samarsky's hotel, the porter refused to admit 'a certain lanky, underfed urchin'. Eventually Chaliapin managed to get in and had a successful conversation with the impresario. Chaliapin did not lay down any conditions: all he asked was that they should give him something to make it possible to get by 'without being too famished'.

Twenty years later, Semyonov-Samarsky said that he had been deeply struck at the time by 'Chaliapin's sincerity and his uncommon desire to be on the stage'.[34] After the signing of the contract Chaliapin looked like the happiest man in the world. A new life was beginning. He was going to work in the theatre!

He did literally everything: he learned the whole of the repertoire in record time, helped stagehands to put up the scenery, cleaned the lights, climbed up to the flies – he simply never left the premises. 'I lived in the house of a laundry-woman, in a small and dirty basement room with a window looking straight onto the pavement. My horizon consisted of pedestrians' feet flashing past and preoccupied hens taking a stroll. A wooden trestle served as bedstead, with an old thin mattress thrown over it. I do not remember anything about the bedclothes but there was definitely a multi-coloured patchwork quilt. In a corner of the room hung a small flyblown, crooked mirror.' And although at the time Chaliapin considered 'that the theatre is only a diversion', he nevertheless experienced 'the proud and joyful feeling of serving a noble cause – the cause of art. I took my work on the stage very seriously.'[35]

To talk of 'serving the noble (or, as they say in Russia, 'exalted') cause of art' may seem somewhat excessive. Is such grandiloquence appropriate? We are after all only talking about choosing the profession of actor, not about renouncing a throne, wealth or high position in the name of 'serving' lofty ideals of good and justice. But look at almost any book or article written by a Russian theatrical authority, read reviews of performances or even letters from theatregoers, and you will soon find in them a similar attitude. The style and the elated tone are the same. We are not concerned here with the Russians' unrestrained excitability, although it is of course in their nature to give free rein to their emotions, in real life as well as on the stage. No, the point is the special place occupied by the theatre in Russian life, in the mental climate of the Russian intellectual. Few other countries could be found where it is revered almost as a holy place, where it is, as the Muscovites called their Maly Theatre, 'a second university'.

Russian theatre began in the middle of the eighteenth century with slavish imitation of the characters popular on the stages of Western Europe, but found its own national artistic identity in an incredibly short space of time.

A hundred years later one can already talk seriously of distinctive features in Russian national plays and acting. More importantly, the theatre was practically the only form of expression open to the spiritual, moral and even the political aspirations of anyone living in Russia at that time. Like literature, it was, of course, strictly ruled by censorship, but the art of performing itself proved impossible to control. A note of truth can always slip between the lines of a text passed by the ruling powers, thoughts which it is not permitted to put into words, feelings which should not be vented. That is why the relationship between the theatre and society is so complex and often so dramatic in Russia. There, every member of society has to live and work according to what he is allowed to do and what he is ordered to do. His compliance assures the perpetuity of the official world, and he, in return, is accorded the right to be registered in it, counted in it, to exist in it. Relations with the system, with society, assume an irrevocable finality. But art, and in particular the theatre, begins where this agreement ends. What is important for actors is to see what goes on 'inside', explore the causes and origins of the situation, discover what inner force feeds it. Moreover, they want to find out what sort of creatures are swarming around underneath when you lift the lid off this world of transactions, obligations, prejudices, possessions and lies. When the result of such investigations is brought to the stage, an intimate dialogue with the spectator takes place, an occurrence regarded as undesirable and unwelcome by the 'system'. Its established conception of the world is submitted to scrutiny and analysis. Discord arises, and society is sharply divided by reactions of love or of hatred.

Is this another exaggeration? Are such extremes really reached? Surprisingly enough, yes. 'The theatre exuded ill-will, the air was heavy with hatred, and I, obeying the laws of physics, flew out of Petersburg like a bomb,' wrote Chekhov to Nemirovich-Danchenko after the first night of his play *The Seagull* at the Alexandrinsky Theatre. Did Chekhov, understandably embittered by failure, somewhat overstate the audience's response? Not in the least. Nemirovich-Danchenko himself confirms what kind of atmosphere was reigning that day: 'The public was indignant. They were shouting "Curtain!"'[36]

Chaliapin had every right then, at the end of his life, to refer to these years as being spent 'in the service of a cause'. Carrying out this service required no small amount of courage, patience and even abnegation. One had to be able to face hunger, cold, humiliation and endless wanderings with no permanent home. One had to be born an artist to follow this path from an early age without hesitation. But that is not all. When Chaliapin, Stanislavsky and many more of their contemporaries talked of the 'sanctity of art', it was no sensational declaration; they believed in it.

Chaliapin speaks for all of them when he says: 'To me, of course, the theatre is a shrine. I enter its doors as I would those of a temple, with little or no interest as to who may be in the audience.'[37]

It is very revealing to see how Chaliapin increasingly returned to this theme in his interviews, articles and books, particularly towards the end of his life. It would be wrong to dismiss this as the discontent of a passing generation, the inflexibility of old age, partiality or even downright conservatism, since we are not now discussing Chaliapin's views on the art of the theatre itself, nor his aesthetic preferences. These questions will be examined later. What upset him was something else: 'the actor's attitude to the theatre has changed.' 'Actors know nothing about the stage, musicians do not really know about music, conductors have no feeling for rhythm or pauses.'[38]

Were these deficiencies unknown in his day, then? Of course not. Chaliapin willingly admits it. What he laments is the disappearance of honest hard work and the use of early successes for quick financial gains at the expense of further artistic development. His last years were saddened by the realisation that these were no longer isolated cases but a general tendency. It may explain his efforts to be as accurate and as frank as possible in describing his own approach to art.

Things were certainly not easy for him, but success strengthened his resolve. After all, he graduated from member of the chorus to soloist in one season. He sang Ferrando in Verdi's *Il Trovatore* and the Stranger in *Askold's Tomb* by Verstovsky, although this was really only the formal launching of Chaliapin's career. At the end of the season, the Semyonov-Samarsky troupe was disbanded and he faced a new spell of difficulties.

When a touring company from the Ukraine arrived in Ufa,* Chaliapin determined to join it. The director agreed to engage him in the chorus at a miserable salary and they left for Samara,† the town his parents had recently moved to. Chaliapin did not know how his family was, only that Astrakhan had been a disappointment. He found them living in a small room in the corner of a dirty courtyard amongst other destitute people. His father had turned into a wizened old man, broken by life; his little brother was pale and emaciated from hunger; when his mother arrived carrying a begging sack on her back, the full extent of their poverty was revealed to him, and the knowledge that he was powerless to help wrung his heart. Chaliapin could only spend two days with them. It was the last time he saw his mother.

Working conditions in the company were extremely hard. Having to sing in an unfamiliar language (Ukrainian) was bad enough, but on top of that the owner was an unpleasant man who behaved abominably to the artists and cheated them financially.

Chaliapin was eighteen years old. An 1891 review is, as far

* Now capital of the Bashkir Autonomous Soviet Socialist Republic.
† Now Kuibyshev.

as is known, the earliest mention of his name in the press: 'The young and talented bass Chaliapin managed to make us forget his rather indifferent powers of acting.'[39] This life went on for nearly two years, during which time he covered the whole of Southern and Central Russia, mid-Asia and the Caucasus. When they reached Baku Chaliapin decided to quit, but the owner refused to hand over his passport to him, saying, 'I'll give it to you at the police station.' 'I must confess that I was terrified. I knew what sort of treatment people received from the police. And sure enough, as if this was intended as a warning for me, when we got there someone was already being beaten, someone was frantically calling for help, begging for mercy. I was so scared I told him that I did not need the passport, that I would stay with the company.'[40]

One day a telegram arrived at the theatre: 'Mother dead – send money – Father.' Chaliapin was penniless and his employer, to whom he had turned for help, just said: 'Somebody is always dying,' and did not allow him to go to the funeral. Several years later, when Chaliapin revisited Samara, he vainly searched for his mother's tomb. She had been buried in a pauper's grave, without even a cross. . . .

Chaliapin's patience had run out: he stopped taking part in the performances. The company departed and he stayed behind without passport and without work. Things improved for a few weeks while he worked with a 'French' operetta company 'where three or four of the singers were French, the rest Jews and compatriots of mine'.[41] He glibly sang in French, another language he knew nothing of, but thus acquired the ability to reproduce the exact pronunciation and intonation of people of different nationalities and even the sound of their voices. He would eventually perfect this faculty to such a degree that it became one of the most valuable assets of his versatile talent.

Unfortunately the operetta company went bankrupt. Again out of work, Chaliapin was forced to sell his overcoat and to subsist on bread and water. He spent some time among escaped criminals on the outskirts of Baku, singing for them in exchange for food. It was not long before they asked him to take part in a robbery with murder. A refusal was impossible: he would have been taken for a police spy and killed. Chaliapin had to run away and look for a safe place. His situation was desperate; moreover, a cholera epidemic was then raging in the city.

Many years later Chaliapin told a French journalist how he managed to survive this grim episode: 'I was so poor that year that I could only eat once every third day. It was made all the more terrible by the fact that if you didn't eat properly, you would suddenly get a taste of ink in the stomach, give a funny hiccup, wheel round right or left and fall down to blacken the snow, like photographic paper in the sun. Sitting down in front of a dead body, I was hypnotised by a handkerchief in its clenched hand, a hand which was blue-black like octopus spawn. I looked at this handkerchief as if in a nightmare and, crawling close to it, I finally pulled this dreadful scrap of fabric from the peeling hand. And when I opened it, Lord of all the Icons, I found in it four kopecks, do you hear, four kopecks, which made me happier than all the hundreds of thousands of francs I have since earned. I was able to eat and leave for another town where there was no cholera, only the plague.'[42]

The town in question was Tiflis.* He secured an engagement to sing the Cardinal in Halévy's *La Juive*, and Oroveso in Bellini's *Norma* – the latter in Italian, another language then completely unknown to him. He also appeared as Valentin in Gounod's *Faust*. This venture was, alas, equally shortlived. 'One of the artists – the devil take him – stole the wife of the theatre's proprietor, he ran away with her and the whole thing collapsed.'[43]

What was he to do, once more alone in a strange town, with neither money nor work? Chaliapin was used to not eating for two days at a stretch, but now it was three or even four. Time was passing, his strength was ebbing, his hopes dwindling. He went through several periods of great hardship in his life, but this one etched itself particularly deeply in his memory. Chaliapin referred to it many times – occasionally with a touch of bitter humour, as in New York in 1910: 'I almost came to the belief that eating had gone out of fashion'[44] – but usually in

---

* Now Tbilisi – capital of the Soviet Georgian Republic.

more sober tones, as when he appealed in the newspaper *Izvestia* on behalf of famine-struck Russia: 'There was just a void in my torn pockets and I did not even have enough to buy a hunk of bread. I could not bring myself to beg. Something held me back; I was ashamed. I tried to sleep as much of the time as possible; this was the only relief I could find from the unbearable torture of hunger.'[45]

Worn out by failure and privation, he decided to end his life. 'I'll go to a gunsmith, ask him to show me a revolver, and when it's in my hand I'll blow my brains out. I very much wanted to live, but how could life go on like this?'[46]

It was in this state, literally on the gunsmith's doorstep, that one of his Italian acquaintances bumped into him, took him home, gave him food and distracted him from his dark thoughts. He soon found work as a clerk in a railway administration where he copied documents day after boring day.

Fear of hunger never left him. 'His favourite pastime,' recalled Fred Gaisberg, 'was to visit the various food and delicatessen shops and gaze at the quantities of sausages and hams on exhibition. Gazing into food shops continued until the end of his life. . . . The well-stocked shops of Paris, London and New York gave him endless pleasure.'[47] This fear prevented him for a while from taking decisive steps to go on the stage. He could not of course go on resisting forever, and before long he would be on the run again, chasing those elusive theatrical shadows. Or so it seemed.

An offer unexpectedly arrived from Kazan. Chaliapin immediately accepted it by telegram, requested an advance to pay for the journey and handed in his notice at work. Fate, however, intervened, and at the last moment before his departure Chaliapin, on a sudden impulse, paid a visit to Dimitri Andreevich Usatov, a famous singing teacher in Tiflis. At Usatov's door, he was greeted by a pack of furiously barking pugs, who flung themselves at his feet. Behind followed a man short in stature, podgy, his moustache twisted like that of an operetta bandit, so close shaven that his face looked blue. '"What do you want?" he asked somewhat abruptly. . . . I explained. "Well then, all right, let's hear how you bellow."'[48]

In those days, Chaliapin's voice, in his own words, 'roamed around somewhere between baritone and bass'. He sang a few songs for Usatov and then began Valentin's aria from *Faust*, when the professor suddenly stopped accompanying him and sat there without a word. Chaliapin was the first to break the distressing silence which ensued. ' "Well? Could I learn to sing?" Usatov looked at me and answered firmly: "You must." '[49]

Usatov gave Chaliapin free lessons and also financial support. The starving youth, homeless and in rags, needed constant help in every conceivable way. Usatov fed him, bought him clothes, taught him some manners. Chaliapin told one of his first biographers: 'Usatov did as much for me as if he had been my own father. He solved my material problems; not only did he not take any money for his teaching, but he also fattened me up. And I badly needed fattening up at that time. I was so thin from hunger that the emptiness of my stomach showed through my ribs without X-rays.'[50]

Varvara Strakhova-Ermans, who was a pupil of Usatov and became one of Chaliapin's regular partners, draws a picture of Chaliapin as a student in her *Recollections of Chaliapin* published in New York in 1953: 'Usatov was very fond of Fedor and gave him all possible assistance. He managed to get him a monthly grant of ten roubles, which was enough to pay the young man's rent, and took care of the rest – food and clothing – himself. Needless to say, there was no charge for lessons. Our new companion quickly won the hearts of the rest of the class. He was cheerful and pleasant by nature, but when he smiled, he just seemed to radiate joy with his whole being. Usatov played an enormous part in the initial stage of Chaliapin's career. It therefore gives me great pleasure to say that Chaliapin had a deep affection for Usatov and always spoke well of him. Later, after Usatov's death, when his wife found herself in straitened circumstances, Chaliapin continued to support her until she died and always made sure that Maria Petrovna had not been forgotten.'[51]

Chaliapin called Usatov his only teacher, and this was the truth. As mentioned earlier, he studied with him for exactly one year. He was self-taught in everything else.

D. A. Usatov, Chaliapin's singing teacher, 1893.

For all the genius of his pupil, Usatov possessed qualities of fundamental importance in helping to make an artist of Chaliapin. Usatov (1847–1913) had won a silver medal at the Petersburg Conservatory in 1873. He attended the classes of a Belgian singer and teacher famous in Russia, Camille Everard. Everard, who had himself been taught by Garcia and Lamperti, could boast of a long list of celebrated pupils, among them Joachim Tartakov, Nikolai Figner and Fedor Stravinsky (the composer's father). Until he turned to teaching, Everard had partnered the greatest singers of his day, including Patti, Lucca, Tamberlik, Cotogni and Mazzini. He could sing Figaro as well as Mephistopheles and had worked on these roles with Rossini, from whom he earned repeated praise, and with Gounod. The precision and the clear conception of his performances were regularly mentioned in press reviews. Everard expected the same level of achievement from his pupils, and Usatov evidently made the most of his teacher's lessons. A report on his final examination is still in existence: 'The voice (tenor), though not particularly wide in range or powerful, is not lacking in pleasant qualities at times and it is wonderfully produced. Usatov makes superlative use (in pianissimo, mezza voce etc...) of his modest vocal abilities, sings with great proficiency, understanding and elegance.'[52]

Usatov's career began in Kiev and continued in Kazan. There he received the offer of an audition from Edward Napravnik, Music Director of the Mariinsky Theatre in Petersburg. His actual debut on the Imperial Stage, however, took place at the Bolshoi Theatre in Moscow, where he went on working until 1889. During that period, Usatov covered some of the main roles in the tenor repertoire: Faust, the Duke of Mantua (*Rigoletto*), Raoul (*Les Huguenots*), Lionel (*Martha*). Some of Tchaikovsky's operatic roles were created by him: Lensky (*Onegin*), Andrei (*Mazeppa*), Vakula (*Chervichiki*). The composer, who thought highly of Usatov's musical talent, dedicated several songs to him, remarking in a letter to one of his friends: 'Usatov, as always, was quite superb.'[53] After giving up the stage, he devoted himself entirely, like Everard, to teaching and chose Tiflis as his place of residence.

Chaliapin was lucky indeed to receive such expert tuition. Usatov's method combined the tradition of bel canto, inherited from Everard, with a profound understanding of the special style required in the performance of Russian music. Incidentally, when, a year before his death, Everard heard Chaliapin sing, he wanted to greet him as the heir to his artistic traditions but, never having truly mastered the Russian language, could only exclaim: 'Ti maya vnoochka!' (You are my granddaughter!)

What exactly did Chaliapin learn from Usatov, and how? Detailed records of this have been left by him as well as by some of his contemporaries. First of all, it must be said that Chaliapin's voice needed little training. He thought so himself, and many of his stage partners tended to agree with him. In 1931, Chaliapin wrote in the London *Evening News*: 'When I was eighteen I went down to Tiflis to study under Usatov, a great and deservedly famous singing teacher. My voice did not give him much trouble: God had been good to me in the matter of tone, resonance and breathing, but it had always been my ambition to be an actor as distinct from a singer.'[54]

The last sentence belongs to a more mature Chaliapin. He could hardly have had such a well-defined conception of his ideals then. And did he have such ideals? It is curious to note that Chaliapin makes no mention of Usatov's teaching system either in *Pages from My Life* or in earlier recollections published in newspaper interviews – the only reference to it appears in his second book, *Mask and Soul*, some forty years after they met. The reason for this may be that *Mask and Soul* is devoted to Chaliapin's artistic pursuits, his views on the theatre and art as a whole. It may also be that when he wrote it, towards the end of his life, the desire to examine the past and to make general observations based on personal experience was much stronger.

To quote once again the memoirs of Strakhova-Ermans: 'If I am asked whether Usatov taught Chaliapin to sing, I answer yes, but I add that Chaliapin's most precious asset was simply a gift from heaven and came without any studying.'[55]

Sir Thomas Beecham's authoritative voice reinforces this judgement: 'Geniuses like Patti or Chaliapin seem from the outset to be endowed with a natural instinct for singing, acting and all else that has to do with their craft, to which the technical lore of the school has little to add.'[56]

Is it quite so simple? Here is, for instance, a press review from the year 1896, two years after he left Tiflis; Chaliapin, by then an artist of the Imperial Theatre, had gone to Nizhni-Novgorod to sing the part of Mephistopheles in *Faust*. 'Chaliapin's voice, uniform in all registers, with a beautiful timbre, made the strongest impression. The only cause for regret is that at times the singer's voice shows vibrations in the middle register. This is a serious defect; it must be eradicated at the very outset so as not to allow it to grow worse in future. The artist's acting, to be frank, did not show any particular originality, but was nevertheless perfectly adequate and closely followed the conventional manner of representing a character full of negation and doubt on the stage.'[57] As can be seen, the provincial journalist noted a 'conventional manner' and some vocal flaws in the soloist from Russia's best opera house. Such reviews were not rare in the early years of Chaliapin's career. Petersburg critics were even more severe: 'As for Mr. Chaliapin,' wrote the *Peterburgskaya gazeta* on April 27th 1896 after his performance in the role of Prince Galitsky, 'he understood the type of the character correctly (his make-up was bad), but his voice sounded somewhat weak (or more correctly, muted) and he had to force it in order to obtain certain effects. He still has a great deal to learn about singing.'

Chaliapin himself never ceased questioning his own achievements, never stopped learning, searching. He was very much aware that craftsmanship is the real cornerstone of art. 'Whatever position I found myself in,' he declared to the correspondent of the American periodical *Etude Music Magazine* in 1936, 'I tried to observe, to learn from both good and bad examples in the work of others, and, most of all, to relate my work in some way to life itself. Things are going on about us at every moment, which may one day make one better able to tell the story of a young man in love, of an old man who has found his peace, of a restless spirit who has not yet come to port. The singing artist must observe these things and then retell them through his own voice and acting. I learn something new every day – something I have never noticed before – something that will make my next performance better than any of the others.'[58]

The fact that Chaliapin understood and assimilated everything very quickly is quite a different matter. This, his genius as an actor, constitutes the 'gift from Heaven' so often mentioned by those who knew him, although the results he obtained were the fruit of steady and serious effort.

Another contributory factor was his early singing practice in church choirs and in provincial opera theatres. 'He had no need to do years of vocal exercises in order to learn to do passage work, perfect staccatos, or evenly sustained notes, and so on. Once he had surveyed this whole arsenal and familiarised himself with it, he was able to master effortlessly those subtleties which cost others years of hard work. One can definitely say that Chaliapin was born with a naturally trained voice,'[59] asserted one of his partners, Sergei Levik.

Let us now take a closer look at Usatov's methods. Chaliapin said that the 'Maestro' taught him vocal technique in a strict and exacting manner. He showed him how to use his breathing as a bow along the vocal cords. He demanded that the sound be free, without any tension, so that each note would be full and equally audible. He not only explained, he demonstrated in a clear and expressive way. If Usatov suddenly felt that Chaliapin's attention was wandering, he flew into a rage and waved his stick at him, sometimes even hit him, and then normal work would be resumed. Usatov, however, was not just teaching vocalism but rather what can be called the art of the opera singer. 'He broke all the traditional rules of dramatic singing,' says a correspondent of *The Times*, quoting an earlier conversation with Chaliapin; 'he also blasphemed the sacred name of Grand Opera, calling it an idiotic display, a mixture of bad singing and meaningless gestures. He tried to give us instead the principles of new musical and dramatic techniques, to show us the possible development of a new sort of opera.'[60] Chaliapin records that in his practical lessons, Usatov tried to apply vocal technique to the solving of artistic problems, and this was of the utmost interest to him. 'How can one control the breath so as to be able to express in sound this or that musical situation, the mood of this or that character, to give the right intonation to the right emotion? I mean,' continues Chaliapin, 'not musical intonation, that is holding a certain note, but *tone colour* [Chaliapin's italics] of the voice, which assumes various shades even in simple conversation. No one can say "I love you" and "I hate you" in the same tone of voice. In each case there will be a different intonation, or *colour* [Chaliapin's italics], which is what I am talking about.'[61] Once the voice had acquired variety in its tone – what Chaliapin calls 'the right intonation' – Usatov next concentrated on facial expressions and on the use of eyes and mouth to convey the performer's meaning. Acting had to be done not only with the face but with the whole body. He even recommended singing in front of a mirror to study one's face and develop its powers of expression.

Usatov used a selection of musical extracts to impress one thing on his pupils' minds: the art of singing knew no limits in its ability to communicate thoughts and feelings. Chaliapin for the first time formed 'serious views' about the theatre, and this is when his acting skills began to develop. As his insight into the character of widely different types of works deepened, the young singer came to feel a special inclination towards the '*musical* perception and the *musical* expression of the pieces performed' (Chaliapin's italics) – in other words, towards what Chaliapin himself regarded as 'the most precious thing', the art of finding a correspondence between music and actual events, real life or scenes from nature. 'Watch,' Usatov would say, 'how music can act on your imagination. See how eloquent and effective a silence or a pause can be.'[62]

How much would be written in future on the subject of Chaliapin's 'audible pauses' – pauses which did not interrupt the action he had set in motion but somehow temporarily consigned it to 'free-wheeling'! 'If I were asked the secret of his magnificent success, apart from the individuality of genius,' wrote an English critic in 1926, 'I would say that it was his wonderful pauses and his perfect sense of when to do nothing at all. Thus do we get the paradox of a singer's fame based largely on the subtle variety of his silences.'[63]

In contrast to straight theatre, the right to a pause in opera is granted by the composer. In Chaliapin's case, however, a pause on the stage flowed naturally from the circumstances surrounding the character he was playing. At such moments, while continuing to experience Chaliapin's projected emotions, the spectator became one with him, participating in a concentrated creative effort to grasp what cannot be said in words. Levik recalls one of those moments with Chaliapin in the role of the Miller (*Rusalka* by Dargomyzhsky) when a 'dead' pause was charged with an ominous warning of impending catastrophe. 'This effect was exciting for the audience, but you never saw their faces display the smile of satisfaction which subconsciously accompanies the thought "How clever he is! How well he does it!" Certainly this "satisfaction" would distract the audience from participating in the Miller's tragedy and would switch their attention and emotional receptivity onto another plane altogether.'[64]

Earlier successes and the pleasure of coming into contact with the stage now seemed superficial to Chaliapin. It dawned on him that 'real art is a very difficult matter', and he even had doubts about his own capacities: 'Is this right for me? And who says that I am an artist? I made that up myself. . .'[65]

Usatov's lessons, combining the teaching of singing techniques and of acting with general education and aesthetic principles, proved exceptionally beneficial for Chaliapin. They gave his powers an early opportunity of revealing themselves to their full extent. Under such conditions, the various facets of his talent continued to grow simultaneously, to complement each other. They evolved in the form best suited to satisfy the demands of a creative approach to stage work. Although, years later, it seemed to Chaliapin that he 'did not learn much' from Usatov, this was nevertheless a time when he started 'vaguely to see something new. What exactly, I still did not know myself.'

'Something new' meant a totally different concept of operatic roles and opera performance, based on the union, the natural fusion, of various artistic elements on the musical stage. 'Each form of art taken separately constitutes a harmonious whole, but by combining several of them, not only did we not disrupt their individual harmony, we also obtained a beautiful, majestic chord,' writes Chaliapin in 1934 in his article 'A Singer on the Operatic Stage'.[66]

Of course, only in fairy tales can the magician transform someone into whatever he wants at the wave of his wand. In real life, even the most accomplished teacher cannot do this, not even with the most gifted pupil. The development of original creative ability presupposes the revision of all anterior modes of thought and, for the actor, of all prior ways of portraying a character. To augment his potential, an artist has to enrich himself by absorbing new knowledge. Time and a certain amount of experience will be needed before the directives he has received from outside in the form of theory and practice of a given aspect of art can be fully assimilated and become active attributes of his talent. It took Chaliapin three years to reach this point after completing his studies with Usatov.

Usatov made yet another contribution to Chaliapin's evolution: he introduced him to the music of Mussorgsky. It may sound surprising that this should be necessary, but at the time, far from being particularly popular, Mussorgsky was not even well-known. The première of *Boris Godunov* in 1874 on the stage of the Mariinsky Theatre and the first performance of the opera in Moscow fourteen years later (1888) were largely ignored by the Russian public and the critics. The works of one of the world's greatest composers were considered heavy, boring and even harmful to the voice. This opinion stubbornly persisted even after Chaliapin's enormous success in *Boris Godunov* in 1898.

Chaliapin and Mussorgsky – this is a momentous encounter. To Chaliapin belongs the honour and the glory of a complete reversal of opinion in favour of Mussorgsky, first in his homeland and then abroad. We will return later to this point, when considering Chaliapin's approach to Mussorgsky. Let us just say for the time being that Usatov's ardent admiration for the composer provoked a deeply felt response in Chaliapin. 'What Usatov played and sang of Mussorgsky's struck my heart with a strange intensity. I felt that here was something extraordinarily close to me, a kindred feeling. Mussorgsky intoxicated my senses with a strong potion of fragrant homegrown herbs. I felt that this was truly Russian. This was something I understood.'[67]

On another occasion, he gave the following account of one of his first performances in Mussorgsky's opera: 'It was during the Inn Scene of *Boris Godunov*. I was playing the frontier guard. And there, when Varlaam began his pathetic and seemingly absurd song, while the Pretender Dmitri was talking to the Hostess, against a background of orchestral chords, I suddenly felt in this strange music something wonderfully familiar, akin to me. It seemed to me that this same music had accompanied me throughout my chaotic and difficult life. It had always been in me, dwelt in me, in my very soul, and even more importantly, was around me everywhere in the world I knew.'[68]

Chaliapin's discovery of Mussorgsky's works was one of the most significant events in his life. The lengthy preparation their performing style demanded brought about a new phase in the development of the singer's individuality and potential. Chaliapin's interest in Mussorgsky also helped him to define the sphere of his own aesthetic ideas and to orientate his tastes.

The public, together with singers and critics, openly showed that their sympathies were not on the side of Russian opera and that they preferred works coming from Western Europe, particularly Italy. Usatov's repeated attempts to instil some enthusiasm for the works of national composers into his pupils were all in vain. Classmates said to Chaliapin, 'Don't listen. Of course our Usatov is a good singer, and what he says may even be true, but "La donna è mobile" – that's just what singers need, and Mussorgsky with his Varlaams and his Mitiukhas is nothing else than deadly poison for the voice and for singing.'[69]

Chaliapin's doubts tortured him to the point of insomnia. Which was the proper path? 'La donna è mobile' or 'Kak vo gorode bylo vo Kazani'?* For the sake of hearing his voice, opera-goers grudgingly forgave his obstinate determination to sing Mussorgsky, but he faced strong opposition from musical critics, as when a well-known Petersburg musicologist told

---

* 'Beneath the walls of Kazan town.' – The first lines respectively of the Duke of Mantua's aria in Verdi's *Rigoletto* and of Varlaam's song in Mussorgsky's *Boris Godunov*.

Chaliapin to his face that the 'Songs and Dances of Death' were 'an abomination, third-rate lightweight music'. At a time when Chaliapin was already a national celebrity, with his triumph at La Scala to reinforce his fame, a review of his concert in Orel (1901) declared: 'The appearance of Chaliapin on the platform brought forth the sustained thunder of general applause, but Mussorgsky's "Trepak", which he sang, had a strangely perplexing effect on the audience, very close to disappointment, not only with the composer but with the singer as well. Even the number of fine Schumann pieces which were given an encore – "I Wept in My Dreams", "I Do Not Complain" and "The Two Grenadiers" – could not soften this impression.'[70]

Chaliapin quotes the words of the Director of the Imperial Theatres, Ivan Vsevolozhsky: 'At the first sound of a Russian overture, the very air of the theatre starts to reek of vodka....'[71]

It took a firm and unshakeable faith in one's opinions not to give way, not to let the pressure of conventional criteria defeat you. Some sort of natural law even seemed to operate: how often in the history of the theatre have authors and works had to wait for the 'right' performer while the normal process of evolution took its course. Creator and interpreter were involved in a common search, pursuing the same artistic goals. That they would finally meet was unavoidable, but it could take a long time. Then a masterpiece until recently ridiculed by the crowds would enter a new life, as happened with Chekhov's plays, which the world discovered through Stanislavsky, Nemirovich-Danchenko and the Moscow Art Theatre. So it was too with Mussorgsky, whose call was answered by Chaliapin. 'Very few artists,' remarked an American critic forty years later, 'attempt Mussorgsky at all, and Chaliapin seems to have been born for the express purpose of being his priest and prophet.'[72]

All this was as yet in the distant future. For the present Chaliapin worked with Usatov on his first operatic roles, earning a living in the offices of the Tiflis railway administration and slowly amassing the rudiments of an education. His new city friends, young and cultured, introduced him to serious literature, and reading gradually became a necessary part of Chaliapin's everyday life. He also badly needed to acquire proper manners, to learn how to behave in society and hold a conversation. He got his friends to agree that if he did something wrong, they would snap shut their cigarette cases. It would be a warning signal that he should stop and think. He was glad to follow their advice, although at first the cigarette cases snapped almost constantly.

Usatov arranged for Chaliapin to appear at the evenings of the Tiflis amateur Music Society, which awarded him a small grant. He also took part in their theatrical performances, mostly in plays by Ostrovsky. The composer Mikhail Ippolitov-Ivanov has described one of these concerts: 'Among the performers was a young man who looked exceedingly undernourished, so thin and pale that he seemed inordinately tall, with a not very big but very pleasing voice. We were struck by his musicality and the sincerity of his performance.'[73] This was the young Chaliapin. His recital on September 8th, 1893, when he sang excerpts from *Faust* and *Rusalka,* was reviewed in the newspaper *Tiflisski listok*: 'Chaliapin's voice sounded superb, it impressed the listeners by its fresh and soft tones allied to a considerable power and well-defined phrasing. The young singer's acting lacks conviction, it is erratic and uneven, but he moves quite well on stage. Those who saw Chaliapin last winter have been pleasantly surprised by his progress over such a short period. There is no doubt that with some further work on his voice, Chaliapin will not be at all bad in operatic roles. He possesses all the required qualities for this: a sonorous, powerful voice, a musical ear, the beginnings of a dramatic talent, and more important than all the rest, youth.'[74]

These occasions gave Chaliapin a chance to start making a name for himself, to gain more experience of the stage, and, above all, the opportunity to put to almost immediate practical use what he had learnt in Usatov's classes.

In Tiflis he still gave pride of place to the vocal side of his roles. As a result, and in spite of Chaliapin's intentions, other aspects of his talent were rarely displayed in actual performances. They occasionally manifested themselves at moments of inspiration, to his own surprise. So far, however, this was not due to a calculated and controlled act but only to chance.

He first experienced such a moment at an amateur concert during the Miller's scene from the third act of *Rusalka*. The story calls for the portrayal of an old madman in rags, so distressed that he is completely out of touch with reality. On seeing the Prince, who has lost his way while hunting in the forest, the Miller seems to recover his senses for a moment and confides to him that he has been wandering in the dark wood for a long time, lonely, hungry and forgotten by everyone. Chaliapin could not be said to resemble an unhappy old man, and his appearance provoked a smile. But after hearing him sing 'Yes, I am now old and silly, it would be nice if someone could take care of me ...', the public was shaken out of its complacency. 'I remember even today how terrifying, how still the hall became after I had sung this phrase. The applause was deafening and when I had finished, the public even stood up... I was deeply excited to feel that something unbelievable had happened to me, something beyond my wildest dreams.'[75]

For Chaliapin, who tended to be introspective, such exaltation could not pass without leaving a mark and without leading him to reflect on its possible causes. These reflections became a sort of 'intellectual catalyst' and acted as a stimulant to his artistic development. If the practical knowledge acquired on provincial stages had produced any tendency towards stereotyped interpretations, it was luckily not irreversible. Usatov took on a student who had much to learn but, what is more important, was ready to learn and capable of thinking for himself.

A mere three years had elapsed since, with tears in his eyes, he had told his Kazan friends that he would one day sing leading roles on the operatic stage and they had almost died of laughter, but events had proved him right, everything happened as he said it would.

In the autumn of 1893 he was appointed soloist at the Tiflis opera house. The theatrical season lasted for five months, and within that time Chaliapin took part in sixty-two performances and learned fourteen new roles. Since he had entered a reputable establishment without a repertoire, it was necessary to acquire one as fast as possible. Modern singers could not even imagine working at such a pace, but the chronology established by one Leningrad researcher gives convincing enough evidence of the fact: September 28th – Ramfis in Verdi's *Aida*; 29th – Mephistopheles in Gounod's *Faust*; October 1st – Gudal in Rubinstein's *The Demon*; 12th – Tonio in Leoncavallo's *Pagliacci*; 16th – Monterone in Verdi's *Rigoletto*; 22nd – Gremin in Tchaikovsky's *Eugene Onegin*; November 17th – Conte de St. Bris in Meyerbeer's *Les Huguenots*; 23rd – Lothario in Ambroise Thomas' *Mignon*; December 18th – Zuniga in Bizet's *Carmen*; February 6th – the Miller in Dargomyzhsky's *Rusalka* (the entire role); 11th – Tomsky in Tchaikovsky's *The Queen of Spades*; 18th – Don Basilio in *The Barber of Seville*.[76]

The list is not complete; apart from the roles mentioned above, he sang minor parts in a number of productions, but even for these time had to be found for study and at least one rehearsal. In addition, Chaliapin eagerly took part in a number of concerts. They were mostly charity affairs, but all that mattered to him was that he was singing, and not where he sang, although circumstances could at times be rather paradoxical, as for instance when he performed Moses' prayer from Rossini's *Moses in Egypt,* 'Dal tuo stellato soglio': 'Chaliapin sang in Italian', states the newspaper *Kavkaz,* 'while the choir, composed of Italians, sang in Russian.'[77]

The transformation of a humble member of the chorus into an opera singer of great promise was watched with amazement by the Tiflis public and critics alike. Even the *Moskovskaya Teatral'naya Gazeta* (*Moscow Theatrical Gazette*) mentioned the successes of the young provincial: 'Chaliapin made a great hit, and if the lure of easily won laurels does not stand in the way of his artistic development, he will, before long, occupy one of the foremost places in the ranks of outstanding artists.'[78]

Praise for his talent was mingled with concern for the obvious and harmful overworking of a voice which was still unsteady. When he was studying under Usatov and performing in the amateur concerts of the Music Society, everybody was sympathetic towards him, predicting a great future. Now that he was a professional, indulgence could no longer be expected. 'I prepared my roles as quickly as you toss a pancake. Sometimes

I was given a role only the day before it had to be performed. Without previous experience of the stage and any idea of how to behave on it, work done under such pressure and in such a rush would undoubtedly have been both agonizing and damaging for me, but I was already an "old trouper". I knew how to keep my wits about me on stage, and I loved my work too much to treat it carelessly. And although I did not have enough time for a thorough study of my roles, I nevertheless managed to learn them as I went along, at night. I was deeply moved by each role.'[79]

Chaliapin's eagerness for creative work, his intuition, the development of his musical memory, as well as the guidance he continued to receive from Usatov, helped him to master his parts quickly in terms of knowing the score and singing more or less on cue in the ensembles. It did not always come off. Here is how a critic viewed Chaliapin's performance in *Les Huguenots*: 'On that particular evening his remarkable musicality let him down: rough passages, excessively open notes next to soft, muted ones, produced an unpleasant impression.'[80] The same critic also had severe words about other interpretations: 'As Mephistopheles, apart from vocal shortcomings, he did not even come close to giving a likeness of the character; in *Pagliacci* he either grossly overacted or else played at being a demon.'[81]

Chaliapin then had a predilection for the role of Tonio in the latter work. As he himself said: 'It suited the range of my voice, and I played the part quite well. The opera was regularly performed and always with great success.'[82] Critical remarks usually have little effect on the public's enthusiasm; whatever a small group of experts may say makes no difference. Chaliapin was no exception: applause, flowers, women shouting 'bravo' till their throats ran dry – he had it all. 'I must say ... that whatever I did, I did for Woman, to win her attention, her love....'[83] Luckily he understood that this was not enough and gradually became more disposed to heed his friends' advice and to go to Moscow, if not to enter its Conservatory, then at least to try himself out on its stages. The cultural climate and traditions of that city would be useful to his rising talent.

Articles were occasionally written by some well-known personalities whose judgement carried weight far beyond the confines of Tiflis, as for instance when Fedor Komissarzhevsky, a leading figure of the Russian operatic stage, friend of Dargomyzhsky and Mussorgsky, came to a performance of *Aida*. 'The High Priest [Chaliapin] turns into a page carrying Amneris' train, and his free and easy way of moving brings to mind a hero of operetta.'[84]

At that time, Chaliapin did not devote much thought to the portrayal of characters, especially with regard to their outward appearance. He was just as casual about this as any other opera singer of the day, and there was still no sign of the extraordinary make-up artist he would become later when his work, on the strength of psychological expressiveness alone, could bear comparison with any other form of visual art. This early carelessness does not seem entirely attributable to lack of skill. It is probable that Chaliapin did not then feel the need to flesh out his creations into full-blooded people or to make them valid in real-life terms. So, naturally, he was not interested in recreating their faces, manners, behaviour, way of walking or other external features. Chaliapin still faithfully followed the beaten track in operatic matters and was far from being a 'revolutionary'. 'My first Mephistopheles in the Tiflis opera (1893) did not then shrink from tinsel effects, and sparks darted from my eyes.'[85]

Nevertheless, Chaliapin's musicality and beautiful voice largely compensated for any other defect he may have had. Would he now rest on his laurels and enjoy himself after such long periods of deprivation and wanderings? Strange as it may seem, success and recognition, which should engender propitious conditions for further growth, often have the opposite effect by giving rise to unexpected subjective difficulties. Inventiveness and energy can dissolve when ambition is sated. The fire burns out, the search is abandoned. Promise and talent are soon reduced to mere craftsmanship. But truly great men are more inclined to be dissatisfied with themselves and with their own achievements. Chaliapin showed this trait early on in his career and it became a major factor in his work. Throughout his life, whenever fate presented him with several courses, he unerringly and clearsightedly chose the one most likely to benefit

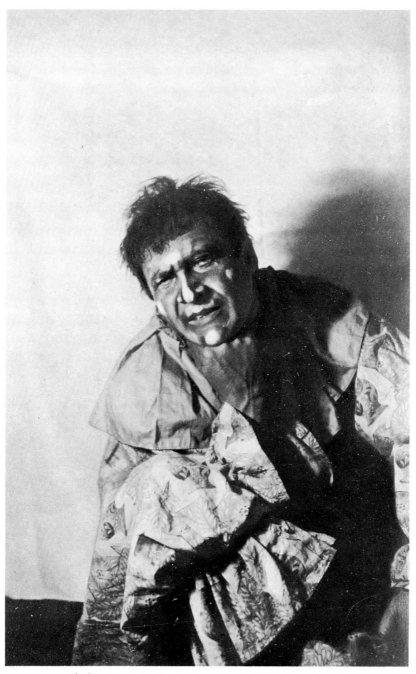

Chaliapin as Tonio, in Leoncavallo's *Pagliacci*, 1918.

his artistry. A clear mind and an iron determination to aim at genuine originality helped him to steer away from anything which, though tempting, might have held up his progress. One must also not forget that in Tiflis he had exacting friends who had high expectations of him. His teacher, Dmitri Usatov was certainly one of them.

At the end of the season, the theatre management decided that as Chaliapin had been a 'greater asset to them than anticipated', they would offer him a benefit performance.* 'I decided at once on two operas: *Pagliacci* and the whole of *Faust*. I was as hardy as a camel and could sing around the clock.' The evening was a great success. Chaliapin was presented with a gold watch, a silver cup and three hundred roubles in cash. 'Usatov removed the words "To Usatov" from a ribbon which had been awarded to him previously, wrote instead "To Chaliapin" and brought it to me with a garland. . . . This made me very proud.'[86]

What next? He no longer wanted to go to the Conservatory. The theatre, Petersburg and Moscow – that was another matter, especially now that the 'dream of a trip to these cities definitely made practical sense'.[87] Chaliapin had some grounds for thinking that he could establish himself there.

In the spring of 1894, Chaliapin left Tiflis, parted with his girl friend, who had refused to accompany him, and set off for Moscow. He had a little money and a letter of recommendation from Usatov to the management of the Bolshoi Theatre. He was not travelling alone; another of Usatov's students went with him in search of success. They had to go as far as Vladikavkaz by horse-drawn carriage, and onwards by train to Moscow. Although Chaliapin was only twenty-one years old, it was not the first time he was embarking for an unknown future. Life had been unkind to him before, and he was not afraid of hardship.

The two young singers tried to arrange some concerts on the way. In Stavropol they were in luck and even managed to make

---

* This meant that the singer could give an extra performance of a work chosen by him and receive part of the profits.

some money, but on the train Chaliapin was lured into a 'little game of cards' and lost nearly all of it.

Moscow, which Chaliapin had intended to 'take by storm' gave him a cool, it might even be said hostile, reception. The administrative director of the Bolshoi Theatre, P. Pchelnikov, did not even receive him, keeping him waiting in his anteroom for two hours. Others (including the principal conductor, Yosif Altani) were more courteous, but still reserved. To perform on the Imperial Stage one had to pass an audition, and this could not be done in the summer; everything was closed. Chaliapin's past successes in Tiflis were of no account here; many others like him arrived every day and all with letters of recommendation from someone or other to someone or other. So, for the time being, there was no hope. He walked around the Bolshoi Theatre, enthusiastically surveying the massive building, or else he climbed a hill overlooking the city. 'From up there I admired the grandeur of Moscow which, like everything else in the world, seemed more beautiful from afar than close to. I would sit there in solitude and think about myself with anxiety and sadness, reminiscing about my past life, Tiflis, where I had spent many happy hours, and a girl, to whom I wrote long letters but whose replies were getting less and less frequent. I was not lucky with the first love of my youth. But what was the point of my sitting there brooding? Apart from which I could not afford this luxury.'[88]

Acquaintances arranged an interview with a theatrical agent. Chaliapin handed him a pile of Tiflis press reviews and stage photographs and sang a few arias. His voice made a favourable impression and, within a month, Chaliapin was invited to meet a new impresario: Mikhail Lentovsky, a former actor of the Maly Theatre known in theatrical circles all over Russia. He was forming a company to play in the Arcadia Gardens of Petersburg. Lentovsky interrupted him in the middle of an aria from *Don Carlos* and there and then offered him an advance of one hundred roubles and the role of Dr. Miracle in Offenbach's *The Tales of Hoffmann*, which he sang in Petersburg a few weeks later, together with Susanin and Mephistopheles. The performances did not manage to attract large audiences and the

Chaliapin as Bertram in Meyerbeer's *Robert le Diable*, 1894.

venture quickly collapsed, but the press singled out 'the beautiful basso cantante of Mr. Chlyapin'[89] – at this stage of his career
his name was not infrequently misspelt.

In Moscow, when nothing else had been in sight, Chaliapin
had signed a contract for the Kazan winter season. The offer
had seemed tempting. After all, it was his home town. What
was he when he left it, and what would he return as! Now,
however, he had no wish to leave Petersburg. 'I liked the wide
streets, the electric lights, the Neva, the theatres, the whole way
of life.'[90] Then someone told him about a new company being
formed for the Petersburg Panaevsky Theatre. According to
Chaliapin, this was 'a remarkably uncomfortable theatre, but
well attended by the public'. The music director of the project,
Truffi, whom Chaliapin had already met in Tiflis, recommended
the young singer and he started work immediately. The Tova-
richestvo (Company), as this association was called, opened on
September 18th, 1894. One of the leading Petersburg newspapers
wrote: 'Mr. Chaliapin (Mephistopheles) has a pleasing bass.
His voice seems to be lacking in strength; towards the end of
the performance it sounded tired (in the church scene and in
the serenade, which however was encored)'.[91]

The repertoire of the theatre consisted of popular operas. All
that was required was that the music should be familiar and
the performance conventional. He would hardly learn anything
there, but work was regular and varied and he began to attract
attention. He met well-known musicians, many of whom took
a genuine interest in his fate. Among those mentioned by Chaliapin is Vassili Andreev, a great expert in Russian folksongs
and founder of the orchestra of Russian folk instruments named
after him, which is famous to this day. Andreev vigilantly
watched over Chaliapin, who still needed to learn many things.
He had no idea how to dress; when he was invited into people's
homes he did not know how to handle his knife, fork or napkin
or how to eat without a great deal of noise. The lessons in
social graces of the previous year in Tiflis had evidently been
insufficient.

The growth of Chaliapin's potential talent was fast acceler-
ating at the contact with Petersburg's intellectual and artistic

circles. 'This world was new to me. Its beauty pervaded my heart. They painted, sang, declaimed poetry, argued about music. I watched, listened and greedily took it all in.'[92]

Once awakened, this veritable passion for improving his mind never abated as long as Chaliapin lived. He quickly and steadily filled the gaps in his education by reading, going to exhibitions, listening to and watching other people. He thoroughly investigated anything which aroused his curiosity, and the depth and range of Chaliapin's erudition began to surprise his acquaintances. Yuri Yurev, a well-known actor from the Alexandrinsky Theatre, remembers a conversation with him which suddenly turned to the subject of Turgenev: 'Chaliapin spoke of his works and their character with such deep understanding of the period in question, he had such a keen perception of everything, that you could not help thinking when you looked at this man who was supposed to have only a thin veneer of culture: where does he get it from?'[93] Sergei Levik came to the same conclusion: 'We all knew that Chaliapin had received very little formal schooling and we considered that in terms of general culture he was not particularly refined and was relatively uneducated. My personal conversations with him led me to form a totally different impression. As is well known, Chaliapin did not, like the rest of us, spend his childhood and youth poring over textbooks. Although he had made no special study of literature, he was extremely well-read. His thirst for learning knew no bounds. Once, suffering from the after-effects of an unsuccessful operation for some infection of either the upper jaw or the nasal cavity, he gave such a detailed account of the progress of his illness, delivered such a lecture on the anatomy of the face, that the resident doctor of the Narodny Dom [a theatre in Petrograd* where Chaliapin often sang], who happened to be present, was reduced to a shrug of helplessness. But Chaliapin could be equally enthusiastic and well-informed on the subject of vegetable growing. He absorbed everything he heard as a sponge absorbs water and all his knowledge was labelled and stored away as tidily as in a conscientious apothecary's shop. He was

---

* As Petersburg was called after the onset of the First World War.

able to produce it on demand with the greatest of ease and it was always to the point.'[94] 'He had a surprising grasp of branches of man's knowledge,' noted Sol Hurok.[95]

It was not just a provincial's curiosity for the celebrities of the capital which made Chaliapin gravitate towards interesting and original people. Such meetings stimulated his powers of observation and of invention and benefited his whole make-up. Whatever the strength and vitality of his nature, however his innate attributes break through and manifest themselves, every human being, especially if he has a creative imagination, is to a large degree shaped by encounters and clashes with others. All friendships, keen interests, struggles, discoveries and losses imperceptibly deposit layers on a man's soul, like the rings of a tree. In this sense, the history of an outstanding figure is, in addition to everything else, the history of the people close to him at various times of his life. Chaliapin's remarkable friends influenced almost every aspect of his personality in its formative years.

Who can say to what extent he would have developed without this 'comprehensive' art school, where there was only one pupil, Fedor Chaliapin, but many tutors, each a master in his own field? Admittedly Chaliapin himself set up this 'school' for his own benefit, actively seeking the company of those who might be useful to his evolution. There again, Chaliapin sharply differed in attitude from many other performers of his (and our) times, stubbornly immured within their narrow professional environment and confining themselves to the discussion of parochial issues and concepts. 'The more I looked at gifted people, the clearer it became to me that everything I knew was insignificant and that I had much to learn,'[96] confides Chaliapin in his memoirs. He continued to enlarge the circle of his acquaintances diligently for many more years, even after universal recognition and adoration had been given to him. Anything showing genuine talent had an irresistible attraction for him and whenever he came across it, he was truly happy. 'It used to be said in Moscow,' reports his friend Ivan Bunin, 'that Chaliapin was drawn towards writers not by the love of literature but by his desire to acquire the reputation of being not only a great singer but also a man of progressive ideals. But it seems to me that Chaliapin did not seek our company out of self-interest. I remember, for instance, how keen he was to meet Chekhov, how many times he talked about it. I, of course, asked him: "What stops you from doing it then?" "What stops me," he answered, "is that Chekhov does not show himself anywhere, I never have a chance to meet him." – "For heaven's sake, why wait for a chance! Take a cab and go." – "But I don't want him to think me rude. And anyway, I know that I'll feel so shy with him that I'll probably look like a complete fool as well. But if you could possibly take me to him ..."

'I did so without further delay and could see for myself that all this was true: when he met Chekhov he blushed to his roots and started to mumble something. ... But when we left the house he was absolutely delighted: "You won't believe how happy I am to have finally met him and how taken I am with him! What a man, what a writer! From now on, all the others will seem like asses to me." "Thank you," I said, laughing. The whole street resounded with his loud guffaw.'[97]

Chekhov for his part liked the young singer and, to the end of his life, whenever the opportunity arose, enjoyed spending time in his company. One can say that they became friends.

Chaliapin was interested in various forms of art and tried his hand at several closely related skills, spending a great deal of time composing poetry and drawing. His improvised stories enjoyed great success. 'To hear him,' recalls a contemporary, 'was a real pleasure. This side of his genius has remained in the shadows, although early in his career, when working in Petersburg, young Chaliapin was on good terms with a very high-ranking court official and well-known Slavophile, Tertii Filipov; it was through him that he met Vladimir Stasov, an equally fervent supporter of Russian talent. Both men listened spellbound to Chaliapin's storytelling, remarked on it and tried in every way to encourage him to persevere with it.'[98]

Press articles started to notice the increasingly natural and true inflections in the singer's voice. 'The public found something original in my way of performing. I was talked of in society as a singer who must be heard.'[99]

Chaliapin at the beginning of the century.

The first and most significant changes showed themselves in concerts and not in opera where, as Chaliapin himself admits, he continued to 'go for stereotyped dramatic effects'. These concerts often took place in private houses. The circle of his acquaintances was rapidly widening; little by little he was making a name for himself and no longer felt out of place. He still remembered one of these occasions, even to its date, some forty years later and described it in *Mask and Soul*: 'There was a big soirée at Filipov's on January 4th, 1895. All the big names sang there. A young boy who had just arrived in the capital played the piano. It was Josef Hoffmann.... I sang Susanin's aria from *A Life for the Tsar*. Glinka's sister, Madame Shestakova, was in the audience and paid me the most flattering attention after my performance. This soirée played an important role in my destiny. Filipov's name carried great weight in the capital ... My performance in his house made a certain impression and rumours of my successes reached the Imperial Theatre. The management called me for an audition.'[100]

He chose the invocation from *Faust*, 'Il était temps! Sous le feuillage sombre ...' The principal conductor of the theatre, Edward Napravnik, was a reserved and laconic man not known for the generosity of his praise, and he listened to Chaliapin without a word. Shortly afterwards, however, the young singer was invited to give a second audition, this time for the Directors of the Mariinsky Theatre. He performed Ruslan's aria and the scene from *A Life for the Tsar*. Ruslan was clearly not well received, but Susanin made a good impression. The leading tenor of the theatre, Figner, came up to him, shook him firmly by the hand, 'and there were tears in his eyes'. Chaliapin was 'offered a contract the next day and became a member of the Imperial Theatre Company'.[101] But that was not all. Chaliapin would have to go through three débuts. If the public and the critics liked him, the contract would take effect. If not – it would be cancelled. These were the rules, and anyone who wanted to be a soloist at the Mariinsky or the Bolshoi had to submit to them. Finally, on the third of February, two days after Chaliapin had celebrated his twenty-second birthday, the contract was endorsed by the Director of Imperial Theatres, Ivan Vsevolozhsky. The document contained fourteen clauses; in each one of them two ominous motifs recurred with regular monotony: 'the management is entitled to . . .' and 'the artist undertakes to . . .' Paragraph five, for instance, stated: 'Chaliapin undertakes to sing without question and at the first request of the management all roles which he is instructed to learn, whether he is to be their sole performer or alternating with other artists. The management alone has the right to assign roles and will neither allow objections to its decisions nor accept refusals on the part of the artist to perform a new role, or one which has already been sung before by another artist, on the pretext that the part is either too high or too low for his voice. The artist also undertakes to perform the role in a manner that accords with the management's instructions.' It was further explained that 'the time allocated to study a role (from one to three weeks) is at the discretion of the management, and the artist does not have the right to raise objections in this matter. If a part has not been learnt by the appointed date, the artist will be liable to a fine of one fiftieth of his entire yearly salary for the first scheduled performance of an opera, as well as for every subsequent postponement he has occasioned.' Moreover, Chaliapin '[did] not have the right to absent himelf from the city for even one day without the written permission of the management, and even if he [went] out of his house, he [had] to leave a note indicating where he could be immediately found.' He was also forbidden to sing outside the premises of the theatre without the written agreement of the management, or to be ill for more than six weeks (and even then, only subject to examination by the management's doctor). Otherwise his salary would cease to be paid until he was fully recovered. Naturally every misdemeanour or act of insubordination was punished by a fine.[102]

Chaliapin would make his debut in *Faust*, on April 5th, 1895, together with two other newcomers. One of them, Ivan Vasilevich Ershov (1867–1943), eventually also became an outstanding operatic singer. Ershov is unfortunately now quite forgotten outside a narrow group of specialists interested in the history of music theatre, although during his lifetime he was no less famous than the great bass, and contemporaries referred to him as 'a Chaliapin among tenors'. Various press reviews commented on the event: 'The third [debutant] was Chaliapin, who was deservedly the most successful. He had to repeat both of Mephistopheles' arias at the unanimous request of the public. We have many times remarked on the quality of this young and talented artist when he was appearing with the ill-fated Panaevsky Company, and we have always pointed out that his place was on a big stage where he would not have to exhaust himself by working every day. Chaliapin has now entered the haven which all artists long for, and we wish him well; his is a really welcome addition to the Mariinsky Theatre. But there another extreme must be avoided: he should not be left completely free of work, as can happen . . . .

'His pleasant voice had a good sound. Chaliapin was, however, weaker in the church scene; he is still unfamiliar with our large stage and with the acoustics of the auditorium. But all this will come with time and with practice. He possesses everything necessary to be fully accepted by the public.'[103]

Another review, although it refers in fact to a later date (the season ended in April, so his second performance as Mephistopheles took place on September 4th), throws a light on Chaliapin's beginning at the Mariinsky Theatre: 'Chaliapin does not perform the role badly where he has an opportunity to let his voice shine, but it is too soft for the part of Mephistopheles; the phrasing of the characteristic recitatives lacked expression and a tone of sarcasm. He interpreted the rondo of the Golden Calf and the serenade with taste and without unnecessary emphasis.'[104] The evening had gone quite well for Chaliapin; most important of all, his voice had pleased everyone. Nothing else was mentioned – there was probably nothing particular to mention for the time being. The next public test took place two weeks later, on April 17th, when Chaliapin sang Ruslan in *Ruslan and Ludmilla*; the third and final one followed on April 19th with the role of Zuniga in *Carmen* which he had already sung in Tiflis.

The management pronounced, albeit with some reservations, that the débuts had been satisfactory, and the contract became

Chaliapin, 1895.

effective. Chaliapin's happiness knew no bounds. 'Just think of it, me, Fedya the tramp, all of a sudden an artist of the Imperial Theatres,' he wrote to a friend in Tiflis.[105] And yet, within a year he would leave the Mariinsky Theatre, giving up what for many was – and for him had seemed – an unattainable dream. Why? Chaliapin answers this question unequivocally in his two books, or at any rate he tries to set the record straight as he sees it. 'What struck me more than anything else when I joined the Mariinsky Theatre was the fact that it was not, as I had naively imagined, the most talented artists who administered the company, but a number of strange people, some with beards, some without, dressed in uniforms with golden buttons and blue velvet collars. Civil servants. As for the deities whose ranks I was joining with a feeling of reverence and joy, they were for the most part people who always sang the same words: "Yes, sir!" at the top of their voices.'[106] Nor did these civil servants restrict their activities to the propagation of 'military discipline and an atmosphere of fear'. Chaliapin says that, like evil spirits, they also interfered with professional matters. Everything had to follow the established pattern. No change, no creative initiative, was allowed. 'I attribute the complete failure of my first attempts to work on the Imperial stage not to anybody's ill-will, but to the dead hand of bureaucracy.'[107]

The last statement is very curious. His attempts ended in failure, and Chaliapin openly admitted it? What is more, every further reference to his fiasco in the roles of Ruslan and Count Robinson (Cimarosa's *Il Matrimonio Segreto*) was calculated to convince us of that fact. He goes so far as to thank Fate for his discomfiture: when all was said and done, it did prevent him from thinking too highly of himself and forced him to be more careful in the preparation of his performances . . . .

The most extensive research has not revealed any other admission of failure. On the contrary, it was something he could not stand, even when joking with friends, playing cards with his children or fishing in the country to relax. At the mere mention of it, he would fly into an uncontrollable rage and take some time to recover. 'He was extremely vain,' says his daughter Lydia Chaliapina, 'and at the same time as impatient and demonstrative as a child. One day ... he invited me to play billiards with him – there were no other games at hand. I was about thirteen then and very keen on billiards. I spent every minute of my spare time competing with my brothers and sisters. "Shall we play?" asked my father nonchalantly, and he added, without waiting for an answer: "I'll give you a twenty-point start, shall I?" "Yes, all right," I answered, taking no chances. I beat him. Then he got very angry indeed and declared coldly: "I did it on purpose, just to be polite." He could not resist adding: "And you play badly." His eyes were not at all kind: they were even unfriendly and had turned "white". He was accustomed to being first, always.'[108]

How then did he feel about rivals? 'When Adamo Didur's impresario started to advertise him before his first visit to Russia as Chaliapin's only equal in the world, Fedor Ivanovich was very upset,' recalls Sergei Levik. 'I was singing Rangoni in Didur's performance and I well remember how during the intervals people close to Chaliapin were reporting, not without astonishment, that Chaliapin was perturbed and was constantly quoting from memory reviews praising Didur. Although he spoke highly of Didur, he nevertheless kept repeating someone's quip that "eagles can stoop lower than chickens, but chickens will never reach the clouds." '[109] It is hardly accidental that when he dwells on his reverses and the bureaucratic, stifling atmosphere of the Mariinsky Theatre, Chaliapin does not name a single one of his colleagues. Nor does he mention them when, three years later, he returns to the Imperial stage in Moscow. Strange that he 'did not notice' Fedor Stravinsky, or Ivan Ershov, Maria Slavina, Ekaterina Mravina, Nikolai and Medea Figner or Leonid Yakovlev. Not a word about Antonina Nezhdanova or Leonid Sobinov, Evgenia Zbrueva or Joachim Tartakov. It would be easy to add more names to this roll of artists who truly represented the pride of the national theatre and were also widely known outside Russia. Chaliapin devotes only one sentence to them in his memoirs: 'The Imperial Opera could not boast of a galaxy of exceptional singers of either sex at any one time, but nevertheless our Russian singers included in their ranks some first-class representatives of the art of singing.'[110]

Chaliapin as Nilakantha in Delibes' *Lakme*.

These anonymous masters of the operatic stage are given grudging and qualified praise – they are only 'excellent vocalists', although quite a few of them were not just singers but artists of the music theatre as Chaliapin understood the term. Some were worthy partners of his; others had prepared the ground for him, and without them his art could not have blossomed. Yes, Chaliapin was destined to be the most striking example of the Russian performing tradition, but this tradition was not new; it had been forming for decades, only he did not want to admit that the time spent on the Imperial stage had proved in any way instructive. And he was neither the first nor the only one seeking to bring about changes; one of his most notable precursors, apart from Fedor Stravinsky, was Nikolai Figner.

According to the conductor Ariy Pazovsky, 'Figner created on stage life-like characters with real, well-defined features and strong passions. Figner's attention to the psychological colour of sound, his consistent efforts to use the spectrum of his timbre wisely, economically and with the most careful deliberation, to a considerable extent anticipated the brilliant "eloquent timbres" of Chaliapin.'[111] There were also similar, though less striking, attempts by others.

Much of what Chaliapin said about the power of civil servants was certainly true: dozens of memoirs by singers, composers and conductors expressed the same views. But it would be hard to find a government-subsidised opera house anywhere in the world where the artist is master of the situation and where the interests of art are given free rein without outside interference. In Russia, at any rate, such a theatre does not exist and never has.

The high standards of the Mariinsky and its huge international repertoire made it one of the best opera houses in Europe. Chaliapin's declaration that the theatre's productions consisted only of 'false notes and varnished mediocrity' does not tally with the opinion of many of his contemporaries. If we are to believe Chaliapin's account, the Czech director of the Mariinsky stage, Yosif Palichek, was a complete idiot. Chaliapin portrays him as a philistine, a ridiculous character notorious for his poor, even comical command of Russian, but who nevertheless took it upon himself to give advice to native speakers. It is equally unlikely that Palichek rudely interrupted Chaliapin when the latter tried to change the interpretation of Mephistopheles in *Faust*. In the spring of the same year, Chaliapin went on tour to Nizhni-Novgorod, where no one seems to have interfered with the free expression of his artistic concepts. The reviews, however, were far from enthusiastic. One of them has already been mentioned in this chapter, but there were others. 'It was just unbelievable, looking at Mephistopheles, that this was the same Chaliapin.... Where had the fine, deliberate phrasing gone to, the skill in showing off his voice, in displaying its best features? There was nothing of this. Just a man walking around the stage, singing to himself. I was assured that he was conserving his voice for the serenade in the fourth act, but this proved not to be the case. The serenade was sung like all the rest – coldly and barely audibly.'[112]

Palichek evidently had nothing to do with Chaliapin's dissatisfaction. Daniil Pokhitonov, who conducted at the Mariinsky for many years, gives an altogether different picture of Palichek: 'I visited him at home when he was rehearsing singers, and I frequently witnessed to what lengths he went to explain the scenic elements of the role performed. I remember Palichek's words which he often repeated when he was working: "First of all, the idea must be there. From the idea comes the facial expression, the characterisation and the gestures; the idea enhances word and sound, imbuing the phrase with the proper expression."'[113]

Palichek's productions raised the standards of the theatre. The fact that some of them, such as his *Prince Igor*, are still performed on the stage of the Kirov (previously Mariinsky) Theatre, makes it obvious that Chaliapin's judgement of this experienced and talented director was lacking in objectivity. 'Things went from bad to worse at the theatre. Various Czechs [Palichek and Napravnik] flatly stated that if Chaliapin were given a role, it would be a "downright disgrace". I deserved this attitude to a certain extent, as I had sung Ruslan badly.'[114]

This account of the situation is given in both versions of his first book and repeated in *Mask and Soul*: 'I sang the performance, but I made a bad impression on the public. For several days afterwards I was simply ashamed to walk in the street or enter the theatre.'[115] According to Chaliapin, another inadequate performance followed with the role of Count Robinson ('neither the opera nor I had any success'), and the consequences were not slow to follow. Chaliapin was given only small parts. Hopes for the future seemed to him practically non-existent, and if his colleague Mikhail Koryakin, who was to sing the Miller in *Rusalka*, had not feigned illness in order to help Chaliapin, things could have continued like this for quite a long time. The theatre reluctantly agreed to the casting change, and the disaster everyone had been expecting turned into a triumph, whereupon the management's attitude towards Chaliapin improved abruptly. (Calling Koryakin 'a real friend, such as one unfortunately too rarely meets in life',[116] Chaliapin nevertheless could not refrain from mentioning that when he sang Tchaikovsky's vocal trio 'The Golden Cloud Has Rested' at a concert with Koryakin and another singer, 'Koryakin pronounced the word "quietly" so loud that the glass rattled in the window-panes.')[117]

Chaliapin attributed his success purely to chance, insisting that none of the theatre's directors had paid proper attention to him and that no one regretted his departure. However, an entry in the hitherto unpublished diaries of the Mariinsky's principal producer, Grigori Kondratev, quoted by the Leningrad theatre historian Abram Gozenpud in one of his books, testifies to the very opposite. 'The bass Chaliapin has left, a gifted young artist who promised to be a worthy successor to Stravinsky.'[118]

The version Chaliapin gives of his beginnings at the Mariinsky Theatre is so convincing that it has been repeated in book after book, article after article. It has also been used as an argument in assessing the artistic standards of the Imperial stage, all the more so after the Revolution, when a negative attitude towards such institutions was encouraged. Until recently there had been no attempt to cast a doubt on what he said or even to verify the facts. The Soviet establishment does not willingly submit to analysis, and what would be the point of it anyway, since Chaliapin himself explains the causes of failures he is the first to admit?

But things are not quite what they seem. To start with, the majority of his contemporaries do not bear out Chaliapin's self-critical tale of 'disgrace' as Ruslan. Kondratev's diaries[119] contain several references to Chaliapin. Here is his assessment of the singer after his début: 'Chaliapin is an excellent addition to the company. He is not a basso profondo, but a true basso cantante; although his lower register is weak, the voice has an overall pleasing timbre and will get stronger if toned down in the middle. His phrasing is very good and he has a natural gift for the stage, where he conducts himself with intelligence.' Another entry, after the performance of *Ruslan and Ludmilla*, reads: 'Chaliapin is a very good Ruslan. He is still young but is quite out of the ordinary as far as exercising self-control and making a pleasant sound are concerned. I believe he has a future.' Pokhitonov's testimony also refutes the story of disaster: 'Chaliapin sang superbly – how could it be otherwise: his voice was beautiful and full of charm, and that's the main thing in such a difficult role as Ruslan. One could certainly see that he had not completely mastered the role. At times Chaliapin behaved in a "non-Ruslan" manner, but there is no question of calling this a fiasco. Say what you will, Chaliapin's Ruslan already showed evidence of the future artist of genius.'[120]

Critics too voiced certain reservations, but they did not in any way consider Chaliapin's Ruslan a failure. On the whole their disapproval centred not on the singing or the musical side of the performance but on his lack of confidence on the stage, his acting. 'Mr. Chaliapin, although he has still not completely mastered the difficult part of Ruslan (its tessitura is too high for a bass and too low for a baritone), promises, however, to conquer it with time: his voice is most engaging. If we take into account the youth of this artist, who has studied under the famous Moscow tenor Mr. Usatov, there is every reason to hope that with hard work Mr. Chaliapin will eventually occupy a prominent place in our company: he is very gifted and has a beautiful voice. Applause followed his singing of the aria "O my field, my field. . . .*' '[121] 'Chaliapin showed serious shortcomings not only in his singing but in his acting. The very appearance of the artist offends the eye: skinny, slouching, his arms dangling like bits of string. Chaliapin will have to take himself seriously in hand and exercise strict self-discipline.'[122]

This renders suspect Chaliapin's assertion that everybody, including the newspapers, declared his performance worthless. What they all mentioned was his as yet unfulfilled potential, in which everyone believed, and the fact that the role had not been sufficiently prepared or learnt (Chaliapin only had two weeks to do this). But even the sternest reviews were not purely negative; they expressed concern for the future of the young singer: '. . . We expected something more consummate, more polished from Chaliapin, who has so far not fully come to grips with the difficult role of Ruslan: there are mistakes not only in his acting but also in his singing; he shows signs of hesitation everywhere, even in the rhythm. What we have here is still only an outline of what the role should really be. We do not want, however, to let such a performance force us to the conclusion that Chaliapin does not work hard any more, although there is already sufficient ground for doing so; to appear like this on the classical stage, in the classical role of a national hero, is not acceptable.'[123]

One can easily imagine the reaction of the proud young singer; even an experienced and well-established artist would find such a review wounding. Whatever had happened? Was the critic showing bias in the excessive harshness of his judgement? Was Chaliapin simply off form on that particular day? Or were there some deeper reasons lying behind the difficulties he had with the role? It is interesting to note that Chaliapin repeatedly returned to the subject of Ruslan, saying to his friends and acquaintances that he had been afraid of the high tessitura of the role. Both Telyakovsky[124] and Korovin[125] confirm this in their memoirs.

One would think that Chaliapin knew best, but we must once again beg to doubt the accuracy of what he said. Firstly,

* First words of Ruslan's aria.

Chaliapin's repertoire contained roles with higher notes than Ruslan, as well as roles with a similar tessitura. He sang various baritone roles throughout his life: Germont père in *La Traviata* as far back as 1891 in Baku; the Demon in Rubinstein's opera of the same name and Tonio in *Pagliacci* during his Tiflis period and later at the height of his career. 'The scarcity of suitable concert material for the bass voice', writes the newspaper *Novoe vremya* on June 26th, 1895, 'compelled the singer to undertake such a thing as the Prologue to Leoncavallo's *Pagliacci*, written for baritone. To everyone's surprise, Chaliapin acquitted himself of his task superbly: clear diction and the ability to sustain beauty of sound and sonority in a high tessitura carried his interpretation far beyond the limits of the ordinary. . . .'

He even sang Onegin* and although, theatrically speaking, the character did not come off, 'the vocal side of the performance was faultless. In spite of the part's high tessitura, which even for a baritone is not always straightforward, Chaliapin sang with extraordinary ease, without effort, giving his magnificent voice its full power. The aria in the garden brought forth a storm of applause and was given an encore.'[126]

Secondly, this talk of tessitura looks very much like an explanation devised for the benefit of others; but Chaliapin himself was not satisfied with it. 'There were many times afterwards when I would have liked to sing Ruslan,' he wrote thirty-five years later, 'but each time I found hundreds of good reasons for avoiding the part. I felt that something eluded me in the role. I can't to this day explain exactly what.'[127]

His disappointment would seem to stem from the personage of Ruslan himself, whose symbolically heroic nature did not offer enough depth of character for Chaliapin, not enough psychological complexity or intensely dramatic moments of conflict.

He certainly needed to work on his vocal skills; there was much to learn and much to digest, but the singer's picture of 'regular fiascos' is not convincing.

Other contemporary evidence casts further doubts on Chal-

---

* Chaliapin performed the title role in Tchaikovsky's *Eugene Onegin* only once, as part of a gala night at the Bolshoi Theatre on February 2nd, 1905.

Chaliapin as Count Robinson, with N. A. Friede as Fidelma, in Cimarosa's
Il Matrimonio Segreto, 1895.

iapin's self-appraisal: 'It is hard to say now, after an interval of
some sixty years, how total was Chaliapin's control of his voice.
(He of course only developed his miraculous mezza-voce with
time.) But when Chaliapin says that his musical competence
was then 'inadequate' and that he did not yet know how to
sing, he is not being quite truthful. His young bass voice sounded
enchanting in *Robert le diable* (Bertram); and in *Christmas
Revels* (Panas); in *Dubrovsky* (Prince Vereisky) and in Cimarosa's *Il matrimonio segreto* (Count Robinson); in all the small
roles entrusted to him at the beginning, and in major parts too,
such as Mephistopheles.'[128]

The sharp note of discontent running through the section of
the memoirs devoted to his first spell with the Imperial Theatres
can be ascribed to a totally different kind of failure; it is not a
question of stage disasters. And anyway, there were no disasters
for him. Kondratev noted down after the first night of *Il matrimonio segreto*: 'Only the aria of Count Robinson (Chaliapin)

and the duet between the Count and Geronimo (Chaliapin and Koryakin) brought forth any applause.' The press also reacted favourably: '. . . Chaliapin upheld the general high standard as the bridegroom/count, but the outward appearance of his fop was neither typical nor original enough. On the other hand, he was in total command of the vocal side of his role.'[129]

There are no complaints about the musical or vocal aspects of Chaliapin's interpretation; on the whole it is again the acting which is regarded as unsatisfactory. Thus, for instance, his performance as Zuniga in *Carmen*: 'Chaliapin was feeble in the role of the lieutenant, in which he was obviously imitating Stravinsky's excellent interpretation.'[130]

'He sang beautifully,' wrote Yurev, who regularly attended Chaliapin's performances, 'but one must say quite candidly that he played badly: he did not know how to use his body or how to move, and one could sense a certain constraint while nevertheless perceiving flashes of genuine originality.'[131] 'If he was not entirely successful in these parts,' discloses the contemporary source already quoted earlier, 'it was not from lack of singing ability but from inadequate acting.'[132]

This stage of his life, full of professional low points and errors, was the harbinger of the vast theatrical reforms which Chaliapin would accomplish before long. He was evolving a whole new concept of operatic acting, although his innovations had not yet reached full maturity. A purely vocal approach to his roles no longer interested him, but he had so far not managed to find more comprehensive forms of interpretation. This urgently demanded the rejection, both conscious and categorical, of all the artistic principles used by the old school of performing. Since he did not know how to achieve his aim, or even how to formulate it, Chaliapin went through an agonising period of crisis. The trouble was that he himself still remained an artist of the old school and had still not found other ways of playing his roles. The conflict between the traditional methods of acting employed at the theatre and the need for a new approach to the preparation of roles hampered his first attempts in that direction. Preoccupation with finding ways of improving his acting skills had an adverse effect on his singing and on his powers of concentration. He became confused and his confidence on stage gradually crumbled. 'I was close to yielding to a cowardly loss of faith in my talent,'[133] recalled Chaliapin many years later. 'And so when I occasionally – two or three times in one season – had to perform roles which I later made mine, my best roles, such as Mephistopheles in *Faust* or Prince Galitsky in *Prince Igor*, I tried to depart from the tedious stereotyped manner of presenting them, but as I was unable to do this really well, I unwittingly produced a somewhat grotesque effect. I was, as they say, "feeling" my way to a new approach, and naturally, it was not easy. In trying to avoid a predictable routine gesture, I perhaps made one which was strange or awkward.'[134]

'Something had gone from my mind, and it went blank. It was like walking along a lovely, wide road; I had suddenly reached some sort of crossing and did not know which way to go. I needed something, but precisely what? I did not know.'[135] It was therefore convenient to accuse the Mariinsky Theatre of every kind of deadly sin, and to draw a veil over certain events. When, in his memoirs, Chaliapin looked back on the far-off season of 1895, he did so from the pinnacle of his career, and it then suited his purpose to turn even relative successes, or at least normal stages of progress, into failures. At the beginning, Chaliapin had only 'felt an instinctive aversion for all that is stereotyped in operatic performances'.[136] This later turned to positive hatred, and the rest of his professional life was devoted to fighting what he considered to be the greatest enemy in the theatre. He could not compromise with 'enemies', as the numerous and widely publicised 'Chaliapin scandals' testify. Most of them were occasioned by his dissatisfaction with some artistic point and were an active expression of strong protest against trite performances.

Working on the Imperial stage convinced Chaliapin that in itself singing, even of the most accomplished kind, was not enough to make a real character out of an operatic role: 'You see, I know some singers with fine voices; they have wonderful control; I mean they can, at a given moment, sing loud and soft, piano and forte, but nearly all of them are just singing notes to which they affix syllables or words. They sing beautifully, take a high C from the chest, pure and smooth, unfalteringly and apparently effortlessly, but if these delightful singers have to sing several songs in one evening, it is practically impossible to detect any difference between them, whatever they are singing about, be it love or hatred. I don't know how the ordinary listener reacts to this, but personally, after two of them I get bored with the concert.'[137]

The extent to which Chaliapin's future pronouncements on the art of opera were elaborated during this period in Petersburg is difficult to determine. Unhappy as he was with his work at the Mariinsky, it nevertheless helped his talent to mature. Perhaps one should bear in mind the fact that an artist of genius, as against a merely gifted one, however great he may be, must be original. The garment already worn by someone else is not for him; he cannot adapt it or copy it; he needs something completely new. The work of others – predecessors or older contemporaries – can only slightly part the curtain concealing the future art he is destined to create. For this he will have to rely solely on his personal conception of the world in general and of art in particular. Imitating another singer held no attraction for Chaliapin; it might have in the early days of his career, but to do so as a rule would have been tantamount to death since it would mean denying his individuality. He couldn't bear to take part in the ready-made productions of the Mariinsky Theatre, where rigid antiquated tradition ruled. His nature uncompromisingly demanded to be allowed to go its own way, although everyone told him, 'Look, lad, don't keep speaking out of turn and annoying people. Stop acting the fool and just get on with the job. The more quietly you get on with it, the further you'll go.'[138]

Ideas are all very well, but in the theatre any novel formula needs, at the very least, to be seen, to prove itself and be given concrete expression. Making fresh demands is not too difficult, but carrying them out is a much more complicated matter. First of all, Chaliapin had to find new techniques and new working methods to assist him.

The dramatic stage offered the closest approximation to

Chaliapin's objective of creating theatrical characters as organic entities. Acting had attracted him from an early age; improvising stories had given him a chance of perfecting his gift of impersonation; from now on he would study 'authenticity on the stage from Russian actors'. He had already been spending all his free evenings at the theatre rather than the opera in Petersburg, and continued to do the same in Moscow later. 'I drank in every detail of the way our greatest actors and actresses played their roles.'[139]

Chaliapin became a regular visitor to the Alexandrinsky Theatre.* 'We were so used to seeing him backstage,' said one of the leading actors, Konstantin Varlamov, 'that when he did not come we felt something was missing.'[140] Chaliapin gained insight into the art of portraying a character by questioning actors who seemed particularly interesting to him. His attempts at uncovering the secret of transforming oneself on stage were untiring. He wanted to discover how this could be applied to his roles and so fulfil his 'most cherished dream of performing opera not just as a singer but as an actor as well'.[141]

The young singer felt strongly drawn towards straight theatre. 'Many times I seemed to be ready to give up opera and turn to the dramatic stage. I say "seemed" because this was of course a mistaken impression. I felt the attraction of the theatre with all my soul.'[142]

At one time or another in Tiflis, and later again in Petersburg, Chaliapin had noticed something important: whenever he managed to enter into the life of his character, the vocal phrase became a logical means of expression. Translated into the hero's words, it communicated his state of mind. But how could one maintain this throughout a whole performance? How could one learn to impart the psychological authenticity of human thought and feelings to one's singing voice? How could the performer use his voice to convince the audience that they were seeing not just a singer in costume and grease paint, but the projection of a real, living person?

---

* Alexandrinsky Theatre (now Pushkin Theatre), where successive generations of the most distinguished Russian actors have appeared.

One of the most interesting and original actors of the Russian theatre, Mamont Dalsky, had a particularly marked influence on Chaliapin. We cannot, unfortunately, dwell here on Dalsky's career; suffice it to say that the young singer saw in him the personification of his own artistic aspirations. Dalsky, whom Chaliapin called 'a Russian Kean because of his talent and his dissipated way of life', was a very intemperate and unbalanced man. He was uncompromising in his views and in his conduct, often abrupt and even rude with people, but on stage he displayed 'the power of a tragic temperament' and this, together with his very subtle psychological character studies, brought the public back to see him again and again. Dalsky's voice was unusual and unique, wonderfully musical, 'with certain old-fashioned accents'. 'In the modulations of his voice, in its nuances, the slipping from pathos into artlessness, lay the strength of the impression he made.'[143]

Chaliapin moved to the hotel where Dalsky was living and spent his days – and sometimes also his nights – with him. It would be wrong to think that they devoted their entire time to talking about art or professional matters. Neither of them missed any opportunity for a drinking bout and they were both very fond of women. They led a boisterous and carefree life, not parting company with other young actors and opera enthusiasts until dawn. Their friendship, incidentally, survived for many years and ended only with Dalsky's untimely death in a stupid accident when, in 1918, he was killed by a tram just after leaving Chaliapin's house.

Dalsky helped Chaliapin to take a critical look at himself. They lived in close proximity for about a year, during which Dalsky instilled into the mind of his young friend the necessity of devoting long hours of mental effort to the preparation of a stage performance. Dalsky explained various methods of building a theatrical personage, how essential it was to behave and think in character. He also showed him how to move on stage, how to exercise control over his body so as to make his gestures expressive and to the point. An acquaintance of Dalsky's remembers once visiting his room to find him and Chaliapin 'half naked and wearing cloaks'. 'Dalsky now spread out the folds of his cloak, now draped himself in it; the cloak came to life in his hands. It did not work for Chaliapin, but he stubbornly, meekly went on trying to do the task he had been set over and over again.'[144] One can surmise that it was Dalsky who made Chaliapin see the need to moderate the impulses of inspiration. While the actor is creating a stage personality, he must also stand aside and watch it perform. This may have been the period when his powers of insight started to unfold and when he understood how to apply them to his work. Dalsky always bore in mind the fact that he was giving advice to an opera singer, not to a dramatic actor. Like Chaliapin at that time, he regretted that 'singing could not express as much as spoken words' and joined in his attempts to find a way of 'combining opera and drama'.

It must be said that Dalsky hated opera and regarded it as an inferior form of theatre. Nevertheless, he undoubtedly speeded up Chaliapin's development. Of course, many other opera singers before Chaliapin had been gifted actors, but in most cases this was a sort of 'accompaniment' to their vocal talents. An operatic performer was first of all a singer, then, when not actually singing, an actor. It did not enter his head at all that he should give particular thought to the character he was portraying, let alone think 'in character'. Using their voices to express conventional, symbolic feelings of passion, anger, jealousy, etc. was enough for them; they ignored the dramatic aspects of the role; and as for blending the music and the acting together, it was not even considered. Chaliapin was never content to treat the singer and the actor as separate entities. He wanted to base his interpretation on the music, practical experience reinforcing his conviction that to portray a vocal character otherwise was impossible. His acting, singing and musical talents were by now ready to merge and only required that link to be forged which could weld them together.

One day, in a conversation with Dalsky, Chaliapin mentioned that he was uneasy about certain aspects of the part of the Miller, where the character seemed to 'slip away' and the role became 'colourless'. To Chaliapin's surprise, Dalsky asked him to read out the text of the Miller's first aria. 'I read it aloud.

All correctly. With all the full stops and the commas – marking not only grammatical pauses but logical ones as well. Dalsky listened right through and said: "The intonation of your character is false – that is the secret. You deliver the Miller's admonitions and reproaches to his daughter in the tones of a petty shopkeeper, but the Miller is a solid fellow, owner of a mill and some land besides." Dalsky's remark pierced me like a needle ... Dalsky's words were in tune with my own vague feelings. Intonation, the shades of meaning imparted to a word – that's what it was all about. The whole power of singing lies in the correct intonation and nuancing of words and phrases! Intonation ... Isn't that why, I thought, there are so many good singers in opera, but so few good actors?"[145]

This was a wonderful discovery for Chaliapin. Inflection was nothing else than the artistic core of the art of singing. Those innumerable psychological nuances were what distinguished it from the competent, practised vocal exercise. An indispensable part of the singer's transformation on stage was that his inflection must match the character's state of mind at any given moment. Perfect control of this had to be mastered before one could attempt to lend one's own voice to someone else's inner feelings. At the same time as realising the importance of inflection, Chaliapin began to appreciate its creative potential. His conviction grew that finding a character's mental state comes only with profound insight into the way he feels and thinks. The musical, acting and vocal elements, combined in true psychological intonation, brought nearer the realisation of Chaliapin's main objective: the indissoluble fusion of acting and singing. 'It is almost impossible', said the *Wiener Zeitung* in 1927, 'to separate Chaliapin the singer from Chaliapin the actor. Each works for the other. Where the singer ends, the actor begins and vice-versa. They are usually both on stage at the same time....'[146] 'He differs from most of his colleagues', wrote an English newspaper in 1914, when Chaliapin was appearing in London, 'in insisting that the actor's first duty is personation. He is not content to show himself in the limelight in easy contempt of the part which he pretends to be playing. He knows that the material of an actor's art is himself, his voice and his gesture, and he handles this material with a courage and variety which place him high above his fellows.'[147]

These articles show Chaliapin as a master of his art. He had by then elucidated his method of work and put it to the test many times, although the quest had been long and painful. But even at the beginning of his career, 'the discovery of intonation' did not escape the notice of the public. In his book *Chaliapin*, published in 1915 in Petersburg, Edward Stark recalls the memorable performance of the Miller he had seen twenty years earlier: 'It was all the more striking because it was quite unexpected. As soon as Chaliapin started singing, the audience pricked up its ears. There was something new in the very sound of his magnificent voice which completely filled the huge auditorium, freely, easily. Success was already assured with the first act. And after that ... we saw for the first time what sort of artist he was. There must be a divine spark burning in him; why has it been smouldering under a bushel so long and burst into flame only now?'[148]

The 1895–1896 season at the Mariinsky Theatre was drawing to a close. The success of *Rusalka* had consolidated Chaliapin's position and he was offered the part of Holofernes in Serov's *Judith* for the following year – 'a difficult and challenging role, unusually powerful. The bait was very attractive, but fate obviously had something different in store for me.'[149] Chaliapin was on the point of leaving Petersburg to spend the whole summer out of town working on the new opera, when in May he suddenly received an invitation to sing with Savva Mamontov's Moscow Private Opera in Nizhni-Novgorod, where the All-Russian Trade, Industry and the Arts Fair was to take place.

Mamontov himself, and the enormous role he and his theatre played in the singer's destiny will be discussed in the next chapter. Chaliapin had no idea then how all this would affect his future career. The very name of Mamontov and his work in the Private Opera were quite unknown to him. He regarded the offer simply as an opportunity to sing a series of major operatic roles, to test his powers in productions where there was more freedom, without the restrictions imposed by conservative traditions; or perhaps he remembered the youth who, five years earlier, wandering penniless and hungry in Astrakhan, had decided to go to the Nizhni-Novgorod Fair to find work in a choir or as a storyteller in a show. At the time, nothing had come of the project.

Chaliapin arrived in Nizhni-Novgorod in May 1896 and, after renting a small room from an old woman, went to look at the town. 'Countless masts, steamers and barges crowded the approaches to the city, and the Fair gave out such a loud cacophony of noise as could only be dreamt of before the invention of radio. At the Fair, the bright colours of Russia mingled with the many hues of the Islamic East. The life of the big bazaar was unrestrained, cheerful, wild; I loved it all!'[150]

The trade fair was the occasion for a lavish programme of cultural activities. Apart from the Private Opera, artists from the Moscow Maly Theatre* as well as a group of singers from Petersburg headed by Nikolai Figner would be appearing. There were plans for symphonic concerts, the opening of an art gallery, spectacular ballets, a gypsy chorus and a circus, and many more traditional Russian fairground entertainments.

Engulfed in a whirlpool of new experiences, Chaliapin soon found new friends and new interests. When ballet dancers arrived from Italy to join the Private Opera, Chaliapin ran all over town to help them find lodgings. 'I remember to this day the wonderfully cheerful hubbub the Italians brought to our theatre. Everything they did, their gestures, intonation, movements – all was so different from anything I had ever seen before, so new to me! Not one of them understood a word of Russian and they were all like children. It seemed to me that my temperament was closest to that of the Italian. I too could yell, guffaw and speak with my hands tirelessly.'[151]

Jolly, energetic, fond of joking and laughing, Chaliapin indeed resembled the ebullient Italians in character. Mutual sympathy grew stronger every day, although the foreign visitors never managed to remember his difficult name. They simply

---

* Opened in 1824 and still in existence. One of the greatest theatres in Russia (the other being the Alexandrinsky Theatre in Petersburg), it played a major role in the development of Russian dramatic art.

called him 'il basso'. One of the ballerinas in particular attracted Chaliapin's attention. She was called Iola Tornaghi. He made no secret of his admiration for this beautiful Italian girl, manifesting his feelings openly and vigorously. 'Being totally ignorant of the Russian language', remembered Tornaghi many years later, 'we had difficulty in understanding our colleagues and they communicated with us mainly by gestures and grimaces. Chaliapin was particularly trying. No sooner had we appeared in the theatre than he rushed towards us, the sides of his jacket flapping in the air, laughing loudly and gesticulating in an attempt to strike up a conversation with us. By evening, my head was swimming with his "efforts" and towards the end I and another girl, if we saw him coming, would shriek "il basso" and hide in the nearest corner.'[152]

When Tornaghi fell ill and did not come to the theatre for a few days, Chaliapin made some chicken broth and set off to visit her. 'He explained, as always by gestures, that it would do me good and that it all had to be finished up. This touching "chicken Nizhni-Novgorod" has forever remained in my memory.'[153]

Before long, during one of the rehearsals for Tchaikovsky's *Eugene Onegin* when no outsiders were present, he made his sentiments clear in a very original way. The Petersburg ball scene was in progress, Chaliapin singing the part of Prince Gremin. 'I was listening attentively. Suddenly, in the middle of an aria, I had the feeling that he had sung my name – Tornaghi. I decided that it must be some Russian word, similar to my name, but all those present in the auditorium started to laugh and to look in my direction. Savva Ivanovich [Mamontov] leaned towards me and whispered in Italian: "Well, Iola, congratulations! Fedyenka has made you a declaration of love." Only much later was I able to understand all of Fedyenka's mischief: he had sung: "Onegin, I swear it on my sword, I am madly in love with Tornaghi...." '*

She was not the only reason for his cheerful mood. The young singer was literally enchanted by Nizhni-Novgorod. An

---

* Chaliapin, taking liberties with an aria whose words are familiar to every Russian schoolboy, had substituted the name of 'Tornaghi' for that of 'Tatiana'.

extraordinary atmosphere reigned in the theatre among the members of the troupe, who would help each other at rehearsals to try to find the most expressive and valid mise-en-scène, and worked together on their make-up and costumes.

Mamontov was always present. Tactfully, never giving any orders, he made pertinent and constructive remarks on the characters, the style of interpretation and the sound of the singers' voices.

Nearly every performance in which Chaliapin took part turned into an extra rehearsal. He made constant changes, cutting here some details, there a whole scene which had so far seemed satisfactory. His obsesssion with pace drove the conductor, Truffi, to exhaustion: he made him check the length of the pauses over and over again, quicken or slacken the tempo. Konstantin Korovin witnessed one of their conversations. 'Fedya, if we were to do everything you want, even if it all turned out perfectly as a result, it would demand such strenuous efforts that afterwards we would have to go to hospital.' Chaliapin said a great deal more and ended with, 'You know, I still can't explain it. It's all right in one way, but all the same, in fact, it's wrong. Everything is wrong. It needs to be "felt". You see, everything is fine, but the flowers have no perfume. You yourself often say when looking at a picture – wrong! Everything has been done, every line drawn and painted – and it's wrong. The scent is still missing. You can admire the workmanship, wonder at the hard work put into it, but love it – no. The bull and the ox work hard, they labour twelve hours a day, but they're not artists. An artist spends his whole life thinking, but works for perhaps half an hour, and he achieves what he wanted ... if he is an artist.'[154]

Chaliapin's performance in the Private Opera attracted a great deal of attention, although, as the reader knows, some comments were unfavourable. These did not deter Chaliapin and he continued to learn avidly as he went along. When he heard Mamontov discuss the merits of Vrubel's paintings, he was quite amazed. He listened attentively, but in his heart he was not convinced. How much he preferred a beautifully drawn apple-tree, especially when it looked exactly like a real one and under it on a bench sat a dashing young man with a girl. ('What a smart pair of trousers! I must get some just like that.') Chaliapin instinctively understood that his perception lacked subtlety, that his culture and his tastes were not sufficiently developed. 'Why, I asked myself again and again, do I feel this way about things, whereas someone else, obviously cultured, intelligent and knowledgeable about art, feels differently?'[155]

When he could spare some time from work he wandered about the town, observing life all around. There was much to remind him of Kazan. The Volga, the men working at the docks, the local accent and the songs – all was the same. As in his childhood, he went to the fair, closely observing the rich variety of people, their ways of walking, of dressing. Everything he saw deeply engraved itself in his memory and would later be used on the stage as a telling detail, perhaps as a gesture or perhaps in his make-up.

This was the sort of life he could understand and to which his heart responded. Korovin remembered going with the singer to a riverside inn. ' "Look at my Volga," said Chaliapin, pointing to the window. "I love the Volga. People are different on the Volga. They're not pennypinchers. Everyone seems to live for money, but on the Volga money is for living." It was clear that this tall, expansive young man enjoyed his fish soup and white bread and was content to sit in the tavern. And I left him there ... When I got back to Mamontov, he was worried to see me without Chaliapin. "He's singing today, you know! The theatre will be full. Let's go and get him." However, we did not find Chaliapin at his hotel, and were told that he had gone rowing on the Volga with some young ladies. At the theatre, the public had already started arriving but Chaliapin was still nowhere to be found. Mamontov and Truffi were getting very uneasy, when suddenly Chaliapin appeared. He briskly stripped off his clothes in his dressing-room and started putting on his cotton padding. While hastily dressing and applying his make-up he said to Truffi with a smile: "Please, Maestro, don't forget my vital fermata." Then, putting his hand on Truffi's shoulder, he said with great seriousness: "My dear chap, remember, it's not on four but on five. Remember the pause." And he gave the conductor a sharp look. Susanin's aria, "They guess the truth", stunned the public. Mamontov led Chaliapin to his box from the stage. Everyone was surprised at how young he was. After the performance, the singers and their friends had supper together; Chaliapin was surrounded by actresses and there was continuous laughter from his group. When supper was over Chaliapin went off with them to row on the Volga.'[156]

He took part in thirty-five performances during the Nizhni-Novgorod summer season. Shortly before the end of his engagement Mamontov suggested that he leave the Mariinsky Theatre for Moscow. Chaliapin could not make up his mind immediately. Such a move was not to be contemplated lightly, as it meant throwing away security, a guaranteed future, a place in society and a pension. On the other hand, Mamontov opened up unlimited possibilities to do genuine creative work.

Stanislavsky, who first heard of Chaliapin through Mamontov, was clearly intrigued by reports of this new talent: 'We chatted all night. Mamontov was a striking figure with his shining eyes, passionate way of speaking and eloquent mimicry. In his nightshirt, open at the neck, he made a handsome subject for a painting. Half-reclining on the bed, he talked about beauty in art. Then he started raving about his new passion ... Fedor Chaliapin: "You can't get him off the stage," he said with feeling. "Today, for instance, he got the boys to rehearse the children's march from *Carmen* with him. Nobody had asked him to: it was entirely his own idea." Savva Mamontov showed the greatest enthusiasm for Chaliapin and gathered interesting people around his protégé. He told me with admiration how Fedor – as he called Chaliapin – "devoured" learning and any information he could use for his roles and his art. Being an actor, he then gave a practical demonstration of how Chaliapin "devoured" learning by using both hands to represent a jaw chewing food.'[157]

What was Chaliapin to do next? And what about Iola Tornaghi? Chaliapin knew that Mamontov had offered the ballerina a contract for the Moscow season and that she had accepted. Nevertheless, he returned to Petersburg and started rehearsing. The atmosphere of strict discipline, Napravnik's cold and (as

Chaliapin and his first wife, Iola Tornaghi, 1897.

it seemed to him) pedantic criticism conflicted with his desire to do things his own way. The freedom to experiment, which Mamontov's theatre offered him, was almost non-existent here. After his summer successes, the raptures of friends and critics, after the warm and sincere support of Mamontov, Chaliapin found this quite unbearable.

Appearing in Serov's *Rogneda* as Prince Vladimir did not improve matters. It was the same story as in the previous year, when he had already found old patterns unacceptable and new ones elusive. 'Autumn, mist and rain, Petersburg with its electric street lights, all lost their attraction for me.'

At this time of uncertainty and regrets, Iola Tornaghi suddenly appeared one morning in his flat, sent by Mamontov to repeat the invitation to come to Moscow: he again reluctantly declined it, but after she had gone, his longing for her and the nagging awareness of lost opportunities won the day. 'I washed my hands of the Assyrian King Holofernes, collected all my belongings and set off for Moscow and Mamontov. Just for Mamontov? I was at that period of a man's life when he cannot help falling in love. My love was in Moscow. . . .'[158]

The contract with the Mariinsky Theatre was annulled, and Mamontov agreed to cover half of the fine imposed on Chaliapin. Yurev recalls meeting Chaliapin by chance in the street at that time: 'He was happy, full of hopes. It was clear that he was gripped with enthusiasm, inspired by his success and the high hopes he entertained for the future. Everything showed that this alone preoccupied his heart and mind. I did not try to talk him out of it anymore.'[159]

Chaliapin had finally turned over a new page of life.

CHAPTER II

Discoveries

'Mamontov said to me: "My dear Fedya, in this theatre you can do anything you like. If you need costumes, just say so and the costumes will be there. If a new opera needs to be staged, we will stage an opera." All this put me in the best of moods and for the first time in my life I felt free, full of vigour, capable of conquering all obstacles.'

Fedor Chaliapin

THE IMPORTANCE OF the Moscow Private Opera in Chaliapin's life can hardly be exaggerated. In the space of his three seasons there, he sang twenty different roles, fourteen of them new creations. Chaliapin regarded this period as most significant and decisive. He wrote many years later: 'This is where I finally found my true path in art, giving definite shape to what had until then been instinctive inclinations.'[1]

Chaliapin was quite unknown in Moscow; even his standing as a former artist of the Mariinsky Theatre and his excellent press reviews in Nizhni-Novgorod failed to draw any attention. The productions in which he took part received no special publicity. He was not a foreign artist, and for Moscow devotees of singing, this meant that he did not count. However, inside the theatre, the same climate of cordial relations and of creativity free from obstruction as during the summer tours immediately surrounded him. No doubt the insidious attacks, petty intrigues, jealousies and squabblings unavoidable in any human association existed there too, but 'everything was somehow coloured by the new trends in art; you were constantly reminded of the questions they posed by the highly gifted people who had come here with their intelligence, knowledge, experience and above all their artistic flair, their lively interest in and enthusiasm for their work. This was of great value and guaranteed the success of the theatre. No one in the company was bored and idle, or short of work: everywhere – in the rehearsal rooms, in the lobby and on the stage – all was throbbing with a nervous, intense and exciting life. Each one of the artists – from the great Chaliapin to the young beginner – was bursting to get into action, waiting for the time and opportunity to show his talent, which no one was trying to smother, but which on the contrary everyone supported and encouraged.'[2]

Chaliapin had found something he could not even have

S. I. Mamontov.

dreamt of: an amazing opera company unlike any other, where one could freely search for a new artistic expression. This was such a happy time that in his declining years, he singled out Mamontov's opera from anything else he had experienced in the course of his life. 'I am still filled with joy at the memory of the wonderful period I spent working in Moscow. The atmosphere of trust and friendship seemed to increase my normal strength tenfold.'[3]

From the very first day every idea of his, every attempt he made to find fresh methods of interpretation received unfailing consideration. Without the support and understanding of Mamontov himself and of a large group of people selflessly devoted to art, the measure of Chaliapin's eventual achievements would have been much more restricted. This does not mean that Chaliapin did not set limits to the amount of advice he was willing to absorb from others, even from those he respected; he accepted it only as long as it did not clash with his views and helped him to understand why he was dissatisfied with a role or a scene. His gratitude to Mamontov for enabling him to experiment on the stage and for his enormous success in Moscow did not prevent Chaliapin from entering into open conflict with his benefactor if he felt he was in the right, or could not alter his performance. When Mamontov complained that Chaliapin was not following his directions at rehearsals, whereas the soprano Maria Chernenko readily complied with everything he said, the stage director of the Private Opera, Peter Melnikov, told him: 'Masha Chernenko's strong points are that she can imitate and is receptive. Chaliapin cannot perform a role as you see it, because he already has his own conception of it. If he deviates from it, he becomes insincere and therefore bad.'[4]

A man of powerful intellect, Chaliapin liked to analyse the motives of a character's conduct in the most minute detail and paid meticulous attention to every element of stagecraft. But however much one values his originality and his unique artistic qualities, he owed, as was said earlier, an immense debt to all those who had set him on the right course at the beginning of his career. And in this respect, Savva Ivanovich Mamontov

(1841–1918) and his group of Russian artists stand next to Usatov and Dalsky.

The activities and creations of the Moscow Private Opera, which span several years, are outside the frame of the present book, and therefore only those events bearing directly on the subject of our narrative – Fedor Chaliapin – will be considered.

Savva Ivanovich Mamontov's talent, enthusiasm and breadth of vision assure him of a special place in the history of late-nineteenth – early-twentieth-century Russian art, whose character and direction were radically transformed by his theatre and exhibitions. He had cultivated his many natural gifts to become an expert in various spheres of creative work. In his youth, he had practised sculpture, studied to be a singer and a pianist, written plays and opera libretti. He had tried his hand at acting, taking part in a number of amateur productions. In Moscow, Mamontov's artistic pursuits were combined with tremendous financial and industrial activity. He was chairman of several railway boards and owned factories and banks. Until the tragedy of his sudden arrest in 1899, Mamontov was regarded as one of the richest men in the country. (He fell victim to the intrigues of Muravyov, the Minister of Justice, who wanted to compromise Mamontov's protector, the Minister of Finances, Count Witte. Mamontov was accused of illegal dealings and misappropriation of shares. After one year, spent first in prison, then under house detention, he was tried and completely exonerated, but by then his fortune had vanished. He died in a suburb of Moscow during the bitterly cold winter of 1918.) Throughout his life Mamontov retained the conviction that neither industry nor the arts could prosper without the support of private initiative. He clung to this point of view in his construction projects as well as in his theatre. The road-building programme he organised in the north of the country saved many people from starvation during the First World War, at a time when Russia found herself cut off from her allies.

In 1870, Mamontov had bought the village of Abramtsevo, and the old and rather derelict country estate took on a new lease of life. Mamontov turned Abramtsevo, which Repin described as 'an ideal place for life and work', into a peaceful haven where he welcomed many Russian painters. Polenov, Vrubel, Vasnetsov, Korovin, Serov and Levitan were regular visitors. It also became a centre for the revival of traditional folk crafts, and samples of popular art were assembled to form a collection. Abramtsevo was the cradle of a new Russian school of painting which would later play a key role in revolutionising scenic design.

'For us,' said Vasnetsov in 1918 at a gathering commemorating Mamontov, 'he was like a brother, he was one of the family. . . . It is not enough to say that he loved art – it was his life and breath, just as it was for us. Without art ... he would not have lived another day. It was his element, as it was ours. Savva Ivanovich was neither a painter nor a singer, neither an actor nor a sculptor, in the narrow and specialised meaning of these words, but there was in him some sort of electrical current which sparked off energy in those who came close to him. God had given him the singular talent of awakening the creative powers of others.'[5]

Certainly, when Vasnetsov, Serov or Polenov painted a picture, when Chaliapin sang a role or when Stanislavsky produced a play, the results were the fruit of their own efforts and no one else's; but would they have been possible, and on such a scale, without the constant promptings and encouragement of the master of Abramtsevo? Anyway, many felt deeply thankful to him. 'I would very much like to see you at the theatre tomorrow as my master of aesthetics,'[6] wrote Stanislavsky to Mamontov on the eve of the dress rehearsal of Alexei Tolstoy's play *Tsar Fedor Ioannovich*, and he mentioned in his memoirs that the Alexeev family* regarded Savva Mamontov as a 'universally accepted authority in matters of art'.[7]

There is at first glance no comparison between Mamontov's achievements and those of, let us say, Tretyakov or Shchukin, who opened art galleries renowned the world over, or Bakhrushin, founder of today's largest theatre museum in the USSR. But how can one measure his generous help, whether he was assisting the re-birth of the forgotten Russian art of wood

---

* Stanislavsky's real name was Alexeev.

architecture, a cause on which he lavished spiritual support, knowledge, wisdom and money, or whether he was protecting dozens of Russian artists unfairly attacked by critics and shunned by uncomprehending crowds, thus enabling them to complete their unfinished works? Are we not grateful to Diaghilev (who, incidentally, carried out Mamontov's idea of Russian seasons abroad twenty years later) for 'discovering' and aiding Stravinsky, Fokine and Nijinsky, to name but a few?

Mamontov was wholly dedicated to any issue in which he was absorbed, and expected the same commitment from others. He was despotic, hot-tempered and impetuous, although the way he treated people was not a matter of personal sympathy or antipathy but of being convinced that his opinion was right. If on the other hand he saw that he was wrong, pride and vanity did not prevent him from admitting it. Dictator and petty tyrant though he was, Mamontov could be gentle and considerate where real talent was concerned.

Mamontov enjoyed giving private performances at his Moscow house. Stanislavsky described these soirées in his memoirs, *My Life in Art*. It was not unusual for some of the leading lights of the Moscow artistic community to get deeply involved in their preparation. And although refinement of taste and interesting experiments were often coupled with negligence and insufficient rehearsal, these theatricals served as a sort of trial run for future presentations on Mamontov's private stage. Again according to Stanislavsky (who was a most active participant), these productions 'had a strong influence on the level of Russian opera as a whole'.[8] And as time would show, not only on opera. The Moscow Art Theatre, founded by Stanislavsky and Nemirovich-Danchenko, was a direct descendant of Mamontov's dramatic circle and its offshoot, the Private Opera. This point was illustrated by Nadezhda Salina, leading soloist at Mamontov's and then at the Bolshoi: 'We knew nothing then of Stanislavsky's school, and very likely Stanislavsky himself was not yet thinking of it. As a relative of Mamontov, he was fairly often present at our rehearsals and watched our work with interest. And who knows but that Mamontov was not responsible for planting the seed of total devotion to art into the heart of twenty-year-old Stanislavsky?'[9]

Even at the beginning of the present century, when the Private Opera was past its heyday, critics still continued to remark on the obvious similarity between Mamontov's and Stanislavsky's objectives. In those years, the name Moscow Art Theatre was synonymous with the most avant-garde methods of staging. The Private Opera did not of course reach full maturity without years of testing and elaborating its artistic principles. For that reason, we will remain a little longer with Mamontov's domestic productions, or to be more precise, with one of them, Alexander Ostrovsky's *The Snow Maiden*. Mamontov had long been personally acquainted with the 'father of Russian theatre', in whose play *The Storm* both of them had even acted together for an amateur performance. The great playwright's views were close to Mamontov's, and the choice of *The Snow Maiden* was a logical one.

Mamontov planned the event with utmost care and even sent the painter Victor Vasnetsov on a special expedition to Tula* to search out examples of national dress and everyday artefacts. The results exceeded all expectations. It was as if a legendary ancient way of life had been resurrected. Vasnetsov's extraordinary designs represented a genuine revolution: conventional flats, used mainly as a background, had been replaced by real works of art, executed in the most striking manner and preserving authentic regional colour. The meaning and the character of the play came through in the design and the production. The costumes equally departed from convention and gave a definite sense of style in a definite period. This new approach would constitute one of the basic principles of Mamontov's future opera company.

When the Private Opera opened in Moscow on January 9th, 1885 with a performance of Dargomyzhsky's *Rusalka*, the interest of public and critics alike centred on the designers. 'They had painted superb scenes,' recalls one of Mamontov's assistants. 'The oak tree in the first set, with the lacy pattern of dark shadows and bright sunlight thrown by the branches onto

---

*Tula: historic city not far from Moscow.

its trunk, really transported you into the world of nature. As the curtain rose, the public was so stunned that there was dead silence for a moment, and then a thunder of applause broke out.'[10]

A new type of artist had arrived in the theatre who instead of just 'painting scenes' now shared the work of the producer as equal partner. Vasnetsov's sketches of the underwater kingdom in *Rusalka* mapped out the blueprint of the mise-en-scène, which was really his own creation. But 'encroachments' on the preserves of the producer were not limited to the drawing of sketches. The new breed of designers no longer tolerated unconvincing acting: a gap now separated the sets and costumes of a production from the rest of its elements. To bridge this gap, and to achieve harmonious unity in a performance, singers would have to take a fresh look at the very principles of acting and of stage characterisation. It was the designers who pointed the way.

In those years, Mamontov's theatre had, strictly speaking, no producer. The members of the cast were left to their own devices, especially in the early days. Mamontov of course devoted all his free time to his pet child, but this could not be called organised artistic direction, as in the case of Stanislavsky and the Moscow Art Theatre. 'Mamontov was not a teacher in the accepted sense of the word,' wrote Salina. 'We did our own work under his all-seeing eye. We made repeated, determined attempts to get a clear picture of some character or other, and something would rub off from our efforts. And then Savva Ivanovich would appear, stand in front of you, watch your movements in silence, with a slightly mocking smile, and it suddenly began to dawn on you that the result of so much hard work was forced and meaningless. And there and then, before your very eyes, he would with an economical gesture or an imperceptible twist of the body give an illuminating portrayal of the character, instantly etching in your memory a graphic, truthful and lifelike picture of it.'[11] This meant that, apart from Mamontov's advice, the artistic direction of the performance was left entirely to the designers. Painters of that period (between 1880 and 1890) paid particular attention to the close study of their environment; they perceived and reproduced life realistically and straightforwardly, and gained expert knowledge of nature and people in the process. The thousands of small but revealing details from which they would build up a likeness remained firmly fixed in their memories. Even if for some it was difficult to convey their wisdom through the spoken word, since painting was their means of expression, no mistake escaped their notice and they unerringly put the singer on the right path. When an actor is dressed in authentic costume and surrounded by scenery which echoes the atmosphere of the work performed, he will instinctively adapt his behaviour to his background.

Compared with the official Imperial stage, all this was entirely new, bold and unexpected to the point of temerity. It was natural that dramatic art, answering the needs of the times, should move towards the radical reform already launched in Russia by the Moscow Private Opera with its transformation of the visual aspect of productions. And so when Stanislavsky himself needed a designer, he wisely turned to one of Mamontov's associates, Victor Simov.

The evolution of the theatre had until then been held back by the 'independent state' of the scenery, its irrelevance to the events taking place on the stage and to the style, character and specific features of the works performed. As we have already seen, isolated attempts to alter the status quo in government-subsidised houses were doomed to failure, and there was undoubtedly a grain of truth in Chaliapin's view that all enterprise was crushed and shattered by the bureaucratic machine. 'Exemplary discipline' reigned in the organisation of theatrical affairs. A high-ranking official from the Moscow Imperial Theatres administration admitted many years later: 'Even in artistic matters, all the power was concentrated in the office, not in the theatre. The office was not in the service of the theatre, but vice-versa, and in the theatre the word office became almost an insult, while for the office, the theatre was a revolutionary element.'[12]

The Private Opera was just the opposite. 'At Mamontov's,' acknowledges Chaliapin, 'I could indulge in daring artistic experiments which would have had my Petersburg uniformed bureaucrats falling about speechless.'[13]

The composition of the repertoire alone demonstrated the difference between the Private Opera and the Imperial establishments. After *Rusalka* followed the premières of *Faust* and Nicolai's *The Merry Wives of Windsor*. These works had been chosen for a very particular reason: their plots came from some of the world's greatest poets: Pushkin, Goethe, Shakespeare. Of course, it would be useless to try to remain strictly faithful to Goethe in Gounod's *Faust*, to Mérimée in Bizet's *Carmen*, or to Pushkin in Tchaikovsky's *Eugene Onegin*. Interesting and promising experiments have been tried, but they have never been crowned with success. An opera based on a literary source becomes an independent work and assumes its own character, with its own aesthetic rules. Invoking a literary 'model' in the preparation of an operatic role is a complex matter, and each attempt has to be treated as a separate case. As far as Mamontov is concerned, however, we are talking of something very different. The introduction of drama to the operatic stage gave rise to a desire to see a role behind every singing part, to feel that every vocal inflection had an inseparable companion – the word – which had to communicate its logical and emotional content. Close co-operation with designers conduced to combining the various components of the performance into an integrated whole and paved the way for a new formula where production reigned so supreme that the artistic concept prevailed over all other elements. The advent of the producer as organiser and creator made it necessary to adopt a new approach.

The performance itself was the outcome of intensive teamwork between actors, producer and musicians. Before it was presented to the public, every one of its details was tested and adjusted. Individual interpretation was no longer a major concern – all that mattered was the creation of a unified artistic whole. Of course, every new trend and style achieved this 'whole' in a different way. Individual attempts characterised a particular group or a particular designer searching for innovatory ideas. Fresh means of theatrical expression replaced old ones which had lost the power of making an impact on audiences. The history of the theatre is, in fact, nothing but a succession of acting methods and directors' experiments, the latter more particularly in the twentieth century. As we know, the concept of a theatre where production takes precedence was not, in the end, realised on the operatic stage. However, Stanislavsky and Nemirovich-Danchenko did not owe their triumph solely to exceptional talent. Genuine equilibrium between all the ingredients is much rarer in opera than in straight theatre, even today. The reason for this lies in the unstable and mixed nature of opera itself. 'For me,' said Chaliapin, 'the special value of opera resides in the fact that it can combine harmoniously all the arts – music, poetry, painting, sculpture and architecture.'[14] But the perfect fusion of such diverse constituents as sight and sound, words and music, action, scenery and lighting, is extremely difficult to attain. The composite nature of the genre, and therefore of operatic art as a whole, is to 'blame' for its relatively poor record as far as production is concerned by comparison with the ordinary stage. Although drama and music are theoretically considered to be of equal importance in the origins of opera – and opera itself is drama written in music – what one sees in practice is often a long way from Chaliapin's ideal. The various resources of opera, instead of working together, compete with each other, robbing the composition of its essential meaning and validity.

The 'operatic code' is founded on the ever attractive notion of synthesis, which proves elusive in reality. Mamontov was the first to attempt this in Russia, and ushered in a new era of performing art, reaching its apogee with Chaliapin. The founders of the Moscow Art Theatre recognised the value of the innovations he made and the extent of his influence. In 1919 they marked the twenty-fifth anniversary of Chaliapin's début with these words: 'For the faith and strength our dreams gained from your artistic achievements; for the use we made in our work of the lessons dictated by your genius; for holding so high the banner of scenic art – our art – on the day we celebrate your twenty-five years of creative work, the entire company of the Moscow Art Theatre, from its youngest to its oldest member, salutes you!'[15] The London *Times* wrote in its obituary of the singer: 'When people advance theories about the inherent defects of opera as an art form, its anomalies and incon-sistencies, one has only to think of Chaliapin to know that such theories do not stand the ultimate test of an appeal to practice, for, given that subtle combination of qualities which make up a Chaliapin, no anomalies or inconsistencies exist. Opera is simply his complete means of artistic expression, and no other would serve. So he has to be ranked with the creative artists rather than with the interpretative.'[16]

Let us go back to the beginning for a moment. After the 1885 opening, Mamontov's enterprise did not survive for long – less than three seasons. Reforming acting and the visual aspect of musical drama, propagating Russian opera and establishing it firmly in the repertoire, were formidable tasks which demanded enormous effort and years of struggle. To prevail upon the tastes and habits of the public was not easy. Next door stood the Bolshoi Theatre, with magnificent, famous and well-loved singers, with a first-class orchestra and chorus, and with an unshakeable belief in the superiority and the canons of European, especially Italian, opera. And so, despite the success of productions and costumes (particularly *The Snow Maiden*), despite the surprised enthusiasm of the more discriminating members of the public at the beauty and originality of Russian operas, Moscow amateurs of singing continued to ignore the fledgling opera house. The production of *The Snow Maiden* itself, which would later be seen as a historical landmark in Russian opera, did not arouse any really serious interest. Some moments were singled out for praise, but that was as far as it went. The first truly integrated performance passed almost unnoticed. 'For *The Snow Maiden*, the theatre was half empty and this further added to the feeling of gloom,' recalled Vasili Shkafer, then at the beginning of his career as an opera singer and later to become one of Mamontov's collaborators and a favourite partner of Chaliapin. 'The public considered that *The Snow Maiden* was a "boring" opera and the box office returns were low. I assumed that the performance I had gone to see at the Solodovnikov Theatre* would also bring me little pleasure. Moreover, the orchestra was rather small, the chorus was not very good and not a single one of the singers had a "well-known" or "famous" name.... But the curtain went up, and what I saw and heard transported me with singular and supernatural ecstasy. It was a sight I had as yet never seen anywhere on the operatic stage – it was a total revelation to me. A miraculous, aromatic and fabulous spring tale gradually unfolded in front of my eyes, suggesting Russian nature with extraordinary delicacy of feeling and giving a deeply poetic view of an immemorial way of life, pagan and rustic, full of beliefs and superstitions.... I saw on the stage artistic truth, a strange forest, the gorgeous palace of Tsar Berendei with intricate decorative patterns painted on its walls and ceilings, a wealth of colours.... Ostrovsky's poetic work, which so genuinely and deeply moved Rimsky-Korsakov, and which is so masterfully evoked by the sounds of his palette and by the canvases, colours and brushes of Vasnetsov, reached an altogether different degree of harmony, where words, sounds, colours, everything blended together...."[17]

Mamontov knew that he needed accomplished singers and musicians. But where were they to be found? By temperament he was more of an improviser than an educator nurturing young prodigies with patient singlemindedness. Savva Mamontov dreamt of a theatre, not a school. A theatre can, it is true, create a school (as in the case of the Moscow Art Theatre), but only after years of continuous development or if vast amounts of money are available. With all his millions, this was beyond Mamontov's powers. 'Mamontov's attempts to blaze a new trail in operatic art with a young generation of singers were neither understood nor appreciated in Moscow,' wrote Salina. 'Other members of his own class thought that he was just "amusing himself"; the public took him for a self-indulgent autocrat, and the press, with very few exceptions, tore his new-born child to pieces. All this was a bad start for our theatre. Huge expenses had been incurred in the production of the first

* Theatre where Mamontov's opera company was performing – today the Moscow Operetta Theatre.

125

operas (*Rusalka*, *The Snow Maiden*, *A Life for the Tsar* and *The Stone Guest*). Public attendance was low. . . . "One cannot conquer alone,"* but Mamontov had no trusted and faithful assistants, and neither he nor his idea attracted many sympathisers. He had to compromise. To make up for his losses and to save our theatre, he decided to start the new season with Italian operas and invited guest artists and famous singers. The Russian operas stayed in the repertoire and were given alternately with the Italian ones.' It really was the only option open. Mamontov's project was facing disaster. The public had to be won over at all costs, and at the same time his 'operatic team' had to be built up. Audiences would also have to be familiarised little by little with Russian works and with the idea that they deserved to share the programme with Italian ones. Mamontov himself tried to present the postponement of his previous plans as necessary in order to allow the young Russian singers to study with masters of the Italian school. This made good sense, as Salina confirms: 'Our Italians were a blessing to us, and particularly to me. When I left the Bolshoi Theatre twenty years later my voice was still good enough to embark on a new singing career without any feeling of shame.'[18]

The practice of guest performances was widespread in the opera houses of Russia. With the exception of the Imperial stage, lengthy tours by individual soloists or entire companies were common occurrences. They were most frequent during Lent, when the main season had already ended, but rare at other times of the year. A visiting artist would occasionally take part in one or several of the regular current productions, which he simply joined; but it was quite different for systematically organised tours and for specially invited guest singers who came with their own repertoire. Then everything depended on them, and all the rest, including the conductor and the other singers, had to take second place. The public was not paying for an opera or an interpretation but for a vocal display and even sometimes just for one striking high note. 'Clubmen who had regular subscriptions to the Italian opera', recalls Stanislavsky,

*Russian proverb.

126

'would play cards all evening while the performance was in progress and come to the theatre for the sole purpose of hearing some renowned tenor's C-sharp. At the start of the first act the front rows would not yet be fully occupied, but shortly before the famous note was due, noises would erupt accompanied by the sound of voices and the creaking of furniture. This was the arrival of the art lovers-cum-clubmen. When the note had been sung, it was given a few encores, and then there was another eruption of noise – the clubmen were departing to finish their game of cards.'[19]

Presentations of this kind were hastily put together and used an assortment of scenery and costumes borrowed from various other productions. It goes without saying that their artistic level was not very high. Isolated successes were entirely due to the talent and taste of particular singers. In most cases, however, their tours enjoyed enormous popularity, because, like today, the public came to satisfy its craving for exhibitions of virtuosity. This habit is so firmly entrenched as to be almost immutable. The custom of paying exclusive attention to the vocal side of an opera has deep and ancient historical roots. It has been the basis of a lasting 'pact' between performers and spectators and in Russia constituted a serious obstacle to the evolution of opera, an area of the theatre where the practice of individual guest appearances was allowed to survive much longer than in others, such as ballet and drama.

Mamontov, however, while taking advantage of the financial rewards offered by this system, continued to regard it as incompatible with his ideals. He had been forced to make a tactical retreat, but at the very first opportunity returned to producing Russian and foreign operas on the principle of integral concept, in sharp contrast with the generally accepted approach. And so, wishing to educate the taste of the Moscow public 'a little faster', he boldly decided to mount Dargomyzhsky's *The Stone Guest*, but despite the care he lavished on its preparation, the public remained indifferent. Mamontov wrote bitterly to Vladimir Stasov: '... some people are, of course, ecstatic, but the percentage is so small that it is sad to mention it.'[20] Any thought of regular performances had to be abandoned. The initial phase in the struggle for 'a new operatic theatre' had been short-lived, but Mamontov's first Private Opera was of exceptional significance. Its role was decisive in preparing the ground for a fresh assault on engrained traditions. The theatre's productions awoke in the spectator a taste for 'truth on the stage'; the scenery did not stand out for its splendour or effects but for its unity of design. The first and fatal blow had been struck against the division between musical and visual impressions, the inconsistency between singing and action, against all the conventions of style which had governed the operatic stage for centuries.

During the Lent seasons of 1889–1892, Mamontov continued to finance performances in which Mazzini, Tamagno, Marie van Zandt, Silva and other famous masters of bel canto took part. Even when these ended, Mamontov did not give up the idea of starting all over again, although this scheme took some ten years to accomplish. Before re-opening in Moscow, he decided to take his troupe to the 1896 Nizhni-Novgorod All-Russian Exhibition of Trade, Industry and the Arts. Chaliapin's encounter with Mamontov and his decision to leave the Imperial stage for Moscow have already been mentioned in the previous chapter. The Private Opera was at that time entering its so-called 'second period', which ended in 1899 with Mamontov's bankruptcy and arrest and Chaliapin's departure for the Bolshoi Theatre. For three years, towards the end of the century, the Private Opera was the setting for numerous important artistic developments; several of Rimsky-Korsakov's works were created there and the full extent of their depth and beauty revealed for the first time; the public started to open its ears to the music of Mussorgsky and Borodin; and Chaliapin's talent reached maturity. After the company's first triumphant season in Petersburg, César Cui wrote: 'We took our leave of the Moscow Private Opera with a feeling of deep gratitude; it has raised the spirits of Russian composers; it has shown that all is not gloom and despair for them in Russia, that their works, provided they are well performed, can find favour and also be appreciated for their true value, and that there is after all an opera which considers it has the responsibility, the duty, to serve the interests of Russian art in Russia. However simple it may seem, the current state of our musical affairs makes this a truly heroic deed, for which praise and glory be to the Private Opera.'[21]

The state-owned theatres finally reacted to the example set by the Private Opera. They were forced to take notice of Russian music, and after that to give some consideration to the style of operatic productions as well. 'The management of the Imperial Theatres evidently felt a little ashamed that *Sadko*, successfully performed on the private stage in Moscow and Petersburg, had been missed by the State Theatres, which had ignored it,' remarked Rimsky-Korsakov. 'On the other hand, since the failure of *Christmas Eve* in 1895, not a single one of my operas had been performed on the stage of the Mariinsky. At all events, Vsevolozhsky suddenly decided to stage my *Snow Maiden* with the magnificence befitting the Imperial Theatre.'[22]

Once again, in Moscow, the Private Opera was not an immediate success. The performances which followed its return from Nizhni-Novgorod had a rather cool reception from the press. The merits of the voices, the quality of the chorus and the sound of the orchestra, which were indeed Mamontov's weak points, attracted most of the comments. He was criticised for neglecting these sides of his productions in favour of their visual aspect – decorative scenery and plasticity of movements.

In his letters Rimsky-Korsakov often lets slip his dissatisfaction with the musical level of the theatre and with Mamontov's methods of work in general. Recalling in his memoirs the first night of *Sadko*, the composer began by praising individual singers but then continued: 'The way the opera had been prepared was a disgrace. In the orchestra, apart from wrong notes, some instruments were missing; in the first scene the chorus sang from the printed score, holding that in their hands instead of the menu.* In the fourth scene the chorus did not sing at all; the orchestra played alone. All this was the result of *hurried preparation* [Rimsky-Korsakov's italics]. But the

---

* The merchants of Novgorod are sitting at a feast.

opera was a huge success with the public, which was what Mamontov needed. I was furious, but I was called up on stage, presented with flowers. . . .'[23]

This state of affairs gave rise to the persistent view that Mamontov was a dilettante who did not appreciate the importance of the musical element in opera. Was this the case? The same critics did not usually complain about the level of musical performance in *Faust*, *Mignon*, *Aida*, and other European operas. Could it be then that Mamontov's carelessness was reserved for Russian operas and that Mikhail Ippolitov-Ivanov was right when he wrote that 'Mamontov was an out-and-out Italomane'?[24] Of course not. It was just that having to stage so many new productions in so little time – and Mamontov was forced to do this – often made it impossible to prepare each one of them with sufficient care. Work would continue even after the first night, during actual performances, and things would not settle down to a smooth run until five or six of them had passed. Moreover, when the opera was Russian, all available rehearsal time, all attention and energy were spent on designs and costumes and on working out a striking mise-en-scène. As a result, the contrast between visual aspect and sound was marked.

The Private Opera had been created for the benefit of the general public. Tickets at Mamontov's theatre were considerably cheaper than at its mighty neighbour and rival the Bolshoi Theatre. A newspaper commented after the opening night of *The Snow Maiden*: 'This venture makes a favourable first impression. The company is very competent, the performance goes without a hitch, the production is entirely satisfying, soloists and chorus thoroughly deserve their success.'[25] A judgement seconded by Semyon Kruglikov: 'The undertaking is, it seems, on the right path. One cannot but welcome the idea of making it possible in Moscow for anyone of relatively modest means to hear at little cost excellent examples of operatic – mostly Russian – art, rarely if at all performed here.'[26]

Setting up a repertoire distinct from the one used by the Imperial stage was an urgent necessity. All the same, Mamontov knew perfectly well that he would never be able to match the

Bolshoi Theatre's chorus and orchestra. He therefore concentrated his efforts in other directions: staging, costume, movements and acting. This shift of emphasis had historical
repercussions. An entirely new style of performing emerged and
revolutionised Russian opera. Later, the new methods were
used for the European repertoire as well, especially after Chaliapin had joined the company.

Critics seized the opportunity of drawing parallels between
the presentations of the Moscow Private Opera and the traditional concerts-in-costume of the Imperial Theatres. Such
comparisons made it possible to criticise more openly and more
severely the policies of the state-owned theatres and the tastes
of their regular audiences. Strange as it may seem today, the
public for *Manon* was not the same as the public for *Boris
Godunov*. To those who wanted to hear a vocal display,
Mamontov's experiments were a matter of deep indifference.
Such people still represented the majority, and there was a long
way to go before the general public became aware of the ideals
of a new operatic theatre.

Some contemporaries of Mamontov did notice that his
'feeling for the beauty of painting, the beauty of imaginative
use of line and colours, the beauty of sculpture and the plastic
arts was remarkably strong and dominant....'[27] It is possible,
for instance, that the decision to mount *The Snow Maiden*
owed more to Vasnetsov's designs than to Rimsky-Korsakov's
music. But if we take a retrospective look at these years, it
becomes evident that the revolutionary changes in theatrical
scenery, costume and make-up had much to do with Mamontov's enthusiasm for the decorative side of a production. There
was a great artist in Mamontov, but an artist 'who was not
specialised. Hence', continues the writer, 'his lack of cohesion:
he fixed his attention now on the costumes, now on the scenery,
now on placing the singers, now on their movements, but least
of all on the music. This habit of focussing his attention and
the power of his imagination on one particular moment and
one particular thing had a definite connection with the fact that
Mamontov, thanks to his energy and the vast financial means
at his disposal, was accustomed to seeing his plans executed

promptly. Hence a certain lack of balance in all his work: exciting moments alternated with dull ones. Much time would be spent on a single character, on a single short scene, while right next to it something important was handed over to a second-rate assistant director. If the initiative did not emanate from Mamontov himself and if the other person's idea did not succeed in firing his imagination, he would refuse to spend anything.'[28]

At the same time, it must in all fairness be admitted that Mamontov possessed all the qualities required of the leader and director of an avant-garde opera company, a fact recognised by a number of discerning people, among them Chaliapin, whose eyes he had opened to the world of art.

Mamontov started to pay more attention to his work with singers, helping them to get to the heart of their roles and to find the appropriate manner of playing them. 'Before every new production,' recalls Mamontov's nephew, 'Uncle Savva assembled all the participants and explained the score to them in detail. This was followed by comments, during the course of which he touched on the historical period, style and artistic nature of the work or libretto. At his insistence, designers commissioned to work on any production had to give the performers a broad outline of their design plans. He knew how to give brilliant practical demonstrations, entering completely into the role he was treating. He knew how to find specific characteristic features for each of them in terms of looks, facial expression and voice, how to give a quick but revealing outline of the character as a whole. He knew how to pick out a distinctive gesture, typical of the personage, and this gesture, the inflection of the voice and the facial expression, would immediately reveal the personality of the character, make it clear and simple. Savva Mamontov's face was extremely mobile; it was the face of a real, if somewhat highly strung, artist who could use his voice, his body and his hands to express anything he wanted to say.'[29]

Vladimir Lossky, then a young singer, later a prominent operatic producer, gives an interesting account of Mamontov's working methods: 'Savva Ivanovich watched, corrected, advised, encouraged or rejected, and then himself showed how to do it. Sometimes we even argued; I dared to go that far, and on these occasions the difference in years and in station ceased to exist; I felt as if I were playing an interesting game with somebody of my own age. When I came to work, Savva Ivanovich devoted the entire day to me: I arrived at 12 o'clock, the two of us had breakfast, lunch and dinner together. I left after midnight. On these days he was not at home to anyone. The telephone would sometimes ring. Savva Mamontov answered it, coldly and tersely dealt with some piece of business concerning railways, sleepers and carriages and crossly asked not to be disturbed anymore "with such trifles", as he was engaged in serious matters.'[30]

The revival of the Moscow Private Opera coincided with the realisation of a project which had long occupied Mamontov's mind – the construction of a railway to the north of the country. Are the two things related? On the face of it they are just two independent facets of Mamontov's activities, but in fact there is a very close connection. Mamontov was not merely using his profits from the railways to further the development of Russian art. He was fascinated by the unique beauty of the north, which became a new source of inspiration for Russian painters, particularly Valentin Serov and Konstantin Korovin. With the latter's help Mamontov had a huge exhibition pavilion erected at the Nizhni-Novgorod Fair and named it 'North'. Works by Russian painters were displayed there among a variety of other exhibits. As for the works of Mikhail Vrubel, which the judges had categorically refused to include, they were, thanks to Mamontov's perseverance, obstinacy and willpower, shown in a specially erected building.

This is where Chaliapin, who was accompanying Mamontov, first came across the art of his future mentors and friends. Discreetly and tactfully, Mamontov explained to the ignorant singer the difference between ordinary painting ('Well, just like on a photograph!') and the works of artists like Vrubel, which he found initially so shocking. 'You are still young. . . . You have seen little. There is *great feeling* in Vrubel's picture [Chaliapin's italics]. I did not find this explanation very convincing, but it troubled me a great deal. I started to go to the arts section of the exhibition and to the Vrubel pavilion in my spare time. Soon I noticed that the pictures accepted by the judges bored me, whereas I liked those of the rejected Vrubel more and more.'[31]

Chaliapin gradually realised that painting was becoming an important and intimate part of his own creative process. He urgently wanted to find a basic structure for the characters he had to portray. Visual arts provided a way of solving this problem, and he started to reflect on their place and their role in the practical work of the opera singer. Unlike most of his colleagues, he attached the greatest importance to such questions. The fact that he begins his recollections of Mamontov's company with this very topic is not accidental. 'In Moscow, as the reader may remember, I had to make up my mind in an argument between a luscious apple tree in bloom, which I liked, versus the unpalatable "Princesse Lointaine"* which Mamontov liked. I want to settle this now once and for all, before proceeding any further with the story of my career. The fact is that this Moscow period . . . is marked by the beneficial influence of several remarkable painters. The effect of painting on my creative life is second only to that of great, true Russian drama. I think if I had retained my naive and primitive tastes in painting, which so amused Mamontov in Nizhni-Novgorod, I would not have been able to create the characters that have made me famous. To achieve my ideals of truth and beauty on the stage, it was essential that I should feel and understand the beauty and poetry of great painting.'[32]

For Chaliapin, 'to look the part is as important as to act the part',[33] but at that time few other singers were interested in the realistic portrayal of an operatic character. Most of them either appeared on stage as themselves or used conventional make-up and costumes fixed by tradition and earmarked for a particular role. Citing Mephistopheles as an example, Edward Stark, author of Chaliapin's first extensive biography, writes: 'Since the time when someone, nobody knows who, invented this

*Vrubel's famous watercolour panel inspired by Edmund Rostand's play *La Princesse lointaine*.

make-up – pointed beard, tightly rolled moustache with sharply upturned ends and eyebrows strictly parallel to the moustache – it has passed into universal use. Mephistopheles' first entrance loses all interest if you already know in advance, down to the smallest detail, what he will look like when he comes through the trap. His very costume was always boringly predictable and not in the least original. The only difference was that one "devil" wore red silk with a black cloak, and another black velvet with a red cloak. But they both invariably covered themselves in gold braid. That was their idea of "characterisation".'[34]

By the time Chaliapin met Mamontov he was already showing a strong dislike for the performing methods which then prevailed on the operatic scene. One of his first attempts to find a different approach was the part of Prince Gremin in *Eugene Onegin*. With the Private Opera he sang it only in Nizhni-Novgorod, since in Moscow Mamontov wanted to avoid duplicating the repertoire of the Bolshoi Theatre. No one before him had ever managed to breathe life into this character. His Gremin was immediately identifiable; he came from a background familiar to the audience. The reserved but dignified conduct, the military bearing, the impression of age – perfectly acted – the amazing pronunciation of each word – everything astounded by its painstaking attention to detail and its naturalness. (The pronunciation gave Chaliapin a great deal of trouble: his provincial accent was not suitable for portraying an aristocrat.) A contributor to the *New York Staats Zeitung*, who had seen him at the Mariinsky, many years later evoked his appearance: 'He stands there in his general's court dress, white stockings and white pump shoes on shapely legs, the broad red ribbon of an order across his green coat, the finest figure of a man ever to tread the stageboards. His mask is the most expressive, the noblest countenance I have yet seen on an old man.'[35] Until then, even in the case of excellent singers, the role had consisted of nothing more than the faultless execution of a concert piece aria. Now it had become the monologue of a real person and contributed to the development of a character actively participating in the action. Every gesture of the old, war-scarred general betrayed the happiness he had found in his declining years. Happiness, remembers a contemporary, 'illuminated even his eyes'. Chaliapin did not stand at the proscenium arch, addressing himself to the audience and looking at Onegin during the pauses (as is still not infrequently done today), but he really confided his feelings to him. This Gremin was genuinely glad to see again a close friend and relative to whom he could open his heart and talk about what he most dearly loved in the world. Sometimes Gremin could not help shifting his gaze to Tatiana, standing on the other side of the stage. A smile with a hint of sadness would soften his stern features. This interpretation of the role added a dramatic dimension to the finale. It became clear why Tatiana, in spite of her love for Onegin and his passionate entreaties to leave her husband, could not bring herself to do this. Not only duty but also an awareness that her departure would be fatal to Gremin forces Tatiana to make such a decision.

A spectator recalled that Chaliapin 'eclipsed all the others with his single aria in the third act. How much nobility and overwhelming love there was in Gremin's declaration . . . "Ah!" said one of my acquaintances. "I understood – how could Tatiana not remain faithful to such a man!"'[36]

Chaliapin's treatment of Gremin, the way he played him (he sometimes sang the aria sitting next to Onegin, sometimes slowly pacing up and down the ballroom arm in arm with him, was used in other productions. Stanislavsky, for instance, borrowed his original idea for the Bolshoi Theatre Operatic Studio in 1922. 'Gremin signalled to Onegin,' recalls a member of the cast, 'inviting him to sit down. They both took armchairs on each side of a small table, and Gremin continued with his aria from his seat. This gave a certain air of intimacy to the whole scene.'[37]

When Chaliapin joined Mamontov's theatre, he began to take a close look not only at the work of his new friends but at the painters themselves. He was struck by their ability to express form and substance in a few words and with two or three gestures. 'This clever way of catching fleeting moments of life appealed to me very much. And looking at them I also tried, on stage and off stage, to be more expressive, more plastic. My repertoire began to seem to me stale, uninteresting, although I did go on working, trying to bring something new to each role.'[38] The painters, for their part, had also noticed that this was an unusual opera singer. Not a single one of his roles was now created without the benefit of their practical advice; not a single detail – however minute – of his costumes and make-up escaped their attention. 'I remember that when I was dressing as a Viking* in the costume Serov had designed, Valentin himself came into my dressing-room, with a very worried air.... "Excellent!" said Serov. "Only the arms ... they look womanish!" So I delineated the muscles of my arms with make-up, and thus accentuated they became powerful, bulging. The designers were very pleased with this; they complimented me: "Good, you're standing just right. You walk well, confidently and naturally! Well done!" These words of praise meant more to me than the public's applause. I was terribly happy!'[39]

Vladimir Vasilievich Stasov, a man of encyclopaedic knowledge, one of the most brilliant and original Russian critics of the nineteenth century, who counted among his friends Mussorgsky, Rimsky-Korsakov and Turgenev, came to see Chaliapin in *Sadko*. A very stout old man with a huge grey beard, he produced an unforgettable impression on the singer, the pages of whose memoirs devoted to Stasov are permeated with a peculiar sense of excitement.

In an article with the evocative title of 'Boundless Joy',† consecrated to the twenty-five-year-old singer, Stasov wrote: 'I was sitting in Mamontov's theatre reflecting on the sad state of Russian opera, and of our music in general, when suddenly ... in front of me appeared an ancient Scandinavian bogatyr‡ singing his "Viking Song". Its power and its rugged tones bring before our eyes the menacing granite cliffs of Scandinavia, with the waves crashing and roaring against them, and in the midst of this timeless landscape the Viking himself suddenly appears, looking as if his bones had been hacked from the cliffs. There

---

* In Rimsky-Korsakov's *Sadko*: the Viking Merchant.

† Sobinin's first words in Glinka's opera *A Life for the Tsar*, and at the time familiar to the ear of every educated Russian.

‡ Bogatyr – superhuman hero of Russian folklore.

Portrait of Chaliapin by Valentin Serov, 1905.

Vladimir Stasov painted by I. Repin, 1883.

Chaliapin as the Viking Merchant in the opera *Sadko* by Rimsky-Korsakov. Moscow, 1899.

he stands, immense, leaning against his enormous axe, a steel helmet on his head, his arms bare to the shoulders, his strong face and drooping moustache, his whole chest covered in steel, his legs bound in straps. His gigantic voice, the prodigious eloquence of his singing, the herculean movements of his body and arms, as if a statue had been given life and movement, the look under his thick frowning brow: all this was so new, so powerfully and deeply real that I could not help asking myself, completely stunned: "But who is this, who is it? What actor? Where can one find people like that in Moscow? What amazing people!" And suddenly in the interval I found out that it was none other than Chaliapin. I was uncommonly surprised and delighted. What a versatile talent! How extraordinary to be able to create such diametrically opposed figures!'[40]

Chaliapin gradually realised that particular expressions of the face, of the eyes, the position of the lips and other visible signs had to correspond exactly to the conception of the character: its inner life must manifest itself in theatrical language through his external appearance. But to integrate the interior and the exterior, the singer himself had to become a designer, and a very uncommon one at that. On the living fabric of his own face and body he had to create the image of whatever character he was incarnating. And if in Petersburg Chaliapin had attempted to combine opera with drama, then in Moscow he was searching for ways of combining it with representational art.

When Chaliapin sang Rimsky-Korsakov's *Mozart and Salieri* and excerpts from *Boris Godunov* at his benefit performance on February 24th, 1899, an astounded critic from one of the Moscow newspapers wrote: 'The make-up of the artist was so skilful that, were it not for his size, it would be difficult to believe that Salieri, Varlaam and Godunov are played by the one and same man....'[41]

As many of his contemporaries attested, Chaliapin's make-up reflected a process of visible transformation. Once the crucial points of the role and its innumerable but precise details had been established, he 'entered' the character with the first touch of make-up and 'came out' of it when the last trace was removed.

'On the day of a performance,' recalled one of his partners at the Private Opera, 'Chaliapin did not have any lunch. He arrived at the theatre between two and two and a half hours before curtain-up and immediately started to put on his make-up. He knew precisely not only each expression and each line of his face but also the shape of his head and even of the back of his head (he not infrequently sketched it in a few quick strokes, and everybody immediately recognised him). He had learnt all the secrets of make-up, and watching him, I said to myself: What an artist! Chaliapin the great painter makes up Chaliapin the great actor. Really, the term "making up" does not do justice to the result of two hours' work in front of the mirror. Chaliapin was able to make the external aspect of the personage he was portraying reflect its true, inner character. . . . When the face was finished, he dressed . . . and always examined every detail: everything down to the smallest fold had to be in its place. When he came on stage, Chaliapin as it were led the spectators out of real life, and it was only when the curtain came down that they returned from the imaginary, illusory world and tore themselves away from the power of the magic charms of his art. Only then did the tragic figure of the unhappy Tsar Boris or the conscience-stricken Ivan disappear. Chaliapin's movements, gestures and poses followed one another in a logical succession. They were all necessary, since after all they were conditioned by the inner life of the character. Chaliapin the actor expressed by his playing the same thing that Chaliapin the singer conveyed to the audience by other means – music and words.'[42]

While sitting in front of the mirror and putting on his make-up, Chaliapin was searching for the true state of mind, the feelings and thoughts of the character whose form he must assume before going on stage. He made a completely fresh attempt at this every time. 'As soon as you start trying to repeat what has been done before, copying exactly the make-up of previous performances,' explained Chaliapin to one of his musical friends, 'and reproducing mechanically everything that has already become firmly established, then while waiting in the wings to make your entrance, you have to search anxiously for the required state of mind, do an "internal make-up". It is not always possible to manage this to a sufficient extent, and then your first entrance, the first minutes and sometimes the entire first scene are spent in organising the role, "growing into" it. But if, while you are applying your make-up, you start to think about doing Eryomka* "this way or that way", to look at him more closely from all angles, he will himself begin to stir within you. You will see something new in him every time, something small, seemingly unimportant, but which immediately sheds a new light on his personality. In such cases you don't even notice passing from your dressing room to the stage. Your very first thought of him brings Eryomka to life – and he continues to live on the stage and not a single minute is lost "getting into his skin". He is right inside you, and nobody can see you watching over him.'[43]

The famous Chaliapin metamorphosis was the result of a complex system of interaction between the singer and his role. It was so incredible that it surprised even his regular partners and people who knew Chaliapin well in private life. Many of them felt that he changed into a completely different person, to the extent of assuming the features and behaviour of the character he was playing. Early in 1918 a large delegation went backstage to see Chaliapin after a performance of *The Power of Evil*. With the help of Gorky, they tried to persuade him to give a charity concert for the sailors of the Baltic fleet in Kronstadt. While removing his make-up and costume, Chaliapin answered the pressing requests of his visitors with irritation and quite ungraciously. He then said sharply: 'No, I won't sing in Kronstadt. I am tired....' 'Chaliapin was sitting in front of the mirror half naked,' recalls one of those present. 'He sounded displeased. We could see the reflection of his face in the mirror, we could see Eryomka's features fading away; bulging, puffy Eryomka vanished and the familiar soft features appeared, the pale eyelashes, the wide-open nostrils drawing in the air. He was removing the make-up of Eryomka, but the mirror still reflected the haggard, terrible face of the vagabond. As this

---

* In Serov's *The Power of Evil*.

Chaliapin as Eryomka in Serov's *The Power of Evil*. Zimin's Private Opera, Moscow, 1916 (*above* and *right*).

figure disappeared and the round features of the singer returned, the tone of our conversation itself changed. When Eryomka had finally gone, when the make-up had been removed and instead of rags, Fedor Ivanovich's stately figure was dressed in a jacket; when he nonchalantly and elegantly knotted his tie, the rather rude and somewhat blustery tone also disappeared, and when he took leave of us Chaliapin turned into an attentive, most agreeable host, who had received guests in a not very friendly manner and who was embarrassed by this incident. He graciously accompanied us to the door; with innate courtesy he took the arm of a lady and, smiling, went to the exit. Could this really be the same man who had appeared before us half an hour earlier as the vagrant, inveterate drunkard and murderer Eryomka? It really seemed a miracle. And on the following day Dvorishchin, a close friend of Chaliapin, telephoned and said: "Fedor Ivanovich asked me to let you know that he would sing in Kronstadt."[44]

Chaliapin was not content to experiment just with make-up and costume. He was of the opinion that indications of a character's temperament and moods should be shown not only in the eyes and in facial expressions, no less important were posture and plasticity of movement, carefully chosen, logically thought out and expressing emotions. He wanted each gesture, fitting both the character's mood and the action in progress, to blend harmoniously with the background created by the scenery.

The study of painting became a necessity for Chaliapin as one of his regular sources of inspiration. He now saw the problems of portrayal, and of theatrical performance as a whole, through the prism of the visual arts. Paintings and sculptures often served him as prototypes for a character or even for an entire scene. Chaliapin would sit for hours looking at portraits which interested him and, analysing the imaginary world of these people, 'try' their features and attitudes on himself. His earlier love of drawing became part of the process. In short and precise strokes, Chaliapin fixed his ideas on paper. Born in the flimsy realm of imagination, they immediately took solid shape in the sketch, making it possible to look at the result 'from a detached point of view'. There were hundreds of these sketches. 'If Chaliapin cared to,' the correspondent of a Petersburg newspaper wrote in 1911, 'he could produce a whole magnificent album out of the drawings he made for each role. Unfortunately, with his usual insouciance, he has given most of these drawings to friends.'[45] Chaliapin would push his pencil along the paper while talking of something else. Or, interrupting the conversation, he would stop during a stroll to draw on the ground with a stick. 'His hands, expressive as a ballet dancer's, beautiful as a sculpture, always held a pencil – as he talked he wrote or sketched,' recalled Sol Hurok.[46] He drew even while waiting to be served in a restaurant. (A friend of his remembers an amusing anecdote. Once, while lunching in a small café in Prague, Chaliapin took it into his head to draw on the tablecloth. The owner of the tavern became annoyed and demanded money as compensation for her ruined property. Chaliapin paid up without argument and asked for the tablecloth. It was rolled up and handed to him. But then one of the guests told the landlady that she had done something silly. A tablecloth with a drawing by Chaliapin himself deserved to be framed and hung on the wall as evidence that the famous artist had visited this modest establishment. The woman then requested Chaliapin to give it back to her, and put in front of him the ten crowns he had paid her. 'Chaliapin shook his head: "Excuse me, madam. The tablecloth is mine. I bought it from you. And now if you want it back – it's fifty crowns...." The woman paid without a word.')[47]

Drawing was not only useful for understanding a stage character; in Chaliapin's view it also helped to assess one's own potential and qualities. 'I really know myself by heart. Very likely I could draw myself even with my eyes shut,'[48] he said later. 'Thanks to painters I gradually came to understand how to inject real life into a character. And when you get the character right, when it is convincing, then the musical phrase also takes on the proper nuance. This is why I say that painters taught me singing.'[49]

The truth of this statement becomes very apparent in the way Chaliapin prepared for his role as Holofernes in Serov's opera

Judith. The composer's son, Valentin Serov, talked at length to Chaliapin about the art and history of Assyria. Chaliapin was not satisfied with the traditional manner of performing the role – most of all because 'you could not feel the slightest whiff of antiquity in it.' He was not merely interested in a 'life-like image of the ancient Assyrian satrap but in one that should be distinctive as well.' He recounts how while studying books on the history of Egyptian, Indian and Assyrian art in Serov's studio, he came across profile portraits of 'kings and commanders, sometimes seated on a throne, sometimes driving a chariot, alone, in pairs, in threes....' The drawings struck Chaliapin's imagination. He conceived the thought of emphasizing in his Holofernes 'the broken line of the arm with two angles; the bend at the elbow and at the wrist'. This helped to convey 'great serenity, royal indolence' and at the same time tense energy and inner strength. He wanted to make him 'stony and terrifying'. Chaliapin was perfectly aware that no one had actually lived or moved like that in the distant past of humanity. It was only a stylisation, an artistic device. 'Not a single gesture stretching out sideways!'[50] he exclaimed.

According to Chaliapin, Serov approved of his scheme but cautioned against exaggeration which might produce a comical effect. Admittedly there are other memoirs which attribute the idea of 'an animated bas-relief' to Serov. 'One evening, while having tea with Mamontov and some other guests, the painter demonstrated his wonderful talent for imitating the gestures of various people. Serov took a finger-bowl from the table and, turning to Chaliapin, said: "Here, Fedya, watch how the Assyrian king must drink, and here (pointing to a bas-relief) how he must walk." Mamontov also agreed, stressing that the movements should be indicated much more sharply than on the sculpture, as one had to take into account that this was on a stage. Chaliapin started to pace up and down the dining-room and then seized the same finger-bowl and reclining on the sofa adopted the very pose seen in the painter Golovin's subsequent picture.'[51]

It does not matter who first conceived the thought – the singer, who, whether on stage or in real life, had an extraordinary flair

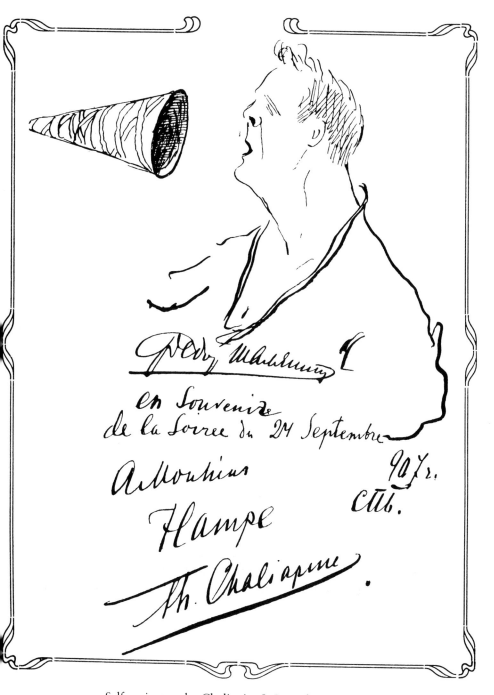

en Souvenir
de la Soiree du 24 Septembre

A Monsieur   907г.

Hampe   СПб.

Th. Chaliapine.

Self-caricature by Chaliapin. St Petersburg, 1907.

149

for truth and could catch its slightest thread, or the painter, who had in effect become director and designer of this production. The important thing is that we have here a remarkable example of empathy and of creative co-operation between two artists.

The costume and make-up devised by Serov and the way he represented Holofernes helped Chaliapin to make this one of the most visually perfect creations of his career. Critics wrote that Chaliapin as Holofernes showed 'wonders of monumental plasticity, with one sculpturesque moment after another',[52] but each attitude, each gesture concealed a definite meaning, dictated by the music.

The well-known music critic Yuri Engel declared after the first night of *Judith*: 'Chaliapin! It is once again very difficult to refrain from using exclamation marks when speaking of the appearance of reality this superior artist has given to Holofernes. What an original figure, risen straight from the walls of an Assyrian sarcophagus! How characteristic this face! As well as the savage, unrestrainable majesty of the warrior, to whom even Judith cannot refuse the name of hero, this face betrays glimpses of a sensitivity peculiar to the degenerate Babylonian satrap. Were this sensitivity not an essential ingredient of Serov's Holofernes, Chaliapin's voice might seem perhaps too soft, too noble for the frenzied and wild "scourge of God" making his triumphant way through rivers of blood. Even the difficult scene of Holofernes' drunkenness, his morbid wild delirium and final paroxysm, which is something of a gamble on the operatic stage, took on in the artist's interpretation the look of real life with its natural mixture of attractive and repulsive elements.'[53] Engel, a shrewd and experienced critic, identified another fundamental principle of Chaliapin's interpretations. In the creation of an operatic role, he worked not only with the music but also with the qualities of voice nature had given him. Chaliapin, who had an unrivalled ability to colour his singing with hundreds of psychological nuances, was nevertheless very careful to adjust his natural timbre according to the behaviour of the character he was playing. Chaliapin's vocal gifts appeared to be ideally suited to that particular role; its 'visible' part was directly based on the quality and resources of his voice and seemed to flow naturally from them. This was one of the things which gave Chaliapin's performances such fascinating authenticity. 'And what wealth of intonation, what expressiveness in the diction of the great artist', says another review. 'Even something which, in the hands of an inexperienced singer, is rather risky – such as the dramatic effect of turning musical declamation into near speech, as for instance in the scene of intoxication and wild ravings during the Act IV orgy – in Chaliapin's case produced a powerful impression without a hint of pomposity.'[54]

The innovations made by Chaliapin on this occasion were not wasted. When he sang Holofernes in 1907 at the Mariinsky Theatre, nine years after performing it at the Private Opera (on November 23rd, 1898), the movements he had devised were used by the choreographer Mikhail Fokine for the dances and the crowd scenes. By then, however, Chaliapin was once again searching for new approaches to the part, trying to broaden the character and refresh his vision of it. All Petersburg was at the dress rehearsal. To the audience's amazement, and to the horror of Telyakovsky, Chaliapin appeared on stage without make-up, wearing an elegant dark grey woollen suit. The surprises did not end there. In the middle of the introduction to Judith's aria, Chaliapin abruptly stopped the orchestra, led the singer of the title-role, Natalia Yermolenko-Yuzhina, to the back of the stage and there gave her some lengthy explanation, punctuated with energetic gestures. Then he gallantly kissed her hand, took her back to her place and signalled to the conductor that he could continue. When Chaliapin's turn came, he sang in a low voice, almost to himself. Another 'Chaliapin scandal' was about to take place. The rumble of discontent almost swamped the sound of the orchestra and the voices of the singers. Chaliapin showed no reaction. He again interrupted the rehearsal, started to shout at the chorus, sent for the terrified assistant director and made him tell them that they should fall to their knees only after Holofernes had said 'Slaves' and not a moment sooner. 'And suddenly,' recalls a spectator, 'he started to sing in full voice, and performed Holofernes' aria in such a

Chaliapin as Holofernes in Serov's opera *Judith*, 1907 (*above*, *right* and *page* 155).

way that ovations shook the theatre. And having finally got exactly what he wanted, Chaliapin quickly crossed the stage with enormous strides.'[55] During the interval, Telyakovsky decided that he would have to reprimand Chaliapin. He went to his dressing-room and to his astonishment found the singer, oblivious of his surroundings, drawing on the wall the make-up and costume of Holofernes with his sticks of greasepaint.... What else was he looking for now? He had already managed to astound everyone by creating the impression of 'living stone, a stern portrait, carved from granite'.[56] This alone would be sufficient to suggest the character of Holofernes. But a new conception of a role meant new movements, new make-up, costume and mise-en-scène. And as long as he had not perfected this new conception, he could not show himself made up and sing in full voice. Incidentally, the gestation of Godunov's first entrance was equally lengthy and laborious, as Chaliapin was trying to find the exact tempo for the Tsar's movements, the carriage of his head, his posture, the way his arms would hold the staff. 'My mistake', said Chaliapin to a friend, 'was that I had no clearly conceived image of what Boris should look like when he uttered the words "Skorbit dusha".* I should have done this as a painter does, and then a suitable walk and a right intonation would have come.'[57]

At the dress rehearsal of *Judith* it looked as if sudden revelation had produced an instant metamorphosis, but appearances were deceptive. Chaliapin's achievements were not only the result of innate talent and chance visitations of inspiration. Work was his most inseparable companion. 'The incident with Holofernes showed me', remarked Chaliapin, 'that gestures and movements on stage, however archaic, artificial and unusual they may be, will nevertheless seem true to life and natural if the artist feels them deeply in his soul.'[58]

The singer's words are especially revealing as his Holofernes was in many respects a product of his imagination inspired by the idea of stylisation. Chaliapin's portrayal owes more to an abstract idea than to psychology. But even in this case he

---

* 'My soul is heavy' – the first words pronounced by Boris Godunov.

concentrated all his efforts on matching the external image of the role to the inner one. Here too, 'the angular lines, the whole severe outline had to suggest seething passion, and every gesture had to reflect definite feelings while remaining strictly in character.'[59]

Chaliapin's interpretation went beyond inventing original physical movements. It had a central concept: crystallising the life and temperament of Holofernes in a visual form, and making it possible to discern in a single character a whole period, an ambience, a people. 'The deep colour of the face, the sharply bent, superbly modelled nose, the sparkling eyes and teeth, the strong, muscular arms, the luxuriantly dressed hair, heavy, black as soot, falling back in waves and tied at the front with an Assyrian bandeau, the enormous beard, carefully crimped and spangled with gold, the archaeological accuracy of the costume, the excellent choice of its colours – everything taken together rivets the attention, creating the impression of a mysterious, eerie apparition.'[60] The contemporary of Chaliapin who has left us this account seems to be describing a painting on the wall rather than a live character on the stage. But the 'pictorial' quality of Holofernes' look served a theatrical purpose. For Chaliapin, the make-up, costume and other attributes of the actor's profession were not simply external devices that united all the members of a cast in sustaining the theatrical illusion together.

'If you but once see this stately figure,' wrote a reviewer, 'draped in a length of precious cloth reaching to the heels, this head with the pale, almost sallow face, the black hair and beard, a pendant-earring dangling from the left ear, but once see the implacably energetic expression of this face with the perpetually restless wandering eyes of a bird of prey, this man whose impetuous movements are wholly unpredictable, down to the murder of a faithful retainer for one word out of line, if you but once see his lifelike image, as mighty as a natural element, you will never forget him. And still, this is only one side of Chaliapin's artistic creation. The other – vocal – one, being closely united with the first, raises the very character to the highest limits of artistic truth. The singer breathed new life into

Serov's recitatives, generally lacking in relief and expression.'[61]

Chaliapin's way of performing his roles made all modern theatre recognise that a character belonged to its own world which was presently being depicted on stage. For him the character's environment, real or imaginary, already contained a certain style of acting. More precisely, reality seemed to be a form of style. He perceived it as a single entity, a visible and audible actuality, where people and beasts, sounds and colours, natural events and everyday occurrences came and went. Chaliapin's brilliant powers of imagination distilled all this into a solid artistic composition. His creations, by their mere presence on stage, managed to suggest the future course of events and their causes, to reveal the essence of the performance. 'It is impossible to see him as Ivan the Terrible, or Boris, without realising that he is steeped in the history of those periods which live again at his will,' said Rosa Newmarch.[62] Expressed in theatrical symbols, the unmistakable truth of real life entered the stage. The scenes in which Chaliapin appeared differed sharply from the others by their *atmosphere*, in the sense that Stanislavsky used the word – atmosphere as indicative of the action in progress.

Holofernes and, incidentally, other of the singer's works displayed this realistic style distinctly and clearly. They carried its quintessence within themselves, as if it had been extracted from life and reproduced on a monumental scale in one unique being.

Chaliapin's ideas could lead him to surprising conclusions. 'Man, with his customs, and nature, in the midst of which he lives, always have something in common,' he said to one of his partners. 'The Ukrainian peasant, for instance, cuts his hair dead straight at the front and at the back, and the roof of his house is similarly neatly trimmed. When I prepared the role of Holofernes, I distinctly imagined a leopard, since Holofernes lived in a country where wild beasts could be found. I tried to imitate the movements of a leopard. For instance, in the drunk scene, when I fight with a non-existent enemy, I fall on the table, I strike the pose of a wild animal: I stretch right out, leaning on my hands as if they were paws.'[63] Pokhitonov, who conducted the opera in Petersburg, recalled: 'Despotic severity was the dominant motif in Chaliapin's Holofernes: everything trembled before him, in constant expectations of outbursts of uncontrollable anger turning into wild rage.... During the feast at the end of the fourth act, Holofernes-Chaliapin was terrifying when, strongly intoxicated by drink and by power, he fell upon his generals with a sword, shouting: "Slaves, dogs, worms! Why, I will crush you in an instant!"; shattered cups fell from the table under which the chorus was hiding in genuine panic.'[64]

Holofernes was not the first role performed by Chaliapin at the Private Opera. Within a few days of joining the company he made his debut as Susanin on September 22nd, 1896; Mephistopheles followed on the 27th and the Miller on October 1st. He had already sung these parts earlier and with considerable success. He had now to do something different, especially with Mephistopheles and Susanin. A remark dropped by Mamontov during a rehearsal had firmly stuck in his memory: 'Fedor Ivanovich, this Susanin is not a boyard, you know!' The comment was thought-provoking but no ready solution was at hand. There was too strong a tradition of performing this hero, who had sacrificed his life for his Tsar and his country, majestically and resolutely striding up and down the stage in red morocco leather boots and in fancy-dress 'peasant' attire.

The initial reaction to his Moscow début in the role was rather lukewarm. The reviews acknowledged Chaliapin's undoubted talent, the sincerity and warmth of his singing, but they also complained of insufficient freedom in the voice, lack of technique in placing the sound and even incorrect intonation. He was not yet completely at ease with Susanin; he had not formed an entirely clear picture of the character, and this affected the musical side of his performance.[65] But within a few weeks the situation had changed. 'Not for a long time have I had occasion to hear and see such a Susanin,' wrote Semyon Kruglikov. 'Before us rose a real, honest figure, absolutely true to life. Every phrase came from the heart, every gesture was in complete accord with the words, every pause expressed a mood. Such a performance can be expected from either a master of

Chaliapin as Ivan Susanin in Glinka's opera *A Life for the Tsar*. Moscow, 1901.

his craft or a natural talent of outstanding originality. We are here, of course, in the presence of a phenomemon of the latter kind...."[66]

Chaliapin continued to make alterations and improvements to this interpretation, as he did to all others, defining something more closely here, adding something new there.

Photographs, recorded fragments (though of a much later date) and, most important of all, eloquent contemporary descriptions, some of them luckily very detailed, help us to imagine Chaliapin as Susanin. 'The typical look of the Russian moujik, a timeless look – as he was in 1613 [the year in which the action of Glinka's opera is set], so he is in 1915,' wrote Edward Stark. 'His powerful, sturdy figure is slightly stooped; his neck is red and chapped; he has a huge spade-like beard which hides his whole face and lends an extraordinary air of dignity to Susanin. His walk is a typical peasant walk; it belongs only to those who do heavy work, who have to walk a long way from the village to the town and back again, walk behind the plough, walk behind the scythe – unhurried steps, with no unnecessary movement, where the feet are almost part of the earth; with this leisurely, shuffling gait our moujiks cover hundreds of versts.... But watch how the inner world of the peasant hero gradually unfolds before the spectator. Everything external, the whole visual accuracy of the portrait, fades into the background as the immense wealth of vocal colours, which is the secret of Chaliapin's fascination and the main tool of his creative genius, takes over. It is not just singing but combined musical and dramatic speech, where each word assumes its own nuance, not only according to the melody but to the feelings experienced at that moment. The sound adapts itself to the dramatic content of each successive moment of the role. These vocal colours are so bright that even people who heard Chaliapin in the role of Susanin only once, a long time ago, can remember the entire musical part with the precise inflections the singer gave it. And I think that were I to live another thirty or forty years, in that little corner of my memory reserved for my most treasured experiences, this voice will always be heard, and the tragic inflections of each note remain alive, as if I had heard them the day before.'[67]

The role of Mephistopheles in *Faust* already formed part of Chaliapin's repertoire; he had performed it more often than any other in various Russian towns. It gave him, however, no satisfaction, neither at the beginning nor at the end of his career – at the beginning because he was following an already established tradition, at the end because, having created his own, whose influence no performer can ignore today, he nevertheless had to confess: 'Mephistopheles is one of my bitterest disappointments. I carry in my heart a character I have simply not been able to portray satisfactorily.'[68] This comment concerned not only *Faust* but also – albeit to a lesser extent – Boito's *Mefistofele*, which Chaliapin sang for the first time at La Scala in 1901. And if he sometimes felt that he had achieved harmony, even if only fleetingly, in some of his other portrayals, with Mephistopheles things stood differently. Anyone watching closely the evolution of Chaliapin's art could see that it was not just a question of broadening and refining an interpretation. 'Mephistopheles does not leave Chaliapin alone for one minute,' remarked Vlas Doroshevich, a journalist well known in Russia at the beginning of the century. 'It is almost his torture, his nightmare. Chaliapin's entire career is his work on Mephistopheles. The character as Chaliapin now plays and sings him almost satisfies his exacting standards. But only "almost".'[69]

'Journalistic hymns of praise', says another review, 'do not explain anything about Chaliapin-Mephistopheles, since hymns are sung only to idols – that is to say, to what is already petrified. There is nothing fixed in Chaliapin's work, and neither is his Mephistopheles, yesterday's or today's. He does nothing final, apart from occasional moments; nothing is clearly stated, except for brilliant flashes of genius which, like lightning, illuminate the character for a minute. The fertility of his talent is staggering. He comes up with new details all the time without pausing to think about the possibility of running out of ideas. He seems to derive his creative power from the theatre boards as Antaeus does from the earth.'[70]

To reduce Chaliapin's 'entire career' to Mephistopheles, as does Doroshevich, is an obvious exaggeration. Nevertheless, from what reviews describe both in Russia and abroad, one gains the impression of a never-ending chase after an elusive ideal. Chaliapin often returned to the subject of Mephistopheles to try to analyse and understand the reasons for his 'conflict' with the role. Chronologically speaking, Chaliapin's own thoughts on this, together with an account of his subsequent appearances in *Faust* and in *Mefistofele*, belong to the next chapter. For the present, the reading Chaliapin offered the Moscow public in the autumn of 1896 will be the only one considered.

The usual operatic Mephistopheles brought to mind an insolent, impertinent rascal. With the agility and expertness of a circus magician, he materialised on stage out of bright tongues of fire and solidified into the pre-ordained attitude which was accepted by everyone as 'authentically' diabolical. Practically the entire role consisted of a set series of movements, which passed like a legacy from performer to performer, from production to production. As we know, even Chaliapin could not immediately overcome the force of habit. 'During the scene in the square, the débutant ... pulled faces, contorted himself, bent in all directions and took the most unlikely poses,'[71] wrote a spectator after a performance at the Mariinsky Theatre. The very look of the 'evil spirit' had also become set once and for all. At first Chaliapin himself adopted the standard: turned-up moustache and short beard; on his head a cap with a cockade in the middle and two feathers sticking out in opposite directions; striped tights of a light colour, close-fitting shirt and over it a short jacket. This is how we see him in a photograph dated 1895, and he is indistinguishable from any other singer in this role (Fedor Stravinsky being a notable exception). The picture gives no hint of the merciless power of evil and destruction which in subsequent years was at the core of Chaliapin's interpretation. What we see is the simple, honest face of a self-satisfied young man cheerfully crooning a love song. The absence of a central concept can be felt even in a drawing Chaliapin made that year: it is just the conventional look of the devil and has nothing to do with portraying a character. True, some critics noticed at this early stage that he was attempting

Chaliapin as Mephistopheles in Gounod's *Faust*, 1895.

an individual approach to the role, although they did not always approve of the results. 'Mephistopheles, the spirit of doubt who knows everything and judges everything, must not take so seriously what is patently human triviality, and show scorn for it.'[72] Chaliapin took exactly the opposite view and later even intensified the devil's contempt for humanity.

The first thing Chaliapin discussed with Mamontov after arriving in Moscow and starting work at the Private Opera was Mephistopheles: 'I see this character in a different way, in a different costume and make-up, and I would like to depart from theatrical tradition.'[73] Mamontov readily agreed, carefully listened to Chaliapin and gave orders that everything should be done as he wished. After they had examined together dozens of representations of Mephistopheles, new costumes were ordered. 'On the day of the performance I arrived at the theatre early and spent a long time searching for a make-up which would complement the costume, and finally it seemed to me that I had found something which harmonized with it. As I went on the stage, it was as if I had found another self, free in his movements, conscious of his strength and good looks.'[74] As with Holofernes, this shows how his search for the right make-up led to a visual representation of the character's personality. It is directly linked with the uncovering of 'another self' – that is to say, the ultimate degree of impersonation. Chaliapin could no longer conceive of any other approach to a role, or of any other reason for being on stage. Working on Mephistopheles, a character even more imaginary and symbolic than Holofernes, Chaliapin gets to the heart of the role through its visible part, movements, costume and make-up providing a starting point for imagination.

Almost a quarter of a century later, in 1928, when singing Mephistopheles in London, he mentioned too that at every performance he tried to give the voice a 'special' quality of sound, and 'weighed each note and found its value with the keenness of a painter mixing his colours'.[75] He confessed in Prague the following year: 'At first I was convinced that Mephistopheles was going to be my great success, but when the time came to appear on the stage in this role, I felt uneasy, without

Mephistopheles in *Faust*. Mamontov's Private Opera, Moscow, 1897.

at the time knowing why. "It's nothing," I tried to reassure myself. "One fine day the right feeling for the role will come, and everything will go swimmingly." But now I know for certain that I will never be a real Mephistopheles on the operatic stage. It is not impossible that one day my Mephistopheles will be praised as "the wonderful creation of a magnificent artist", but this does not prevent me from saying that this role is a theatrical absurdity.'[76]

Chaliapin's contemporaries did not agree with him, and his Mephistopheles was a revelation to them. 'Moscow has hardly ever seen on the operatic stage a Mephistopheles so originally and intelligently conceived, so boldly interpreted and in such a completely novel manner,' wrote Kruglikov. 'He comes straight from the canvas of a first-class painter, from the best illustrations to Goethe's *Faust* – the long, bony and bloodless face itself, with its rather thin beard, continually twitches in a sarcastic grimace. The artist sings with his characteristic brilliance of phrasing, in this case simply saturated with savage irony and contempt....'[77] The distinguished critic Nikolai Kashkin was no less enthusiastic: 'Chaliapin sang Gounod's *Faust*, and the others in the cast sang the latest version of what can be seen on any stage, the difference between them being such that Chaliapin seemed to sing the music of one composer and everybody else the music of another. One may disagree with Chaliapin on some details, but neither in Russia nor abroad have we heard a more consummate and well-thought-out Mephistopheles. The strength of the young performer lies in his refusal to imitate other well-known exponents of this role.'[78]

Sometimes there is, unfortunately, little information to be gleaned even from lengthy reviews. The critics more often tend to express enthusiasm or displeasure, approval or disapproval of what takes place on the stage; they rarely enable us to 'see again' a performance which has vanished into the past. They talk of a 'menacing, demoniac look', but what does that mean? And also, where is it in Gounod's music? This explains why the singer felt it necessary to imagine a background for the mighty ruler of man's and nature's dark forces, as well as the ruler himself. It would enable him to express the philosophical alle-

Mephistopheles in *Faust*. Petrograd, 1915.

gory in concrete dramatic form while preserving the clarity of the idea and the depth of the concept. And Chaliapin could not stop trying to 'understand' the nature of this inhuman character. According to him, Mephistopheles, fashioned out of the dark, instinctive aspects of the human spirit, cannot experience towards people anything other than boundless scorn. Yet is he, perhaps, for all his might, vulnerable and weak? For instance, is this why he is so sad and despairing when he realises the immutability of human vices? And so is there more to his behaviour than just sarcasm and hatred?

Professor Gozenpud has found a curious review written in 1897 when Chaliapin sang in Kiev: 'In his general interpretation the artist revealed an original concept of the role, adding to it some lyrical and sentimental touches. This was a Mephistopheles full of compassion and even sympathy for his victims; instead of demonic evil and sarcasm, something like a secret feeling of concern for people stirred in him. In the recitative, Chaliapin resorted to rapid patter, which removed the illusion of serious evil even further. Such a Satan, more frightening in appearance than in essence, was dramatically speaking insufficiently bold and powerful, but on the vocal side he made a good impression by the absence of any musical exaggeration or caricature.'[79] It is difficult today to say what suggested such a conception. Mephistopheles' words in Goethe's *Faust* may have provided a starting point: 'That power I serve which wills forever evil yet does forever good.' As the above review shows, the singer lacked confidence, and this was probably just one of the many attempts he made to find a solution to his 'most intractable role'. At any rate, Chaliapin persevered with the idea of trying to show a Mephistopheles feeling pain and regret at what he had done. 'I carried away an ineffaceable picture of Lucifer "fallen from heaven", a devilish cruelty in the eyes, a smile that froze the blood, yet sometimes, in the half-open mouth and quivering chin, an agony which seemed to suggest that once, before his fall, the soul of this murderer of souls had itself been white as snow,'[80] wrote a spectator to *The Times* after Chaliapin's performance in London in 1928.

Chaliapin felt no uncertainty as the Miller (*Rusalka*) in which he had triumphed at the end of the previous season on the Petersburg Imperial stage. Moscow reviews were more restrained but nevertheless favourable: 'We have already mentioned his exceptional talent for the stage and the sincerity of expression with which he won the hearts of the spectators in the roles of Susanin and Mephistopheles. He displayed the same qualities on this occasion. In his interpretation, the Miller came out as a quite vivid character; also the wonderful voice of the singer is perfectly suited to this role in range and in the character of the registers. The mad scene made a very powerful impression.'[81] The Miller's behaviour was dictated by unbounded love for his daughter, but, as one would expect from a Russian peasant who has amassed property, he was cunning and wily. He tried to ingratiate himself with the Prince, enjoyed money and presents, yet behind his outwardly cheerful conduct one could sense a vague unease, a premonition of disaster. Towards the finale of the first act, the tone grew increasingly sombre; from an ordinary sort of person, the Miller becomes a tragic figure. Stunned by the death of his daughter, Natasha (learning that the Prince had abandoned her, she throws herself into the river), he goes mad, then falls into a faint. This abrupt fit of insanity lasted only for a brief moment, but it was played with such conviction and authenticity that at the end of the performance the curtain regularly came down in complete silence and a few seconds passed before the applause started.

The climax of the role came in the third act, when the Miller, who by then had completely lost his mind, met the Prince. 'Instead of the respectable, sensible Miller, some awful thing is there, some monster from the forest, only half human: dim eyes, long beard untidy and unkempt, fluttering tufts of grey hair mingled with straw, arms helplessly stretched out sideways, like wings, with tightly hooked fingers, rags covering his shoulders.'[82] 'This strange creature in rags, with an insane look in his vacant eyes, resembled in fact a prophetic bird. "I am a raven, a raven!" he repeated mechanically over and over again. Then suddenly he remembered something, his head cleared for a brief instant, and so as not to lose what sense he had left, he rushed to tell the Prince about his dead daughter; but his

Chaliapin as the Miller in Dargomyzhsky's opera *Rusalka*. Petrograd, 1917 (*above* and *right*).

madness returned, and after that, however hard he tried to remember, moving his lips, hesitating or pulling his hair, nothing happened . . . .'[83]

'I don't think Moscow had ever seen a Miller like Chaliapin's,' wrote Semyon Kruglikov. 'The artist possesses the secret of a real talent to stun crowds by a phrase pronounced without a shade of tragic pathos, with no peals of thunder, no forced sound or ear-splitting note. On the contrary, his voice drops just when he has to convey to the listener what is most touching in the role, he risks losing a worthwhile passage, but what actually happens is quite different: you have taken notice of everything that should be noticed. You share the sorrow of the old man, you are upset, and you realise that it is Chaliapin who has upset you, that he has overcome your dull indifference to everything.'[84]

This is perhaps one of the first reviews no longer regretting in Chaliapin the absence of the customary, and therefore expected, 'thunder-like' sound of a bass. Searching for the right psychological intonation and for a way of uniting vocal and visual elements was by now an established feature of his method of work. Chaliapin's experiments in trying to combine contrasting ideas and feelings into a delicate and complex whole anticipated in a practical form the main principles of Stanislavsky's future system: 'When you play a wicked man, search for what good there is in him.'

On November 15th Chaliapin sang Vladimir Galitsky in Borodin's *Prince Igor*. It is not a big part, being limited to a prologue (in which Galitsky sings only a few phrases) and two scenes in the first act. Nevertheless, Stasov considered that it was worth seeing and hearing the whole opera for Chaliapin alone, 'even if not for all the other countless delights of Borodin's masterly work.'[85]

The curtain rises on the market-place of the old Russian town of Poutivl, where the people are gathering to see Prince Igor and his warriors off to the war. They are joined by Prince Galitsky, brother of Igor's wife Yaroslavna. Distress is general: all are anxious about the outcome of the campaign and the lives of their kinsmen. Galitsky alone shows no interest in either the

Chaliapin as Prince Galitsky in Borodin's opera *Prince Igor*, 1910.

solemn and sad farewells, the war itself or the fate of Russia. The most perfunctory glance at Chaliapin was enough to make this obvious. Vladimir Galitsky stood stock still, staring darkly at what seemed to him an excessive and futile display of affection and agitation. The Prince had apparently not yet quite recovered from his regular drunken orgy. He sometimes staggered in a strange way, winced as if woken by some internal shock, but instantly fell back into a state of unimaginable deadly boredom. The handsome face, framed by a golden red beard, betrayed signs of every conceivable vice: it was clear that no moral limits would stop this man if he wanted something. Whenever Chaliapin sang Galitsky, this scene invariably produced an unforgettable impression. 'His gestures, his revealing touches, his look, his silences and his very immobility give a striking vividness to the character and explicitly illustrate the situations,' wrote a French newspaper in 1932. 'How, without a word, without a movement, just by the expression on his face, the way he listens, he manages in the prologue to outline clearly the personality of this lout of a Prince Galitsky! This is not just art, but truly it is genius as well.'[86] Thus Chaliapin's mere presence on the stage as Galitsky prepared the way for the two scenes of turbulent gaiety and the violent argument with Yaroslavna which follow the prologue. In the first of these, he is not without a certain charm; there is a daring, impetuous youthfulness and strength in every inflection of the voice, in every movement. 'His eyes sparkle full of life and fire, and with a drunken twinkle of mischief, his herculean chest is shaken by loud laughter and yells, the whole of his body moves and dances.'[87] Prince Galitsky has many desires, and each word of the famous aria 'I must confess that I cannot stand boredom ...' was embellished by Chaliapin with a myriad of nuances, and the sound of it all poured out, like a cheerful, sweeping Russian song. 'Chaliapin's singing is superlative,' says one review, 'and so is the way he has assimilated his role. Great talent simply shone in everything. You watch, you listen, and just cannot tear yourself away.' It ends with the already familiar refrain: 'Chaliapin is a Galitsky the like of which has never been seen either in Moscow or in Petersburg.'[88]

Chaliapin as Khan Konchak in Borodin's opera *Prince Igor*, 1930.

Chaliapin was very fond of this role, and of the entire opera. In 1906 he sang in *Prince Igor* at the Bolshoi Theatre, and a few years later, in 1914, he took the part of the Polovtsian Khan Konchak. After this, he often performed both Galitsky and Konchak in the same evening, dazzling the spectators with endless changes of personality and with a fantastic, complete metamorphosis unprecedented in operatic theatre.

'To portray dissolute and cruel Galitsky,' wrote a Parisian opera-goer, 'Chaliapin gave himself a seductive mask: short-curled blond hair, frizzy beard, but avid and harsh glance. Fur cap, sumptuous frock-coat trimmed with heavy white embroidery, white leather boots. There was something at once attractive and repellent in his appearance, a great feline ready to bite savagely.

'This cad was nevertheless a great lord, and his height towered over the timorous herd of women and the sorry band of his drinking companions. But in the act of the Polovtsian camp, a striking figure appeared: tanned complexion, almond-shape slit eyes, tightly plaited hair, all Eastern litheness. A wide-necked, embroidered coloured shirt was held at the waist by a belt into which a leather whip was stuck. It was really impossible to think that this was the same interpreter who had just incarnated Galitsky; how could the brutal, gigantic Slav have metamorphosed himself into a wily Oriental? And the voice was also transformed: rough and violent for Galitsky, it was all caressing and troubling inflections for the speech of Khan Konchak.'[89] An American critic commented: 'As the Tartar chieftain in *Prince Igor*, he has but few lines to sing, but his gestures during the performance of the ballet, which he has arranged for his guests, in fact his actions throughout the single act in which this character appears, are stamped on the memory as definitely as a figure in a Persian miniature. And the noble scorn with which, as Prince Galitsky, he bows to the stirrup of Prince Igor at the close of the prologue to this opera, still remains a fixed picture in my mind.'[90]

There are creations in the life of every great performer which suddenly throw a new light on an already well-established talent. Such roles reveal the scale of the artist's gifts, and in the eyes of contemporaries, interpreter and character merge into one. This happened with Chaliapin in Rimsky-Korsakov's opera *The Maid of Pskov* on December 12th, 1896, during the finale of the second act's first scene, when a horseman enters the stage. The people of Pskov, massed in the market-place, anxiously await the arrival of Ivan the Terrible. They all know that he has just seized Novgorod and plunged thousands of innocent victims into rivers of blood. Now their turn has come. 'Fear was mounting. In a moment the scene became charged with nervous tension, which quickly transmitted itself to us, the public,' recalls the painter Mikhail Nesterov. 'Everything stood still. A moment later all prostrated themselves. To the right, a white horse in rich harness appeared round the corner of the street, advancing at a slow pace. On the horse could be seen the profile of the Tsar's weary figure, deeply sunk into the saddle.... The Tsar was wearing heavy armour; under his lowered helmet his sombre glance surveyed the submissive population. The horse came to a halt. The mighty sovereign gazed pensively at his slaves.... It was a terrifying instant. The fateful hour had come. What was now happening on the stage struck terror into the whole audience. The silence was deadly. The stillness of the scene, where not a sound was heard, was unforgettable in its tragic simplicity. The curtain fell slowly. The whole theatre was in a state of shock.'[91]

'That unforgettable first entrance in *Ivan the Terrible*,' wrote the London *Times* eighteen years after the Moscow première, 'is a marvellous contrast to his entrance in the coronation scene of *Boris Godunov*. In the latter case we spoke of him as being at the apex of the crowd: in *Ivan*, so far from being the apex, one is given a curious sense of anti-climax which is precisely what is needed. After the nervous apprehension of the citizens, the choruses of greeting, the march of troops, one is tensed to expect the arrival of a commanding hero, when, behold, an old man bowed upon the saddle, gazing with suspicious eyes upon the crowd, betraying a terror answering theirs.'[92]

Chaliapin's triumph in the role of Ivan the Terrible revealed to the Russian public yet another undeservedly forgotten masterpiece. *The Maid of Pskov* had had an unhappy record on the stage. It was first performed at the Mariinsky Theatre in 1873 but was soon dropped from the repertoire. The second version of the opera was never performed, and the third was given, with little success, by the St. Petersburg Musical Society with the participation of singers from the Mariinsky Theatre. There is some speculation that Chaliapin saw this production; indeed, it was first performed on April 6th, 1895, the day after his début on the Imperial stage. In any event, he 'knew that Rimsky-Korsakov had composed an opera called *The Maid of Pskov*. When I suggested staging it so that I could play the part of Ivan, everyone in the theatre, including Mamontov himself, received the idea with scepticism.'[93]

It may be what actually happened, although Chaliapin's subsequent accounts of the work's production at the Private Opera contain many inaccuracies.

Let us take first the claim that to prepare this complex role, which had eluded him for so long, he was left to his own devices and that only the designers 'explained a little and gave some help in understanding the period and character of Ivan the Terrible'.[94]

Chaliapin also writes that he 'produced the opera'. Neither of these statements corresponds to reality. *The Maid of Pskov* was produced by Savva Mamontov, and, as usual, he gave Chaliapin invaluable support in his work on the character of Ivan the Terrible. The photograph inscribed by Chaliapin two months after the première is eloquent proof of this: 'Souvenir from your slave Ivan. To my dear and beloved teacher Savva Mamontov as a token of gratitude and devotion from his F. Chaliapin, 15th February 1897.'* Mamontov would certainly not have left the young singer to the mercy of fate when he was undertaking the performance of a major role on which the success of the production depended. It is also strange that when talking of Ivan, Chaliapin not only forgot about the advice of the eminent Russian historian Professor Vasili Kliuchevsky but even remarked with regret: 'At that time I did not have such an excellent teacher as V. O. Kliuchevsky, who helped me to study

---

* There is a reproduction of the portrait in the archives of Abramtsevo.

the role of Boris Godunov.'[95] However, contemporary memoirs as well as an interview given by Chaliapin himself in 1898 clearly show that he had extensive consultations with Kliuchevsky.[96] The deep and subtle analysis of Ivan's personality given by the professor exerted a strong influence on Chaliapin: Kliuchevsky stressed in his books the suspicious nature of the Tsar's disposition, his mistrust of his associates, his malice and vindictiveness. 'He was more receptive to bad impressions than to good ones: his first thought on meeting anyone was that this was an enemy. Having clashed with the boyards and lost all trust in them after his illness in 1553 ... the Tsar overestimated the danger and took fright. ... Then the question of public order became a question of personal safety for him, and like a man who is scared out of his wits once his eyes are open, he started to hit out right and left, without any distinction between friends and foes.'[97] 'Tsar Ivan Vasilievich is not a bit ashamed', said Chaliapin, developing Kliuchevsky's conclusions, 'if the river is flowing not with water but with human blood....'[98] Such a conception of the personality of Ivan the Terrible was firmly established in the cultural awareness of Russian society at the end of the nineteenth century, and it also prevailed in art. The traditional view, originated by Karamzin and accepted by literally everyone who touched upon the theme of Ivan the Terrible's reign, inspired a variety of portrayals: in plays by Alexei Tolstoy and Ostrovsky, paintings by Schwarz, Nevrev, Repin and Vasnetsov and sculpture by Antakolsky. Mamont Dalsky in Petersburg, Alexandre Sumbatov-Yuzhin in Moscow and the Italian actor Ernesto Rossi, who often toured Russia, had created the stern and powerful figure of a Tsar-tyrant. Chaliapin went further than his predecessors, adding much that was new to the concept of the character.

In *The Maid of Pskov* Ivan IV is in the last period of his reign. Although he is only forty years old, his life is almost over. Ivan the Terrible is seen only three times in the opera, but in these scenes Chaliapin managed to let the audience feel in every word and every action of the Tsar the indelible marks of his past deeds, marks left by disasters and crimes, violent passions and spiritual emptiness.

Chaliapin read in Kliuchevsky that after his illness Ivan was consumed by anxiety and aged rapidly. He who had until recently been tall, slender and strong became senile; his gait altered drastically; every phrase he uttered was accompanied by laboured breathing; his eyes grew dim. At first, Chaliapin probably over-emphasised the premature deterioration of Tsar Ivan. A critic objected to the fact that the singer 'more than anything else presents to us a tumbledown ruin, barely able to sit on a horse – a ruin clad in armour.... If Ivan had become as weak as Mr. Chaliapin portrays him, he would not have wanted to sit on a horse. He ... would have had himself carried on a litter....'[99]

His interpretation rested on solid ground: Chaliapin had made a careful study of contemporary memoirs and conformed to their descriptions. But he was not simply governed by a desire to remain faithful to history. Other reviews make it clear that the sickly state of the Tsar was in fact only a mask. Ivan deliberately pretended to be weak and almost incapable of holding on to power. It is easier to watch what is going on through weary, half-closed eyes. Then those around you are not so nervous and take less care to hide their real feelings and intentions. Later Chaliapin 'gave back' some strength and energy to the character: he made a dashing entrance on a horse – bursting upon the stage at a gallop, it stopped in front of the petrified crowd and reared.

This Ivan was remarkable for the regal magnificence, lasting and absolute autocratic power imparted to him. 'What unlimited sense of authority over others,' wrote Chaliapin, 'and what unimaginable confidence in one's rightness!'[100]

Ivan regarded people as his slaves, but he was also afraid of them. Such was the view propounded not only by historians but also by psychiatrists, who were showing great interest in the personality and mental condition of Ivan the Terrible. Some specialists in particular explained the Tsar's cruelty by the fact that he suffered from paranoia.[101] In Chaliapin's interpretation, fear became Ivan's dominant feature, from which all his other attributes sprang. It determined his conduct, the way he moved, the expression on his face. Chaliapin went about the stage taking short steps and made frequent but unexpected stops, his eyes constantly darting around. When he stopped, he listened intently to the deadly silence. At moments like these, his eyes would narrow and he would incline his head slightly to one side. The great and invincible sovereign, who had subjected people to cruel torture and terror, seemed to live in expectation of an attack from any corner, afraid even of his own shadow. 'How much suspicion, mistrust and anxious cowardice there is on the face of Ivan the Terrible,' writes Stasov, describing Chaliapin's first appearance in the role, 'what a mixture of formidable menace and secret pusillanimity emanates from him as he looks around, scanning the crowd in Pskov; in vain do they offer him bread and salt,* in vain are the tables laden with honey and beer, and the inhabitants of Pskov on their knees. This entrance was a pure chef d'oeuvre.'[102] Two words stand out: the 'formidable menace'. For all his symptoms of morbid behaviour, Chaliapin also saw Ivan as 'a man consolidating the strength of centralised power, extolling the benefits of auto-cracy.'[103]

In Rimsky-Korsakov's opera, however, Ivan is not motivated solely by political interest and the struggle for power. After entering Pskov, he faces the greatest tragedy of his life: the chance encounter with his daughter – Olga, whose existence he did not even suspect, awakens in his heart long-forgotten human feelings. The transformation, albeit temporary, of a tyrant and murderer into a loving and deeply grieving father became an important detail in Chaliapin's interpretation. Olga perishes at the time of the skirmish between Ivan's troops and the rebellious defenders of the town. Nothing can now save the Tsar from knowing the loneliness of the grave before his death, from enduring pangs of conscience and agonies of fear at the prospect of imminent retribution. The singularities of Ivan's nature, as Chaliapin played him, manifested themselves in unexpected and odd combinations: constant readiness to do the most savage deeds alternated with spurts of piety, cruelty with feigned mag-nanimity, perpetual mistrust and cunning with a desire to find

---

* Traditional Russian way of welcoming guests.

(*Above* and *right* and page 187) Chaliapin as Ivan the Terrible in
Rimsky-Korsakov's opera *The Maid of Pskov*. The sketch is by Chaliapin
himself, 1914.

out the truth whatever the cost. From separate features and details a complete character took shape in Chaliapin's imagination; it was as if he could see Ivan's face, the way he walked, his gestures, how he sat, ate, stood and looked at people. At this stage of his work, painting and sculpture had again a special role to play. 'For the actor, or more exactly, for the plastic portrayal of a certain type, and even more so for Ivan the Terrible, it was not enough to have read all the books.'[104]

Chaliapin studied Repin's painting of 'Ivan the Terrible and His Son Ivan'. It shows a Tsar distraught with sorrow, holding in his arms his dying son, covered in blood. Nearby on the carpet rolls the staff with which Ivan, in a fit of anger, has just struck him on the temple. 'And although the episode of his son's murder was not actually part of the role, the spirit of Ivan was portrayed exactly as I wanted to do it, as Human Spirit. Under the despotism and the brutality, deep, deep down, I could see a glimmer of love and goodness.'[105]

Chaliapin also looked with great care at Antakolsky's statue. He was startled to see an Ivan absorbed in thought. In the immobility and the unusual sadness of the cruel ruler, the sculptor had tried to feel the impulses of a soul, the state of a man when he is at his most honest with himself. 'This old, wicked and sick man,' wrote Ivan Turgenev about Antakolsky's work, 'is at one and the same time a typical Russian and a Tsar from head to foot – no less impressive than King Lear.... What is particularly striking here is the felicitous combination of the domestic, the everyday and the tragic.'[106] Chaliapin also studied the paintings of Schwarz, but what really fired his imagination was the portrait of Ivan by Victor Vasnetsov. 'The face of Ivan is shown in three-quarter view,' wrote Chaliapin about the painting. 'The Tsar's fiery dark eyes are looking somewhere to the side.'[107]

Chaliapin's interest in these artists' works extended beyond looking for realistic details. The indications of Ivan's character that he read in them helped to give him a deeper understanding of the relationship between the Tsar's outward appearance and his inner world. This Ivan incorporated everything Chaliapin had learnt, all the impressions he had accumulated in examining historical sources, literature and works of art, but at the same time it was also a new and original figure, which astonished his contemporaries and has a place among the greatest Russian artistic and scholarly accomplishments. Rimsky-Korsakov, who was a stern critic and did not give praise freely, wrote after the performance: 'The success of *The Maid of Pskov* was due to the great talent of Chaliapin, who created an incomparable Tsar Ivan.'[108]

This effect was not accomplished without effort: despite the exceptional enthusiasm with which Chaliapin started rehearsing, the role eluded him. The music of the opera pictures Ivan as being by nature impulsive, perhaps even unrestrained in all his actions. The strange and terrifying figure of this murderer and dictator must undergo a visible change before he can be capable of experiencing a spiritual shock at the sight of his daughter's dead body. Chaliapin was only twenty-five years old, and it was no easy task for him to paint a realistic and expressive portrait of this many-sided, complicated character and to cover the complex gamut of his feelings. It is interesting in this connection to quote from one of the first reviews of *The Maid of Pskov*, written by a well-known Russian music critic, Herman Larosh. He considered the music of the opera to have an 'extremely unhealthy character.... Such music, it seems to me, would suit a plot taken from Dostoevsky's *Crime and Punishment*.'[109] Larosh's paradoxical remark accurately pinpoints a similarity between Rimsky-Korsakov's Ivan and Dostoevsky's heroes, however odd and surprising this may at first seem. Is there a connection between the power-hungry tyrant, who holds the fate of others in his hands, and the humble and perpetually starving inmates of Petersburg's damp basements? The similarity resides in the vehement feelings which rule them both and are indivisible from one another: mockery and tenderness, cynicism, incomprehensible cruelty and tormenting pangs of conscience; in their unrestrained ambition to gain power by any means; and in their expectation of eternal punishment.

It was important for Chaliapin to define clearly the psychological motives of Ivan's conduct at any given moment of the story, to give more substance to the role and turn an operatic character into a real person. 'I did not undertake the role of Ivan without misgivings . . . despite the fact that I had extensively consulted all available sources, I often chose the wrong tone, and finally I tore up my part in despair and decided not to play it,' said Chaliapin in 1898.[110] He reminisced about this later in his books, and scanning his memory for the most important moments of his life, he listed among them the agonising rehearsals of *The Maid of Pskov*, which made such an impact on his development. 'I knew that Ivan was a hypocrite, and therefore the words "To enter or not to enter?", which he utters on the threshold of Tokmakov's mansion and with which the drama opens, I pronounced quietly and humbly, but with hidden malice. I continued in the same tone. Boredom and gloom filled the stage. I felt it, and all my colleagues felt it. I tore up the score, broke something, rushed to my dressing-room and in despair burst into tears. Mamontov came in, patted me on the shoulder and advised in a friendly manner: 'Stop fretting, Fedyenka! Take yourself in hand . . . and make the first phrase a little stronger.'[111] This comes from Chaliapin's first book; the same episode is treated in far greater detail in the second. 'My first scene has Ivan standing on the threshold of the Governor of Pskov's house, the boyard Tokmakov. "To enter or not to enter?" is my first phrase. This question has the same importance in the role of Ivan as Hamlet's "To be or not to be". It must immediately reveal the character of the Tsar and bring to the surface his inherent cruelty. It must be made clear to the spectator who has not read history, and even more to the one who has, why the boyard Tokmakov trembles at the mere sight of Ivan.

'I sing "To enter or not to enter?", but the phrase falls flat, it has no effect. And the whole act is like that, boring and colourless. Mamontov comes up to me and quite casually, as if in passing, remarks: "There is cunning and hypocrisy in your Ivan, but terrible – he is not." This single remark of Mamontov's illuminated the whole thing for me like a flash of lightning. "My intonation is wrong!" I instantly realised. I make the first phrase, "To enter or not?", sound malicious, hypocritical,

sarcastic and vicious. This creates a weak, characterless picture of the Tsar. The lines and the shadows on his face are there, but not the face itself. I now understood that this first phrase must express the very essence of his nature. I started again from "To enter or not to enter?" This time, to hurl my question, I used a resounding voice, charged with menace and cruel mockery, like a blow from a metal rod, while casting a fierce glance at the room I had entered. The effect was immediate; everything around woke to life. The entire act became vivid and created a strong impression. The correct intonation of a single phrase had transformed a venomous snake (the image suggested by my first intonation) into a ferocious tiger.... I had long ago realised the significance and the importance of correct intonation in a role – perhaps as far back as during my studies with Usatov, and certainly after my conversation with Dalsky about the role of the Miller. But with the production of *The Maid of Pskov*, I had to work very hard to put my knowledge into practice. In conventional terms, I had sung Ivan impeccably. I had performed the musical intonations with mathematical precision, i.e. I had sung an augmented fourth, a second and a third, major and minor as indicated; but even if I had had the most magnificent voice in the world, it would still not have been sufficient to produce the artistic effect the role demanded. That meant – and I had finally grasped the point – that mathematical precision, even with the most perfect voice, is lifeless unless mathematics and sound are transfigured by feeling and imagination. It meant there was something more to the art of singing than the brilliance of bel canto. . . .'[112]

Some moments of his performance come to life for us through contemporary memoirs. The dreaded Tsar, 'eagle nose, cruel mouth accentuated by a short drooping moustache and goatee, long and dishevelled hair, the eye at once weary and ruthless,'[113] pausing on the threshold, scrutinised the interior of the chamber. His first words, loaded with menace and irony, 'made the blood curdle; one felt terrified for the fate of those to whom they were addressed. He entered the chamber. Everyone was thrown into disarray.'[114] Once inside, he removed his helmet and, seeing the ikons on the wall, crossed himself. Tokmakov

and the boyard Matuta respectfully took his arms to escort him
to the seat of honour. Ivan's recent fear before entering Pskov
had now turned into cruel vindictiveness. His rage erupted
suddenly like flames from ashes; he roughly rejected his hosts,
literally flinging them aside. 'My thanks, truly!' he hissed. 'Two
of them to offer you a seat! And in proper Christian style; on
the right an angel, on the left a devil.' One incautious word and
the Tsar would destroy them. But once he had settled in the
armchair, his temper cooled down just as suddenly as it had
flared up. A mask of gentleness and submissiveness descended
on his face; he had the air of a man who is weak and finds
it difficult to speak. However, this was only a pretence. He
threatened again: 'I will tear everything down!' He then
enquired with practical curiosity whether Tokmakov had a
wife, but when he heard 'No, only a daughter,' he asked: 'Is she
young?' The inflection of Chaliapin's voice and his expression
clearly indicated the hidden meaning behind the question. His
eyes lit up; he started to run the fingers of his right hand through
his beard – there was no mistaking the direction of the Tsar's
intentions. Olga entered. With eyes downcast, she offered the
Tsar a cup of mead. But Ivan, full of mistrust, shrank from it
and insisted that his host should drink first. Tokmakov drank
to the sovereign, who, brightening up, accepted the refreshment.
'All right then, give me some too,' said Ivan to Olga, '– and
don't just bow to me, give me a kiss as well'; but as he raised
his head, he recoiled slightly. The lascivious grin vanished
to give way to visible astonishment; his whole body shook
repeatedly – and he said, almost in a whisper: 'Holy Mother!'
    'He was thrown into confusion. Ivan the Terrible was in a
state of confusion! Human feelings had awoken in him; invisible
threads of love had joined the pure heart of a maiden to another
heart ... Whose? That of Ivan the Terrible! An almost imperceptible shadow crossed the Tsar's face; the corners of his
mouth gave a little quiver. "Don't you want us to kiss?" But
now these words had a different meaning. ... '[115] Trying to hide
his agitation, he affected loud laughter. Servants brought him a
pie and some wine. Ivan broke into the crust of the pie, pulled
out some of the filling, raised it to his mouth, then smelt it and

abruptly turned to Tokmakov and Matuta standing beside him. Chaliapin-Ivan motionlessly commanded them with his eyes to try the pie; finally satisfied that he was not being poisoned, he started to eat.

Alone with Tokmakov, the Tsar asked the name of Olga's mother. Tokmakov did not hide the truth. Olga was the daughter of his late wife's sister, Vera Sheloga, but who her father was remained a mystery. Ivan was deeply affected by the tale. He crossed himself, pensively hung his head; then, leaving his armchair and drawing himself up to his full height, he pronounced words of mercy: 'Let all the carnage cease. God save Pskov!'

Act Three, scene two. A quiet moonlit night. Everyone is fast asleep except the Tsar. The encounter with Olga, the return to the familiar places of his youth have revived thoughts about the past. He also thinks about Russia, about the need to unite her, 'to bind her in a law as strong as armour'. Chaliapin found this monologue of Ivan's particularly difficult, not only at rehearsals but even during performances. 'I sing Ivan the Terrible ... and at the beginning of the last act of the opera I am unable to go on as I should. What is the matter? This: At first, Ivan is sunk in meditation. He recalls his youth, his meeting Vera, Olga's mother, long ago in a nut grove, how his heart throbbed, how he yielded to his latest torrent of passion. But at that very moment, right after this, his thoughts take a very different turn. "Only that kingdom is strong, mighty and great where the people know they have but one leader, as a flock has but one shepherd." The dreamy lover ... suddenly becomes a mature political thinker.... There is an abrupt transition from one state of mind to another – it needs either a pause, or perhaps there should be a change in the pace of the music, but the composer has not done this. I had to ask the conductor to hold the orchestra on the last note, to draw it out so as to give me the opportunity, and the time, to change my expression and my manner. I talked about this to Rimsky-Korsakov. My admiration for him is boundless, but it must be said that Nikolai Andreevich did not like to hear about his mistakes. And he was not particularly keen to hear me either. He said sullenly: "I'll see, I'll think about it...." A short time later be brought me a new aria for this scene. He had dedicated it to me ... but I sang it only once – at the rehearsal. The original recitative, even with its mistakes, was superb, while the aria with which he wanted to replace it was quite unsuitable: an "aria" was not what I wanted on the lips of Ivan the Terrible. I felt that an aria would interfere with the normal development of my role.'[116]

We can see how vital it was for Chaliapin to maintain at all times of the action this unbroken contact between the performer and the thoughts and feelings of the character he was playing. Scrutinising the motives and the logic of Ivan's conduct enabled Chaliapin at the same time to form a clear impression of his external appearance, which in turn facilitated the changes of emotional states demanded by the action. Once he had deter-mined the psychological motives of Ivan, Chaliapin succeeded in making his voice 'capable of answering the slightest emotional and intellectual demands of its master. Not a single word, not a single sound is wasted in his Ivan. There does not seem to be any feeling in the music of Ivan which the singer could not express.'[117]

'In this strange figure there is nothing of Chaliapin,' wrote a London critic in 1914, 'the ruthless Emperor is represented as the Oriental that he was. He appears before us old and awkward and suspicious. His thin parted beard, his hooked nose, his Mongolian lips are a sure index of his character. There is a studied clumsiness in his movements which you are sure belonged to the man himself. When he drinks you can hear his teeth rattle on the winecup. His fingers dissect the food set before him with a savage curiosity. He comes before us in such a guise that nothing he says or does can surprise us. The differences of his wayward nature are subtly harmonised. His cruelty and his tenderness are alike made credible. His heavy-lidded eyes deliver, before his tongue, the message of his elemen-tal passion. And in spite of diversities the Emperor's dignity is constant and unchanging.

'His first entrance upon the stage – it is in the second act – is a very miracle of pompous tranquillity. You are prepared by the crowd for a terrible apparition, and Ivan appears upon his white horse, Eastern and sardonic, a monument of disquieting quietude.

'Thus with shifting emotions his dignity remains immutable. When he finds a daughter he is still a despot. He pardons the city, bidding cease the massacre, with the sudden graciousness of a tyrant. Even his grief at his daughter's death is the more bitter because it is the grief of a monarch still unapproachable. Here at any rate is a consistent portrait which, for those who have seen it, will survive ineffaceably with memory itself.'[118]

In the scene with Olga he was unrecognisable. Here the severity was only pretended, to hide tenderness, fondness and admiration for his daughter. While she was down on her knees before Ivan, telling him about her life, he bent over her, and although he so much wanted to press his lips on her head, fearing to give himself away, he just cautiously passed his hand over her hair. But the transformation was short-lived, just a few moments. 'When the young people of Pskov, whom he hated and feared, could be heard approaching, his bitterness came back; he flung his metal staff at them heatedly, wildly pulled out his sword and, brandishing it, yelled to his forces in a voice full of despair: "Death to them all!" and then cravenly ran from one tent to another, fearfully looking out to see how things were going and wondering whether they were not turning against him. But then the body of his daughter, accidentally shot in the midst of the fighting, was brought in and laid down at his feet. This was the beginning of a dreadful tragedy for Ivan. His beloved daughter was already beyond saving: a learned foreign doctor had humbly declared that only a miracle could revive her, and so the Tsar tried for one moment to resort to the ultimate means at his disposal. He prayed; he crossed himself before the ikon, attempted to raise his heavy hand and his lifeless eyes towards it – to no avail. He snatched a prayer-book, feverishly turned the leaves, wet his finger to try and find the page with the most potent prayer – but no, this did not help either, all was in vain. Then he abandoned everything and, with all hope gone, fell on the ground beside the body of his daughter, like a subjugated, stricken beast. The inflections of his voice everywhere, the way he spoke and the music, the poetry, the tragedy – it is impossible to give anyone an idea of all this.'[119]

The public reacted to Chaliapin's Ivan the Terrible in the same manner as it had reacted to his Miller: 'His sobbing and lamentations amidst the muted singing of the chorus of townspeople had such a powerful effect that the theatre remained plunged in stunned silence for some time after the curtain had fallen, and then exploded in tumultuous applause. You should have seen Chaliapin in the wings while the curtain was coming down. One could tell that he was tired, that the scene he had just played had cost him a great deal of effort, a great deal of nervous excitement, but he quickly pulled himself together and took his curtain calls. Once in his dressing-room he became his usual self again, clowning, pretending it was all child's play for him.'[120]

'Chaliapin took a long time to answer the tempestuous calls of the audience. He suddenly appeared before us without make-up, without helmet, in his heavy battle-armour and real coat of mail. He seemed rather clumsy. We had in front of us a good-humoured, flaxen-haired lad of gigantic stature, standing there and bowing. He smiled naively, and how far all this was from what had recently taken place here, on this stage! The contrast was striking. It was hard to believe that the man we had seen earlier on and the man we now saw were one and the same person. After this the Russian public remained for many years under the spell of this enormous talent, which reached moments of pure genius on the stage.'[121]

Chaliapin's interpretation gave his audiences much more than a triumphant performance of the role; it was an innovation whose importance reached far beyond the limits of operatic theatre to affect Russian scenic art as a whole. It also marked a stage in Chaliapin's artistic development: this was the young singer's first real encounter with a new way of constructing the vocal phrase, with new answers to the question of 'word and music'. The idea of combining the two was at the origin of opera, and in subsequent periods manifested itself frequently and with great variety in the works of all manner of composers; but in Russian music, and particularly in the compositions of members of the 'Moguchaya Kuchka',* this ancient concept took on a different character. The 'Moguchaya Kuchka' left no treatise on their work comparable to Gluck's preface to *Alceste* or to Wagner's writings. However, Cui's wide-ranging critical output, Rimsky-Korsakov's articles, remarks scattered among Balakirev's and Mussorgsky's letters, make the ideals of the new Russian school sufficiently clear. Their aesthetic aspirations were based on 'musical truth'. This expression, coined by Mussorgsky, was frequently heard among the group: as for instance when Rimsky-Korsakov said that Cui's opera *William Radcliffe* contained moments of 'life and action, not to mention musical truth', or when Cui wrote that he saw in Verdi's operas 'a disregard for musical truth'. What exactly did the 'Moguchaya Kuchka' want to say by this rather vague notion? 'Truth means that the music throughout the opera faithfully expresses the action taking place on stage, remaining as close as possible to local colour, the spirit of the period and the development of the musical character of the protagonists,' explained Cui.[122]

One of the conditions of 'musical truth' is that melody and text should be intimately related. 'The phrasing must be natural, each phrase pronounced correctly, the voice being raised and lowered where needed; each note must intensify the expressiveness of the text so as to make a strong impression on the listeners.'[123]

However, the text used as the basis of an opera was not to be treated as a framework on which to hang a melody but as a dynamic structure, whose 'components are filled with poetical charm'. The inflection of the voice in this case becomes the basic pivot in searching for 'musical truth': it is a sensitive indicator of the smallest currents stirring in a man's soul. The whole effect can sometimes even rest on the word, since

---

* 'Moguchaya Kuchka' ('the Mighty Handful', known in the West as 'the Five'). An association of Russian composers, also called 'Balakirev's group' and 'the New Russian Musical School'. The name was given to them by their spokesman and ideologist, Vladimir Stasov. The association was finally formalised in Petersburg in 1862 and consisted of Mily Balakirev, Alexander Borodin, César Cui, Modest Mussorgsky and Nikolai Rimsky-Korsakov. It ceased to exist towards the middle of the 1870s. Continuing the tradition of Mikhail Glinka and Alexander Dargomyzhsky, the 'Moguchaya Kuchka' accomplished a revolution in the history of Russian music.

emotional and psychological nuances, as well as the general course of the action on the stage, flow through it.

'Taking human speech as the basis of my work, I arrived at the melody created by this speech; I arrived at the conversion of recitative into melody.... I would like to call this reasoned, justified melody,' wrote Mussorgsky to Stasov in 1876.[124] This idea of 'musical truth' also coloured the views of 'The Five' on the question of form free from biased tradition. The ideal form of construction in music theatre was for them one 'where the composition's plan derived directly from the theme of the text, of the dramatic situation.'[125]

These words of Rimsky-Korsakov define the principles which guided him for *The Maid of Pskov*, but Stasov and Mussorgsky, who took an active part in the writing of the libretto and in discussing the plan of the opera, naturally shared the same belief. The musical language of *The Maid of Pskov*, with its extensive crowd scenes, its small number of solos and the predominance of declamatory recitative in the main roles, demanded a new type of singer with a new performing style: the operatic stage was now peopled by characters who sounded natural, behaved naturally. Chaliapin proved to be such an interpreter. 'Russian singers were kept away from Russian operas by their musical formation and the interests of their career, and even if a few outstanding artists among them were prepared to give some of their time to Russian music as well, they often introduced alien and distorting artifices into their way of performing it,' wrote Yuri Engel in his article 'Russian Opera and Chaliapin'.[126]

Chaliapin astonished his contemporaries by the effects he produced; the precision and the accuracy of his singing gave the impression of human speech. 'The realism of his declamation was amazing; I sometimes found it positively unbelievable that I was listening to a phrase which had been learnt from written-down music. It was live, free speech, adapting itself to convey all the shades of emotion. In the part of Ivan the Terrible, not a single word was wasted, not a single one of the composer's intentions was lost sight of.... Such talent seems to have been especially created for the striking declamatory style of Mussorgsky,'[127] wrote another reviewer, who soon proved to have been prophetic in his observations.

At the start of the following season Chaliapin was singing Dosifei in *Khovanshchina* and a year later *Boris Godunov*. He would subsequently show himself at his best in roles which were either, like Ivan the Terrible, linked with real historical figures or with a definite period of history and to some extent representative of it. In *The Oprichnik** by Tchaikovsky, Prince Vyazminsky is Ivan the Terrible's companion at arms, the accomplice in the Tsar's crimes who carries out his bloody commands. Vyazminsky was usually played as a melodramatic villain, thus depriving the character of elementary psychological cogency. Chaliapin gave him the recognisable features of a man who believes in a system. Anyone who disagrees with it is an enemy and must be destroyed. The cruelty with which he mocks defenceless people does not stem from diabolical evil. Vyazminsky has become an executioner because of his convictions. He knows no other way. The photograph of Chaliapin in the role shows a stern face ravaged by passions, a face one cannot forget.

The first night of *The Oprichnik* took place on January 23rd, 1897, a month after *The Maid of Pskov*. Two weeks before, Chaliapin had sung Colline in Puccini's *La Bohème*, and in November 1896, Nilakantha in Delibes' *Lakmé*. The season lasted only six months, but he appeared in five new roles, took part in more than eighty performances, and on almost every occasion the evening ended with the members of the orchestra banging their bows on the music stands or even honouring him with a fanfare. In Moscow theatrical circles and on their fringes the name of Chaliapin was on everyone's lips; opera lovers did their utmost not to miss a single one of his performances. Time passed at a meteoric speed, and although much was accomplished, Chaliapin felt no fatigue. On the contrary, he wanted to go on, to test further the innovations he had tried out at Mamontov's. When the performances had to end in Moscow, the only solution was to go on tour. At the beginning

---

* See note page 48, Chapter I.

of March he left for Nizhni-Novgorod, where he gave two concerts. He found trying to hold the interest of the public while performing a succession of unconnected pieces of music without singing partners, without costume or make-up, even more challenging. All the singer can rely on is the eloquence of his voice.

A review – possibly one of the first to comment on his concert performances – wonderfully catches the essential qualities of his art. 'Chaliapin is an artist with an exceptional gift for the stage, blessed with a voice of rare beauty, strength and softness, which he uses with amazing flexibility. The singer's acting style is remarkable for its sensitive taste, restraining him from exaggeration, even when a certain amount of caricature would seem unavoidable, as for instance in Mussorgsky's comic songs. The phrasing is dignified and unpretentious, which does not in any way detract from its expressiveness. The diction is clear and precise. Chaliapin is equally good whether pathos or plain straight singing is required. He is equally at home with humour and with musical declamation. The latter in particular is notable for the refinement of its presentation. . . .'[128] The article ends on an interesting remark: 'Moving on to the defects – this word would be too strong; rather, to the weak points – in Mr. Chaliapin's singing, one might express the wish that the artist should give more care to perfecting his voice in purely vocal terms, that he should free himself from such mistakes as the tight sound which occasionally manifests itself in certain notes, or accidental vibrato, etc. . . .' The advice did not go unheeded. When his tours finished (after Nizhni-Novgorod came Kazan, Kharkov and Kiev), Chaliapin went abroad for the entire spring and summer, not only in search of new impressions but also to take singing lessons. He was himself aware of the need to improve his vocal technique.

This was Chaliapin's first voyage to Europe, and, like that of many of his fellow-countrymen, his knowledge of it rested on traveller's tales. Two of his friends were particularly insistent that he should undertake the journey: Stasov and Mamontov. Chaliapin recalled one of his conversations with the critic: 'You, my friend, must go to England! They are wonderful people, the English. You must show Ivan to them, you must! Go to

Chaliapin as Prince Vyazminsky in Tchaikovsky's *Oprichnik*. Moscow, 1899.

England!' – 'But surely one needs to know foreign languages for this!' – 'Nothing of the sort. Who needs languages? Play in your own language, they will understand everything!'[129] Chaliapin would not be visiting England for quite a while yet – in fact, not until the Diaghilev season of 1913 – but afterwards, in his memoirs, in letters and conversations with friends, he would often confirm that Stasov had been right. England became second to Russia in Chaliapin's heart.

For the time being Chaliapin decided to follow Mamontov's advice and start by taking a look at Paris, especially since his friend the producer Melnikov lived there and since Mamontov was planning to join him later on. On the whole, though, he really did not care where he went first: for an inexperienced Russian, it was all covered by one attractive but rather imprecise word – abroad. He had no pre-arranged programme, no keen interests in any particular direction; he simply wanted to see new facets of life, breathe a new air, have a rest. He had no intentions of asking himself awkward questions, but they nevertheless intruded on him almost as soon as he had crossed the border. Chaliapin could not help constantly contrasting what he had found outside Russia with what he had left at home. He travelled by train, and 'already in Warsaw ... I was struck by the sharp difference between everything I had seen in Russia and everything I was now seeing. ... Everything was marked with the stamp of a different life, different habits and customs.' And he went on: 'I did not sleep until I reached Paris, three nights and two days; with every hour I felt that I was getting closer to a fairy tale.'[130]

It was indeed like a fairy tale. Men in blue blouses and aprons were pouring water on the streets and scrubbing the pavement the way sailors scrub the decks of a ship. ('If only one could get them to do the same in Moscow! Or even better – Astrakhan!') Although he was wide-eyed with amazement at all he saw, much struck him as 'pleasantly familiar, as if I had been there before'.[131] He liked everything; he was impatient to 'rush somewhere, anywhere, my heart was bursting with joy.' He saw everything there was to see in Paris, observing a way of life unknown to him, wandering through the Louvre 'thoroughly

Chaliapin in Moscow, 1897.

Chaliapin with statuette of Vladimir Stasov, late 1920s. Courtesy EMI Music.

intoxicated by its treasures', delighted to find his room so clean, everything so cosy and comfortable, and the food so cheap and tasty. But he was perhaps just as impressed by the Parisian crowds, the free and open style of living. After Russia, after the eternal look of fear, the perpetual circumspection and admonitions, it was a bitter-sweet pleasure to watch, on clear warm evenings, people sitting in the open air around tables, in squares and on the pavements, leaning back in their chairs while they read newspapers, loudly discussing the latest political news, arguing, laughing, singing in the streets. For a Russian, who had learnt at his mother's breast that none of this was allowed, it was all forbidden, one had to conceal desires and even thoughts ('What you don't want to tell your enemy, don't say to your friend,' sadly says popular wisdom) – this was at first very puzzling; he did not know how to react. He did not know how to behave in a free and unconstrained manner; he did not know how to conduct himself with dignity and self-respect but without arrogance. 'When I look at Europeans I envy them – what freedom and ease in their movements and in their speech!'[132]

Not only ordinary people but European actors too seemed to Chaliapin less inhibited. On the stage, 'they simply had greater freedom in the way they moved.' His observations led to some melancholy conclusions: 'This was in all probability due to the fact that Russians have for too long been kept under strict surveillance, that they have too often been told: Shut up, nobody asked you anything.'

The happy days in France quickly came to an end. It was time to return to Moscow to get ready for the forthcoming season. On the journey home across Germany, he watched from the window of his train compartment the towns, villages and fields rush past. 'The nearer I got to my homeland, the more the colours faded, the sky became greyer and greyer, the people lazier and sadder. A nagging, disturbing feeling gnawed at me: why was it that abroad people lived a better life than we did, more cheerful, more enjoyable? Why could they treat each other with more trust and more respect?'[133]

In Moscow news awaited him at the theatre: Mamontov had engaged a young composer named Sergei Rachmaninov as

Fedor Chaliapin and Sergei Rachmaninov, circa 1900.

second conductor. On October 12th, one week after rehearsals had begun, Chaliapin and Rachmaninov started to work on the same production – *Samson and Delilah*, in which Rachmaninov made his début. Both men were of the same age, and despite their differences of character, upbringing and temperament they quickly became firm friends. 'Watching these two Russian geniuses,' recalled a contemporary, 'I was struck by their "dissimilarity": Rachmaninov – concentration, calm, absorption. Chaliapin – talked incessantly, gesticulated, "acted". Rachmaninov just listened and smiled his gentle smile.'[134]

Chaliapin literally worshipped Rachmaninov to the end of his life and retained for him a feeling of particular respect; this respect was so great that it bordered on 'religious fervour'. 'Rachmaninov is the only man in the world Fedor Ivanovich is afraid of,'[135] affirmed Iola Tornaghi. Chaliapin also regarded the composer's authority as absolute in musical matters. 'When Rachmaninov is at the piano accompanying then what I have to say is not "I" am singing but "we" are singing,' he often repeated.[136] And Rachmaninov in turn appreciated and admired Chaliapin's talent more than anyone else. 'Sergei Vasilievich cherished him as a person, cherished him as a magnificent singer and artist, and as a "big difficult child"' (as Rachmaninov called him). A mutual acquaintance recalled Rachmaninov saying: 'My association with Chaliapin is one of the strongest, deepest and finest experiences of my life.'[137] Chaliapin, with his explosive temperament, his inexhaustible humour, his inimitable talent as raconteur and, when he felt like it, his irresistible charm, made a powerful impression on the reserved, unsociable and highly strung Rachmaninov: the mere presence of the singer seemed enough to dissipate his lugubrious moods. In the summer of 1916 the Chaliapins and the Rachmaninovs went on holiday together in the resort of Yessentuki in the Caucasus. 'Rachmaninov was depressed. . . . He sometimes went for walks with Chaliapin and then he looked better, more cheerful. He was very punctual at meal times. In the dining room he sat opposite Chaliapin, who either did not come at all or arrived twenty or thirty minutes late. . . . From the lobby, where he was hanging up his hat, Rachmaninov's cold grey eyes searched for

Chaliapin's place; if the latter had taken his seat, which rarely happened, Rachmaninov would go in smiling, cheerfully exchange greetings, sit down and strike up a conversation, giving the impression all the while that he was only waiting to hear Chaliapin's voice. But if Chaliapin was not there, the composer remained sullen, bored; he turned round every minute to look at the balcony, like an ardent Romeo waiting for Juliet – "And isn't Fedya here?" "Where can Fedya be?" "Has no one seen him today?" "Has he overslept again, or has he gone to Kislovodsk?" "Or did he get stuck there yesterday?" He plied his table companions with such questions. "Here he is! He's here!" rang out the voice of Rachmaninov, who was the first to notice the arrival of the singer. At table, he did not take his eyes off Chaliapin; every movement, every word of the artist was reflected on his face; he obviously derived aesthetic pleasure from seeing and hearing the famous actor in person, the inflection of his voice and his play-acting. He smiled, laughed, till tears ran down while listening to his jokes and funny stories. . . .'[138]

From the very beginning Chaliapin and Rachmaninov frequently met outside of their work in the theatre. They enjoyed playing music and giving concerts together, but best of all they liked to play and sing in the company of friends. 'I cannot name a single artist who has given me such deep and pure artistic pleasure. To accompany him was the greatest joy of my life,' said Rachmaninov.[139] These occasions, which were often impromptu, have been described in dozens of memoirs, all overflowing with words of rapture at the way in which these 'two giants stimulated each other, and literally produced miracles. This was no longer singing or music in the generally accepted sense of these words. This was inspiration breaking out in two great artists.'[140]

It would be difficult to decide which of them benefited most from their association. Rachmaninov, whose musical culture was greater, helped Chaliapin to polish his performing style. Chaliapin for his part revealed to him that truth of intonation, that secret of combining declamatory expressiveness with the cantilena, 'the conversion of recitative into melody' which formed an important and characteristic part of his vocal talent.

Rachmaninov was, to a certain extent, one of Chaliapin's music tutors: 'He was a great artist, a magnificent musician and a pupil of Tchaikovsky: it was he who urged me to study Mussorgsky and Rimsky-Korsakov. He taught me some of the basic principles of music and even of harmony. He tried, generally speaking, to give me a musical education.'[141]

Rachmaninov understood the importance of a serious musical base for Chaliapin. In the summer of 1898, at the end of their first and last joint season at Mamontov's theatre, they took up residence in a dacha near Moscow. Under the terms of his contract with the theatre, Rachmaninov had to prepare the soloists (many of whom were also staying nearby) for *Boris Godunov*. Here, while Chaliapin was free of rehearsals, he 'covered with Rachmaninov the Conservatoire's entire course on the theory of music. . . . The pupil was exceptionally bright, he was quick to learn, but he did not shine by his patience or his zeal. Rachmaninov, who was very witty, teased some of those present mercilessly, and most of all Chaliapin. The latter was very touchy and painfully sensitive to ridicule. He started to prepare his lessons, to get up earlier, although he loved to stay in bed.'[142]

All in all it was a wonderful summer. Chaliapin had proposed to Iola Tornaghi; she had accepted him and obtained her parents' consent in Italy. They were married in the local village church at midday on July 27th. After the ceremony virtually the entire Moscow Private Opera company celebrated the event late into the night. 'We had arranged a merry feast, something à la turque: we sat on carpets on the floor and romped like small children. There were none of the things considered indispensable at a wedding: no richly decked table laden with all kinds of foods, no eloquent toasts, but a lot of wild flowers and lots of wine. In the morning, at about six o'clock, an infernal noise erupted outside my bedroom window – a large group of friends led by Mamontov himself performed a concert with kitchen utensils, iron stove-lids, buckets and some sort of shrill tin-whistles. "Why the devil are you asleep?" shouted Mamontov. "People don't go to the country to sleep. Get up, let's go into the woods to look for mushrooms." And they again banged their pieces of metal, blew their whistles – this chaos was conducted by Sergei Rachmaninov. . . .'[143]

In spite of his many friendly and professional ties with the Moscow Private Opera, Rachmaninov decided not to return to the theatre. There were many reasons for this, which do not fall within the scope of the present work. Our main interest is the enormous influence exerted by the composer on the formation of Chaliapin as a musician, and also the fact that three major roles in his repertoire – Dosifei, Salieri and Boris Godunov – were prepared under the direct guidance of Rachmaninov. When in 1900 Chaliapin was invited to sing Boito's *Mefistofele* at La Scala, 'Rachmaninov was the first' with whom he 'shared his pleasure, his fears and his plans'. Chaliapin recalled with gratitude that 'he at once expressed the desire to go to Italy with me, saying: "Splendid, I shall work on music there and in my spare time I will help you to prepare the opera."'[144]

As mentioned earlier, Chaliapin had been introduced to Mussorgsky's music in 1892 by his teacher Usatov. 'We, his pupils, gathered around him while he sat at the piano and played various pieces, pointing out the difference between some opera of the Italian school and . . . a typically Russian one. He certainly did not deny the merits of Italian music, but he said that simple, popular melody predominated in it. "It is", he explained, "as if it had been written for a musically gifted mass audience who, after hearing it, memorise it, to sing its pleasing airs at sad or joyful moments of life. Russian music, Mussorgsky's for instance, is quite a different matter. Melody is not absent from it, but it is in a completely different style. It suggests atmosphere, expresses drama, it talks of love and of hate much more reflectively and penetratingly. . . . Take *Rigoletto*", he continued. "The music is beautiful, light and tuneful and at the same time evocative of each character's personality. Nevertheless, the characteristation remains superficial and exclusively lyrical. . . . Now, gentlemen, listen to Mussorgsky. This composer depicts the *psychology* [Chaliapin's italics] of each character through the medium of his voice. In his *Boris Godunov*, for instance, there are two voices in the chorus, with two short, seemingly insignificant musical phrases. One voice sings: "Mitiouk, eh!

Mitiouk, what are we yelling about?", and Mitiouk replies, "And how should I know?" And the music gives you a clear and distinct picture of the two fellows. You can see: one is an arguer with a red nose, a hoarse voice and a fondness for drink, and you can sense that the other is a simpleton.'[145]

This lengthy excerpt from Chaliapin's memoirs helps us to understand the change in his tastes and interests which led him to what was then called 'new Russian music', and how his efforts paved the way for the recognition of this music. Moreover, in this account of Usatov's lessons we hear Chaliapin's own views, although he was admittedly expressing them much later.

Chaliapin eventually came to realise that 'the whole course of his career and his artistic future were bound up with the works of Russian composers'.[146] At first, 'something instinctively drew me to Mussorgsky'.[147] But what? Chaliapin provides no straightforward answer to this question, and in any case, it is hardly possible to put such things into words; but from comments he made at one time or another, certain conclusions suggest themselves. Thus, confiding his thoughts on Mussorgsky to Stasov, he wrote in 1899: 'Take for example the inn scene: the song of the Hostess, Varlaam, Missail, Grigori and the Guard; I chose this scene first because the whole inn is firmly planted in my mind and I am indeed familiar with it....'[148]

He frequently returned to the subect of the inn scene; thirty years after the above letter, *Mask and Soul* opens with this very theme – or more exactly, with the story of the wandering pilgrim he once encountered on one of Russia's endless roads. There was, it seems, nothing particularly remarkable in this man: his clothes were threadbare and grey; his beard was grey; he wore gaping felt boots 'although it was summer'. Not a single word passed between them. But Chaliapin knew a great deal about the old man; he was full of understanding and sympathy for his fate and his vagabond way of life. 'From time immemorial such people have existed in Russia, always on the move. They had neither home nor shelter, no family, no trade. Something drove them on. They were not gypsies, but they lived like gypsies. They roamed over the vast territories of Russia from place to place, from district to district. They went from one hostel to

Chaliapin as Varlaam in Mussorgsky's opera *Boris Godunov*.

another, stopped at a monastery for a while, dropped in at a tavern, drifted into fairs. They rested and slept anywhere. It was impossible to understand the purpose of these travels.... They seemed to be searching for something. They seemed to harbour the confused idea that there was some mysterious land where life was fairer and sweeter. Perhaps they were running away from something? But if they were running away, it could only be from *toska*, that nostalgia which is so peculiarly Russian, utterly inexplicable, utterly indescribable and often without reason.'[149]

The tale about the pilgrim he had met so many years ago, when still in his youth, only served as an introduction to his reflections on Varlaam, who, for Chaliapin, personified Russia, destitute, nomad, forever wandering and restless. 'This is, of course, not a complete portrait of Russia, but it is an important part; without it life would have been more difficult, emptier for Mussorgsky and for all of us too.... It is one of the most remarkable although perhaps one of the saddest aspects of Russian life. Mussorgsky conveyed with incomparable art the abysmal nostalgia of this vagabond.... It is so strong in Varlaam that the only thing he can do is to hang himself, or failing that, then laugh, invent something wild and tipsy that will look funny. Varlaam's bitter humour is wonderfully portrayed by Mussorgsky, a humour in which deep tragedy can be felt. Varlaam's awareness of his worthlessness lacerates his soul. Go where he will, he carries with him the certain knowledge that no one wants him. When Varlaam crosses himself, it is to clean his heart from the stain left by nostalgia, by life. But nothing will remove it: neither dancing nor singing. Fathomless Russian nostalgia ...'[150]

Even if one is not familiar with Chaliapin's biography, it is obvious that these words come from a man who has himself trodden the long and bitter path of the wanderer. His analysis of Varlaam shows a deep sense of doom and hopelessness in the whole Russian way of life, of the persistent note of unhappiness which so often pervades the accents of Mussorgsky's heroes. Is Boris Godunov, attired in the garments of Russia's ruler, not suffocated by loneliness and suffering? Does Dosifei, uncompromisingly faithful to his beliefs, not perish powerless to defend them? There is no peace on earth, no consolation for any of them, neither for the people of Russia nor for her rulers. And everything blends together so inextricably, so strangely and painfully, grandeur with pettiness, generosity with cruelty, profound wisdom with futility. The affinity Chaliapin felt with Mussorgsky, soon turning to positive adoration, is not surprising: the nature of their genius and their understanding of the Russian character and of Russian life have much in common. The tragic power of Mussorgsky's music is matched by the tragic power of Chaliapin's art. 'It is one of the greatest regrets of my life that I never met Mussorgsky. He died before my arrival in Petersburg. Unfortunately for me. It is like missing a train on which your fate depended. You reach the station, and the train pulls out in front of you – forever.'[151]

Chaliapin had to work hard to master Mussorgsky's musical language. The 'Song of the Flea' proved particularly difficult. Some others of the composer's works also gave him trouble, but he did not give up and 'sang his music at all the concerts he gave'. He later blamed his difficulties on not finding the right intonation, the right tone for the words in order to convey their descriptive meaning. 'I sang his songs ... according to all the canons of singing – I used my ribs for breathing, kept the voice in the mask and, generally speaking, conducted myself like a pretty good singer, but nevertheless the result was lifeless.'[152]

It must be stressed again that Chaliapin's experience in performing the works of Russian composers such as Dargomyzhsky and Rimsky-Korsakov enabled him to master Mussorgsky's vocal style. But it was in Mussorgsky that Chaliapin found a satisfactory solution to his attempts at combining expressiveness and psychological truth in singing. Chaliapin, with his extraordinary flair for distinguishing the genuine from the false, real substance from mere form in musical and spoken intonation, regarded Mussorgsky as an ideal composer. In the 1930s, he reacted to the admiration provoked by his interpretation of *Boris Godunov* with these words: 'It has often been said ... that my talent animated the character of Boris, that I brought him to life, made him immortal. It is not true! I am ready to do the same with any of Mussorgsky's characters to prove it: it is possible to breathe life into every one of them; each one of them can be made relevant to our own time, for Mussorgsky has been able to give all of them authentic colours of dramatic truth.'[153]

How and to what extent Mussorgsky's songs anticipated his operatic dramas is a question which requires special analysis. Suffice it to say for the moment that in these songs, the 'personal' tone of the composer seems to disappear entirely and all is concentrated on the authenticity of the action and on individual characterisation. Chaliapin's tireless efforts to understand and assimilate the special quality of Mussorgsky's songs at the beginning of his career gave him mastery of control over imperceptible inflexions of speech and over the colours of his timbre. These many songs, all different from each other, unorthodox in subject and in style, exposed the realities of Russian life in an artistic form. Their separate voices would eventually unite in the composer's operas, especially *Boris Godunov*. But by the time Chaliapin encountered Mussorgsky's operatic heroes, he would already have sampled in his music both spiritual isolation and a sharply observant eye; the delicate unfolding of emotions inside outwardly clear-cut characters; lofty, poetic feeling and prosaic reality; breadth of vision, philosophy, profound thinking and meticulous attention to the smallest details.

The discoveries Chaliapin made through Mussorgsky soon affected his approach to other composers, Western as well as Russian. They formed at once the basis and the apex of his art.

After hearing Glinka's 'Midnight Review', a critic tried to convey his astonishment to his readers: 'Chaliapin has a sound which I could not call anything but "a sound heralding the dawn". I simply have no other words to describe the beauty and the charm of this sound. When you hear it, you see before you winter, dawn; the light of day is faintly breaking through the windows, and somewhere, far away in the garden among the leafless trees, a muffled, long-drawn-out dying sound is heard.'[154]

In 1897 *Khovanshchina* gave Chaliapin his first taste of a major operatic work by Mussorgsky; *Boris Godunov* followed in 1898. These two events are of unequal importance in the singer's career, but despite a not entirely successful production the part of Dosifei paved the way for his historic début in *Boris Godunov*.

When the Moscow Private Opera decided to start work on *Khovanshchina*, Semyon Kruglikov, on Mamontov's instructions, asked Stasov to act as consultant. Stasov eagerly accepted the proposal and wrote: 'I deeply rejoice at the birth of such a theatre which can and wants to do something good and important for Russian opera. When *Khovanshchina* was staged here* the two of us – Rimsky-Korsakov and myself – were called in and Rimsky-Korsakov's directions exerted a strong influence on the musical side, while I also had something to do with the way it was produced. ... As you of course know, I had made up the plot of the opera and then I regularly worked on it with Mussorgsky himself, almost until the end of his life. As for Chaliapin, I have seen him many times and deeply admire his originality and his talent. The rest of your artistic team also holds great promise and therefore ... command, I am at your service.'[155]

Stasov and Kruglikov must have met during the summer of 1897, and this is presumably when their conversation about *Khovanshchina* took place. Stasov was not directly involved in the production, although some of his suggestions were taken into consideration. He continued to take an interest in it from Petersburg, where he lived. 'Do you expect censorship to be less severe in Moscow than it is here? I think you know that both Rimsky-Korsakov and I had to sit through an entire evening and most of a night to alter many words and replace them with new ones – otherwise permission was going to be refused. Perhaps after so much time, and especially in Moscow, the censor will be more tolerant and lenient, and it will be possible to reinstate all, or as many as possible, of the original words Mussorgsky wrote. All this worries me in the extreme.'[156]

Mamontov directed *Khovanshchina* himself. As usual, all the

---

* The opera was first performed on February 9th, 1886 by a dramatic and musical amateur society in Petersburg; *Khovanshchina* was subsequently performed in Kiev (1892) and Petersburg (1893 – Russian Opera Company). The work, scorned by the Imperial Theatres, was seen only on private stages.

participants were gathered for a talk before rehearsals started: the performers had to familiarise themselves with the historical facts on which the opera was based. The production's designer, Appolinari Vasnetsov, proved particularly helpful on this occasion. It was he who had the idea of an 'excursion' to the Old Believers' community near Moscow 'where much was preserved from ancient times. . . . We came to a temple', recalled Vasili Shkafer, 'next to which was a small cemetery. . . . A slim, slender woman in a black sarafan and wrapped in a big shawl went by. Someone said: "That's Marfa".* The eye could pick out typical figures and faces among those present. . . . These people really exist, religious fanatics, they still live, deep faith in their creed still burns in them. . . . At the cemetery gate stood an old caretaker . . . a colourful character, the live replica of an ikon painting, his face deeply creased by wrinkles. His expressive eyes looked at us penetratingly, intensely and searchingly. In a voice trembling with age, he started to talk of the old faith, of the way they were being tormented and hounded. The Old Believers have often been persecuted and their churches closed by order of the police. The words of the old man rang with the truth he so firmly defended and believed in. It made a powerful impression on us and we were deeply disturbed by it, mentally and emotionally. Of course, this was not the authentic Russia of before Peter the Great, not an authentic fragment from the epoch of 'schism'; but we needed no more than traces, hints, marks left by a way of life, and we found them, we felt something, and our journey was not wasted. We returned to the theatre to tell everybody all we had seen and heard.'[157]

What was the overall concept of the production? In the first place, the theatre was unreservedly on the side of the dissenters – this is understandable in the context of the period. It was common knowledge that Old Believers were deprived of civic rights. An official publication of the time declares: 'To protect by law total freedom of dissent in all its religious and social practices would mean legitimising and protecting by law the most bitter enemy of orthodox believers.'[158]

* Marfa – heroine of *Khovanshchina*.

215

The censorship to which *Khovanshchina* was submitted, the constant alterations to the text mentioned by Stasov, are to a large extent attributable to the fact that the opera, ending with a scene where the dissenters burn themselves to death as an act of protest, could arouse the sympathy of the spectators. At the end of the nineteenth century, performers and public regarded Dosifei, Marfa and their confederates not so much as enemies of Peter the Great's reforms as people protesting against the repression of spiritual freedom and the violent persecution of their faith. No one got excited over Dosifei's ideas and arguments about the new and the old Russia anymore. It was all part of distant history and known to every schoolboy. The dissenters in Mussorgsky's work departed somewhat from historical reality and became the repositories of virtue and moral strength. Moreover, the topicality of the opera's finale was unexpectedly and tragically confirmed. On two occasions (at the end of December 1896 and in February 1897) groups of Old Believers drowned themselves and their children in the Dneistr near Tiraspol.* They left behind them an open letter saying that they preferred to die rather than obey the new laws.

Dosifei-Chaliapin was the focal point of the opera, although when he began to work on his role, the singer had no very precise idea whom he was going to portray on November 12th, 1897, the first night of the opera, or how he was going to do it. 'Dosifei was not clear to me. I once again turned to Kliuchevsky and he was kind enough to talk to me in vivid detail about Prince Khovansky, Prince Myshetsky,† the Streltsy‡ and the Tsarevna Sofia.'[159]

Painters, particularly Korovin, once more gave invaluable assistance. Chaliapin could listen endlessly to his lively and colourful tales about the dissenters' customs, their religious rites and songs of prayer (Korovin came from a family of Old Believers). They planned Dosifei's appearance together. Korovin drew several alternative sketches of him: as a wrathful

---

* In the south of Russia, now Moldavian Soviet Socialist Republic territory.

† Dosifei's name before entering the church.

‡ Body of Russian troops, composed of infantry, raised by Ivan the Terrible and abolished by Peter the Great.

bigot, a burning fanatic, a good shepherd. On Korovin's advice, Chaliapin repeated again and again the passages in his role which did not satisfy him.

The part of Dosifei is distinguished by subtle variations of mood. His manner of speaking changes according to the situation: when addressing princes, it is majestic, as befits a prince; with Marfa it is full of genuine kindness; in his sermons he shows passionate zeal and even fanaticism. The inflections of his voice are loaded with the weight, the significance of each sound, of each word. Laconic in its melodic line, often bordering on the psalmodic style, Dosifei's part reaches moments of great tension and intensity. It has the accents of Russian religious music, and this generates a feeling of sublime peace; it imparts nobility to the character of the religious leader.

Critics greeted Chaliapin's Dosifei with a rapturous chorus of praise for the depth of his understanding of the music, his wealth of psychological nuances, the high level of his artistry and the uniformity of his style. 'Chaliapin created a very ... complete figure of Dosifei, his wisdom and his fanatical conviction in the rightness of his actions, his entirely human streak of sympathy for Marfa's sufferings, and the heavy depression of this old man conscious of his impotence in the struggle and of the unavoidable destruction of his confederates.'[160] 'Dosifei made a really tragic impression, especially in the last act, where Chaliapin brilliantly conveyed the inner serenity of a man who has irrevocably decided to leave the world, confident that there – beyond the grave – a better life awaits him.'[161]

Unlike other performers, who found Mussorgsky's recitatives difficult to cope with, Chaliapin revealed from the very first rehearsal a fine grasp of the composer's style. *The Maid of Pskov* had been most instructive, particularly in the art of producing expressive and natural phrasing. But if in the role of Ivan the Terrible Chaliapin had searched for truth in musical declamation, for a way of conveying through recitative the complex inner life of the character he was embodying, in Dosifei he had additionally to master the aria form, which gives the melody such dramatic force.

Judging by the scant reviews of the 1897 production, Chal-

(*Above*) Self-portrait of Chaliapin as Dosifei, 1911.

(*Right*) Chaliapin as Dosifei in Mussorgsky's opera *Khovanschina*, 1912.

iapin was extraordinarily successful in suggesting the depth and intensity of Dosifei's emotions behind a reserved, even severe exterior. His gestures and movements were sparse and restrained but radiated strength, energy and dignity. 'Although this character, in a sense, dominates Mussorgsky's great opera,' wrote an American critic, 'there is little opportunity for the display of histrionism which Boris presents to the singing actor. By almost insignificant details of make-up and gesture, the bass creates before your eyes a living, breathing man, a man of fire and faith.'[162]

Dosifei, as Chaliapin played him, had nothing of the meek, humble hermit who has renounced the vanities of the world. This was a man of great experience, who knew the worth of life and of people, although he was still agitated by strong passions. Prince Myshetsky was not dead in him, and at times this broke through, although Chaliapin's interpretation (at any rate in 1897) did not emphasise the characteristics of an accomplished politician, and the quarrel scene between the princes (Act Two of the opera) was severely cut. This Dosifei demonstrated instead an unshakeable faith in the rightness of his beliefs: through rational thinking as well as great suffering, he had formed the conviction, ringing in his voice and in every word he uttered, that there was only one possible path for Russia. He therefore regarded any outside interest or any disagreement in the ranks of the confederates as a dereliction of duty. Dosifei-Chaliapin believed in the sanctity of the fight for the triumph of the 'true faith', but he was also aware of final doom. He did not offer his companions any false hopes; on the contrary, he warned of the extreme ordeals which could lie ahead. By indicating, from his very first entrance, an underlying theme of tormenting thoughts and anxieties, Chaliapin prepared the audience for the concluding monologue and the finale. 'The climax of his [Chaliapin's] realistic, mesmerising and startling interpretation was the scene in the forest. His imploring voice, unaffected but penetrating to the heart, his absolute faith in salvation through fire, and finally the brilliant portrayal of agonising yet stoic death, the gentle look in his eyes, filled with the consciousness of being right – it was unforgettable.'[163] The author of the review also added that the scene of silent death was performed with such tragic intensity that the stunned audience could not bring itself to break the silence of the auditorium with applause immediately after the curtain had come down – a reaction by now familiar to the reader.

Three months after the first night of *Khovanshchina*, in mid-February 1898, Chaliapin and the Private Opera went on tour to Petersburg. Within a few days his name had become as popular there as in Moscow. In the words of César Cui, Chaliapin had a 'stupendous success, possibly surpassing Mazzini's and Battistini's . . .'[164]

The astonished critics of the capital seemed to be witnessing the birth of a new talent. 'His fine, strong bass has become even firmer, while his gift for acting has developed to an extent one would not have thought possible earlier on.'[165] 'He became the latest vogue in Petersburg – so much so that people even talked of "the days of Chaliapin" at the time!' recalled Yurev later. Old friends and acquaintances were joined by new ones, and he now saw Petersburg itself and everything else around him with different eyes. Rimsky-Korsakov, with whom Chaliapin was gradually forming a close friendship, often came to the theatre. 'At his soirées Nikolai Andreevich [Rimsky-Korsakov] always greeted Chaliapin most cordially and with sincere pleasure, and always thanked him touchingly for his performance, something I witnessed myself a number of times. Nikolai Andreevich demanded from his interpreters accurate intonation, tempo and rhythm; he did not tolerate arbitrary cuts, fermatas, hums or shouts, and so on. But my father never accused Chaliapin of any of these things, neither to his face nor behind his back,' wrote the composer's son.[166]

During one of his visits to the theatre, Rimsky-Korsakov said: 'I have written a little thing in the spirit of Dargomyzhsky's *The Stone Guest*, called *Mozart and Salieri*. I have brought it to show you.' He sat at the piano and started playing it to the singers who had gathered around. Chaliapin began to sing the part of Salieri and Rimsky-Korsakov that of Mozart.[167] The opera immediately went into production. Chaliapin's partner in the role of Mozart would be Vasili Shkafer; the producer,

Savva Mamontov; and the designer, Mikhail Vrubel. This last name was particularly important, as the painter was a great expert on the period in which the work was set. The costumes, the scenery and even the singers' make-up plunged the spectator straight into the atmosphere of the opera, filled him with a sense of imminent tragedy. Vrubel was both a great painter and a great director. His designs created a uniquely original picture. By enlarging some details and cleverly discarding others, he managed to give the illusion of space on the stage. His ability to think in truly theatrical terms and his unerring sense of proportions were accompanied by an exceptional sensitivity to the nature of musical sound, to vocal characterisation and orchestral colour. Chaliapin found not only his drawings but also his advice very useful. Vrubel, a highly strung and impressionable man, could see into people's souls and decipher their innermost thoughts. According to one of the designers working for Mamontov, 'Chaliapin's interpretation of Salieri was entirely based on Vrubel's comments and on his sketches.'[168]

Many of Chaliapin's contemporaries regarded Salieri as one of his greatest creations, the power and scale of his portrayal making it superior even to *Boris Godunov*. It may be pointless to set up a ranking order of his roles, especially since Chaliapin himself could not stand the idea of a 'favourite character' and often repeated: 'For me the best role is always the one I am singing today.'[169] However, recalling his first encounter with the part of Salieri, he wrote: 'This was a task much more complex and difficult than all the previous ones.' Experience had already taught Chaliapin that 'in opera, the performer must not only sing, he must also play the role, as it is played in drama. In opera one must sing as one speaks. I noticed subsequently that singers who wanted to imitate me did not understand me. They were not singing as one speaks but speaking as one sings.'[170]

As mentioned earlier, Chaliapin went to Rachmaninov for help. In terse phrases, he reveals what a titanic labour both of them accomplished in the creation of Salieri. 'And how Rachmaninov rebuked me for the smallest inaccuracy!'[171] 'I sometimes suggested to Rachmaninov making changes to one movement or other. He would say to me: here it is possible, but here it is not. And without distorting the intentions of the composer, we found the right style of interpretation to bring into clear relief the tragic figure of Salieri.'[172]

'Chaliapin was really inspired, full of fire, and achieved a wonderful make-up which created a perfect illusion,' declared Mamontov in a letter to Rimsky-Korsakov after the première. 'It was a man belonging entirely *to that epoch* [Mamontov's italics], without any imitation props. Such personification is possible only to people of strong creative powers.'[173]

Rimsky-Korsakov's opera, whose plot is taken from one of Pushkin's 'Little Tragedies', preserves (with negligible omissions) the entire text of the original. This may explain why contemporary writings stressed above all that Chaliapin was giving a superlative interpretation of Pushkin's character. 'If you examine Rimsky-Korsakov's new opera,' wrote Yuri Engel, 'you see that this, more than any other work, demands unusual singers, able to mobilize all the resources of musical declamation to which the composer resorts in order to enhance and reinforce the power and the eloquence of Pushkin's tragic verses.'[174]

Such words do not belittle the qualities of Rimsky-Korsakov's music (although Chaliapin was inclined to think that 'it did not measure up to Pushkin's text'), nor are they evidence that the singer himself showed a preference for the dramatic side of performing in his art. This attitude will seem perfectly logical if one bears in mind the literally universal adoration in which Pushkin is held in Russia. Russian literature is not short of writers of outstanding talent, even of genius, but not a single one enjoys such unanimous worship, no one receives such unquestioning admiration, as Pushkin. All others can be subjected to analysis, one can argue and sometimes disagree with them, they can be liked or disliked, but not Pushkin. At the mere mention of his name, differences of opinion and taste melt away; the most sincere love is immediately expressed.

Chaliapin, who was no exception in this, once urged: 'Read Pushkin, read him at all times – when you are in good spirits and when you are not, when you are ill and when you fall in love. In Pushkin you will always find an irreplaceable companion and friend.'[175] In 1935 he told an acquaintance in America: 'My best roles were his [Pushkin's] heroes. I gave them real life. Pushkin and I created Boris Godunov, the Miller, Salieri ... I dreamt of singing Herman* although the part is for a tenor, but believe me, this would have been my greatest creation! Listen, in two years' time it will be the centenary of Pushkin's death. Of course, this will be celebrated all over the world, wherever there are people with hearts and minds. I want to mark this date in my own way, at the same time as my forty-five years on the operatic stage. ... It will be my farewell to the stage, to the public, to the theatre ... I want to play Pushkin himself. I have been nurturing this dream for years.'[176]

While recognising in Rimsky-Korsakov's opera 'a new type of scenic art, successfully combining music and psychological drama',[177] he nevertheless relied almost entirely on Pushkin's play for his conception of the character. 'I don't know whether Alexander Sergeevich [Pushkin] played an instrument. I don't think he did. Neither in his lyrical works nor in his correspondence is there any indication of this. So he was not a musician, and yet how deeply he felt the very spirit of music. Everything he says about music in *Mozart and Salieri* is absolutely right. How well he understood Mozart ... in his deepest essence, in his very substance.'[178]

The curtain slowly rises to the music of the overture. Salieri, his back to the audience, sits at a desk piled with books, music, papers and pens.† Salieri's day begins not at the harpsichord, open nearby, but here at his desk. The candles are burning low.... 'He is holding a sheet of music covered with writing and corrections – the unsatisfactory result of a long and agonising night of toil. But his hand moves. It points to the music and a sort of spasm shakes his whole body – while the orchestra plays a trill, on the upbeat preceding his first notes, Chaliapin slowly turns round, and at full volume, *a piena voce*, his voice ringing with the metallic clang of violent anger, he begins his mono-

---

* In Tchaikovsky's *The Queen of Spades*.

† Chaliapin sometimes started his performance differently: the public would then see a man, his face distorted by anger, who despairingly tore up the music he had written, threw the pieces to the ground and stamped on them with his feet.

Chaliapin as Salieri in Rimsky-Korsakov's opera *Mozart and Salieri*, 1915.

logue: "Everybody says there is no justice on earth. But there is no justice higher up either." Keeping strict rhythm, adhering rigorously to the rhythmic pattern, in spite of the pause in the orchestra which allows this to be sung *ad libitum*, adds particular force and even nobility to the feelings expressed. Now we can see his face, his eyes: everything in him shows outrage, indignation. He is not pathetic; no, this is a big, strong and courageous man. Time, hard work and suffering have laid their heavy hand on him but not broken him. We are immediately charmed by him, we trust him, we find him handsome – a hard-working, dignified old man, elegant even in a dressing gown and without his powdered wig, his straight ginger hair dangling like wire. "For me this is as plain as a simple piano scale!"[179] This was sung and played in a way which left no room for doubt; the thought now expressed had presented itself long before, although he was perhaps putting it into words for the first time. And the scene itself had also begun long before the curtain went up. This was what had tormented him all night, and all the other nights and days, days and nights.... But why this bitter condemnation of people and of God, this complete denial of hope? People were not so important after all; they had always been and always would be just rabble for him, a frivolous and foolish crowd, with a taste for silly gossip. It is terrible, there has been a monstrous error up there. The great gift of genius, truly a gift from heaven, has fallen on an "idle time-waster", a ne'er-do-well, an unworthy man. The music which this Mozart writes is not the fruit of sleepless nights, of pains-taking and laborious work. Didn't he, Salieri, devote his entire life to art, serve it like a priest, selflessly and faithfully? Genius is the only possible reward for such heroic zeal; it must be, it has to be. And yet, he has not received it! Now he has to watch it being squandered on that fool Mozart. Certainly, he is a genius. ... A genius who has no right to be one, for the simple reason that he does not follow the path of industrious, per-severing and wearying work, like Salieri and many others. The injustice one could somehow bear; but he is dangerous: by creating a great and new art he dethrones the old one, the one to which Salieri has consecrated his whole life. He cannot rise to the level of Mozart's genius. There is no formula, the most precise calculations are useless, in order to reach the heights which Mozart attains so easily, without effort.

'So only one solution is left. Salieri will have to correct God's mistake here on earth. With Mozart dead, normal order will return; the rules of law, logic, common sense and all the others which Salieri knows so well will again be observed. Colossal effort will, as before, guarantee to make you a genius. The calm is broken. Like a wild animal, freed from its chains, Salieri darts off, rushes all over the stage. "Sublime work and idleness cannot dwell together." No! No! He will not allow it. The frenzied tempo of his movements corresponds exactly to the frenzy of his feelings, to the timbre of his voice and to his expression. "O Mozart, Mozart" – the accursed name has finally been pronounced; now Salieri will either choke with rage or kill him, but no ... 'he is petrified, his eyes widen in utter terror, he cannot breathe.'[180] Salieri does not understand immediately who has just entered the room and is speaking to him and that Mozart, the real Mozart, has surprised him at this most intimate moment with his soul laid bare and on the brink of committing a crime. What has he heard? What has he understood? Wetting his parched lips, Salieri whispers hoarsely: 'You are here! How long?' He looks anxiously for any sign in his unexpected guest's behaviour, in his clear eyes, in the sound of his voice that Mozart has heard his last words and seen into the secret, forbidden abyss. Did a few moments mercifully elapse between his cry and the visitor's arrival?

'In spite of the entrance of a new character, which always distracts the attention of the audience from what is already on stage, in spite of Mozart's noisy joie de vivre, bursting into the gloomy study with light and sunshine, it was utterly impossible to tear oneself away from the motionless, stony figure of Chaliapin, from his face distorted by malice and horror and making agonising attempts to smile.'[181]

Mozart is not alone. On his way to Salieri's he has heard a blind violinist near a tavern, and has brought him along. 'Play us some Mozart,' he cheerfully tells the musician. And it really is funny to hear what your own music sounds like under clumsy fingers. Don't you agree? Mozart, beating time with his head, now and then smiles at Salieri. ... But the latter, barely recovered from the nightmare of his painful thoughts, is slow to realise what is happening. When the false notes finally penetrate his ear, Salieri shudders as if he had received a blow, raises his eyes and encounters Mozart's glance. An almost imperceptible grimace of contempt crosses his face, giving way to downright indignation. He leaps to his feet, noisily moves his armchair aside and throws himself on the violinist with clenched fists. 'At the last moment Salieri contains himself and with an abrupt gesture accompanied by an orchestral sforzando, he interrupts the playing.'[182] His rage is so terrible that Mozart stops smiling. He looks at his friend with surprise and alarm, not understanding what has angered him. He just wanted to have a little fun. ... Fun? How can one find pleasure in ridiculing the pure art to which he, Salieri, has devoted his whole life? What makes this layabout laugh? Watching some dauber 'soil Raphael's Madonna' with his dirty paws, or a wretched mountebank 'dishonour Alighieri' with his parodies?

Mozart is really embarrassed: he had no intention of hurting the feelings of the great Salieri. He has a high opinion of him as a musician and had come to show him his latest composition. Nothing serious, of course – just that last night he could not get to sleep for some reason, and 'into his head came two or three ideas. ... But you can't see me now....'

Salieri suddenly calms down. Perhaps his agitation really is unfounded and this boy is not dangerous. 'Two or three ideas....' It can hardly be anything important. And Mozart's explanation before he starts to play does not show any great depth either: a trivial theme of good and evil, light and shadow. 'I am in a cheerful mood.... Suddenly a sepulchral apparition, darkness all at once, or something like that....'

The scene during which Salieri listens to Mozart's fantasies left an indelible impression on anyone who heard Chaliapin in this role. Settling into his armchair, Salieri takes a cup of coffee and, stirring it lightly with a little spoon, prepares to listen to the new 'creation'. As Mozart plays Salieri's whole look changes. He is happy and cannot not hide it. In some per-

As Salieri in *Mozart and Salieri*. Mamontov's Private Opera, Moscow, 1898.

formances Chaliapin would stand up, go to the harpsichord
and look in amazement now at Mozart's face, now at his hands,
as if to make sure that it was not a dream. 'The wrinkles on his
face smoothed themselves out; suspicion, uncertainty and pain
disappeared; he listened and was freed from the burden of his
conflicts. Suffering, envy – all was forgotten. He listened and
his eyes grew warmer, illuminated by a soft glow of kindness.
This worn-out body was invaded by an immense joy bringing
release and peace.'[183]

He now worships Mozart, and for the very thing which had
caused his hatred of him. The greater his delight in the perfection
of Mozart's music, the stronger Salieri's conviction that he must
kill him . . .

Shaking off the delusion, Salieri says, barely audibly: 'You
came to show me this and you could stop off at a tavern to
listen to a blind violinist? Mozart, you are not worthy of yourself!' God, does he really not understand what he has written?
He is not even capable of recognising greatness and genuine
accomplishment. He cannot see what he is doing, nor can he
comprehend what has just happened. 'You are a god, Mozart,
and don't know it. But I know it, I know it.' Mozart does not
argue. All right then, if that's the case . . . perhaps it's not
bad. . . . 'Well, my divinity is starving . . .' he rejoins casually.

'A perfidious plan suddenly occurred to Salieri. A malicious
spark blazed in his eyes; a shadow crossed his face, the last
vestige of his fleeting qualms: a spell-binding and terrifying
moment in Chaliapin's acting.'[184]

'Instant transformation. Everything is different: the figure,
the hands, the face, the eyes, the cruel steely eyes, the piercing
glance of fixed pupils.'[185]

'Listen, let's have dinner together at the Golden Lion Inn,'
proposes Salieri. Mozart leaves to warn his wife not to expect
him that evening. Salieri, alone, stands immobile. He cannot
detach his eyes from the instrument Mozart has just touched.
He glances at the ring on his index finger, but the harpsichord
draws him back with a kind of magnetic power. Salieri forces
himself to turn away and concentrate on the signet ring: it
holds some poison, it holds Mozart's death. And truly, God be

witness, it is no longer possible to resist what fate has preordained. He is certain that he has been chosen to stop the
senseless destruction of music. And so, the sooner this 'cherub
who has brought us a few heavenly songs' disappears, the better.
Salieri's every word and action now betray his obsession with
the ring. Eighteen years ago, a beloved woman had left it to
him to use as a last resort in case of extremity. Many, many
times, Salieri has feasted with people he hated, but not once has
he felt the desire to open the terrible jewel. But – 'Now it is time!
Cherished gift of love, pass today into the cup of friendship.'
Chaliapin's voice sounded triumphant, free and joyful. Not only
has Salieri found a solution; he has found an ally, a faithful and
loyal friend. This ally – death – will help him. It understands
that he is doing the right thing.

The prelude to the second act ends. 'Ominous shadows
thicken around Salieri; inexorable truth has already raised her
hand. . . . In this dispirited state, as if crushed by the weight of
evil intent, we find Salieri in the second scene dining with his
friend. Here Chaliapin even eats in a special manner, somehow
mechanically, as if his mind were beset by an obsessive thought
which nags and nags him all the time.'[186] On stage is a table
with the remnants of a meal and a great number of plates and
dishes. Salieri sits on a sofa. 'Below the powdered wig, his
ravaged and envious face with the thick eyebrows, the clean-
shaven chin, brought to mind the intensity of one of La Tour's
pastels. Classic coat, opening on a splendid waistcoat, large
black bow of the necktie, lace cuffs from which emerged feverish
(and soon to be criminal) hands.'[187] His eyes unremittingly
follow every one of Mozart's movements. Strange; why is he so
sad? The answer makes Salieri wince: Mozart is writing a
Requiem recently commissioned by a mysterious visitor in
black, and has uneasy feelings about it which he cannot explain.

Motionless as a stone, Salieri listens to Mozart. Fearing to
give away his agitation, he restricts the conversation to short
and sharp questions: 'What?' 'How?' 'Any minute now he could
be unmasked. Salieri makes enormous efforts to contain his
nervousness; his hand convulsively grips the arm rest; he leans

forward.'[188] With his other hand Salieri moves aside the lighted candles and covers his eyes. 'And now too, it seems to me that he is with us – sitting here,' confesses Mozart sadly and quietly. Salieri can delay no more: he jumps to his feet; a huge shadow, thrown by the flame of the candles, flutters on the wall like a large bird. Chaliapin, moving slowly but with assurance and deliberation, takes off his ring. At that precise moment, Mozart strikes up an air from Salieri's opera *Tarare*. 'There is a tune in it, I always hum it when I am happy. ...' Salieri sits at the table; he takes a glass into which he pours some wine and keeps fingering his ring over it. Suddenly Mozart asks: 'Salieri, is it true that Beaumarchais once poisoned somebody?' A pause follows. Salieri turns his head sharply. Fear, terrible fear, seizes him. He searches Mozart's face, trying to find out whether this is just an idle remark. Mozart adds another blow: 'But he is a genius, like you and me. And genius and evil-doing – the two things are incompatible.' Someone else would be unable to go through with this, yet Salieri does not hesitate for a moment. 'You think so?' In one swift motion, he openly empties the contents of the ring into the glass, knocking it in his agitation. It answers with a slight tinkle. 'Well, drink!'

'In Chaliapin's interpretation,' recalled Edward Stark, 'the figure of Salieri assumed grandiose proportions and the tragic element which Pushkin had imparted to it was so vividly outlined as to become awe-inspiring. In a brief instant, the whole gamut of complex, contradictory emotions passes before the spectator, revealing the psychological intricacies of a being who can no longer bear the blinding glare of genius. Chaliapin-Salieri had great dignity. Another interpreter would probably have played this down and thus removed some of his fascination. This would be wrong. Hatred and envy are human feelings and can both develop to a degree where they lose their narrow ordinary character as trifling manifestations of human nature, to assume the kind of grandiose and pure beauty found in all natural impulses....'[189]

'Listen to my Requiem, Salieri.' Salieri is overwhelmed by this renewed encounter with Mozart's genius. Weeping shakes his whole body; his head hangs limply; his hands dangle

As Salieri.

ROYAL ALBERT HALL
LONDON

Manager ∴ ∵ ∴ ∵ ∴ CHARLES B. COCHRAN

CHALIAPINE

in

"MOZART and SALIERI"

Opera in Two Acts
by
RIMSKY-KORSAKOFF *from a story by* POUSHKINE

And the Inn Scene from Act I of

"BORIS GODOUNOFF"

By MOUSSORGSKY

∽∾

The London Symphony Orchestra
and The Royal Choral Society
Conductor -- -- ALBERT COATES

- - UNDER THE DIRECTION OF - -
CHARLES B. COCHRAN

October 11th & 13th, 1927

OFFICIAL PROGRAMME

Printed and Published by
FLEETWAY PRESS LTD., 3-9, DANE STREET, HIGH HOLBORN, LONDON, W.C.1

aimlessly, holding a handkerchief wet with tears. Salieri is crying while listening to the music of the man he has just poisoned. Mozart stands up: '... I am ill today. I feel unwell. I'll go home and have some sleep.' 'Salieri has walked to the door to see his victim out, over whom the languor of mortal sickness is already beginning to creep,' wrote Sir Desmond MacCarthy, recalling a performance of the opera at the Royal Albert Hall in 1927. 'His back is turned to us; Mozart has disappeared. What would the murderer's face be like when he turned round? What would he *do*? [D. MacCarthy's italics]. Chaliapin did not move; he thrust his hands down violently in the pockets of his long-skirted coat and the resolute gesture was like a cry, *"It's done"* [D. MacCarthy's italics]; then he wheeled to show a face distorted with grinding immitigable misgivings. One second's acting this; let it serve as an example of a series of continuous inspirations.'[190]

Some of the scenes were recorded at that time.* One of them begins with Salieri's last words: 'You will sleep for a long time, Mozart!' This was sung in a whisper; he really was afraid that death would deceive him and not come to his assistance. Then sharply, horror-struck: 'But can he be right, and I am not a genius?' After Mozart's murder, feelings of guilt and remorse are not the only things Salieri has to face. He has to accept once and for all the fact that he is not a genius and never will be, and that his entire life has been but a futile attempt to reach the unreachable. ... He keeps turning over Mozart's words, which are consuming him; he tries out the letters and syllables of each of them on his tongue, on his teeth, on his lips: 'Genius and evil-doing – the two things are incompatible.' – 'Not true!' The armchair crashes loudly to the floor. The fateful thought that Mozart had expressed begins to penetrate his consciousness. Not only is he not a genius; he is an evil-doer, a murderer.

'I thought about more than envy and hatred yesterday,' wrote the famous critic Amphiteatrov after seeing a performance in St. Petersburg. 'I thought about the terrible anguish which inhabits Salieri's soul, about the dreadful loneliness and disillusionment of a man who has exhausted all the resources of

* See Discography.

natural intellect, of natural energy, in loving efforts towards an ideal, and is all of a sudden thrown from the heights he has reached and reduced to dust by a supernatural occurrence.'[191]

Salieri rushes to the harpsichord, puts his fingers on the keys but cannot press them, cannot repeat the sounds of the music which have vanished. Then, totally destroyed, his dead eyes staring vacantly into space, he sinks onto the sofa and his loosely hanging arms fall heavily on his knees. 'Chaliapin was magnificent here, with his hysterical terror at this new doubt, by now the doubt of a criminal. He wanted to sneer, but his guilty conscience showed him the damning truth and choked him with tears. And to the tearful laugh of an unhappy man, half-crazed, crushed by his own acts, the curtain falls....'[192]

Chaliapin retained the role of Salieri in his repertoire for many years, practically to the end of his career. With the passing of time it gained in polish, refinement and unity. A critic compared his earlier impressions of Chaliapin's Salieri with those of a later date: 'Since then the singer has made progress by working out in significantly greater detail both his acting and his singing.'[193] But the basic lines of the character were drawn in 1898.

'If there were no Chaliapin among the constellation of Russian artists,' wrote Nikolai Kashkin in 1901, 'then we do not know whether Rimsky-Korsakov's *Mozart and Salieri* could have been seen, and even more important, remained, on the stage. Now that the character has been created musically and dramatically, we regard it as accessible to any artist of talent who has not sunk into routine, but the creation itself was a new term in vocal and scenic art, and it was Chaliapin who stated this term.'[194]

The 1898 season was a busy and momentous one: on December 7th, two weeks after that of *Mozart and Salieri* (November 25th), came another première, when Chaliapin sang *Boris Godunov* for the first time. This production ranks among the most outstanding events in the history of the Private Opera, along with the *The Maid of Pskov*, *Sadko* and *Mozart and Salieri*. It also marked the beginning of a new stage career for the opera, which entered the regular repertoire of Russian and international houses. Two people have to be thanked for rescuing this little-understood work from almost total oblivion: Rimsky-Korsakov and Chaliapin.

Rimsky-Korsakov completed the new version of *Boris Godunov* in 1896. Comparisons between this and the original are beyond the framework of the present book, but certain general remarks seem nevertheless to impose themselves. As is well known, Mussorgsky himself wrote two versions of the opera. The first one (1869) was rejected by the administration of the Imperial Theatres. The composer then wrote a second one (1872); but instead of being a revision of the first, this turned into a completely independent work. Mussorgsky had made many changes in the second *Boris Godunov*; he introduced new episodes, created the role of Marina and took out the scene 'In front of the Cathedral of St. Basil the Blessed'. It was replaced by the so-called 'vagrants' scene' (now called 'scene near Kromy'), a sort of tragic epilogue where the endless troubles of Russia are heralded in the Simpleton's lament. Presenting the two scenes in the same performance is nothing other than the mechanical merging of the two versions, and the commonly heard professions of 'faithfulness' to Mussorgsky used as justification are quite irrelevant.

In the 'vagrants' scene' the people believe the Pretender to be the true Tsarevich Dmitri and so follow him to Moscow shouting 'Death to Boris'. Outside St. Basil the Blessed's Cathedral the Simpleton expresses the feelings of the people towards Boris, telling the Tsar to his face: 'You murdered the little Tsarevich.' The desire to introduce the public to yet another example of Mussorgsky's genius is perfectly understandable, but the theatre is not like a restaurant where to satisfy the client one must set before him everything the kitchen has to offer. When it is only a question of music, everything is relatively simple. The stage, however, has its own laws which cannot be ignored.

After many long discussions, and at Chaliapin's urgent request, Mamontov finally agreed to start work on *Boris Godunov* and chose the Rimsky-Korsakov score. It was probably the only decision possible at the time. At the end of the nineteenth century, the composer's own version would hardly have found favour with either the critics or the public. Mamon-tov was well aware of the sad fate of the opera on stage: in eight years (1874–1882) it had received twenty-five performances in Petersburg, and even fewer in Moscow, and had subsequently been withdrawn altogether from the repertoire of both cities. Nowadays too, in spite of the slogan currently in vogue in the West of 'Return to Mussorgsky' and the repeated accusations that Rimsky-Korsakov distorted the concept of the opera, the quarrel about the viability of the composer's version has not abated. In his homeland, at any rate, it still persists: witness to this is the orchestration prepared by Shostakovich. However, this too has failed to supplant the edition produced by Rimsky-Korsakov, who, working on the opera of a very dear friend, tried to remain as faithful as possible to the original while bringing the work closer to contemporary aesthetic and artistic tastes.

Contrary to what many people think, the revised *Boris Godunov* was not an ideological or political compromise. It simply represented Rimsky-Korsakov's concept of historic opera at that time. The conductor and musicologist David Lloyd-Jones, who has spent many years researching and restoring authentic manuscripts of Mussorgsky and to whom English-speaking audiences owe an excellent translation of *Boris*, is mistaken when he says that Rimsky-Korsakov's alteration of *Boris Godunov* was motivated by the demands of censorship. 'After several performances the so-called "Revolution scene" was cut, while the scene in Pimen's cell was never staged during Mussorgsky's lifetime because the censor disapproved of any representation of clergy on the operatic stage.'[195] In fact, these scenes were omitted not on the censor's orders but to please the principal conductor of the Mariinsky Theatre, Napravnik, who thought the opera long and boring enough without them.[196] If the authorities had objected on religious grounds, not only would the scene in the cell have gone but also the inn scene (Varlaam is a monk, too), the 'Polish act' (Rangoni) and Boris' death (arrival of Pimen). Lloyd-Jones further states: '... Although my edition has recently been published in the Soviet Union I can't help feeling that sheer convention will make the Russians the very last people to jettison Rimsky.'[197] Refraining from further comment, one can only remark that any extreme opinion is bad for art. Preference for one version or another is a matter of personal taste, over which it is futile to argue. Both sides can line up large and impressive forces. Thus among the opponents of the composer's version we would see, for instance, Alexander Glazunov ('Mussorgsky's music is not always playable; in the original orchestration it lacks colour and is dull'),[198] and among its supporters Claudio Abbado ('In the original version the measure of Mussorgsky's genius and his unique individuality are much more in evidence').[199]

Naturally, when attempts were made in Russia to return to the 'original' Mussorgsky, Chaliapin's possible reaction was a constant topic of discussion. Most people were convinced that Mussorgsky's greatest interpreter would have been among the first to welcome them. 'If Chaliapin knew of the discoveries made in the score, he would be overjoyed,' Stanislavsky confidently predicted.[200] The singer stated his views on the subject in 1932 during an interview in Prague; it aroused a great deal of interest and was reproduced by several Western newspapers. When asked whether he intended to re-create the character of Boris along the lines of the composer's manuscript, he replied: 'Let's get one thing straight first of all. When I was studying my part more than thirty years ago I used the original conception of *Boris Godunov* in order to stay as close as possible to Mussorgsky's ideas. As a whole, this original version is not adapted to the stage. The performance would have to begin at 4 p.m. in order to finish by 4 o'clock the next morning. When Rimsky-Korsakov gave the work a new version, he was acting in the interest of Mussorgsky, to whom he was deeply attached and whose talent he valued highly. In doing so, he may have smoothed over a few places, but on the whole he didn't do any damage to the work – he merely helped it on the way to a long, let us hope eternal, life on the stage.'[201]

A theatre which opts for the first version of *Boris Godunov* cannot avoid abridging it – in other words, doing exactly what Rimsky-Korsakov is now blamed for. The cuts are necessitated not so much by the length of the composition (some of Wagner's

operas are even longer) as by the desire to present a homogeneous work; in practice the original version inevitably ends
up as a series of isolated incidents with no strong dramatic link
between them. As an actor, Chaliapin instinctively realised the
advantage for the stage of Rimsky-Korsakov's classic treatment.
That edition of *Boris Godunov* was intended for the Mariinsky
Theatre, although it was once again rejected. Professionals and
amateurs then joined forces to perform the opera, and Rimsky-
Korsakov himself conducted the orchestra and chorus.

Mussorgsky's friends and admirers were at first reluctant to
accept the idea of a new version, but after seeing it many of
them, including Stasov himself, renounced their uncompromising attitude. 'Ah, what a pleasure it was,' exclaimed the stunned
critic, 'to be present at the performance of such a great thing!
... What pleasure to feel in every move the inspiration and the
astonishing power of the great departed master, what pleasure
to feast on the extraordinary beauties of Rimsky-Korsakov's
orchestration!'[202]

Chaliapin started to study the part of Boris during the summer
of 1898, but rehearsals of *Judith* and of *Mozart and Salieri*
temporarily interrupted work. We know from the singer's own
words that he was increasingly fascinated by the role. Mamontov wrote to Rimsky-Korsakov that Chaliapin was 'simply in
love with the role of Boris'. It would be difficult to find a more
accurate expression. It defines his attitude not only to the part
but to the entire opera. 'Every word, or more exactly every
musical phrase, enlivened by Pushkin's genial word, is extraordinarily beautiful in Mussorgsky. If you knew ... how I revere
and love Mussorgsky; in my opinion this great man was created
on the same mighty scale as one of Michelangelo's statues,'
declared Chaliapin in 1898.[203] And later, in his memoirs: 'I liked
Boris Godunov so much that, not content with learning my
part, I sang the whole opera, all the roles: male and female,
from beginning to end. When I realised how useful it was to
study a complete opera, I started to do this with all the others,
even those I had sung earlier. The deeper I delved into Mussorgsky's opera, the clearer it became to me that in opera it is
possible to act even Shakespeare.'[204]

The singer's life-long veneration of Mussorgsky was nowhere more in evidence than in the meticulous care he bestowed on every performance of *Boris Godunov*. 'I played Prince Vasili Shuisky opposite Chaliapin many times,' recounts Vasili Shkafer. 'I saw ... that things would annoy and irritate him: the cast as well as the sound of the chorus.... This was fertile ground for breeding various kinds of misunderstandings with conductors. I think – and in fact it is true – that Chaliapin knew not only every bar of every vocal part but also the parts of the musicians playing in the orchestra.'[205]

Thorough study of the score, memorising the whole work from beginning to end, penetrating the inner world of a character and the interrelation of all the parts ('the seemingly insignificant phrase of someone of no importance, some "second guard" at the palace gates, can unexpectedly throw a light on a crucial moment of the action,' said Chaliapin), trying to imagine in advance the general atmosphere of the finished production – at the turn of the century these things were absolutely new to operatic art.

Chaliapin thus gradually evolved his method of approaching roles, which rested on achieving mastery of the composer's artistic principles and style. He added to it over the years and reached a broader perception, but the basic rule remained invariable: study and analysis always preceded the work of creative imagination.*

'If the character is a fictitious creation of the composer's mind, I know all I need to know and all it is possible to know about him from the score – he is entirely contained within the work. I shall not find any other light on his personality nor will I try to. It is another story if the personage is historical. In that case I must consult history as well. I must make myself familiar with the events which took place around him and those which happened because of him, what distinguished him from other people of his time and environment, how his contemporaries saw him and how historians depict him. What is the point of this? It isn't history I must play but a character in a particular

---

* This point will be discussed in Chapter IV.

Chaliapin's self-portrait of himself as Boris Godunov, 1911.

Chaliapin as Boris Godunov in Mussorgsky's opera *Boris Godunov*.

work of art, however far it may depart from historical truth. Yet this knowledge is essential, and the reason is this: If the author has been entirely faithful to historical truth, history will help me to gain further and deeper comprehension of his intentions; but if the author deviates from history, if he is deliberately contradicting it, then in this case even more than in the first it is important for me to know the true historical facts. It is precisely this deviation from historical truth which enables one to grasp the most intimate essence of the author's thoughts. History hesitates; it does not know whether Tsar Boris is guilty or not guilty of the murder of Tsarevich Dmitri at Uglich. Pushkin makes him guilty; Mussorgsky follows Pushkin and gives Boris a conscience in which his wicked soul* rages like a caged wild beast. I of course can learn far more from Pushkin's work and Mussorgsky's conception of the character of Boris if I know that this is not an incontrovertible fact but a subjective interpretation of history. I am faithful, I cannot be other than faithful, to Pushkin's intentions and to Mussorgsky's – I play a *wicked* [Chaliapin's italics] Tsar Boris; but my knowledge nevertheless enables me to put some nuances in my acting which would otherwise not be there. I cannot say this with absolute certainty, but it is likely that my knowledge helps me to make Boris more tragic – sympathetic. This explains why, while I was studying the part of Boris, I went to our eminent historian V. O. Kliuchevsky for directions and advice.'[206]

As the reader may recall, the young singer had already met the venerable old scholar: his expertise had proved invaluable when Chaliapin was creating Ivan the Terrible and Dosifei. And so, now that he was working on Tsar Boris, Chaliapin did not begrudge the lengthy journey from Moscow to the country place near Yaroslavl where Kliuchevsky was living. Chaliapin never forgot those days; in numerous interviews, at rehearsals, in conversations with acquaintances and in his memoirs, he constantly returned to his talks with Kliuchevsky, reliving them in

---

* In the original Russian text of *Mask and Soul* the word 'muka' (torture) has been used, but this is clearly a printing mistake; the sense indicates it should be 'dusha' (soul).

his memory again and again as one of his most precious and treasured recollections.

What did Chaliapin find so attractive and astonishing in the 'eminent scholar'? His vast knowledge? The originality of his views on the period known as 'the Time of Troubles'? No doubt, but more than that. A great deal of contemporary evidence shows that Kliuchevsky combined the attributes of a scholar with those of an artist for whom the past existed in almost tangibly real scenes. Kliuchevsky did not 'fictionalise' accounts of historical events and did not turn strict scientific research into a fascinating novel. In his narratives the past put on real flesh and blood, became familiar and simple. Kliuchevsky was tremendously popular, not only through his books but also through his lectures at Moscow University. Students from various faculties regularly attended them and were joined by ordinary members of the public, one of whom recorded in his memoirs: 'There entered a modest professor, not very tall, with greying hair and in a buttoned-up black jacket. The whole amphitheatre gave a sort of gasp and showed signs of excitement; it was Kliuchevsky. He started his lecture in a low voice, as if reluctantly. After a while, he was transformed: he seemed to grow taller, his voice was firmer, the figures he was evoking became clearer and clearer and we could distinctly see scenes of the ancient past. Kliuchevsky was lecturing on the period of Ivan the Terrible. This was not a lecture but something for which there is no name – a brilliant reconstruction of a bygone life. The lecture ended. Vasili Osipovich became again a modest, shy man, carefully descending from the rostrum to the furious thunder of applause of the entire room.'[207]

The effect produced on the impressionable Chaliapin by his conversations with Kliuchevsky is not hard to imagine. The true actor readily admits that he sees everything around him as a never-ending performance and that he finds elements of the art of the theatre in every act of cognition. For him, such penetration to the heart of a situation is tantamount to an acting 'experience'. The actor regards it as a first move towards metamorphosis, or at any rate as one of its prerequisites. For this reason, the erudite historian seemed to Chaliapin to possess a natural gift for the theatre. 'When I asked him [Kliuchevsky] to talk to me about Godunov, he suggested that we went for a stroll in the woods. I shall never forget this marvellous walk among the tall pine trees on the sand full of pine needles. The little old man with a pudding-basin haircut and a little white beard, his narrow, wise eyes shining behind his glasses, walked beside me. He stopped every now and then, and in an ingratiating voice, with a cunning grin upon his face, he re-enacted for me, just as if he had witnessed the event himself, the dialogue between Shuisky and Godunov, then talked of the police officers as if he knew them personally, of Varlaam, Missail and of the charm of the Pretender. He talked a great deal and it was so wonderfully picturesque that I could see the people he was portraying.'[208] His talent for this seems to have been so great that Chaliapin regretfully exclaimed: 'What a pity that Vasili Osipovich can't sing and play Prince Vasili with me.' And later, when performances were already under way, he said again about the role of Shuisky, 'Ah! If only Vasili Osipovich Kliuchevsky was playing this part.'

For young Chaliapin the most important thing was to understand what he was going to show to the public; the rest would follow. And so he had no difficulty in imagining the old professor from Moscow on the operatic stage, although the latter gave no evidence of any singing talent. Kliuchevsky understood Shuisky intellectually, and as far as Chaliapin was concerned, that meant that he was already interpreting him, since he was forming a mental picture of his nature and of his behaviour. 'It seemed to me at times that Vasili Shuisky had risen from the dead and was himself admitting his mistake in destroying Godunov.'[209]

We can assume that during this visit in the summer of 1898, Kliuchevsky also acquainted Chaliapin with the views expounded later in his voluminous publication *The Course of Russian History* (1903–1906), and therefore refer to this source in our attempt to reconstruct the gist of their conversations: Chaliapin never made a secret of the fact that Kliuchevsky's stories strongly influenced his understanding of the character of

Godunov and his concept of the role.

'Despite his many years' experience as a ruler, the mercy he generously extended to all classes after his accession to the throne and his governing abilities, his popularity remained shaky. Boris was one of those ill-starred people who attract and repel at the same time – attract on account of evident qualities of mind and of talent but repel owing to invisible flaws of heart and of conscience. He could provoke surprise and gratitude but not inspire trust in anyone: he was always suspected of duplicity and perfidy and thought capable of anything. Undoubtedly, the dreadful school of Ivan the Terrible, through which Godunov has passed, had left on him an indelible bad mark.'[210] Kliuchevsky, of course, put special emphasis on Godunov's psychological traits in the analysis he gave Chaliapin. The singer remembered in particular how Kliuchevsky stressed his loneliness. 'I listened and felt sincere pity for this Tsar, who possessed great strength of will and mind, wished to do good for Russia, yet created serfdom. . . .'[211] The words 'sincere pity' are very revealing and significant. They do not concern only the role of Godunov; some feeling of sympathy towards the character he was playing was perhaps one of the permanent features of Chaliapin's art. It is not a question of justifying tyranny and crime (Holofernes, Ivan, Salieri, Boris, Eryomka, King Philip) nor (as it is frequently seen) one of trying at any price to find some positive qualities in the nature of the 'evil-doer'. In Chaliapin, this sympathy was the result of careful analysis and came from his grasp of the multiple influences which had fashioned the personality he was incarnating. The power and the irresistible fascination many of them possessed raised their conflict with life to the level of real tragedy, on a scale which reminded contemporaries of the acute and bitter anguish found in Dostoevsky's novels. The singer once dedicated a photo-album entitled 'Chaliapin on Stage' to Gorky with these words: 'Your faithful friend, suffering sincerely for everyone who is here.'[212] The results of such an approach did not pass unnoticed: a review following the first night of *Boris Godunov* said: 'Again, a clear-cut type, once more intelligently conceived and amazingly, brilliantly portrayed. He has so far never repeated himself, such is the versatility and variety of this singer's talent. Many were in tears at the end of the performance, so true and sincere was Chaliapin's portrayal of the mental tortures racking Boris and leading to his death. In the earlier roles of Susanin, Mephistopheles, Salieri and others, we saw a different person each time, but we never noticed Chaliapin; he reveals himself only in one thing: the unusual sympathy he shows for the character he is playing – one might call it love. This love is the proof of the genuinely artistic nature of Chaliapin.'[213]

The role of Boris, with its psychological depth and the richness of its subject matter, was probably Chaliapin's greatest challenge so far. In Ivan, Dosifei, Susanin and even Salieri, he had had to play a fully developed character: almost everything in these roles revolves upon a progress towards a last and decisive trial of fate. But Boris is different. The slow and agonising disintegration of a gigantic personality must take place in front of the spectators: from his accession to the throne to the barely audible 'forgive' before his death, the Tsar is haunted by an unbearable suffering which consumes him. Neither the titanic strength of his will nor his intelligence nor his burning lust for power can protect Boris from the tragic retribution inexorably drawing near.

Rehearsals went on for long hours every day, but there was still not enough time. In addition to three premières in rapid succession,* Chaliapin had to sing almost every night.

He was nervous. Boris' first entrance in the Prologue was giving him particular trouble. When he heard Mamontov exclaim once more 'No, it's not right!', Chaliapin could not contain himself and left the stage. Mamontov, who well knew the temperament of his favourite singer, went after him. 'Fedya! What's the matter with you, calm down! Well now, you must understand that, in the words of Pushkin, you have "attained the highest power". Why should you behave like a boyard who plumes himself on his title, position and birth? Why should you try so hard? Make your entrance more simple.'[214] Chaliapin gradually regained his composure, although he just could not

* *Judith* – November 23rd; *Mozart and Salieri* – November 25th; *Boris Godunov* – December 7th.

get the rhythm of his step right. Many years later, Chaliapin wrote in an American magazine: 'When Tsar Boris is seen moving majestically across the stage, the young artist is not conscious that he had to spend months – possibly years – in learning to walk that way; that at one time, he even had to learn the very beginnings of walking.'[215]

According to one of the production's designers, Chaliapin was also dissatisfied with his costume of black brocade with silver flowers and a violet lining. He started to object, saying that it looked like mourning, to which Mamontov replied: 'How can you fail to understand that all *Boris Godunov* is a mourning for Russian history.'[216]

Let it be added in passing that for once Chaliapin was not convinced by Mamontov's words. Soon after leaving the Private Opera he discarded the black brocade for a gold one (as we see him, for instance, in the famous portrait by Golovin).

However, in spite of all the difficulties, it was quite clear to Mamontov that Chaliapin was preparing another artistic triumph. In an unpublished letter to Rimsky-Korsakov he wrote a few days before the dress rehearsal: 'Chaliapin is immersed in the role and he will be superb.'[217] He was not mistaken; everyone who saw him went into raptures over Chaliapin, even those who considered that 'from the musical point of view, the role of Boris was not the best in the opera'.[218] His effect on the public is most vividly illustrated by contemporary descriptions: 'From the moment the newly elected Tsar first appears on the parvis of the Uspensky Cathedral, the attention is riveted on his majestic figure, betraying signs of preoccupation and secret forebodings. An inexorable fate already hangs over his head, and the rest of Chaliapin's interpretation will be all of a piece, marvellously consistent, with the degree of tension only he can create by intensifying tragic colours in a continuous crescendo.'[219] 'Chaliapin in the role of Boris Godunov', says another, 'rose to new heights of musical and dramatic interpretation rarely seen on the operatic stage. In the monologue "I have attained the highest power", his acting, his facial expressions, the versatility of his intonations, the profusion of dramatic nuances and the strength of the psychological portrayal reached such a level of artistry that the critic can only silently bow to the artist together with the enthusiastic crowd.'[220]

'One must give first place to the superb and astonishing Chaliapin, who gave an entirely consistent and completely convincing interpretation of Boris. His monologues, full of dramatic effects, of bitterness and of a sense of dread at the prospect of the punishment prophesied to him; his scenes of repentance and of tormenting despair at the memory of his evil deeds and, on the other hand, the realisation of his superiority over the throng of base, smooth-tongued boyards; and finally the struggle between the magnificent actor Tsar Boris in fact was and the man with a tender heart but a will of iron – all this is wonderfully combined in Chaliapin's creation.'[221]

The reviews of Chaliapin's first performance in *Boris Godunov* unfortunately include few factual details of his interpretation. Such accounts do exist, but only in articles written at a later date, when musical criticism, influenced by the changes which occurred in Russian opera at the beginning of the twentieth century (changes exemplified chiefly by Chaliapin's art), began to show interest in the question of harmonious stage characterisation. The reviewers had an additional reason for analysing the singer's work with such attention: Chaliapin's performance in *Boris Godunov* put an end to the many lingering doubts about the qualities of the opera and of Mussorgsky's music as a whole. The conflict between bel canto and the 'new' Russian school of composition, which had torn Chaliapin apart five years earlier in Tiflis, no longer existed. He now knew how Mussorgsky should be sung, and this was a revelation not only for Chaliapin but also for other singers and musicians, as well as for the general public. A critic who heard him during one of his guest appearances in Kiev reported that the singer had 'found the right approach to Mussorgsky's style and understood it perfectly. He has identified himself with this style and found the secret of interpreting it. Chaliapin makes Mussorgsky's grandiose conceptions comprehensible. ... With what sublime dramatic effect, and at the same time how simply and naturally, does Chaliapin sing.'[222]

But he was not only searching for a new solution to the

'vocal' side of the problem. 'The more I played Boris Godunov, Ivan the Terrible, Dosifei, the Viking Guest and the Hetman in *May Night*, the more convinced I became that in opera the artist must not only sing but also act his role, as actors do in straight theatre.'[223]

There seems to be nothing new in Chaliapin's declaration. He had already given some thought to the idea of 'playing opera like straight theatre' earlier. What was new was that characters from Russian operas had become the basis of his argument and that his conviction was particularly strong where the works of Mussorgsky and Rimsky-Korsakov were concerned. There was simply no other way of approaching them. The composer's intentions were clearly indicated, and this in turn led to only one possible form of theatre – the theatre of artistic ensemble. 'It was difficult to act if your partner did not respond in the tone which was right for the mood of the scene,' recalled Chaliapin.[224]

It cannot be said that the Russian stage had never seen this type of work before Mamontov and Stanislavsky. In dramatic theatre and even in opera, such ensembles existed, but they consisted of good actors or singers on whose creative powers they were totally dependent. If two or three of the performers were less gifted, or followed a different style, it was enough to disrupt everything, and all the public saw then was the collective performance of a variety of guest artists who happened to find themselves together on the same stage at the same time.

The situation began to change with the productions of the Moscow Art Theatre, when the very concept of ensemble gradually took on a new meaning. Flawless 'concert' performing gave way to communion of mental outlook and of feeling, showing the actors' spiritual unity. In the 'theatre of like-minded people', as Stanislavsky later put it, unity of mind does not mean that everyone must think alike but quite the opposite: everyone must think for themselves, only the aim being common to all. And if the actors are not just puppets but artists, then by the time work on a production has been completed, this common aim must have become clear and evident to all. Then an ensemble can be formed even if it is made up of extremes.

Chaliapin never managed to appear in such a theatre and with such an ensemble, although he continued to dream of it to the end of his life. His book *Mask and Soul*, for instance, ends on a note of regret: 'Mamontov represented for me everything bright and creative in life. I have not created my theatre. Others will come and do it.'[225]

But if he had any regrets, what were they exactly? Perhaps he remembered how, long before the end of his third season with Mamontov, five days after the huge success of *Boris Godunov* (i.e. on December 12th, 1898), he went to see the recently appointed Director of the Moscow Imperial Theatres, Telyakovsky, and signed a three-year contract with the Bolshoi Theatre. And also that he did it in secret, without breathing a word of it to anyone at the Private Opera, although news of his departure was already leaked through the press in January 1899.[226]

At first sight, such an act seems unbelievable: Chaliapin owed everything to Mamontov's theatre – he had until quite recently been almost totally ignored by the Imperial stage in Petersburg. He is clearly ill at ease when referring to the circumstances surrounding his discussions with the Bolshoi Theatre and seems to try to justify himself. He explains his decision to move by saying that Telyakovsky inspired in him 'a warm feeling of deep sympathy.... It was clear that this man understood and loved art, and that he was prepared to serve it faithfully. Somehow, I immediately started to tell him about my dreams, about what I would like opera to be. Moreover, Telyakovsky said, "Gradually we shall do everything you consider necessary!"'[227] But hadn't Mamontov used the same words? And what is more, he had already provided Chaliapin with extraordinary conditions for his work. Varvara Strakhova-Ermans, rightly observed: 'The years Chaliapin spent at Mamontov's theatre must be regarded as a period of extreme intellectual exertion and great fecundity.... This was the moment when his genius burst forth. This is where he made his brilliant stage creations, and this is where and when Fedor Ivanovich became *Chaliapin* [Strakhova-Ermans' emphasis], a name which subsequently came to be so universally acclaimed.'[228]

Could it be because of rumours that Mamontov's affairs were doing badly, that he was going to be bankrupted and put on trial? No, that was not the case. Chaliapin says: 'When the season started at the Private Opera, I felt sorry for my companions and for Mamontov. I decided to remain with them.'[229] The fact is confirmed by Telyakovsky in his memoirs,[230] and other sources indicate that Chaliapin made several unsuccessful attempts, up to and after Mamontov's arrest, to annul his contract with the Bolshoi Theatre.

Chaliapin left at the same time as Rachmaninov; Korovin had gone even earlier. All this (and Chaliapin was perfectly aware of the situation) could only end in total collapse for Mamontov's theatre. And so it did. The Private Opera – or under its new name after Mamontov's arrest, the 'Company' – was already beyond recovery. Its days were numbered. Many contemporaries, as well as subsequent generations, blamed Chaliapin for this, and he himself, as some of his previously quoted comments show, did not feel that his decision had been entirely right. Had Chaliapin remained at the Private Opera, he might have assumed its artistic direction, and then at the end of his life perhaps there would have been no need to regret that he had not created his own theatre. He probably thought that way many years after the event, but in December 1898, at the age of twenty-five, he saw things differently, and it is difficult to criticise him for leaving. A variety of reasons contributed to his decision: Telyakovsky offered him significantly better financial conditions, and of course the possibilities of the Bolshoi Theatre itself – first-class orchestra and chorus plus practically unlimited resources for staging operas – no doubt attracted the young singer. 'Actors, and as a whole all members of staff, at the Imperial Theatres were well provided for,' wrote Chaliapin. 'An actor had ample opportunity to live, think and work free from worry. Nobody counted the pennies. Spending was on a large scale. The costumes and sets were so lavish as to be beyond the dreams of private promoters. And no wonder, since the patron of these theatres was none other than the Emperor of Russia himself.'[231] Also, in the Private Opera, in spite of his success and the gratitude he felt to

Mamontov, Chaliapin was growing increasingly dissatisfied with the musical level of the productions. 'Judge for yourself,' he wrote to Stasov after the première of *Boris Godunov*, 'is this a way to behave, for example, towards Mussorgsky? I mean that for all his protestations that an opera as magnificent as *Boris* demands a meticulous production, it seems that Savva let it go after only two or three rehearsals with the full cast. Really, is it possible? What the hell is this, that by the last rehearsal almost no one knows his role properly.... You decide, Vladimir Vasilevich, whether a man sincerely devoted to art would allow this purely so as to hang over the box office the notice "sold out". Eh? Surely not. Isn't that right? But in our theatre they are capable of it. And, of course, we poor artists must, out of pride and most of all out of love for the work to be performed, bend over backwards to avoid ruining the opera, and yes, all right, we do it, and jolly well too, and although, thank goodness, we manage to do it, one or two of us, perhaps five even – but the rest, the chorus, the orchestra? I will say, like Boris, "My soul is heavy." '[232] It has to be admitted that Chaliapin was not alone. Many others including Rimsky-Korsakov and Rachmaninov deplored this state of affairs and found it intolerable.

Chaliapin now needed to expand his range and find a higher professional level.

At the beginning of March, he went on another tour with the Private Opera, visiting Petersburg, where Rimsky-Korsakov noted in his *Chronicles* that 'Chaliapin was a huge success',[233] and then his home town of Kazan to play the Miller, Susanin, Galitsky and Mephistopheles. Chaliapin makes no mention of this anywhere, although there again the theatre was packed and 'during his stay in Kazan he was the subject of noisy ovations'.[234]

Upon his return to Moscow in the autumn of 1899, Chaliapin gave some farewell performances at the Company (as it was already called by then). His last appearance took place on September 21st. Three days later he was to sing in *Faust* at the Bolshoi Theatre; three days later he would once again become a member of the Imperial Theatres. 'A mood of sadness pervaded the Private Opera yesterday on the occasion of his departure,' wrote a Moscow newspaper. 'With the last sounds of

Chaliapin's voice in the brilliantly performed death of Godunov, the public was saying goodbye not only to a pleasing talent but also to the Russian works that had remained in the repertoire of the Private Opera only thanks to the presence of such an artist as Chaliapin. It will no doubt take a long time for these operas to reach the Imperial stage, and they are not likely to remain in the repertoire of the Private Opera: under the previous management (Mamontov) losses did not matter, and with Chaliapin there were no losses anyway, since the box-office returns for the performances in which he took part were sufficient to cover the losses of other productions. . . .'[235]

This was more than a simple acknowledgement of his success: Chaliapin had become a national glory.

CHAPTER III

Back to New Ground

'I will go and listen to him, even if the only words he sings all evening are "Lord, have mercy". Believe me, he can sing these words in such a way that God, if he exists, is bound to hear, and to have mercy there and then on everyone and everything, or else turn the earth to dust and ashes. That will depend on what Chaliapin wants to put into those words.'

Maxim Gorky

SOMETHING INCREDIBLE WAS happening during Chaliapin's first performance at the Bolshoi Theatre; 'even the old habitués couldn't remember anything like it'.[1] The ribbons of the innumerable garlands and bouquets brought onto the stage at the end of every act, or just raining down from the darkness of the auditorium, which 'had become a sea of furiously clapping hands',[2] bore inscriptions like 'To the pride and glory of Russian opera', 'Hail to an artist and singer', 'To a great artist'. That evening Chaliapin took no less than thirty curtain calls.[3]

The scene was repeated three months later at the Mariinsky Theatre. 'We cannot recall such a success since the time of Patti. The house, packed to capacity, was in an uproar,'[4] declared the *Peterburgskaya gazeta*. Strangers exchanged enthusiastic remarks and delighted looks with each other; the same words echoed everywhere: 'A wonder!' When, before the start of the second act, Telyakovsky entered his box, he received an ovation: many people knew how much patience, intelligence and diplomatic skill he had shown so as to obtain the return of Chaliapin to the Imperial stage. Telyakovsky, smiling, said that 'he was very grateful to Petersburg for letting Chaliapin go, since he was not needed there. But now Moscow, where he was very much needed, would occasionally let him go to Petersburg for two or three performances.'[5]

This was a reversal of normal procedure: Moscow soloists did not usually sing in Petersburg. Soloists from the capital traditionally appeared at the Bolshoi Theatre: some of them to raise the box-office returns, others because they were not considered good enough for Petersburg, though perfectly adequate for Moscow. However, things were changing; opera lovers readily undertook the long and uncomfortable journey to Moscow for the sake of hearing Chaliapin. They thought nothing of queueing up for two or three nights to get tickets for his performances, even in the middle of the bitter Russian winters. Not that the crowds were attracted by the prospect of seeing yet another star in the operatic firmament: Chaliapin categorically rejected the very notion of 'famous guest performer'. But the level and the principles of his artistry acted as a sort of catalyst on the singers and on the spectators, forcing them to take a fresh look at the unexplored potential of musical theatre. 'He added special excitement and lifted all our scenes to unprecedented heights,' wrote Telyakovsky. 'His presence soon made itself felt not only in opera but in our other theatres. Real artists were ashamed and embarrassed to play or sing badly in front of Chaliapin; I was ashamed to put on a poor operatic production if he was in it; the same was true of the designer, the costumier, the hairdresser, the chorus, the orchestra, the stagehands – in a word, anyone who came into contact with him in one way or another. The *corps de ballet*, too, danced better and with greater zeal in his presence, and even the usher was unwilling to let in latecomers, because "Chaliapin is singing today." '[6]

The time has come to make the acquaintance of a man who played an important part in Chaliapin's life – and, one must add, not only in Chaliapin's but in that of the entire Russian theatre during its last pre-revolutionary decade.

Vladimir Arkadevich Telyakovsky (1860–1924) was the son of a well-known military theorist and received a broad education at home. Equally gifted in science and the arts, Telyakovsky studied languages, painting, piano and mathematics with equal enthusiasm. In his parents' house he frequently met many artists, actors and musicians. Among them were Tchaikovsky and Liadov, Fedor Komissarzhevsky and Anton Rubinstein. The latter's brother, the renowned Nikolai Rubinstein, founder and first director of the Moscow Conservatoire, enjoyed playing piano duets with young Telyakovsky. However, his father was determined to send him into the army. He had to obey and reluctantly joined the Corps des Pages* and later served in the Horse Guards. The years went by. Telyakovsky graduated from

* Privileged Cadet School in Petersburg.

the Academy of the General Staff with the rank of colonel, but his interest in music did not lessen: at one time he even seriously hesitated between the careers of professional musician and regular army officer. Telyakovsky's inclinations were known at court. In May of 1898 he was appointed Director of the Imperial Theatres in Moscow, and within three years he became their sole director in the two capitals. 'This caused amusement in theatrical circles: "What an idea! The man's been in charge of horses and now is going to be in charge of the actors,"' recalled Chaliapin.[7] But the new director turned out to be a far-sighted and shrewd man, who was a good judge of art. Always on the lookout for anything new and promising, Telyakovsky showed himself an ardent supporter of the Moscow Art Theatre from its very beginnings. He repeatedly asked Stanislavsky to work for him, and finally persuaded him in 1915 to give regular classes for young singers of the Bolshoi Theatre. Ignoring the active opposition of the majority of leading actors, the desperate outcries of the press and the disapproving silence of the court, he appointed the 'decadent, anti-Christ and iconoclast' Vsevolod Meyerhold principal producer of the Imperial Theatres. To take such a step required no small amount of courage and confidence. In 1907 few could foresee that Meyerhold's productions would one day be regarded as immortal gems of Russian theatre which had opened fresh and infinite perspectives in acting methods for future generations.

Among the new names Telyakovsky brought into the lime-light one must also mention Mikhail Fokine, launched on his career by the new director in spite of the slander spread against him by envious people. Within days of taking up his appointment in Moscow he managed to entice Korovin away from Mamontov and began to take a close interest in Chaliapin. The details of the secret negotiations with the artist have come down to us through Telyakovsky's own memoirs: 'In the autumn of 1898, having just assumed office ... I heard Chaliapin for the first time. I was struck not only by Chaliapin's voice but by his acting, his appearance, the way he conducted himself on stage, his diction and, generally speaking, his musical performance of the part. I was even more struck to learn that Chaliapin was a

former singer of the Mariinsky Theatre about whom I had so
far heard nothing, either from the public, from singers or from
my superiors. His departure from the Imperial stages was obviously the result of some misunderstanding. I felt instinctively
that such an artist ... was important for the management, being
not only a very gifted singer but a man capable of raising the
standards of our opera. I was told, however, that there was no
possibility of engaging Chaliapin at the moment, that he was
under contract until the following year, and that the management was hardly likely to agree to breaking a contract, and
furthermore to paying a price for that, so soon after Chaliapin
himself had paid one for joining Mamontov's opera.

'The situation was awkward: Chaliapin had been released by
Vsevolozhsky, the old and experienced Director of Imperial
Theatres, with the full knowledge of the old and experienced
conductor Napravnik, and now the young and inexperienced
cavalry officer Telyakovsky, who had just been appointed director of the Moscow office, wanted not only to take him back but
was even ready to pay a fine for it. It was therefore useless
even discussing it with the Petersburg management; one had
somehow to act without regard to the authorities and not ask
anything. But there was another difficulty: a contract comes
into force only when it has been sanctioned by the director –
and what if Vsevolozhsky did not sanction it? And this could
easily happen, since at the Mariinsky Theatre Chaliapin
received 2,400 roubles a year – so if they let him go it meant
that they had found he was not worth this amount. Chaliapin
was now getting 6,000 roubles at Mamontov's, so he wouldn't
come to me for less than 10–12,000.

'I decided to act, leaving the Petersburg management in the
dark by not bringing it to their notice, moving promptly and
giving, if need be, my inexperience as an excuse. I had to meet
Chaliapin in secret and as if by accident. Discussions as to how
to carry all this out went on for several days. All the details had
to be fixed in advance, since, as we were meeting in secret, we
could only do it once, and if everything was not signed and
sealed immediately, Moscow and Petersburg would of course
find out that Chaliapin was visiting me (and with my kind of

entourage I could count on my secret being uncovered). And if they found out, Mamontov's opera would of course take steps to keep Chaliapin and I would receive from Petersburg the "friendly" advice not to engage him.... I entrusted this diplomatic mission to V. Nelidov, who was a born diplomat and who was at that time handling some special assignments of mine. I explained the importance of the matter to him, asked him ... not to go to Chaliapin's flat but casually arrange to meet him at the Slaviansky Bazar restaurant, treat him to the right kind of meal and from there come straight to my flat when the theatre office's staff had left.* On December 12th, 1898, after a good dinner and some wine, Chaliapin and Nelidov appeared in my study, and at the end of lengthy negotiations Chaliapin finally signed a three-year contract at a fee of nine, ten and eleven thousand roubles per year respectively. I was told that "a bass should not be paid such large amounts of money", to which I answered that we had not engaged a bass but an outstanding artist. The management was not happy about Chaliapin's appointment, that was clear....'[8]

Telyakovsky was not at pains to please the theatrical powers of the capital and had no intention of letting them dictate to him. Moreover, he was so convinced that he was doing the right thing that he wrote in his diary on the same evening: 'Chaliapin made a very favourable impression on me. We haggled for a long time, he wanted time to think; but I didn't and ... I could not rest until he had signed the contract. He knows what he is talking about, but he has as yet no idea of his own worth. Now, if only Petersburg ratifies it – I will have accomplished something big in my life!'[9]

It took two weeks to obtain Vsevolozhsky's consent, but then Chaliapin's guest performances in Petersburg with Mamontov's opera, and his triumph at the Bolshoi Theatre, swept away all doubts. 'Chaliapin's joining the theatre has now become a reality,' wrote Sobinov to a friend. 'Fedor's voice sounds magnificent and seems even bigger. The management is simply wooing him and the artistic directors are ready to make any

---

* Telyakovsky's flat was in the same building as the office of the Imperial Theatres.

concession. As the saying goes, his every wish is their command.'[10]

When Chaliapin suddenly fell ill three days after his début, the public refused to accept another singer in his place, 'expressed their displeasure at the box-office and demanded their money back'.[11]

Fate seemed to be favouring the young singer more than ever, blessing him with financial success, recognition from critics and public alike, sweet smiles from the theatre directors and a happy family life. It is interesting to note that he writes about these times in his memoirs without even a trace of the bitterness and irritation which fill the accounts of his first season at the Mariinsky Theatre. Chaliapin, deeply disillusioned, had then abandoned Petersburg for Mamontov without regret. But now he was placing great hopes on the Imperial stage, and he certainly had good reasons for doing this: the operatic resources of the Bolshoi Theatre were vastly superior to those of the Private Opera, and Telyakovsky had given his personal guarantee that 'little by little we will do everything you consider necessary'.[12]

This explains why in the American edition of *Pages from My Life* (this passage does not figure in the Soviet version of the memoirs), Chaliapin writes: 'Those who have never been in Russia cannot possibly imagine what a magnificent institution the Royal Imperial Theatres and their schools were. Nowhere in the world, except perhaps in France under Louis XIV or during the Empire, was the theatre so pampered and caressed. The care bestowed upon them and the goodwill of the Tsars placed the Russian Imperial Theatres in an extraordinary position. Having been in their service and having travelled all over the world, I have never found any stage that could be compared with them from the artistic point of view. The beauty of their productions of drama, opera and ballet inspired many great musicians, and it is common knowledge that they produced not only exceptional composers, but great and serious dramatists. The traditions of the Russian Imperial Theatres were so powerful than not even revolution could crush them, and so during the great revolutionary conflagration the Russian stage stood like a knight in indestructible armour, ready to meet any and every enemy.'[13]

And what about the routine, the lack of interest in a lively art form, the officials giving orders to the actors as if they were soldiers in barracks? Perhaps all this had vanished during the three years he had spent at the Private Opera? Not at all; no striking changes had taken place. But a different light now fell on the picture, and the scenes it illuminated did not look quite so sad. The background against which the action was taking place had also significantly brightened. It is difficult to believe that he could not remember what conditions had been like with Mamontov or that when he did, he made no comparisons. The atmosphere of artistic experimenting, of creative enterprise which Chaliapin had many times described so ecstatically, evidently did not reign at the Bolshoi Theatre. 'We were not looking for kindred spirits who might achieve something for art by acting together and in unison,' recalled Nadezhda Salina. 'No, we did not care. We lived apart, and our interests were simply the interests of employees. They were far removed from artistic quests. The chorus was grouped according to voice and, entering the stage as an entity, its members took up prescribed positions and paid very little attention to the action that was unfolding in their presence. There was no one to watch over the chorus, and gestures and movements, instead of following the logic of the action, were the result of guesswork and performed carelessly, often going against the sequence of events. The chorus stood facing the public, not taking their eyes off the conductor's baton and as close as possible to the footlights. The costumes, wigs and even the footwear were often selected arbitrarily, because those in charge of such matters had no idea of the style or the period of a certain production. You could see the chorus in the opera *Prince Igor* wearing the Ukrainian costumes from *Rusalka,* and the necklaces of the Polovtsian maidens on the peasant women in *Eugene Onegin*.'[14] All this naturally annoyed Chaliapin, and heated arguments with conductors, soloists, chorus and even the orchestra began to flare up.

Even with Telyakovsky's full support, the fight was not an easy one, but Chaliapin had no intention of giving way and showed himself unyielding in his demands regarding the productions in which he was himself taking part. He was essentially right and was not trying to find a tactful way of saying it; the number of people feeling offended and of people brushed aside grew like mushrooms after the rain. Not surprisingly, his enemies vastly outnumbered his friends. For older members of the theatre, used to considerate treatment in the past, all this was particularly incomprehensible. Salina herself, who devoted several enthusiastic pages of her memoirs to Chaliapin, wrote: 'The Bolshoi Theatre is Chaliapin's private domain, where he can do all he pleases, punish or pardon whom he likes.'[15] The situation became more and more strained. Chaliapin did not, could not compromise: after three years with Mamontov, he had formed a clear idea of the artistic standard he expected to see in opera productions. And if those around him did not want to understand, then it was better to leave and not to sing at all. On September 27th, 1900, Telyakovsky wrote in his diary: 'I was informed today that Chaliapin came to the Bolshoi Theatre at 11 p.m. and said that he was ill and unable to sing *A Life for the Tsar* on Friday.* Upon investigation, it turned out that Chaliapin was in good health but simply did not want to sing Susanin, as he considers that he still hasn't got the part right. Chaliapin refused to see the doctor sent on stage to examine him and locked himself in his dressing room, and none of the producers dared enter. Then I sent Nelidov, who soothed Chaliapin and brought him to me. Chaliapin was in a state of nerves, cried, pleaded that he could not sing, but in the end he came round. At the same time he asked me not to plan further performances of *A Life for the Tsar* immediately. Chaliapin represents a rather difficult type and requires special treatment. Like all nervous people, when he gets angry he does not know what he is saying or doing. He is a man of impulse, and this has to be taken into account.'[16]

The press unexpectedly rallied to Chaliapin's side. All sorts

*September 29th.

of Moscow and Petersburg newspapers started to voice regret about his departure from the Private Opera, saying that by moving to the Bolshoi Theatre he had condemned himself to a very monotonous diet in his repertoire. Some critics (among them Kashkin) were of the opinion that working on the Imperial stage could prove disastrous for him. After hearing *A Life for the Tsar*, Kashkin came to the conclusion that Chaliapin and the productions in which he had to appear were ill-assorted. He compares the young singer to new wine poured into old wineskins: either the wine makes a hole in the mouldy sides or it turns sour. By the end of the season reviewers spoke even more bluntly: 'We consider that Chaliapin at the Bolshoi Theatre irretrievably lost a year of his artistic life.'[17]

'I believe', wrote another, 'that with Chaliapin's recall from the Private Opera, the latter has had its head chopped off, and if the body still lives then it is only thanks to its firm desire to do so and to the enormous love of the public, fervently supporting the Private Opera in its noble national mission. There is only one way to bring the Private Opera back to life – bring back its head, return Chaliapin to it!'[18]

Russian musical circles seemed really upset. Chaliapin, still only at an early stage of his career, found himself placed in the controversial position of leader of a new performing school and in danger of being treated as a piece of public property.

In the first place, the singer's repertoire was regarded as unsatisfactory: neither *The Maid of Pskov* nor *Mozart and Salieri* nor *Boris Godunov* figured on the placards of the Bolshoi Theatre. Even *Rusalka* and *Judith*, regularly seen on the Imperial stage, were for some reason absent from it that season.

Deprived of his best roles, Chaliapin risked becoming 'a permanent guest artist constantly travelling between Moscow and Petersburg with three or four parts, and thus put an end to his artistic development.'[19]

If this happened, the size of the tragedy would be incalculable, since Chaliapin was not only an outstanding singer 'but a phenomenon on whose destiny hangs the future of Russian opera'. This is exactly what Yuri Engel was saying in his previously mentioned long article entitled 'Russian Opera and

Chaliapin'. Engel, one of Russia's most judicious musicologists, was convinced that Chaliapin was a giant, born to create something hitherto unknown. Fate had chosen him to lead a multitude of followers and to turn a new page in his country's cultural history.

Engel's essay is probably the first serious attempt at subjecting the basic components of Chaliapin's talent to analysis, at explaining the reason for the triumphs of the young bass, before whom 'public, singers and press all bow their heads'.[20]

Everything was systematically and rigorously examined: voice and physical attributes, musicality and acting ability, artistic temperament and make-up. 'For all its brevity,' wrote Engel, 'Chaliapin's curriculum vitae shows that we are dealing with someone who possesses a natural talent, one of those who belong to the elite and, as the Latin proverb says, "non fiunt – nascentur".* Like so many great Russian singers, Chaliapin is a bass. An extremely interesting parallel can be drawn between this fact and the predilection Russian composers have shown for basses in their operas: it is precisely for this voice that their best, most characteristic roles were written. No further proof of it is needed than Chaliapin's repertoire. *A Life for the Tsar* (Susanin), *Rusalka* (the Miller), *Boris Godunov* (Boris),† *Judith* (Holofernes), *The Maid of Pskov* (Ivan the Terrible), *Prince Igor* (Vladimir Galitsky),‡ *Mozart and Salieri* (Salieri), etc.... The singer's voice is one of the most attractive in terms of timbre that we have heard. It is powerful and even, although by its very nature (bass-baritone, basso cantante) its sound in very low notes is less full, steady and powerful than in high ones; on the other hand, at the top, it is capable of mighty upsurge, of rare brilliance and range. One only has to hear this voice in such parts as Susanin, Vladimir Galitsky, Nilakantha and others to realise how much pure beauty of sound it has, how easily broad cantilena, what is known as bel canto, comes into it. But what constitutes the very special quality of this

---

* Are born, not made.
† Varlaam was added later.
‡ He later performed the role of Khan Konchak as well.

voice, what lifts it above dozens of other voices equal or even superior to it in terms of texture, is what may be called its inner versatility and its feeling. When you listen to this voice, even without words, the general character of the emotion or mood being expressed is never in doubt, and neither, in most cases, are its particular nuances: you hear in it old age, infirmity and fading youthful vigour, monastic humility and regal pride; the very colour of the sound indicates whether a remark is intended for others or only for oneself.'

What Chaliapin most specially valued in everything Engel said (and we have quoted only a small part of his article) was perhaps the observation about the nuances of the sound, through which the state of mind and the personality of an operatic character could be perceived. This was precisely what he had not long ago discovered with Dalsky and had since then been confirmed many times in the preparation of his roles at Mamontov's. He called it 'correct intonation', encapsulating his own personal definition in a narrow musical term. In this, he was now firmly convinced, lay the 'whole power of singing'. So he was on the right path, and the main thing had been achieved! It could of course be done better, with greater precision and depth, but Chaliapin would always remain faithful to the principle that the art of controlling the voice is the art of singing. 'I do not dispute the fact that in comparison with Russian music Western music is more suited to bel canto, which attaches very great importance to mastery of technique,' he wrote shortly before his death. 'But *all* [Chaliapin's italics] music always one way or another expresses emotion; a mechanical interpretation leaves an impression of dreadful monotony. The most eloquent aria will sound cold if the singer has not given an intonation to every phrase and if he has not coloured the sound with the necessary shades of feeling. *That intonation of a sigh* [Chaliapin's italics] which I have deemed indispensable in the interpretation of Russian music is also needed in Western music, although there are fewer psychological fluctuations in the latter.'[21]

Chaliapin's 'intonations' were remembered as something totally unique. No one mentioned the brilliant notes or the

269

expressive phrases, although his voice had rare charm and beauty, and his singing, from the technical point of view, was amazing. What engraved itself on the mind was Chaliapin's ability to paint in sound the mental state of a person. 'In the summer of 1931 I heard Chaliapin in London,' said the British conductor Arthur Hammond to the author of this book. '*Boris Godunov* was being performed. From the depth of the stage the doleful figure of the Tsar slowly advanced. And then, the first phrases: "My soul is heavy, some involuntary fear...." They sounded like deeply hidden, unexpected thoughts. He made it clear that what he was saying could not be heard, and you were perfectly aware that no one else on stage could hear it. He was standing there thinking, and as far as the public were concerned he was silent. I subsequently heard many interpreters of Boris, but nobody could do this. With the others it was just a *piano*, a better one or a worse one.'[22]

In Engel's opinion, 'this peculiar quality of Chaliapin was only one side of his colossal talent'. Chaliapin was the first opera singer 'in whose dramatic interpretation there was nothing conventional, affected, pompous. Every one of his gestures, attitudes, movements – everything was in the highest degree simple, true, powerful. What is striking is the ease with which the artist passes over vocal, as well as acting, difficulties: he utters words in song with the same facility as a dramatic actor does in talk. The same freedom distinguishes his gestures and movements, which remain closely linked not only to the word but often even to the orchestral indications.'[23]

The article proved literally prophetic in its final conclusions: 'Russian opera and such artists as Chaliapin (we are, of course, talking not of the measure of his talent but of its general complexion) are made for each other, and it is precisely in this sense that one can regard Chaliapin as "the first" Russian singer and the leader of the new-born Russian school of singing bred and reared on Russian opera, and in turn feeding it and driving it forward.' And indeed, Chaliapin's name came to symbolise the achievements of Russian performing arts. When in 1914 Rosa Newmarch was making preparations to publish in England a collection of essays on Russian composers, she dedicated it to Chaliapin and put his portrait at the beginning of the book.[24]

The fear that Chaliapin's move to the Bolshoi Theatre would mean the end of his artistic development was unwarranted. This could have happened with anyone else, but not with him. 'If I credit myself with a certain merit,' wrote Chaliapin, 'and allow myself to consider my example worthy of imitation, then it is in the tireless, ceaseless force which drove me. Never, not even after the most brilliant successes, did I say to myself: "Now, my friend, rest on your laurels with their magnificent ribbons and superlative inscriptions." For all the frivolity of youth, the love of pleasure, the bliss of being lazy after wild nights out with friends, when not a little vodka would be consumed and not a little champagne ... I remembered that my Russian troika was waiting for me by the porch ... that I had no time for sleep – I must go on.'[25]

Slowly and reluctantly the Imperial stage started to realise that the presence of Chaliapin in the troupe demanded an exceptional repertoire, chosen especially for him. *Judith* was revived in 1900, then in 1901 *Boris Godunov* and *The Maid of Pskov*. The season also included *Mozart and Salieri* and César Cui's *A Feast in Time of Plague*, Chaliapin playing the part of the Priest. At his insistence, the Bolshoi Theatre staged such contemporary Russian operas as *The House of Ice* by A. Koryeshchenko (Biron, 1900) and *Dobrynya Nikitich* by Alexander Grechaninov (Dobrynya, 1903).

Nor was Chaliapin idle between performances. On December 15th, 1899 he gave a concert (together with Rachmaninov) at the Hall of the Assembly of Nobility in Moscow for the benefit of the Women's Charitable Organisation for Prisoners. Kashkin saw this 'as a step forward in his artistic progress', declaring Chaliapin 'a first class Lieder singer'.[26] In addition, Chaliapin decided to 'take another look' at some of his 'old' parts, which he was still singing and which were his most resounding successes with the public – first of all, Mephistopheles in Gounod's *Faust,* a role that, as we know, worried him particularly and still failed to satisfy him.

Chaliapin made constant changes, never stopped searching

Chaliapin as Biron in *The House of Ice* by A. N. Koryeshchenko. Moscow, 1900.

at literally every performance for new ways of performing the character of Mephistopheles. 'The stage is for him an arena for improvisation,' remarked a critic. 'Here an art which is constantly being re-born, and effects which are forever being renewed destroy today what they had erected yesterday.'[27] Unlike many who thought the role of Mephistopheles (and incidentally the whole of *Faust*) superficial, shallow and without any of Goethe's wisdom and philosophy, Chaliapin did not have an unfavourable opinion of the opera. 'One must not reproach a great master who had the soul of a lyric poet for developing in *Faust* the theme of love. This does not give us the right to claim that Gounod does not seem to feel the greatness and the dimension of Mephistopheles. In my view Gounod's *Faust* can be played without deviating from the essence of the original Goethe,'[28] he declared to a correspondent from the French periodical *Musica*. Mephistopheles, as Chaliapin played him at the beginning of this century, was unmistakably related to the literary original. Some even attributed his success in *Faust* to this very fact.[29] On the whole, though, the reviews agreed with Kashkin when he wrote that 'Chaliapin's creation, carefully planned in musical and theatrical terms, faithfully observes the directions of the composer.'[30]

A small dissenting minority managed to make its voice heard above the loud chorus of those convinced that this was yet another glorious triumph for the young singer, and their views should also be mentioned: 'Chaliapin's Mephistopheles is far from perfect, in both the vocal and the visual sense. We see only the contours of the fictitious character which Chaliapin has chosen for himself. He is evidently no admirer of the French Mephistopheles, although the opera is French and in our opinion he should be portrayed as being French. This Mephistopheles must be refined, adroit, elegant, graceful. Chaliapin rejects all these traits; he clearly wants to impersonate Goethe's character. Chaliapin forgets that realism, which is widely used in the operas of Mussorgsky, Rimsky-Korsakov and others, is totally out of place in French opera.'[31]

Chaliapin, who usually avoided engaging in polemics, answered his critics on this occasion with what was for him uncharacteristic restraint: the role needed to be re-thought over and over again and continued to give him trouble: 'I keep hearing that in *Faust* Mephistopheles must conduct himself nobly and has to be portrayed as *un gentilhomme*. Why? It must not be forgotten that everything Mephistopheles does or says, he does and says with irony. As soon as you have realised the irony of the first line, it must colour for you the whole tonality of the character.'[32] Analysing the reasons for his difficulties with the character of 'the evil spirit', he came to the conclusion that rigid performing tradition was the main problem. 'I am hindered by the greatest assortment of extraneous circumstances,' Chaliapin complained as early as 1901. 'The production of *Faust* needs a complete change; it wants new scenery, a totally different interpretation of the other roles. . . .'[33] In conversations with friends and colleagues he said that he dreamt of staging *Faust* not for his own sake but 'for art's sake'. The project, unfortunately, never materialised, although Korovin made particularly interesting sketches for the costumes and scenery. Chaliapin based his theatrical concept on the universal, symbolic nature of Mephistopheles, and he also saw the conflict opposing the opera's main characters in bleak and severe tones. 'Marguerite, who is usually presented to us as a young society beauty, going to a ball in fancy-dress, is in reality a simple and modest girl. In the last act she wears a peignoir, which is so becoming! In fact, she should be in rags, her body showing through the holes, although there must be nothing in her to suggest any ambiguity.'[34] As for Mephistopheles: 'It seems to me that for the portrayal of this figure, which is so remote from *life* [Chaliapin's italics], from reality or unusual situations, a figure totally abstract – the only suitable means of expression is sculpture. No amount of colour in the costume, no touches of make-up can, in this case, replace the sharpness and mysterious coldness of the sculptural line. A sculptural element is usually inherent in the theatre – it is present in every gesture – but in the role of Mephistopheles sculpture pure and simple is the first principle. I see Mephistopheles without theatrical props and without costume. Just sharp bones in continuous sculptural effect.'[35]

Chaliapin's performance was a revelation to the public. What had happened to all the things an old opera habitué looked forward to: good singing, rich costumes, sitting in a comfortable velvet armchair to listen to pleasant and familiar tunes? Then you could pick out what pleased you and treat yourself to your favourite arias, as a child picks out currants from a bun. But now, the accepted notion of opera as concert in costume had been dealt a severe blow. Instead of a dressed up performer, the all-powerful ruler of nature's and man's dark forces himself had suddenly appeared; there was no stage and no theatre anymore; 'at times the proximity of Satan produced a feeling of fear',[36] and anyone who 'saw this figure only once would never forget it'.[37] 'Watching Chaliapin's interpretation,' wrote Edward Stark, 'one is struck by the extent to which it is inspired by sculpture. This massive figure is like a bronze cast: there is not a single blurred line in it; everything is definite, everything clearly imprinted. And at the same time one senses that beneath this solid armour hide extraordinary flexibility and mobility.'[38] He has had a long life, this strange newcomer, and therefore he knows the worth of earthly joys and of people's lofty intentions. Having experienced everything, the devil believes in nothing and wants nothing: he is neither sad nor cheerful – rather he is impassive. The world holds no mysteries for him and no surprises. All the noise and the arguments about the complex nature of man are a waste of time. Nothing is simpler than people. Weak, cunning and shallow, they are his subjects to the end of time. The only thing man deserves is contempt. What is stronger in him; what dominates – reason, striving to know eternal truth and to make it triumph, or the treacherously weak life of the body?

The fear of death, of losing the pleasures of life, governs all his acts, compels him to accept the inscrutable nature of the universe and shackles his thinking and his inspiration. The conflict within mankind of opposing forces was the basis of this new treatment of Mephistopheles. The devil does not come from somewhere outside; he is permanently inside man himself. 'Mephistopheles', thought Chaliapin, 'is the symbol of earthly affairs, human passions, man's virtues and vices.'[39] He is nothing other than 'a small part of Faust's soul, his secret alter ego'. 'Faust himself', continues Chaliapin, 'summoned him by the power of his will, of his passions, of his tormenting anguish. This explains the enigma of man, in whose soul forces of light and darkness struggle, of man hesitating between poles of good and evil.'[40] So wrote Chaliapin in his article 'The Singer on the Operatic Stage' in 1934, but the idea of Mephistopheles as Faust's double had attracted him for many years. In a newspaper interview (1901) he said: 'In the first scene, I would like Mephistopheles to be on stage all the time, from the very beginning. To Faust he is invisible, but the audience must see him as if through a mist. At first his presence is only felt. Then the figure of the devil must appear more and more clearly. And so Mephistopheles must not be far away when Faust sinks into bitterness and despair. At Faust's frenzied behest, he simply becomes visible to him, quietly sitting on the other side of the table.'[41]

It is interesting to note that Chaliapin gave up this idea after only a few attempts to put it into practice. The reason may have been the inadequacy of the technical equipment available at the time, in particular the lighting. The answer is perhaps to be found in the singer's sad admission at the end of his conversation with the correspondent from *Musica*: 'My interpretation on its own cannot run counter to the established style of staging *Faust*.'[42] Nevertheless, tradition had been shaken, as newspapers were quick to notice enthusiastically: 'What a gulf lies between [this Mephistopheles and] the Mephistopheles of 1894 at the Panaevsky Theatre, the next stage of development at the Mariinsky, and even the more recent creation at Mamontov's! Then there were many ingenious touches, but now this is an entirely polished character; watching it makes one want to exclaim with Goethe's Faust:

> "Into one Whole how all things blend,
> Function and live within each other!" "*[43]

The journalist was drawing somewhat hasty conclusions in saying that the character was 'entirely polished': Chaliapin

* Translated by Louis MacNeice, Faber & Faber, London.

Sketch by Chaliapin of Mephistopheles.

continued in fact to work on it for many more years. 'One can get an idea of some details of interpretation', remarked a contemporary in 1915, 'from article excerpts, although these details obviously refer only to the artist's performances about which reviews have been written. The details in question could easily be missing on other occasions, and instead there would be some completely different ones....'[44]

Act One. The sounds of the chorus, which stopped Faust from taking his own life, have died away. In a fit of rage Faust flings his heavy, useless books to the floor, and his desperate cry seems to come from the depths of a dark pit: 'A moi, Satan! A moi!' (Come to me, Satan! Come to me!) 'Me voici!' (Here I am!) 'At Faust's incantation, a huge red apparition materialised in a flash on the right wall. It had grown unnoticed from behind the wings, reached the edge of the stage and was clinging to the scenery. The tone of the first phrase was supremely simple, in truly regal simplicity. The bearing and the manners denoted a person of great authority. Mephistopheles' way of speaking betrayed covert sarcasm about human weakness for trivialities and, at the same time, serene awareness of his own worth. The sound produced by the voice was of the greatest beauty, and the beauty of this voice contrasted with the ugliness, not of the features, which were sculpturally majestic, however sharp, but with the ugliness in their expression. It was a beauty that symbolised an essentially colossal power.'[45] The fascination of vice immediately focussed all attention on the creature which had just appeared. Everything hinted at patent and gross inhumanity, albeit cleverly concealed: a negative energy, hatred and destruction. 'This force, this calm confidence makes itself felt in all the poses, the deliberate movements with which Chaliapin gradually unfolds his enormous black cloak. That cloak of his is astonishing. It just seems that as he unfolds it the spirit of evil is actually born out of the primeval darkness of elemental chaos. And finally, on the last descending scale, the cloak is completely unfolded and falls to the ground....'[46] When Faust voices doubts that he can satisfy his desires, a 'barely perceptible grimace crosses Mephistopheles' face', but at the words 'Je veux la jeunesse' (I wish for youth) he smiles for the first time, though

Chaliapin as Mephistopheles in Gounod's opera *Faust*, 1915.

this smile is not a sign of pleasure signalling that he has forgotten his sinister occupations. The main thing now is not to let Faust notice that he wants to conquer his soul. And so Mephistopheles conjures up Marguerite's image and, watching the astonished old scholar from the corner of his eye, settles quietly, even with a faint air of ennui, in an armchair by the desk, picks up a book from the floor and studies the achievements of the human mind, a light sneer periodically curling his lips. With his other hand he takes up a skull lying on the papers and slowly turns it around on its axis as if saying to Faust: 'This also once lived, suffered and thought, and look how it all ends. . . .' Presenting the parchment scroll to Faust for his signature, he asks almost reluctantly: 'Eh bien! Que t'en semble?' (Well, what do you think?) 'Donne.' (Give it to me!), shouts Faust.

In the second act Mephistopheles behaves quite differently. According to Chaliapin the devil does not just take part in events; he also 'directs' them. 'The fair must bubble with life; there must be a lot of people of all kinds and the revels must be in full swing. Everyone is dancing – old and young, fat and thin, dancing not only on the ground but on the tables too.'[47]

As time passed, Chaliapin's Mephistopheles changed look. Instead of a gallant, ironical and at times sarcastic devil, a doleful figure, bored with the infinity of human stupidity, entered the stage. Mephistopheles' bilious intonations, the peals of his caustic laughter, now had a ring of tiredness and suppressed bitterness. Mephistopheles had in his mind, it seemed, 'an ideal Promethean conception of mankind', but every new encounter with the human race only brought further proof that the age of Titans was past. Each line uttered by Chaliapin in existing recordings of the first act[*] makes this distinctly audible. 'When Mephistopheles is sitting in Faust's study,' wrote a Petersburg critic, 'deadly tedium and weariness with the endless repetition of human stupidity are written on his face.' Any show of emotion on the part of human beings looks like a sorry parody of real suffering and real love. 'Watching the meeting of Faust and Marguerite, he is full of scorn for what he foresees

[*] I refer to recordings of an actual performance at the Royal Opera House, Covent Garden, June 22nd, 1928, available on EMI RLS 742.

as the inevitable end of an old tune, and yet at the same time his heart sinks. Chaliapin's Mephistopheles destroys, but with pity; he corrupts, but with regret.'[48]

At the fair (Act Two) Mephistopheles is enjoying himself. He looks with satisfaction at the drunken, sweaty crowd dancing clumsily. Then, interrupting Wagner's song with a resounding slap on the back, he says 'Pardon' (Excuse me), takes up the pose of a gallant dancing partner at a ball, makes a slight bow and invites him to descend from his perch with a slow movement of the right hand. Sweeping the drinking mugs off the table in one sharp blow, Mephistopheles nimbly leaps onto the table at the first chord of the orchestral introduction to his song or he sometimes stays where he is and waves people out of the way, seeming to surround himself with an impenetrable though invisible wall. 'During the "Song of the Golden Calf",' said Chaliapin, 'the chorus must not join in the refrain loudly as if celebrating a festive occasion; it must be done differently. The devil goes up to one group after another and mockingly, tauntingly shouts his sarcastic and savage words straight at their faces. They retreat in fear and confusion, repeating his last words in an undertone, mechanically, almost in a state of hypnosis, in as many different ways as possible.'[49] Mephistopheles stands with his back half, or even completely, turned to the audience and with a barely noticeable movement of the body directs the bewitched crowd in the square. Tossing the last word to the sky, he suddenly changes again. The previous gloating vanishes without trace, and a sunny, cordial smile lights up his entire face – the odd stranger himself seems to know that the song is only a joke and that life is in fact sweet and pleasant. Like an agile circus clown he begins to mix with the crowd, insulting someone here, making dire predictions there. 'As he moves about a crowded stage, threading his way among the chorus, chucking the girls under the chin, digging the men in the ribs, he seems to be the only real live person present,' wrote *The Observer* in 1928.[50] 'A pimp, an adventurer and a usurer lived together in this red devil. He operated a stock exchange, arranged discounts, rigged the market, made contracts and took bribes, opened pawnshops, lending shops, gambling dens and bawdy houses. He made ... grimaces of scorn and loathing, jeering at the very passions which had been fomented by him, Mephistopheles.'[51] When the furious Valentin draws his sword against him and it breaks, Mephistopheles 'swiftly draws a magic circle around himself and thus protected stands motionless, arrogantly conscious of his power.'[52] But the students guess who he is and point the cross-shaped hilt of their swords at him. Reviews and contemporary memoirs indicate that Chaliapin made particularly frequent changes in the behaviour of Mephistopheles in this scene. 'In 1903 in Kiev,' writes Sergei Levik, 'he immediately hunched himself up and wrapped himself hermetically inside his cloak. After a few bars of music, and keeping his face covered, he turned his back to the public, now and then lifted a panel of the cloak to look at Valentin and did not straighten up until after he had gone. In 1909 Chaliapin did not cover his face but, on the contrary, leant towards the sword, as if his gaze were riveted on it. At first there was fear in his eyes; then terror dilated his pupils. He was motionless, but after Valentin's exit he shook himself violently, like a man who has thrown off a whole pile of unpleasant experiences.'[53] Later still, towards the end of the 1910s, Chaliapin again rearranged the scene; he took a few short steps forward and abruptly stood up, 'positively growing before your eyes'. The strange guest who had been suddenly transformed by the intensity of his hatred and his destructive power into something inhuman was so frightening that retreat was the only solution for Valentin and his friends. 'I can understand', wrote Ernest Newman, 'some people disliking Chaliapin's Mephistopheles for its decidedly unpleasant flavour. There have been Mephistopheles whom one could like in spite of their wickedness. Chaliapin shows us a devil so filled with the sheer lust of evil, so pitiless to every human weakness, that one shrinks from him as from some horrible, ruthless animal.'[54]

If Chaliapin had earlier regarded the 'scene of the swords' as the victory of faith over evil, he later emphasised more and more strongly the theme of an open clash with the will of heaven: scorn dominated every one of his gestures. Only once was he really shaken by a fit of temper into losing his self-control: when Valentin tried to get close to him, overstepping the line drawn by the devil. This sealed his fate. (In the fourth act, Mephistopheles' intervention in the duel with Faust did not seem to be caused so much by his wanting to help his ward as by the desire for revenge.) A phrase full of hidden menace was hurled at the backs of the retreating students: 'Nous nous retrouverons, mes amis! Serviteur!' (We will meet again, my friends! Your servant!) Mephistopheles does not fear God; later, he has no qualms about entering a church to torment the soul of the unhappy Marguerite even in the middle of her prayers. And so, 'crossing his legs, he held his sword between them and, leaning against the table, his head slightly bent forward, stood perfectly still waiting for this importunate little soldier, Valentin, to finish his threatening speech, which did not in the least frighten him. I thought', continues Levik, 'that he would at least shrink before my last thrust, but the opposite happened. He suddenly swung his head round (if one can put it this way) in such a wide arc and gave me such a look that the sword faltered in my hand and I was not sorry to hurry out of sight behind the wings.'[55]

Mephistopheles needed only a few seconds to assume his mask of cheerful hail-fellow-well-met. When Faust enters and asks, 'Qu'as-tu donc?' (What is the matter with you?), he answers in a relaxed tone, 'Rien' (Nothing), and then, after a brief dialogue, he deftly catches Siebel and carries him off in a waltz. 'The lanky devil seemed to twist himself into the earth, like a corkscrew, sank lower and lower and vanished altogether into the depth of the square. Flapping his black cloak, which was somehow wrapped around him, he quickly sank. The spectator was left with the impression of having seen a huge sinister bird flapping its wings.'[56]

During the third act applause and bursts of laughter often broke out in the auditorium: Mephistopheles was inimitably funny. Infinite irony pervaded every movement, every intonation of the voice. Watch him making advances to Martha: offering her his hand with great courtesy, 'an indescribable expression on his face', he slowly took her deep into the garden. This is the devil pretending to be a human being. The devil mocking woman's credulity, men, who take advantage of it, and lastly, love itself. 'Mephistopheles makes Martha, who is not at all shaken by the death of her husband on the battlefield, fall in love with him,' writes Giacomo Lauri-Volpi. ' "La voisine est un peu mûre"* with this "ripe" said through clenched teeth, almost unintelligibly, and accompanied by a most eloquent gesture of the right hand, Chaliapin, as they say in the theatre, put the public in his pocket.'[57] 'Later on, Chaliapin's acting was superb when Faust, looking at Marguerite while she is talking to the stars, is filled with desire for her, and Mephistopheles, pretending to hold him back, is in actual fact pushing him into Marguerite's arms. At this point Mephistopheles is really playing with Faust like a cat playing with a mouse.'[58] 'The impression was reinforced by the coolly malevolent and chilly face of the singer, on which the moonlight and his bright red clothes threw bluish reflections.'[59] Having got rid of Martha, Mephistopheles, 'stretching out like a snake in the sun', settles himself on a garden bench, preparing for a long wait: this love nonsense will evidently drag on for some time. Then, seeing Faust's indecision and Marguerite's resistance, he suddenly jumps to his feet, takes a step forward. 'He somehow grows larger and larger' with every word he addresses to the mysterious and dark powers of nature. The smooth vocal crescendo, mounting imperceptibly from phrase to phrase, reached a frightening intensity in the finale of the incantation. When, unable to resist temptation, Faust and Marguerite fall into each other's arms, Mephistopheles bursts out into such loud guffaws that 'long after the curtain has come down, this satanic laughter goes on ringing in your ears'.[60]

'I once sang Marguerite in a festival performance in which he was singing,' recalls Lotte Lehmann. 'The impression he made was indescribable. After the scene where Mephistopheles challenges nature to help him in corrupting the innocent Marguerite, he stood like a tree, perfectly still against the background. He gave the impression of *being* [Lehmann's italics] a tree, and then, quite suddenly, he had disappeared, as

---

* The neighbour is a bit ripe.

if blown away. I did not see him sneak off, and I have no idea
how he managed it, but it was like black magic. At the end of
the act, in the embrace, a tall figure appeared above me that
twisted its way along the window like some frightful spider,
seeming to encircle Faust and me. An indefinable terror made
me go cold. This was no longer opera, this had turned into
some terrible reality. And when the curtain came down, and
Mephistopheles changed back into Chaliapin, I breathed a sigh
of relief.'[61]

According to Chaliapin, the scene of Marguerite's prayer
must take place not inside but near a church, as Goethe wrote
it. He performed Mephistopheles for many years and always
insisted on this. Wherever possible, he had his way. 'The church
is full of people,' said Chaliapin, 'the flock of the faithful crowds
its wide-open doors. The service is already in progress, and all
the parishioners, assembled in front of the church, are deep in
prayer and pay no attention to what is going on behind them.'[62]
'Meanwhile, more and more people keep arriving, amongst
them Marguerite. She tries to get closer to the doors of the
church.'[63] She is followed by a tall figure in a black cloak.
Mephistopheles has changed from his red costume into a dark
one so as to be able to mix with the believers unnoticed. 'In this
guise he was more like a monk. He did not differ sharply from
the others in appearance,' remarked Chaliapin.[64] 'In the church
scene,' observed the Milan *Gazzeta dei teatri* in 1904, 'traditional Mephistopheles are unable to leave aside the character
they are playing, and they perform a duet with Marguerite. But
Chaliapin understood that Mephistopheles' words in this scene
are nothing other than the voice of Marguerite's conscience.'[65]
The devil now looks as if he had been spun out of darkness, 'the
twirling motion of his cloak enveloping him like a whirlpool'. At
times, when he swings round very abruptly, its edges part to
reveal a fire-red lining 'like tongues of flames'. The audience
could not forget 'the awful face, so set it was terrifying'. 'Whenever the church choir is heard, he averts his face, his whole body
makes a half circle, sags and freezes into immobility. At the
last moment, Chaliapin completely sinks inside the folds of
his cloak ... and vanishes, just like a black whirlwind.... No

one before Chaliapin had achieved such a picturesque effect in this. . . .'[66]

In the following scene, Mephistopheles moves very little. His gestures are few, his body turns slowly and smoothly. At the very last moment his arm shoots out like lightning to stop Valentin's sword from entering Faust's chest. 'When, after the duel,' wrote the French periodical *Comoedia* (1932), 'Mephisto picks up his scarlet cape with the tip of his sword and waves it in the air like a trophy as he runs away, a huge infernal blast sweeps the stage.'[67] 'Probably not within living memory has such a Mephistopheles appeared at Covent Garden,' wrote the *Daily Telegraph* in 1928. 'Whether you agree with it or not, there could be no denying the sheer domination of it. It is in no sense derogatory to the work of other artists to say that when this new Mephistopheles was on stage he completely occupied and ruled it. No Faust or other desperate hero in the whole operatic gallery could have a dog's chance for a moment against such a magnificent, forceful personality.'[68]

In retrospect, Chaliapin's choice of new roles appears to have been determined not only by his successes but also, and paradoxically, by the dissatisfaction he almost invariably experienced to some extent after each one of them. As he himself admits, this was particularly pronounced in the case of Mephistopheles and explains why when, at the beginning of May 1900, Chaliapin was suddenly invited to appear in Boito's *Mefistofele* in Milan, he at first did not know what to do and 'could not bring himself to give an affirmative answer'. 'I spent two whole days in a turmoil, not sleeping, not eating; finally I had a look at the score of Boito's opera and found that his Mefistofele suited my range. But even this failed to give me confidence, and I sent a telegram to Milan asking for 15,000 francs in the secret hope that the management would not accept this. But they did!'[69] The prospect of singing in a language which was not his own, at La Scala, the citadel of operatic art (as it was then considered, in Russia at any rate), was not the only reason for Chaliapin's hesitation. He had to bring himself to confront this enigmatic, diabolic character again – and not in the popular and universally loved *Faust*, where everybody

Chaliapin as Mephistopheles in *Faust*.

will shout 'bravo', if not to the singers, then to their favourite melodies, but in a work with a relatively short and not too happy stage record. 'I vacillated between feelings of rejoicing and anxiety,' recalled Chaliapin later. The latter was understandable: he could foresee the reaction of Italian singers, the press and the public.

For more than a hundred and fifty years the numerous exponents of bel canto had been regarded in Russia as arbiters of good taste and represented the sole criterion in evaluating the art of singing. The term 'opera' applied exclusively to Italy. All the rest could be entertaining, even pleasing, but still only second-rate. Giulio Gatti-Casazza, then director of La Scala, recounted that after he had signed Chaliapin's contract, he was accused of being a 'traitor to his country'. 'It is a disgrace to Italian art. We have Mefistofeli and to spare, and if the director of the Scala doesn't know this, it means that he is an ass who doesn't know his business.'[70] Reactions of this nature were also reported by Vlas Doroshevich. His article 'Chaliapin at La Scala' had as epigraph a remark made to him: 'What are you so excited about? Exporting a Russian singer to Italy! Isn't it just the same as if we started exporting wheat to you?'[71]

Chaliapin was not due to arrive for another ten months, and agitation in the theatre grew. Really, why had they chosen him? Who among the directors or the artists of La Scala had heard Chaliapin? It became clear that neither Toscanini, nor Caruso, who was to sing the part of Faust and had recently returned from engagements in Russia, nor even Gatti-Casazza himself knew anything about him. As always in such cases, fantastic, and therefore all the more believable, tales soon replaced lack of real knowledge.

'What things were said and invented! Some people who had been in the Russian theatres circulated a rumour that Chaliapin had no voice and was only an old chorus man who had achieved a certain notoriety through his facility in make-up. In short, he was a lightning-change artist rather than a singing actor,' recalled Gatti-Casazza.[72] After all this, it is not surprising that Toscanini, alarmed, kept asking the theatre's management to clarify the situation: he could not forget how long it had taken to obtain the agreement of Boito, who was always deeply affected by every failure of his favourite opera on the stage, and he did not want to take any risks. But what could be done? The first attempts at sound recording were not of sufficient quality to silence the rumours once and for all. The only thing to do was to wait patiently for Chaliapin's arrival in Milan some time towards the end of February 1901. The singer, for his part, was still full of anxiety, although he had started serious work on his Italian début almost a year in advance. The reader no doubt recalls from the preceding chapter that Chaliapin asked Rachmaninov to help him and that the composer readily agreed. They chose to work in the small town of Varazze, not far from San Remo. Rachmaninov at first stayed with the Chaliapins, then moved to a room in a boarding-house. The composer's own work was not going well. He could not write anything, and he was in a murderous mood. 'Since my visit to you in Kline,' he wrote to Modest Tchaikovsky, 'two years have passed, and in these two years, apart from one song, I have not squeezed a single note out of myself.'[73] However, faithful to his friendship and to his promise, Rachmaninov visited Chaliapin every morning for a month and a half and worked with him until lunch. The rest of the day, Chaliapin studied the language, which, as he himself wrote, he 'assimilated very quickly'.

Autumn soon came and it was time to return to Moscow. 'During the season at the Imperial Theatre I felt very nervous, thinking only of *Mefistofele* and Milan. Boito's opera I had studied in its entirety during the summer and, as usual, knew not only my own part but all the others as well,'[74] confessed the singer in his memoirs. Now that he had learnt the musical side of the role, he began to search for its character. What should this Mefistofele be like? Chaliapin did not want to repeat himself, but neither could he simply break away from what he had already done in *Faust*. These two roles were prepared by him with equal thoroughness and assiduousness, but the variety of views he expressed about the character of Mephistopheles does not always make a clear distinction between what refers to Gounod and what refers to Boito. There are probably more dissimilarities between the two operas than similarities, and

Chaliapin as Mephistopheles in Gounod's *Faust*.

Chaliapin's self-portrait in the same role.

Chaliapin was well aware of this. The libretto of *Mefistofele*, written by the composer himself, includes (admittedly in a very condensed form) both parts of Goethe's tragedy; but in Boito the conception of the characters and of the conflict opposing them is as far removed from Goethe as it is from Gounod. The change of title itself is no mere accident. Boito's Mefistofele is the centre of all events, of the whole universe, one might say. The contrasts Chaliapin achieved between the two Mephistopheles, and which so amazed contemporary audiences, were not immediately apparent to him. To begin with he had to use their common points as a springboard for his imagination, 'a popular legend, recreated by the genius of Goethe'.[75] From this came the idea of an abstract character, of 'cold, bare sculptural lines'.

'My conception of the part of Mefistofele', said Chaliapin in an interview with the *Daily Chronicle,* 'might be described as being inspired by the Beelzebub of Milton. I think that explains it admirably.'[76] The structure of Boito's opera made it possible to embody these ideas more precisely and more fully than in *Faust.* On the other hand, preparing for the Milan première influenced his re-interpretation of Gounod's Mephistopheles. Both processes developed simultaneously by an intricate system of collaboration and opposition between characters so close and yet so far apart. Chaliapin discovered that, unlike the devil in *Faust,* his new role did not present a great variety of features. It was based on 'resentment, omniscience and hatred'.[77] Boito's music suggested 'a special sort of physical movements and the wish to play Mefistofele naked: a devil in costume is not a real devil.' He had a vision 'of some iron figure, something metallic, mighty'.[78] The music also prohibited the use of concrete elements of staging and costume, an unusual situation for opera at the beginning of the century. The action had to unfold in empty and dusky space, where there was neither beginning nor end. Transitions between scenes had to be reduced to nothing. As reality was absent, it could not provide motives or be used to make any kind of statement. The conflict and the very course of the action resulted from spiritual problems and not from a change of circumstances. The factor of negation and evil in Boito's Mefistofele is so great that losing the battle for Faust's

Chaliapin as Mephistopheles in Gounod's *Faust*.

soul seems more like a concession to the exigencies of Goethe's tragedy than a logical consequence. Alongside this Mefistofele Chaliapin envisaged a Faust whose every movement was illuminated by thought, thought which even if it had reached its limits was neither cowed nor disillusioned with itself. It flew high, but without hope. Sooner or later it would have to come down and smash against inanimate, cold and sharp stones.

Chaliapin asked painters to give him some advice. Alexander Golovin made a few sketches for him, although the design could not be carried out entirely. In those days the theatre still knew certain bounds, and it was not possible to appear on stage naked.

Chaliapin started rehearsing immediately upon his arrival in Milan. He was so worried that he could not sleep, and one thought kept nagging him: 'How am I going to sing in this huge theatre, in an alien language and with alien people?'[79]

His first meeting with Toscanini did nothing to reassure him. 'The young conductor seemed to me very ferocious; he was sparing of words, did not smile like all the others and corrected the singers quite harshly and tersely.'[80] Chaliapin himself, who had started to rehearse in a low voice, was just as severely interrupted by Toscanini, who demanded that he sing as he would sing at a performance. 'I started to sing in full voice and when I had finished, Toscanini paused for a moment, his hands still lying on the piano keys, inclined his head a little and said in his hoarse voice: 'Bravo!'[81]

The only one with whom Chaliapin immediately established cordial relations was Caruso. He was so taken with the tenor's cheerful and easy manner that he even gave him an entire line in his memoirs: 'He had a generous nature, Russian style, was exceptionally kind, sympathetic and always glad to give unstinting help to his comrades in the difficult moments of their lives.'[82] Conditions improved gradually; the Italians liked Chaliapin. Toscanini stopped giving him advice on how to play the devil and agreed to let the singer do what he wanted. The Maestro is quoted in Gatti-Casazza's book as saying: 'My dear Chaliapin, you have everything to turn out an excellent

Mefistofele. We shall work together and arrive at something out of the ordinary.'[83]

The theatre management also made some concessions – Chaliapin was allowed to wear his own costumes and to use his own make-up. 'At the dress rehearsal,' recounted the singer to one of his biographers in 1903, 'everyone was so amazed that they even took me close to the light to try to decide whether this was really me. It seems that what struck them above all was that my make-up as Mefistofele differed totally from the one they were used to. Boito himself was very pleased with the results of the dress rehearsal and paid me heaps of compliments, saying that this was just what he imagined Mefistofele to look like, but that until now he had not found such an interpretation.'[84]

The first night, on March 16th, 1901, was a triumph for Chaliapin. Let us once again avail ourselves of Gatti-Casazza's memoirs; Chaliapin excluded, he is the only participant to have left any recollections of the event. 'Chaliapin studied and prepared his role with the attention and diligence that characterise the few members of that select company of artists who look after everything, think of everything with perfect conscientiousness. His Mefistofele turned out a new thing, without precedent, breaking all traditions. His make-up and costume have since been copied by everyone, but above all were his great authority, mobility of countenance, richness of expression and incredible acting. In a word, it was one of those few occasions when the much-abused word "creation" could be applied with perfect justice. So it was that Boito said: "My dear Gatti, wasn't I right when I insisted on a real Mefistofele? Only now do I realise that I never had, up to this time, any but poor devils. . . ." 'To say that Chaliapin won a success at the première is to put it mildly. He won the battle to such a degree that the public, which had come to the theatre full of diffidence, and even prejudice against him, finished by driving out some disturbers who dared attempt to hiss.'[85]

Gatti-Casazza's last words refer to an episode recounted in detail in *Pages from My Life*.[86] Five days before the dress rehearsal some strangers called upon Chaliapin and offered to arrange a triumph for his first night at a price. When the

As Mefistofele in Boito's *Mefistofele*. Milan, 1901.

infuriated singer threw them out, 'they left, declaring that Signor Chaliapin would be sorry'. Later, recalling the day of his first appearance at La Scala, Chaliapin thought that the word 'nervousness' was inadequate to express what he had really been going through. 'I was trembling as at the time of my first début in Ufa in *Halka*.* Once again, I could not feel the stage beneath me and my legs were like cotton-wool. Through a haze I saw a huge auditorium packed tight with spectators.'[87] The performance started 'in deathly silence'; Chaliapin sang 'without feeling anything, giving as much voice as I could'. He did not have enough breath; everything was swaying and floating around – 'there was a mist before my eyes.' But no sooner had the sounds of his voice died down than a volley of applause thundered in the auditorium. Everything stopped; the Prologue was interrupted. Chaliapin, breaking the inflexible tradition of La Scala, took a bow in the middle of the act. 'I felt as if I had turned to water, as if I was going to collapse, I could not stand. Agitation even made me a little hoarse. I felt that I was not singing quite in tune in the last acts and resorted to various flourishes in order to hide it. I felt weak, I had no strength left.'[88] But no one noticed any of this; 'the public went berserk.' 'In the boxes they all jumped to their feet. There was shouting, howling, handkerchieves were waving. The stalls were roaring.'[89]

The famous tenor Angelo Masini,† for whom Chaliapin had the greatest admiration, wrote after the performance: 'The deep impression made by Chaliapin is quite understandable; this is an excellent singer and an outstanding actor, and in addition his pronunciation is worthy of Dante – an extraordinary phenomenon in someone whose mother tongue is not Italian.'[90]

The local press reacted no less enthusiastically. 'Signor Chaliapin showed himself to be a genuine and great artist in the

---

* Opera by Stanislaw Moniuszko.

† Konstantin Korovin relates that at lunch with Chaliapin in Paris shortly before his death, the conversation turned to Masini. Chaliapin's eldest son, Boris, asked him: 'And tell me, Papa, was Masini a good singer?' Chaliapin looked at his son and said: 'Masini was not a singer. I, your father, am a singer, but Masini was an angel of God.' (Korovin, Konstantin: *Chaliapin: encounters and life together.* La Renaissance, Paris 1939, p. 33.)

fullest and widest sense of the word. In addition to his remarkable costumes and make-up he is magnificent as a singer and
inimitable as an actor. Chaliapin created a convincing and
original character, using the most economical means. He does
not resort to "satanic poses", which are more like the poses of
circus athletes but of which so many performers of Mefistofele
make excessive use."[91] 'New to La Scala and indeed to Italy was
the Russian bass Chaliapin, performing the far from easy role
of Mefistofele. The curiosity this artist provoked in everyone
was great, and it is not clear which was uppermost in this
interest – expectancy or incredulity. But Chaliapin totally conquered us. He conquered us by his make-up, then he enchanted
us by his brilliant and at the same time natural acting, and
finally by his singing.'[92]

'To begin with, he looked the part,' said Beniamino Gigli,
recalling their joint performance in New York in 1922. 'With
his towering, lithe figure, his half-bared breast, and the cruel,
terrifying expressions in which he cast his mobile features,
the appearance he presented was quite unnervingly diabolical.
Diverging at many points from what I knew by now to be the
traditional Met interpretation of the role, his own rendering of
it seemed to me invariably truer and artistically more coherent.
In the "Prologue in the Heavens", for example, instead of
emerging among the clouds, he entered from below, huge and
menacing, shambling about like a great spider, his long black
hair gathered into a sort of scalp-lock that gave his face the
look of a Japanese devil-mask. And at the end, instead of
descending hurriedly into the pit, he pawed feebly at the celestial
rose-leaves that were searing his flesh, crumpled slowly to the
ground, and lay sprawling and motionless. Faust had won.'[93]

An even more illuminating appraisal could be found in the
Observer (London, 1926): 'Where Boito had given him anything
to sing, he sang into it that world of meaning a composer hopes
for, but seldom gets. Where there was – as generally – nothing
to sing, he declaimed it with a singing or a speaking voice, a
mutter or a roar, as occasion asked. As the singing merged into
the speaking, so both merged into acting and the acting into
being himself. People sometimes think the devil is an easy part

As Mefistofele.

to act: you have merely to let yourself go (in a certain direction) and there you are. But the prince of darkness is a gentleman; although he has a cloven hoof, it is not the cloven hoof of vulgarity and it is because there is not a shadow of cheapness or blatancy that Chaliapin's devil is so great.'[94]

Chaliapin remained in Milan until the middle of April and sang eleven performances, all to packed houses. 'Thank God,' he wrote to a friend in Russia, 'the battle has been won brilliantly. I am having a colossal success and it is even going crescendo.'[95]

Chaliapin gave a farewell dinner to all the members of the production before his departure and at the end of the evening, 'overcome by emotion', ordered two cases of champagne and invited everyone who happened to be in the restaurant to his table. He arrived in Moscow a day earlier than expected so as to avoid noisy demonstrations at the station. He reached his house unnoticed and remained there for two uninterrupted days, until it was time to go to the concert he was giving. 'The disappointed Chaliapin fans rushed to Chaliapin's flat and laid siege to it.'[96]

However strange it may seem, he did not like stormy displays of enthusiasm outside the confines of the theatre auditorium and as far as possible avoided habitually crowded places. Unless it was on business, he did not like going out of the house alone and always tried to surround himself with a group of people whom he knew well and with whom he felt at ease. This almost totally excluded his colleagues at the theatre. Relations with them, especially after his return, grew more difficult. The simplest explanation would be plain jealousy, but the actual facts were far more complicated. Chaliapin did not regard his success at La Scala as another trophy to be added to his earlier ones. Universal fame was of little interest to him. His victory in Milan meant, above all, the triumph of new methods of approaching operatic roles and their interpretation on stage. This was the triumph of the innovations made at Mamontov's – innovations which, he was firmly convinced, it was high time to introduce into the everyday practice of opera.

In Italy – as Chaliapin could not help noticing – all eyes had

As Mefistofele in Boito's *Mefistofele*. Bolshoi Theatre, Moscow, 1902.

been on him; people were unable to hide their naive astonishment: a barbarian from Siberia, from some incomprehensible wild land of snows and bears, suddenly turned out to be
an artist who eclipsed Toscanini and Caruso.

'I was in a splendid mood,' he recalled later. 'I felt I had
achieved something and not only for myself.'[97] 'I was proud that
it had fallen to my lot to have the good fortune of representing
Russian art, which still did not have the prestige it deserved in
the West.'[98]

Astonishment, however, was followed by a desire to understand, to penetrate the secrets of his method, and if possible, to
try to learn to do the same thing. His partners in Boito's opera
manifested this curiosity from the very beginning. Caruso, who
was not a good actor, studied the Russian singer very carefully.
Two weeks after the première, a reviewer remarked that the
subsequent six performances reinforced 'the wonderful impression produced by Signor Chaliapin in the main role' and
that 'the tenor, Signor Caruso, made significant improvements
to the vocal and visual aspects of the role of Faust'.[99]

Naturally, upon returning to Moscow, Chaliapin wanted to
perform *Mefistofele* on his home ground – and not just to
distribute the roles amongst the soloists and then deploy them
on the stage in the manner routine prescribed but to include
everything that could not be done in Milan. Chaliapin, as usual,
was not satisfied with merely giving a successful interpretation
of his own role. Boito's *Mefistofele* seemed to him to offer an
excellent opportunity for trying out his long-cherished ideas
about opera production, and he thought he knew how to achieve
the desired result. But Chaliapin's first attempts to attract other
singers to his approach were, on the whole, received with
irritation: 'What is he teaching us for? What right has he to
teach us?'[100] Rights, at any rate formal ones, he certainly had
not. Chaliapin was not in charge of the productions, and the
Bolshoi Theatre was not taking orders from him in either
financial or administrative matters. Unlike Mamontov or Stanislavsky, Chaliapin, as far as his partners were concerned, had
little ground for giving advice. Mutual displeasure quickly
developed into a regular 'Chaliapin scandal'. The reason was

As Mefistofele.

not hard to find: Chaliapin had a penchant for telling people what he thought straight to their faces, without trying to clothe his judgement with diplomacy. 'The work of the artist is one of nerves,' he wrote, recalling the rehearsals of *Mefistofele*. 'I was not brought up in drawing-rooms, and although I know how to behave, I do not always remember it. I am by nature unrestrained, I am sometimes abrupt.... Moreover, I am impressionable; surroundings have a very powerful effect on me; with "gentlemen" I can also be a "gentleman", but with ruffians – begging your pardon – I become a ruffian myself.'[101] Boito's opera was not an isolated case. Chaliapin bitterly cites, in several pages of his autobiography, repeated examples of the absence 'in theatrical people of deeply felt love for their cause; this cause demands it and without it it is dead.'[102] In another passage he lets slip a remark that has nothing to do with memoirs but is simply a cry of despair such as one could hear from the lips of some hero of Russian literature: 'I have quite often wailed and howled like a wolf.... I know that it is useless. But, good heavens, I feel unbearably wretched at times. What you want and what you get are two vastly different things. It is not easy or pleasant ... to feel surrounded by the most malicious narrow-mindedness, by offhand and bureaucratic attitudes towards your sacred beliefs. Singing is not a trifle for me, nor an amusement; it is my life's hallowed work.'[103]

At first, Chaliapin had strong hopes that he would be able to reorganise the Bolshoi Theatre along the lines of Savva Mamontov's Private Opera. But how could one change century-old habits, kindle in the singers the desire to work together for a common artistic goal? This demanded, above all, a producer who understood the particular nature of operatic performance and a conductor who gave equal place to the music and to the stage. In his diaries and memoirs Telyakovsky recounts the frequent conversations he had with Chaliapin on this subject. They once sat up for most of a night in the company of Korovin and 'Chaliapin exposed with genuine humour the ways and means used by contemporary operatic producers who wanted to get rid of the existing Italian routine and tried to subject the production of operas to new influences of "naturalism" and "stage realism".' But when the director offered Chaliapin the opportunity to assume these responsibilities, the singer answered that 'it would be difficult for me as an artist to devote much time and energy to this.'[104] Telyakovsky did not insist: he knew that Chaliapin was right and secretly agreed with him. At the time, there was no such notion as 'producer of music theatre'. The profession, in its present-day sense, was only just beginning to become established, a deciding role in this being played by Mamontov's Private Opera and by the Moscow Art Theatre. The latter was particularly influential on all aspects of theatrical art. And so it came as no surprise when Nikolai Kashkin, surveying the musical season, called upon the operatic stage to take a closer look at what Stanislavsky and Nemirovich-Danchenko were doing in Kamergersky Lane.* 'The people who ran the Art Theatre', he wrote, 'understood that the art of our time must be an art of ensemble. For contemporary opera this principle of perfect ensemble is incomparably more important.'[105] The article by this eminent critic appeared in 1907 and was considered both significant and opportune. But Chaliapin had raised the subject much earlier. He was keenly attuned to what the times demanded of operatic theatre and by his mere presence on stage defined the spirit and the character of a whole work, so that his participation meant, in the majority of cases, that he took over as director.

'The figure created by Chaliapin in Boito's opera', wrote a critic after the Petersburg premiere of *Mefistofele* in December 1902, 'shone with such a blinding light that everything around him on the stage seemed coloured by this radiance.'[106] 'About Chaliapin in the role of Mefistofele,' remarked another, 'it is not right to talk of interpretation; one must call it incarnation.'[107]

Despite the enthusiastic reviews and the rapturous audiences, the singer remained dissatisfied with the production. Once again, as was so often the case, everything disintegrated into individual parts, well or not well sung. And, although he did his best to control himself, his feeling of resentment persisted. Chaliapin had moved to the Bolshoi Theatre three years earlier,

---

* Site of the Moscow Art Theatre.

and this was not the first disagreement with his colleagues. The agitation and the difficulties which arose during the rehearsals of *Mefistofele* paled into insignificance compared to what he had had to endure in the previous season when they were working on *Boris Godunov*. Chaliapin had been particularly sensitive at that time. He was just back from Milan and, inspired by his success, had been yearning to devote all the energy and the powers of emotion he possessed to his favourite opera and to a composer whom he literally idolised. It was well known that Chaliapin had repeatedly raised the subject of re-introducing *Boris Godunov* into the repertoire of the Bolshoi Theatre, while he continued to perform it in guest appearances all over Russia. Now, he was offended by every trifle and refused to make any concessions. During one of his regular clashes, he bluntly declared to the hurriedly summoned director of the theatre that if he had his way, he would 'not let the curtain rise on a production until it had reached the right artistic level'.[108] Telyakovsky did not doubt this and kept trying to maintain a reasonable balance between Chaliapin's uncompromising demands and the actual resources of the theatre. Moreover, not a single rehearsal passed 'without various incidents and annoyances' provoked by Chaliapin's cutting remarks. Here again one had to find the right words of appeasement, explaining to the malcontents that Chaliapin was right in essence and that one should not feel hurt by him: it was just his manner. . . . The chorus posed even greater difficulties. They simply did not understand what he asked of them: what was this 'acting' he wanted, what did a 'realistic crowd scene' mean? Everything had always been very straightforward: you put on the costumes the wardrobe gave you, you went on stage when called, and after you had sung your piece, you returned backstage. And should anything really be changed when the conductor himself told Chaliapin that 'if the chorus fails to sing with the orchestra, it is because they are concentrating more on acting than on singing'?[109] As for the soloists, they grumbled: 'He is not the producer but a singer just like everyone else, and has no right to give lessons and demonstrations.'[110] Telyakovsky, having seen Chaliapin at work in the rehearsals of *Boris Godunov*, was

Chaliapin and his son Boris, 1911.

of a totally different opinion. 'Only then did I understand', he admitted later, 'what a real operatic producer means – that is, a producer whose concepts are all based on the music. His extraordinary memory and knowledge not only of his own part but of all the others was something quite astonishing. Whether he was speaking to the singers, the chorus or the orchestra – everything was so clear, consistent and logical; everything seemed so simple and natural that I could not help asking myself why others could not understand this and do it. This is how a work should be analysed. It is not just that he has studied carefully and knows it well; he feels it and he transmits his understanding to others.'[111]

Chaliapin first performed the role of Boris Godunov at the Bolshoi Theatre on April 13th, 1901, in a revival of a ten-year-old production with very tired-looking scenery. At his urgent request, Chaliapin was allowed to make a few changes to the scenes in which Boris appears. 'I remember what torment I endured with the first staging of *Boris Godunov* in Moscow,' said Chaliapin in 1911 to the correspondent of the *Peter-burgskaya gazeta*. 'The way the roles were assigned was enough to prove that no one was taking the style of the opera into consideration. Neither the producer nor the conductor wanted to know anything. It was all the same to them whether it was Gounod or Mussorgsky.'[112]

Chaliapin was not in the least exaggerating when he spoke of the indifference shown by many singers. The critics wrote that, regretfully, the expectations of Muscovites thirsting to see again the opera which they had so much liked at Mamontov's had been far from satisfied. Even Chaliapin, whose interpretation was as usual remarkable for its careful planning and depth, seemed at times less interesting than before. The reviewers attributed this to the absence of a genuine ensemble, to the fact that the other members of the cast failed to take an active part in what was happening on stage. 'Let us take, for instance, the last scene,' wrote one newspaper, 'when Shuisky tells the boyards about Boris' distress. Shuisky told his tale so dully, unfeelingly and indistinctly that he did not prepare the entrance of Godunov, and the terror of this entrance lost half of its power. He made the previous scene with Boris even less exciting. The singer did not project the character of Vasili Shuisky at all. Against such a background it was impossible to show everything Boris was experiencing.'[113] Still, despite the lack of artistic conception and of worthy partners in the production, Chaliapin, particularly in the solo scenes, was always Chaliapin. The role sounded perfect in every nuance; its unprecedented scale and tragic power were staggering. 'I left after *Boris*', recalled Semyon Kruglikov, 'positively thrown off balance. My mental equilibrium was disturbed. The death I had only just witnessed had left me with a feeling of awe. Before our eyes the criminal usurper had fallen: the man of powerful gifts and strong will had fallen, tormented by mental anguish, by the implacable punishment his conscience was inflicting on him. I had seen Chaliapin in the role of Boris many times, but never had he carried me away to this extent. His mastery of the part and of the role was now incomparable. We were seeing the portrait of a man mentally ill, crushed under the weight of a severe psychological shock.... Chaliapin's Boris was already undermined by this sickness at the time of his first entrance, when the people acclaim Godunov as the new Tsar. His jaundiced face bore distressing traces of some destructive anxiety. Seven years later Boris is old and grey, he has hallucinations, his gaze is half-dead.'[114]

At the end of the Bolshoi Theatre season Chaliapin left for the countryside with his three children, his wife and his mother-in-law, who had come from Italy for a short visit. He always preferred the countryside for his holidays: it was what he was used to, what he knew best; each time it was like going back to his childhood. Chaliapin was planning to remain there until the end of June, but at the beginning of the month a telegram arrived. His father was feeling unwell and wanted to see him. The journey took ten days on the interminable, chaotic Russian roads. 'In the *izba* it stank horribly of rotting matter; it was swarming with clouds of flies and cockroaches scurried about. In a corner, on a wooden bench, my father, as thin as a skeleton, lay among the dirty rags, his nose protruding sharply, his cheeks sunken....'[115] It was a painful scene. He had so many times

tried to persuade his father to live with him in Moscow. He had
sent him money to buy a house in the country, but also in vain.
His father immediately squandered everything on drink and
never had a penny to his name. Chaliapin took him to the
hospital, where he was put in a clean private room. 'The doctor
even said that perhaps it was not so bad after all; perhaps he
would pull through,' but on the 13th of June his father died.
Chaliapin was already back in Moscow by then. An engagement
in Petersburg at one of the celebrated Pavlovsk concerts* had
prevented him from prolonging his stay in the country. Stasov
was at one of the concerts and remained long after under
the spell of this 'encounter with great art'. 'Chaliapin,' wrote
Amphiteatrov, 'is the only one who, when I listen to him, never
makes me feel that the impression I have of art suffers a painful
comparison between past and present: on the contrary, the more
I listen, the more convinced I become that this is new, fresh and
incomparably more vigorous than anything that has gone before
on the lyric stage. This is an artist such as has never been before,
the begetter of a new force in art, a reformer creating a new
school. He has come to the surface like a nugget. He has no
precursors. Will he have followers? There are plenty of good
voices in the world; even on the Petersburg stage there are basses
whose vocal resources would be more than enough for several
Chaliapins. But this is the crux of the matter: when you go to
hear Chaliapin, you don't even remember that you have gone
to hear a "bass". What you want is Chaliapin, not his ability
to sing loud or soft notes in the order required by the part but
his extraordinary talent for *thinking in sounds* [Amphiteatrov's
italics] – a wonderful new revelation which the arrival of this
strange man has brought to singers.'[116]

In July he was back in Moscow to sing at the Hermitage
summer theatre, mostly *Faust*, and in between *Prince Igor*,
Rusalka, *A Life for the Tsar* and also (twice) *Boris Godunov*,
which to Chaliapin's delight was a great success. He spent the
entire summer, right up to the beginning of the new season at the
Bolshoi Theatre, making guest appearances. He was working

* Pavlovsk – one of the country residences of the Russian tsars, holiday resort of
the Petersburg aristocracy.

Chaliapin with a group of Russian writers: seated, from left to right: L. Andreev; F. Chaliapin; I. Bunin; N. Teleshov; E. Chirikov; standing: Skitalets (S. Petrov); M.Gorky.

incredibly hard, almost without a stop. Even taking into account the vigour of youth, one cannot help wondering how he could manage it all: not only performances and concerts but meeting countless people, tirelessly continuing to educate himself, talking all night long in restaurants or in friends' houses, where he usually ended up singing indefatigably for hours. All those who knew Chaliapin at that time were astounded by the irre-pressible, tempestuous energy which seethed in him. He was always in motion; there was no sense of measure in his actions. His close friend Ivan Bunin recalled how once during some banquet 'at the door of the hall the huge figure of the blond-haired Chaliapin suddenly appeared. He surveyed the orchestra with what is known as an "eagle" eye and all of a sudden, waving his hand, he joined in what they were playing and singing. Needless to say, ecstatic rapture seized all the diners at this unexpected "royal" favour! That night we drank almost till morning; then, when we left the restaurant, we stopped on the stairs of the hotel to say goodbye and he said to me out of the blue: "I think, my dear Vania, that you are very drunk, and so I have decided to carry you to your room on my shoulders, since the lift has already stopped working." – "Don't forget," I told him, "I am on the fifth floor and I am not exactly small." – "Never mind, my friend," he answered, "I'll get you there somehow!" 'And he really did, however much I tried to fend him off. And this done, he played the "Herculean hero" to the end: he sent for a bottle of hundred-year-old burgundy, costing all of one hundred roubles. . . . In truth God gave him "all that the earth can offer". And also gave him great physical strength, which only cracked after forty years of wandering all over the world and every possible earthly temptation.'[117] Chaliapin retained this ability to look like a giant to the end of his life. He probably seemed taller and stronger than he really was, but the impression of meeting something colossal in every sense of the word was instantaneous and remained fixed forever in people's memories.*

'Chaliapin was a man without inhibitions,' declared Sir Neville Cardus; 'everything was overdone. He was enormous of stature and enormous in personality. He had a truly wonderful bass voice, as rich as any I have ever heard in my life. I cannot differentiate between Chaliapin the man and Chaliapin the artist. He was always and everywhere the same, expressing the same bigness, the same geniality, the same gusto.'[118] Yet Chaliapin's indisputable greatness, which was the object of universal admiration, concealed a tragic impasse of which he was at first unaware. With time his genius matured; in his unswerving search for artistic synthesis he managed to achieve with increasing subtlety and originality the fusion of singing, physical movements and words. But, strangely enough, the brighter his fame shone, the deeper his loneliness grew. The uniqueness of his art isolated him, and the only way he could continue in the theatre, whether in Russia or abroad, was as a star performer, when all he wanted was to create or to find a

---

* 'Contrary to all descriptions I have read of him,' says the singer's daughter Marfa, 'my father was not a giant. He was barely six feet two. It was his way of projecting his personality which dwarfed other men and deluded them into believing he was outsize.' ('Reminiscences of Chaliapin by his daughter Marfa.' Broadcast January 24th, 1950. BBC Archive, Reading. Script, page 6.)

theatre where everything would be unified. By the last pages of *Mask and Soul* he kept asking himself 'Where is my theatre?' and answering sadly: 'I had *my roles* [Chaliapin's italics], but *my theatre* [Chaliapin's italics] I never had, not anywhere.'[119]

Chaliapin, as we know, often clashed with other singers, with conductors and producers. He was rarely, very rarely, satisfied. But perhaps it was not a question of obstinacy on their part, of laziness or of obeying a static performing tradition. What if he asked of them more than they had to give, although they tried in rehearsal and in performance to go to the limits of their abilities? There is every likelihood that this was the case, and the shrewdest observers of Chaliapin's art gradually came to this conclusion. 'Always immeasurably superior to others,' as one of the articles written in 1915 to celebrate the singer's twenty-five years on the stage put it, 'Chaliapin fatally disrupts the general effect. In creating, Chaliapin destroys. And so great is the power of his talent for the stage that even a minor part, when Chaliapin undertakes it, immediately rises to a gigantic height. Chaliapin is crushed by the force of his own talent. He can only play opposite Chaliapin, or reconcile himself to the position of solitary guest artist....'[120] Was this not the source of his frequent outbursts of anger, his uncontrollable irritation and perpetual clashes? Was all this not a reaction to the painful realisation that the theatrical resources available to him were of disappointing mediocrity? It seems very probable. After all, he had no difficulties with Rachmaninov, Toscanini, Caruso, Titta Ruffo, Sobinov or Gigli. 'When he came across a real master on the stage, it was as if it electrified him and it made him rise to the full splendour of his genius. There was no talk of any scandals,'[121] affirmed one of his regular partners.

'He was such an enormous, abounding personality on the stage,' recalled Sir Neville in 1973 on the occasion of the centenary of Chaliapin's birth, 'he dwarfed an ensemble. It was as though he was the only man on the stage; and all the other artists just appeared and disappeared, running round him as though round the legs of a great colossus.'[122]

Sir Neville was not alone in his judgement. 'Through an accident of nature,' affirmed the San Francisco *Chronicle* in

Chaliapin as Farlaf in Glinka's opera *Ruslan and Ludmilla*, 1901.

1935, 'this Russian giant was endowed with one of the greatest voices of all time, but if he had never sung a note, Chaliapin would nevertheless have been one of the great men of our day. He has the personality and the physique of a commander and would have dominated any department of activity he might have entered.'[123] 'He dominates the scene even when he simply appears and says nothing,' wrote the London *Jewish Guardian* in 1926. 'When he first appeared in London and simply walked across the stage to his coronation in *Boris* he had an over-whelming effect on the audience at Drury Lane [1913]. When he appears as the Grey Friar, who simply sidles up to Faust, we have eyes only on him, and when he appears in the Brocken scene and dominates the witches' revels with a broomstick, etc. the effect is electric.'[124] But Yuri Engel, reviewing Chaliapin's first performance in *The Power of Evil* at the Bolshoi Theatre in 1902, was one of the first to notice the possible dual effect of Chaliapin's magnetic personality: 'Eryomka was incomparable, straight out of a novel by Gorky, vivid and lifelike from head to foot, from his first word to his last. Yet Chaliapin's per-formance had rather an important deficiency, though a very unusual one: he made a minor part assume too central a place and thereby disrupted the unity of the general perspective.... This "deficiency" was noticeable earlier too, and will recur for as long as Chaliapin appears in insignificant parts or until his partners become other Chaliapins.'[125] Rimsky-Korsakov perhaps had the deepest insight into the problem. He always gave the great singer his due, but nevertheless considered that he 'distorted by his genius the proper ratio of musical values (composer–performer) and diverted the attention of the public from the work to himself.'[126] Several sources indicate that Rimsky-Korsakov categorically refused to re-write the baritone part of Gryaznoi in *The Tsar's Bride* for Chaliapin. This decision was no doubt motivated by the same fear that Chal-iapin would switch the centre of attention to himself, thus displacing the intended emphasis and overshadowing the other characters of the opera. 'What am I to do?' he complained to Igor Stravinsky, who was telling him about the 'extremely powerful impression' Chaliapin had made on him in *The Maid* *of Pskov.* 'I am the composer, and he does not take any notice of what I say.'[127] 'I discovered in myself', admitted Rimsky-Korsakov, 'unequivocal signs of some sort of "Salierism". I find myself somewhat irritated, for instance, by Chaliapin's successes and I feel more kindly disposed towards a talented mediocrity.'[128] Nevertheless, after the première of *The Maid of Pskov* at the Bolshoi Theatre on December 10th, 1901, he wrote in his diary: 'The performance was good, but Chaliapin was unique.'[129] Even he, normally reserved and sparing with praise, had to give in to the irresistible nature of Chaliapin's gift. This leads us to think that Telyakovsky was not right when he said that after his trip to America in 1908, 'the singer of genius, unable to live with the fame he had won and to resist the fantastic temptations offered to him, eventually gave way completely to the universally acclaimed guest artist weighed down by an international glory. Gradually Fedor Ivanovich devoted increasing amounts of his time to the acquisition of money and of valuable property ... his appearances at the Mariinsky and the Bolshoi theatres became rarer and rarer, and he sang more and more often in the private operas of Zimin* and Aksarin.†He tried to acquire advantageous goods, property and land ... he was always going on lucrative trips, whose attraction increasingly turned to another direction.'[130]

It was not a matter of money, or rather not just a matter of money. The future proved that to his dying day Chaliapin never abandoned his artistic principles and the theatrical ideals he so ardently expressed in conversation and in writing. But fate, unfortunately, decided for him: after his three years at Mamontov's, Chaliapin just could not find his 'niche'. As previously indicated, the Imperial Theatre, for all its financial advant-

---

* Zimin, Sergei Ivanovich (1875–1942) founded in 1904 a Private Opera in Moscow, continuing Mamontov's tradition. Such works as Wagner's *Die Meistersinger*, Rimsky-Korsakov's *The Golden Cockerel* and the original version of Bizet's *Carmen* received their first performance on a Russian stage at Zimin's Theatre. Zimin employed outstanding singers, designers and conductors. His producers were P. S. Olenin and F. F. Komissarzhevsky. The latter subsequently became well known in England. Zimin's Theatre ceased to exist in 1917.

† Aksarin, Alexander Rafailovich, owner of a private operatic concern in Petrograd.

ages and Telyakovsky's support, never became 'Chaliapin's Theatre'. He was particularly aware of this in the productions of Mussorgsky's works, when the gulf between hope and reality seemed unbridgeable. Mussorgsky, in Chaliapin's opinion, demanded a totally different approach, breaking away from tradition. However much he tried to explain, suggest, demonstrate, Chaliapin found himself in the position of a man who wants to move the earth. He sadly realised that the number of people who loved and understood Mussorgsky was small. Most singers as well as most of the public would have subscribed to the views of a critic reporting on Chaliapin's guest appearance in Nizhni-Novgorod in the autumn of 1901: 'There is here (in *Boris Godunov*) a great deal of musical realism, but the excess of discordant colours and the confusion in a music depicting grotesque characters and comical situations in the end get on your nerves.'[131]

Provincial impresarios (and the same is true of the administration of the Imperial Theatres) were yielding to the obstinacy of the singer rather than following their own inclinations when they included *Boris Godunov* in their programmes. The public after all came just "for Chaliapin": it was a pity that it was not *Faust* or *Lakmé,* but what could you do if he liked this heavy, unbearably boring music? True, he plays Boris well: it is in effect like straight theatre – and anyway, thank God, it is not performed so often. In Nizhni-Novgorod, for instance, it was given only once and with extensive cuts at that. Even on the occasions when the critics treated Mussorgsky's work more kindly in their articles, the note of doubt as to the advisability of expending such incredible efforts on staging this opera persisted.

'*Boris Godunov*,' wrote the newspaper *Kievlyanin,* 'is not very popular. It requires from the listener that he should have some knowledge of the music and the intentions of the composer. Furthermore, it needs performers with the ability to interpret the work. *Boris Godunov* is very difficult for singers; so many different qualities are expected of them that only a few are equal to what is required.'[132]

Petersburg critics were of the same opinion. 'In Mussorgsky's opera,' wrote one of them, 'the visual aspect, the acting, eclipses the vocal aspect of the role. The only striking effect that the part of Boris produces is the ability to use recitative freely, which has little appeal except for those interested in the fine points of this art, and to which most people usually pay no attention. Above all, therefore, the audience was judging Chaliapin as an actor and was moved to tears by his realistic portrayal of human suffering.'[133]

Chaliapin found all this incredibly irritating, but what could he do? You cannot explain to those who cannot understand. And anyway, what is there to talk about when even among singers an overwhelming majority considers that 'singing proper' has no practical significance in performing Mussorgsky, that what counts is 'the ability to strike a balance between speech and song'? Similar views were also expressed later in the West, as this extract from an article written during Chaliapin's stay in New York in 1921 shows: 'Vocally, Boris is not a part to disclose the power and beauty of Chaliapin's noble organ, though it does bring into play all his skill in tone-colouring.'[134] Could they not hear that even when he had to declaim, going beyond a certain pitch of sounds, he never lost the liquidity of his flowing melodiousness? That it was always there, as a solid, permanent base? 'The quality in which he used to be supreme in the operatic world,' wrote Ernest Newman, '[was] the way he had of making every psychological expression a matter of musical tone; a sneer, a curse, a bit of irony that other singers would have made the excuse for stepping outside the boundaries of pure singing never ceased to be the purest singing with Chaliapin.'[135]

Chaliapin himself categorically opposed replacing song with speech. When he came across people who shared his attitude to Mussorgsky, he could talk, demonstrate and sing for hours, heeding neither time nor fatigue. These were usually unprejudiced young musicians, who could easily throw aside the established way of looking at operatic performance. One of them remembered Chaliapin's words: 'It seems to many people that in *Boris Godunov* I sometimes do not sing. I always sing, even if I am talking – both in rhythm and in key. That is the secret of singing and one of the laws of the art. I want to give this impression. If the singer does not hear the music of the words, then neither will the listener hear it.'[136] And he seemed to be summing up many years of quarrels when he wrote in *Mask and Soul*: 'Mussorgsky is usually described as a great realist in music. I am not such an authority that I can give a final verdict in this matter. But in my humble opinion as a singer who feels music with his soul, this definition is too limited for Mussorgsky and by no means embraces the whole of his greatness. There are those summits of art where all formal definitions lose their meaning and become of secondary value. Although Mussorgsky is certainly a realist, his power does not lie in the fact that his music is realistic but in the fact that his realism is *music* [Chaliapin's italics] in the fullest sense of the word. Behind his realism, as behind a curtain, there is a whole world of emotions and feelings which do not enter the realistic plane at all. I don't know about the others, but for me even Varlaam, who appears realistic through and through – indeed he simply "reeks of vodka" – is not just realism but something else beyond it: soul-sickness and fear expressed in the infinity of music.'[137] Chaliapin had only to show himself on stage for this to be immediately recognised by everyone, even those who did not know a word of Russian and had no actual knowledge of Russian life. 'On very special occasions such as at a gala in London four or five years ago,' wrote the *New York Herald Tribune* in 1932, 'this peerless artist abandons his own role of Boris and sings instead the relatively minor part of Varlaam. To read what the singer says of Varlaam now is to understand the electrifying effect he makes in that role: and a very great deal of the Russian genius in music and literature is implicit in it. It is pure Russian – no ordinary operatic basso should ever be permitted to sing that matchless scene at the inn – and Chaliapin understands it magnificently, with every ounce of energy and imagination in his huge body.'[138]

No other role equalled the importance of Boris Godunov in Chaliapin's life. He sang it for almost forty years, and chose it for his farewell to the stage, ten months before his death. He naturally modified his interpretation over the years; a new touch would be added or something taken away and replaced by an entirely fresh detail. What remained invariable was the organic structure of the character, the carefully planned conception, and the impression Chaliapin made on his audiences all over the world, leading them to ponder on the eternal, but insoluble, problem of 'crime and punishment'. Again and again contemporaries referred to Chaliapin as Pushkin's and Mussorgsky's full partner in the creation of the historic figure of Tsar Boris.

However, unlike Gounod's Mephistopheles, Rimsky-Korsakov's Salieri or Massenet's Don Quixote, where the features of the original literary characters were a determining factor in working out their stage counterparts, Boris Godunov, as Chaliapin interpreted him, belonged strictly to Mussorgsky. And it could not be otherwise: while preserving both the meaning and the basic plot of the tragedy, the composer rearranged the order of the parts making up Pushkin's great and multi-layered drama, in which the fate of Boris, tightly interwoven with the other themes of the play, is nevertheless only one of them. In Mussorgsky, the tragedy of Boris is strongly emphasised as the tragedy of a personality situated at the very heart of the narrative; it symbolises the idea of incompatibility between good and evil. In Pushkin's play, the action continues after the death of Boris. In the opera this looks like an artificial addition. With the Tsar's last words the story comes to a majestic close. Pushkin's Boris shows above all the mind, will and strength of character of a great sovereign, whereas Mussorgsky's Boris is characterised by suffering, pangs of conscience, madness and the search for expiation. Pushkin's Boris is an imperious and omnipotent Tsar whose misfortune lies in the Russian people's hatred of any kind of authority. Godunov's destiny is entirely dependent on this forever restless herd, hungry and tormented but also senseless and vacuous. The fact that the Boris of the opera is a Tsar has no vital significance: his destruction is preordained not by the hostility of the mob but by the fire of human suffering smouldering within him. Boris is much less complex in the opera than in the play. There the cries of his wounded soul are muffled under various strata; whenever they surface they are immediately concealed behind solemn reflections, momentous decisions and finally the Tsar's own actions. In Mussorgsky, on the contrary, Godunov is entirely consumed by personal grief and suffering.

In Pushkin, Boris is first seen addressing the patriarchs and the boyards – one of the several occasions when he talks with boyards, with Shuisky, Basmanov and others.

In Mussorgsky, Boris enters the stage in the coronation scene absorbed in self-contemplation and in his preoccupation with the growing unrest. Mussorgsky from the very start places the Tsar in a kind of isolation; even in his conversations with his children, with Shuisky or with the Simpleton, Godunov's loneliness makes itself heard like a persistent leitmotiv. Against the background of various scenes – when the people acclaim him, in the Kremlin chambers, at the Council of Boyards – Boris is shown locked inside the world of his constant fears. The musical part is constructed like a chain of monologues; the tragedy of Boris, which lies within himself, unfolds in the privacy of his own soul and seems like a unique kind of mono-drama. The relationship between the melody of these mono-logues and every word, every phrase, has been worked out with supreme care and with great attention to its 'stage effect'. The aim is to bring out the imagery and the expressiveness of the word, not just to characterise its pronunciation. This is why interpreters of the role of Boris who do not speak Russian, however gifted they may be, are unable to feel the dramatic vividness of the lines properly. Mussorgsky indicates through the music the hidden meaning of words, sentences and situations, thus clearly defining both the reality of the action and the development of the characters, their psychological and emotional make-up. At times one can even catch in it the faithful reflection of certain individual traits of the characters, an expression, a gesture or a way of walking. Mussorgsky found for Boris a manner of speaking which is unique to him. Its melodic line is at times classically clear, with a well-defined outline, but at other times it is fragmented, uneven in rhythm and broken. To express moments of extreme nervous tension he constantly divides phrases into sections: the masterful, truly regal intonation suddenly degenerates into chaotic mutter-ings, into an alarmed and uncontrollable flow of words. The harmony, like the melody, registers every emotional tremor in the heart of Boris. The fusion of the musical and verbal elements of the character is so effective that the spectators easily see the picture of a tormented man exhausted by suffering. Mussorgsky's score, to a certain extent, is already a 'producer's score'.

According to Chaliapin, the ability to 'compose' a visual image from the music is essential for anyone taking part in an operatic production. He rules out illustrating the music by the action; instead, the staging must bring out the dramatic substance contained in the music. The very fact that Chaliapin applies the word 'compose' to the visual aspect of musical performance is significant. Instead of reiterating on stage what is already in the work, the concept and the intentions of the composer are interpreted and recreated by theatrical means to form an original artistic whole. Chaliapin explains this by citing the example of 'a producer putting on *Boris Godunov*. He has read in Karamzin that the pretender Grishka Otrepiev fled from the monastery in the autumn, in September. So when he stages the inn scene with Grishka and Varlaam, he leaves the window open and displays behind it an autumn landscape of withered vegetation. Chronology triumphs but the scene is ruined. Mussorgsky composed a *wintry* [Chaliapin's italics] music for this scene. It is doleful, intense, subdued. An open window destroys the atmosphere of the entire scene.'[139] These few remarks of Chaliapin's, even the two words '*wintry* music', are sufficient to resolve the question of how to stage the entire inn scene: a single, small frosted window, letting in a faint ray of pale light; beyond the window a dusty highway along which Varlaam wanders, grimy, fat and flabby, as do thousands of other, similar vagrants. A 'doleful, intense, subdued' music and ... the jolly song of the Hostess of the inn. But is it really jolly? One often sees a well-dressed mezzo-soprano on the stage with the playful smile of a courtesan crooning 'Poimala ya siza seleznya'* ... and even dancing. But shouldn't this be a show of 'excessive mirth' just to stop yourself from shrieking out loudly, from

* I caught a grey duck – first words of the Hostess' song.

hanging yourself, in despair at the endless monotony of a grey, vegetating existence? And besides, it is difficult to imagine a person in that situation suddenly breaking into a merry dance.

From his careful study of the score Chaliapin obtained a detailed picture of each moment of the drama. Steady, thorough analysis of the role led to the creation of a concrete character, expressing himself in music.

Kashkin wrote after a performance: 'Chaliapin in the title role, which is the opera's main role, can serve as a model of artistic perfection. What we like in the singer's technique is how closely it blends with the music, which produces a natural interpretation such as no other means could achieve. Chaliapin never interrupts the musical phrase for the sake of a stage effect and always reserves for the music the primary importance due to it in the opera; but all his movements and his facial expressions are so closely synchronised with the music that they may seem to flow naturally from the given situation. This is the summit of the art which an opera singer can reach, and Chaliapin has full mastery of it. It would be safe to say that in the entire opera you will not notice anything stereotyped, conventional. In this he differs from all other – even the most talented – singers that we know of in Europe.'[140] 'This artist-psychologist is, one might say, musically experiencing the sufferings, the hesitations and the conflicts of Boris. Such a combination of actor and musician can hardly be found anywhere else.'[141]

This theme of Boris' conflict with everyone, including himself, was very important to Chaliapin. What, indeed, are state and historical necessity? How do they correspond to the dictates of the soul? What makes the painful sound of weariness destroying this man so clearly audible in Boris' voice and even in his breathing? In his brilliant, genuinely tragic Boris, Chaliapin presented a minutely analysed study of a man devoured by feelings of guilt, from which only the grave can deliver him. To inner suffering the Tsar adds hatred of his entourage. 'There is great strength in Boris Godunov,' wrote the singer, 'in this person whom I like best in my whole repertoire. But this wretched man, although he is a despotic Tsar, is like a huge elephant surrounded by savage jackals and hyenas, whose brute force finally overcome him. Instinctively feeling the elephantine power of Boris, and fearing it, the boyards prowl around with their tails between their legs, gnashing their teeth. But they are only temporarily quiet. At the first opportunity the cowardly but treacherous, lawless and rapacious pack tears the elephant to pieces.'[142]

As the Kremlin bells ring out ceremoniously, Boris Godunov, preceded by boyards, Streltsy and in some productions the clergy, and leaning on the arm of Vasili Shuisky, slowly and majestically emerges onto the parvis of the Uspensky Cathedral.* The procession usually looked 'imposing and peaceful, with no display of insolent arrogance. Boris is not deviously plotting anything against the rest of the world. A great problem confronts him: to save Russia from sedition and the people from disaster. Will he be able to cope with this immense task?'[143]

Robed in brocade and gold, Boris takes another step or two forward, then stops, absorbed in his own thoughts. 'And who has seen *Boris*', wrote the *Daily Mail* on the occasion of Chaliapin's 1914 guest appearance in London, 'and can forget the first glimpses of Chaliapin and that haughty yet hesitating step as, his mantle stiff with gold, he crosses the Kremlin courtyard for the Coronation? His pride and troubled soul are in his gait and air before he has uttered a word. Then words are uttered, a very few, but the mood straightaway is infallibly fixed.'[144]

The opening words of the monologue, 'Skorbit dusha' (My soul is heavy), are sung with the utmost degree of concentration; their sound is low. Each note betrays a sense of the anxiety which has clearly long been besetting the soul of this man. It is as if an iron hand were constricting his throat. He continues in a slightly more muted *piano*: 'kakoi to strakh nevol'nyi' (some instinctive fear). The 'a' of the Russian word for 'fear' ('strakh') is very slightly drawn out and lingers for a brief moment before dying away. The subsequent phrases about the 'ominous foreboding which rivets [his] heart' are tinged with various shades of confusion and anxiety. At the beginning of his short speech

---

* Cathedral of the Assumption.

Chaliapin as Boris Godunov in Mussorgsky's opera *Boris Godunov*, 1915.
Couresy EMI Music.

Chaliapin-Boris stands almost completely motionless. His right hand firmly clasps the tall staff and indeed seems to be the only support propping him up. This is power: this is a dream come true but at the price of a crime. The figure of the newly elected Tsar is reminiscent of a statue: his left hand tightly pressed to his heart shows the only discernible sign of life. The way it lies across the chest and the occasional clenching and unclenching of the fingers are a clear and tangible indication of extremes of pain and stress. This odd use of the arms made a lasting impression on the public.

Later on, during the scene in the *terem** when he is talking to his son, his right hand will rest on a map of Russia while the left tenderly and wistfully strokes the boy's head. How long will this land, which his young heir has drawn on a sheet of paper, remain under the dominion of Boris? 'Sometime, and perhaps soon, this whole kingdom will be yours. . . .' The swollen-veined hand resting on the map has already lost some of the powerful grip that was so much in evidence at the time of the coronation. And in his final scene, before he tumbles from the throne and hoarsely gasps out his dying words 'O zlaya smert' (O cruel death), the lifeless right arm (it very much looks like hemiplegia) will hang like a limp whiplash, while the left weakly stretches out towards the terrified and crying tsarevich to give him a last blessing and beg once more, 'Forgive. . . .'

All this, though, is still a long way off. Boris is now ascending the throne, and all vestiges of doubt are swept away when he intones words of prayer. 'O just God! O almighty Father! . . .' He prays with devotion and ardour, since he believes that he committed his crime for the good of his suffering country and hopes that his sins will be absolved. Only once his prayer is said does he really believe in the success of his deed, and in a clear voice, with gentle yet regal gestures, he orders, 'Summon the people to a feast, all, from the boyards down to the last blind beggar.'[145]

Boris' prayer seems to have given him inner strength: a new spirit of self-assurance and solemn commitment to his chosen

---

*Tower chamber – here, living quarters of the tsar and his family.

As Boris Godunov, 1915.

path already animates him. Anxiety, fear and doubt are dispelled when he fully realises the pomp and splendour of the occasion. Casting his eye over the square, and seeming to notice for the first time the rejoicing crowd, Godunov opens his arms wide as if trying to embrace them all. His voice soars joyfully, deliberately emphasising certain words with renewed vigour: 'All ...', 'for all ...', 'all ...' And indeed: 'All are welcome guests!' Never again will God grant him another moment of happiness, but at this particular time.... 'If only you could hear this richness of sound and this extraordinary expression of warmth.'[146] 'He is not only perfect as Boris, he *is* Boris – in voice, manner, gesture, everything.'[147]

More than five years have passed since Boris' coronation when we next see him entering a chamber in the Kremlin. 'I would tell any young actor,' said Sacha Guitry, 'if you want to study how to dominate the stage and move on it, go and see the nursery scene in Boris. The children are playing; Boris enters through a low door at the back of the stage. Immediately the atmosphere changes from gaiety to brooding tragedy. He walks across the stage without singing a note and pats one of the children on the head. If you want to know how to walk on the stage, study that walk – only a supremely great actor could do it.'[148] But how markedly this man has changed, almost beyond recognition! 'His face is deeply lined, his beard and his slightly dishevelled hair are decidedly grey. His body is wasted, his breathing laboured, and he walks slowly.'[149] The low door forces him to stoop, and it clearly costs him a great deal of time and effort to straighten up again. And yet he still has some reserves of strength; Boris is still mighty and, if need be, can terrify his enemies 'with his tall, commanding figure, his kingly bearing, the striking face with the high cheek-bones of a pure Tartar, and that Oriental look in the eyes – imperious, piercing and at the same time calculating.'[150]

'The young people who were there will talk of Chaliapin's acting to their grandchildren of the dim future,' said the London *Evening News*. 'A man with no ear for music would have been impressed by the great artist's declamation. A deaf man would have been enthralled by merely watching his facial expression, so revealing was it of the conscience-tormented Tsar's poisoned soul and physical undermining.'[151]

Godunov's unexpected arrival interrupts the children's merry games and frightens the Nurse out of her wits – she slumps to the ground in panic. 'What? So a ferocious beast has startled the hovering hen?' he enquires in a friendly, almost jocular tone, and yet the phrase has sombre overtones. 'Bitter thoughts had swept away the last vestiges of happiness from his soul.'[152]

Brushing aside the Nurse's explanations, Boris looks intently at his daughter. Dear God, will she also have to pay for what he has done? His unhappiness deepens at the idea. In an effort to console Xenia, Boris fondly and with loving care clasps her to his breast. Their dialogue is very short – a few sentences in all – but it is a difficult one for Boris. 'The voice of the Tsar abruptly lost its virile, masterful tone and literally started to quiver with deep-felt tenderness.'[153] His parting words to her – 'Go, my child' – are sung softly, pensively. Chaliapin often asked the conductor to hold the chord accompanying Xenia's exit until it died down naturally, and it was only the subsequent *sforzando* that aroused Boris from his reverie.

'And you, my son, what are you doing? What is this?' When he speaks to Fedor, his tenderness is edged with a hint of firmness: this is after all the heir to the throne, the future Tsar of Russia. It is easy to see that Godunov not only loves Fedor but is also extremely proud of him. He is genuinely amazed by the ease and confidence with which the little boy explains to him the distribution of towns and rivers on this incomprehensible piece of paper covered with strange drawings. The way Chaliapin played this scene showed that Boris was illiterate but had a kind of fearful reverence for education. Perhaps it was the cure for all the evils threatening him, or perhaps a source of power for governing, although that was unlikely. . . . For him, at any rate, there is no salvation. Surprised and frightened, Fedor, from the corner of the room, watches his father's eyes, ringed by sickly shadows, growing swiftly dim; he sees his smile fading and his face altering beyond recognition: it is now so pinched, troubled and sad that looking at it becomes unbearable. 'Paternal pride and delight soften his voice for a brief moment,' wrote a Vienna newspaper, 'but then he once again gives in to anxiety, to the terrible vision which finally crushes this man vainly trying to preserve his balance. The sobbing wrung from him by the fear of death is of terrifying authenticity.'[154] Even with his own children he has to wear a mask to hide the relentless pain burning inside him. This mental torture has confined him to the darkest regions of hell. His efforts to find happiness on the throne and in his family have been wasted – they brought only hatred from the people, mutual mistrust between him and the boyards and grief for his daughter.* What will the next blow be?

'I have attained the highest power. . . .' The first words of the monologue ring like the tragic summing-up of an entire life. This is not 'thinking aloud' but a painful re-living of the past and the present, the futile due of a lonely man fighting with himself and with the rest of the hostile world. How can he bear to go on living when he is blamed for the deluge of never-ending misfortunes which shower down on Russia? What is the reason for such evil, what has brought it about? Even if he is a criminal, does he have to pay for everything that happens? The music of the monologue is written as separate episodes which have no precise endings comparable to 'full stops' in literary terms. On the contrary, the impression gained is of a relentless succession of thoughts. This prevents any slackening of the emotional intensity, communicating the unbroken tension of his inner turmoil to the scene. Many of those who wrote about Chaliapin in the role of Boris remarked on the fearful confusion of his soul and his desperate perplexity in the face of incredible human suffering. They were struck by the amount of psychological and emotional content he could often squeeze into a few words. 'The singer makes us forget all the operatic conventions,' wrote the Petersburg periodical *Theatre and Art*. 'Singing even seems like natural speech.'[155] 'Chaliapin as singer and actor in the role of Boris is beyond compare,' reiterated a Paris critic at a later date. 'He excels equally in both. We know of no other instance where singing and gestures are combined with such unexampled

---

* Her husband-to-be died before their wedding.

As Boris Godunov.

power of expression and feeling. Chaliapin does not sing; he conveys the life of the character he is performing through singing. He spurns conventional methods; he is dramatic truth personified.'[156]

When recalling the murdered tsarevich, Chaliapin utters the words 'krik yevo pryedsmyertnyi' (his dying scream) and clasps his head in his hands, as if trying to protect himself from the wail which has taken possession of his brain. It fills the nocturnal silence, it hounds him everywhere, but there is no escape. 'O Lord, my God. . . .' Unable to endure the stress of his emotions and of his sombre thoughts, Boris, drained of all energy, lets his head sink forward onto the table. When a boyard enters to announce Shuisky, Godunov has still not completely regained control of himself. 'His features show traces of unwonted weariness.' He averts his gaze while listening to the boyard's denunciation of Shuisky, and then, after he has given the order to seize the messenger, making a great effort to summon all his will-power, he addresses Prince Shuisky 'with a show of outward composure'. Boris has always hated and feared this man; he has always known that when it comes to brains and duplicity he has no equal. 'I realised', wrote Chaliapin, 'that when such a master of dissimulation as Shuisky is speaking, I, Boris, must listen to him as one would listen to a wily schemer, and not as to an honest courtier making an honest report!'[157]

But the news which Shuisky brings is so startling that Boris leaps from his chair as if stung. 'Dmitri!!' Nothing could be worse! 'Tsarevich, be gone!!' Feverishly, hastily, not even trying to hide his trembling and the agitation which grips him, he blurts out the peremptory order: close the frontier with Lithuania 'so that not a soul can pass beyond the border'. His voice breaks, the words seem to stick in his throat; he is clearly unwell. 'Get out!' And suddenly, shaking all over as if struck by lightning, he takes one prodigious step towards the retreating figure. 'No, wait! Wait, Shuisky.' His voice grows more powerful with each successive word; Boris strains every nerve, ready at any moment to pounce on Shuisky and tear him to pieces. His enunciation also becomes unpleasantly grating and excessively precise. It seems for a moment that Boris has lost his mind – at any rate

As Boris Godunov.

his sudden 'horrible, forced laughter' gives Shuisky a start. Then, pausing after every word, he asks: 'The ... little one ... who ... was killed ... was it ... Dmitri?' 'It was,' Shuisky raps out. But this is not sufficient for Boris; he wants a detailed account of the bloody events at Uglich. Boris clasps Shuisky tightly, then flings him to the ground. His back turned to him, he says in a hollow voice: 'I am waiting for the answer.' 'It was clear from the Tsar's face that he would have given anything for the question to be left unanswered.'[158]

Shuisky obeys the command with relish, slowly driving every sentence into the heart of Boris like a knife, savouring the details and obviously enjoying the spectacle of his suffering. 'Enough,' cries Boris. Shuisky vanishes instantly, like a ghost, and Boris, utterly exhausted, sinks into his seat. The stage darkens. The faint, bluish light of the evening dusk filters through the small window, casting a pale and wavering pool on the floor. Godunov has difficulty in breathing and rips open the collar of his silk shirt. 'Ah, I am stifling! Let me get my breath....' At the back of the chamber a clock strikes. To the rhythm of its muffled chimes, Boris starts to chant his words monotonously and plaintively, deliberately accentuating every one of them. The scene becomes unbearably terrifying.'[159]

Chaliapin first performed this 'clock scene' in 1908 at the Paris Opéra.* When Chaliapin arrived at the Opéra on the morning of the dress rehearsal, he realised that the stagehands would not be able to erect the scenery in time, and that some of the costumes were not ready. The singer, who was in an irritable mood, declared: 'Since you are not ready, neither am I. I won't put on my make-up or my costume; I shall rehearse in my jacket. And that's what I did.'†[160] The atmosphere, already tense, became highly charged. Even Diaghilev, the organiser of the 'Russian seasons', who had the reputation of being able to find a way out of the most awkward situations, seemed to have

---

* Until then, the episode of 'Boris' hallucination' followed immediately upon Shuisky's exit, as in the 1896 version. It was Diaghilev who had the idea of reinstating the scene.

† Alexandre Benois records in his memoirs that Chaliapin did, in fact, wear one of his costumes for this dress rehearsal – the one for the coronation scene. (See Benois, *My Memories*, Moscow 1980, vol. 5, pp. 487–88.)

lost patience. It was understandable. Huge amounts of money, energy and time had been spent on the production of *Boris*. Chaliapin's gold brocade costume for the Prologue alone was studded with eighteen thousand precious stones, pearls, rubies, emeralds, topazes and other gems. It weighed over 27 kilograms. The fate of the entire season hung on this rehearsal: the auditorium was already filling up with 'the flower of Parisian society'.... Years later Alexandre Benois could still remember the impression Chaliapin had produced in the clock scene. According to him, a miracle had taken place on the stage. 'I was not the only one to feel a shiver going down my spine when in the semi-darkness, moonlight shining on the silver clock, Chaliapin started to "recite" his monologue. I could tell by my neighbours' faces that they were also shuddering, that they were all terrified beyond endurance. Such extraordinary moments of pure genius happen in the theatre.... Its miraculous effect is strong enough to overcome all obstacles, as in this case, when both the abnormal nonsense of the empty stage and Chaliapin's inappropriate garb were suddenly forgotten.'[161]

Boris' fevered mind imagines seeing the spectre of the murdered tsarevich, Dmitri, in the flickering shadows of the clock. 'What is it, there, in the corner?' 'At that moment,' writes Chaliapin, 'I was startled by a strange noise in the auditorium. I glanced sideways to see what was happening and this is what I saw: the audience had risen to its feet – some were even standing on their seats – and were staring into the corner.... I was singing in Russian, a language which they did not understand, but from the look in my eyes they had sensed that I was very afraid of something.'[162]

Glimmers of the nightmares inexorably looming over Boris flash through the music. The Tsar sinks heavily to his knees, digs his fingers into his dishevelled hair, and then, crying out into the darkness of the room, 'Be gone, child, be gone!', he hurriedly crawls away from the apparition towards the opposite corner, where the ikons are hanging. As he drives off the vision, he tries to justify himself. Even with the imperfect technical quality of the contemporary recordings still available today, one gets the impression that Boris treats the vision as if it were

As Boris Godunov. Bolshoi Theatre, Moscow, 1911.

a real person. He begs for mercy, sobs, mutters incoherently. 'Mustering his last remnants of strength to defend himself, Godunov seizes an ornately covered stool and with all his might hurls it into the corner.'[163] At the moment when it hits the floor, a short, thunderous roll from the orchestra abruptly signals the end of his torment. Breathing heavily, Boris 'attempts to make the sign of the cross, but his hand refuses to obey him; it seems to have turned to stone so that the unfortunate Tsar is denied the solace of even this soothing balm....'[164] Boris is utterly spent, all his energy drained. He remains lying on the floor in a semi-conscious state.

An opera-goer remembers seeing him in the role at Covent Garden: 'It must be forty years or more since I last heard Chaliapin's Boris, but my spine still chills enjoyably as I recall his Clock Scene, where the Tsar, who has murdered his way to the throne, sees the ghost of the child he has murdered. And he did the whole thing with a chair and a red handkerchief; a monumental and solitary figure in a splendid costume of brocade and fur, he scarcely made a movement at first, only the agitation of the red handkerchief in his hand showing his growing uneasiness and his incredulous horror. Then at the moment when he actually saw the child, he would take the chair on which he had been sitting and try to keep off the figure, unseen to all but him. And we, sweating with heat and terror in the gallery, could have sworn in the end that we saw the child too. That was acting!'[165]

Finally, the concluding scene in the Granovitaya Chamber.* The Council of Boyards is holding a special session.† Everyone gathers around Shuisky to listen in disbelief to his account of what happened to the Tsar the previous evening. Shuisky has barely finished repeating Godunov's words 'Be gone! Be gone!' when from somewhere deep inside the chamber Boris himself is heard saying 'Be gone, child, be gone!' Such unexpected confirmation of Shuisky's story astounds the boyards. They

---

* Hall with facets. The walls are cut like diamonds or facets similar to the interior of a pomegranate.

† Irrespective of whether the scene near Kromy was played or not, performances in which Chaliapin took part ended with the death of Boris.

stand aside as the figure of the Tsar appears in the doorway. Unaware of their presence, he enters backwards, waving his arms in the air in fear of something. When he reaches the centre of the stage, Boris turns round and, looking over the heads of the boyards, asks, stressing each syllable with deliberate clarity: 'Who says I am a murderer? There is no murderer! The child is alive, alive! . . .' His appearance has deteriorated overnight. His eyes are completely sunken; his face is now indelibly furrowed by deep lines of suffering. 'A new tingle crept over his Boris,' noted the critic of the London *Sunday Times* in 1929. 'If it is now less forceful, less terrible, it is far more subtly pathetic: the oncoming madness is no longer in the physical but [in the] spiritual substance of the brain.'[166] His right hand convulsively grips the chain of the cross hanging round his neck. 'The blessing of the Lord be upon you,' obsequiously whispers Shuisky in his ear, but several seconds have to pass before anything can penetrate his consciousness. Boris listens attentively, then mumbles 'Eh?' He looks around, scrutinises the dumbfounded boyards, and a look of sanity returns to his eyes. Then, catching sight of the throne, with a tremendous effort 'he slowly drags himself' towards it.

'I have called you, boyards, I rely on your wisdom. . . .' The veiled irony which Chaliapin imparts to the word 'wisdom' is audible in the recording of this scene made in 1928 during an actual Covent Garden performance.* And truly, what can he expect from them other than stupidity and treachery? Only a moment ago, they could not manage to discuss what to do about the Pretender without quarrelling and interrupting each other, and, unable to come to a positive decision, had to admit: 'Pity that Shuisky is not here, without him everything seems to go wrong.'

Laboriously ascending the dais, Boris continues: 'In times of trouble and crisis you have always been my help, boyards.' The end of the sentence is sung in a low, faint voice: 'help' indeed – such as you would not wish on an enemy. Before lowering himself into the armchair, he hears out Shuisky's suggestion

---

* Available on EMI RLS 742.

that he should give audience to a 'humble old monk' who wants 'to reveal a great secret'. 'Nothing now matters to the Tsar: he can foresee no harm in this visit, and – who knows? – talking to the old monk will perhaps quiet the secret unrest of a tormented soul.'[167]

Boris listens to Pimen's tale quietly. 'His glance reveals nothing; he is recovering from his terrible fit in a state bordering on prostration,' recalled a spectator.[168] This is how Chaliapin sometimes performed the role, though other accounts give a different description. Boris Asafev, after hearing Chaliapin in this scene at Stasov's house, wrote: 'I remember how, before Pimen's monologue in the last act of *Boris Godunov,* Chaliapin sang the line "Tell me everything you know, old man ... keep nothing from me," and how this was accompanied by a deeply intent gaze, penetrating through space to where Pimen was supposed to be.'[169] Pimen's speech flows steadily, and Boris probably does not even hear all of it, sunk as he is in his own thoughts. Only the mention of Uglich kindles a slight sign of anxiety. 'A wry smile flits across Boris' pale face. He sits as if riveted to the throne, but one can see his hands digging into the armrests. Boris remains frozen in this attitude. To continue watching him is almost unbearable.'[170] He inhales deeply; he is short of breath. His left hand convulsively plucks at the collar of his clothing to try to free his neck. Unable to endure any more, Godunov draws himself up to his full height and, interrupting Pimen with a despairing gesture, cries frantically: 'Oh! I am suffocating, suffocating. . . .' Ezio Pinza, reminiscing about his joint appearance with Chaliapin in America (1927) wrote: 'I was happy to sing Pimen and watch Chaliapin as Boris. He was a superlative actor, so compelling that only my professional experience and perfect knowledge of my role saved me time and again from missing my cues, so absorbed was I in watching him act. What impressed me most was the intelligence with which he limited his movements and gestures to psychological necessity. They were very sparing, but when Chaliapin moved, the whole stage shifted with him.'[171]

After Pimen's departure, Boris moves forward; his foot misses the step and he falls, like a felled tree, into the arms of the

(*Above* and *right*) Chaliapin as Boris Godunov. Moscow, 1911.

boyards, who catch him just in time. Someone brings an arm-chair and Boris is carefully settled into it. 'The Tsarevich ... quickly! ...' he says in a soft, frail voice. When Fedor runs in, Boris feebly draws him into his arms and presses him to his bosom.

'When you looked at Boris at this moment, you could see his entire life passing by. Here he was at the Uspensky Cathedral for his coronation, now with his son and daughter in the second act, and then on his knees in the hallucination scene. Before Boris died, Chaliapin made all this flash past in his intonations, in his movements and in the expression of his eyes.'[172]

In the brief instant granted by God for their farewell, Boris manages to say a great deal to his son. But the end is near; exhortations and behests are over. Leaning on Fedor, Godunov slides from the armchair onto his knees, to appeal to heaven for the last time. He now prays only for Fedor, but the effort exhausts the dying man. The sound of the voice, 'immaterial', detached, suddenly fades, trailing off to nothing. Deep in prayer, Boris remains on his knees, motionless, holding his son tightly in his arms. The silence is broken by the tolling of a bell. Boris shudders and turns his head abruptly. Another spasm convulses his face. He croaks ominously: 'A bell! The passing bell!' The ringing grows stronger and the distant sound of a dirge gets louder. Still leaning on Fedor, Boris stands up, manages to reach his armchair and stretches himself in it, trying with all his might to overcome the pain which racks him. But when monks in black habits, boyards and choirboys enter the Granovitaya Chamber with lighted candles, Boris suddenly rises towards them. He takes a few uncertain steps and with extraordinary force shouts straight at them: 'Wait! I am still Tsar!' His cry builds up to a crescendo, and on the top E of the word 'Tsar' Chaliapin made a fermata. This lengthening of the sound comes to an abrupt end: the cry has exhausted Boris' already depleted strength. The second 'I am still Tsar!' is much weaker; the words trail off, almost spoken, not sung.

'All of a sudden his right leg gave way under him and, reeling, he stumbled sideways in a half-circle, clawing at the air with his hands in the hope of staying on his feet, and then, turning his face towards the public, he collapsed to the floor as if mown down.'[173] 'What a Shakespearean actor the man is, what a Shylock, Macbeth, Lear, Othello! The dying Boris, still an eagle among sparrows, tousled and tormented, shot at from all directions by fate, and dying with a grandeur beyond pathos. He looked as though nature had meant him to be an emperor and as though he had never worn anything but such superb Elizabethan clothes,'[174] wrote the *Daily Mail* after one of the 1928 Covent Garden performances.

A second later, he raises himself a little with the help of his left hand and tries to point at Fedor with the right one: 'There! there is your Tsar! ... the Tsar! Forgive!' Boris does not finish his final 'Forgive!'; his throat can only manage a hoarse, stifled 'aaaa....'

Here again, contemporary accounts indicate that Chaliapin sometimes played this differently. 'In the final scene,' wrote a Petersburg critic in 1911, 'Chaliapin has given his death a "new look" – in other words, he has found a new way of expressing royal death, by petrifying in the sculptural pose of a fallen colossus before the eyes of the spectators.'[175] One of Chaliapin's compatriots, who happened to see the singer in the role of Boris both at his peak and again later, in his declining years in Paris, mentioned yet another version: 'This was a different Boris: he was not a strong and wise man, fatally wounded by remorse for the crime he had committed. From his first appearance on the stage, this was a dispirited man, tormented by death, by mortal disease, and suffering deeply. This new image contained an echo of Chaliapin's personal tragedy.... The astounding words "I am still Tsar", in the circumstances, were not taken so much as the words of Tsar Boris but as the plaintive cry of a singer who felt his own end drawing near – and indeed he did not have much longer to live.'[176] The French musicologist Bernard Gavoty gives a detailed description of the Tsar's last moments: 'Chaliapin's hands went to his neck, as when a man is choking; he made a dash for the top of the throne as if only up there might the dying Tsar have found some oxygen to breathe. In the last thrust, he rose on tiptoe, remaining like this as if suspended between heaven and earth; then suddenly, like

As Boris Godunov. Moscow, 1911.

an oak sawn at the base, he fell down flat on his back, with a rustle of fabrics clutched by magnificent hands. Of this giant, proudly erect a minute earlier, there was now only a shapeless little heap of furs and jewels. At the same time as his soul, the material shell of the Tsar had disappeared.'[177] 'When he lay dying in the hall of the Duma,' wrote the *New York World*, 'his great frame stretched prone as a fallen oak, his glazed and blinded eyes turned for the last time upon his little son, men and women watched him with unashamed tears trickling down their cheeks.'[178]

Naturally, some of his performances could not exactly have been called great artistic events, and at times like these he had to rely above all on his technical skill. 'It is possible', wrote Richard Capell in 1929, '(if comparisons are wanted) that Chaliapin was a little more reserved, vocally, last night than of old. But those who saw *Boris* for the first time last night need not pay attention to any laudator temporis acti. Let everyone who was there count himself lucky. He saw something that is not matched on the rest of the contemporary stage – something that is a compensation for not having lived in the age of Garrick, Siddons, Talma or Rachel.'[179] Even then, Chaliapin was still Chaliapin. 'I have watched people in the stalls at Covent Garden', recalled Sir Neville Cardus, 'when he was in the throes of the death scene and I could see their hair bristling.'[180] It cannot be denied that the singer's powers and his voice occasionally let him down, especially towards the end of his career. But his place in the history of the theatre is not determined by these bitter hours; to this day no interpreter of the role of Boris has been able to escape Chaliapin's influence. Some excel in portraying a criminal's pangs of conscience, others the inescapable loneliness and doom of the Tsar, while a third group (the treatment most favoured by Soviet theatre) regards Godunov's impotence against the people's hatred as the cause of his downfall. Singers of strong individuality try not to copy Chaliapin's intonations or imitate his particular moves, but their search for a personal interpretation shows how much they are indebted to Chaliapin – that is, to his talent for injecting the spark of real feeling into an abstract artistic concept, his ability to colour every word and gesture with the truth of the emotions experienced by the character he was playing. 'It is impossible not to surrender to the power of this demiurgic will,' wrote Boris Asafiev, 'not to re-live again and again the tragedy of this clever, ambitious man, who has achieved his aim, but at such heavy cost: the loss of inner peace right to the end of his life. From Chaliapin-Boris' first entrance to his last convulsive cries, this gnawing mental suffering never ceases to affect the way he looks, what he says and what he thinks; the man who is moving and talking in front of the audience is a man doomed to destruction. He cannot fight, and there is nothing that can arrest the terrible events which are engulfing him. He has been his own judge and has ravaged his own soul.... He has not been able to justify the means to his chosen ends. Boris no longer believed in his own rightness, became frightened at what he had done and perished. This helplessness, hopelessness and impotence are all reflected in the genius of Chaliapin's intonation, and it is impossible to find words to describe the depth, the vividness and the versatility of all its nuances, for how could one possibly describe the process of life which goes on inside a man?'[181]

In his memoirs Gatti-Casazza sums up Chaliapin's interpretation of Boris: 'He was an enormous success. No one will ever reproduce this impersonation. Someone may do as remarkably, in a different way, though that seems far off. But there will never be another Chaliapin.'[182]

'One wonders,' wrote the *Graphic* in London in 1928, 'what will happen to *Boris Godunov* when Chaliapin becomes too old to undertake the responsibilities of the title role. Needless to say, the opera has been given in many theatres without him, but in the mind of the public Chaliapin and Boris are so intertwined that many people will find it difficult to think of one without the other.'[183]

Chaliapin's first contract with the Bolshoi Theatre, signed three years previously, ran out in September 1902. Telyakovsky worried about this 'fateful' date for a year; he knew perfectly well that securing a new agreement was not going to be a simple matter. Chaliapin was no longer the naive young man whom it

ROYAL OPERA
:: COVENT GARDEN ::
Lessees: Covent Garden Opera Syndicate, Ltd.

THIS EVENING'S PERFORMANCE

Monday, June 17, 1929, at 8

MOUSSORGSKY'S OPERA

BORIS GODOUNOV

In Italian

Boris	FEODOR CHALIAPINE
Theodore	NADIA KOVACEVA
Xenia	ELENA DANIELI
Nutrice	MARIA CASTAGNA
Prince Chouisky	ANGELO BADA
Tchelkalov	ARISTIDE BARACCHI
Pimen	LUIGI MANFRINI
Dimitri	FRANCESCO MERLI
Marina	IRENE MINGHINI CATTANEO
Varlaam	SALVATORE BACCALONI
Missail	GIUSEPPE NESSI
Ostessa	MARIA CASTAGNA
Innocente	OCTAVE DUA
Ufficiale	MICHELE SAMPIERI
Boyard	LUIGI CILLA
Lavretsky	DENNIS NOBLE
Tcherniakovsky	ARISTIDE BARACCHI
Conductor	ALBERT COATES

had been relatively easy to entice from Mamontov. He was now a singer of universal fame, who constantly threatened to go abroad if the Imperial Theatres did not meet his demands. Telyakovsky entirely concurred with some of Chaliapin's views about the repertoire and the standard of the productions, but he was unable to change everything at once. Other conditions which the singer wanted written into his contract were simply impossible to fulfil. For example, Chaliapin wanted two complimentary tickets in the front rows of the stalls for every performance in which he took part. He also wanted his stage costumes to become his personal property at the end of the season. On another occasion Chaliapin tried to get a 'travelling allowance' for the dresser who accompanied him everywhere, and for himself the right to go on holiday during the season whenever he felt like it. Moreover, he would continue on the Imperial stage only as long as Telyakovsky was director. One had to hear all this out patiently, never argue, agree about everything 'to try and persuade Chaliapin to sign just the rough draft now and to discuss the small print later on with legal experts at his leisure'.[184]

Telyakovsky had even greater difficulty with Chaliapin's third contract in September 1907. He had very little hope of success. Whenever they met, Chaliapin did his best to avoid discussing the issue. He stubbornly gave the same answer to every question: the terms of a new contract with the Imperial Theatres depended on his guest tour of America at the end of the following year. There was, however, a little trick the director had already resorted to in the past. While the contracts of all the other singers terminated on September 1st, Chaliapin could not officially consider himself free until after the 23rd. Things had been arranged that way at the signing of the first agreement in the winter of 1898. This chance circumstance, to which no one had paid much attention at the time, now forced Chaliapin to take part in performances for a further three weeks after the beginning of the new season. 'I put him on the billings,' recalled Telyakovsky, 'and thus, by keeping him in the thick of events, I slightly improved my position for finalising the new contract.'[185] Moreover, the director had no objection to the financial demands of the singer, since he knew that 'no matter what price you ask for Chaliapin – the house will always be full'. Nevertheless, Telyakovsky constantly had to give endless explanations: the notorious 'Chaliapin fees' were of interest to everyone, including ministers of the Imperial Court. Nobody would have objected had such sums been paid to an Italian singer, but to pay them to a Russian, and one who was not even a tenor, meant asking for serious trouble. The fact that Chaliapin was not in favour 'in high places', where the director's partiality towards him was not shared, further weakened Telyakovsky's position.

The press also watched Chaliapin's every move: in its columns many of his most innocent actions were transformed into political issues. Possibly no other Russian artist had to experience such persistent harassment and persecution from every side. All sorts of groups and factions wanted to be able to claim Chaliapin as 'their man', and as a result insults and threats never stopped raining down on him, someone somewhere was always dissatisfied. . . .

In the autumn of 1906, Chaliapin contracted a mastoid infection. He underwent a painful and unsuccessful operation, which prevented him from singing in *A Life for the Tsar* at the opening of the season. Telyakovsky reports that 'a countless number of anonymous postcards of the most shocking nature addressed to Chaliapin started arriving at the Bolshoi Theatre where everyone could read them. Chaliapin was depressed by the mass of letters he had received from both left and right, the former railing at him for intending to take part in *A Life for the Tsar*, the latter for not taking part in it. All this rendered the atmosphere utterly impossible. No one believed that his refusal was due to illness. After thoroughly discussing it with Chaliapin, we came to the conclusion that he would have to sing Susanin, albeit just once, but that in view of the particularly critical situation in Moscow, it would be better for him to sing this opera in Petersburg. . . .'[186]

Newspapers did not hang fire either. Every morning Chaliapin could read that he was 'a lout who had crawled out of the gutter' and that it was 'high time he was booted out of the

349

Chaliapin, Moscow, 1902.

Imperial Theatres'.[187] Chaliapin was spared absolutely nothing: his friendship with Gorky, his peasant descent, his lack of respect for the Tsar, his large fees. Telyakovsky was summoned to Petersburg to account personally to the Minister. Poor Chaliapin! The only thing he had ever wanted was to be just a singer and keep out of politics. It is significant that at the time when this row flared up, Chaliapin refused to sign a declaration that he was not a member of any illegal political association. He refused not because he wanted to hide the truth but because he believed that a man's convictions belonged only to him and were therefore a purely private matter. 'In Petersburg every one of the singers has signed,' Telyakovsky assured him, trying to damp down the flames a little. One must give Chaliapin his due – he always, whatever the circumstances and whatever regime was in power, knew how to maintain his sense of dignity and self-respect.

'One day,' relates Chaliapin, 'I received a case containing a present from the Tsar: a gold watch. I looked at the watch and it seemed to me it did not sufficiently reflect the generous nature of the Russian sovereign. I dare say this gold watch, decorated with little roses, would have given great joy to the worthy doorkeeper of some rich household. I put the watch back in its case and sent it to my dear Telyakovsky with a letter in which I explained in full the reason for my action. It created a "scandal". In the old days no one would have dared refuse a present from the Tsar, and now I...'[188]

Telyakovsky's memoirs reveal how often he had to intervene in Chaliapin's arguments with his fellow singers, conductors, chorus and even with the government. The vast majority of these disputes arose from Chaliapin's inability to accept the limitations of ordinary ideas, ordinary people. Dismissing him from the theatre was unthinkable; neither the management nor the public would have allowed it. So his enemies' only alternative was to engineer a situation in which the highly strung and volatile Chaliapin would not be able to control his emotions and would 'make a scene'. 'A scene today, a scene tomorrow; perhaps he will eventually leave and the operatic repertoire will run smoothly. And so they took every opportunity to behave in a manner which would irritate Chaliapin and drive him out of his wits, and then he would do the rest himself and do his best to show how unsuitable he was for any state-run establishment. In addition, the more people were embroiled in the story, the better,' observed Telyakovsky.[189] Luckily for Chaliapin, Telyakovsky understood that 'men of exceptional talent were always unacceptable in the eyes of the management, since they were demanding and intractable. Square pegs of even size and weight fit more easily into the administrative box.'[190] Telyakovsky did not regard the inevitable passions, conflicts of interests and of aspirations inherent in the theatre as something evil but rather as part of the nature of things and did everything possible to avoid wasting creative energy on futile squabbles over trivialities. All the same, trivialities so often make life unbearable, poisoning its otherwise normal course. The amount of gossip, slander and unfair allegations Chaliapin had to put up with was incalculable. Witness to this are the tales of his pathological meanness and his total indifference to the needs of others which turn up in memoir after memoir. 'He was niggardly, mean and begrudged every kopeck,' recalled one of Chaliapin's impresarios. 'He never gave anything to anyone. "Whoever gave me anything?" he would always say.'[191] Even some of the singer's close friends spoke little better of him, and Konstantin Korovin, for one, seems to have taken particular delight in accumulating 'proofs' of Chaliapin's avarice in his book.[192] Ivan Bunin, too, quotes Chaliapin's supposedly invariable reply whenever asked to participate in a charity performance: 'Only birds sing for free.'[193]

Was this true? Behind its dry enumeration of facts, the *Chronicle of the Life and Career of F. I. Chaliapin*[194] recently published in Leningrad, paints a very different picture of the man. At times not a month would pass without Chaliapin sending money to someone and singing in some charity concert. One of these, for instance, was to aid the family of a French baritone with whom he had worked at Mamontov's theatre and who had suddenly collapsed and died on the stage.[195] On another occasion, he distributed everything he had earned in Rostov-on-Don during the summer of 1903 to Jewish pogrom victims.[196]

Programme cover for Chaliapin's charity concert. Albert Hall, London,
October 2nd, 1921.

He made a donation to the Mikhail Glinka Memorial Fund, sent cash to the ailing composer Kalinnikov (anonymously, for the sake of Kalinnikov's pride), gave a concert for the benefit of the Society for the Prevention of Cruelty to Children.[197]

'Hundreds of students owed their education solely to the material support they received from Fedor Ivanovich,' said his daughter Irina.[198] During the First World War he opened two hospitals for wounded soldiers entirely at his own expense. After emigrating, he gave a large sum to the head of the Russian Church in Paris for starving children. . . .

It is astonishing how hardy the seeds of malicious rumour are and how readily people believe what they hear. Ordinary envy was exacerbated in this case by Chaliapin's indifference to the impression he produced on others and by his dislike of giving detailed explanations whenever he had to say no to something. And he had to say no, because he lacked the time and energy to satisfy every request.

Those who had known him for a long time without being really close to him, or who had not won his respect, describe him as arrogant rather than open and approachable in his relationships. In these reminiscences one can often detect a slight note of pique: he had not given something; he had not been sufficiently obliging, at any rate not as was expected of him. Those few who had managed to get through the almost impenetrable barrier of Chaliapin's mistrust of people, or those to whom he had taken a liking because they were good at their jobs, were of a different opinion. 'A great deal is said about Chaliapin, and he is often censured for his abruptness and his neurotic whims,' wrote Karl Walz, for sixty-five years a technical director at the Bolshoi Theatre. 'Chaliapin rarely gets annoyed for personal reasons. His bad moods are usually associated with the interpretation of some part or other, and these are grounds which entirely justify the indignation they provoke. In his private life Fedor Ivanovich is a totally different person; he is most amiable.'[199] 'Much has been said and written about the clashes he had with conductors, colleagues and singing partners,' recalls Strakhova-Ermans, who had known Chaliapin from his early youth. 'Yes, there were incidents which he would always regret later, once he had calmed down. He was short-tempered, but the real cause of all the misunderstandings was Chaliapin's total intolerance of "hacks", specially in artistic matters.

'With his knack of making an impeccable analysis of any work he was performing in its totality, and not just within the limits of his own role, this super-artist was indeed sometimes at variance with his conductors or partners, or rather, I would say that they did not always keep pace with him; they had a different way of understanding and feeling what was written in the score. This would result in a scandal, and he, making a gesture of helplessness with his arms, would ask in all innocence: "What is the matter?" When he found himself sharing the stage with a really great artist, he would spring up as if electrified to show the full radiance of his genius, and there was no talk of scandals.... Chaliapin was said to be rather miserly, but that is untrue. He was by nature a kind and responsive man, and I know of instances when he gave generous help to those who had asked for his assistance. But, from the years of poverty in his childhood and in his youth, he had retained a feeling of "respect for the five-kopeck piece", of which he had been so short then. He never forgot those times and, I might add, was still afraid even after he had amassed relatively large wealth: just suppose that he became unable to work – poverty would set in and his family was, after all, a large one!'[200] To be accurate, he had two families. The second one, rapidly expanding, had started in 1910, when the first one was already sizeable. For several years Chaliapin supported as many as twelve to fourteen people at one time. 'Wherever you look, there are children,' he wrote to Gorky in 1913. 'In Peter* there are four of them† and in Moscow five. True, in Peter only two of them are mine, but I love these little imps, all of them, the others as well as my own.'[201] Chaliapin's attitude to his children was remarkable. He continued to look after them even when they were grown up and had children of their own. The correspondence of the

---

* Colloquial abbreviation of Petersburg.

† Maria Valentinovna Petzold, with whom Chaliapin was living and who eventually became his second wife, already had two children from her first marriage.

Chaliapin with his children in the country, 1912.

singer with his eldest daughter, Irina, published in the Soviet Union, gives eloquent proof of this. 'It seems that Mama* is coming to Russia soon,' he wrote to her from America in 1926. 'I am awaiting her instructions and will soon send every member of the family some money to live on.'[202]

Fred Gaisberg wrote that during the hard times suffered by Russian emigration, 'Chaliapin and his family were always most generous and considerate to their servants and helpers, and were in turn worshipped by them all. I remember the number of quiet old people who haunted the servants' quarters of the Chaliapin home, seemingly with very little to do and yet living on his bounty. At their table there were always two or three elderly governesses or nurses whom they would call "Nyaniushka" or some other affectionate diminutive.'[203]

One of the many 'Chaliapin stories' wounded the singer particularly deeply, and he never forgot it. The incident in question seemed to split Russia into two camps and was discussed by everybody. No one could remain indifferent, and everyone considered it his duty to express approval or disapproval, not just of the motives but of the action itself, although Chaliapin had in fact taken no part in it. On the evening of January 6th, 1911, Nicholas II went to hear *Boris Godunov* at the Mariinsky Theatre. That morning the Tsar had conferred on Chaliapin the highest honour a singer could aspire to at that time, the title of 'Soloist to His Majesty'. These two events must be borne in mind. The fact that they happened to coincide was later used to draw unjustifiably far-reaching conclusions.

Busy with the preparations for this crucial première, and as always feeling very nervous, Chaliapin did not notice anything unusual when he arrived at the theatre a few hours before the beginning of the performance. Absorbed in his own thoughts and oblivious of his surroundings, he quickly went to his dressing-room and proceeded to get ready for his entrance. The dress rehearsal had taken place the previous evening, and although it had been an enormous success for Chaliapin, he

---

* Chaliapin's first wife, Iola Tornaghi, who was abroad at that time.

was still not satisfied with the production as a whole. His relationship with Meyerhold, who was responsible for the revival of Mussorgsky's opera, was almost hostile. His mood communicated itself to the rest of the cast – there was a feeling of tension behind the scenes. For Meyerhold the situation was rendered all the more bitter by the fact that he regarded Chaliapin as an ideal performer and frequently cited him as an example not only to singers but also to actors. 'After the coronation scene,' Chaliapin recalled later, 'the noise in the auditorium had nothing to do with the opera: people were exchanging greetings, chatting and gossiping. . . .'[204] This seemed odd: the effect of the grandiose crowd scene was usually assured. Also, why were the members of the chorus whispering continually amongst themselves and exchanging glances with one another? Could it be that they, too, thought the production 'squalid and disastrous'? The real reason was quite different: the chorus, who had long been asking the administration to raise their pension, had decided not to wait any longer and, taking advantage of the Tsar's presence, to deliver a petition to him. After the third act, right at the start of the interval, when the entire cast, including Chaliapin, had taken their bows and were beginning to disperse to their respective dressing-rooms, loud voices in the auditorium suddenly demanded: 'The national anthem!' Behind the curtain, the chorus immediately started to sing a capella 'Bozhe, tsarya khrani' (God Save the Tsar). There was chaos as the musicians, who had already left the orchestra pit, rushed back, the curtain went up and the chorus, down on their knees and their arms stretched out in the direction of the Imperial box, continued to sing with mounting fervour. At the sound of the anthem, Chaliapin and the other soloists returned to the stage. It was the rule that when the national anthem was being sung all the singers had to join in it. Seeing the chorus on their knees, Chaliapin started to back away, but some of the members blocked his exit. 'Chaliapin looked in the direction of my box,' recalled Telyakovsky, 'as though asking what he should do. I shook my head to show that he could see for himself what was happening. Whatever he did would be wrong. If he knelt, people would ask why he had done so. And if he did not kneel – why was he the only one to remain standing? If he continued to stand while everyone else was kneeling, this would be construed as a political gesture. So Chaliapin knelt on one knee.'[205] After repeating the national anthem six times, the chorus finally made a move towards the wings – it was time to resume the performance. 'The whole episode', writes Chaliapin, 'left me with a very unpleasant impression.... But I felt neither shame nor humiliation for having knelt or not knelt before the Tsar. Not a whit of it. It did not even enter the remotest cells of my brain that I had done something improper, betrayed something, departed from my dignity or my instinct for liberty. For all my failings, I have never been and will never be either a slave or a lackey ... I was not kneeling *before the Tsar* [Chaliapin's italics]. On the whole, I did not feel any involvement in the incident.'[206] The next day Chaliapin left for an engagement in Monte Carlo and the event completely slipped his mind. He had no idea that all this would lead to rifts with many people, insults, persecutions, and sleepless nights, culminating in a nervous breakdown and the desire to leave Russia forever. To Chaliapin's 'sad and indignant astonishment' the tales about what had happened were snowballing, new 'facts' being added all the time. Every Russian newspaper (and later on some European ones as well) was talking of 'the unprecedented and impulsive outburst of patriotism and the demonstration of devotion to the monarchy which had been so unexpected and so stirring'. Chaliapin was naturally accorded pride of place in these reports. No one was interested in the fact that the chorus' 'impulsive outburst' had been dictated by purely material interests: no mention was made of the other soloists who had also knelt. No, the main theme was that of 'the peasant singer, now Soloist to His Majesty', who had demonstrated the inveterate love of the simple man for his Tsar.

'Not a single paper,' affirmed Telyakovsky, 'reported the story as it really happened. The more that was written, the more entangled the whole thing became. Chaliapin, moreover, utterly weary, harassed and anxious to justify himself about something of which he was, in actual fact, completely innocent, talked to representatives of the press from various countries about it in such a way that, by omitting some details and muddling up others, he actually laid himself open to further attacks.'[207] By now, Chaliapin was under a constant deluge of anonymous abuse and threats from all quarters. A group of Russian students, coming face to face with him on a train in the south of France, shouted 'Lackey! Rogue! Traitor!' His close friend the painter Valentin Serov sent him a curt and offensive letter breaking off all further contact between them. Suddenly Chaliapin felt himself ostracised. With few exceptions, everyone had turned against him. Telyakovsky was one of the first to rescue Chaliapin from his sad reflections on people and on Russian mores. He did everything possible to pacify the singer, tried to persuade him not to pay attention to 'hissing vipers' and to forget the very idea of cancelling his contract with the Imperial Theatres. After receiving the director's letter, Chaliapin began to calm down, although he still would not return to Russia. 'I think that they will cause scandals and trouble for me there, and since my nerves are already strained to breaking point, I am terribly afraid of myself: I mean I am afraid I might do something horribly silly,' he answered.[208]

Chaliapin had every reason to worry: he well knew what his fellow-countrymen were capable of. His apprehension was not unfounded – during a performance of *Don Quixote* in Paris there was whistling in the audience, accompanied by insulting adjectives about the singer. It turned out the shouting came from a group of Russian emigrés. Chaliapin was extremely upset. 'He struggled through the rest of the performance somewhat apathetically.'[209]

'I shall not try to hide the fact', said Chaliapin in an interview with the newspaper *L'Intransigeant* 'that I feel very hurt. First and foremost because I am the victim of a mistake and of vile slander. Moreover, I cannot reconcile myself to the idea that my friends believed the slander without even giving me a hearing. I was born a peasant, went barefoot and hungry, my mother died of starvation. . . . Such things cannot be forgotten. . . . And then came success. I asked for nothing. The title of Soloist to His Majesty, or the Cross of the Légion d'Honneur – all these descended on me as gifts from heaven—and I frankly admit that I received these marks of distinction with pleasure. I looked upon this as the crowning of my artistic career. Is that a crime?'[210]

Russia is a country where everything takes on extreme, and therefore distorted, forms. People seldom respect the limits of civilised conversation when expressing divergent views, especially in the domain of ideology. Any exchange with someone of a different opinion is usually brief and generally ends in uncompromising hostility. In Chaliapin's case, no one cared about the fact that he had nothing to do with politics and did not belong to any party. Left-wing, anti-government attitudes of mind seem to be an essential part of the intellectual elite's way of thinking. Whichever government is in power does not matter as much as what upbringing and fashion dictate. A. Amphiteatrov, for instance, an ardent admirer of Chaliapin, sent the singer an angry, accusing letter in which he severed all relations with him. Unable to contain his righteous indignation, he called the Tsar a butcher and a murderer and advised Chaliapin not to sink so low as to make people 'laugh at him with scorn'. Amphiteatrov circulated his letter to all the newspapers and to many private individuals. High-mindedness and loyalty to the ideals of freedom were thus forcefully displayed. True, at the moment of victory for these very same popular masses, whose bitter fate Russian liberals debated so passionately while sitting by their warm fires in their cosy drawing-rooms, Amphiteatrov, like many others, quickly lost interest in the problems of equality and justice and emigrated abroad. Neither is it important whether Chaliapin was in favour of the monarchy or of revolution, whether he was willing or not to sing the anthem on his knees, or even what he himself said and thought about this. 'He was too large a figure,' justly observed Telyakovsky. 'His fame was great and his name legendary, and because of this the right and left tried to fit him to their own views, giving their own interpretation of his true inclinations.'[211] As in the case of *A Life for the Tsar*, Chaliapin found himself at the centre of a political argument and was not allowed to be 'just a singer'.

The struggle for the right to claim his allegiance continued in Russia (by then the USSR) even after Chaliapin's death. The recent transfer of his remains from Paris to Moscow (1984) is further proof of this.

In these unhappy times, one question preoccupied Chaliapin more than any other: What did Gorky think of all this? But Gorky, then living in Capri, remained silent. In *Mask and Soul* Chaliapin says he decided to obtain his friend's permission before going to see him. 'Gorky answered that he was really upset by the rumours.... He therefore wanted me to write to him to explain what had actually happened. I did so. Gorky answered, requesting me to go to him without delay.'[212] In fact, Gorky did not ask for any explanations; he believed the rumours and wrote to Chaliapin: 'You evidently do not realise what a wicked deed you have committed; you are not ashamed of yourself – we had better not see each other, and don't come to me.'[213] Only after Chaliapin had sent him a detailed account of the events of that ill-fated evening did Gorky agree to a meeting. According to the memoirs of one of Gorky's wives, the actress Maria Andreeva, Chaliapin arrived 'depressed, worn out, on the brink of suicide. It was painful to see him. Fear made him wonder if everyone wasn't against him.'[214] Talking to Gorky brought a certain relief, although the experience left permanent scars. 'Under the influence of unrelenting distress,' wrote Chaliapin later, 'I acted contrary to my real personal feeling; I refused to participate in the tercentenary celebrations of the House of Romanov. I behaved like this only because the memory of the persecution I had undergone had deprived me of my composure. The thought that it might be repeated in any form made me faint-hearted.'[215]

Whenever Chaliapin had to discuss the conditions of his contract with Telyakovsky, he brought up the question of his future repertoire. They also frequently talked about it during the season. Chaliapin would call on the director at home after a performance and stay long past midnight.

During one of these visits he expressed the wish to sing the role of the Demon in the opera of the same name by Anton Rubinstein. Although he had already sung it early in his career,

the singer's suggestion was not at first received with great
enthusiasm. The part, written for a baritone, was one of the
most popular in Russian music. Chaliapin's contemporaries
heard famous Russian and European singers in it: Leonid
Yakovlev, Pavel Khokhlov, Joachim Tartakov, Mattia Battistini, Eugenio Giraldoni, Titta Ruffo. A beautiful vocal timbre,
an ideal smooth sound – 'noble', as it was then called – was
what was required above all from the performer of the Demon.
In Rubinstein's opera, based on one of Lermontov's greatest
poems, it is the lyrical motives which are most eloquently
expressed. At the heart of the work lies the Demon's aspiration
to find redemption in the love of a mortal woman, Tamara.
The contrast between the rebellious Demon, who refuses to
accept the laws of heaven, and the pure Tamara, ignorant of
devilish misrule and mental anguish, is perhaps the only thing
left of the poem in the opera. The music of *The Demon* is
uneven. It contains some superb pages, but they are interspersed
with a good deal of rhetoric and transitional passages. *The
Demon* owed its success to the charming melodies which in
most places embellish the parts of the main characters and
to an emotional and sincere representation of love, nostalgia,
loneliness and spiritual anguish. What innovations could Chaliapin bring to this over-sung role, which had become a comfortable tradition? Even with the great freedom of his upper register,
some alterations were unavoidable. Was it really worth the risk?

'This was truly a terrible moment, like sitting an examination,' wrote Vlas Doroshevich, describing the atmosphere at
the Bolshoi Theatre on the day of the first night. 'If Chaliapin
had been bad in a bass part, everyone would have said "He's
ill – it's an accident," because everyone knows from the newspapers that Chaliapin is a bass. The public dislike dare-devils.
The Philistine is himself timid. Daring seems to him an impertinence and an insult. And when a dare-devil breaks his back,
there is no greater pleasure for the public. They have learnt
from the newspapers that Chaliapin is not a baritone. You can't
fool them!'[216] A number of musicians also had doubts about
this choice. 'Even assuming', they said, 'that the part of the
Demon is not incompatible with Chaliapin's vocal abilities,

what about the natural timbre of his voice?' Everyone knew and admired Chaliapin's virtuosity in colouring his intonation with innumerable nuances; he did it in such a way that the listener was left in no doubt about the true meaning of any musical idea. The recognition of timbre as a psychological nuance, as an eloquent and not just a physical attribute of tone, was now firmly associated with Chaliapin's art. What worried both his admirers and his detractors was something else: Chaliapin was a typical basso cantante, and however easily he managed the upper notes of the baritone repertoire, his voice could sound normal and full-blooded only within the limits of the bass tessitura. The care lavished by great singers of the past on the natural texture of their voices is well-known: in many respects the character of their interpretations depended on it, as well as the logic of their acting. In Chaliapin's case contemporaries often mentioned how the singer invariably endeavoured to 'start from the voice' in his stage creations. It meant that undertaking to sing the Demon would cost him no small amount of effort in order to 'justify' a bass sound in the role whose emotional and psychological structure is delimited by the resources of a different register. But many critics, including someone whom Chaliapin greatly respected – Professor Nikolai Kashkin – found this also unacceptable. 'We do not rank the part of the Demon among the best in Chaliapin's repertoire,' he declared after the première.* 'It seems to us that the overall complexion of the part does not quite match the quality of the singer's voice, and although he sings everything very freely, with extraordinary art, the resulting impression is nevertheless something like the one produced, for instance, by a very skilful double-bass player playing a piece written for the cello.'[217] In the three arias of the Demon that Chaliapin recorded, his voice sounds completely natural and does not prompt any criticism, but it was probably different in the theatre. A 1919 review says, for instance, 'The first phrases of Chaliapin–the Demon, if one takes the term "baritone" in its old, customary sense, initially startle the ear somewhat, but the versatility of the voice and the

---

* Chaliapin's début in the role of the Demon at the Bolshoi Theatre took place on January 16th, 1904.

extraordinary expressiveness of the phrasing make it quickly adapt.'[218] As if to contradict Kashkin, Semyon Kruglikov wrote: 'Chaliapin's high notes are free and brilliant, and what is low for a baritone sounds bright and clear for this bass, because each phrase, and this is the main thing, has been touched by exceptional talent. All right, you heard "Don't cry, child . . ."* half a tone lower; some minor alterations were made here and there; some of the top notes were left out. But that does not worry me at all now. It is of course a pity that the bass could not avoid all this. But it would be an even greater pity for Chaliapin not to sing the Demon, not to show how he can be sung and how he can be portrayed, what character one can give him. I am not only talking of course about external appearance but about everything he did in *The Demon*. . . . For the first time the figure of the Demon was before you – powerful, fantastic and original. Nobody had ever conceived it like this before.'[219] 'Chaliapin's talent', says another review, 'has given back to Lermontov's sublime poem its sublime meaning. Chaliapin was not a pretty boy, nor a voluptuous seducer, like the previous Demons, but a real creature of darkness, the incarnation of the damned, the external exile.'[220] Everyone was by then used to finding that reviews of Chaliapin's performances devoted a great deal of space to detailed descriptions of the physical appearance of the character he was playing. In this case too, music critics were at pains to find colourful and surprising details which could illuminate for the reader the art of this actor of genius and the way he never failed to bring the unique magic of the theatre to the operatic stage. It is also interesting to note that in evaluating the singer's work, they generally remarked on its links with Lermontov's poem and Vrubel's painting, whereas Rubinstein's opera tended to be referred to as merely providing Chaliapin with a good opportunity to search for a new Demon. One cannot help remembering how articles about his Mephistopheles and his Mefistofele named Goethe first rather than Gounod or Boito.† But if the comparison with a

---

* One of the Demon's arias.
† Leonid Sobinov, who sang with Chaliapin in Berlin in 1907 (in Boito's *Mefis-tofele*), told an acquaintance: 'After the performance the Kaiser decided to con-

literary character was undoubtedly to Chaliapin's advantage, references to Vrubel were not so unanimously well received. Vrubel's art, imbued through and through with the dramatic spirit of the period, its aches and hopes, was almost totally rejected by contemporaries. His paintings seemed utterly alien not only to the faithful supporters of academic order (which was only natural and to be expected) but also to people of progressive views. Among Vrubel's many detractors were Gorky, Benois, Stasov, Lanceret ... it would be quicker to list those who were not openly critical of him. On the rare occasions when Vrubel's works were exhibited, sarcasm and at times even anger at such 'decadent rubbish' (Stasov's words)[221] were quite commonplace in press reviews. The Nizhni-Novgorod exhibition of 1896, where Chaliapin first saw Vrubel's paintings, has already been mentioned in the first chapter of this book. At that time, Mamontov was almost alone in recognising him as one of the greatest Russian artists.

Mamontov's mantle was taken up by Diaghilev, who invited the ostracised painter to participate in the 1902 'World of Art' exhibition. The controversy which instantly flared was conducted with the same bitterness and jeering as a few years before in Nizhni-Novgorod. Only this time on the wall instead of the 'Princesse Lointaine' hung the 'Fallen Demon' – the picture all the critics later would allude to when they spoke of Vrubel's influence on Chaliapin.

He willingly confirmed the truth of their obervations: 'My Demon is taken from Vrubel,' he declared in *Mask and Soul*. Mamontov's lessons had not been wasted: the singer was quick to discern in Vrubel's almost universally derided masterpiece a tragic cry of loneliness. His Demon reflected the bitter thoughts of neglected genius on the clash between the individual and the rest of the world. Only someone with Chaliapin's artistic sense could proclaim his admiration for Vrubel's art in the face of the enormous chorus of dissenting voices (which included some of his own friends). But others were slow to realise their mistake.

gratulate the leading performers in person. The Kaiser talked to Fedor for a long time and said to him straight off that it was such a pity Goethe could not see him in this role.' (Leonid Vitalevich Sobinov. *Letters*, Moscow 1970, vol. 1, p. 411.)

Chaliapin as the Demon in Rubinstein's opera *The Demon*. Painted by A. Golovin in 1906.

Benois was one of the first to do so and mentioned Vrubel many times in his articles and books. 'I charged Vrubel', he wrote, 'with a certain amount of affectation in his desire to "play the genius". I was wrong. Vrubel was without question a pure and sincere artist, and he really is a genius. But what I mistook for affectation, the grimace which distorts the face of his art, is not devised; it is not the eccentricity of a man who tries to startle the crowds at any price but the mirroring of the burning suffering which has dogged all of Vrubel's creative life.'[222] And in the obituary he wrote in 1910, Benois seemed to continue with the same theme: 'All his life Vrubel offered himself to everyone. By constantly returning to the "Demon" in his creations, he was only giving away the secret of his mission. He himself was the Demon, the beautiful Fallen Angel, for whom the world was an endless joy and an endless torture, for whom human intercourse was both fraternally close and hopelessly distant.'[223] Naturally the controversy provoked by Vrubel's picture flared up again and affected the judgements passed on Chaliapin. Those who did not accept Vrubel's work also disapproved of the character created by the singer. 'If the Demon,' wrote a critic, 'appeared to Tamara in the form Chaliapin has given him, she would simply faint or die of fright.'[224]

Some people tried to show that the influence of Vrubel was minimal and therefore could not mar the enormous effect produced by the singer. However, neither Chaliapin nor Vrubel needed any excusing, and the most perceptive section of the Russian intelligentsia understood this. 'We do not mean', wrote a Moscow newspaper, 'that Chaliapin took the entire character from Vrubel; but his Demon is very Vrubelian in his titanic force. The striking individuality and the power of Chaliapin's own imagination ensured that his Demon, though related to Vrubel's, was entirely original.'[225]

Rubinstein's opera begins with a prologue in which only the Demon and an Angel take part. A storm is raging in the mountains of the Caucasus. Dark clouds scurry across the sky; furious gusts of wind rock the trees; rivers burst their banks. Only the gigantic cliffs stand firm: no one can disturb their peace. The wailings of infernal spirits can be heard over the stormy din.

They know who has conjured the elements and impatiently wait for their master. 'Above snowy peaks, nocturnal darkness. Through the gloom irregularly angular shapes of glaciers are softly outlined. You sense, rather than see, a presence on the left crag, while the invisible chorus sing their hymns. But light pierces through the thick fog and reveals for the first time the figure of the Demon – mighty, fantastic, primeval,' wrote Semyon Kruglikov.[226] Rejected by God and humans, he cannot find refuge anywhere. He has long tired of sowing destruction and evil: everything obeys his commands; nothing can resist him. Mighty nature, the work of the Creator, does not inspire in him any admiration – on the contrary, this 'damned world' is hateful to the Demon. 'There is something elemental in the very sound of his voice, cursing the universe,' recalled another eyewitness; 'there is crushing contempt and sarcasm in every word, in every note.'[227]

'The Demon's first phrases', recounted Evgenia Zbrueva, who was singing the role of the Angel, 'made the whole audience prick up their ears. A dazzling white light illuminated the clouds and I appeared, as if descending from a great height. The duet – or to be more precise, the exchange of lines, one after another – begins. I thought that I would find it difficult to sing. I was wearing a structure weighing no less than a pood* (a corset with four wings: two pointing downwards and two pointing upwards), but once I had started singing, I no longer felt its heaviness. I forgot about the theatre, the public and my wings – all I could see was the real Demon in front of me. I heard his voice – powerful, impassioned and imperious – and I answered him, feeling and realising at the same time that I had to answer just as I did. Such was the hypnotic force which emanated from this man of genius.'[228]

'There is something of the fantastic in the whole interpretation: the proud profile; the deeply sunken eyes burning with an ardent glow; the tightly compressed, snake-like line of the lips. A mop of tousled hair, heavy, thick and black as soot, frames a handsome face with an irresistibly attractive enigmatic

---

* 16 kg, or 36 lb, approximately.

air. Many thoughts have lain on this lofty brow; a sea of suffering has devastated this pale countenance, with its fixed look of severity. It is the figure of Prometheus. This is who Chaliapin resembled when, against the gloomy background of the Caucasian mountains, his huge and massive figure, shrouded in darkness, materialised before the spectators. The Demon seemed to have been hewn out of this rock, to be part of it. The bare left arm, strong and muscular, is lying on the rock, and its clenched fingers convulsively snatch at stones, as if he were making a terrific effort of will to restrain himself under unbearable torture. The admirable gesture of placing the other arm behind the head is full of immense, boundless despair, and everything is stamped with kingly majesty and conscious strength. It is a live sculpture carved by the chisel of a master.'[229]

The Angel tries to persuade the Demon to repent; then the recreant will be forgiven. But why aspire after a doubtful heavenly bliss if in exchange you have to renounce your freedom and be untrue to yourself? Enraged, the Demon-Chaliapin draws himself up to his full height and cuts short the Angel's attempts to reconcile him with heaven. 'Silence ... slave!' The Angel, frightened, hides behind the rocks.... The Demon expects thunder and lightning in retaliation. But the skies remain silent; his challenge is not taken up.... He slowly sits down on a rock. Storm clouds obscure his now sagging figure; as the orchestra plays the final coda, the curtain comes down.'[230]

In the second scene the Demon looks down on the picturesque valley of the river Aragva. The ancient castle of Prince Gudal stands on its bank. Maidens descend into the Aragva to fetch water, among them Gudal's daughter, Tamara. The Demon is moved by the sight of the young princess and cannot take his eyes off her. Tamara is seized by a sudden and inexplicable fear: she seems to hear a strange voice. Who is calling her? Who is promising her eternity and worldly power? Strange words of love, unlike any human ones, were inflaming her heart, stirring her and robbing her of peace. 'There was indeed in his voice some bewitching power, some magic. The Demon opened up before Tamara a vision of extraordinary splendour and became himself intoxicated by the beauty of the spectacle which was unfolding. His eyes blazed with rapture; the first gleams of brightness illuminated his mournful face. Here, an unbroken stream of flowing and soft sounds poured out. The breathing was imperceptible; there was no unevenness or careless jolt which might have ruined this radiant picture.'[231] The conductor Daniil Pokhitonov compared Chaliapin's singing to the work of a painter, and heard Rimsky-Korsakov call it 'a sound to contemplate'.[232]

A rich caravan travels along the mountain path: Prince Sinodal is hurrying towards his bride, Tamara. A landslide bars the way, delaying the impatient young lover and forcing him to camp in this wild gorge. The Demon appears. From the cliff top he scrutinises the face of his rival, who will not dream of his beautiful bride much longer. Tartars are on the prowl, and hardly anyone will escape death. 'When the figure of the Demon stands on a rock above the sleeping prince,' recalled A. Ossovsky, 'and threatens, "The darkness of the night is fraught with danger, but your enemy is right here!", Chaliapin imparts a real demonic force to the words. This is what fate has decreed. And indeed when the Demon returns a few moments later as a silent vision, he is now towering over Sinodal's dead body like the image of fate itself – terrifying and aloof. The silent scene is extraordinary. Not a single word, only the pose and the rigid expression, but the impression produced is colossal....'[233]

In Gudal's castle a great feast is being prepared for Tamara's wedding. The bridegroom is late, but his messenger assures Gudal that he will soon arrive. Loud cries of despair suddenly rend the air. The stunned guests watch the body of Sinodal being carried into the great hall. The bride bitterly laments over her lifeless lover: 'All is finished; the hopes are ended.' From the corner of the sky a soft, soothing voice rings out. 'Who are you?' asks the girl, but the only answer is: 'I will return every night and stay till morning.' 'Here is the exile from heaven, the fallen angel; here is the Demon himself,' wrote Victor Kolomiitsov. 'The dream now has tangible form; illusion has become reality. How much inhuman evil and diabolical hatred there was in the voice of the Demon when he was by himself or when he angrily rebutted the radiant cherub, heaven's envoy!

But my God, how this voice changed when the Demon, transported by a different, long-forgotten feeling, promises Tamara "golden dreams"! How much sadness, how much tender and beguiling passion in these unearthly sounds! And the oath, which could rock the universe, and at the end the hopelessness of his despair! Where were we yesterday – was it really at the opera?'[234]

In great distress, Tamara begs her father to let her enter a convent.

Love for the beautiful princess has transformed the Demon: immortality and universal power have lost all meaning for him. He has only one wish now: to be with Tamara and through her to find salvation. Nothing can prevail against him, not even the walls of the nunnery. He is not afraid to enter a place where God rules; his soul is ready for redemption.

With Chaliapin in the title role, the scene with the Angel at the gates of the nunnery became one of the highlights of the work. The singer's partners were themselves as astonished as the public and the critics by this 'volcano of emotions, this storm of passions of such force and intensity that nothing could resist them'. 'It was with an absolutely genuine feeling of fear', recalled Evgenia Zbrueva years later, 'that I took a step backwards to let Chaliapin enter Tamara's cell when he rushed towards the entrance I was guarding, saying: "She is mine!" '[235]

In the final scene of the second act, the cloister is silent. Only one window shows a pale flicker of light. It is Tamara's cell. Alas, even here she can find neither peace nor oblivion: the same figure continues to pursue her relentlessly. Always and everywhere, during her prayers and in her sleep, Tamara hears the strange voice, summoning her to mysterious, faraway places. Who is it? Suddenly, the Demon is standing in the doorway, and pleasant curiosity gives way to terror. The Demon tells her who and what he is: the spirit of evil, heaven's foe and the bane of nature, hated and cursed by everyone on earth. But since he has encountered Tamara, everything has changed. With a single word she can bring the Demon back to goodness and to God. He sees the whole of paradise in Tamara's eyes. The nun is perturbed. Such language is dangerous – God might hear it!

The Demon answers with a wry smile: 'He will not look at us; he is busy with heaven, not with earth.' 'And punishment and the torments of hell?' cries out Tamara. 'But you will be there with me,' he answers. The Demon's sincere and passionate words conquer Tamara: she feels pity for the 'proud outcast'; she is ready to believe him and to follow him wherever he commands. Let him only swear that he will forget his evil intentions, repent, make his peace with heaven. Let him start to believe in goodness, to love, to pray and to repent what he has done.

Lermontov's oath of the Demon is one of the summits of Russian poetry. The strict rhythm of the verse, the profundity of the words and the precision of their choice, the spirit of abnegation and the faith which pervade them, have made this section of the poem particularly dear to the heart of every cultured Russian. 'I swear by the first day of Creation, I swear by its last day....' But in Rubinstein's music there is not even a flicker of the powerful and sombre fire of this inspired poem. Insipid and dreary, it lacks colour and sounds stilted. From the opera's very first performance, the oath had never excited a great deal of interest. This time, too, no one was expecting any revelations from it. But at the dress rehearsal, noted Salina, 'Chaliapin amazed everyone with his interpretation. What he did was extraordinary and passed comprehension. It was as if a vortex of the elements was swirling by out of the chaos of the universe, and it gave the oath a ring of menace and despair. Chaliapin sang, scanning every word, and as he sang, all of us on stage were rooted to the spot stunned while the orchestra, continuing to play, rose as one man from their seats to look at him in astonishment and enthusiasm. When he had finished, carried away by a common impulse, we all started to applaud and shout; the musicians stamped their feet and tapped their bows on their instruments, and this was an ovation without precedent, a tribute of our admiration for his genius. It is not hard to imagine how much I was waiting for the last act at the actual performance. When, after my aria "The night is silent, the night is warm", I turned round and saw in the doorway of my cell the tall, sombre figure with its tousled dark curls above a pale, lofty brow: when I saw the strangely arched eyebrows and below them the severe, piercing glance of these eyes, enormously enlarged by special make-up, my cry, Tamara's cry, was for real, not acting. I froze, convinced at that moment that the evil apparition which had arisen from another world was going to harm me, and I trembled with the realisation that neither praying nor imploring for mercy would save me from his power. I was shaking as he came towards me, and I was concentrating all my nervous energy on trying to shield myself from his burning glance, not to hear the words "Love me", which sounded menacingly. And when Chaliapin took me into his arms, drained of strength from genuine emotion, I slipped from his embrace, which was so terrifying for me, and fell at his feet, unable to sing the last few words.... That is the sort of Demon Chaliapin was.'[236]

Other accounts, among them Yuri Engel's, confirm Salina's reaction. 'Everything in the Demon and around him was trembling and singing, the sort of trembling and singing which can happen only in the face of perdition.'[237] This foreboding of final perdition, just when happiness so long awaited by the Demon is finally near, made a strong impression on the public. 'One had to see and to hear', wrote a critic, 'how he finished the line in the oath "I want to believe in good" to understand and appreciate all the versatility of this wonderful singer's talent. As he was pronouncing these words, he seemed to shrivel all over and his face took on a gloomy, dejected expression.'[238] But heaven proves stronger; his self-denial is in vain. At the Demon's very first kiss, Tamara falls dead. 'Cursing both God and the universe, the Demon rushes out of the cell with the force of a storm. He cut a superb and awe-inspiring figure at this fateful moment, frenzied and ready to smash everything in his way at the prospect of renewed torments for all eternity.'[239] The audience's noisy cheers, steadily rising during the performance, turned by the end into 'collective madness'. 'Howls, sobs, shouts, stamping of feet accompanied me as far as the exit doors,' recalled an opera-goer.[240]

The same scene was repeated when Chaliapin sang *The Demon* at the Petersburg Mariinsky Theatre, two years later.

In spite of his nervous state on the eve of the première ('... Chaliapin was a sorry sight; he was as dejected as a child'[241]) it was a stunning success. 'This was one of those rare, unforgettable performances from which you go home joyful, filled with wonder and rapture at the power and magnitude of real art: words cannot be found to formulate the fullness of one's impressions, to express one's gratitude to the singer for the magical gift he has received from heaven.'[242] Reviews of this sort became more and more frequent. It seemed that the most outspoken and rigorous critics fell under his spell as soon as he appeared on stage. They, who had until recently subjected Chaliapin's performance to meticulous analysis, were now turning into naive and enthusiastic spectators, who frankly admitted that they had neither the ability nor the means to explain the cause of their enthusiasm. In Kharkov, where the singer was making guest appearances, they wrote: 'This man is capable of everything. His soul, his voice contain every emotion, every nuance and every sound: sombre and profound, solemn and prayerful, impetuous and heroic, cheerful and jolly, gentle and tenderly sad, like the complaint of a lonely soul, like the lullaby a pining mother sings to her child. And above all, in everything, the stamp of genius, the stamp of pure beauty.'[243] 'Is there anything new to add to what has already been said many times about the vocal and dramatic sides of his magnificent interpretation? Any work of classical literature can be read and re-read many times, and the pleasure loses none of its strength; on the contrary, it seems to grow. Chaliapin's acting possesses the same properties. There are no roles in which Chaliapin would be bad; his discrimination, his artistic flair protect him against any wrong move, any false touch.'[244]

From the early part of the century Chaliapin was greeted everywhere in Russia with cries of rapture and endless applause. Everything connected with his name was the object of tireless curiosity. The faceless mob is usually quite tactless in its manifestations of interest and treats any event, even a sad one, as just another sight to gape at. At Chekhov's funeral in Moscow on July 9th, 1904, a newspaper reported: 'A huge wreath of gorgeous roses, orchids and lilies attracted general attention.

Chaliapin, 1915.

Everyone rushed to look at the ribbons. They bore the following inscription: "In great sorrow. Chaliapin. To dear, unforgettable A. P. Chekhov."[245] 'From the Nikolayevski Station to the Art Theatre,' said Gorky later, 'I walked among the crowd and I heard them talking about me, and saying that Chaliapin looked like a minister of the church, that having his hair cut did not suit him ... but no one said a word about Chekhov. Wherever I and Chaliapin showed our faces, we were both immediately subjected to persistent staring and touching. It was unbearably distressing. Chaliapin was crying and started to swear: "And it's for that scum that he had lived, for them, all his teaching and exhorting!" I took him out of the cemetery. Once we had got into our carriage the crowd surrounded us, smiling and looking at us. Someone – one in a million – shouted: "Go away! This is indecent!" But of course they would not go.'[246]

Chaliapin's fantastic, unprecedented success at home was given an additional boost by the reports of his fame abroad. From 1901 onwards, after his triumphant visit to La Scala, Chaliapin regularly sang in various European countries. Milan, Rome, Monte Carlo, Orange, Berlin, Paris followed one after another.

Chaliapin retained particularly warm memories of his visits to the French capital. They began in April 1907 when Sergei Diaghilev invited him to perform in the historical Russian concerts. In *Pages from My Life* Chaliapin writes that he was immediately attracted by Diaghilev's idea and that his answer was unconditional and positive. Moreover, he had no difficulty in visualising what others thought a doubtful enterprise: 'This was the start of something serious.'[247]

It seems likely, however, that these observations were made by Chaliapin much later, when not only the concerts but also the Russian seasons which followed them in Paris and London had brought him secure universal acclaim. But there is evidence – for instance – in the correspondence of Sobinov, whom Diaghilev repeatedly tried to involve in his plan, that at the time 'Chaliapin was not very keen on the project and did not show any great eagerness towards it.'[248] Chaliapin pertinently remarked about Diaghilev: 'There was almost more movement and life around him than on all the streets of Paris.'[249]

The energy, the breadth of vision, the enterprise and the boldness of Sergei Pavlovich Diaghilev are undeniable, but more than business acumen was needed here. Artistic taste, great erudition, an understanding of the problems of contemporary art as well as the demands of the public were also essential. Diaghilev's sense of time and place was one of his most valuable assets. Like all great reformers and military commanders, he knew that in making the right decision timing was all-important. Iron logic and certainty of intent guided most of his actions. Diaghilev faced the hazards of fate without panic, and no obstacle could stop him. The unshakeable confidence he had in the rightness of his views made him invulnerable to even his most powerful enemies. Chaliapin could not help noticing such energy and such a larger-than-life personality, reminiscent in many ways of Savva Mamontov. Strictly speaking, he had nothing to lose, especially with Scriabin, Rachmaninov, Rimsky-Korsakov and Arthur Nikisch also taking part in the venture. The occasion might warrant his making an exception and he might relax his fee. Instead of the customary 2,000 roubles per performance Chaliapin agreed to 1,200. He had no cause for regret later: he clearly enjoyed himself in Paris, where his invariably cheerful behaviour astonished everybody who knew him.

At times, it even went beyond the limits of propriety: Chaliapin was not well known for his moderation. One day, as Alexandre Benois recalled, 'around midnight Fedor Ivanovich suddenly presented himself to me as God had created him, descending the back stairs from his room to Diaghilev's.'[250] (Most members of the company were staying at the Hôtel Mirabeau.) 'True,' continues Benois, 'it was murderously hot....'

The cause of Chaliapin's undisguised joy was known to many people: 'His love affair with the woman who would one day become his wife and life companion was past the stormy stage.'[251]

Rehearsals took place at the hotel. Accompanied by Diaghilev, 'Chaliapin sometimes sang what he was preparing for the public in a low voice as if to test it, but sometimes also with all the power he then had.'[252]

At the very first concert on May 3rd (16th) Chaliapin received a spectacular ovation. 'The success surpassed all expectations,' reported a Russian correspondent to Petersburg. 'Galitsky's aria and the second scene in Act One of *Prince Igor* were a triumph both for the composer and for Chaliapin. He had to take countless curtain calls; he was applauded by everyone, but especially the ladies, with an enthusiasm unprecedented here. Roses were even thrown to him from the boxes. After Chaliapin had been duly honoured, Artur Nikisch returned to the platform to conduct the last piece: "Kamarinskaya".* At that moment renewed and persistent cries rang out shrilly from the gods: "Chaliapin! Chaliapin!" But Chaliapin had already gone; it was after midnight, and still the stubborn and persistent cries continued from the gods. Then Nikisch, annoyed by this hysterical shouting and very pale, dismissed the orchestra and left the stage himself. . . .'[253]

'Chaliapin was in good form that day and showed himself to the Parisians in all his elemental vigour,' noted Alexandre Benois. 'Somehow he immediately subjugated the audience and put such conviction into his role that, in spite of the tail-coat, the absence of make-up, the restraint in movements and facial expressions imposed by the concert platform, the effect was perfect, vivid and enchanting. He achieved such a success as I don't think the walls of the Académie Nationale de Musique have ever seen.'[254] It must be added in all fairness that Chaliapin was not the only one to earn the Parisians' approval. The concerts won a victory for Russian art as a whole, acting as a magnificent prelude to the many future visits of Russian artists, painters and composers to the West. The doors were now wide open to welcome them. Even before the end of the tour, Diaghilev was deluged with offers to make a regular tradition of the event. The talks began in Paris during the summer of 1907 and culminated in February of the following year with the

---

* Symphonic work by Mikhail Ivanovich Glinka.

signing of a contract for the production of two Russian operas: *Boris Godunov* and *Sadko*. A much broader operatic programme was being planned for 1909, with a repertoire including *The Maid of Pskov* (now renamed *Ivan the Terrible*), *Prince Igor, Ruslan and Ludmilla, Judith* and of course, once again, *Boris Godunov*. For a number of reasons, which have been exposed in detail in many memoirs and studies devoted to Diaghilev, the outcome proved far more modest than had been anticipated. Opera was squeezed out by ballet. But Benois was absolutely right when he wrote years later: 'Deep down, inside the real Diaghilev, there was nothing of the "balletomane"; ballet interested both him and his close friends, but only to the same extent as other theatrical forms and other fields of art in general. We called our periodical *The World of Art*, and it was our wish to cover art as a whole. It is not our fault (and least of all Diaghilev's fault) if in the end everything was reduced to ballet – an enjoyable and splendid branch of art, but a branch nevertheless, in which all of us, and most of all Diaghilev, felt cramped.... Diaghilev, who had started with exhibitions and art books, and then consecrated himself almost exclusively to the theatre, complained to me many times in the last years of his life that his work had been narrowed down and reduced to some sort of ballet management by the vagaries of fate. He made repeated attempts to break free from this specialisation and to widen his programme, if only by including operas in his productions. His last try at this was an operatic production in Monte Carlo in 1924.'[255]

However, for all his perspicacity, Diaghilev had not been able to foresee this. 'The great onslaught of Russian opera' seemed to him to be the major artistic event of the time: recognition and appreciation of the true value of the greatness and beauty of Russian music were long overdue in Europe. He naturally assigned the leading role in this 'campaign' to Chaliapin. To a Petersburg newspaper reporter who asked him, 'Which artists have had the greatest success?', Diaghilev answered: 'Chaliapin and Rimsky-Korsakov.'[256] Diaghilev's verdict is endorsed by the composer himself; in *Chronicles of My Musical Life* one can read: 'The greatest success was reserved for Chaliapin.'[257] Every-

Rimksy-Korsakov drawn by Chaliapin, 1908.

one knew it: when news came shortly before the start of the second Russian season that illness had forced Chaliapin to cut short his performances at La Scala and that he might not be able to attend the dress rehearsal of *Boris Godunov*, the magazine *Teatr i iskusstvo* (Theatre and Art) openly admitted: 'Without Chaliapin, the whole of S. P. Diaghilev's venture loses most, if not all, of its interest.'[258]

After a much-needed period of rest and recuperation in Italy, Chaliapin returned to Russia to open the new season (1907–1908) at the Mariinsky Theatre and get ready for a lengthy tour of America. Further engagements awaited him: Monte Carlo in February, Milan in March and Paris in May. From Paris he would go to America. Chaliapin did not return home for eleven months; he had never been away for so long. The crossing from Le Havre to New York took six days, but thoughts about appearing in the stern land of "businessmen" so preoccupied the singer that he remembered practically nothing of his first journey over the ocean. Chaliapin's notions of America were rather hazy. The picture which emerged from the tales of the few travellers who had visited it was that of a country 'where some fantastically energetic people were making millions upon millions with greater ease and speed than we in Russia could make rope sandals and where they intrepidly built sixty-floor-high towers of Babel'.[259]

The Americans for their part were just as ignorant of Chaliapin as he of them. His arrival had been preceded by announcements that 'one of the strangest personalities at the Metropolitan will be the sensational Russian basso, who acts *Mefistofele* with bare arms and neck and (if rumour does not lie) sings remarkably.'[260] The success earned by Chaliapin in this role was explained by 'the barbaric instinct of his race, together with the artist's careful study of detail'.[261] His knowledge of detail had an equally simple explanation. In the words of *Musical America,* 'he saw so much of hell on earth years since, in his youth, when he toiled and starved in the company of his friend Gorky, that he has earned the right to be regarded as an authority on that subject'.[262] Notwithstanding the fact that Chaliapin and Gorky did not know each other at the time (they only met many years later), almost every article written about Chaliapin's forthcoming visit mentions the name of the writer. In the majority of cases, this friendship with Gorky 'was not considered a good thing'. For instance, the critic, Henry Krehbiel, reviewing the singer's début in *Mefistofele* wrote: 'It calls to mind more than anything else the vulgarity of conduct which his countryman Gorky presents with such disgusting frankness in his pictures of Russian low life.'[263] Some newspapers declared that 'the singer is quite as much of a reformer as the novelist'.[264] Some simply referred to him as an 'ardent revolutionist',[265] others, to the utter bewilderment of American opera lovers, asserted that 'Chaliapin was a functionary of the Government and at the time of the Moscow riots was a member or perhaps head of the terrible Secret Three, whose vote condemned men to death at the far end of the Empire.'[266]

'Chaliapin interviews' also contained some very curious things. He had allegedly given one in Petersburg on June 8th, 1907. What Chaliapin had said proved so 'interesting' that the very next day American readers were able to discover the following facts: 'Like a good many of his compatriots Chaliapin has been in prison. "It was", he explains without any emotion, "the result of a judicial error. They knew that I was a friend of Gorky and I did not conceal my sympathy for those of my unfortunate countrymen who demanded a better regime." '[267] It is perhaps unnecessary to give further examples of 'irreproachable' journalism. Suffice it to say that Chaliapin spent the summer of 1907 in Italy and would therefore have found it very difficult to give an interview in Russia.[268]

No wonder that his mood deteriorated from the very start. One week after the beginning of rehearsals in New York he was writing to Gorky: 'I liked the countryside, but I cannot say the same of the city. The statue personifying liberty has been exiled out of town and stands outside the gates; it is evidently offended and has come out in a rash of dark hatred. In my opinion, her eyes look towards Europe, and she must think that in that faraway place there is some slight hope and that if only she could, she would cross the waves of the ocean to come to us in Europe. Although I have not been here long, I already feel bored. People have no soul here; one's whole existence is at the service of the dollar. I have been to a concert (symphonic) and to the opera. To judge from their stupid faces nobody understands anything, but they all come. Even if they are very interested, they get tired. They are in a sweat from trying so hard to understand whether it's good or bad. There were three rehearsals at the theatre. I controlled myself for two, but at the third I swore and shouted.... In the Brocken scene in *Mefistofele* the costumes are very strange. If I had not been hearing Boito's music with my own ears, no one could have persuaded me that this was an opera house. The girls dance in such costumes as are used in the lowest grade of café-chantant. Poor, poor art.... One ought to get more dollars out of this place. Perhaps this year it won't work, but on the other hand if I am successful, I will fleece this scum – the damn hypocrites!'[269]

Chaliapin's fees did not escape the attention of the press, either. '1,250 dollars for a performance – a salary far in excess of anything previously paid to a bass in the history of opera,'[270] a newspaper complained indignantly. 'Fedor Chaliapin the Russian bass will draw a salary of U.S. $40,000 for his present season with the Metropolitan Opera Company,' calculated another one sadly.[271] The dissatisfaction was, it seems, mutual.

Chaliapin left America feeling humiliated and offended. After his return to Europe and another triumph at La Scala in March 1908 he wrote to Telyakovsky: 'Yes, America is a rotten country and everything they say at home about America is complete and utter nonsense. They talk of American freedom – heaven forbid that Russia should one day be reduced to that kind of freedom. Even breathing freely is difficult there. One spends one's whole life working – working like a convict.... There the sun, the stars, the sky and God – all is forgotten. Love does exist, but only for gold. I am so glad to have left this rough, intellectually worthless country – left it and forever. Even if they offered me fantastic sums to return, I would be delighted to refuse.'[272]

It must be said that Chaliapin eventually revised his opinion of America. By the middle of the 1920s, he saw it as a great country with a great future: 'Yes, from America there will come much that is true, beautiful and great – in time!' he told a correspondent in 1929. 'America will some day teach the Old World instead of learning from it. For my part, I will never forget that it was in America that I received a warm and lasting welcome, and that this country has repaid me with the genuine gold of true appreciation as well as with the gold of Wall Street.'[273]

However, his first visit left him with a lingeringly bitter aftertaste. Little space is given to it in the Russian edition of *Pages from My Life*. The tone is milder in comparison with the letters to Gorky and Telyakovsky, but the attitude remains the same. 'People were rushing, tearing along, snatching newspapers from the hands of vendors as they ran past, reading them as they went and dropping them under their own feet, pushing each other without apologising because time is too short, smoking pipes, cigars and emitting billows of smoke, as if they were on fire. The sun shone through the smoke and dust. It had a pained and despondent look, as if thinking: "I'm not wanted here." It was a very boring life and I dreamt of the day I would be leaving for Europe.'[274]

In the Russian version of his autobiography Chaliapin writes that the press treated him 'with indulgence' but nevertheless declared that he 'was not an artist for America'.[275] Later, in the 1927 New York edition (from which all traces of ironical or derogatory remarks concerning America and Americans have vanished), he is more explicit. 'My stay in America was short* and far from happy. My artistic ideals were misunderstood; my performances were adversely criticised and, in general, it seemed that I was looked upon, artistically, as a barbarian. Complete ignorance of the English language prevented me from establishing sympathetic contact, to any extent, with natives of the great country, America.'[276]

Chaliapin's ignorance of the English language did not prevent him from finding out what most reviews were saying about him. The singer was simply stunned by the critics' pronouncements. In all his years on the stage Chaliapin had never before encountered such unanimous hostility to his way of performing.

---

* Chaliapin's first guest tours of America lasted in fact over three months.

Chaliapin sailing from New York to Europe, May 10th, 1924.

The interpretation of a role naturally produces divergent views. It is perfectly normal to prefer one detail to another, and even to disagree with the treatment chosen by the artist. Memoirs devoted to Chaliapin show quite clearly that he was always prepared to listen to convincingly argued objections and neither liked nor respected people who were always praising him. But what was being written in America looked like some malicious plot, the reason for which he could not fathom at all. It was all the more incomprehensible when he compared it with the reaction of the public. 'His audiences,' wrote an American musicologist, confirming Chaliapin's impressions, 'were as large and enthusiastic as they are anywhere.'[277] 'It took the audience but a brief moment to see that an unusual artist was before them, and when his voice rang out the ear emphasised the impression of the eye,'[278] wrote a newspaper after the première of *Mefistofele*. But this had practically no effect on journalists. 'He was badly treated by the press,'[279] recalled Gatti-Casazza. 'The reaction of the New York critics puzzled me,' confessed Sol Hurok.[280] If others felt the situation so keenly, it is not difficult to imagine Chaliapin's reaction in reading, for instance: 'He is a very ordinary basso, who sings in a vulgar way, without polish or refinement, and who has a very bad tremolo. As an actor he is only fair, always taking advantage of his great height, his massive limbs, his fine chest and magnificent stage scenery and the limelight. His method of taking the odd curtain calls naked and the even ones in fun is but part and parcel of his manner of singing.'[281] 'Chaliapin made a dirty, vulgar boor and buffoon out of the part of Leporello,'[282] commented the *New York Tribune* after the singer's first appearance in *Don Giovanni*. Leporello was a recent addition to Chaliapin's repertoire. Who knows? Perhaps he could not feel Mozart's style and find the right approach to the character. But what is one to make of the devastating reviews on his *Mefistofele* when six years earlier it had been so warmly praised by the composer himself? 'He makes of the fiend a demonic personage, a seething cauldron of rabid passions. He is continually snarling and barking. He poses in writhing attitudes of agonised impotence. He strides and gestures, grimaces and roars. All this appears to superficial observers to be tremendously dramatic. The present writer much prefers a devil who is a gentleman. But one thing more remains to be said about the first display of Mr. Chaliapin's powers. How long did he study the art of singing? Surely not many years. Such an uneven and uncertain emission of tone is seldom heard even on the Metropolitan Opera House stage, where there is a wondrous quantity of poorly grounded singing. The splendid song 'Son lo spirito che nega' was not sung at all in the strict interpretation of the word. It was delivered, to be sure, but in a rough and barbaric style. Some of the tones disappeared somewhere in the rear spaces of the basso's capacious throat, while others were projected into the auditorium like stones from a catapult. There was much strenuosity and little art in the performance. And it was much the same with the rest of the singing of the role.'[283]

Anyone who had witnessed Chaliapin's American débuts could see how biased were the opinions expressed by New York critics. Even if one takes into account that he was unwell for his first performance, this still exceeded any reasonable limit. Nowadays, after so many years, it is difficult, and perhaps even not so important, to examine closely the real reason for the press's disapproval. One can in the end agree with an American critic of the time who thought that the initiative was coming from the all-powerful director of the Metropolitan Opera, Heinrich Conried, 'who had no desire to retain in his company a bass who demanded sixteen hundred dollars a night, a high salary for a soprano or a tenor'.[284]

Another question springs to mind: why were only adverse reviews translated for Chaliapin? Why did the people escorting him on his tour deliberately (there is no other possible explanation) keep from him the notices which were favourable? Some of them were not only enthusiastic about Chaliapin's art but also answered his detractors' objections. 'Chaliapin's interpretation of one of the characters in which Mefistofele is placed on the operatic stage is realism in art; it is masculine and therefore it offends some people. It is beautiful, it is vigorous in all its movements and it is very satisfactory, considering the place, the circumstances and condition under which it appeared, namely, on the Brocken among the other inhabitants of the low world. It is no more offensive than Gustave Doré's tableaux; no more offensive than other representations of Dante's *Inferno* or Goethe's *Faust* or Rabelais, or other equally intense poetic figures, transported across the Styx.... His is one of those unique appearances that challenge the usual criticism and that make a tremendous effect because of originality of conception, a very broad view of the character and magnificent stage equipment and youth and brain work together with musical ability.'[285] 'In a comedy part—that of Basilio, the music teacher in *The Barber of Seville*—Mr. Chaliapin, the Russian basso, earned a clear-cut success last night at the Metropolitan Opera House. His was an original conception of the character, and he kept the audience in laughter throughout the performance. Vocally too, his performance was excellent, so that in every way he deserved the plaudits showered upon him.'[286] Generally speaking, critics (those, that is, who were willing to give serious consideration to what the "Russian bear" was doing) were struck by Chaliapin's artistic range and by the infectious quality of his art. 'Thanks primarily to Chaliapin, the best performance within memory of Rossini's *The Barber of Seville* was given at the Metropolitan Opera House last night. In the characterisation of Basilio the newcomer showed that he was not only able to sing, but that he was a comedian of exceptional merit. The audience, which was a large one, fairly bubbled over all the time that he was on stage. His tall figure with the semi-serious, comical face and big sprawling expressive hands was too much for everybody's risibilities. Peal after peal of laughter followed his utterances. For once the artificial situations seemed real and the action not altogether impossible. In this young man whose commanding figure as Mefistofele startled and awed and interested us at his first appearance, Mr. Conried would seem to have found a real artist.'[287]

Chaliapin knew nothing of this. A few days after the première he received 'an anonymous letter with some press cuttings. They tore me to pieces in abusive language,' recalled Chaliapin in his memoirs. 'The same theme ran through all of them and went something like this: "It is painful and shameful to see this

Siberian barbarian profane religion with his portrayal of a priest."[288] The critics found my Don Basilio a dirty, repulsive creature. One man even said that I was offensive to another singer on stage!'[289]

It would be wrong to think that Chaliapin had never met incomprehension and hostility before visiting America. In an interview with the correspondent of *The New York Times*, he declared: 'I have been sometimes adversely criticised during the course of my artistic life. The most profound of these criticisms have taught me to correct my faults. But I have learned nothing from the criticisms I have received in New York. After searching my inner consciousness, I find they are not based on a true understanding of my artistic purposes.'[290] Not wasting time on superfluous words to soften the outspokenness of his remarks, Chaliapin gave his views on the Metropolitan Opera with his customary bluntness: 'The contemporary direction of this theatre believes in tradition. It is afraid of anything new. There is no movement. It has not the courage to produce novelties, and the artists are prevented from giving original conceptions to old roles.'[291] According to the correspondent, this statement 'created a small sensation in operatic circles', while Chaliapin himself proved an even greater 'sensation'. 'Exuberant is the word which best describes him off the stage. The interview which ensued was the longest I have ever had with anyone. It began at 11 o'clock in the morning and lasted until a like hour in the evening – it might have lasted much longer – and during this whole time we sat at table in Mr. Chaliapin's own chamber at the Brevoort ... while he consumed vast quantities of food and drink. I remember a detail of six plates of onion soup. I have never seen anyone else eat so much or so continuously, or with so little lethargic effect. Indeed, intemperance seemed only to make him more lighthearted, ebullient and Brobding-nagian.'[292]

Chaliapin makes no mention anywhere of his return journey to Europe. In his memoirs and letters all references to his stay in America come to an abrupt end from the moment he left: he was reluctant to talk about the months he had spent there. There were occasions, of course, when he had to answer the endless questioning. He did so with unconcealed irritation. Time had not yet softened his bitterness; on the contrary, it was even stronger. Actors, singers and dancers are much more affected by unfair criticism than members of any other profession: the material used for their roles is, after all, their own person, their physical and personal attributes. When their creations are attacked too savagely, not only is their work destroyed but their own selves as well, their bodies, their faces, their voices, their human essence. Of course, any artistic creation is addressed to an audience and therefore presupposes that it will be judged. Whatever form the work takes, the dangerous possibility of a painful disagreement between artist and public is always present. But of all the arts, 'the art of the live being', as Stanislavsky liked to say, is the most vulnerable. Other artistic professions offer to the verdict of the crowd something already created, finished before it is submitted to readers or spectators. Performing arts are quite different. When an actor goes onto the stage he produces (or at any rate should produce – what else do we go to the theatre for?) an immediate sense of reality. Before our very eyes, it takes on the convincing quality and appeal of a living character, irresistibly attractive. The expectant darkness of the auditorium faces the actor, carefully measuring him up. In the darkness, in this mysterious unknown, hides the ever-present threat of destroying what has taken so long and so much effort to erect. Neither is a lifetime of experience any guarantee against failure: the prospect of appearing before an audience chills anyone's inspiration. Therefore, and this is hardly accidental, one of the basic concepts of Stanislavsky's system was 'the circle', the conventional definition of a limited space within which the actor is placed. Inside its confines he is safe, he has a centre, he can perform and live his role. He can look for a way of escaping from his subjections to the people who are here to look at him and from their exigencies. This 'ivory tower', stubbornly re-erected every time, rests on the actor's 'belief in the given circumstances' (Stanislavsky's expression) and the absolute inner conviction that the way he has chosen to act on stage is exactly the one demanded by these circumstances; the absence of this certitude is tantamount to professional death. 'The actor must firmly believe in the character he has created and insist that this and only this is the real truth. The character lived exactly like this, and no other way, and died exactly as I do it,' wrote Chaliapin.[293]

In the course of his long career in the theatre he had more than once had occasion to verify the humiliating fact that in his profession results depend almost entirely on how the spectator reacts to what is offered to him. If, for instance, he is bored, yawns, coughs, talks to his neighbour, the tension of the performance slackens; its pace changes and it loses its sense. Then the actor has to try feverishly to find in himself the resources and the emotions to save the scene which is falling apart.

One wonders whether reviewers realise all this as they laboriously churn out their murderous lines. Chaliapin was perhaps right when he said: 'It has always seemed to me that criticism and ill-will are closely related.'[294]

Chaliapin reached Le Havre in mid-February and proceeded immediately to Monte Carlo, where performances were due to start within a few days. Although tired, he was glad of this; the rapturous reception he received from both public and critics helped to 'heal the wounds' and made him regain faith in himself. Some crucial appearances awaited him – first in Milan, then in Paris. He was particularly worried about the latter. How would the French react to his beloved Mussorgsky? With the exception of a small circle of professional musicians, the habitués of the Grand Opéra knew absolutely nothing about *Boris Godunov*. He still had not forgotten how it had been rejected not just by the Russian public but by his own colleagues too. What then could one expect from foreigners to whom the whole thing, from the language to the historical facts, was totally unfamiliar? In 1929, shortly before his death, Diaghilev recounted to a journalist how Chaliapin suddenly came into his room on the eve of the dress rehearsal of *Boris Godunov*. ' "Sergei Pavlovich," he said, "where could I lie down here? I can't stay alone in my room." I had a tiny little sofa. Chaliapin curled up on it and fell asleep.'[295]

The Paris première of *Boris Godunov* provoked some unusual criticism. Alongside wild enthusiasm for the interpretation one could find in the same article sharp rejection of Rimsky-Korsakov's version and of the cuts and changes in the order of scenes made by Diaghilev. Those who were familiar with the score published in Russia in 1874 were in favour of the composer's own version. Rimsky-Korsakov was accused of distorting Mussorgsky's intentions. It was said that he had corrected and re-written his friend's work as a form-master does the essay of a schoolboy.[296] The unpopular stage version differed both from the original and from Rimsky-Korsakov's arrangement. The inn scene and the first scene of the Polish act were excluded from the production. The omission of the inn scene seemed quite illogical; it made it impossible to understand the sudden appearance of the usurper at the Mniszek castle and the transformation of a poor monk into the pretender to the Russian throne. The continuity of the action also seemed odd. In Mussorgsky, the coronation scene follows the scene in the courtyard of the Novodevichy Monastery. But Diaghilev introduced the scene in Pimen's cell between the two scenes of the Prologue. Pimen, in this case, as a critic aptly remarked, cannot know of Boris' accession to the throne. The whole chain of events in the opera, already not too coherent, loses all logic. Yet another change consisted of putting the Polish scene by the fountain before the scene in the Tsar's apartments. Diaghilev had conceived the idea that the Pretender should first be shown in Poland and that only then should Boris be warned of the danger threatening him.

What Rimsky-Korsakov thought of Diaghilev's rearrangements has not been recorded. He can hardly have approved, but he was already too weak to fight the energetic and self-assured young man. The composer was seriously ill and died one month after the Paris première of *Boris Godunov*. On the other hand, it is known that another, ever-zealous 'guardian of Mussorgsky's interests', Fedor Chaliapin, did not raise any objections. We can now only conjecture as to why in Russia he obstinately went on quarrelling over every inaccurate note unconcerned with his colleagues' reactions, while suddenly here, in Paris, where 'he regarded this production as a test of Russian maturity and originality in art',[297] he was willing to make concessions. True, the success obtained by the producer, the conductor, the Bolshoi Theatre chorus and the individual soloists was quite exceptional, but he could not have known this in advance.*

Referring to the omission of the inn scene, Chaliapin writes that it needs such singers 'as we, in spite of all the wealth of talent Russia possesses, could not find'. 'In my youth,' continues the singer, 'I more than once sang both Boris and Varlaam in the same evening, but I could not bring myself to do it here.'[298] It is hardly necessary to disprove this explanation by enumerating the names of those who could have taken the role of Varlaam without endangering the splendid performance of Mussorgsky's opera. Moreover, Chaliapin knew the real reason for the removal of the inn scene. Benois mentions it in his *Memories of Diaghilev*: 'This cut was the result of an attack of fear to which Sergei, for all his bravery in general, was occasionally prone. When he was in the grip of some fear, no argument could prevail upon it. It suddenly seemed to him *impossible* [Benois' italics] to show something so coarse and "dirty" to the elegant, fastidious Parisian public.'[299]

However, notwithstanding all the errors of judgement observed by the press, the performance was a triumph. The chorus and Chaliapin were the centre of attraction. 'One is astounded by the naturalness of the singing and the realism of the acting and of the crowd movements in the opera,' wrote the correspondent of *Le Gaulois*.[300] 'As a singer and as an actor, Chaliapin is beyond praise,' enthusiastically declared *Le Théâtre*. 'Never have we heard and seen in opera word and movement combined with such unexampled strength of expression and depth of emotion. Chaliapin is not simply singing his role: he communicates the life of the character he portrays through singing, communicates his torments and his

* Producer, A. A. Sanin. Conductor, F. M. Blumenfeld. Scenery from sketches by A. Y. Golovin realised by K. F. Yuon, E. E. Lanceret and S. P. Yaremich, except for the scene by the fountain, which was designed by A. N. Benois, Costumes designed by I. Y. Bilibin. Apart from Chaliapin, the cast included: Pimen – V. I. Kastorski; Shuisky – I. A. Alchevsky; the Pretender – D. A. Smirnov; Marina – N. S. Ermolenko. Chorus of the Bolshoi Theatre; chorus master, U. I. Avranek. Orchestra of the Opéra.

sufferings. He spurns conventional devices and personifies dramatic truth on the stage.'[301]

'The artistic simplicity of the interpretation is amazing,' concurred the critic of *Le Figaro*. 'The most pathetic and intense scenes became totally natural – so convincingly true was everything he did. It would be truer to say: Chaliapin became one with the character of Boris and lived his emotions on the stage.'[302]

As already mentioned, Chaliapin produced his most striking effect not on the first night but at the only half-ready dress rehearsal. Contemporary sources indicate that Diaghilev had not managed to assemble all the members of the company in Paris until the last minute. The performance had been prepared in a nervous atmosphere and was always on the brink of collapse. The chief scene-shifter of the Opéra was doing his best to ruin the performance of the Russian artists.[303]

'The stalls were packed,' recalled an eyewitness. 'Music critics sharpened their ears, disaster was in the air: what could one really expect from singers without costumes, against a makeshift "backdrop"?' And the inspiration of the production, the famous bass singer – would he, however impeccable his singing, be able to metamorphose himself under the conditions of a working rehearsal, without make-up, without the attributes of the Tsar's role? But a miracle took place. From the moment he appeared amongst the throng of the choristers to the accompaniment of bells pealing, until the final death scene in the fourth act, Chaliapin held the audience in a state of near trance. Unable to take their eyes off him, they forgot both about the absence of Kremlin chambers and the poverty of modern dress. Chaliapin surpassed himself. The voice convinced by its intonations and the acting conquered by its majestic plasticity ("C'est comme une statue mouvante,"* exclaimed a French opera-goer sitting nearby), the plasticity of sparse "regal" gestures and of mounting dramatic tension.... The scene with the ghost of the murdered tsarevich plunged the sceptical Parisians into a state of idolatrous rapture. Chaliapin was staggering, moving, fright-

---

* It is like a moving statue.

Chaliapin in London, 1913.

ening, entrancing, his presence illuminated, recreated everything in his own way, elevated, transfigured. The orchestra, the chorus and the soloists followed the public in surrendering to his magic. . . .'[304]

On May 22nd, the day of the last performance of *Boris Godunov*, Chaliapin received the Légion d'Honneur.* 'I am not so much delighted by my personal success', he said to a friend about the occasion, 'as immensely happy over the triumph of our great genius Mussorgsky. How sad that he is not among the living.'[305]

Chaliapin remained in Paris for another week. A long journey again awaited him: performances were scheduled in Buenos Aires for the end of June. He was billed in the same operas he had recently sung in the United States: *Mefistofele*, *The Barber of Seville* and *Don Giovanni*. The atmosphere of the bustling, colourful southern city immediately transported Chaliapin into 'utter rapture'. So at any rate say the memoirs. 'They had a European outlook on how to do things, and the performances, well-staged, were a great success.'[306] However, in one of his regular letters to Telyakovsky during the tour, his tone was quite different. The inhabitants of South America, like those of North America, are described as 'ignoramuses'; the theatre is just as boring and devoid of elementary imagination as many other opera houses he had frequented. 'All in all, to hell with them, their money and their applause!'[307]

Chaliapin left as soon as his engagement ended. In *Pages from My Life*, he tells about his return journey on an English ship, the strong impression made on him by the natives of St. Vincent island and the misfortune which befell an old French friend who was travelling with him, when all his life-savings were stolen from his hip-pocket in Buenos Aires. Chaliapin adds that he immediately replaced the missing sum. It is remarkable that, loving travel and knowing how to give interesting accounts of his many foreign tours, Chaliapin rarely writes about them. On the whole, he restricts himself to his first visits to France,

---

* The certificate of award is in the Central Theatrical Museum named after A. A. Bakhrushin, Moscow. Archive no. 303, folio 262, no. 272009/47.

Italy, America and England. The last is given particular attention; he retained his enthusiastic love of Great Britain to the
end of his life. There was nothing surprising in Chaliapin's
anglomania; generation after generation, the overwhelming
majority of educated Russians attached to the adjective 'English'
a very particular connotation. It became synonymous with the
word 'excellent'; to this day one can hear the expression 'English
taste', 'English honesty', 'the word of a gentleman' used in a
complimentary sense. The roots of this hypnotic condition
are no doubt lost in the distant past. But Chaliapin was not
disappointed when he visited England. 'These congenial people,'
he writes of the English, 'cheerful, modest, grew dearer to me.
I left London very happy – I had seen some very special
people.'[308] The American edition of *Pages from My Life* contains
many more passages devoted to England which disappeared in
the Soviet publication. Here is one of them: 'I have been all over
Europe and have visited North and South America. Everywhere
I have seen liberty, but nowhere greater freedom than exists in
England. The meetings in Hyde Park surprised me especially.
One hears socialists and anarchists speechifying almost side by
side. The crowd listens with equal attentiveness and respect to
both of them. A Catholic defends religion with fiery zeal and,
not far away, an atheist deprecates all faith no less ardently. I
was very much astonished at some of the speeches that were
translated for me by my friends, and my Russian habits of
thought made me involuntarily wonder what the police would
have to say about it. At times I even felt like asking the park
policeman how he could listen to such things unmoved! What
an incredible phenomenon it seemed that a policeman should
be the free servant of a free democracy.'[309]

But it was the attitude of the English public which Chaliapin
found most amazing of all. From his very first 'Russian season'
in London (1913) he had felt the atmosphere of concentrated
attention with which the audiences followed everything happening on stage. It seemed that not a single word, not a single
intonation was lost. The auditorium's reaction to the smallest
artistic details was immediate and unerring. And yet on this
occasion Chaliapin's repertoire was not offering any familiar

works; the Diaghilev company was playing *Ivan the Terrible,*
Khovanshchina and *Boris Godunov* at Drury Lane.

The visit was repeated a year later, with the addition of
Borodin to Mussorgsky and Rimsky-Korsakov. In *Prince Igor*
Chaliapin now sang two roles: Galitsky and Konchak. 'Speaking
to me of his London experience,' recalls Rosa Newmarch,
'Chaliapin was evidently deeply moved by, and not a little
astonished at, the enthusiastic welcome accorded to him and to
his compatriots. He had, of course, been told that we were a
cold and phlegmatic race, but he found in our midst such
heartfelt warmth and sincerity as he had never before experienced outside Russia.'[310]

Chaliapin must often have been reminded of what Stasov had
told him many years before: 'Go to England. Play in your own
language, they'll understand everything!'[311]

Stasov's prediction turned out to have been prophetic. The
more Chaliapin heard the views of English critics,* the more
convinced he became that in terms of depth of analysis, ability
to distinguish between the trivial and the important and to
communicate the impression produced by a performance, they
had no equals. They had an extraordinarily clear grasp of what
constituted the basis of his artistic method, what he had spent
some twenty years stubbornly fighting for.

The majority of reviewers were not content to observe that
the performance had been a success; they also tried to explain
why. 'The distinction seems elementary, but in London, at any
rate, it must be made. Every step, every movement of Mr.
Chaliapin belongs not to himself but to the man who for the
moment he represents. He knows no single vice of the popular
actor. He never rants, he is incapable of rhetoric. He does not
mar his representation by false emphasis or elaborate gesture.
His tones and movements are alike harmonious. He does not
destroy at his first entrance upon the stage the possibility of
subsequent emotion. He has a reserve of force, upon which he
does not call in vain. His art, like that of the writer or painter,
is an art of expressing something outside himself. He does not

---

* 'The English is translated to me; I can't read it myself,' he wrote to his daughter
Irina. (*Fedor Ivanovich Chaliapin*, vol. 1, p. 479.)

show us Chaliapin with weary iteration. He shows us Ivan or Boris or Don Quixote, interpreting for us as he goes the meaning and idiosyncrasy of each. Whatever be his part, he plays it with a dignity of restraint, a sense of character, an elimination of self which have not been seen in any actor of our time.'[312] 'Chaliapin's subtle changes of expression,' said *The Times,* 'his gestures, always very restrained, save in the real emotional climaxes, his way of standing, of eating and drinking, of doing the commonest things, all express character so eloquently because they are the outcome of the character which is his for the moment. He has no symbolic acting as most operatic artists have. His acting comes out of him, and is not superimposed upon him.'[313]

Wonder at Chaliapin's talent 'to disappear, to empty himself of all personality' so as to recreate that of another being did not overshadow interest in his vocal mastery. But what was foremost was not the singer's technique or the fullness and beauty of his voice but the fact that Chaliapin 'does not separate the art of his voice from the art of personation'. 'For Chaliapin the singer,' observed Richard Capell, 'the tone-colour is all that counts and for the sake of heightening the dramatic colour on a word he willingly sacrifices beautiful tone – which to an Italian singer would seem madness. And the truth and directness of his singing are such that one forgets it is singing, singing usually implies some strain or effort, but Chaliapin's seems the most inevitably natural utterance. Perfect breath control is, of course, an element of this effect, but this is not enough to say. Other singers have perfect breath control, but who else has the lustre and indefinable depth of this voice?'[314]

'It was a theatrical and musical sensation without parallel since the coming of Wagner,' declared the *Musical Times.* 'London was spellbound by the revelation of a new order of vividness in operatic music and operatic acting. Chaliapin's portrayal of the chief parts in *Boris Godunov, Khovanshchina* and *Ivan the Terrible* was unlike anything that the operatic world of the day had experienced in the normal round of German and Italian opera.'[315]

King George V was present at the final performance of *Boris*

Godunov on July 8th, 1913. 'After the hallucination scene,' recalled Chaliapin, 'Beecham excitedly rushed into my dressing room and announced that the King wanted to see me. I had to go through the auditorium to reach the Royal Box, still in my costume and make-up. The public stood up to stare at Tsar Boris, who had just been having fits of insanity. When I entered the box, the King rose without a word, and a few seconds of silence went by, to my great embarrassment. It then occurred to me that the King might be shy and I decided – although this was against etiquette – to start the conversation with him myself. I said I was indescribably happy to play in the presence of the King of such a splendid people as the English. He kindly spoke to me of his pleasure at this wonderful opera and expressed surprise at the simplicity with which I played the role. Smiling good-naturedly, he said he hoped that this would not be the last time he would see Russian opera in London. I heard later from Beecham that the King had left highly satisfied with the performance and had asked for his thanks to be conveyed to all the members of the company.'[316]

'The English way of life puts me in a situation to which I am, of course, not accustomed,' he wrote to his eldest daughter, Irina, in Moscow, 'and so I can't help getting a little tired, namely: I have had to meet a lot of Englishmen here – they invite me to breakfasts, lunches, teas and dinners. It means having to get up early, answer various letters, and on top of that, go and pay visits. I, of course, know no English at all, and although all my acquaintances speak French, I feel rather awkward and for this reason this winter I want to learn English, which I also advise you to do – it seems to me the most essential language, and so all of you – Lydia, Tanya, Fedya and Borya – must learn English. Tell them this.'[317]

His intuition frequently astonished, even frightened people. Dealing with the same facts as most of his contemporaries, Chaliapin, unlike others, had the ability to read their hidden meaning. And in this letter too, sent to his children from London in 1913, he seemed to be looking through a crystal ball. Everything turned out as he said: every one of them, except for Irina, who remained in Moscow after the Revolution, would need to speak English. They would need it fairly soon, and as time showed, permanently.

His second visit to London was no less successful, but for Chaliapin it was forever associated with the First World War. On his way back from England, he was held up in France; trains had already stopped running, and he had to go on foot a good part of the time. 'To facilitate the return to Paris, I opened my trunks and distributed all the things, all the clothing to poor people, leaving for myself only the barest essentials.'[318] Moving from country to country (he had to go through England again, then Norway, Sweden and Finland), Chaliapin finally reached his homeland at the beginning of September.

He was soon reclaimed by his old life: performances, concerts and receptions succeeded one another. But the atmosphere was different. Behind the war spreading over Europe and the mood in Russia, Chaliapin sensed disaster. The changes inescapably setting in would not be for the better....

CHAPTER IV

Mask and Soul

'The actor lives, cries and laughs on stage, but while crying and laughing he is observing his own tears and laughter. And in this dual life, in this balance between life and play — lies art.'

Tommaso Salvini

THERE WERE AT first no obvious signs of deterioration; everything seemed to go on as usual. 'The shops were open, carriages were rolling along the roads, street lights illuminated the Morskaya.* The theatres were in full swing and filled to capacity,'[1] recalled Chaliapin. True, trips abroad were no longer possible; he could now only sing in Petrograd, Moscow or the provinces.

From time to time, rumours sweeping the country broke the regularity of everyday life. They veered from panic – with tales of one thousand officers and soldiers being lost in a single day's fighting – to enthusiasm for the invincible valour of the Russian army. Patriotism became a fashionable word read on every page of the newspapers and heard in every conversation.

But as the war dragged on, assuming a depressing monotony, Chaliapin started to think that what was happening was nothing other than collective madness. In a world which had visibly run amok, stifling the voice of reason, calls for new sacrifices and for new victories grew increasingly vociferous. The simple and normal language of human emotions lay buried under official jargon. People themselves were changing, or perhaps just revealing their real nature. The bitterness of defeat, mingled with admiration for the brave defenders of the homeland, produced a very sobering effect. Sad reflections upon the future invaded drawing-rooms, literary debates, card games and festive gatherings. There was a general mood of expectancy, fear and uncertainty. Anyone capable of interpreting facts was forced to realise, to a greater or lesser extent, that 'a storm was gathering, which no one dared to call a revolution'.[2]

More and more men had to join the army regardless of position or importance. Chaliapin escaped call-up as he was

* Morskaya: street in Petrograd.

over the age limit of forty. He was intelligent and lucid enough
to see that almost everyone was tired of the widespread cor-
ruption and confusion, the blaring manifestos, the boastful
claims of newspapers too revolting to soil your hands with,
the reports of successes when in reality military debacle was
complete. Chaliapin could have ignored the latest news, taken
no notice of events, avoided worrying or thinking about
anything, but he was incapable of it. 'My heart was torn by
what was going on at the front. When war is declared it is not
the people who want it, but the leaders. I am for people, always
the people, regardless of religion or nationality, and the people
were being butchered,'[3] he wrote later. He did whatever was in
his power, giving all his free time to charity performances. His
name ensured the participation of other famous artists and, of
course, good box-office returns. 'Wishing to be useful one way
or another and to make up for my absence from the trenches,
I opened two hospitals – one in Moscow, the other in Petersburg – for some eighty men in all, whom I fed and supported
at my own expense. Many patients passed through my hospitals
during the war years. I visited them and sometimes entertained
them with singing.'[4] Hearing of the countless disasters which
had befallen the Poles, he went to give a free concert in Warsaw,
once again in order to 'somehow help poor people'.

Nevertheless, Chaliapin's despondent mood at this time could
not be entirely explained by the war and the grimness of the
situation. He knew himself that many reasons contributed to
it, that one thing exacerbates another while the root of the
problem remains hidden. For Chaliapin the most important
thing was always the THEATRE, however strained relations
might be there and whatever difficulties might arise. Only this
time it was not a matter of obstacles to overcome. That stage
of his life was long since past, and Chaliapin now had at his
disposal all the resources of the Russian operatic stage: he chose
the repertoire, decided on the number of performances and
named his own fee. But he still had not found the answer to the
question any true innovator asks himself periodically: 'What
next?'

Although irritable, hot-tempered and unpredictable in his

reactions, Chaliapin was mentally a very stable man, with his two feet firmly on the ground. He could not avoid moments of hesitation, doubts and disappointments, but constant soul-searching, depression and diffidence were not in his nature. He was more inclined to be cheerful than reserved and sad; he was sure of what he wanted and knew how to get it. At any rate, this is how his family and the narrow circle of his friends saw him. Nevertheless, as with all artists, and more especially actors, at times what he had so far accomplished suddenly felt like a deadweight. And not necessarily because it seemed now worthless or outdated: the objective on which inspiration depends had simply vanished from sight. The next performance became a tedious repetition, and the theatre itself, only yesterday a unique, magic place, appeared today irritatingly ordinary.

There is perhaps no greater calamity for the actor than to play a role which does not fire his imagination, to find that everything is becoming mere technique, even if it is brilliant. The public continues to shout and rave, the performances are still sold out, but the performer regards his acting career as finished.

Chaliapin was passing through such a phase, but luckily his talent was too great to collapse under the weight of the gloom provoked by his usual dissatisfaction with the state of operatic affairs. This had tormented him for many years, and more strongly now than ever. Prevailing conditions and age made it imperative to take stock.

The problem was never resolved to Chaliapin's satisfaction. In 1932, when he was finishing his second book of memoirs in Paris, he wrote: 'I must regretfully admit that I have seen as few real opera singers abroad as in Russia. There are some good, even remarkable, singers, but there are no great masters of vocal art, no operatic artists in the full sense of the word. One way or another, music always expresses some emotions, and where there is emotion, a mechanical interpretation leaves an impression of dreadful monotony.... If I am playing Holofernes, I try to do something that looks like that period. But what about my surroundings? What about the chorus of Assyrians, Babylonians, Jews and all the other people around

Holofernes? They have put dark make-up on their faces, stuck black beards on their chins and wear whatever costume could be found. But none of this will let you forget that just before the performance they were eating Russian cabbage soup. And now I think of all the years, all the seasons that have passed in my life, all the roles I have played – comic and tragic, in the various theatres of the world. These were my *roles* [Chaliapin's italics], but a *theatre* [Chaliapin's italics] of my own, I have never had, not anywhere. In Rimsky-Korsakov's opera, for there to be a perfect Salieri his partner must also be a perfect Mozart. A production in which, for instance, Sancho Panza is outstanding and Don Quixote execrable cannot be called a success. Each one of the musicians – to say nothing of the conductor – has a share in the making of a performance! I have often despaired of my art and believed it to be sterile....'[5]

Most striking in the above passage is a strong sense of dissatisfaction with himself. It cannot be blamed on the querulousness of advancing years or on waning success – this, after all, he enjoyed right up to his very last appearance. 'I know what fame is,' Chaliapin often repeated. 'I have experienced it. What *real happiness* [Chaliapin's italics] does fame give, apart from material gain and occasionally agreeable pleasures of worldly vanity?'[6] The reason lay elsewhere; he had long felt the need to pass on to somebody what he had accumulated, to teach what he had discovered for himself in the theatre, to share it with young singers prepared to wage war on routine.

The essence of these discoveries consisted in giving maximum emphasis to the individualisation of the human character on the operatic stage. Chaliapin's central idea was to search for the life of 'this' particular person, its idiosyncrasies, the sum of its details – whether internal or external, behavioural or psychological, concealed or unconcealed, as well as the interplay between 'this' same person and other people, the rest of the world.

From this flowed the new concept of 'the character of the environment', the character of a man's surroundings, the influence of which determines his mentality and his emotions.

Audiences in the early years of this century were not surprised to see a faithful replica of the conditions in which the action was taking place. The productions of the French director André Antoine in Paris and of Stanislavsky in Moscow, the evolution of positivism in philosophy and of naturalism in literature had all played their parts. These new ideas had been very quickly assimilated, even by theatres in remote Russian provinces. Chaliapin, however, took a bold step forward – and inwards. He not only introduced into operatic performance the representation and interpretation of a man's environment but – and this was the most important element – he laid bare this man's ties with the world, nature and society, and through the understanding of these ties he produced a method of studying operatic roles.

He could, of course, have written everything down (indeed he did to a certain extent in *Mask and Soul*), but then he had neither time nor patience for essays on the theatre.

At rehearsals, Chaliapin often could not resist trying to convert others to his ideas, and he would suddenly start telling them what to do and how to do it. The advice, as we know, was not always well received. Some were grateful and gladly took from him what they could; others, of little ability or indifferent to what he was saying, continued to concentrate exclusively on the sound of their voices and asked to be left alone. Chaliapin reacted to this very badly – not out of wounded pride and runaway megalomania, as some thought and said, but because he could not accept that some artists were not interested in art. What can someone without an atom of creativity be doing in the theatre? 'In the professional domain, there is only one path to my heart: Whatever your place, do your job properly,' he constantly affirmed.[6] 'Legends abounded of Chaliapin's love of work,' recalled Sergei Levik.[7] In 1911 Chaliapin wrote from France to Gorky about a thought which kept worrying him: 'In Russia I have often dreamt of my own theatre. But for me this is not feasible! One must have administrative abilities, which I do not possess at all, and life being as it is now, with everybody thinking only of how they can best cheat you, and blackmail you, too, you would lose your health and your voice.'[8]

To this day, it is not widely realised that the creation and the success of the Moscow Art Theatre, so readily attributed to Stanislavsky, would not in fact have been possible without Nemirovich-Danchenko's iron determination, clarity of mind and organising talent. Genius and a wide-ranging imagination are invaluable in any human undertaking, but it is the theatre's, and even more opera's, misfortune that, unlike poetry, painting or music, it cannot fully develop in poverty or in solitude. These two art forms are, more than any other, dependent on financial considerations.

Of course (and such cases are not rare) every material requirement can be available – a building with a row of columns, an orchestra, scenery painters, stagehands, administrative staff and even money – yet this is not the Theatre. But a small cart rolls out onto a village square, as in *Pagliacci*, a piece of carpet is spread out for the actors, and the magic of the acting may take everyone's breath away. Nevertheless, on that piece of carpet there will never be anything more than a troupe of wandering players; art itself will not significantly change course.

Chaliapin had no Nemirovich-Danchenko. An artist who also possesses the qualities of a military commander is a very rare combination. So one must again express regret: under different circumstances, Chaliapin's influence on twentieth-century opera would have had greater impact and in a greater variety of areas. Productions today would then perhaps look different. The shameful past of the operatic stage would be gone forever. No more would nondescript, irrelevant costumes be worn by people with crude, stereotyped make-up on their faces, singing without showing any trace of intelligence, logic or artistry, their eyes lovingly fixed on the conductor, themselves as though rooted to the floor. Straight theatre has after all been transformed by the productions of Stanislavsky, Nemirovich-Danchenko and Meyerhold. 'Those who saw him [Chaliapin] at work at rehearsal at Covent Garden or at Sir Thomas Beecham's season of Russian opera at the Lyceum Theatre in 1931 realised that his instinct for mise-en-scène and theatrical effect would have made of him a supreme producer or stage régisseur if some misfortune had rendered him incapable of singing or acting,' wrote Richard Capell after the singer's death.[9] The onset of the war dashed his hopes of creating a theatre.

Chaliapin missed no opportunity of airing his views on the art of the operatic singer whenever he could find an attentive ear. 'I called on Chaliapin at about two o'clock,' recounted one of his acquaintances. 'He was lying on the bed drinking tea; his young companions, a pianist and a violinist, sat by the window. After we had exchanged greetings, Chaliapin resumed the speech my arrival had interrupted; the young men listened with great attention. He spoke for a long time, quite fluently, in a didactic tone; he sometimes used aphorisms, old memories. ... "The main objective is to convey the spirit of the work. We are taught technique, technical devices. But that is not enough, it's not all, it's not the main thing. One must know how to convey the spirit." He talked passionately of the vocation of singer, of understanding the sense of an opera, of the means by which to communicate this sense without resorting to technical processes.'[10]

There was a marked change in the relations with his colleagues in these years. Chaliapin learnt to be more patient in his explanations and demonstrations, and singers, in turn, seemed more inclined to accept his lessons.

In 1911 Chaliapin persuaded the management of the Imperial Theatres to stage *Khovanshchina*, absent from their repertoire for many years, and undertook to prepare the singers himself.* He was now officially entitled to advise others, to agree or disagree with what they were doing. Various tales immediately started to circulate in Petersburg; the press took good care to report on the presumptuous dictator who was bending the poor soloists to his will. Chaliapin did not bother with denying this and maintained a cautious silence. Shortly before the première, one of the capital's leading newspapers printed an interview with members of the cast. The general public was surprised, after hearing so much about Chaliapin's insufferable character and his many scandals, to find that the singers were full of undisguised admiration. In their opinion, Chaliapin the director

---

* Melnikov was in charge of the general mise-en-scène and of the crowd scenes.

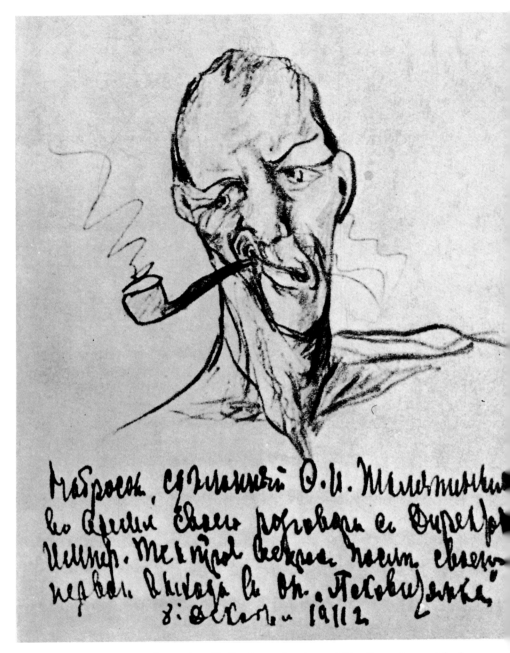

Self-caricature drawn by Chaliapin at the time of his discussions with the Director of Imperial Theatres about his first appearance in *The Maid of Pskov* in the 1911 season.

was equal to Chaliapin the singer. 'It is something incredible,' said Joachim Tartakov. 'What he teaches at rehearsals should all be written down and published in book form. Chaliapin shows the same genius whether demonstrating the visual or the musical side of a role. He feels the situation immediately in his head and in his heart, and moreover he possesses to perfection the gift of conveying to someone else his understanding of the role.'[11] 'Chaliapin is staging the opera wonderfully,' added Ivan Ershov. 'See him showing Marfa how to sing a phrase. His face is now a woman's face: he immediately becomes smaller: his gestures, his stance are those of a woman. Now he turns into Dosifei – and suddenly before your very eyes he grows thinner, his eyes take on a vacant look, his voice changes; the man singing now is completely different from the one who was singing Marfa only a minute ago. If he was given the opportunity of staging our entire repertoire, to what heights wouldn't the Mariinsky Theatre ascend!' These remarks should not delude us, they are not signs of idyllic friendship and mutual understanding, although Chaliapin himself declared: 'Everything went well.'[12]

Indeed, major conflicts were avoided in Petersburg; but when he staged *Khovanshchina* in Moscow a year later, Chaliapin caused another tremendous rumpus, the like of which had not been seen for a long time. The press and the public had been invited to the dress rehearsal on the morning of December 10th. 'In the middle of Act One,' recalled Daniil Pokhitonov, 'because of rhythmic "vacillation" in the choral ensemble, Chaliapin stopped the action. "When is there finally going to be some real rhythm in this theatre?" he shouted from the stalls to the auditorium (he was not rehearsing; the part of Dosifei was sung by V. R. Petrov). There was an unpleasant exchange with Josef Suk,* after which the offended conductor put down his baton and left the rostrum. Everyone dispersed. The rehearsal was ruined.'[13]

Pokhitonov's accounts show that 'Chaliapin directed with enthusiasm, putting into his work a great deal of patience and

---

* V. I. Suk – conductor of the Bolshoi Theatre.

self-control. He did not impose his own will and allowed the singers complete freedom.'[14] The tenor Andrei Labinsky was even more explicit: 'Chaliapin did not in any way hamper the performers. He was the first to be sincerely glad when one of them explained to him why he conceived or performed a certain passage in a certain way.'[15]

The above may seem obvious if one forgets the fact, already mentioned, that in the early twentieth century directing, as an independent theatrical profession, was only just beginning to gain recognition and success, and even then mostly on the dramatic stage. In opera, methods of directing were still far removed from any sort of system; the example of Meyerhold's or the Moscow Art Theatre's productions was as yet to be emulated there. In Russia, only a handful of people were seriously dedicated to operatic direction. In comparison with the actor in a drama, the transformation of a singer into an artist passionately involved in the general concept of the performance is, as a rule, a much more difficult and lengthy process. Chaliapin knew this better than anyone else. He saw in the practical work of many contemporary directors a danger of destroying the actor's individuality. He categorically rejected any abstract idea, however original, which was not in the spirit of the work and was a substitute for the actor's art.

Everything on the stage is there for the sole benefit of one person – His Highness the Actor. Nothing must stand between him and the public. Amongst the innumerable details of the surroundings, one should select only those which illuminate the continuity, the inner life of the play's or opera's hero. It is for this reason that Chaliapin so adamantly declared that the producer must also be an actor. 'He must not only be able to tell you where to go, right or left, and what sort of helmet to put on; he must also be able to play all the roles. He must show how a character speaks, thinks, laughs and cries. What is a contemporary producer? A critic, at best an armchair strategist. He will tell you clearly and precisely in which museum and where this or that portrait hangs, explain to you the style and the structure of a role, but he is hardly capable of giving a practical demonstration of what Ivan the Terrible, Dosifei or

Don Carlos must be like. I, as a producer, never look for small details, even if they are historically correct; I am not even all that interested in how a given character was dressed. But I consider it indispensable to explain to the actors and to give a visual demonstration of how to experience and then convey what Vera Sheloga, Marfa, Galitsky, etc. ... were feeling.'[16]

One can easily detect a tone of irritation in Chaliapin's remarks. What had provoked them? Were they really aimed at producers? Perhaps the great singer, the soloist, was defending the time-honoured concept of the theatre as a purely performing art and insisting that it should only be judged on that criterion. The aim would then be a kind of orderly concert with perfectly polished solo numbers and participants all in their proper places. The action is reduced to entrances and exits, to the 'apparition' of widely disparate characters. Each actor plays within his own limits, taking little interest in what goes on inside his neighbour's territory. The mise-en-scène is in this case simply a convenient way of placing the actors on the boards, regardless of what events are being represented and who is taking part in them.

No, with Chaliapin the question was more complex and more subtle. The aggressive acerbity of his statements was not denying the role of the producer, whose profession had evolved from the simple duties of supervising and co-ordinating the work of the actors. Chaliapin's efforts at establishing contact at all levels with his partners – with the conductor, the designer, the electrician, with anyone involved in the production – his attempts to persuade them to search for the substance of the opera not only within the work itself but beyond its limits, in real life, show his new concept of staging. To be more precise, the life of the performance consists not only of individual roles and individual actors but also of nature, of things, of the circumstances which join and separate human destinies in the play, and of the life which the composer is not showing in the character he creates but which enveloped him when he was writing the work and which continues outside the walls of the theatre. The public sitting in the auditorium comes from this life, adding its share of active participation to what is taking place on stage. This is a crystallised perception of emotions and of the essence of reality and is the producer's supreme goal. Work with the actors is only a preliminary stage in the creation of a unified picture of actuality. Chaliapin's brief and sporadic experience as a producer was limited to this first link in the chain. He did not manage to go any further.

With the advent of the 'producer's theatre' at the beginning of this century came a new way of conducting rehearsals. The development of the action on stage was no longer based on the principle of adding separate elements of the play's mechanism to each other, but on blending them, letting them flow into one another. There was a desire to harmonise the events and the characters of the play or opera: nothing existed by itself; everything was a transition. What has only just taken place and what one is expecting to happen are reflected in what is happening now.

The two possible ways of achieving this were conflicting and moreover competed for dominance in the theatre from the very first steps taken by professional producers. These first steps were not easy; those who attempted them were accused of the blackest sins: they were slave-drivers, dictators, animal-tamers depriving actors of all freedom. The hostile suspicion with which the Petersburg Alexandrinsky Theatre company received their newly appointed Principal Director, Meyerhold, was typical. From time immemorial, every newcomer possessed of great knowledge and ability has been received with mistrust. He is perceived as having power which he can, if he likes, use for evil instead of good. People become instruments on which the devil plays his tune. He does nothing himself; rather he forces others to embody his ideas. Thus Svengali takes over the soul of his victim, Trilby, in George du Maurier's novel.*

The alternative approach presupposes that the director and the actors drink from the same cup for their beliefs and their inspiration. Teacher and pupils have equal rights to be understood and to try out new ideas. The design is not imposed; it

---

* The analogy is that of Naum Berkovsky, in the collection *Theatre and Literature*, Moscow 1969, p. 270.

grows from a joint effort. Discipline is also necessary here, but orders and blind obedience are ruled out. Helped by the producer, the actor examines his inner world through the role, searching in it for means of creating his character. This method relies on freedom, open-mindedness and acting in the grand style. One can afford to discard any superfluities, large or small. One is not afraid to destroy and, if need be, to start all over again. Being capable of taking a fresh look at one's work every time engenders the uncommon ability to appreciate this in others too. The play or score isn't simply transferred to the boards; it is re-created through mastery of the theatre as a synthesised art form.

Which type of director was Chaliapin? Did he search for solutions together with the singers or did he imperiously order them to follow him? Both – partly because in the early days, the producer was inevitably a dictator. Stanislavsky, for instance, would carefully prepare a precisely drawn-up plan, arriving at the unity of the production through absolute rule. Like Chaliapin, he taught actors by practical demonstration; but as time went by, Stanislavsky departed more and more from this, whereas Chaliapin, talking about production with various journalists, deliberately equated the word 'demonstration' with the word 'explanation'. He worked by meeting the singers half-way, arousing their artistic initiative by all the means at his disposal. When 'explanation' was not enough, Chaliapin used 'demonstration'. In this persuasive and effective method, however, lay a hidden danger. Chaliapin's brilliant improvisations looked like fantastical transformations, but almost no one else could repeat them. Not that he was asking for imitation; his 'demonstrations' took into account the potential of the performer.

Chaliapin started the rehearsals of *Khovanshchina* with a talk on the general concept of the opera and on the interpretation of the various roles. His analysis showed clearly that he was not trying to adjust Mussorgsky's work to his own view of the world, to subject it to the rules of his personal emotions. Everything he suggested was evidence of a clear and profound insight into the composer's intentions and was rooted in the logic of the dramatic action. A thorough grasp of both the words and the music of the opera enabled Chaliapin to peel off carefully the layers which made up a uniquely original monolith. This was not easy to do. *Khovanshchina* lacked cohesion to an even greater extent than *Boris Godunov*. The action unfolds loosely, like an epic tale, where there is no boundary, no well-defined interrelation between the various parts, no clearly drawn story line. The composer, moving from subject to subject, dwells arbitrarily on events of great historical importance or on insignificant details of everyday life. The central characters of the opera, Ivan Khovansky, Galitsin, Dosifei and Marfa, appear and disappear like episodic figures. Not a single role has a determining importance in the development of the plot. And if the beginning of *Khovanshchina* expresses the idea of life's eternal beauty triumphing over events, the finale on the other hand conveys the rejection of everything earthly. The last act, enveloped in the pathos of death, is not terrible but sublime, exultant. There is no sign of confusion; it is a departure from the world in the proud consciousness of faith, without fear and without mercy.

In *Khovanshchina* Chaliapin had a marked preference for Marfa – not because he saw in her the key to the whole opera but simply because the character attracted him. He was taking the part of Dosifei, but this seemed to occupy him least of all. At any rate, his memoirs, written twenty years after his début as producer, make no mention of it. On the other hand, several pages are devoted to Marfa. It may also be because he had not forgotten his clash with Evgenia Zbrueva, who was singing Marfa. 'There are times', he patiently repeated to her, 'when a singer has to sing words which do not reflect the mood of the character at that moment. He sings one thing but thinks about another. These words are like the outer shell of another emotion, which is underneath and simply does not show through.'[17] It is a pity that mutual understanding proved so difficult with this particular singer. Zbrueva, an experienced and accomplished mezzo-soprano with an outstanding voice, who gave original interpretations of many roles, was on good, friendly terms with Chaliapin (they even used the familiar form of speech to each other), but on this occasion nothing could persuade her to give up her reading of the character. Not so much the whole character, but one scene: 'Marfa ... sits on a log outside the window of Prince [Andrei] Khovansky, who at one time deceived her. She sings what seems a simple tune, in which she recalls her love for him: "I wandered as a maid over meadows and marshes...." These words have the ring of sad indifference, and yet Marfa is not a mindless little lamb. She ... pensively counts out old memories like beads, thinking not of the past but of the future. Her soul is filled with the sense of the martyrdom for which she is preparing herself. With her beloved Khovansky, she will soon ascend the pyre – they will burn together for their faith and their love. This means that Marfa's song must be sung so that the audience from the very beginning can feel the secret underlying it. Their thoughts must not be of beads but of the ramblings of a soul disguised by the melancholic movements of the fingers.... The public must realise that something is going to happen. Marfa's soul seethes with carnal love, passion, burning sin, intense jealousy, religious fanaticism, ecstasy and purifying faith. All these contradictions are resolved above the flames of the pyre.'[18] 'If Marfa's inner feelings,' Chaliapin continued, 'do not filter through her song, then there will be no Marfa. There will just be a plump or not so plump lady, singing, more or less well or badly, words of no interest to anyone. ....' Complete concentration, stern reserve, no complaining and no weakening – that above all is what Chaliapin saw 'in this extraordinarily complex and deep nature that only Russia, it seems, can breed, and which only the genius of a Mussorgsky can express.' As always, attaching the greatest importance to the choice of the right psychological intonation, Chaliapin regarded Marfa's song as the key to her personality.

Zbrueva reasoned differently. 'If Marfa were not alone, then she would probably not sing this song at all, or at any rate she would not confess her anguish in public and would not shed tears. But since she is quite alone and no one can see her tears, why shouldn't she sob out her sorrow? She is, of course, a strong woman, but a woman nevertheless and moreover one who loves and suffers.'[19] Her views found support among some singers, although the difference in approach was obvious to most of them. Chaliapin had reached his conclusions by analysing the musical composition of the opera, while Zbrueva followed the path of emotional imagination, based on common logic. However, there was a limit to how far one could argue with Chaliapin. During one of the rehearsals, Zbrueva had scarcely finished her first stanza when from the darkness 'boomed the gorgeous bass': 'This is really boring! Merely notes! What is it? Tears? Don't you understand that Marfa won't cry?'[20] Zbrueva felt that what had been said sounded 'loud and rude'. Offended, she left the stage in silence and her understudy had to take her place. She no longer came to rehearsals conducted by Chaliapin. In the theatre they started to think that Zbrueva would not sing on the first night; but time passed, professional pride gradually asserted itself and Chaliapin's remark seemed to lose some of its edge. She reappeared before her astonished colleagues just as suddenly as she had disappeared. She said in her memoirs that she 'sang it her own way' and that from the depth of the theatre, the same voice boomed: 'Bravo! Bravo! Excellent!'

A year later Yuri Engel, reviewing the first night of Chaliapin's production of *Khovanshchina* at the Bolshoi Theatre, observed: 'Madame Zbrueva is very good as Marfa; she has grown extraordinarily since times long past in Moscow,* both as an actress and as a singer.'[21]

Generally speaking, the critics were delighted with many of the roles, calling Chaliapin 'the greatest teacher of opera singers and an inspiration to them'. As for the performance itself, it marked the beginning of 'an era in the history of operatic production'.[22] The reviews adopted a similar tone for Chaliapin's Dosifei, but new shades of opinion were added to the usual enthusiastic approval. Perhaps for the first time in the many years Chaliapin had spent in the theatre, no mention of a difference between him and the other singers was made. The soloists, united by a common goal, had turned from mere acquaintances into real partners. Chaliapin, incomparable as ever, became an integral part of the ensemble, which realised the

* Zbrueva had started her career at the Bolshoi Theatre.

concept of the producer, completed it, upheld it and developed it further. 'Yes,' wrote *Novoe vremya*, 'this was his greatest achievement – harmony. Can the producer be at one and the same time an actor? Chaliapin proved it yesterday. He sacrificed himself to the opera. He has been fighting for the production for a long time, worked out its plan and produced it. Not only has he refrained from giving first place to the role of Dosifei, but he even gave up its advantageous position to improve the ensemble. This modesty, this flexibility, this "heroic deed" I put as the greatest merit of the singer. To be on stage, to act and not once overstep the limits of personal interest is a positive miracle.'[23] Yuri Belyaev, the distinguished Russian critic who wrote the article, had put his finger on one of the most important of Chaliapin's performing methods: the absolute necessity of being attuned to one's partners. And this apparently was not a question of modesty. According to Chaliapin, an actor's appearance, make-up and costume must, apart from anything else, take into consideration the other members of the cast. When he plays his role, the singer does not have the right to forget what it looks like in relation to those who are on the stage with him. Travelling all over the world for his guest appearances, Chaliapin would often meet the other singers only on the day of the performance, but he was always faithful to the idea of 'playing as a team'.

Describing Chaliapin's performance in *The Barber of Seville* (Covent Garden, 1926), Ernest Newman wrote: 'With an artist less scrupulous than Chaliapin, Basilio could easily have become a star part in the worst sense; with his commanding abilities, and the attention of the house centered on him, it would have been so easy for him to have played wholly for his own glory. The admirable feature of it all was that, great as he was individually, he never once stepped out of the picture, never once asserted himself at the expense of his colleagues; he was Basilio, not Chaliapin.'[24]

Although in those years it was fairly rare for the public to retain a lasting memory of an opera performance as a whole rather than just of the singing, this pleased Chaliapin far more than personal success. 'I am, of course, very happy about *Kho-*

vanshchina,' he wrote to Gorky. 'It is not going badly; the singers and the chorus have done all they could, and this is a great reward for all my pains – and pains there have been, so much so that I did not find time to shave: daily rehearsals plus regular performances, of which I have already sung some twenty.'[25]

Everyone was amazed that he had managed to do the impossible and set the apathetic Imperial stage in motion. From all quarters, the press as well as acquaintances, the same question could be heard: 'Will he go on with staging?' Perhaps things were really beginning to change, and not just in straight theatre. Chaliapin's satisfaction was mingled with sadness as he understood that it was impossible to overturn everything all at once; the desire had to be mutual, and a different concept of operatic performance was also needed. This could not be achieved without a fundamental re-adjustment in the singers' artistic consciousness, and that took time. Even at the Imperial theatres, where Russia's best actors were to be found and where serious interest could long ago have been shown in, for instance, the work of Stanislavsky and Nemirovich-Danchenko, things continued as before. Telyakovsky tersely remarked in his diary after a preview of *The Merry Wives of Windsor* at the Alexandriinsky Theatre in 1904: 'Just as the Japanese are now beating us in Manchuria,* so the Art Theatre in Moscow is beating the Imperial one. There, there is work, discipline, doing one's duty, method, technique and tolerance. In the Imperial Theatre, there is routine, complacency, playing as it comes, lack of order, no discipline. The old theatre, with its traditions, is played out, it has nothing left, everything is faded, and to raise its level, or just to improve it, is impossible.'[26] And how much more difficult this is with opera, which is far less homogeneous than a dramatic production....

We now know that Chaliapin did not manage to do all he wanted. Contracts in Russia, foreign tours, then the war, the Revolution and emigration – these left no time for reforms: he had a large family to support; he had to start rebuilding his life. In spite of all that, he still could not change. Wherever he

* 1904.

went, he asked for additional rehearsal time, tried to convince conductors, colleagues and managers that opera houses were not meant for voice demonstrations but for giving performances. The truly marvellous faculty the actor has of instilling into the musical intonation, into the word, his own emotions, his thoughts, intuition, voice and charm, was always for him the essence of the Theatre: to turn a part written by someone else, handed to him by the producer's office as odd sheets of music, into his own flesh and blood and imbue it with his attitude to life and to people, his attitude to the past and the present; to understand the composer's intentions by lifting off the veil from someone's life, which for a few hours must become your life, and make the audience live it with you.

Chaliapin succeeded in his aims to some extent, although if he could not obtain a satisfactory result, he was quite capable, even now, of leaving, declaring that he would never set foot in the place again. During his stay in Copenhagen in 1935, for instance, unable to reach common agreement in Gounod's *Faust*, he cancelled his guest appearance. 'I don't want to make an impression as a soloist but to act in a proper production. People who pay high prices to hear me in a theatre, and not in a concert hall, expect to see not only me but also a polished artistic performance. And I always have difficulties; art is not easy, you know,'[27] he told various Danish newspapers.[28]

'In Chaliapin's great days,' recalled Ivor Newton, 'he would unofficially supervise the entire production of any opera in which he sang, select the costumes and decide the lighting. His eye for detail missed nothing even down to the rings he was to wear.'[29]

His visits did not, of course, always win him admirers and friends. Singers, being generally impressionable, credulous, excitable and childishly touchy, were easily divided into warring factions, who either championed Chaliapin or were up in arms against him. On the other hand, if he saw a desire to 'resolve professional matters', he rehearsed tirelessly and without sign of irritation. In a very short space of time the production was unrecognisable. 'I am like a fly that haunts the theatre. Chase it through the window, it gets in by the door; that's the way I

Chaliapin. Courtesy of EMI Music.

am indissolubly bound to the stage,' said Chaliapin.[30]

Nevertheless, his effect on singers and conductors also depended in no small degree on their own ability to 'think clearly, understand, be creative' (Chaliapin's words). One cannot easily assess in each particular case who contributed what, but there are fortunately descriptions which give an idea of the size of Chaliapin's 'share'. 'It was stated,' reported the London newspaper *The Referee* in 1926, 'that Mr. Chaliapin himself rehearsed the witches' Sabbath scene. Nothing more convincing has been seen at Covent Garden. The sepulchral dell of rocks, the mass of whirling grisly figures in half-lights, the rising and falling of waving arms and clutching fingers, with Satan standing above commanding obedience and hommage with a besom as sceptre, his fiendish glee in the terror displayed and his wild dance in the Bacchanalian-like revels were horrible but unforgettable.'[31] And again, a review from the Prague news-paper *Narodni listy* (1934): 'He has not come here merely to excel by his own performance without regard to his surround-ings. He does not derive pleasure, as others might, from the fact that this environment is artistically far below him. Chaliapin's aim is that an opera in which he appears should be performed as perfectly as possible, as he alone feels and lives it. Hence, in rehearsals he actually teaches those with him; he leads the singing and the production.'[32]

Reading Chaliapin's interviews, letters, books and the con-temporary memoirs which mention him, one cannot help feeling deep respect for a man so unswervingly faithful to his ideals. The way he speaks and writes late in life not about his own place in art but about art itself never ceases to surprise. Evaluating the past, scrutinising the present, he wants to know what will happen to people's spiritual life tomorrow, what will become of his beloved THEATRE. In his mature years when he freely confided his thoughts in regular interviews, Chaliapin some-times seemed able to see into the future. 'If I had the necessary money,' he was quoted as saying in *Musical America* (1929), 'I would myself form an organisation to produce for screen and sound the great operas. This is assured of a great future.'[33]

Generally speaking, his plans were always on a large scale,

but as time passed he wisely learnt how to choose among them – one could not say with caution, but certainly with careful deliberation. An artist who has gained fame in the early stages of his career is often later unwilling to take any risk with the public and the critics. They both look at him with jaundiced expectancy and measure every subsequent move of his on the Procrustean bed of his early successes. Appearing on the stage in a new role is difficult for anyone, but it was particularly so for Chaliapin, who had to bear the added burden of being treated as a genius. He knew very well that success quickly becomes common property but that the bitterness of failure has to be endured alone. At such times, recent allies and admirers turn into enemies. 'The days when our father was giving a concert or a performance were the most difficult ones for our family,' says Irina Chaliapina. 'He felt very nervous on those days; one had to try to keep out of his sight. At moments like those we children would be scolded for nothing at all. But we did not mind; we knew the reason for it: our father's nervous excitement before a performance.'[34]

Nor did Chaliapin's agitation vanish once he was on stage. 'From the wings of the Mariinsky Theatre, I had many occasions of observing Chaliapin making his entrance,' recalls Boris Asafev. 'If he saw that he was being watched, he would do "something funny", "show off". If no one was taking any notice, this was a man concentrating, very tense, his whole body braced. In the opera which one would think the most familiar to him – *Faust* – Chaliapin, a shapely and lithe Mephistopheles, goes into the wings after the first act. I greet him. As he offers me his hand I feel that it is slightly trembling. I study him: the face is anxious, the voice seems to falter. "Fedor Ivanovich, even you are so nervous?" – "Ah! How could it be otherwise? If I don't quite make it, if I do a little less than they expect – after all, from me they'll demand a hundred, a thousand times more because I'm 'Chaliapin' – they'll say: his voice has gone, Chaliapin is finished, past his best, he has taken to drink", and he left, almost stooping. He then knew me only from seeing me at Stasov's; I was a nobody in the theatre, only a pianist – repetiteur de ballet; he did not need to pretend with me – and he said this simply and sincerely.'[35] It may be of interest to add that Asafev later came to be regarded as the doyen of the Soviet school of musicologists.

Chaliapin's relatively limited (for the times) and slowly expanding repertoire should not be attributed to cowardice, laziness or complacency, although many people, some of whom knew him well and were supposed to understand him, did just that. 'Fedor Ivanovich Chaliapin remains now the same fine artist and singer, but as an active artistic force he has already ceased to exist. He is no longer tearing ahead as he did before.'[36] These words were pronounced in 1910, and not just by anybody but by Savva Ivanovich Mamontov. The former owner of the Private Opera could probably not forget the days when Chaliapin was working in his theatre and sang twenty roles in three seasons. And before that, when he was wandering all over the provinces, he would, if need be, learn a major part in one day and perform it the same evening. All this was true and could not have been otherwise – not only because he was driven by youthful vigour and robust health and because everything seemed to beckon him onwards but also because he was obliged to reconcile his own interests with those of the theatre where he was employed. Even in his privileged position at Mamontov's, Chaliapin sang many things to which he subsequently never returned. The greater Chaliapin's freedom of choice, the more he narrowed the once long and varied list of his roles, comprising some sixty-seven titles in all. He took his time to add new parts and prepared them with great pains. Each addition was motivated by very careful reasoning. Creative talent changes as it matures, and so do its objectives. Certainly, Chaliapin was not always entirely guided by purely artistic considerations. There is no other explanation for his taking part in such featureless operas as Raoul Ginsberg's *The Old Eagle* and *Ivan the Terrible*.*

But these are really mere trifles in either the destiny or the art of Chaliapin. At some time after 1904, his repertoire could be divided by and large into two groups: the Russian characters (Susanin, the Miller, Galitsky, Farlaf in *Ruslan and Ludmilla*,

* Monte Carlo, 1909 and 1911 respectively.

Boris Godunov, Varlaam, Dosifei, Salieri, Eryomka, Ivan the Terrible, the Demon, occasionally the title role in Rachmaninov's *Aleko*, Gremin, Konchak) and the European ones (Mephistopheles and Mefistofele, Don Basilio, Don Quixote, King Philip, occasionally Tonio and Nilakantha).

After his departure from Russia in 1922 he further reduced it to five or six roles. The last addition, Don Quixote, was made in 1910; Chaliapin's contemporaries never ceased to wonder at this and deluged him with questions and suggestions. They thought, and quite rightly, that he was ignoring dozens of extraordinary characters well worth his attention. Chaliapin's disinclination to sing Wagner was the first and greatest shock. Surveying the 1901 season, the singer's future biographer Edward Stark reflected in the newspaper *Rossiya*: 'It seems to us that for such a master of subtlety as Chaliapin Wagner's musical dramas hold a huge, untouched territory of artistic pleasure. Take Wotan, for instance, a bottomless well for the creative powers of a great singer. Chaliapin has to be the first Russian singer to plumb its depths. Or Hans Sachs. This is a very complex part; they can barely manage it on our Mariinsky stage. Let us hope that we will eventually see Chaliapin in these roles. They require a perfect combination of vocal qualities and dramatic talent. However, the whole question is to what extent he is himself attracted by the Wagnerian repertoire. ...'[37]

Gorky, hearing of Chaliapin's new production plans, enthusiastically wrote to a friend: 'If you see him, tell him that I am terribly glad of *Khovanshchina*'s success and that his ideas seem to me brilliant and as up-to-date as can be. He is finally getting down to his proper business. I am absolutely certain that he will accomplish a great deal. I can imagine how he will stage *Die Meistersinger* and how he will sing Sachs!!'[38]

Chaliapin was not trying to avoid giving explanations, but they varied according to circumstances. When Kaiser Wilhelm decorated him on the occasion of his guest appearance in Berlin (1907), he politely and respectfully answered, 'Yes, I sing [Wagner], but only in concert; his operas I still dare not sing.'[39] 'I like Wagner very much; I always listen to his operas in Germany. Shall I myself sing in German, I do not know. Doing an opera ideally is possible only in its original language,' he declared in a 1911 interview with the *Peterburgskaya gazeta*. A few years earlier, in 1907, he had been more specific in the same paper: 'I would very much like to appear in the *Nibelungen* – Wotan, that is a role after my own heart. I think that one day I shall do Wotan the way I see him. Only I don't know where. I don't, after all, speak German and will never bring myself to sing in German.' Talking to the London *Morning Post* in 1923, he expressed the desire to sing Hans Sachs, but at the mention of Wotan 'he demurred': ' "If I sing Wotan I must follow my own conception of the part. The Wagner tradition as regards acting, such as Madame Cosima Wagner and Siegfried Wagner uphold at Bayreuth, does not appeal to me. The actors move in squares. First one stands here in this attitude, and then one stands there in that", and Chaliapin moves about to show his meaning. Could he breathe a new spirit into the dramatic action of the *The Ring*? It seems to you that his volcanic personality might achieve this. But as he puts off Wotan and subsides into a Russian dressing-gown (our talk took place in the forenoon), he deprecates the wish to be such a reformer.'[40]

Where does the truth lie? It is not easy to find it in Chaliapin's own words. No one prevented him from doing Wagner 'his way', just like his other roles. The excuse of not knowing German is equally unconvincing: he had for years been singing Rossini, Gounod and Verdi in Russian. In recitals, even abroad, he sang Schumann, Schubert and Brahms in his native tongue, and it is in this language that he recorded their songs. Neither was timidity one of Chaliapin's distinguishing traits, so that it is rather difficult to take seriously his humble 'I dare not' to the Kaiser. He gave perhaps his most honest answer in an informal conversation with Sergei Levik. It was brief, sharp, and somewhat irritated: 'I don't like it.'[41] The nature of likes or dislikes in art is not something that can be explained. They are, in the last resort, entirely a matter of personal taste. It may be interesting to analyse them in the case of some outstanding person, but the problem remains essentially the same. 'Anyone can feel drawn towards Mozart or Wagner,' wrote Chaliapin. 'The personal motives for such a preference may be different, but even the most naive amongst them will subjectively be cogent.'[42]

Wagnerian heroes were not the only ones missing from Chaliapin's repertoire. Although he had a high regard for Rimsky-Korsakov's music, he never even gave a thought to Dodon in *The Golden Cockerel* or Saltan in *The Tale of Tsar Saltan*. He might have tried Kochubei in Tchaikovsky's *Mazeppa*, Procida in Verdi's *The Sicilian Vespers* or Fiesco in his *Simon Boccanegra*, or looked further than Don Basilio and Leporello* in the works of Rossini and Mozart. He could ... but he did not, and there is hardly any point now in trying to find out why he behaved in this manner and not differently. Building theories is not all that difficult, especially when one is determined to do so. Then facts and details are of no importance; making conclusions is the only thing that matters. Boris Asafev, for instance, decided that 'no one understood how difficult it was for him to select roles, for all his sensitivity, his striking ability to distinguish between true and false, form and substance in musical and vocal intonation. The whole music had to be right for what he required, for the character he was creating – and in his creation both intonation and body movements were in unity: that is, the music's intonations, the entire emotional and conceptual sides had to correspond to his ideas. This is not entirely possible, since rare is the composer who does not, during the course of some major part, "break" into a completely different type, or, at best, into a completely neutral form.'[43]

If one were to agree with Asafev's views, how could one explain, for instance, one of Chaliapin's greatest creations – Don Quixote? Massenet's music is unremarkable, and since the death of the singer, the opera is not very often performed. And does it mean that the many roles he did not sing, including Wagnerian ones, do not satisfy 'exacting demands of musical and vocal unity'? Many other composers could be named, but the question remains open. Would it not be better to let Chaliapin speak for himself, especially since he made everything

---

* Chaliapin sang Leporello for a few performances in North and South America in 1908, and never again.

clear to his detractors, at least as far as Wagner is concerned? He did this at the very end of his memoirs, with a fantastic little sketch: a young musician at the beginning of his career decides to obtain the autographs of two geniuses – Mozart and Wagner. Chaliapin's tale is in the first person. Mozart is there only as a contrast. Easy-going, warm, kind and simple, he is the antithesis of Wagner, in the gloomy hall of whose house all is 'majestic and cold'. Every word of the host, who has appeared like a god, is weighty and important; what he says is truly memorable. 'But when the massive oak doors closed behind me, and I saw the sky and the ordinary passer-by, for some reason I felt relieved – as though the heavy load which was oppressing me had been lifted. There is a grandiose battle of centaurs in Wagner. It has great, almost superhuman, force. But I have no liking for the spears with which one must pierce the heart to draw from it some sacred blood.'[44]

One may disagree with Chaliapin, but what is important here is that he is not hypnotised by great names; he is not afraid to speak out against what he considers an unacceptable course in art, what he simply has 'no liking for'. At times like these nothing could influence him – neither storms of applause from the public nor favourable reviews from the critics. 'As could be expected, Wagner's music gave the singer the opportunity to display to us the whole might of his genius,' wrote the Petersburg newspaper *Molva* after a concert performance of Wotan's final scene in *Die Walküre*. 'One could, it is true, argue with some of the tempi, with the arbitrary slowing down of certain phrases. But these are just trifles compared with the majestic picture Chaliapin gave us. What we had was a real god singing, a god full of sorrow and suffering but who can still make everybody tremble. ... It was magnificent!'[45]

In fact, while the press and his admirers continued to regret 'his lack of interest and his indolence', Chaliapin never ceased seeking to enlarge his repertoire. The inner motive behind his search is not easy to decipher, and it is difficult to reach a final judgement. One thing is perhaps clear – he looked for characters with dramatic depth, a complex and strong mixture of emotions. 'Grandeur, nobility, impressiveness, and, by inversion, sordidness, bestiality, an awkward ugliness fall easily within his ken,' shrewdly remarked an American reviewer in 1921.[46]

The idea of Oedipus, for instance, kept haunting him. There was no opera on this subject, and Chaliapin, with astonishing perseverance, tried to persuade first Rimsky-Korsakov, then Glazunov, to compose one. When this failed, he wrote to Gorky, asking him to talk to a mutual acquaintance about the libretto while he looked for a composer abroad. Chaliapin's desire to play Oedipus was so great that he even considered a theatrical performance, but after lengthy and, as witnessed by contemporaries, agonising doubts, he lost his nerve. 'If someone wrote the opera, I would help him. I would even invent something, perhaps come up with a tune. But as for drama – that's terrifying!' he said.[47] (It is sad to read in Georges Enesco's memoirs that when he had completed his *Oedipus*, he approached Chaliapin as a possible interpreter. 'Shortly before the great singer's death I went to see him at the theatre. *Don Quixote* was on that evening. Chaliapin pronounced a sentence which seemed strange to me at the time: 'I only want to look at the libretto.' Later, I understood that before forming an opinion on the music, he wanted to know what the amount of work involved was, whether his health would permit him to undertake it. Convinced that he did not have the strength to remain on stage for so long, he silently gave the text back. My heart sank. What an Oedipus he would have made!')[48]

A good role gives an actor the chance to stretch himself, and Chaliapin could clearly see the rich selection offered by dramatic theatre. Nor did he forget that a singer's voice is capricious and can change at any moment. This thought settled more deeply into his consciousness as time passed. The cold and hunger of his childhood and youth, always present in his mind, turned a natural concern into a nightmare. It seemed desirable from all points of view to have a second string as an insurance. Material and artistic rewards seemed to be waiting round the corner. He was surrounded by tempting talk which would not die down. Many, including his friends in the theatre, thought that it would cost a genius like him little effort to add another jewel to his crown. After Chaliapin's performance as Don Basilio on the Covent Garden stage in 1926, the English newspaper *Truth* wrote: 'He played with a drollery and subtlety which made it the outstanding performance of the evening. His make-up alone was enough to show what an actor of genius Chaliapin is, and if he ever loses his voice – which there is fortunately no reason to fear – he could easily become one of the greatest of living actors. He could make a magnificent Othello and Macbeth and a wonderful Falstaff.'[49]

Moreover, the dramatic stage was no terra incognita for him. This was how he had entered the theatre, acting in various types of plays. And Chaliapin could not have feared that this kind of performing might harm his singing. It is well known that he could tell stories for hours without tiring, and if he was in a good mood, he continually chatted, performed little numbers and entertained guests in his dressing-room even during the intervals. The critics reacted at length and favourably to Chaliapin's rare but, as was immediately evident, successful attempts to gain a foothold in this 'neighbouring province'. When he read Byron's *Manfred* at a recital in 1902, music critics devoted a larger portion of their articles to him than to Schumann. 'Chaliapin is richly endowed with a talent for the stage,' wrote Nikolai Kashkin. 'If he decided to appear on the dramatic stage, it would arouse enormous interest. We do not say that everything would be equally good, but never before have we received a better general impression from a reading.'[50] 'Some roughness, unevenness was noticeable here and there in Chaliapin's performance,' conceded Yuri Engel, 'but the overall tone of speech, so well caught (a certain amount of elation, called for by the character of the plot and of the language, combined with simple and sincere intonations), the uncommon power and the expressiveness of the recitation – all this would have done credit to a first-class dramatic actor.'[51] Gorky declared after attending two concert performances: 'Fedor Ivanovich read well the first time, but the second time he read magnificently.'[52]

Such admissions undeniably flattered the singer, letting him hope that he would not have to give up his beloved art until his last day. On November 10th, 1918, he took an even more decisive step when he performed on the stage of the Alexandrinsky Theatre. The occasion was a gala celebrating the hundredth anniversary of Turgenev's birth. The long programme included an adaptation of his tale *The Singers* with Chaliapin as Yashka Turok. And though singing was the most important part (the story revolves around a contest between Yashka and another folk singer), making the character credible and becoming an integral part in an ensemble of actors was not easy. Once again, it was a triumph. 'I cannot even say how the performance went, so bewitched were we all by Chaliapin,'[53] recalled a member of the cast more than half a century later. It is approximately at that time, as Yurev indicates, that he 'agreed to play Lucifer in Byron's *Cain* and planned to undertake the role of King Philip in Schiller's play *Don Carlos*'.[54] He was also contemplating Shakespearian parts, Bolingbroke in *Richard II* and King Lear, as well as Boris Godunov in Pushkin's tragedy. 'When he read in an undertone, all was well,' continued Yurev. 'One could not wish for anything better. The whole interior line of the character was pictured so movingly, expressively and with such limpidity that I thought: "Ah! How wonderful this is going to be!" But as soon as he started to read in full voice, everything collapsed. The singer's habit of producing sound with the diaphragm rendered his speech unnatural; his voice resounded too intensely in the cavity of the mouth. The result was quite unsuitable for drama. The phrases have no clarity or distinctness; it all spreads out as on blotting paper. . . . We began the preparatory work and started to practise in hexameters. Our work went on steadily and he was already close to his goal. The last lesson took place on the eve of his final departure abroad in the spring of 1922.'[55]

It is interesting to compare these memoirs with an interview Chaliapin gave in 1925 to the correspondent of *The Ladies' Home Journal*. 'My stressing of the art of the actor in opera sometimes brought me queries as to my ambitions in regard to the dramatic stage. It is true that I have sometimes felt that I perhaps had it in me to play Othello or Lear or Shylock on the stage. I have even studied their characters. I have considered how they should be represented. But . . . in the opera I am

Chaliapin as Yashka Turok in the stage adaptation of Turgenev's story, *The Singers*, 1919.

entirely at home, I know just how softly I may sing and yet be heard all over the house. When I speak, while I can modulate my voice with equal precision, I do not know how it will reach my audience. No, I shall never turn actor. Opera has claimed me for three decades, and I am content.'[56]

And so the conclusion is self-evident: Chaliapin, for all his passionate desire to master the profession of dramatic actor, did not succeed because he could not learn the laws of acoustics of stage speech. Strangely, neither three years of studying with Yurev nor the natural gift which in other cases never let him down was of any use here. Uncommonly receptive to the expressiveness of sound, Chaliapin proved unable to cope with what an average drama student finds relatively easy.

It seems that one must once again question the persistent and generally accepted stories told by Chaliapin's well-informed contemporaries, as well as disagree with the singer himself. To begin with, Chaliapin 'knew how to speak'. The extant recording of Nadson's* poem 'Reverie' and Pabst's film *Don Quixote* give proof of this. His manner of pronouncing words and constructing phrases is another matter. This today sounds somewhat affected, even pompous, and therefore old-fashioned. Meyerhold, who saw the film in France sometime in the mid-1930s, confided later to a friend: 'I did not recognise him: he was timid, mawkish. If *Don Quixote* somehow comes over here I don't recommend seeing it – you won't be able to understand what the great actor and singer Chaliapin represented in the theatre.'[57] But even there, in what is perhaps Chaliapin's most notable artistic failure, the contrast between 'spoken' and 'sung' episodes is striking: in the latter he is simply transformed. Every note is filled with emotion and meaning; a gesture which had just before seemed embarrasingly exaggerated now looks essential: sublime idealism becomes the individual characteristic of a real man.

Chaliapin's views on opera and on how it should be performed are expressed in his autobiographical books, his articles and interviews. He never separates music from theatre. 'A great

---

* Nadson, Semyon (1862–1887). Russian poet, many of whose verses were set to music.

deal of the intimacy and the power of his appeal comes directly through his voice,'[58] observed a *Times* correspondent in 1914. 'Typically, if people talked to him only about acting, he remained indifferent to praise, but if they admired the singing, he was genuinely pleased,' recalled Ariy Pazovsky.[59] 'If Chaliapin had become a dramatic actor,' writes Sergei Levik, 'he would no doubt have been a great, outstanding artist, unique of his kind. But he would not have become the Chaliapin who surpassed everything ever known before or since in the art of the theatre. Chaliapin was born a singer of genius, and he was not a genius in anything else.'[60] 'I think that the prodigious phenomenon which Chaliapin remains', says the theatrical authority Professor Pavel Markov, seemingly putting an end to all arguments, 'could only have happened in opera.'[61]

Any study of the singer must of necessity mention his voice and his vocal skills. An opera supremely well-staged, with an excellent orchestra and conductor, wonderful sets and costumes, but badly sung, will be regarded as something unpalatable, incomplete. This popular belief has a grain of sense. Chaliapin's striking records may, of course, give a clue to the sort of voice he possessed, to what constituted his vocal mastery, but it is regrettably difficult to rely solely on them to form a general opinion – regrettably because they were of enormous importance to Chaliapin. In a letter to the public, now in the archives of EMI, he wrote: 'I am very particular about my records. When I sing for the gramophone, I give my best, and the records are part of me – I feel almost that they are my flesh and blood. No matter where I sing my songs, I always feel as if I am the father of those song-children.'[62]

To this day, some of Chaliapin's unpublished records (dissatisfied with his own performance, he did not allow their release) keep coming to light among collectors. There is, moreover, abundant evidence that Chaliapin's voice and performing style had undergone noticeable changes as time passed. 'Recordings made in the 1930s give a particularly false idea of his singing up to 1922,'* wrote Sergei Levik.[63]

---

* The year he left the USSR.

'That is no longer his voice,' the correspondent of the *Daily Express* overheard old stagers saying in the foyer of Covent Garden in 1929. ' "Marvellous, marvellous!" shouted the younger generation, who have no memories.'[64]

There is of course another alternative – to seek the help of those lucky enough to have heard Chaliapin in person and who left descriptions of his singing, though this also presents its own difficulties. If one studies reviews of his appearances, one notices that comments on the qualities of Chaliapin's voice and on his vocal schooling are of a most general nature. It might be assumed that articles devoted to an opera singer would feature an extensive analysis of the principal weapon in his armoury, but these authors often concentrate on something else. 'How does one talk about this, how?' exclaims a critic from the town of Kharkov in the Ukraine. 'What words can explain how Chaliapin sang. . . . As if it were possible! One can only sing it. And only one person can sing about Chaliapin's singing – he himself. What is the point of talking about the power of Chaliapin's voice, about his upper and lower notes, and of discussing how long he can hold his breath? Is that what matters? Is that what Chaliapin means? When one looks at the Venus de Milo, does one ask oneself what kind of marble she is made of; or when one looks at a Raphael painting, what kind of brushes and paint were used? It is so perfect that one does not notice these things, and it does not prevent one surrendering with all the power of one's emotions to the thought, to the live spirit which the artist has embodied in his creation. This spirit is in Chaliapin's singing; it is how he sings. This is what his genius consists of.'[65] 'Chaliapin's voice flowed amply and freely,' said a colleague of his in the newspaper *Caucasus*, trying to pierce the mystery of the singer's success, 'at times astonishingly powerful and metallic, at time shot through with the soft glow of velvet, smoothly and unexpectedly passing from a mighty forte to a soft *piano*. In this wonderful voice you can hear the powerful, deep sounds of a true bass, as supple as a baritone's, as tender as a tenor's. All this thrills, enchants. This is a diamond, blazing with all the colours of the rainbow.'[66]

The memoirs of Chaliapin's compatriots offer nothing better.

With the exception of Sergei Levik's book, excerpts from which have already been quoted, they do not contain any critical examination of his vocal art. Learned comparisons and literary associations, carefully selected, give a measure of the listener's enthusiasm rather than help to understand what Chaliapin did as a singer and how he did it.

English reviewers writing in 1913 were the first to treat this subject seriously, but by then Chaliapin had already been on the stage for almost a quarter of a century. Later, in the 1920s, interesting observations were made in America, when Chaliapin was over fifty. As far as is known, the earliest review about him is dated 1893. Here it is: 'Mr. Chaliapin, a pupil of Mr. Usatov, probably due to some misunderstanding considering himself a bass when he is clearly a baritone. His lower register is extremely weak, but the upper notes are sonorous and attractive. It was enough to hear him perform Gremin's aria to be convinced that bass parts are just not for him.'[67]

Chaliapin, only just turned twenty, did not spend a great deal of time wondering whether the critic was right. Did it matter – baritone or bass – if the big, strong (according to certain reports, these were the qualities which subsequently 'suffered considerably') voice seemed to know no limits?[68] Despite Usatov's warning, he was not afraid of a mixed repertoire; worries about the future were meaningless when his whole life was before him. And there were so many beautiful concert arias for baritone which he enjoyed singing. The great Battistini heard him in one of these performances. 'Several years ago,' he recounted to a newspaper correspondent in Kiev, where he was appearing in 1903, 'I found myself in the house of a Petersburg acqaintance. The lady of the house introduced me to a tall young man with almost no sign of hair on his face. After dinner he was invited to sing. And we heard the Demon's aria. The voice was indeed big, beautiful and soft, the young man sang expressively, with feeling. When he had finished, I conveyed to him my sincere pleasure at his interpretation, congratulated him on his rich vocal resources, but said: "You undoubtedly have a future, but why, my friend, do you sing baritone parts when you have a genuine bass? Never mind that the pitch of your voice allows you to take high baritone notes: you are nevertheless a bass and this you must remember." The young man [it was Chaliapin] entirely agreed with me. We parted and have not seen each other since.'[69]

So, in spite of many attempts at roles in the baritone's repertoire – even if some of them came off – Chaliapin remained a typical basso cantante. On the whole, it is not pitch but timbre which determines the type of a voice, and the memoirs and testimonies of the singer's contemporaries leave no possible doubt on this question. The enormous effect which Chaliapin produced on people, both on stage and in real life, created the legend of a voice of unprecedented volume and force. However, as early as 1897, a Moscow critic remarked: 'Chaliapin has power not because of the loudness or sharpness of his sound but because of the spiritual quality of the melodic phrase, the delicacy of the phrasing.'[70] 'The power of his sound', concurred Levik, 'was not innate but was the result of Chaliapin's exceptional skill in arranging light and shade in his performance.'[71]

Many agreed with this observation. 'The power of his voice, like its compass, is not really extraordinary,' wrote the *Musical Times*. All the singers above-named [Edouard de Reszke, Pol Plançon] could produce louder, broader outbursts of open-vowel tone and more resonant deep notes than Chaliapin, who has none of the heavy reverberating timbre of the typical Russian bass. But to make up for it he can mount to the loftier regions of a genuine baritone with the smoothness inseparable from a faultless scale, while his attack in that part of the voice is equally clean and true. His 'effects', consequently, are always safe and interesting to listen to. Whether spontaneous or studied, they obviously belong to the equipment of the clever vocalist no less than of the accomplished actor.'[72] 'Chaliapin was a great singer,' wrote *The Listener*. 'By that I don't mean that he was endowed by nature with a phenomenal voice. There have been more powerful, more resonant basses than his, but I doubt whether there has been in our time one that became so sensitive, so subtle, so flexible an instrument for the purposes of a great actor-singer.'[73] And Sergei Levik summed it all up: 'Chaliapin's voice was not a phenomenon in the purely *psycho-*

logical sense, like for instance A. P. Antonovsky's voice, the Pole Silikh's, or the Italian Navarini's. But as an *artistic* phenomenon, it sounded ampler, more powerful and sparkling than these singers'. We often said to each other that not one of us had ever heard *such* a voice.' (Levik's italics)[74]

Time did not erode this impression – quite the contrary. 'Most musical executants, however brilliant, pass away and are as though they have never been, but the name and the reputation of this extraordinary man – of his kind the greatest artist, with his combination of vocal and histrionic genius, of the lyric stage of our time, and possibly in the whole history of music – will never be forgotten,' reflected Richard Capell after Chaliapin's death.[75] Purely as a singer he was supremely gifted, with a basso-cantante voice of a range, power, flexibility, expressiveness and technical accomplishment that today has not its like in the world. 'Even those of us who have a slight knowledge of the Russian language', commented Ernest Newman on Chaliapin's 1921 concert in England, 'were very glad to forget it and give ourselves up to the sheer joy of Chaliapin's singing. In the old days what made him so remarkable was not only the glory of his voice, but his extraordinary command of it. Last night this art of his was as wonderful as ever; it really seemed as if we had heard no real singing since he left us in 1914.'[76] 'Chaliapin's singing was as great as his acting,' affirmed Gigli following their joint appearance the same year in America. 'His voice was beautiful in texture, perfectly produced, thrilling in range and power, his vocalism was an outstanding exhibition of breath control, tonal production and phrasing.'[77] 'Then he began to sing,' recalled Arthur Rubinstein, 'with a voice of unique quality; powerful and caressing, soft as a baritone's and flexible as a tenor's, it sounded as natural as a speaking voice.'[78] 'A voice that never breaks the musical line, yet brings into pure singing a wealth of expressions which speech with its greater freedom, has never in my experience been able to achieve,' says the critic of *Time and Tide*, echoing the famous pianist.[79]

What was Chaliapin's singing like? What made it so original? 'Above all, Chaliapin's voice came out of the larynx without the slightest effort. In the loudest *forte* passages the tension of the cords, it seemed, did not exceed the limits of their usual state in normal speech. It was impossible under any circumstances to detect signs of forcing. Dilation and contraction of the respiratory flow – that was all one could imagine, but only imagine, and not perceive as something tangible and audible. Like a piece of dough which can easily be rolled into the thinnest sheet, the voice just as imperceptibly swelled without a single jolt into a volcanic torrent of sound of extraordinary force. And however long the note had to be sustained, there was not one dent in the ideal line, not one "kink" along the way. Always and everywhere, crescendos and decrescendos rose and fell ideally.'[80] 'It has in a remarkable degree the capacity for a voice of infinite delicacy, a lovely *fil de voix* that can be attenuated and prolonged to a gossamer film of sound without losing either continuity or charm. No other bass or deep baritone now before the public possesses this exquisite mezza voce in the measure that Chaliapin does. He uses it with discretion, that is to say, only when occasion demands; and with all the greater effect because his amazing control of breath-pressure enables him to either swell or diminish tone from or to this "thread of voice", so that it runs through the whole gamut of strength and volume of which his elastic organ is capable.'[81] 'The chief factors in Chaliapin's marvellous combinations of quantity and quality are enormous chest depth, a singularly domed roof of the mouth and perfect co-operation of sound-modifying muscles and natural resonances. Chaliapin appears to hold back his breath till the last possible moment, so that when at last it leaves his moulded lips the tone soars forth on the strongest possible breath impulse. Thus the note seems to explode, as it were, on the lips, and the result is that almost thunderous hollow tone peculiar to Chaliapin. Then there are wondrously plaintive soft notes, in which he gives the impression of leaning so elastically on the breath. They are not produced, as with many singers, entirely in the head, but always have a continued chest-depth'.[82] 'The outstanding features of his unique art are the beauty of his *pianissimi*, which are the particular privilege of tenors. The glorious tone he achieves in the greatest effects, the expressive control of the melodic line, the calm and complete mastery and richness of his performance – these are qualities which are rarely found all together in such pre-eminence. They are, however, merely Chaliapin's stock-in-trade as an interpreter. He is one of those artists who are able to penetrate into the most secret corners of the human soul, who can reach down to the very source of feelings and yearnings.' [83] 'Chaliapin was in full possession of his voice, one of the noblest basses ever heard here [New York, 1922]. His use of that voice technically, especially as regards breath support and legato, was lessons to all aspiring vocalists. His singing was also notable for its variety of shading, its command of style, and the perfect ease and clearness of the diction – a diction so pure, in fact, that even one ignorant of the Russian language might almost have written down the words phonetically.' [84] 'One of the most striking features of his technique is the remarkable fidelity of word utterance which removes all sense of artificiality, so frequently associated with operatic singing. His diction floats on a beautiful cantilena, particularly in his mezza-voce singing, which – though one would hardly expect it from a singer endowed with such a noble bass voice – is one of the most telling features of his performance. There is never any striving after vocal effects, and his voice is always subservient to the words. This style of singing is surely that which Wagner so continually demanded from his interpreters. His technique is of that high order that never obtrudes itself upon the hearer. It is always his servant, never his master. His readings are also his own, and it is this absence of all conventionality that makes his singing of the "Calumny" aria from *Il barbiere* a thing of delight, so full of humour is its interpretation, and so satisfying to the demands of the most exacting "bel cantist". The reason is not far to seek, for his method is based upon a thoroughly sound breath control, which produces such splendid cantabile results. Every student should listen to this great singer and profit by his art.' [85] 'I doubt whether in any other artist at any time, speech and song have ever been welded into so indivisible a unity. In its supreme moments the phenomenon baffles analysis; how, we alternatively ask ourselves, can the man sing with his mouth and lips and his palate in the shapes and positions they must be in to simulate thus the qualities of speech, and how does he succeed in giving us the impression that he is chatting casually with us when he is so obviously producing a fine round singing tone?'[86] 'His art, like that of all the greatest artists, seems so simple because it is so complex. Many threads have gone to the weaving of that wonderful texture. Every phrase, every part of every phrase, is modelled upon the words. The mystery is how, with this close fidelity to verbal literalism, he contrives to make his voice sing with the freedom of line and infinite variety of shading of a great instrumental player. He plays upon it like an instrument; in its noble pathos it suggests a cello.'[87] 'There is a haunting and lingering loveliness about the long-drawn-out threads of sound that one can hear from no other singer.'[88] 'A voice whose range allows all nuances and gives us a glimpse of what the language of the gods might be: singing which would be as natural as speaking is for humans.'[89]

The above may sound like a monologue but is in fact a compilation of writings from various periods and various corners of the globe. The two concluding examples are taken from reviews of Chaliapin's performances in England and France when he was nearing the age of sixty. However, the effect produced is not that of a multi-coloured patchwork but rather the reverse. A sole desire suffuses everything: to solve the secret of Chaliapin's vocal mastery, and through it, if possible, of his whole art as well. 'In our time,' wrote Levik, 'we singers listened very carefully to the way Chaliapin emitted sounds. How did he open the larnyx? Did he throw the high notes to the back of the head or, on the contrary, did he place them against the teeth, i.e. "take" them in the "famous" mask? Did he raise his collar-bone or did he breathe through the diaphragm? Didn't his tongue, which sometimes stuck out a tiny bit, bother him? And we invariably came to the conclusion that there were no straightforward answers to these questions. With Chaliapin, purely technical moments melted away within the complex of his interpretation. The details of various schools were all present, but there was no variation of style. It was impossible to talk of one school in particular, but it was equally unthinkable to say that there was no school at all. Because, if

Chaliapin's colours of timbre were a unique treasure house, his vocal technique was just as original, rich and totally incomparable. With such singers as the tenor Dimitri Smirnov, loudly acclaimed for his voice and his school of singing; with Everard's best pupils, Tartakov and Obraztsov; with the excellent vocalists and past masters of bel canto Sibiriakov, Kastorsky and others, we could always see that their school of singing had much in common with the exponents of one manner of performing or another – in addition, of course, as fashion decreed, to the Italian one. We compared Smirnov to Anselmi, Kastorsky to Navarini, Sibiriakov to Arimondi.... To compare any of them – even remotely – to Battistini would have been regarded as the highest form of praise. But I remember perfectly that in the years when the authority of Italians was still unquestioned for the average mass of singers, at the performance of *Maria di Rohan'* * with Battistini, many of us already thought that at times (only at times) he sang like Chaliapin. The yardstick against which we all measured ourselves had lost its accuracy.

'I think that it was precisely Chaliapin who was the *first* [Levik's italics] Russian singer to fuse in his singing all the techniques and all the schools to the extent that they ceased to exist as independently recognisable features of the art of singing. The sphere in which Chaliapin's beneficial influence started to make itself felt almost immediately was that of taste and a sense of proportion. Perhaps it was from him that others borrowed economy of sound. It is obvious that many good singers before him had skilfully used *mezza voce, piano* and *pianissimo,* as they did not consider battering *forte* to be the only way of making an impact on the public. But until Chaliapin, they saw in this not only a means of conveying emotion but an additional arsenal of purely vocal effects. Their methods had in most cases a different philosophy.

'During the first decade of our century, Titta Ruffo quite frequently visited Russia. He shone by a unique voice, the richest I can remember. In addition, he had at his disposal a great variety of timbres, or "intonations", as Chaliapin said, which

---

* Opera by Donizetti.

he used cleverly and with tact. But ... between him and Chaliapin there was an enormous difference. Titta Ruffo found colours for each given section of the role and adroitly superimposed them on the foundation of his voice. And we always said: "What a voice Titta had in such an such a passage!" It was wonderful but fragmentary. When we talked of Chaliapin, however, we would say: "What a voice Chaliapin had as Boris (or the Miller, Mephistopheles, Basilio)." ' [90]

The amazing powers of transformation of Chaliapin's voice are perhaps the only vestiges left of the great singer's art. Whatever the date on the disc's label and the merits of the vocal performance (and they are naturally unequal), the first sound clearly indicates the mental state of the person. The many voices addressing you are strikingly unlike each other, but they make you believe in the reality of these people's existence and so believe their words and their emotions. Through the hiss veiling the imperfect recording technique of 1912, you make out noble Don Silva,* barely containing his indignation as he says 'Che mai vegg'io', and then, moved by the sad 'Infelice! E tuo credevi', you see, you really see, that Silva is old. And the sighs of Don Quixote's death scene, betraying his utter exhaustion; the surprise, jealousy, pain, thirst for revenge, loneliness, all in the one note crowning Aleko's† aria; Salieri's chilling 'You will sleep for a long time, Mozart'; or the simple worldly wisdom which the good-natured but naive and dull-witted Miller teaches to his daughter.... The basis of Chaliapin's 'credibility' was his voice, which seemed new in each new role. Quite often, writers of memoirs recreating his performances in their minds realised to their amazement that in the scenes that had struck them as particularly tragic, Chaliapin hardly moved, did not 'act' in the literal sense which the average member of the public gives to the word. The character revealed his thoughts and his emotions above all through his singing, and this created the feeling of an unforgettable theatrical event taking place on the operatic stage. A friend of the singer remembers that while they

* *Ernani* – Verdi.
† *Aleko* – Rachmaninov.

were holidaying together in the Caucasus, he 'managed to make him speak many times about art, about the "secrets" of his musical and dramatic interpretation'. Chaliapin, when he was in the mood, answered questions willingly, but he mostly talked of voice, of how it has to be controlled to represent accurately the personality and the actions of a character. 'About acting he said much less, as if he even did not quite understand why it made such an impression.'[91]

'In opera, portraying the life of a person means singing,' Chaliapin was fond of repeating.[92] This saying is mentioned in the book of the late Emmanuel Kaplan, professor at the Leningrad Conservatory. The author also records that during one of his conversations with Chaliapin, the talk turned to Caruso, 'whose vocal genius', according to Kaplan, 'made one forget his unprepossessing appearance and most mediocre acting abilities. He produced an indelible effect even in the short phrase "C'est moi" in the fourth act of *Carmen*. It seemed that we were dealing with a tragic actor of colossal dimensions. Small, stout, outwardly unattractive, he turned into a menacing symbol of death. His whole person, transformed, exuded the sinister and terrifying coldness of the grave. This icy blast scorched me, and recounting my impressions to Chaliapin, I asked him: "Why is Caruso thought to be a bad actor?" And Chaliapin said with a smile: "Who told you that Caruso was a bad actor? That is nonsense. Caruso has a thousand voices, and each voice has such an abundance of colours and shades! He uses them like a painter. He who can sing like Caruso can act like Salvini."'[93]

'I like to think of a singer as a teller of stories,' declared Chaliapin in an interview with the American *Etude Music Magazine*. 'To sing with a singing voice alone means nothing. It will never enhance the singer's progress in art; and it never will reach his hearers' hearts. But to tell the different stories of human life and emotion through the voice: Ah! That is another matter! Anyone can sing notes and syllables as they appear on the printed page. Some can even penetrate into the music enough to sing melody and words. But only the very few learn to sing the song itself with all its human emotion, all its joy and suffering. Those who do are artists. They devote themselves to portraying the truth of life through their voices.'[94] And as if continuing the same conversation, he added in London: 'It is a small thing to sing a song or ballad. What is indispensable is to understand the sense of the words one utters and the feelings that dictated the choice of these words. In opera one should sing as one speaks.'[95]

It is curious that in his articles, comments and recollections Chaliapin never concerns himself with the purely technical problems of the art of singing. This is partly due to his lack of faith in the existence of some definitive school, suitable for all. ('Every throat is built differently and every singer must find his own best means of development. The best method is the one that feels easiest and most natural. I have been very careful to watch for my own vocal needs, and equally careful about prescribing for the needs of others!')[96] But most of all it is because he considered that the means and the language of art must not become an end in themselves. On their own, they cannot serve as a source of inspiration and creativity. Applied to singing, this meant that the most brilliant vocal gifts were 'an accident, a gift of God' and that 'an unusual voice may, perhaps, make a star – never an artist.' Mastery of one's profession was something to be much more esteemed and valued, but even that was only 'the foundation of his future work'. 'Indeed, it is only after the voice is so well trained, so pliable, so easy that tone production has become second nature that one is ready to begin artistic work. While the singer still has to indulge in conscious concentration on producing a good B or B-flat, he is not ready for full stage-work. The singer who sings self-consciously gives but poor effects. One's younger years are taken up in learning to use the mechanical technique upon which art must be built. There must be the learning to use the voice, to gesture, to walk; there must be the learning of the values of different historical epochs – how the people of various lands and ages looked, how they dressed, how they thought and felt. One must learn what to do with one's arms and legs, how to handle a sword, a goblet or a rose. Each thing must be learned separately, and none of them has the least meaning until they are all fused together with such complete technical mastery that one is conscious not of all of one's actions, but only of the human, emotional effect one wishes to project through these actions. Precisely there is where art begins.'[97]

The advice Chaliapin was giving in his decline to the rising generation was the fruit of long years of experience. He had himself recognized early the necessity of transforming the singer into an operatic artist, of turning operas from 'concerts in costume' into musical drama, and he had achieved this on a scale unsurpassed to this day. 'There are singers whose voices are better than his ever was. Yet there is no voice in the whole world to which the passage of time and the inevitable deterioration that accompanies it matter so little. The explanation is merely that – HE IS CHALIAPIN,'[98] affirmed the *Evening Standard* on the occasion of his 1928 London guest appearances.

Is it then possible to define his greatness, to explain what made contemporaries set Chaliapin entirely apart from anything else they had ever seen in the theatre? 'Probably, if he had been asked to place the constituents of opera in order of their importance,' reflected Edwin Evans in *Time and Tide*, 'the first place would have been given not to music, not to the singer's art, but to drama, as being the source of all else – the source of the poet's text, of the composer's music, of the singer's inflections, his gestures, and the painter's scenic inspiration.'[99] The exceptionally perspicacious English critic was pointing at the very essence of Chaliapin's aims. The state of shock his performances induced in his audiences was not due to great acting, vivid, expressive make-up or a wonderful voice, although all these were undoubtedly present. Chaliapin presented to the spectator what he had discovered in the character. Appreciation of the performer, admiration for him involuntarily gave way to personal involvement. A real feeling of participation in the events taking place seized the public. For opera-goers this 'impression of being present' was startling and absolutely new. Stravislavsky's famous 'fourth wall' had ceased to exist, and they could swear that they had seen 'Ivan the Terrible, Mephistopheles, Dosifei, Boris Godunov in person, and not Chaliapin in the roles of Ivan the Terrible, Mephistopheles, Dosifei,

Boris. . . .'[100] Art was after all not as exciting as the fate of the people whose form he was now assuming.

Here are some more extracts from English and American reviews of the 1920s: 'This colossal genius gets so completely inside not only the clothes and the skin but the very heart and soul of Tsar Boris that it will not be surprising if one day he really does see ghosts and give up the ghost on stage, and so end a career of make-believe that borders amazingly upon reality.'[101] 'Feodor Chaliapin brings something to the opera that is greater than singing, greater than acting. He brings drama, that perfect realisation and illusion of life for which singing and acting exist. He sang Boris at the Metropolitan last night. One says "sang" because it is the conventional word and the most easily comprehended. It is not adequate. He lived Boris, he was Boris. When he strode upon the stage, all sense of artifice of the theatre vanished. As long as he was there the other singers, the scenery, the audience, even Mussorgsky's great music – all were blotted out. One saw only the Czar Boris Godunoff, living, triumphant, agonising and dying.'[102] 'Anyone who has seen him on stage will know that the word "created" is here used advisedly; each of his impersonations was far more than a reproduction: he did not act so much as live the character he was representing.'[103] 'Interpreters at once very profound and very intuitive, who really create life on the stage, have always been very rare; they seem inhabited by a sort of spark which, as soon as they have entered the skin of their character, enables them to find spontaneously the most natural gestures and the most appropriate way of speaking. This was the first impression Chaliapin made as soon as he appeared; no art as such, no method, no effects. The actor, the singer had disappeared; only the character lived before us, and it was his thought which could be glimpsed, which commanded this gesture or that facial expression. The same feeling regarding his lyrical interpretations. Whatever his vocal abilities and the mellowness of his warm bass voice, soft and powerful, whose timbre was always even and smooth and which was admirably produced and used, whatever flexible and subtle art controlled it, it was never the singer who showed himself, who dominated in him. Singing seemed to be for him only one means of expression among others, or rather he sang only because this was the way the character he was incarnating expressed himself.' [104] 'With Chaliapin on the stage we neither watched nor listened – we experienced with him.' [105]

Chaliapin's ability 'not to seem but to be' subjugated not only the public and the experienced critics but even, as we have seen, his partners. 'When Chaliapin, as Philip II of Spain, orders Elizabeth de Valois from his presence she (Slobodskaya) took one look into his fiery eyes and fled with genuine terror into the wings. She was later complimented on this realistic piece of acting.' [106] The 'transformation' was so imperceptible and so immediate that those who witnessed it retained a feeling of mystical awe from it. This other creature who had completely supplanted Chaliapin bore no resemblance whatever to its maker. His place had been taken by a new being, first seen only in outline, then fully revealed, and which started at once to talk, act and use its own reasoning. Innumerable, life-like signs of a new personality looked like natural traits instead of laboriously planned and selected details. 'At the time of one of the performances of *Boris Godunov*,' recounts Levik, 'we were in Chaliapin's dressing-room with other singers and guests. He was celebrating a family event on that day and some members of his family were there. Fedor Ivanovich was in an excellent mood, offered fruit to everybody and chatted endlessly. He was recounting some episodes from his childhood and was utterly fascinating. As always on these occasions, things did not end without two or three risqué stories, which he told in a masterly fashion, his lips closed to keep certain words out of the children's hearing. But the bell rang, announcing the end of the interval. Chaliapin stopped in the middle of a word and turned sharply to the mirror in his chair to check his make-up. I left for the foyer but was held up two steps from the open door. Chaliapin added a couple of strokes to his face, slowly and majestically got up and made his way to the stage. I flinched; Tsar Boris was advancing on me. Nothing remained of the witty charmer of a moment ago, neither in his eyes, nor in the set of his mouth, nor in his gait. . . . Some huge thing, full of might, of power, of a thunder-like force was advancing. He went past, literally transfixing me with his glance as if he were seeing me for the first time. I am not fond of exaggerated comparisons, but his glance really flashed like lightning. "Please," I wanted to say, "it's me, the baritone Le——" but I did not say anything, I understood what was the matter. It was not that Chaliapin had seen a man but that Tsar Boris had seen his potential enemy – the Jesuit Rangoni. This glance made my hair stand on end and my heart miss a beat.'[107]

As mentioned earlier, the way Chaliapin could make 'everything apart from him look dead on stage, everything not connected with him lose interest' was something which already puzzled his contemporaries. 'What is it,' worried young Leonid Sobinov, observing Chaliapin during his Mamontov period, 'hard work or inspiration?'[108] Many came to the conclusion that most likely 'it was not him creating all this but an elemental force which controlled him, operating through him, and he was only its involuntary expression. One senses something irrational, which does not lie within the bounds of comprehension in Chaliapin's creative work.'[109] Such an explanation seemed all the more plausible in that the most painstaking efforts at imitation invariably ended in failure. Chaliapin's creations, an indissoluble blend of imaginative thinking and genuine feeling, became clichés, even if skilful ones. Compared with the original, the sight was unbearable. Well, 'the Lord giveth and the Lord taketh away.' Genius is not something one can learn.

The apparent ease with which Chaliapin usually rehearsed helped to reinforce this view. Even if difficulties arose, they usually involved only minor details. It was thought that he spent an irritatingly long time over these, trying them out and studying them from every angle. Moreover, on stage and on the concert platform, he was liable to change the mise-en-scène or the tempi without warning, putting his partners, the conductor or the pianist in an awkward situation. 'The accompanist,' writes Gerald Moore, 'far from being carried away, had to keep the coolest head; his senses had to be alert as he tried to anticipate what the singer would be doing next; was he going to hurry a certain phrase, neglecting to take the breath in the middle of it as he sometimes did? This next note, was he going to make a *fermata* on it or was it to be abandoned quickly? Was it going to be made the climax of the phrase or would it become a *subito pianissimo*? It was all a question of mood – not the mood of the music but of the singer and whether he considered himself in good voice or not. Yet there is no doubt in my mind that I was playing for a great singer, who could lift the audience out of their seats and thrill them as few basses before or since have been able to thrill. Certainly I have never been associated with a more exciting artist.'[110]

This gave birth to the idea of someone ruled by sudden impulses, as unexpected to him as they were to others. But after the first chapter of *Pages from My Life* there was no longer any room for doubt. It said in black and white: 'However much I prepared myself, the main work still took place during the course of the performance, and my insight into the role deepened and broadened each time I performed it.'[111] 'He told me once', reported an American journalist, 'that his interpretation of a part was never twice the same.'[112] And indeed, the press never ceased to wonder at the wealth and the variety 'of the details which Chaliapin always brought to his stage impersonations'.[113] But in fact this was not the main point at all. In the theatre, nothing can serve a purely external purpose; it must represent some essential inner characteristic of the events or of the protagonists. For a long time, the costume sewn in the workshop for the future première is just a piece of tailoring, but if it is made according to the design of a genuine artist, there comes a moment when it changes into a symbol, in its way a token of the personality assumed by the actor. New details *per se* never had any interest for Chaliapin. Contrived, and not born with the character, they remain the product of training and technique. The value of a detail can be judged by its relevance to the deeper meaning of one episode, of the other episodes, of the work as a whole. If it can be replaced, moved or discarded altogether, that means that the performer is trying to cover up lack of substance. It is like a false testimony which obstructs the truth.

With Chaliapin's performances, audiences encountered what

is perhaps the most·worthwhile attribute of the theatre: they saw decisions being taken, choices being made, people going to victory or to death, passing through radical changes of fate as the action progressed. He knew how to present a man who was not a fabrication but a real person, and how to try to play him anew each time without recalling what he had done in the same opera a few days before. And so the very essence of Chaliapin's art turned out to be the very essence of theatre – improvisation. It, and only it, can convey the pulse of life, give credibility to the words, the actions and the thoughts of the dramatis personae; but without it, all the cumbersome, agonising toil of the actor, all that has been assembled, analysed, weighed up, and yet fails to produce something that deserves to be called the art of the theatre, will be mercilessly exposed. And improvisation preserves authenticity in the theatre, guards it from clichés. If the performance goes exactly as rehearsed, if from beginning to end it repeats what has been done earlier, then the people sitting in the auditorium are served a laboriously warmed-up dish passed off as something fresh. 'One can enter into the feelings of the role just once, or several times,' said Stanislavsky, 'in

Queue for Chaliapin's first appearance at the Royal Opera House, Covent Garden, May 25th, 1926.

order to observe the external form of this natural display, and having observed it, learn to repeat it mechanically, with the help of trained muscles. This is representing the role.'[114] As is well known, Stanislavsky distinguished between the theatre of 'experiencing' and the theatre of 'representing'; moreover, he considered that the first was more universal and that it always included the second as well.

As mentioned earlier, Chaliapin, unlike Stanislavsky, did not write any theory on the process of acting. In the only chapter of *Mask and Soul* devoted to these questions he avoids giving definitions. In his opinion, both types of theatre are only the two sides of the same coin. Chaliapin does not believe in a clear division between them, since neither exists in its pure form. If this must be discussed, then one can only talk about what lends itself to being formulated in words and analysed intellectually. All the rest lies, as he put it, 'on the other side of the fence'. 'How an actor creates a stage character can only be explained in an approximate manner. I must say, however, that the conscious part of an actor's work is of extreme, perhaps even decisive, significance. It stimulates intuition, fertilises it. To fly in an aeroplane to the mysterious heights of the stratosphere, one must take off from a strip of terra firma, sensibly chosen for this purpose and known to be suitable for it. What sort of inspiration will strike the actor as he gets further into the role will be seen later. This he cannot know, nor must he think about it. It will come without his realising it; he cannot predetermine it by any amount of zeal or will power. But he must know for certain where he is taking off from on his creative flight. All following remarks about my method of work concern exclusively the conscious and volitional side of the creative process. Its secrets are not known to me, but if I sometimes, in the most sublime moments of spiritual élan, dimly feel them, I can nevertheless not express them. ....'[115]

The conviction that on stage every emotional state must be entirely controlled by thought led Chaliapin to a whole series of vital conclusions. They are directly concerned with the preparation of a role and with its performance. A supreme master of theatrical synthesis, he was not afraid to take to pieces

455

the delicate mechanism of an artistic creation. In the careful elaboration and perfecting of all its elements, temporarily disassembled, Chaliapin saw the only right path towards 'experiencing' a role. Everything in Chaliapin's theatre has been considered many times, everything calculated, rehearsed again and again. There comes a moment when, joined together, these elements become individual features of the personality which has been brought to life, when they are united by the artist's imagination. 'Imagination helps to overcome the mechanical and the lifeless, it is the basis of *freedom* [Chaliapin's italics] in creative work. But freedom, in art as in life, is only good if it is restricted and reinforced by inner discipline.'[116]

According to Chaliapin, making the audience believe in the authenticity of what is taking place on stage can be accomplished only through a carefully maintained sense of balance, when all 'the intonations and gestures are made in the exact measure corresponding to the given situation and the given character'.[117]

What is perhaps most remarkable in Chaliapin's theory is that he never tells the performer to resort directly to emotion or even to search for it in himself. Emotions, which are of course the main objective and for whose sake an enormous amount of preparatory work is accomplished, cannot be rehearsed. They come of their own free will, as if allowed total liberty, and their answer to the actor's summons must be entirely voluntary but nevertheless come just when it is needed. Their principal quality is spontaneity; if they are played to order, they become a grimace. The accuracy of the sets, the authentic style and period of the costumes, the minute analysis of the living conditions of the dramatis personae – all these have only one purpose: to create a complex system along which, as if along a wire, run the impulses of an 'uncontrollable' progress of events. Studying would seem to preclude entirely any kind of improvisation, kill it at the root, and if it still manages to break through the thick layer of painstaking deductions, then this is not because of the work done but in spite of it. Chaliapin insisted, however, that the two 'halves' – preparing and performing – had to be indivisibly joined and, in addition, that the cumbersome fruit of research, of rational effort and exercise, had to be entirely subordinated to theatrical improvisation without letting any traces of planning show through.

The singer's daughter Irina recorded in her memoirs a curious statement of her father's. The conversation had turned to the Moscow Art Theatre and its clumsy attempts at achieving 'real-life truth on the stage'. While acknowledging great artistry in many of Stanislavsky's productions, Chaliapin nevertheless remarked: 'It's amazing how they want to simplify all the time. Moreover, they "act" simplicity, and the result nearly always rings false: I see an actor behaving "simply", "carelessly" unbuttoning his waistcoat, or whistling "simply", or "simply" shooing off a fly, and I can see that he has contrived all this simplicity. And you know, it suddenly becomes so complicated, trivial, prosaic details push the character into the background and interfere with the basic line.'[118]

But how can the contradiction be resolved between rigidly prepared performance and improvisation, live emotion born of the instant – the very vitals of theatre? How can everything achieved at the cost of so much time and effort be hidden from the public? Stanislavsky went so far as to threaten actors that one day he would force them to play against a new, unexpected set of circumstances every time. 'I dream of such a performance,' he said, 'where it will not be known which of the four walls will be open today.'[119]

Chaliapin had the answer to these questions. It was necessary, he thought, not to play a part but to live the character. That way one can continually discover something new in the thoughts and acts of the man one is impersonating, and so look again for ways of conveying his existence. As he explores deeper and deeper the endless variety of traits belonging to a real-life character, the actor will get further and further away from prearranged *devices*. More exactly, they take on a different meaning; and even if they look the same, they sound different.

'The main point of my theory', wrote Stanislavsky, 'is that the actor must not repeat *forms* but must each time recall and feel the *essence*, the *substance of the role* [Stanislavsky's italics throughout].'[120] Chaliapin entirely agreed with him; the man who goes onto the stage must be created by the performer but be unlike the performer. This last point is of particular consequence for the actor since it concerns the cardinal problem of his art – impersonation. It is an art and not a craft. Chaliapin is in no doubt about the importance of the distinction. Penetrating the mind of another being, not giving a picture of it, that was the only way he accepted in the theatre. But how is one to feel what the character felt? How can one experience his pain, his hopes, his tears and his happiness?

One of the most prevalent methods is to enter the role starting from oneself, to go from the actor's personality into the character he wants to play. The interior world of this other person is reached by asking oneself how one would behave in his place (in Stanislavsky's definition, 'in his given circumstances'). This method relies on the assumption that each one of us possesses every possible feature and attribute needed to portray any personality, however complex. We can all be naive and cunning, kind and envious, vindictive and magnanimous. That means that if one digs deep into oneself and if one imagines the situation clearly, the character is ready.

Chaliapin has a different point of view. The imagination must concentrate not so much on the situation as on understanding the 'state of mind' of the character at every moment of the action. [121] Similar circumstances make totally dissimilar types of persons. Getting the environment right, carefully researching the period – these are only the first stages on a long and tortuous journey into the labyrinth of someone else's mind.

To work on a role, Chaliapin took the character as his starting point, drawing on its destiny and its inner world to compose its mental and physical portrait. What he had to show was not the general reaction of the performer to the surroundings, but of that 'new' person, the play's or the opera's hero. He had to show him walking, feeling, eating and laughing. In that case, the actor does not go on stage to speak or sing a role that someone has written for him, but through it to make contact with a real person in a real environment. Stanislavsky called this environment 'implied circumstances', for the actor, and under his influence the public too, must believe in them.

This is, incidentally, another inexhaustible source of improvisation. Even within an already established plan of performing and mise-en-scène, such a dialogue has practically no limits.

In 1914, while appearing in London, Chaliapin told Rosa Newmarch: 'At the crises of feeling there may be tears if you like, but in the eyes of the spectators only, *never* [Chaliapin's emphasis] in those of the actor. Art to be great must be almost purely objective, and the least attempt to read his own personal sufferings instantly decreases the actor's hypnotic power over his audience.' [122]

Twenty years later he returned to the same subject in *Mask and Soul* and even recounted the events which had led to his conclusions. 'Sometime in my youth,' writes Chaliapin, 'during one of my tours of southern Russia, I found myself in Kishinev one day, and on my evening off I went to hear Leoncavallo's *Pagliacci*. The performance of the opera was indifferent, the audience rather bored, but when the tenor broke into the famous aria, everything became strangely animated: he started to cry on stage, and the public began to giggle. The more dramatic the tenor became, the more he cried and the more the audience roared. I also thought it was very funny. I bit my lips and contained myself as much as I could, but inside I was shaking with laughter. . . . But the act ended, the public departed for the foyer to continue their laughter and I went backstage. As I passed the tenor's dressing room, I decided to go in and say good evening to him. And what did I see? Tears still running down his cheeks he said "Good ev-vvvening!" with an effort. – "What is the matter with you?" I enquired anxiously. "Are you ill?" – "No . . . I'm . . . well." – "But why are you crying then?" – "I can't help crying. Every time I experience an intensely dramatic situation on stage, I can't hold back my tears, I we-eep. I feel so sorry for the poor clown." I realized what was the matter. This singer, perhaps not altogether without talent, was ruining his part simply by the fact that the tears he was shedding over a broken love affair were not those of the clown but his own, those of a too sensitive man. . . . The result was ridiculous because the tenor's tears were of no interest to anyone.' [123]

The idea of building a character out of the actor's personality still prevails in current theatrical teaching. One can argue interminably about the degree to which another person's mind and feelings can be understood by asking oneself 'How would I have acted in his particular circumstances?', but a character based on the performer's personal world cannot really be called a creation. Chaliapin never asked himself in what respect he resembled the character or how he would have behaved in his place. Instead he thought about this other person's objective essence. Such an ability to incarnate human beings and their complex mental states, down to the smallest detail, is what distinguishes true acting talent from mere craftsmanship. 'When I sing a character,' said Chaliapin in an American interview, 'I am no longer Chaliapin. So whatever I do must be in keeping with what the character would do. Any artist who gets all his characterisation from the opera score in his hands, fails at being a real artist by just that much. When I have to portray Philip II in *Don Carlos* it is necessary that *I be Philip II* [Chaliapin's emphasis]. It is not enough for me to put on the costumes and say '*I am Philip II*' [Chaliapin's emphasis] and then sing the music Verdi wrote. I have to become the man himself. "How is this done?" By study and by thought and by observation ... and then go over the role with yourself in the character and say constantly: "What would Philip do here?" or "How would Boris look when he said this?" '[124]

So the 'modelling' of a character (Chaliapin, like Stanislavsky, often compared the actor to a sculptor) and, after that, the process of acting itself are based on control. 'The ideal correspondence of means of expression with artistic aims', one can read in *Mask and Soul*, 'is the only condition under which a harmonious and well-balanced character, with a life of his own, can be created. Through the actor, of course, but independent of him. Through the actor-creator, independent of the actor-individual.'[125]

He had reached these conclusions long before the publication of his second book of memoirs. His eldest daughter, Irina, who as a teenager had dreamed of becoming an actress, recorded practically the same words in a conversation with her father: 'To bring truth through the actor-creator, and not through the actor-individual – that is what art is about. That, it seems to me, is where Kostya Stanislavsky and I part company.'[126]

Indeed, however great the illusion of authenticity, the spectator always feels the actor behind the role, and in moments of most intense involvement it is to him, above all, that he relates. To Stanislavsky's idea that 'the actor and the character must blend together' Chaliapin opposes the principle of a 'deliberate split in two'. 'When I sing,' he wrote, 'the character I embody is before my eyes all the time, I sing and I listen, I act and I watch. I am never alone on stage. One of me plays, the other checks. I never let go of my consciousness on stage for a minute; not for a second do I lose the faculty and habit of controlling the harmony of the performance. I see every quiver, I hear every rustle around me. The boot of one of the choristers creaks and I already feel a prick. "The lazybones," I think, "his boot squeaks," and at the same time I sing: "I'm dying. . . ."'[127]

Chaliapin did not try to disappear into the character he was playing; on the contrary, he never relinquished his own physical identity. In answer to the questions of one of his young partners, he maintained that 'while performing he remains totally aware of himself at every minute, to the extent of knowing the position of the little finger of his left hand.'[128] Fairness compels one to say that the theoretical limits set down by Chaliapin and Stanislavsky in practice easily give way before genuine talent. Neither approach exists in an absolutely pure form. To begin with, when a man truly believes that he is not himself but, let us say, Tsar Boris, this no longer denotes great acting but mental illness. On the other hand, to make a total split and dissociate entirely one's personal emotions and experience of life from the thoughts and emotions of the character is equally impossible. But both methods can be subjected to explanation and definition. Their principles merely offer the actor two different routes.

When Stanislavsky declared, as quoted earlier, 'My system is taken straight from Chaliapin,' it certainly was not intended as a casual remark. 'Dramatically, there really were two Chaliapins,' commented the correspondent of the New York Sun after a performance. 'One was the singer who seemed to completely lose himself in a part, so that he became that personage, as was true of the Chaliapin Boris. One forgot then that he was acting, as one forgot that he was singing. There was no thought of consciously applied technique. The other Chaliapin was the technician who could saunter through a role like Mephistopheles in the Gounod opera, planning and executing, seizing bits of business, like the by-play with the sword in the scene when the hilts of reversed weapons are raised in a forest of crosses against the evil intruder. Both Chaliapins were superb artists but they left curiously opposite impressions as to what it was that lifted the singer high above his fellows.'[129]

Recollections of people who observed Chaliapin from behind the scenes or shared the stage with him occupy a special place in the memoirs written about the singer. They are of undoubted value, partly because most of their authors worked in the theatre and thus enable us to draw on their professional judgement when talking about Chaliapin but also because they give us a unique opportunity to peep into his creative workshop, to come closer, if not to solving, at least to being well acquainted with the mystery of his transformations.

These commenced long before the performance, when, after arriving at the theatre, he set about 'attuning' himself to the role, re-adjusting his ideas and his feelings about it. In these first few hours he became intensely absorbed and uncommunicative, reluctant to answer questions, entering deeper and deeper another world known only to him. Later on in life, before going on stage, he could be more sociable, but his train of thought, his way of speaking and of moving, all his reactions were those of his role. Nevertheless, throughout the course of the action, he retained, even in highly dramatic moments, such absolute control of himself that he astonished even his most blasé partners. In the intervals, all depended on whether 'it was working or not'. Trying to convince him was useless; he relied only on his own impressions. 'There is in me a sort of critical controller, far harder to please than any other critic,'[130] he confided to a London correspondent. When the curtain finally came down and he slowly left the stage – usually behind all the other members of the cast – for his dressing room, he again needed time to return from his journey into another life to his usual appearance and behaviour.

Let us imagine such an evening. Right from the morning Chaliapin would be restless; he was himself nervous and irritable and got on the nerves of everyone else in the house. From time to time he would make someone telephone the theatre to cancel the performance; he was not in voice today and nothing would persuade him to sing. Having driven everyone to hide in his or her corner, he would 'gloomily wander around the rooms, tease the dog and push a few balls at billiards'.[131] Then he would calm down, go to the piano and start to warm up his voice. Perhaps it was not so bad; perhaps he would go to the theatre after all. There, no sooner had he installed himself at his dressing-table than someone knocked on the door. 'Peering intently at his reflection in the mirror as if it was something unfamiliar, he reluctantly said "Come in!" Entered Elvira de Hidalgo, a Spanish singer, and Sol Hurok, our tour organiser. De Hidalgo was leaving New York in the evening and wanted to discuss some business matter. Chaliapin asked her to postpone the conversation until the second interval. The visitors sat down behind Fedor Ivanovich and could clearly see him in the three-sided mirror. Chaliapin looked as if he were slowly sinking into a succession of thoughts. Constant changes of mood corresponding to these thoughts showed on his face, and his hand obediently fixed in light touches the still photographs of the character's life visible only to him. It was undoubtedly Fedor Chaliapin before us, but with a new "inside" in the process of being born. It was impossible to separate Chaliapin from the Mephistopheles making his appearance. The clear pale-blue eyes turned into needle-sharp, piercing, devilish coals of fire. Common human standards did not apply to these eyes, inscrutable to others but seeing through everything. There was a loud knock on the door. Nobody answered. Chaliapin was alone with Mephistopheles, and we were under the spell of the great artist. The knocking nevertheless brought us round. The Spanish singer, the impresario and I quietly left the room without a word for fear of breaking Chaliapin's concentration.

'At the door we found two singers; it was they who had been

knocking. De Hidalgo, not letting them speak, said in a peculiar, tragic-sounding whisper: "You are going to Mr. Chaliapin? Don't – it's not possible, a devil has taken possession of him and sees through his eyes!" This was said so persuasively, so seriously and with such conviction that the two singers followed us in silence. I very much liked what de Hidalgo had said, pronouncing it like an incantation. I repeated her exact words to Chaliapin when I went to take my leave of him during the last interval. He went into raptures over it: "Well done, señora! There is no better way of putting it. I certainly could not wish for a better one. That's just it, the devil should see through my eyes but I should not change into him. The outside does not mean anything, but when the inside is right, everyone will understand." I had already witnessed a similar act of creativity. I once had the good fortune to be in Chaliapin's dressing-room with my father, then conductor of Zimin's opera company, before a performance of Serov's *The Power of Evil*. Fedor Ivanovich suddenly interrupted his conversation with my father and, speaking more to himself than to those present, he said: "You conductors often complain that I am difficult, that I rarely sing twice the same way, that you have to be on the alert all the time, that no one knows what I am going to do next to 'amuse' you. This comes from the fact that now and then I take another look at my Eryomka, Holofernes or Boris – here at my dressing-table, in my dressing-room." '[132]

Always remaining in character, feeling and living every moment, Chaliapin demanded total concentration from the rest of the cast and the conductor. It goes without saying that the accuracy of the musical performance was not in question, but Chaliapin insisted that the conductor should feel himself closely involved in what was taking place on stage. 'Apropos of this,' writes Pokhitonov, 'I recall an interesting conversation he had with Blumenfeld. "Fedya, you are often angry with us conductors for not holding your pauses long enough or for holding them too long," he said to Chaliapin. "But how are we to guess the length of these pauses?" "Very simple," he answered. "Feel them with me and you'll hit the mark." '[133]

In 1921 a special medical commission was set up to investigate 'what an actor's organism expended in the process of creativity', and so a Dr. N. A. Popov appeared in Chaliapin's dressing-room. The records he made are kept in the archives of the Leningrad Theatre Museum.

'February 5th. Opera: *The Power of Evil*; role: Eryomka. Clumsy, strapping, slow-witted type, strong, rough, not too many thoughts in his head, a drunkard and a lecher. A slovenly man, physically and morally dirty. Type of blacksmith with no morals, or cabby. Chaliapin, rather in low spirits, depressed by family worries. Anxious about his sick daughter in whom tuberculosis has been diagnosed. Expresses indignation that there are difficulties about his going abroad. Curses the Russian God who had him born in Russia. While making up intently studies his own face, goes through a series of exceedingly complicated facial expressions. Makes up with extraordinary art. When he appears on stage, there is no longer anything left of Chaliapin. We have before us the real Eryomka – heavy drinker and profligate. The scene of progressive intoxication and of his display of drunkenness was amazingly played. His gait was unsteady, uncoordinated. Even off stage his behaviour reminds one of a man who is slightly tight. Noticeable is the uplift in the mental state, the cheerful humour, loud voice, tipsy jokes.

'February 17th. Chaliapin: Salieri. After the first act, remains under the impression of acting, hums to himself some passages of the opera he has just been singing. While I was taking his pulse, the voice of a tenor passing along the corridor could be heard through the door. Chaliapin immediately shudders, his pulse becomes arrhythmic, irregular, intermittent, his face is distorted by wrath and suffering, the nostrils flare, the respiration quickens, the hands become sweaty and cold as well. This lasts 20–30 seconds, then F.I. regains his self-control.'

Of late his room is now always crowded with people. Relatives, friends, some are here on business, others just to have a look at the famous singer. It is not easy, but what can one do? Take today, for instance. A book about Chaliapin is in preparation and needs some good illustrations. So he has to give his first photographic sitting, that means no rest in the intervals; instead he will have to do over and over what the

photographer finds most expressive. And who is the photographer? How good is he? Chaliapin has never heard of him
before – a certain Shperling – although he does know the editor
of the book, Sergei, son of the painter Makovsky. As it happens,
Sergei Makovsky is also feeling uneasy: 'On the way to the
theatre, I considered it necessary to warn Shperling of possible
misunderstandings with Chaliapin. "He can be very abrupt
where artistic matters are concerned, simply unbearably rude.
In that case you'll have to be content with a few shots and wait
for the next time." But Shperling had a strong belief in his lucky
star: "What are you saying? Abrupt, with me? I'm a man of
talent. He will understand immediately who I am when he sees
me!"

'At the theatre, the crowd of visitors made the dressing-room
warm. Seated at the mirror brightly lit by a hanging lamp was
Chaliapin in the costume I knew so well of Don Quixote
designed by Golovin. He was putting the last touches to his
make-up, glueing a tuft of grey hair to his cheek-bones. A small
table stood nearby with a bottle of champagne and some glasses.
The guests were chatting happily. Catching sight of me and of
little Shperling in the doorway, Chaliapin smiled hospitably
and, shaking his dishevelled head, greeted us from afar in a sort
of unctuous voice: "Hello, hello, my friends! I was waiting for
you. Only don't get angry – it's not going to be very convenient
to work, the lighting is not very good. . . ." When we had seated
ourselves, he continued in the same apologetic tone: "I don't
know, is it worth taking pictures? The make-up is not working today. . . ." Shperling took photos in all the intervals.
Chaliapin's manner towards him did not change; he was
just as courteously kind and obliging. Whatever pose
Shperling intended was immediately taken up by Don Quixote,
who instantly guessed what the photographer wanted. And he
posed extremely well: he stood or sat like a statue. On the way
back from the theatre, Shperling was exultant. "You see," he
said with a rather smug smile, "how right I was! Birds of a
feather flock together. . . ."

'The next day he was singing *Boris Godunov*. Shperling
lightheartedly, even somewhat offhandedly, had already entered

Chaliapin's dressing room ahead of me, but ... catching sight of him, he stopped at a respectable distance. The informal "Good evening, Fedor Ivanovich!" died on his lips. Before him stood Tsar Boris in his robes of ornate brocade, a short mantle on his shoulders. Godunov's glance was imperiously severe, his head slightly retracted; his bejewelled hands held the back of the chair. Chaliapin pronounced his words coldly and commandingly. Poor Shperling shrank and I am ashamed to say that I, not wanting to witness Chaliapin's imperious treatment of him, left the theatre on some pretext and abandoned Shperling to his fate. When I went to visit him a day later to have a look at the negatives, the cocky little photographer was unrecognizable. Frowning disconcertedly, he took the plates out of the fixing solution. "Well, how did you get on the other day?" I asked, assuming a carefree manner. "Was Chaliapin friendly?" – "You know very well he wasn't!" flared up Shperling. "You saw what a cold shower he gave me? And then he wouldn't let me open my mouth. All he did was give orders. And at every trifle he banged his staff. Terror seized me. Absolutely as if he was an almighty ruler...." '[134]

Chaliapin's difficulty in controlling his stagefright and the surprise this caused to those who happened to witness it have been mentioned before. Equally well-known is the fact that his heightened sensitivity, his inability to make concessions at the expense of art often resulted in serious clashes. 'In moments of anger,' recalls Nikolai Golovanov, principal conductor of the Bolshoi Theatre, 'Chaliapin was terrifying. The stage would resound with terrible shouts if his partners did not satisfy him. He had a nasty look, his eyes threw sparks, foul language escaped him; he was not in control of himself and was at the mercy of his ungovernable temper. These outbursts cost him dearly.' But this very same Golovanov (and in this he is not alone) also paints the portrait of a totally different Chaliapin. 'His acting technique was consummate; it surprised and amazed. It was nothing for him, for instance, to tell funny stories to members of the chorus during pauses (which I, as a young chorus master, found very disturbing) and then within a few seconds run out to the stage with a crazy look on his haggard face: "Keep away, keep away from me...."* Or during the performance of *Don Quixote*, in the death scene in the forest (at his request I would quietly prompt him from the wings), Pasha Tikhonov was silently sobbing at his feet and he would say softly: "Pasha, don't shake your belly or I'll burst out laughing," and this while the whole auditorium was in tears.'[135] Beniamino Gigli told of the night Chaliapin was singing an opera in Russian and suddenly remembered something he had forgotten. Without stepping from character, he addressed his servant in the wings, singing: 'Go to the hotel immediately. Get the two bottles of good wine I forgot in my room and bring them here, as we leave immediately after this damned opera is over.'[136]

The French writer Jean Goury reports an anecdote he heard from Louis Musy, who sang Sancho Panza to Chaliapin's Don Quixote. 'In the third act of Massenet's opera, after Dulcinea has told her Don Quixote that she is not for him and rejects him, the singer would withdraw with great dignity to a corner of the stage and cry alone, silently. Surprised to see on his face an expression of such intense desolation and affected by the sight of his real tears, Louis Musy went up to him and – a move which they had not worked out together – very gently took his hand in his own. Fedor Ivanovich "responded" immediately. He looked at his servant and, without changing the expression on his face, said to him: "Sancho, I have no handkerchief." Musy had a red handkerchief in his pocket. He took it out and started to wipe his eyes carefully. This time Chaliapin whispered to him: "Very good idea, this. Must do it every time."' 'He managed to enter into his character to the point of shedding real tears,' commented Goury, 'but did not for one instant lose control of his acting.'[137] 'I watched Chaliapin many times and at close range,' notes Mikhail Fokine. 'I witnessed many occasions when Chaliapin, infuriated by the mistakes of other singers or the conductor, virulently whispered swear words, curses or protests totally out of tune with the feelings of the role. Where had his state of mind gone to? What was happening to his

---

* In the hallucination scene in Act II of *Boris Godunov*.

creation at that moment? Was he going to wreck the character he had made with this momentary outburst inconsistent with the role? No, his next phrase already sounded totally convincing in artistic terms. Does this mean that everything he did was learnt and could be performed without feeling? I am certain that at any moment Chaliapin, while talking to you, can give you any phrase from any of his roles with the utmost expressiveness. He neither needs to "feel inspired" nor to "get into the mood" for this. I am equally certain that he has never sung a single phrase which was not produced by his inspiration and his genius for setting a mood at the moment when he worked it out.'[138]

Fokine touches here on an important point of Chaliapin's art: improvisation, and therefore the very existence of the character, is possible only if one is going to search every time for a key to the role and not reconstruct mechanically something already done. During a performance of *Don Carlos* at the Metropolitan Opera, the action was stopped by tumultuous, unrestrained applause. After a long wait, Chaliapin, breaking the established tradition, 'finally came forward to the footlights, told the conductor where to begin again and straightaway repeated the last stanza of his monologue – with what effect upon dramatic illusion need not be described. He did it differently, as if to show that his resources were not used up. No doubt he could have done it a third time still differently, and the picture having once been shattered, he might as well have.'[139]

But where is the 'true' Chaliapin? In terms of Diderot's classification, in his *Paradoxe sur le comédien*, to which category of actor does he belong? One of them believes only in a well-rehearsed and carefully thought out performance, but free of passionate feeling at the moment of execution. The other believes only in those who indefatigably 'create' in front of the public; inspiration comes as the performer goes on stage and does not abandon him for a minute. Chaliapin himself thought neither the one nor the other, and yet both at once. It was almost impossible to locate the exact moment when a certain feature of the role had revealed itself to its performer and it had become clear how it should be played. Every link in the chain is equally important and cannot be removed. It could be when he first studied the material and when he began to try it out at rehearsals: it could be when he went on stage, or even when he looked back on the performance afterwards. The interplay with the character, by which Chaliapin set such great store, was built on searching each day for a greater, more precise truth than the one taken as incontrovertible the day before.

One often hears that the actor's profession is wearying and boring; two hundred times in succession, every night the same Romeo or Don Quixote. Chaliapin knew how to avoid monotony and fatigue, how to make the actor's lot a happy one. In principle, unlike writers, composers or painters, the actor does not have to suffer the sadness of parting with his creation. The character, born for the stage, remains inside the performer. The bonds between them makes it possible to resume a past association, start all over again and experience afresh the thrills of this acquaintance.

Chaliapin laid special stress on the fact that the role must be born, created, and not fabricated. Then it has the indispensable inconstancy of a live organism; it is subject to the natural course of events, to inequality of conditions. For this reason, its external features too can emerge only as the result of detailed research – more exactly, of understanding the character's inner world. 'If you can imagine the inside of a man, then you can also accurately guess what he looks like physically,'[140] writes Chaliapin. 'To imagine means to see suddenly. To see clearly, precisely, correctly. The outer image as a whole, and then the typical details. Facial expression, posture, gesture.'[141]

Attention is drawn to the word 'suddenly' in these observations; the character, long in gestation, reveals itself all of a sudden. First slow assimilation, digestion; various, often agonising attempts to find one's way into an unknown world, to get to know it and its people as a whole and as individuals, and finally, the 'sudden' spurt when you manage to leap into the role, to crawl inside somebody's skin, knowing without hesitation what the man will do, why and how he will do it. 'In a word,' says Chaliapin, 'I know him as well as I know a schoolmate or a regular bridge-partner.'[142]

A contemporary memoir records some wonderful remarks of Stanislavsky's on how an actor enters into an imaginary life. It is worth quoting a small extract from it: Chaliapin would certainly have endorsed the views of his friend. 'The other day I attended the reading of a new play. I remember the people in it. I remember them, but they are half alive in my mind, they are still shadows and not people of flesh and blood. . . . I become more closely acquainted with the play; I want to see not only the people in it but everything around them, to see, feel every object. I can already see myself as part of a familiar environment. And finally, I occupy a place inside the play – I do not look on as an observer but from within; I know everything intimately! That ultimate moment is what I call "I am". You know of course how this happens, when . . . suddenly it's off, everyone starts to feel warm and everything comes to life. It means the actor has got his "I am". It happens in an instant: "Pop! The buds have burst open and one fine morning the tree is green with life." '[143]

However, the subsequent stages of work on a character cannot be reached by means of a simple translation: first immerse yourself in his mental state and then choose in the vocabulary of the theatre suitable means of expressing it. 'By appearance,' wrote Chaliapin, 'I mean not only make-up, colour of hair, etc . . . but also *comportment* [Chaliapin's italics] of the character: how he walks, listens, talks, laughs, weeps.'[144] And he goes on to say: 'Individuality is a very valuable thing, but only in spirit, not in flesh. I will go even further. No make-up will help an actor if from inside of him do not emanate the spiritual colours peculiar to this character, that is to say, his psychological make-up. If the emotions portrayed do not blend with the make-up, then they exist independently of it. There may be no make-up, but the emotions which relate to it will nevertheless show through if the performance is sincere and not mechanical. From the "hero's" first entrance, the spectator will certainly understand his character, provided the actor has deeply felt his part and imagined it correctly.'[145]

Chaliapin himself proved this more than once. One of the most memorable instances of it was described in the previous

471

chapter, when he came on stage with neither make-up nor costume at the dress rehearsal of *Boris Godunov* in Paris. 'I was singing in Russian, a language which they did not understand, but from the look in my eyes they sensed that I was very afraid of something.* Well, would make-up have made the impression more vivid? Hardly.'[146]

Stanislavsky expressed similar views. He told his colleagues: 'When you play Hamlet, for instance, and his complex psychology leads you to murder the King, will the problem be resolved if you have a real sharp sword in your hand? And if one can't be found, will you stop the performance? Let your imagination burn and sparkle; then you'll kill the King without a sword and you'll be able to light a fire in the chimney without matches.'[147]

Chaliapin never forgot that make-up is only the actor's assistant and is needed above all to hide the individual features of the performer. 'My face is as unsuitable for Tsar Boris as my jacket would be for him.' When you look at stage photographs of the singer and then at his drawings, you see that the unique pictorial quality of Chaliapin's portrait-like make-up comes from his knowledge not only of the character but of himself. This knowledge of every line, every peculiarity of his face and body as they changed with the years, allowed Chaliapin to make the most of his innate gifts when he worked on a character. He constantly fixed on paper what he was seeing in imagination; the picture either reinforced and amplified his idea or categorically rejected it. 'Standing at a desk,' writes a *Peterburgskaya gazeta* correspondent after a talk with the singer, 'he would run his pencil over the white paper. He would correct a sketch, then throw down the pencil and stride across the room. Without interrupting the conversation, he would return to the desk and finish the outline.'[148]

However strange it may be, even when there was no physical similarity between Chaliapin and the character he was creating, he nevertheless used his own features as a starting point. The make-up of Don Basilio, Ivan the Terrible or Mephistopheles

---

* He is referring to the hallucination scene.

was not done without regard to the form of his head but was based on it, on the position and the movements of each muscle and line of his face. 'Just as clothes must not interfere with the body's movements,' affirmed Chaliapin, 'so make-up must be done in such a way as not to interfere with the movements of the face.'[149]

Friends and relations themselves would often find it difficult to believe that it was not Don Quixote, Mephistopheles or King Philip sitting there drinking tea during the intervals and calmly discussing domestic affairs but the Fedor Chaliapin they knew so well. 'I was greeted by Chaliapin-Boris,' recalls Skitalets, 'with his usual, typical good-natured jokes, but I could not talk with him freely: the careworn face of the unhappy Tsar was looking at me. Chaliapin made up with such artistry that even at close range it was the real face, true to life and terrible, of a doomed man.'[150]

Once he had imagined and then created the features of his future character, Chaliapin would turn his thoughts to the way he would move. This, with him, implied much more than just gestures in the literal sense; it included the whole psychological complex of existence. 'A gesture is not a physical move but a move coming from the inner spirit,' he told a young actor seeking his advice. 'If, without making any movement, I set my lips in a smile, that is already a gesture.'[151] On stage, the gesture must accompany the work, not illustrate it. The actor's body is for Chaliapin an ideal instrument 'on which any melody can be played'.[152] Paying particular attention to the rhythm and the tempo of the acting, he insisted on exploiting the body's means of expression to the full. 'I admired not for the first time his perfect physical control,' commented *Time and Tide* on the performance of the fifty-three-year-old Chaliapin, 'the lack of all strain in his movements and gestures. A body at the beck and call of the slightest demand of the will, never in the way, and never out of the way.'[153]

On the whole, Chaliapin's method rests on the conviction that a man's external behaviour and his inner state are not only indivisible but also liable to have a constant effect on each other. 'Chaliapin lives every part he plays so completely that his inaction is as eloquent as his action,' declared *The Times* in 1914.[154]

Entering inside another being, adopting his appearance and his view of the world, Chaliapin passed into the stream of someone else's mentality and someone else's actions. It is undoubtedly an immutable rule of true impersonation that what belongs to one character cannot be torn away from it and used for another one. The main thing, says Chaliapin, is to catch the general tone, the colour; to stick to the whole and not let go of it. 'Superfluous details must be avoided in make-up as in acting.'[155] And if the essence of the role, the fundamental nature of the person depicted are understood, then the slightest nuance becomes a shrewdly observed trait of character. A London critic wrote of Chaliapin in 1926: 'I wish he could give a performance of it [Don Basilio] to members of the dramatic profession, so that they might learn what can be done with expressive movements of the hands.'[156]

Chaliapin's powerful art left no one indifferent, though it was not always admired. Even in his most exceptional successes, there were always people who disagreed with what they had seen: had the actor correctly understood the author's intentions? Was he faithful to what the writer or the composer had in mind? Unanimity on an author's intentions and on the real meaning of his works is rare, even if he clearly indicates the characteristics of the dramatis personae and of the events.

Why does the public go to watch others act? What in the final analysis is the point of these people's activities? Is it really to learn by heart speeches thought up by someone else and then to bandy them with each other? Of course not. 'Notes are just a written record,' said Chaliapin. 'One has to make them into music as the composer intended.'[157] The essence of what the author wants to say is not in conventional, dead signs, letters and notes but in the emotions of the characters, in the changes these emotions undergo, in the clashes of thoughts, desires and feelings. When they are brought to life by the art of the performance, they lead the spectator to analyse the conditions of life at the source of the author's inspiration. As they develop his views on stage, actors prove that without interpretation the theatre does not exist. Chaliapin wanted a performer-creator and not a performer-illustrator, even if he was equipped with the highest technique.

The Gospel says in its great simplicity: 'What you sow does not come to life unless it first dies.' He who has spent all his energy on expounding the author's material, trying not to change a single comma, who is incapable of showing even an atom of independence, is not an artist. For the seed planted in the actor's mind to start a new life on stage, the author's idea must first die in him. The play or the score then becomes the foundation on which the performance is built. When in 1914 Stanislavsky thought of playing Salieri in Pushkin's play, he asked Chaliapin to help him. They were often seen together, and Stanislavsky, listening attentively, made notes on a writing pad. 'Chaliapin read me Salieri drily, coldly, but very convincingly,' he recalled of these lessons. 'This is what I felt then: a man as gifted as Chaliapin can make Pushkin his servant, but an untalented one will himself become Pushkin's servant.'[158] Actors who make the author their 'servant' turn out in the end to be the ones most faithful to him. Because they are capable of interpretation, they bring to light the hidden meanings of the work, the secrets it holds, the slowly maturing ideas.

'For all the uniqueness of Chaliapin's characters,' writes the conductor Ary Pazovsky, 'for all the originality of their vocal and visual interpretation, the singer never departed from the composer's *basic idea* [Pazovsky's italics], treating the essence of the music with wonderful consideration. Nothing he introduced of his own ever contradicted it. At a rehearsal of the scene between Yaroslavna and Galitsky* Chaliapin asked me to take Yaroslavna's phrase 'You forgot that I am a princess ...' with more animation and energy than written in the score. (The tempi, admittedly, have not been marked by Borodin himself but by the opera's editors, Rimsky-Korsakov and Glazunov.) The very first trial convinced me that the deviation from the tempo indicated in the score requested by Chaliapin was entirely justified, permitted to depict more expressively Yaros-

---

* *Prince Igor* by Borodin.

lavna's state of mind (and consequently the scene as a whole). Without disrupting the logic of the music, this deviation underlined even more clearly the contrast between Yaroslavna's noble anger and the drunken Galitsky's cynical calm. The tradition of performing the scene in this way has continued in many opera houses up to the present time.'[159]

Real theatre is not satisfied with showing only what happened. It has to show also how it happened, to understand the events which inspired the author's ideas. 'If it were otherwise,' affirmed Stanislavsky, 'spectators would not rush to the theatre; they would stay at home and read the play.'[160] One can of course argue with Stanislavsky and say, for instance, that the number of people able to read greatly exceeds the number of those who can perform a symphony or an opera at home. Music, more than any other art, needs an intermediary between creator and public. But in principle, Stanislavsky's assertion is irrefutable. Creators are just as far apart from illustrators in singing as in drama – only in the former they are much rarer. . . .

Chaliapin's biographers usually leave three roles – Don Basilio, King Philip and Don Quixote – for the end. From the chronological point of view, this makes sense, since they indeed conclude the list of his stage works. Strictly speaking, he had already sung in *The Barber of Seville* in Tiflis when he was studying with Usatov, but his first serious encounter with Don Basilio took place in 1907. *Don Carlos* entered his repertoire in the same year and *Don Quixote* in 1910. Then, for some three decades, the list of Chaliapin's roles remained unchanged.

There is of course another reason for putting these three parts in a special category: all were created not by a young beginner but by an accomplished artist. The way Chaliapin worked on them and the way he analysed them in his memoirs indicate a precise method, a confident progress towards a clear goal, displaying great experience. Gone are the earlier fits of despair, the tears, the sleepless nights, the diffidence at one time associated with Ruslan and Mephistopheles, Boris and Ivan the Terrible. Gone too are the previous attempts to explain why something did not come off, to restore the thwarted dreams. For the 'composition of the character' – as always difficult and laborious – he could now at least depend on knowing how to combine wishes and actual possibilities. Chaliapin's mature genius was at its zenith. 'The whole performance was an extraordinary character study,'*[161] wrote the London *Evening News*. 'It was a fantastic study, faultlessly finished,' echoed the *Daily Mail*.[162] 'I noticed too', the *Evening Standard* correspondent informed his readers, 'the way members of the orchestra, whose normal attitude is, not surprisingly, one of rather bored indifference to the feats of the stage performers, stood up in their places, when not actually playing, to catch a glimpse of the great man's antics. They were well rewarded.'[163] And, in truth, continuous explosions of laughter greeted his very entrance, his every gesture after that and his killingly funny faces. At times even his partners had great difficulty in keeping their self-control and could do so only by a great effort of will. 'It was incredibly funny!' recalls Toti dal Monte,[164] for many years his regular Rosina. 'Of enormous height, he had to fold himself in half to enter; his head, covered by a battered wide-brimmed hat, and the upper half of his torso emerged from behind the door; it looked as if his eye had been glued to the keyhole before he came in; then he pushed the door with his hand and straightened up once over the threshold.'[165] 'He gradually grew taller in the doorway, from which his figure derived a certain titanical and at the same time sinister character.'[166] The new arrival was indeed an astounding sight. 'We shall not forget in a hurry', wrote Richard Capell, 'that awful old face with its monstrous nose and one tooth, nor those lank hands. He was got up like a terrible old begging friar, unshaven, slow-witted and leering.'[167] 'He secured on his head a false, pear-shaped skull, with a crown of sparse, oily hair; he then put on a false chin which jutted out, a false nose, a sort of disquieting snout curved like the beak of a bird of prey. Overall, a yellowish foundation which he decorated with a network of small wrinkles. Under the nose a suspicious shadow, as if snuff always left there some dirty dribble. The make-up of the neck was equally careful; then came the turn of the hands, which

---

* Don Basilio.

seemed enormous by contrast with the too-short sleeves. Black under the nails, black on the teeth. Same meticulous attention for the costume: a sort of filthy cassock exposing huge and muddy boots which left no doubt that the feet inside were bare and smelly; a light mantle with a greasy collar, reaching down to the small of the back. Very high, almost under the armpits, a broad leather belt covered with scratches. And stuck in it a red kerchief which would be used for amazing antics.... Sometimes enormous, sometimes miraculously shrunken, turning his kerchief into a necktie, or into a bandage for some hypothetical toothache, brandishing an (also red) umbrella.'[168]

In *Mask and Soul*, and in many interviews, Chaliapin explained why his Don Basilio looked so paradoxical. 'He says: "Just give me money and I'll do anything." All of Don Basilio is in this phrase. The audience must realise at first sight what an old pro this is, what the man is capable of. Just from his bearing, before he has uttered a word. My imagination suggested to me that the less rigidly realistic he was, the more spectators would believe in him, and in performing this role I abandoned strict realism for the grotesque. My Don Basilio is sort of pliable; he is, if you like, as elastic as his conscience. When he appears in the doorway, he is small like a dwarf, but immediately, before the public's very eyes, he uncoils and grows into a giraffe. From a giraffe he can again contract into a dwarf if need be. He can do *anything* [Chaliapin's italics] as long as you give him money. This is the reason why he is at once both funny and terrifying. The public already expects anything from him. Even his figure is a eulogy to calumny.'[169] Irina Chaliapina's recollections complete this explanation: 'Mother would tell how somewhere in France she and Father were on a train on their way to some resort when a Catholic priest entered the compartment. The weather was bad and he was evidently not feeling very well. His neck was wrapped in a long knitted scarf. He was holding an umbrella, soaking wet with rain. After clearing his throat for a long time, he finally started to unwind the scarf, which he did quite slowly. My father watched him intently, then softly asked my mother: "Iola, can you knit me a scarf like that?" "Of course, but what for?" – "You'll find out later...,"

Chaliapin as Don Basilio in Rossini's *The Barber of Seville*. Bolshoi Theatre, Moscow, 1913.

answered my father enigmatically. And so it was that in the performance Fedor Ivanovich entered in the last act holding a wet umbrella and muffled up to his eyes in a scarf; and this scarf he unwound interminably, and when he left the stage, he started rewinding it again, and the scarf had already taken on a symbolic meaning. . . .'[170] A detail of clothing he had noticed on a man he had met accidentally had unobtrusively become a detail of the character's appearance. The lanky, huge Don Basilio who was only just now occupying so much space suddenly disappeared, became quite inconspicuous and did not take up any room. The snake-like scarf, supple and seemingly endless, provided an astonishing visual means of representing his remarkable faculty of stretching out and shrinking back at will, of being there and not being there as he pleased or as it pleased others – he could be whoever and whatever circumstances demanded. This scarf, by turns rolled and unrolled, is both the body and the soul of Don Basilio, his outer skin and his inner self. The scarf is also a leitmotiv, an accompaniment to the musical portrait of the man: the mounting energy and tempo of its unfolding announces the Calumny aria, Don Basilio's credo. Inviting Bartolo to take a seat with an imperious gesture of the hand, Don Basilio settles himself in his host's armchair. The head is sunk into the shoulders, the body bent and huddled, the narrow, piercing eyes sharply fixed on his interlocutor: Will this idiot understand all the significance of his great system? 'La calunnia è un venticello. . . .' The very first word is pronounced with a multitude of nuances. The initially mild, gentle tone alters on the 'u', the sound of the double, nasal 'nn' gives a foretaste of the final unpleasant open 'a', frightening Bartolo. Corresponding changes of expression cross the music teacher's face. Distended in a sweet smile on 'la calu', it then becomes severe and stony. A shiver ripples through his body and his whole person alternately freezes and revives as he slowly straightens up. By the second half of the monologue, Don Basilio is already on his feet. He is transported by ecstasy; a veritable surge of inspiration seizes him; he is in his element. What bliss to talk about what is near and dear to your heart! 'This black, enthusiastic champion of slander, who sings its praise with such

As Don Basilio.

relish – he is himself its living embodiment. The black shadow seems to have dimmed the light. Someone is already trapped under this thick blanket of calumny and suffocates. One instant more and perhaps his very life will go out, overcome by calumny's pernicious poison.'[171]

The all-triumphant 'sì, va a crepar' which has just rent the air dies down, and after a satisfied glance at poor Bartolo flattened in his chair, Don Basilio is once again smiling broadly. He is pleased to have produced the right impression, and moreover, he can already see how to take advantage of the situation.

The proximity of Count Almaviva seriously worries Rosina's guardian, and he is willing to go to any expense to get him out of the way. Don Basilio stealthily creeps up behind Bartolo and, bending down to his ear, quickly lifts up the side of his wig and whispers in an inimitable manner: 'Give me money and I'll fix everything for you.' 'In some of his concert songs,' wrote Ernest Newman, 'especially the satirical or cynical ones of Dargomyzhsky, Chaliapin has given us a hint of his comic powers; but not until we saw him as Don Basilio could we realise that the great tragedian is equally great as a comedian. There was once more the feeling – so rare in the opera house! – of a character expressing himself with perfect ease and naturalness in every gesture, every modulation of the voice. Basilio has comparatively few big singing moments, apart from the famous "calumny" aria. We were not sorry for it, for it gave Chaliapin unlimited opportunities for the exercise of that faculty in which he is supreme, the phrasing of a musical sentence with all the changing colours, accents and inflections of the speaking voice. And Chaliapin is as great a master of the comic in gesture and facial expression as in speech and song.'[172] Edward Stark remarked that Chaliapin's acting was 'peppered with hundreds of comic touches'. In the finale of the second act, for instance, Bartolo, stunned with astonishment, stands stock still holding his open snuff-box. Don Basilio, who has noticed this, slowly moves to his side, one big step at a time with a pause between them, never taking his eyes off Bartolo. His face with the long nose of a fox sticks forward; he is crouching, nervously fingering the folds of his cassock. At one point he somehow manages to bend down and, without stopping, pick up a small piece of paper. When he is near Bartolo, Don Basilio quickly empties the contents of the snuff-box into the paper. Bartolo shows no signs of regaining his senses, and Basilio, his deed done, retraces his steps backwards in the same manner and melts into the crowd of onlookers.

'Basilio is generally presented as a somewhat lugubrious figure,' wrote the *Westminster Gazette*, 'but Chaliapin makes him frankly jovial, with an irrepressible sense of humour which is reflected in every twist and turn of his movements and ever-changing facial expressions. Needless to say he did not fail to make the most of his famous "calumny" solo while later he played his part in the ensemble with unlimited gusto and irresistible effect, at the same time being careful always, like a true artist, to keep within the picture and not to magnify unduly what is only a subordinate role.'[173]

Of course, the interpretation was not received with universal approval. One could perhaps not go as far as calling the doubts expressed by Western critics a rejection, but it was obvious to Chaliapin that many of them found it difficult to accept his bitingly satirical reading of the role. 'The interpretation of this immortal Rossinian character,' reflected the *Corriere della sera* correspondent, 'whose very elastic conscience is ready to bend wherever the tinkling of gold can be heard, seemed, of course, totally different in spirit and in style. From Chaliapin's figure, gestures and voice emerged the caricature-like comical character who was at times irresistible and often far from what had been the tradition or, at any rate, the stage custom.'[174]

In America, as already mentioned in the previous chapter, reaction was far more critical. 'He got much applause as a fun-maker in Rossini's *Barber of Seville*, although there were not a few who, while admitting that his impersonation of the Spanish music master was doubtless realistic and true to the time in which the story is placed, objected to certain Zolaesque details, such as the use of his sleeve instead of a handkerchief.'[175]

As usual, Chaliapin's response was couched in less than diplomatic terms. '"*The Barber*'s Don Basilio is conceived as a low, tricky, dirty rascal," he cried. "But because he wears a

As Don Basilio.

friar's costume these musical donkeys want him to be treated as respectfully as the Pope. Never! Write down that I will not wash his face or improve his manners or give him a clean silk handkerchief for his nose, not for the *Sun* or the *Tribune* or the *Times*. Write down that the New York *Sun* should be banished to Siberia!" His emotions at this point so overpowered him that his hand swept a vase off the table beside him. It crashed to pieces.'[176]

Unlike their overseas colleagues, some British reviewers saw in Chaliapin's treatment not the influence of Zola's naturalism but 'a Russian conception'. The *Evening Standard* decided that 'Chaliapin's Basilio is in the main a comic figure of no particular nationality and, above all, not primarily Italian.'[177] Ernest Newman, who started his review by saying 'The great thing of the evening, of course, was Chaliapin's Basilio,' continued: 'He would probably be able to produce historical evidence that every detail was correct. But what we are sure of is that however Italian the get-up may have been, Chaliapin made it look thoroughly Russian; it would have done quite well for one of the drunken Friars in *Boris Godunov*.'[178]

'Not that he is bad,' conceded Francis Toye in the *Morning Post*, 'in a sense he is quite good, but in this quintessentially Latin opera, with all these Latin artists animated by century-old Latin tradition, he can hardly expect to be in place. And he is not. His Don Basilio is a villainous mendicant friar, not an "out-at-elbows" Spanish priest.'[179] Seeing another performance a week later did nothing to change the critic's opinion. 'His nationality, his methods are, despite his extraordinary gifts, a handicap to perfect success in the part. He certainly was not as good as either Badini or Malatesta, who had the advantage of being Latins and being imbued with the century-old traditions of playing this essentially Latin opera.* But I honour him artistically for so doing, in the first place because he thus proves his superior taste in appreciating the genius of Rossini, in the second

---

* Ernest Newman, to quote a last excerpt from his article, remarked: 'I fancy his example stimulated the other players also to their best possible. Badini's Figaro and Malatesta's Bartolo are always rich in humour, but I have never seen them play so well as on this occasion.'

because he shows thereby a desire to shine as an interpreter of comedy as well as of melodrama, as an artist of parts instead of one part only.'[180]

Opinions sometimes seem to exist for the sole purpose of differing. Nevertheless, the views of all eyewitness are of value to the historian. There is no need here to decide who is right by comparing their impressions, but it is interesting just to know what they thought when they heard and saw a Russian singer in Italian opera. Moreover, independently of whether they were of the opinion that Chaliapin joined naturally in the ensemble with the other performers or that he did not, English critics caught with exceptional clarity the very essence of his conception and the method on which his Don Basilio was based. The complex, exaggerated characterisation he gave to an unassuming comic figure could really be traced back to one of the traditions of Russian artistic culture. Witness a review by one of Chaliapin's compatriots dated 1913: 'Finally, all Moscow has had its long-awaited musical feast: at last it has seen Chaliapin in the role of Don Basilio. The interpretation of this part represents an absolutely outstanding composition in the art of the stage and of opera. The subtlety of its polish, the integrity and the vividness of the type he was playing go far beyond the limits of criticism. This Don Basilio, the like of which has scarcely ever been seen, is at once funny, repulsive and terrifying. Before he even opens his mouth, he has about him the air of both the comic, petty, venal rogue and the profound horror which we encounter in the types of Dostoevsky.'[181]

Recalling that the first centenary of Chaliapin's birth had been celebrated in 1973 prompted Sir Neville Cardus to remark: 'He sang with a natural peasant geniality and he had the power to present beyond life-size, and with regal authority, the Russian peasant's view of the human tragi-comedy. He is in the company of Mussorgsky and Dostoevsky in being able to express and sum up the Russian character of his period.'[182]

Certainly the difficulties besetting the presentation of opera are so great that a first-rate performance of music earns our gratitude. One can be equally certain that Chaliapin and his partners in the Covent Garden production did their best to

Programme for Chaliapin's first appearance at the Royal Opera House,
Covent Garden, May 25th, 1926.

follow the composer's directions with the utmost care, and from the point of view of 'faithfulness to the music', in the literal sense of the term, there was hardly any difference between them. On the level at which they understood their performing task and Rossini's intentions, each one of them did everything he thought necessary and everything he could. But it was precisely there, as Edwin Evans of *Time and Tide* observed, that their union ended. 'It was not the vanity of the actor that caused him to "steal" the opera and make Don Basilio its outstanding personage. He could not help himself. He merged himself into the character, playing for all it was worth, and if the others had done the same the proportions would not have been disturbed. It was not his fault that they failed to do so. Nor, in all fairness to them, was the fault theirs. It was inherent in the accepted conventions of classical opera. Traditionally they could claim that right was on their side and that Chaliapin was out of the picture.'[183]

When, in the spring of 1907, before the start of his Monte Carlo tour, Chaliapin announced that he wanted to sing King Philip, the choice was enthusiastically welcomed by his friends and by the press. The part seemed to have been written for him; one could not imagine a better interpreter for it: another tyrannical ruler, a tragic figure concealing agonising spiritual strife behind the mask of a cruel despot. A man who can decide the fate of entire peoples with a wave of his finger, but inside, an old husband consumed by jealousy, hoping that love will ease his conscience stained with the blood of innocents. A truly Chaliapinesque character, in which he could display his tragic genius. No one doubted the success; this would be on a par with Ivan the Terrible and Boris Godunov.

It was, indeed, a considerable success and endured for many more years, wherever Chaliapin sang in *Don Carlos*. But it is strange that when he discusses some problem or other of interpretation of his roles, he never cites this one as an example. You cannot tell from his memoirs how he saw Philip, what he would have liked to uncover in his harsh destiny. Not a word even of his customary researches in libraries and archives, his visits to picture galleries and his conversations with specialists in the history of the period. 'Imagination must feed on real life, on observation,' he wrote in *Mask and Soul*. 'To play a Spanish accordionist you have to go to Spain. At the time when I was composing Don Basilio, I had not yet been to Spain. But I had been to the Spanish border, in France.'[184] He seems to be trying to explain himself to his public, to prove that his imagination had roots in firm soil – not that of Spain, of course, but still, not far from it. And for the part of Philip there was even no need for this. As if all he had to do was to slip on whatever costume he was given, knit his brows so as to stress the gloomy mood of the King, and go on stage just like any other singer.

Should one be tempted to accept such an unlikely idea, it would soon be dispelled by contemporary reviews. In Moscow, for instance, a newspaper wrote: 'Philip II is carefully and thoroughly thought out, and of course the singer has not drawn from Verdi's opera alone what he needed to know to allow him to resurrect this terrifying and cruel character.'[185] And in Petrograd: 'Chaliapin remained Chaliapin in this role too: refraining from trying to find in it anything specifically "effective" with which to shine, he combined all the traits and features into one wonderfully harmonious and truthful whole. Philip's weary and hardened soul could be felt both in the restrained and severe inflections and in the stony mask of the face. A stout soldier, his red hair greying, the face square, with coarse features, immobile as a statue, the gestures imperious and unhurried – such was his King Philip.'[186] 'It was easy enough to say that Mr. Chaliapin looked like a great historical portrait, or like such a portrait come to life,' said a New York writer, 'but words of that sort convey scarcely so much as a faint notion of his achievement. His Philip was at once the proudest, the craftiest and the gloomiest of monarchs, and likewise the most imposing to see. Gloves of as white a kid as ever graced the hand of man or woman were positively sinister as he wore them. He lifted a single one of his ten digits and it was as the royal sceptre raised on high. The very curve and angle of his silken knees held the fate of peoples balancing. His face was the cloistered, tortured visage of Mad Joan's grandson, and the whitening russet of his hair betrayed that Spanish house of Austria which sought peace through bloodshed, and burned all heretics, to the greater joy of an approving God. Could Mary Tudor, whose heart in the years of his strength and beauty he had broken, have looked down on this old and broken vestige of a man, his kingly pride cast from him as a useless garment, when in soliloquy he laid bare his soul, wounded to death because his young queen loved another, she would have had to believe that retributive justice does issue from an avenging heaven.'[187]

One can see that the role was planned with great care and painstakingly constructed in Chaliapin's usual manner. So why is he not as enamoured of this clearly brilliant piece of work as he is of others? And why did he sing the part so rarely, not to say so reluctantly? One cannot help thinking that Chaliapin did not find enough dramatic power and depth in King Philip for his taste, and this impression is reinforced by his interpretation.

Eyewitnesses can again help to recreate it to some extent. 'At the back of the stage, amongst the trees, one could glimpse a shadow, which suddenly turned into an ominous figure. Cold and gloom emanated from the colossal statue, dressed in black velvet with a heavy gold chain on his chest. The hand, gloved in white kid, regally rests on his walking stick; from under the brim of his tall black hat peer out heavy, leaden eyes with a fixed look.'[188] 'He crosses the stage diagonally, takes in everybody with a sullen glance, looks back, pauses and exhales a barely audible sigh. The public froze for a second and suddenly a thunder of applause broke out.'[189] 'In this silent scene one could understand everything going on in the King's mind: his tragic love of the Queen, his jealousy of Don Carlos – everything was mirrored in his expression, which said more than words and sounds could.'[190] 'You still do not know his tragedy, this is your very first acquaintance with *Don Carlos*, but you can see that this man is unhappy.'[191] 'Cold air was blowing from the stony face. "Why is the queen unattended?" Chaliapin asked the lady-in-waiting in a metallic, biting sound, striking terror in her with a piercing glance. His eyes then shifted to the Queen. In this glance one could now read jealousy and inquisitorial suspicion.'[192] The severity of the lady's punishment causes surprise. Banishment for just a breach of etiquette? Philip sees how deeply upset the Queen is, but this does not alter his decision. Chaliapin-Philip goes off stage while she takes leave of her friend, and returns only just in time to join in the small ensemble. Deeply absorbed in thought, he has clearly been scouring the garden in search of Don Carlos. Perhaps as he arrived he had noticed his son in the distance. However that may be, his rage is not caused by the violation of court rules but by burning jealousy. During the ensemble he scrutinises his wife's face, looking for confirmation of his suspicions. He finds none but feels no better for it. "She seems to feign a noble heart....' Taking Elizabeth's arm, Philip moves out of the garden and suddenly notices Posa. He stands rooted to the spot for a second, then, freeing her arm, waves away all those present and turns to Rodrigo. The way Chaliapin conducted the scene left no possible doubt as to the real interests of its main character. He is clearly trying to be pleasant to the marquis. He endures Posa's impertinence almost with indifference, patiently answering all the terrible accusations laid against him. Even when he talks of matters of state, saying that only through terror and blood can peace be restored to the country, the King remains rather moderate. He is allowing unprecedented conduct and being surprisingly frank with Posa only in order to find out whether his wife is unfaithful to him. And it is clear that at that moment jealousy and not the fate of the crown is on Philip's mind. 'Two or three times Philip's anger flares up, he even brandishes his cane at Posa, but this was not Chaliapin's real anger – terrifying for the spectators, murderous for his partners – this was formal anger. Yes, he is treated with rudeness, he is the King and this is insolence, but he needs this man and so will tolerate everything.'[193]

Beginning of the fourth act. 'Words cannot convey the sense of tragedy in this sad, mute pose; what darkness of the soul could be read on Chaliapin's face and in his lifeless eyes! He "simply" sat in an armchair, he "simply" kept silent, but we, the public, could feel in his rigid figure, in the head bowed in royal sorrow, in the hands resting on the chair, the King's steady flow of agonising emotions and thoughts. Long before he uttered any sound, Chaliapin made you hear the doleful melody of his next aria.'[194] 'Rarely is it given to any mime of song or speech to utter the syllables of the last despair as the Russian basso did in the King's "Ella giammai m'amò!" The single line "Dormirò sol nel manto mio regal", no one who heard it is likely ever to forget. Other basses have sung this air, some of them extremely well; Chaliapin lived it.'[195] Thoughts of the crown and of treason have crept back, only to be engulfed in the unending stream of his melancholy reflections and inhuman weariness. Chaliapin is not playing the statesman, although his desk is piled with maps and papers and nearby stands a huge globe which Philip turns mechanically. The King is still waiting for Posa's report, and so when the Grand Inquisitor arrives, he tries to defend Posa. His blood-curdling 'No, never!' rocks the house. But the Church is stronger than him, and Philip has to give in. The Inquisitor is already at the door when the conversation ends and he quickly disappears. Philip leaps up from his seat with a jerk, rushes to the door watching him go and wondering whether he should call him back. So caught up in his uncertainties is he that he has not noticed the arrival of the Queen until he hears her 'Justice, sire!' In the brief, stormy explanation which follow, Chaliapin was literally choking with spite. 'The voice lost all restraint and steadily rose in an unbroken crescendo.' And just after shouting the words 'adulterous wife!' to her face, Philip suddenly wilted before your eyes, turning into a devastated, very weak old man. In the succeeding scenes his earlier look of an 'animated marble statue with a heavy slow tread' had returned, but at the same time one could sense a crack in him. He regrets Posa's death not because he valued him but because he took with him the last hope of finding out the truth about the love of Elizabeth and Don Carlos.

Chaliapin's interpretation had many other vivid and memorable moments, but, generally speaking, the role did not excite him. It could be that what he saw as the central motif of Philip's conduct – the pathological jealousy of an old man for his young wife and son – did not seem to him a sufficiently serious, worthwhile base for the creation of a powerful character. If an

Chaliapin as King Philip II in Verdi's *Don Carlos*, 1920s.

opera did not furnish him with enough material, he was usually
able to find something useful in literature, history or paintings,
which he could then add to and re-arrange as he wanted.
But this time the search was fruitless. Chaliapin found little
source of inspiration in either Friedrich Schiller's play or in
the historical events (from which the author, by the way, widely
departs).

Inspiration returned to Chaliapin in his last great creation –
Don Quixote, Knight of the Doleful Countenance. The immortal hero of Cervantes, distorted beyond recognition first by the
playwright Le Lorrain, then by the librettist Henri Cain and the
composer Jules Massenet, came back to life with the Russian
singer's brilliant feat of acting. 'Its [the score's] only conceivable
excuse for survival is that it gives Mr. Chaliapin a stalking-
horse for a superb impersonation,' wrote the *New York Herald
Tribune* in 1926. 'This extraordinary artist has gone beyond
Massenet. He has gone, evidently, to the figure of the nobly
fanatical dreamer as he exists for all of us in Cervantes, and
has recreated him almost in defiance of the shabby trio who
defaced a masterpiece. In Chaliapin the true Don Quixote comes
alive across the footlights.'[196]
   The reaction to his performance was practically unanimous.
Chaliapin's joy knew no bounds. He genuinely loved the role
of Don Quixote; the figure of the noble hidalgo had long
attracted him. In one of his letters to Gorky he declared that in
the spring of 1909 he had had only 'two fine days' in Paris,
when listening to Massenet's music and Cain's libretto. Both
seemed to him wonderful; he felt so affected that he could not
contain his tears. He confided in *Pages from My Life*: 'By the
time he had reached the beginning of the last act I was sobbing
so hard that Massenet stopped playing, looked at me and
exclaimed: "Chaliapin, please, please! *Calme-toi!* Control yourself! Let me finish!"' He seems embarrased at the memory of
this display of hypersensitivity and goes on to say somewhat
apologetically: 'I could of course mention many other composers who have written more profound music than Jules Massenet. Yet I must confess that I never remember being more

intensely moved than by his interpretation of the score as he
played it to me that day for the first time.'[197]

As if thrilled at meeting at last a friend he had long been
waiting for, Chaliapin continued in his letter to Gorky: 'If God
makes me wise this time too, then I think it would be a good
thing to play Quixote as "you" and also to play him a little as
"myself". Who knows, maybe I won't be able to do anything
after this and the role will by my last.'[198]

This confession – there is no other word for it – contains
much to make one ponder. Apart from yet another frighteningly
accurate prediction – 'I won't be able to do anything after this' –
it is the only instance of a desire to identify, even if only partly,
with the character he was to play. He had, after all, always
rejected such a course, and if one must look for common features
between Chaliapin's personality and his roles, Don Quixote is
hardly the first to spring to mind. 'In this part,' wrote Sergei
Makovsky, 'Chaliapin left a particularly deep impression. In
fact, how opposed it was to everything which characterised
Chaliapin as a person! Why was Chaliapin so great in this
role, he who was not noted for kindness, sentimentality or
disinterestedness? Why was he so fond of this role and why did
he take the Knight of La Mancha so much to heart that he cried
every time?'[199]

When you are trying to re-create a person's life and destiny,
it is not easy to argue with his contemporaries. Unlike you, they
knew him, and your work is based on their tales, memoirs,
diaries and letters. And yet one must disagree with Makovsky
here. The fact that Don Quixote is sentimental whereas Chaliapin was not is beside the point. Chaliapin's personal traits are
in this case of no significance whatever; what matters is not
whether the singer resembles Don Quixote but what in the
character attracted him as an artist and what he wanted to say
through him. Chaliapin created his Don Quixote not so much
out of Massenet's opera but almost in spite of it. 'The wonderful, moving, majestic figure is entirely the result of Chaliapin's
work,' asserted V. Karatygin. 'It does not rest upon the flaccid
melodies of the French composer but soars high above them.
Let us imagine that one day someone will invent a way of

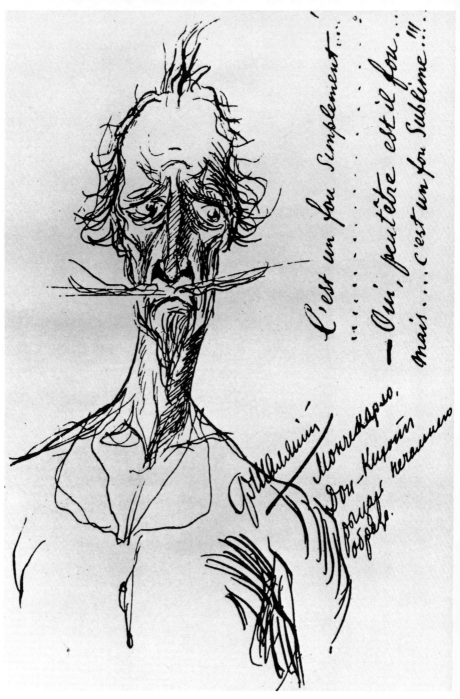

Above: Self-portrait as Don Quixote, 1910.

Right: Chaliapin as Don Quixote in Massenet's opera *Don Quixote*, 1910.

representing acting by notes. If this were done, then if one laid the musical score of Chaliapin's impersonation against Massenet's melody line, one would see that between them they made a superb counterpoint. Chaliapin performs the main theme, and Massenet only accompanies him in the minor voice.'[200]

What does Chaliapin himself say? The music which had made him cry when he first heard it really had very little part to play in the composition of the role. He had possibly never so openly relied on literature; for him the opera was just a good occasion to work on this character. 'Don Quixote – I have no idea what he is like. After reading Cervantes attentively, I close my eyes and form an idea, I can get the general impression of Don Quixote. I can, for instance, understand that this introverted dreamer must be slow in his movements, he must not be agitated. I understand that his eyes must not be cold and sober. It is clear that his appearance must suggest at the same time imagination, helplessness, childish weakness, the pride of a Knight of Castile, and the goodness of a saint. Don Quixote's inner nature made me see his external aspect. I pictured it in my mind and, feature by feature, I steadily continued to model his image, which from a distance produced a great effect but was comical and touching when near.'[201] 'With his barber's tin that serves him for a head-dress, with his lance in hand, with his cuirass blackened and rusty, his emaciated figure, his scrawny calves, his long beard, Chaliapin succeeded in bringing to life a silhouette of Don Quixote which combined the depth and geniality of a Goya, the epic grandeur of a Gustave Doré, the subtle esprit of a Léandre,'[202] says Massenet's biographer Louis Schneider, completing for us the portrait of the knight. All those lucky enough to see Chaliapin's Don Quixote agreed on one thing – he came straight out of Cervantes. It would be more accurate to say that he came from an interpretation of the novel influenced by the cultural and philosophical thinking of nineteenth-century Russia, which led Turgenev, for instance, to pronounce his famous speech on 'Hamlet and Don Quixote'. And sixty years later one of Chaliapin's models for Don Quixote, Maxim Gorky, wrote in the preface to the Russian edition of Romain Rolland's *Jean-Christophe*: 'They say that

Romain Rolland is Don Quixote. From my point of view, nothing better can be said of anyone.'[203]

The degree of Gorky's quixotry is a question which can be left aside; but what matters is that Chaliapin saw these traits in his friend ('I think it would be a good thing to play ... "you"). The singer's memoirs show that in the years of the Revolution, Gorky acted in a manner worthy of Don Quixote, tirelessly interceding at all levels with the Bolsheviks newly risen to power – and sometimes with Lenin himself – for the release of innocents arrested and condemned to death.

Like Faust, Don Juan and Hamlet, Don Quixote had long turned from a literary hero into an allegory. Successive generations continue to attribute to him their own concept of the meaning of life, using him to define vague, eternally evasive notions of good and evil. But what is he like, this great knight inherited by Chaliapin from Belinsky, Turgenev and Dostoevsky? First of all, very little is comic in him. Don Quixote is not funny. He is unlucky, he is deceived, but he is always right. He is deeply naive. Since he loved Don Quixote, Chaliapin made this into a positive quality. A man has the right to be naive. It is not his fault if his fellow human beings are incapable of accepting him and greet him with rude words. Don Quixote–Chaliapin wants a world where things are what they seem, where lies, violence, cunning and deceit do not exist. This is still only a hope, but Don Quixote is certain that one day it will come true. He keeps his conscience pure; armed with a rusty old lance, he goes to 'fight forces hostile to mankind'. He is always solitary – an army of Don Quixotes is unthinkable. He struggles against evil selflessly, at his own risk and peril. On the road to Truth, he takes the side of the first thing he encounters; this is the only way he can behave. The reality he sees through the prism of his own ideals is strongly distorted, but he never mistakes wrong for right. Don Quixote asks no one's help; he relies on his own strength and on God's final victory. The intensity of his faith looks to others like madness, but it awakens in them lofty dreams and turns their minds towards higher purposes. 'His is a faith in something immortal, unshakeable, a faith in the truth that exists beyond the individual, difficult to

As Don Quixote.

attain, demanding devotion and sacrifice. To live for oneself, think of oneself, would be regarded as shameful by Don Quixote. He has no vestige of egoism; he does not worry about himself, he is all self-sacrifice. Of humble heart, he is great and daring in spirit.'[204] 'Chaliapin's Don Quixote as we saw it on Friday in the National Theatre,' wrote the Prague newspaper *Narodny Listy* in 1934, 'does not present the tragi-comic figure of Cervantes' knight but a being completely infused with ideals of humanity and justice, an apostle of love and good. Hence the very convincing nature of his performance as he overpowers the robbers and pours scorn on Dulcinea's suitors. This enthusiasm for an ideal is the core of Chaliapin's hero, whether he expresses it in song, words or acting. Chaliapin's Don Quixote is a figure totally consumed by his *idée fixe*, down to the last quiver of his nerves, and this has a compellingly powerful effect on spectators. Every detail of the character, every intonation, every gesture – even a movement of the fingers – is in perfect harmony with the psychological conception. Chaliapin's personal attitude as a Russian dramatic artist is clearly in complete agreement with this reading of Don Quixote as an expression of humanitarian ideology and almost fanatical idealism pitched against the reality of life.'[205]

In Cervantes' novel, Don Quixote sometimes finds himself in humiliating circumstances. He can be weak; this ascetic and idealist suddenly develops the healthy appetite of the common man. The great champion of truth even tells lies at times. But Chaliapin's Don Quixote is cleansed of weaknesses and defects. He is outside ordinary life, and this aloofness makes him imposing. After passing through all the thorns of this earth, he leaves life as a saint. 'The highest moment was undoubtedly the scene of Don Quixote's death, which Chaliapin performed standing against a tree: a heroic death, like Cyrano's, but even more, a mystical death with the arms, suddenly raised and stretched out, suggested (with what respect) a crucifixion,' recalled a French opera-goer.[206] 'In *Don Quixote*, Chaliapin was intensely moving – his helpless humanity was stunning,' writes Pavel Markov. 'My sister was with me at the theatre, and she cried from the moment Chaliapin appeared to the end

As Don Quixote. The Bolshoi Theatre, Moscow. 1910.

of the performance. At the Bolshoi Theatre Chaliapin staged *Don Quixote* himself; there was no great inventiveness in the production, but everything was very carefully done, especially the final episode. Don Quixote stood by a tree towering over the centre of the stage in a pose associated with the crucifixion; his outstretched arms and sorrowfully inclined head left an imperishable, indelible impression on the memory.'[207]

Chaliapin brought to the concert platform what he brought to the operatic stage: theatre. But here he created it all by himself, without the aid of costume, scenery, make-up, partners or stage lighting. The pianist Ivor Newton, who worked with him on many occasions, observed: 'He found a recital far more taxing in itself than any role; in essence he was an actor, and recital gave him more personalities to assume and many more characters to create.'[208] Inside each song performed by Chaliapin there was someone real, with a definite personality. The concert piece turned into a personal monologue, delivered like a spontaneous confession, declaration of love, objection or protest.

The kaleidoscope of images succeeding one another produced in truth an incredible effect: 'The listener had to prod himself to make sure he was not dreaming.'[209] 'Think of Chaliapin', wrote Oda Slobodskaya, 'and how he sang, hear him interpret four or five different songs, and you would think it was four or five different singers.'[210] 'This great legendary giant with just a flip of his fingers, a wave of his expressive hands, assumed dozens of shapes during the evening; he was the disappointed, spurned lover weeping into his beer; the cold, ruthless maiden who danced and laughed and drank when her lover was hanged; the prophet with his dire warnings; the Volga boatman with his haunting song and strained face; the gay, rollicking Don Juan with conquests aplenty; the barbarian Khan Konchak reproving his restive guests; the Russian convict mourning the life he is about to depart and the love he cannot wrench from his heart; the young flirtatious girl whose kisses become realistic when mimicked by the great Chaliapin; in the one English song he sang, which seemed to be something about a "lovely chat with you", he was the contented friend, and he made the whole ghostly assemblage of Napoleon's troops pass in review. He was all these characters and many more ... and his impersonations seemed effortless,' wrote the *Seattle Times*. 'His singing was all the power and glory and fire of Chaliapin of the great Russian Imperial Opera, Chaliapin of the Metropolitan and Chaliapin of the Chicago Civic Opera Company. In fact, after we heard him last evening we didn't mind growing old. If your interests can stay as alert, your friendliness as warm, and your public hypnotism as great as Chaliapin's then we could move the age of life's beginning up to sixty-two instead of forty. For this great basso seems to be the perennial concert singer ... the man whom youth cannot forsake, the man who today can draw the third largest audience of Seattle's entire season ... and that at sixty-two, and at the end of the season. His buffoonery, his pathos, his art and his charming villainy (stage variety of course) still hold thousands enchanted.'[211]

His anxiety was greater before a concert than before a stage performance; it often persisted even once he had started singing. 'Chaliapin would pace up and down the artist's room like a tiger determined on escape, creating an atmosphere of enormous tension,' recounted Ivor Newton, 'but when his moment came, he would rush, all smiles, on the platform and everyone, except the accompanist, could relax.'[212]

The singer made an impact on his concert audience from his very entrance. 'In his economy of movements he was uncommonly plastic, even elegant. Every gesture he made engraved itself on the memory. The auditorium thundered with ovations; extending his hands clasped in each other towards the audience, Chaliapin greeted the public.'[213] 'To achieve the maximum of expression he had no need to make himself up either as Boris or as Don Quixote,' declared the Italian newspaper *La tribuna*. 'Tall, with a mobile face, by turns severe, cunning, contemptuous or gentle, he can, without opening his mouth, without uttering a single word, say everything he wants.'[214] 'The act of singing seems to freeze many people stiff. Chaliapin sings like a public speaker, turning now to the right, now to the left, and even right round, so that no one shall feel out in the cold. He walks about the platform – now four paces one way, now four the other, and when he thinks he has done something particularly good he will walk out of the limelight altogether and chuckle to himself at the wonder of it. He must have walked a good mile and a half yesterday afternoon. And his hands are a study. His favourite pose is to rest one on the piano and the other in his trouser pocket, but he never stays like that for long. He conducts his accompanist as Sir Thomas Beecham conducts an orchestra.

'He cracks his fingers like castanets. He throws a high note into the air like throwing a toy balloon. He ends up each song with a motion like snapping a spider's web. His hands act all he sings, they are as much part of the performance as his incomparable voice, which Time forgets to lay his hands on.'[215]

'The arts of magic are not dead; they are still potent and still dangerous,' warned *The Times* in London in 1925. 'To make the worse song appear the better – or not quite that but at least as good as the best – to subvert the youth by giving them an alluring example of dramatised lieder, is to earn the cup of hemlock, while to bind spells on an audience by the magic of personality which uses art as a tool is akin to witchcraft, for which the penalty is burning. Chaliapin was guilty on both counts at the Albert Hall last night, and the sentences should by rights run concurrently. But what can one do? He turned a huge crowded hall into an intimate music room; he treated every song as freshly as though he had never sung it before . . . . If any Leporello sang the Catalogue aria as he sang it, no one would have any further interest in Don Juan, yet it did no violence to Mozart.'[216]

The power of his personality was perhaps even more evident in concert than in the theatre. Those who rejected his manner of interpretation and disagreed with his treatment of individual numbers were nevertheless unable to resist him. 'In the light of my experience,' affirms Gerald Moore, 'I say that Chaliapin was not a first-class lieder singer. A song by Schubert or Schumann would be distorted out of all recognition by his wayward rhythm and his own personal interpretation of the poem. . . . The most discriminating devotee of Schubert and Schumann would be swept temporarily at least off his feet, against his better judgement, by the man's histrionic mastery and the power of his personal magnetism.'[217]

Similar opinions can be found in almost every review in the West, but critics' reactions differed in Russia. His compatriots rated Chaliapin's concerts as highly as his operatic performances. 'He is the most intelligent, talented singer I have ever heard in my life,'[218] noted Lev Tolstoy's wife, Countess Sofya Andreevna, in her diary after one of them. 'This man is, to put it mildly, a genius,' declared Gorky. 'What a Mephistopheles! What a Prince Galitsky! But all this pales by comparison with his concert. My friend – it was something extraordinary, I have never experienced anything like it.'[219]

Europe and America tended to think that 'the Titan Chaliapin' imperiously forced his will on the public; his success did not come from exposing the composer's intentions but, just the opposite, from destroying them. Chaliapin razed everything to the ground and on the smouldering ruins erected his own, no less great, creation. 'A universe of drama opens up,' says the *San Francisco Chronicle*, 'and if music is slighted in the process, much the worse for music. The distortions of melodic line that Chaliapin habitually commits in the "Catalogue" aria and the "Calumny" aria, both of which he sang last night, may shock the purists, but they do not shock his audiences in general and for very good reasons. The stupendous personality carries everything away with it, including the notes written by Mozart and Rossini. But what of it? Here is literally a case where the King can do no wrong!'[220] 'He takes more liberties with the text than ever,' commented *The Times* in 1924, 'and some of his songs have as much right to be labelled Schumann-Chaliapin as other pieces Bach-Busoni. Opinions vary about this; after some wavering we should be inclined to vote with the ayes; it seems the right thing for the right person, like, let us say, Turner and Whistler.'[221]

Descriptions of Chaliapin's concerts clearly show that his comportment on these occasions was not the same in Russia as abroad. He was more restrained at home; the public, speaking the same language and sharing the same cultural background, did not need additional explanations, accents and gestures to

Royal Albert Hall

MANAGER :: :: :: HILTON CARTER, M.V.O.

Tuesday Evening

NOVEMBER 3rd

1925, at 8 o'clock

*Positively the only appearance
in LONDON this year*

OF

CHALIAPINE

"The World's Greatest Lyric and Dramatic Artist."

ASSISTED BY

ISOLDE MENGES *(Solo Violin)*

MAX RABINOWITSH *(Pianist)*

CHAPPELL GRAND PIANOFORTE.

TICKETS (including Tax): Grand Tier Boxes £5 15s. 0d. Loggia Boxes £4 12s. 0d.
Second Tier Boxes £2 12s. 6d. Stalls 15s. and 12s. Arena 12s. and 10s. 6d.
Balcony 7s. 6d. and 5s. 9d. Orchestra 5s. 9d. and 3s. 6d. Gallery (Promenade) 2s. 4d.
May be obtained at the **ROYAL ALBERT HALL,** the usual Agents and
L. G. SHARPE, 25, Haymarket, S.W.

Telephone: GERRARD 5564. A stamped addressed envelope must accompany all orders for tickets.

Vail & Co., Printers, London, E.C. 1 **P.T.O.**

amplify the words. It was a subtle interchange between people
with deep common roots. Also, in Russia, he could permit
himself any outburst of temper, openly display any caprice. For
his Moscow farewell concerts before leaving the USSR in 1922,
he insisted on the following warning to the public: 'Fedor
Ivanovich wants it made clear that no personal requests should
be shouted from the auditorium or else he will not sing. There
was some grumbling in the audience but it quickly abated.
Tense silence reigned, but there was still no sign of Chaliapin.
Time was dragging on ominously slowly. . . .'[222] The grumbling
was not without justification: he had himself instituted the
tradition of requests from the auditorium; he often very willingly complied with them, sang endlessly and then even recited
poetry. At another of the concerts, 'somewhere in the middle
of a song, Chaliapin evidently forgot the words. He was holding
the music – he took his lorgnette, had a look, but obviously
turned over to the wrong page. . . . So he stopped the pianist;
putting his hand on his shoulder, he crumpled the music and
flung it under the piano, then stared fixedly at the auditorium.
The silence there was sepulchral, everyone was transfixed with
terror, it did not enter anyone's head to give some expression
of their bewilderment. . . . Towards the end of the concert,
someone in the audience, forgetting the warning, shouted: "Sing
'The Flea'*". Chaliapin with inimitable majesty shifted his glance
to the upper box, next to Glinka's portrait, and looked in that
direction for a long time – the pause was so strained that the
public held its breath in the expectancy of a row. And suddenly,
the singer smiled widely. The house burst into applause. And
then Chaliapin just said: "Well, all right, 'The Flea'. . . ." '[223]

In the West, he seemed to try to protect himself against
audiences' lack of comprehension. Before the start of a concert,
what an English journalist wittily described as 'hymnbooks'
were distributed with translations of his whole programme.
'Each song was announced by its number immediately before
it was sung, as if the singer were obeying the whim of the
moment.'[224]

* Song by Mussorgsky.

His very relations with the public took on a different form outside Russia. What came naturally in his native land had to be artificially fabricated abroad. In London, Paris, New York and Rome he tried to create the atmosphere of a gathering of old acquaintances who found pleasure in each other's company. Whatever the size of the hall and of the audience, Chaliapin wanted his recitals to have 'the charm of a private rehearsal, of intimacy'.[225] 'It has been said,' commented a *Daily Telegraph* correspondent, 'that it is chiefly as a dramatic artist that Chaliapin excels. That is only half the truth. As an exponent of dramatic force he is certainly without parallel among singers, but this power is only one side of his make-up. He is essentially a medium – a universal medium. He not only has the power of giving, but – what is far more important – of receiving, and there in his mind are stored all kinds of experiences, big and small, which when expressed can create the most intimate relation between himself and his audience.'[226]

This always cost him a good deal of effort, but it proved particularly difficult at the beginning of his new life in the West – for instance, when he returned to sing in England in the autumn of 1921 after an absence of seven years. He came to give five Famine Relief concerts* for his country, although he was very run down and felt he had reached his limit. He had not been seen there since before the war, and although that was not so far away, how distant the Diaghilev tours and those happy, unforgettable days now seemed. . . .

Chaliapin had long been thinking of leaving Soviet Russia. Already in 1920, when H. G. Wells had visited Petrograd, Chaliapin had asked him to carry a confidential letter to Fred Gaisberg saying that 'I was doing my best to get out of the country and when I got out I should be awfully broke and probably in no fit state to conduct my own affairs properly.'[227]

Gaisberg, meeting him in Riga, was deeply distressed by what he saw. He never forgot 'how the train pulled into the station and discharged a threadbare and bewildered Chaliapin from a crowded carriage. He cried with joy at seeing me and kissed me

---

* Two concerts in the Albert Hall and the others in Birmingham, Sheffield and Liverpool.

Chaliapin in concert, 1934.

on each cheek Russian fashion. To celebrate the occasion and to placate the Soviet agents who were watching him, he threw a supper party. It was a primitive affair with plenty of good Riga vodka and beer. The principal and indeed the only dish was an Irish stew served in one big vessel placed in the centre of the table. From this we helped ourselves with the spoons we had brought with us. We soon arrived at the stage where we embraced and called each other "Tovarich".'*[228] 'His wardrobe was in rags and tatters and he looked most forlorn in his threadbare clothes ... his voice seemed to be more sensitive to colds, due to the hardships of the Revolution. . . .'[229]

No opportunities to arrange an operatic performance (which would, of course, have been much easier for Chaliapin) offered themselves, and so he had no choice but to agree to the huge Albert Hall with its disastrous acoustics; he had to perform in public and make a success of it at any price. Chaliapin was very moved to see how well English people understood all the difficulties of the situation. Not that it surprised him: he had always admired their delicacy and sensitivity. 'No one knew better than he', wrote the *Musical Times*, 'that in this huge amphitheatre he was out of his element: for he is essentially a shining light – or whatever may be the masculine for *diva* – of the operatic stage; nor can he with all his talent sing in the concert-room save at a serious disadvantage. Still, there was no other course open to him if he was to appear in London at the present juncture, and successfully fulfil his self-imposed task of making money on behalf of his starving countrymen. That he should have achieved it with such brilliant results was remarkable in many ways. An audience of ten thousand would never, to begin with, have been drawn to the Albert Hall to hear a solitary singer, a stranger here for years and a celebrity in practically a different line of his art, unless the "stunt" had been worked with unusual skill. Neither, again, would that audience have listened, silent and enraptured, to group after group of "selected arias" – all sung in the unfamiliar Russian language, not one of them advertised or announced by name beforehand –

* 'Comrade.'

Chaliapin in 1930. Courtesy EMI Music.

had not the singer possessed an extraordinary personality as well as the requisite genius to conquer on the initial attack all the drawbacks and obstacles of the situation. It is this last point which is really the crux of the matter; not the question how the mere name of Chaliapin – the obscured reflex of an interrupted glory, the half-forgotten creator of a memorable experience – sufficed to draw the crowd, or the secret spell with which he held them enthralled during every instant that he stood before them.'[230]

From England, Chaliapin went by boat to America, where illness lasting over a month forced him to postpone the start of his performances until the beginning of December 1921.

Neither his wife nor his children had been allowed to join him on his tour, and so he returned to Soviet Russia in the spring with the firm intention of breaking free. On June 29th, 1922, Chaliapin left his country again, this time with part of his family.* Officially, it was only for a limited period; in reality, it was forever. And although many contracts were awaiting him, his heart was heavy. He did not want to live under Soviet rule ('There is little enough of the pleasant to remember,' he said of those days to an English newspaper),[231] but his whole life had been and would remain closely tied to Russia. You cannot throw away the past, especially when you are nearing the age of fifty.

* 'My daughter,' he wrote, 'my first wife and my sons remained in Moscow.' (*Mask and Soul* p. 304.)

With the exception of his eldest daughter, Irina, the rest of Chaliapin's family eventually left the USSR. The last one of them to do so was Iola Tornaghi, who did not return to her native Italy until the end of the 1950s.

EPILOGUE

Exile

'Chaliapin is certainly one of the most wonderful things in Russia at the present time.
He is the ARTIST, defiant and magnificent.'

H. G. Wells

For the rest of his life Chaliapin would be tormented by uneasy, gnawing feelings about the country he had left behind. It is no accident that he so often dwells on what happened in his native land after the Revolution, on why he decided to leave for the West and whether he would sometime return. The exceptionally stormy events of those sombre days and nights had become as if tangled up in a tight skein; to unravel its strands and assign everything its proper place required time – not so much to understand oneself as to make others understand. This was something which worried him a great deal, though at first Chaliapin was obviously trying to evade all attempts by journalists to winkle the truth out of him. His silence was clearly deliberate. Was it because he did not want to talk about the Soviet authorities or was it because he *could* not, for reasons known only to himself? The press did not fail to remark on the strangeness of his conduct. 'It is a difficult matter to question Chaliapin on politics,' wrote the *Sunday Express* in 1926. 'He will drink with you, laugh with you, play games with you, and quarrel with you. But he will never talk politics with you.'[1]

In the American edition of *Pages from My Life*, published a year later, he talks of the sufferings brought on by the 'horrible revolution' (searches, confiscation of property, famine), but on the whole he was still unwilling to speak out more specifically. 'Can I look critically at life as I saw it during the years of the revolution? Certainly not. It is not for me to pronounce judgement as to who was right and who was wrong....'[2] And in 1927, when events took a decided turn for the worse – he was stripped of his title of 'People's Artist' and was even threatened with being deprived of his citizenship (or at any rate so the papers informed him) – the correspondent of *The Referee* remarked after an interview: 'As regards Mr. Chaliapin's cat-

and-mouse relations to the Soviet, it is difficult to find out how exactly he stands with the rulers of Moscow.'³

The decision of the Soviet authorities had in fact stung him to the quick. 'Fedor Ivanovich only raised his arms in perplexity, but his eyes turned white with anger,' recalled Andrei Sedykh.⁴ In Austria, though, he suddenly could not contain himself and ironically commented on the situation at a press conference: 'There is only one title of which I am proud – that is the title of "Artist". This title was given to me by God, and only God can take it away from me.'⁵

When four years later Chaliapin finally decided to make his views public and to submit his detailed account of life 'under the Bolsheviks' to the judgement of his contemporaries and of future generations, he once again returned to the decree of the Committee of People's Commissars of August 24th, 1927, which had so distressed him. Reflecting on what had happened led him to compare the conduct of Nicholas II, who had made him, a son of the poorest of peasants, 'Soloist to His Majesty', with that of the so-called people's power. When Chaliapin had refused to participate in the gala concert celebrating the tercentenary of the Romanov dynasty, no one had thought of punishing him. But now, as the singer wrote, they had taken back the gift they had given him. 'Only the representatives of proletarian culture could have thought of such an idea,'⁶ he remarked.

Reading today Chaliapin's description of events more than half a century old, one sees what a sincere and naive desire he had of proclaiming his innocence, how much he wanted above all this time (and how many times before!) to be believed. Is it really a crime, he seems to be asking the reader, to help the starving Russian children he had noticed behind the fence of the Russian church in the rue Daru in Paris? Had he done anything more than to invite a priest home and give him five thousand francs to be distributed to hungry families? A few weeks later Chaliapin was summoned to the Soviet embassy to explain himself. The information from Moscow stated that the donation had been made for the benefit of White Guard organisations. He had to put in writing that he took no part in

The first Golden Disc presentation to Chaliapin. Savoy Hotel, London, 1933.
Courtesy EMI Music.

politics, that nothing in his action was against the interests of the communist regime in Russia; he added that 'it was difficult to determine with certainty which children were White and which were Red'.[7] 'My letter,' continues Chaliapin, 'left the Kremlin very displeased. I do not know what they expected of me.' He found out as soon as the Soviet newspapers started to discuss his stay abroad. A short but active campaign culminated in an article by Anatoly Lunacharsky, the member of government responsible for culture and education. (According to Marina Chaliapina, he had earlier been among those who had urged her father to leave.)[8] The trouble, it seemed, was not so much what Chaliapin had written, since, although he had answered somewhat evasively, 'he had at least shown that he had no intention of seeking any deliberate break with the current regime of his country.'[9] It was more his staying away which provoked the indignation of the authorities, and demands that 'he should come back and redeem by his stupendous talent a separation which had already lasted far too long' were growing steadily louder. Chaliapin's unique popularity placed the Soviet government in an embarrassing position. His prolonged absence had either to be justified in some way, or else he had to be punished as befitted his crime. And if a People's singer did not want to sing for the people, then he had no place in a country where socialism reigned. One never ceases to wonder at the way lying can disguise itself as truth, using the same inflections, the same vocabulary. It can rise to the level of genuine inspiration; by a slight shift of emphasis or by substituting here and there causes for effects, it attempts to seize the very right to control life. 'The papers published articles saying that Chaliapin had joined the counter-revolutionaries. Actors, circus artistes and other servants of the arts protested as they discovered that I was not only a bad citizen but a worthless actor as well, while at meetings "the popular masses" banished me from my country.'[10] Even the singer's death* failed to calm their seething anger. *Izvestia* devoted only a few lines to one of the greatest artistic losses ever suffered by Russia. As the press was under

---

* Chaliapin died on April 12th, 1938 at 5.15 p.m.

Royal Opera House
Covent Garden

Lessees : Royal Opera House Company, Limited.
Secretary and Business Manager : C. A. BARRAND

**Thursday, February 18, 1937
at 8.30 p.m.**

UNDER THE PATRONAGE OF
THEIR MAJESTIES THE KING AND QUEEN

In aid of the National Council of Social Services in the Distressed Areas.

CHALIAPINE
Assisted by LOUIS KENTNER
At the Piano - **IVOR NEWTON**

PROGRAMME AND BOOK OF WORDS   Copyright by F. W. GAISBERG (1925)

the control of the state, nothing was added to the announce-
ment, but at the same time readers could not be left without
guidance. It had by then long been the fashion to publish public
opinion comments. A letter from a Bolshoi Theatre singer,
Mark Reizen, kept the tradition alive. 'In the prime of his
powers and of his talent,' he said, 'Chaliapin betrayed his
people; he exchanged his native land for easy money. All his
appearances abroad had a casual nature. Chaliapin's colossal
talent had dried up long before then. He departed this life
leaving nothing behind, without bequeathing to anyone the
benefit of either his methods of work, or his extensive experience. Chaliapin's literary heritage offers nothing of interest to
art. It is a chronological account of various episodes, remarkable
only for the poverty of its ideas.'[11] However, even at the height
of the terrible Stalin years, when the mere thought of disagreeing
with the official point of view could have fatal consequences,
Reizen's letter produced an unexpected result: the artists of
the Bolshoi Theatre organised a silent boycott against him.
A retraction was issued within a few days; the newspaper
correspondent talking to Reizen on the telephone had, it seemed,
grossly distorted his words, and he had, naturally, been severely
disciplined.

The years passed, yet the desire to bring back even a dead
Chaliapin still persisted. Previous unsuccessful attempts and
Chaliapin's own words 'I will not go to Russia. Enough!'[12] were
forgotten. The new generation of Soviet citizens knew nothing
of all this, and Chaliapin's continued residence abroad was
now put down to his greed for money, to the contracts which
completely enslaved him and did not let him get away from the
capitalist mire.

The life of the singer in the West and his death there were
regarded as a 'tragedy'. He was weak, had no character, and
had fallen under an evil influence, but he had nevertheless not
said anything against Russia's new rulers. As for some hundred
pages or more of *Mask and Soul*, that contradiction was easily
explained: everything about art and published in the Soviet
Union had been written by him, everything about politics had
been interpolated. 'The book contains many falsehoods, many

hostile attacks, which have clearly been inserted by someone else,' affirms M. Yankovsky in his monograph *Chaliapin*.[13] The author of this brilliant study, a well-known expert on Russian opera, is not alone in casting such aspersions. This was what everybody had to think.

'He never did anything against his own people, against the Soviet state,'[14] writes the tenor Ivan Kozlovsky in an article on the occasion of the centenary of Chaliapin's birth.

The last stage in the fight for the transfer of Chaliapin's remains to the USSR had begun. But the wishes of the Soviet Union were not enough in themselves; the consent of Chaliapin's children was required for a re-interment. Not all of them agreed,[15] it was necessary to wait until those who refused had died and the rest had been persuaded. 'For quite some years the Soviet regime put pressure on us in order to get my father,'[16] declared his daughter Marina Chaliapina in an Italian magazine interview. 'Putting pressure' gradually became easier; the children were growing older, and the arguments of the Soviet authorities were no doubt beginning to seem reasonable to them. In Paris, where Chaliapin was buried at the Cimetière des Batignolles, who would look after the grave? Tatiana, Fedor and Marina now live in Rome, and Marfa in Liverpool.

In the Soviet Union, however, Chaliapin is still worshipped. Possibly there were other considerations, too, but speculation is pointless. Chaliapin's children had, after all, the right to allow their father's bones to be removed to a country he had chosen to leave and to which, in spite of all his misgivings, he had declared he did not want to return.* Contemporary memoirs report such words, as the example cited above shows, and his son Fedor repeated them, though not to the correspondent of *Izvestia*, of course – to the latter he said what the authorities wanted to hear: 'The decision to transfer the ashes of our father home is entirely in accordance with both my own and my sister's wishes. I hope that Rachmaninov's remains will also be buried in his native land. I am ready, while I have the strength, to help in this noble task.'[17] He gave a different answer when questioned

* Chaliapin's ashes were re-buried in the Novodevichy Cemetery in Moscow on October 29th, 1984.

Chaliapin with his second wife, Maria; her daughter from her previous marriage, Stella; and their daughter, Marfa. St Jean de Luz, France, mid 1930s. Courtesy Isabella Wallich.

by a Russian-language newspaper in New York: 'What do you think, if your father were still alive today, would he go to the USSR?' – 'Only for guest tours. . . . He hated the whole style of life in Soviet Russia. . . . My father could not have lived there. My father was persecuted even after his departure; taxes were imposed on him, he was stripped of his title of People's Artist, he was vilified. Now the scoundrels need him. But they do not matter – his people need him. Fedor Ivanovich's grave must be where his people live. The Soviet authorities have used this for their propaganda, but regimes come and go, whereas Russia remains. I regard the USSR as a form of monarchy, but I would define it as a monarchy of louts. They restore a few outward signs of the old culture so as to proclaim themselves its heirs and win popularity. . . .'[18]

These words of Chaliapin's son pose many questions which tear at the hearts of Russian people. And the most important one of them, which faced Russian emigrés from the start, was their attitude to a Russia now taken over by Bolsheviks. It probably concerned everyone, those who stayed as much as those who left. The former, provided they did not disappear in concentration camps, eventually paid with their conscience and with constant fear; the latter, in many cases, with nostalgia and even doubts as to whether they had made the right decision. Those who stayed decided on a blatant compromise or tried to convince themselves that they could maintain their dignity and honour while working for communism. The ones who emigrated were taking Russia away with them; it lived in them and was their life. Some of them, unable to endure the separation from their past, rushed back as fast as they could. They believed that they were going home, but again the price was violent or, at the very least, spiritual death. Chaliapin was no exception. He too knew the consuming power of doubt, before and after leaving Russia, although he was more shielded from the blows of fate than many hundreds of thousands of his compatriots. He passed through both revolution and emigration with relative ease. He clearly recognised this, and wrote in Paris, recalling those terrible years of starvation in Petrograd: 'From time to time I still performed here and there outside the theatre, and would be given either flour or some other provisions. Considering the conditions then prevailing, this troubled me somewhat. It was painful to feel in a rather privileged position.'[19]

However, lack of food was not his greatest problem. To put it simply, the further the Revolution developed and the stronger the new regime became, calling itself the state of the workers and peasants, the further Fedor Chaliapin wanted to run away from it. This was hard for him to accept; he could not forget that not so long ago he had actually wanted the fall of the Tsar and through Gorky had helped the Social Democrats in every possible way. He had even thought of joining the party of Russia's future reformers, but Gorky himself had told him: 'You are not fit for this. And I beg you, remember once and for all: do not join any party, but be an artist, as you are. This is quite enough from you.'[20]

Chaliapin realised that he was not a born revolutionary. In

the preface to *Mask and Soul*, he warns the reader: 'Everything I will be recounting and recalling will be connected one way or another with my life in the theatre. I intend to judge people and events not as a politician or a sociologist but as an actor, from an actor's point of view.'[21] This is a clever stratagem; Chaliapin is really saying: Don't be severe in your judgement if I have not understood something, or if I have not correctly evaluated it. I am only an actor – what do you expect of me? For me the world is like a great stage on which mankind plays its roles, bad ones and good ones. But 'the role a man has to play in life is always more difficult than any role which one can imagine in the theatre'.[22] This is why people make so many mistakes, choosing to personify a character which does not correspond to their potential; and not only do they suffer as a result, they also make the captive audience which fate has forced to take part in the performance suffer. Just as in the theatre, the tone is wrong, the artificial inflections and gestures 'produce a bad impression' and end in fiasco.

In art, of course, this is not so dangerous, even if a vast amount of time, money and energy has been wasted. But it is another matter when the role of Tsar, for instance, is badly played in history. Then 'people cannot help asking in a hoarse half-whisper: "Is that really a Tsar? ... He didn't feel the atmosphere right, he is a failure. His kingdom is burning." '[23]

Looking back into the past to try to determine what had originally driven him finally to abandon his country, Chaliapin writes that he finds it difficult to draw a dividing line between the three Russian revolutions.* He sees them as a chain of tragic events, dragging everything which stood in their path faster and faster into a precipice, like a stone falling from a mountain and gathering momentum. Russia's uncontrollable dive into the abyss might have been averted, but not for the first time, Chaliapin sadly explains that a Russian knows no measure in anything: 'in submission as in revolt, he must go to the very limit. ...'[24] The evil, anarchy and inhuman cruelty of those 'accursed days', as Bunin called them, deeply traumatised Chal-

---

* 1905, February 1917 and October 1917.

iapin: the fanaticism of the socialists, the weariness and the inability of the provisional government to control the wild, bloodthirsty outbursts of the popular masses. 'In their hatred and their passion to exterminate, they killed not only people, but even animals,' recalled an eyewitness. 'On an estate I knew, the racehorses on the stud-farm were beaten on the spine with crowbars because they belonged to a landowner.'[25] Another writes that 'revolutionary people' plucked 'gentry' peacocks bare and set the featherless birds loose, shrieking and bloody. 'There is no need for peacocks now, everything is working class now, not gentry.'[26]

Chaliapin could himself have cited several similar examples, but unlike some of his friends, he believed in the Revolution at first. He was not prepared to surrender his integrity and bow to a new regime in order to stay alive, but he thought: 'Now is the time when the gods I have worshipped will come to power and make a good life – a good life for all; a life with a purpose, a just life....'[27] Later he would blame himself severely for his unforgiveable naiveté. Sixteen years after the Bolshevik Revolution he was still grieving over it and said to Bunin in 1933: 'I thought that they really wanted the good of the people. I am after all a peasant, a moujik.'[28] And once again one cannot help noticing how objectively he judged himself. Anyone familiar with the facts of his life will not be surprised that he should want justice, that he should feel sorry for those who worked from morning to night to bring home a few kopecks and did not know how to feed their families. True, Chaliapin had not thought of ways of changing the established order of things. He only came into contact with ideas of reform in the capital, when he started his career as a young soloist at the Mariinsky Theatre. In Petersburg, and then in Moscow, he had met 'educated people', as he calls them, 'people of progressive ideas'. 'I began to sympathise with them more and more – especially when I saw that they were genuinely ready to sacrifice themselves for the people. I was sincerely angry when the authorities arrested such people and threw them into jail. In this respect, a man who exerted a particularly strong, I would say decisive, influence on me was my friend Alexei Maximovich

Peshkov – Maxim Gorky. It was his ardent conviction and his example which tightened my links with the socialists; I had more faith in him and in his enthusiasm than in anyone else in the world.'[29]

It was at Gorky's that Chaliapin met Lenin, and through him that he made the acquaintance of other future rulers of Russia. The sketches he draws of Stalin, Trotsky, Zinoviev and Kamenev in *Mask and Soul* are as remarkable for their laconic style as for their accuracy. He spent about five years under the new system, treading the path to a 'new life', but he understood its character from the very outset. If he had joined the Bolsheviks, he would have received everything the Soviet state had to offer in exchange for freedom – if he had learnt not to speak his mind in front of the authorities.

In his memoirs, Chaliapin says that he paid no attention to Lenin when he first met him and did not recognise him later when he saw him again. Bunin, however, noted in his diary that Chaliapin's acquaintance with Lenin and Trotsky had not remained superficial; he used the familiar 'thou' with both of them.[30] Around his dining-room table, where previously Stasov, Rimsky-Korsakov, Korovin, Stanislavsky and Rachmaninov had been sitting, there lounged new guests whom he would later 'hate to remember':[31] commissars of all ranks and sizes in leather jackets; members of the secret police, now the Cheka, headed by Dzerzhinsky; newly fledged officers of the new Red Army; and some others whose names Chaliapin forgot. One had to welcome them with a smile and some vodka at all hours of the day or night; they came without warning, announcing their arrival by a loud knock on the door – the same knock as their men used when they burst in to make searches and confiscate the last remnants of silver or paintings which they fancied.

Chaliapin tried to cover himself by undertaking various official duties and became a member of numerous committees on artistic matters, genuinely attempting to introduce theatrical reforms. But it was the same story: 'Russian theatre was swarming like flies with all sorts of revolutionary figures. Day by day the work became more difficult and more unpleasant.' He did not like hearing that 'the art to which opera singers devote themselves is a bourgeois art and the proletariat does not need it.'[32]

Hopes of any improvement quickly vanished, and a clear picture started to emerge from the welter of events and facts: this regime was not for him. The much-vaunted democracy was in fact turning into a party bureaucracy. Although neither *Animal Farm* nor *1984* had yet been written, Chaliapin was intimately familiar with the conditions Orwell would describe. Everything was tainted with elementary fear as one after another of his friends and acquaintances perished in the torture chambers of the prisons. 'My very sleep became restless and troubled. Every minute I held my breath to hear whether the Cheka van had gone past or stopped at my door.'[33] Pleas or personal protection were of little avail. Many things he already knew; many were told to him by Gorky, who was 'positively ill with horror'. Sometimes the two of them simply gave money to people and helped them to escape abroad. Gorky no longer hid his feelings and openly decried Bolshevik demagogy. 'I very quickly realised', recalled Chaliapin, 'how disillusioned Gorky was by the trend of events and by the rising leaders of the Revolution.'[34]

How could he possibly forget all this? That is why he was so surprised and upset when Gorky called him back. At first gently, but with increasing firmness, Chaliapin rejected his advice.

'I simply cannot imagine that this man could do anything dictated by base motives. Everything which has happened lately to my dear friend, I think has some explanation which neither I nor anyone else knows and which is in keeping with his personality and his character.'[35] He treats all this quite mildly in his book, continuing to regard Gorky as an honourable man and his closest friend, but his youngest daughter, Dasya, remembers her father being quite furious: "Gorky persuaded us to leave, and now this time Gorky calls us back!" Even Mother could do nothing. Not about going back, of course. But she did not want Father to judge Gorky so severely. After all, he was my godfather. Perhaps he had been forced to do this? Perhaps it had been written for him and he had only been made to sign?'[36]

Anyone familiar with the history of the Soviet system will not think Dasya's suppositions far-fetched. But Chaliapin probably preferred not to believe this. There are certain things which one cannot bear to part with. Gorky meant too much to him – above all the time, now gone forever, when they had met and become friends so quickly and lastingly. That was in 1900. On that occasion they had spent only a few hours together. And then, the following year, Chaliapin was singing *A Life for the Tsar* in Nizhni-Novgorod in August, and Gorky had appeared backstage at the end of the performance. 'From the very first handshake,' recalls Chaliapin, 'we, or at any rate I, felt a mutual sympathy.' 'We met comparatively late, we had already made our reputations by then; but Gorky always seemed to me like a childhood friend.'[37]

To the end of his life Chaliapin retained his fervent gratitude to him. In spite of Gorky's conduct and his abusive letters, he kept happy memories of him which never altered. When Gorky died, Chaliapin was deeply affected. 'Now that he is no more, every breath of his and about him is dearer to me than it ever was,'[38] he wrote to his daughter Irina in Moscow, asking her to send him the book collection Gorky had left him.

Past memories kept flooding in. It was particularly sad that their estrangement should have been caused by the accursed Soviet authorities, that he had been abrupt with Gorky at their last meetings. One of them took place in Berlin in May 1928, when Chaliapin was appearing with the Latvian National Opera company conducted by Emil Cooper.* That the meeting took place at the Adlon Hotel is confirmed by Sol Hurok.[39] 'At this dinner,' writes Gaisberg, 'Gorky again tried to get Chaliapin to return to Russia to take up a position as leader of Russian art.

---

* There are two handwritten notes in Fred Gaisberg's archive which look like drafts for a letter or perhaps fragments of memoirs. They were probably made many years after the events they describe; neither the time of year nor the year itself corresponds to the facts of Chaliapin's biography. 'Winter 1925. Adlon Hotel. Mr. and Mrs. Chaliapin gave a dinner party for Mr. and Mrs. Gorky. I was present. The Chaliapins were in Berlin for a Russian opera season.' However, in the winter of 1925, Chaliapin was touring in America. He had, it is true, spent about three weeks in Germany prior to this, but only to give concerts; and in any case, Gorky was then in Italy. The meeting to which Gaisberg refers actually took place in May 1928.

Chaliapin refused the invitation. This caused the split between them. Gorky was very serious over his responsibility to the Soviets.'[40] A few lines from Gaisberg's book *Music on Record* complete the picture: 'Gorky pleaded with him for two hours, setting forth the honours, position and rights the Soviets were prepared to guarantee him if he would return. Chaliapin replied that he was not young or adaptable enough to risk the change.'[41]

The years passed, but the Soviet Union had not forgotten Chaliapin. The scandal over the publication of his memoirs and the lawsuit in Paris already mentioned did not seem to shake the resolve of the authorities to get him back at any price. Sol Hurok recounts a curious episode in this connection. 'The year before Chaliapin died I was in Moscow and I carried away with me a message for Chaliapin from Premier Stalin. Nemirovich-Danchenko, the brilliant stage director and administrative head of the Moscow Art Theatre, and also organiser of the Musical Studio, presented me to the great man of the Soviets one night at the theatre, in an intermission of Bulgakov's *The White Guard*. In those days, before the treason trials, Stalin was not inaccessible, especially not to artists of the music and theatre world and their managers. He went constantly to the theatre, the ballet, the opera, and it was in the lounge next to Stanislavsky's office, reserved for high Government officials and their guests, that I stood, among a dozen Soviet celebrities, in Stalin's presence. Nemirovich-Danchenko presented me as Chaliapin's American manager. "What is Chaliapin doing?" Stalin asked. "Why doesn't he come to Moscow?" "I suppose," Nemirovich-Danchenko offered, "he needs quite a lot of money to live these days. He makes money abroad." "We'll give him money, if it is money he needs," said Stalin. "Well, then, there's the matter of housing. He has a large family, you know." The housing shortage in Moscow was one of the favourite subjects for feature stories in the European and American press in those days. "We'll give him a house in Moscow. We'll give him a house in the country, too. Just tell him to come home." I gave the message to Maria Valentinovna, Madame Chaliapin, whom I met in Paris. Chaliapin was in Baden-Baden, and since this was 1936, I would not set foot in Hitler's Reich. Chaliapin did not live to accept the invitation.'[42] From what we already know, Hurok is mistaken in thinking that, even had he lived longer, Chaliapin would have gone back. When he heard Stalin's words, he gloomily muttered: 'You'll give me a house? You'll give me a country cottage? And what about my soul? Can you give me back my soul?' 'And at this,' continues someone who witnessed the scene, 'I was moved by tears of pity for him. Such an eagle! And they had clipped his wings. What an original mind and heart they had stopped beating!'[43]

Many of those in regular contact with him knew that in spite of success, money and freedom of movement, he had some very difficult moments. 'Chaliapin was Russian to the core and it was a cruel fate that sent him to live and die in exile,' shrewdly observed Fred Gaisberg.[44] 'His forced break with Russia, with his native soil, with Russian theatre, was painful for him to endure. He would sometimes ask: "Tell me, why do I have to sing in Bordeaux, or in Munich, and not at home, in Saratov?",* recounted Andrei Sedykh.[45] Such 'occasional bouts of nostalgia', as his daughter Marfa called them, increased towards the end of his life. His wife saw in them a sign of approaching death. 'He was a robust man and on the whole enjoyed good health,' said Marfa in a BBC broadcast. 'So I was surprised when in the spring of 1937 I received a letter from my mother saying that she was convinced Father would not live long, for he had an unreasonable desire to return to Russia. No doctors could find anything the matter with him. But Mother's premonition proved to be right: next spring a pernicious anaemia had drained him of vitality in six months, and in April we were summoned to his bedside. It was strange to see how the disease had altered his appearance: he lay there looking most aristocratic; his straight and rather rounded nose had become eagle-shaped, his ruddy complexion a waxy pallor. We were all in the room, some of the doctors with us. Father asked for a drink and insisted on holding the cup himself. Then, turning to my mother, he said: "Why is it so dark in this theatre, Masha? Tell them to turn up the lights." '[46]

---

* Saratov – town on the Volga.

Chaliapin was suffering from terminal leukaemia. His life expectancy could no longer be reckoned in years but in days or even hours. Time flew faster than ever. He knew he was dying, often talked of death but without fear, quietly, lightly. 'He didn't particularly want to die, but he didn't want particularly to live, being weaker and disabled and drowsy.... He used to make a lot of jokes about his death which seemed to be quite natural for him.'[47]

The artistic world stubbornly refused to believe the rumours; in Paris an 'International Committee for Chaliapin's Jubilee Celebrations' was working with the utmost energy. Fifty years on the stage was not an everyday occasion, and the organisers considered that 'the celebration of this jubilee will be not only an act of homage to one of the greatest artists of our age, but also an event of international importance in the world of music and drama. Sir Thomas Beecham, Bart. has kindly accepted the chairmanship of a similar committee which is being formed in London. It is intended that a concert and a banquet will be organised in London.'[48] But Chaliapin's condition was steadily deteriorating, and the thoughts which he confided to his eldest daughter were anything but festive in mood. It seems that he had started to make a final inventory, as if he had already done all he was capable of on this earth. In the same letter, he tells her of his intention to start writing a book on the art of the theatre; but his hopes for the future do not sound very positive and he is lost in melancholy reflections on the past. 'The crackpots! Somewhere they have already decided that my anniversary must take place any minute now. And I, meanwhile, am gasping like a fish. I have been telling my fortune – silly, but the cards say that I will get well by May. But actually, all my teeth have started to come loose and my gums bleed. Generally speaking, it looks like I am dying slowly but surely. Bear in mind that I say this without complaint or sadness.... *Tout casse, tout passe, tout lasse.* Enough, I am already sixty-five. I have lived – I have seen a great deal, much of it bad, but even more of it good.'[49]

His last letter to Irina, dated March 28th, 1938, had to be dictated, for his strength was fast ebbing. Within a week,

Chaliapin and his daughter, Dasya, Paris, 1936.

telephoning Moscow, he begged her to come to him: 'I am in great pain. Whom do I have to ask so that you can be allowed to do this?'[50] She managed to obtain a visa and left immediately but was stopped at the border: she was told that her documents were not in order and that she could not leave. However much she implored, repeating over and over again that she was going to her dying father, it was of no avail.

Chaliapin certainly had no cause to complain of solitude. If the doctors had authorised it, there would have been an endless succession of visitors in his large flat on the avenue d'Eylau. Someone always wanted to see him to express sympathy. On April 10th, two days before his death, Rachmaninov called again. 'As often in the past, I managed to distract him a little, and just before my departure, he started to say that he wanted to write another book for artists on the subject of the art of the stage. He spoke of course very, very slowly. He was panting! His heart was barely working! I let him finish and said, standing up, that I also had plans; that as soon as my performances were over I was going to write a book too, the subject of which would be Chaliapin. He gave me a smile and patted my hand. On this we parted. Forever! The next day, April 11th, I came only in the evening. They had given him injections of morphine. He was in a semi-conscious state and I did not see him. I decided to tell his wife that I had to go away tomorrow but would return in ten days. I felt that he did not have many more days to live! She thought the same. And then for the first time she, who had behaved magnificently all these days, broke down and as we said good-bye, she started to cry. I left hurriedly.'[51]

Rachmaninov did not attend the funeral; to see Chaliapin in his coffin was more than he could bear. An enormous cross of white flowers with the simple inscription 'To my friend' was his farewell.

The whole world mourned Chaliapin's death. Not only Russians grieved; anyone who had anything to do with the arts knew that the loss was irreplaceable. 'The history of the theatre', wrote Serge Lifar in *Le Figaro*, 'must record his disappearance as a fact equal in significance to the fall of the Empire in the history of mankind.'[52] *The Times* of London was one of many

Chaliapin's funeral cortège outside the Paris Opera, April 18th, 1938.

expressing similar feelings: 'This statement', said the obituary, 'is not likely to arouse jealousies. The popular favourites of the opera house who have reached their several pinnacles of fame by unique qualities of voice, mastery of vocal technique, or the charm of a winning personality, will probably be the first to recognise that his art differed from theirs not in degree but in kind. It was for no one of these or kindred qualities that one went to Chaliapin.'[53]

And now he was no more. Night and day, people were streaming to the house where he had died, filling the street outside. For twenty-four hours his colleagues and friends formed a silent guard of honour around his coffin. 'At the entrance of the apartment stood a little table with a massive inkstand and a visitors' book on it. Before the funeral, it looked as though all the great men of France and of music had called to pay homage; the lying in state might have been that of a king.'[54]

The funeral took place on a sunny but crisp Monday morning.

Regardless of the early hour, several hundreds of people were silently waiting at the house. At 9.15 singing could be heard; 'The famous Afonsky Choir and the Russian Opera Chorus' were intoning a final send-off to Chaliapin. The coffin, draped in crimson brocade embroidered with gold, was placed in the black limousine. The procession, swelling as it went along, slowly made its way to the small Russian church in the rue Daru. It was not large enough to accommodate all those who had come to say good-bye to Chaliapin, but people stood in the courtyard, in the street, overspilling into neighbouring side streets; their number seemed incalculable. The crowd stretched as far as the eye could see. The burial service ended at 11.30. The last notes of the Russian hymn 'Eternal Remembrance' died away. The procession resumed its march, stopping by the Opéra, where the choir sang the prayer again three times; the line of cars moved off once more, this time for the Batignolles cemetery. Chaliapin is said to have chosen his ultimate resting place himself. It was some distance from the entrance and shaded by chestnut trees rustling in the wind.

In the last months of his existence, when already almost entirely bedridden, Chaliapin had had many strange dreams. He sometimes described them to his family. The vivid and dramatic pictures he painted were very meaningful. In one, he was standing on the stage of the Bolshoi Theatre in the crown and mantle of Boris, in his golden imperial robes. The chorus was singing his praises and bells were ringing. Then he glanced back; no one was there ... not a soul either in the auditorium, or in the orchestra, or on stage, and he was standing alone at the very edge of the footlights, as if on a precipice, abandoned by all. And all around, the empty theatre, huge and silent, glittering with dark gold.... The past was gradually taking the place of the present. What until so recently had been the life he loved so much was now just a collection of memories. Their number grew day by day. One thought which had preoccupied him for years became an obsession: would anything remain after him? It seemed that while he did not fear death, he feared oblivion. Of course, time is time, and no sooner is it with us than it is gone, sweeping along in its train the greatest events

Chaliapin's grave from 1938 to 1984 at the Batignolles Cemetery, Paris.

Chaliapin's tomb in Moscow.

and the greatest people. In the past half-century since the singer's death, more than one generation has grown up to whom he is known only through records, photographs and published material. And yet for once, Chaliapin's intuition let him down: his fear of being completely forgotten was unfounded. The innovations he had made in the theatre remained an inexhaustible source of new experiments and new discoveries for others. 'Art may pass through periods of decline,' said Chaliapin, 'but it is as eternal as life itself.'[55] These words are his title to lasting glory.

Discography

by Alan Kelly and Vladimir Gurvich

Introduction

This Discography lists all the records made by Chaliapin, in so far as these can be traced. Extensive use has been made of the files of the two recording companies – The Gramophone Company Ltd of London and The Victor Talking Machine Company of Camden, New Jersey – without whose help the discography could not have been written. Other information has come from label copy, and much has been supplied by many individual collectors.

The format of each discography entry is as follows. Every recording was given a matrix or master number at the time the wax was cut and this number is unique to that recording, no two recordings having the same matrix number. The number is visible on all European and some American pressings. Before 1924, celebrity records were issued single-sided but after 1924 they were coupled in pairs, back to back. Thus early records may have up to four catalogue numbers, a single-sided and a double-sided in Europe and another single-sided and double-sided in America. For example, the first recording in Session 21 has the following details:

a Cc549–1   2–022005 DB103   88644   6416   The song of the flea
                                                     (Mussorgsky)

Cc549–1	is the matrix number;
2–022005	is the single-sided European HMV catalogue number;
DB103	is the double-sided European HMV catalogue number;
88644	is the single-sided American Victor catalogue number;
6416	is the double-sided American Victor catalogue number.

This pattern is followed throughout, except that when single-sided numbers ceased to be used, those columns were omitted. Catalogue numbers placed in brackets were allocated but not actually used.

Domestic issues by the Victor Company of Japan are listed in Appendix I, German domestic and export issues in Appendix II. Records with numbers beginning 15–1000, VA, VB, AGSB, HMA and HMB were issued as parts of special 'historical' series for collectors and others.

Records made before 1925 were recorded by the 'old' acoustic process using a horn and mechanical linkage to the recording stylus. Those made in and after 1925 (Session 41 onwards) were made by the 'new' electric process using a microphone and amplifiers.

Acknowledgements:

A fuller and annotated version of this Discography will appear at a future date in *The Record Collector*.

The compilers and the publishers would like to record their debt of gratitude to: EMI Ltd and the late J. M. Hughes; RCA Victor Ltd and W. R. Moran; Dr Boris Semeonoff; the Victor Company of Japan and M. Kumatori; Victor Garmash.

FEDOR IVANOVICH CHALIAPIN – A Discography

1. *Circa 1897–1901. Unnumbered private wax cylinders. With piano.* [Moscow?]

a   NERO Act 1 (Rubinstein)
      Vindex's epithalamium – Glory to Thee, God Hymen

b   SADKO Scene 4 (Rimsky-Korsakov)
      The Varangian Merchant's song – On fearful crags

c   PRINCE IGOR Act 1 (Borodin)
      Galitsky's song – I can't conceal that I dislike boredom

d   FAUST Act 3 (Gounod)
      Mephistopheles' invocation – Il était temps

e   Nochen'ka (folksong)
      (Night)

f   The prisoner, Op 78 No 6 (Rubinstein)
      (I sit behind cold prison bars)

g   Ich hab' im Traum' geweinet Op 48 (Schumann)
      (Dichterliebe No 13)

h   White, fluffy snowballs (folksong), unaccompanied

i   I have worn my eyes out (folksong), unaccompanied

j   Unidentified folksong, unaccompanied

2. *January, 1902. Hotel Continental, Moscow. 10" red label Gramophone. With piano*

a	572x	When the King went to war Op 7 No 6 (Koenemann)
b	573x	Ah, thou red sun Op 10 No 1 (Slonov)
c	574x	Elegy (Korganov)
		(Serene moonlit night)
d	575x	FAUST Act 2 (Gounod)
		Mephistopheles' couplets – Le veau d'or (Gounod)
e	576x	Disenchantment Op 65 No 2 (Tchaikovsky)
	(22824)	(The sun was still shining brightly)
f	577x	The nightingale Op 60 No 4 (Tchaikovsky)

3. *January, 1902. Hotel Continental, Moscow. 10" red label Gramophone. With piano*

a	621x	Nochen'ka (folksong), unaccompanied
		(Night)
b	622x	A LIFE FOR THE TZAR Act 4
		Susanin's aria – My dawn will come (omitting recitative)
c	622½x	As above
d	623x	Disenchantment Op 65 No 2 (Tchaikovsky)
		(The sun still shone brightly)

4. *24th September, 1907. St Petersburg. 12" orange and pink label Gramophone. With orchestra (Bruno Seidler-Winkler)*

a   270m   A LIFE FOR THE TZAR (Glinka)
                  Aria (unspecified)

b   281m   The song of the needy pilgrim (Manykin-Nevstruev)
                  (I walk through meadows), with chorus only

c   283m   When the King went to war Op 7 No 6 (Koenemann), with piano
                  accompaniment by P P GROSS

d   288m   MEFISTOFELE Prologue (Boito)
                  Ave Signor (in Italian)

e   289m   FAUST Act 4 (Gounod)
                  Mephistopheles' serenade – Vous qui faites l'endormie

f   290m   The song of the flea (Mussorgsky)
                  (Once upon a time there was a King)

g   291m   FAUST Act 2 (Gounod)
                  Mephistopheles' couplets – Le veau d'or

5. *October, 1907. Milan. 12" Gramophone (all unissued). Unaccompanied*

a   1290c   Eh, Vanka (folksong)
b   1291c   Dubinushka (folksong)
                        (The oak cudgel)
c   1291½c   As above
d   1297c   Eh, Vanka (folksong)
e   1298c   Luchinushka (folksong)
                        (The little birch torch)

545

6. *7th April, 1908. 15 rue Bleu, Paris. 12" pink label Gramophone. With orchestra (I P ARKADIEV)*

a	RUSLAN & LUDMILLA Act 2 (Glinka) Farlaf's rondo – Oh joy! . . . The hour of my triumph is near			022109	607i
b	IL BARBIERE DI SIVIGLIA Act 1 (Rossini) Don Basilio's aria – La calunnia è un venticello, in Italian			052222	614i
c	A LIFE FOR THE TZAR Act 4 (Glinka) Susanin's recitative & aria – They guess the truth . . . My dawn will come	DB629		022111	615i
d	LAKME Act 2 (Delibes) Stances de Nilakantha – Lakmé, ton doux regard	DB617	15–1041	022112	616i
e	RUSLAN & LUDMILLA Act 2 (Glinka) Ruslan's aria – From the dark shroud of eternity (Omitting recitative 'Field, o field')			022113	617i
f	Dubinushka (The oak cudgel) (folksong), with chorus only			022114	618i
g	Arise, red sun (folksong), with chorus only			022115	619i
h	Luchinushka (The little birch torch) (folksong), unaccompanied			022129	621i

7. *26th August, 1910. Moscow. 12" pink label Gramophone. With the Chorus of the Imperial Moscow Opera (M I SEMENOV)*

a	In the meadows, by the birches (Ukranian folksong), with male chorus only	DB617	022180	2003c
b	THE POWER OF EVIL Act 2 (Serov) Eremka's song – I'll amuse my hostess . . . Merry Shrovetide			2004c
c	As above, with chorus and piano	DB610	022181	2004½c
d	1) Down Mother Volga (folksong); 2) From under the oak, from under the elm (folksong), with male chorus only	DB610	022182	2005c
e	Nochen'ka (folksong) (Night)			2006c

f	2006½c	022159		DB620	As above, unaccompanied
g	2007c				ASKOLD'S TOMB Act 1 (Verstovsky) The Unknown's aria – In olden days our forefathers, with male chorus & piano

8. *29th August, 1910. Moscow. 12" pink label Gramophone. With orchestra*

a	2008c				FAUST Act 4 (Gounod) Church scene: Seigneur, daignez permettre, with sopr. MARIA MIKHAILOVA, organ & orch.
b	2008½c	024039		DB618 VB1	As above
c	2009c	022183	15–1041	DB618	FAUST Act 3 (Gounod) Mephistopheles' invocation – Il était temps
d	2010c				Die beiden Grenadiere Op 49 No 1 (Schumann)
e	2011c	022184			Eh, Vanka (folksong), unaccompanied
f	2012c	052292	15–1045		DON CARLOS Act 4 (Verdi) King Philip's aria – Dormiro sol, in Italian
g	2013c				BORIS GODUNOV Act 1 (Mussorgsky) Varlaam's song – In the town of Kazan
h	2013½c				As above
i	2014c	022185		DB622	The tempest rages (Sokolov), with piano

9. *31st August, 1910. Moscow. 12" pink label Gramophone. With the Orchestra of the Imperial Moscow Opera (M I SEMENOV)*

a 2016c   BORIS GODUNOV Act 1 (Mussorgsky)
                  Pimen's monologue – Yet one more tale

b 2016½c 022157 As above

10. *1st September, 1910. Moscow. 12" pink label Gramophone. With Chorus & Orch. of the Imperial Moscow Opera (M I SEMENOV)*

a 2017c   THE DEMON Act 2 (Rubinstein)
                  Demon's first romance – Do not weep, child

b 2018c   Now let Thy servant depart in peace, Prayer (Strokin)

c 2018½c   As above

d 2019c 022186 DB620 Dubinushka (The oak cudgel) (folksong), with chorus only

e 2020c 022187 DB108 Arise, red sun (folksong), with chorus only

f 2021c 022188 Russian prisoner's song (folksong)
                  (The sun rises and sets), with chorus only

g 2022c 022189 Luchinushka (The little birch torch) (folksong), unaccompanied

h 2022½c   As above

11. *30th September, 1911. St Petersburg. 12" pink label Gramophone*

a 2451c (022209) BORIS GODUNOV (Mussorgsky)
                  Aria (unspecified on recording sheet)

b 2452c (022210) Die beiden Grenadiere Op 49 No 1 (Schumann)

c 2453c (022211) BORIS GODUNOV Act 1 (Mussorgsky)
                  Varlaam's song – In the town of Kazan

d 2453½c 022208 As above, with orchestra

e	2454c	(022212)	Mashenka (folksong) (They won't let Masha walk by the brook)
f	2454½c	022213	DB104 — As above, unaccompanied

12. *15th October, 1911. St Petersburg. 12" pink label Gramophone*

a	2492c	(022221)	BORIS GODUNOV Act 4 (Mussorgsky) Boris' farewell – Farewell, my son, with orchestra
b	2492½c	022222	As above
c	2493c	022223	BORIS GODUNOV Act 4 (Mussorgsky) Death of Boris – The bell! The passing bell, with chorus & orchestra
d	2494c	022224	PRINCE IGOR Act 1 (Borodin) Galitsky's song – Have you enjoyed yourself, Prince . . . I can't conceal that I dislike boredom, with chorus & orchestra
e	2495c	022225	DB611 / AGSB8 — THE DEMON Act 2 (Rubinstein) Demon's first romance – Do not weep, child, with orchestra
f	2496c	022226	DB108 — Now let Thy servant depart in peace, Prayer (Strokin), with chorus only
g	2496½c	(022227)	As above

13. *13th November, 1911. St Petersburg. 12" pink label Gramophone. With orchestra*

a	2534c		Die beiden Grenadiere Op 49 No 1 (Schumann)
b	2535c	022261	As above
c	2536c	022262	AGSB8 — THE DEMON Act 2 (Rubinstein) Demon's second romance – On the ocean of the air, with sopr. MARIA KOVALENKO & orchestra
d	2537c		As above
e	2538c		It is not autumnal drizzle (folksong)
f	2539c	022263	DB622 — As above, with male chorus only

14. *26th November, 1911. St Petersburg. 12" pink label Gramophone. With orchestra*

a	2548c	022252	BORIS GODUNOV Act 4 (Mussorgsky) Pimen's narration – Once at eve
b	2548½c		As above
c	2549c		IL BARBIERE DI SIVIGLIA Act 1 (Rossini) Don Basilio's aria – La calunnia è un venticello [in Italian]
d	2549½c		As above
e	2550c		MEFISTOFELE Prologue (Boito) Ave Signor [in Italian]

15. *26th April, 1912. Milan. 12" pink label Gramophone. With LA SCALA CHORUS & ORCHESTRA (CARLO SABAJNO)*

a	613m	052353	DB106	88462	15-1042	NORMA Act 1 (Bellini) Oroveso's aria – Ite sul colle, o Druidi (in Italian)
b	614m	052354				IL BARBIERE DI SIVIGLIA Act 1 (Rossini) Don Basilio's aria – La calunnia è un venticello (in Italian), without chorus
c	615m	052355				MEFISTOFELE Prologue (Boito) Ave Signor (in Italian), without chorus
d	615½m					As above
e	615"m			88461		As above, transfer from 615m
f	616m	052356				LA SONNAMBULA Act 1 (Bellini) Count Rodolfo's recitative & aria – Il mulino, il fonte . . . Vi ravviso (in Italian)

16. 26th October, 1912. St Petersburg. 12" pink label Gramophone. With orchestra

a	2692c	052387	DB106	ROBERTO IL DIAVOLO Act 3 (Meyerbeer) Bertram's recitative & aria – Le rovine . . . Suore che riposate (in Italian)
b	2693c	052388	DB403	LUCREZIA BORGIA Act 2 (Donizetti) Don Alfonso's cavatina – Vieni, la mia vendetta (in Italian)
			VB72	
c	2694c	052389	DB403	ERNANI Act 1 (Verdi) Don Silva's recitative & cavatina – Che mai vegg'io . . . Infelice (in Italian)
			VB72	
d	2695c	032260	DB629	Chanson bachique Op 27 No 1 (Glazunov) (Pourquoi donc se taisent les voix) (in French)
e	2696c	032261		La Marseillaise (Rouget de l'Isle) (Allons enfants de la patrie) (in French)

17. 5th July, 1913. 21 City Road, London. 10" pink label Gramophone. With the PETERSBURG [vocal] QUARTET (M M CHUPRINNIKOV, N I SAFONOV, N N KEDROV, K KEDROV), or piano by D I POKHITONOV

a	y16736e	4-22579	The tale of Il'ya Muromets (folksong arr N N Kedrov), with quartet
b	y16737e		SADKO Scene 4 (Rimsky-Korsakov) The Varangian Merchant's song – On fearful crags, with piano
c	y16738e	HMA46	Sapphische Ode Op 90 No 4 (Brahms) (I plucked dark roses), with piano
d	y16739e	4-22581	She laughed (Lishin), with piano
e	y16740e	(4-22582)	Ballade (Rubinstein) (Before the voivode), with piano
f	y16741e	4-22583	The nightingale Op 60 No 4 (Tchaikovsky), with piano
g	y16742e		When yesterday we met Op 26 No 13 (Rachmaninov), with piano

17. *5th July, 1913, 21 City Road, London. 10" pink label Gramophone. With the PETERSBURG [vocal] QUARTET (M M CHUPRINNIKOV, N I SAFONOV, N N KEDROV, K KEDROV, or piano by D I POKHITONOV)*

h	y16743e	sADKO Scene 4 (Rimsky-Korsakov)
		The Varangian Merchant's song – On fearful crags, with piano
i	y16747e	The tale of Ivan the Terrible (Lyapunov), with quartet
j	y16748e	The mother-in-law had seven sons-in-law (folksong), with quartet
k	y16749e	1) The green oak has perished (folksong), with quartet
		2) A great big gnat (folksong), with quartet
l	y16750e	As above

18. *12th January, 1914. St Petersburg. 10" pink label Gramophone. With piano*

a	53ooae	A word of farewell (Slonov)
b	53o1ae	The prisoner Op 78 No 6 (Rubinstein)
		(I sit behind cold prison bars)
c	53o2ae	A swan Op 25 No 2 (Grieg)
		(Oh, gentle swan)
d	53o3ae	On the hills of Georgia Op 3 No 4 (Rimsky-Korsakov)
e	53o4ae	When yesterday we met Op 26 No 13 (Rachmaninov)
f	53o5ae	4–22669
		Sapphische Ode Op 90 No 4 (Brahms)
		(I plucked dark roses)

19. *4th April, 1914. St Petersburg. 10" (ae) & 12" (af) pink label Gramophone. With piano*

a	5928ae	The prisoner Op 78 No 6 (Rubinstein)
		(I sit behind cold prison bars)
b	5929ae	A swan Op 25 No 2 (Grieg)
		(Oh gentle swan)

552

c	5929½ae	(4–22723)				As above
d	5930oae					On the hills of Georgia Op 3 No 4 (Rimsky-Korsakov)
e	5931ae					A word of farewell (Slonov)
f	5931½ae	4–22722				As above
g	5932ae					A swan Op 25 No 2 (Grieg) (Oh, gentle swan)
h	5932½ae					As above
i	5933ae					The tempest rages (Sokolov)
j	5934ae					1) Parting Op 4 No 3 (Grieg) 2) Verses in an album Op 25 No 3 (Grieg)
k	5934½ae					As above
l	309af		HMB37			When the King went to war Op 7 No 6 (Koenemann)
m	310af		HMB32			Aufenthalt (Schwanengesang No 5) (Schubert)
n	311af					The tempest rages (Sokolov)
o	312af		HMB32			A LIFE FOR THE TZAR Act 4 (Glinka) Susanin's recitative & aria – They guess the truth . . . My dawn will come

20. *9th October, 1921. Hayes. 12" red label Gramophone. With piano by MAX RABINOWITSCH*

a	Cc540–1					The last voyage Op 17 No 2 (Alnaes)
b	Cc540–2					As above
c	Cc541–1					Oh, could I in song tell my sorrow (Malashkin)
d	Cc542–1	(2–022014)				1) An old song Op 4 No 5 (Grieg); 2) Verses in an album Op 25 No 3 (Grieg)
e	Cc543–1					Russian prisoner's song (folksong) (The sun rises and sets)
f	Cc544–1	2–022015		DB757	6532	The Nightingale Op 60 No 4 (Tchaikovsky)

21. *10th October, 1921. Hayes. 12" red label Gramophone. With orchestra (PERCY PITT)*

a	Cc549–1	2–022005	DB103	88644	6416	The song of the flea (Mussorgsky) (Once upon a time there was a King)
b	Cc550–1	2–022006	DB105	88655	6058	The prophet Op 49 No 2 (Rimsky-Korsakov) (Parched with spiritual thirst)
c	Cc555–1					In questa tomba oscura (Beethoven) (in Italian)
d	Cc551–2					As above
e	Cc551–3					As above

22. *11th October, 1921. Hayes. 12" red label Gramophone. With piano (MAX RABINOWITSCH) or orchestra (PERCY PITT)*

a	Cc540–3	2–022013	DB757		6532	The last voyage Op 17 No 2 (Alnaes), with piano
b	Cc541–2	2–022012	DB104		6533	Oh, could I in song tell my sorrow (Malashkin), with piano
c	Cc556–1	2–022007	DB102	88645	6057	Die beiden Grenadiere Op 49 No 1 (Schumann), with orchestra
d	Cc557–1	2–022008		88646	6061	When the King went to war Op 7 No 6 (Koenemann), with orchestra
e	Cc558–1	2–022009	DB102	88656	6057	The midnight review (Glinka), with orchestra

23. *12th October, 1921. Hayes. 12" red label Gramophone. With piano (MAX RABINOWITSCH) or orchestra (PERCY PITT)*

a	Cc543–2					Russian prisoner's song (folksong) (The sun rises and sets), with piano
b	Cc543–3					As above
c	Cc541–4	2–052212	DB107	88657	6059	In questa tomba oscura (Beethoven) (in Italian), with orchestra
d	Cc560–1	2–022010	DB101	88659	6061	Songs and Dances of Death (Mussorgsky) No 1 – Trepak (Still in the forest), with orchestra

27. *9th October, 1922. Hayes. 12" red label Gramophone. With orchestra (GEORGE W BYNG)*

a	Cc556–2					Die beiden Grenadiere Op 49 No 1 (Schumann)
b	Cc1890–2	2–022017	DB103	88666	6416	SADKO Scene 4 (Rimsky-Korsakov) The Varangian Merchant's song – On fearful crags
c	Cc1891–3					Ei ukhnem! (folksong arr Chaliapin & Koenemann) (The song of the Volga boatmen)
d	Cc1891–4	2–022016	DB105	88663	6058	As above
e	Cc1891–5					As above

28. *23rd October, 1922. Hayes. 12" red label Gramophone. With orchestra (GEORGE W BYNG)*

a	Cc541–2					Oh, could I in song tell my sorrow (Malashkin)
b	Cc543–4					Russian prisoner's song (folksong) (The sun rises and sets)
c	Cc551–6					In questa tomba oscura (Beethoven) (in Italian)
d	Cc551–7					As above
e	Cc543–4					Russian prisoner's song (folksong) (The sun rises and sets)
f	Cc556–3					Die beiden Grenadiere Op 49 No 1 (Schumann)
g	Cc556–4					As above
h	Cc2015–1					BORIS GODUNOV Act 1 (Mussorgsky) Pimen's monologue – Yet one more tale
i	Cc2015–2					As above
j	Cc2015–3	2–022018	DB612		6489	As above
k	Cc2016–1					She laughed (Lishin)

29. *22nd November, 1922. Camden, New Jersey. 10" (B) & 12" (C) red label Victor. With orchestra (JOSEF PASTERNACK)*

a	C26104–3					DON CARLOS Act 4 (Verdi) King Philip's aria – Dormiro sol (in Italian)
b	C26104–4					As above
c	B27088–1					LA SONNAMBULA Act 1 (Bellini) Count Rodolfo's recit. & cavatina – Il mulino, il fonte . . . Vi ravviso (in Italian)
d	B27088–2	7–52229	DA101	(87378)	981	As above
e	B27089–1					MEFISTOFELE Prologue (Boito) Ave Signor (in Italian)
f	B27089–2	7–52227	DA101	87355	981	As above
g	B27090–1					Eh, Vanka (folksong), unaccompanied
h	C27090–1	2–022019				As above
i	B27091–1	(7–22012)	DB691	87361	558	PRINCE IGOR Act 1 (Borodin) Galitsky's song – I can't conceal that I dislike boredom

30. *23rd November, 1922. Camden, New Jersey. 10" (B) & 12" (C) red label Victor. With orchestra (JOSEF PASTERNACK)*

a	C26104–5	DON CARLOS Act 4 (Verdi) King Philip's aria – Dormiro sol (in Italian), with cello by LENNARTZ
b	C26104–6	As above
c	C26104–7	As above
d	B27089–3	MEFISTOFELE Prologue (Boito) Ave Signor (in Italian)
e	B27089–4	As above

31. 26th June, 1923. Hayes. 10" (Bb) & 12" (Cc) red label Gramophone. With orchestra (EUGENE GOOSSENS)

	Matrix				Work
a	Cc3153-1				BORIS GODUNOV Act 2 (Mussorgsky) Boris' monologue – I have attained the highest power
b	Cc3153-2	2–022021	DB612		As above
c	Bb3154-1	7–22011	DA100	6489	PRINCE IGOR Act 1 (Borodin) Galitsky's song – I can't conceal that I dislike boredom
d	Cc3155-2				ALEKO Act 1 (Rachmaninov) Aleko's cavatina – All the gipsy camp is sleeping
e	Cc3155-2	2–022026	DB691		As above

32. 2nd July, 1923. Hayes. 10" (Bb) & 12" (Cc) red label Gramophone. With orchestra (EUGENE GOOSSENS)

	Matrix				Work
a	Cc3197-1	2–022020	DB100		BORIS GODUNOV Act 4 (Mussorgsky) Death of Boris – The bell! The passing bell, with chorus
b	Cc3197-2			6455	As above
c	Bb3198-1	7–32080	DA554	960	FAUST Act 2 (Gounod) Scene & Couplets – Pardon! . . . Le veau d'or (in French), with chorus
d	Bb3199-1	7–32081	DA554	960	FAUST Act 4 (Gounod) Mephistopheles' serenade – Vous qui faites l'endormie (in French)
e	Bb3199-2				As above
f	Bb3200-1				DON GIOVANNI Act 1 (Mozart) Leporello's catalogue aria (pt 1) – Madamina (in Italian)
g	Bb3201-1				DON GIOVANNI Act 1 (Mozart) Leporello's catalogue aria (pt 2) – Nella bionda

33. 7th July, 1923. Hayes. 10" red label Gramophone. With piano (FREDERICK W GAISBERG) or orchestra (GEORGE W BYNG)

	Matrix				Title
a	Bb3229-1			1050	Dubinushka (folksong) (The oak cudgel), with male chorus & orchestra
b	Bb3229-2	7-22013	DA621		As above
c	Bb3229-3				As above
d	Bb3230-1				Arise, red sun (folksong), with male chorus and piano
e	Bb3230-2				As above
f	Bb3230-3				As above

34. 25th September, 1923. Hayes. 10" (Bb) & 12" (Cc) red label Gramophone. With orchestra (JULIUS HARRISON)

	Matrix				Title
a	Bb3200-2				DON GIOVANNI Act 1 (Mozart) Leporello's catalogue aria (pt 1) – Madamina (in Italian)
b	Bb3200-3	7-52246	DA555	1105	As above
c	Bb3201-2	7-52247	DA555	1105	DON GIOVANNI Act 1 (Mozart) Leporello's catalogue aria (pt 2) – Nella bionda (in Italian)
d	Bb3201-3				As above
e	Cc3504-1				A LIFE FOR THE TZAR Act 4 (Glinka) Susanin's recitative & aria – They guess the truth . . . My dawn will come
f	Cc3504-2	2-022027	DB758	6534	As above

35. *3rd January, 1924. Camden, New Jersey. 10" (B) & 12" (C) red label Victor. With orchestra (ROSARIO BOURDON)*

a	C29246–1		15–1045	ROBERTO IL DIAVOLO Act 3 (Meyerbeer) Bertram's recitative & invocation – Le rovine . . . Suore che riposate (in Italian)
b	C29246–2			As above
c	C29246–3			As above
d	B29247–1			LA BOHEME Act 4 (Puccini) Colline's aria – Vecchia zimarra (in Italian)
e	B29247–2	AGSA11		As above
f	B29248–1		1004	Pilgrim's song Op 47 No 5 (Tchaikovsky) (Blest be these forests), with violin by SCHMIDT
g	C29249–1	DB881	6512	Le Cor (Flégier) (in French), with harp by LAPITINO
h	B29250–1			ERNANI Act 1 (Verdi) Don Silva's cavatina – Infelice, e tuo credevi

40. *9th October, 1924. Hayes. 12" red label Gramophone. With orchestra (ALBERT COATES)*

a	Cc5200–1		BORIS GODUNOV Prologue (Mussorgsky) Coronation scene (pt 2): I am oppressed
b	Cc5200–2		As above
c	Cc5200–3		As above

560

41. *26th October, 1925. Hayes. 12" red label Gramophone. With chorus and orchestra (ALBERT COATES)*

a	Cc7064–1		BORIS GODUNOV Prologue (Mussorgsky) Coronation scene (pt 1): Long live Tzar Boris! (music for Shuisky, chorus & orch only)
b	Cc7064–2		As above
c	Cc7064–3	DB900	As above
d	Cc7066–1	DB900	BORIS GODUNOV Prologue (Mussorgsky) Coronation scene (pt 2): I am oppressed
e	Cc7067–1		FAUST Act 4 (Gounod) Church scene (pt 1): Seigneur, daignez permettre (in French), with soprano FLORENCE AUSTRAL
f	Cc7067–2	DB899	As above
g	Cc7075–1	DB899	FAUST Act 4 (Gounod) Church scene (pt 2): Quand du Seigneur (in French), with soprano FLORENCE AUSTRAL
h	Cc7075–2	DB899	As above

42. *5th November, 1925. Hayes. 12" red label Gramophone. With orchestra (JULIUS HARRISON)*

a	Cc7193–1		THE DEMON Act 2 (Rubinstein) Demon's second romance – On the ocean of the air
b	Cc7194–1		THE DEMON Act 3 (Rubinstein) Demon's third romance – I am he to whom you listened in the night

43. *20th May, 1926. Hayes. 12" red label Gramophone. With orchestra (EUGENE GOOSSENS)*

a Cc8412–1A DB932 IL BARBIERE DI SIVIGLIA Act 1 (Rossini)
   Don Basilio's aria – La calunnia è un venticello (in Italian)

b Cc8413–1 Die beiden Grenadiere Op 49 No 1 (Schumann)
c Cc8413–2A DB933 6619 As above
d Cc8414–1 The song of the flea (Mussorgsky)
   (Once upon a time there was a King)

e Cc8414–2 DB932 As above
f Cc8415–1 Ei ukhnem! (folksong arr Chaliapin & Koenemann)
   (The song of the Volga boatmen)

g Cc8415–2 As above
h Cc8416–1A DB933 6619 The midnight review (Glinka)

44. *21st May, 1926. Small Queen's Hall, London. 12" red label Gramophone. With orchestra (EUGENE GOOSSENS)*

a CR374–1 BORIS GODUNOV Act 4 (Mussorgsky)
   Death of Boris – The bell! The passing bell, with chorus

b CR374–2 As above
c CR375–1 DB934 6724 BORIS GODUNOV Act 4 (Mussorgsky)
   Boris' farewell – Farewell, my son

d CR376–1 Now let Thy servant depart in peace, Prayer (Strokin), with chorus only

45. *27th May, 1926. Small Queen's Hall, London. 12" red label Gramophone. With chorus & orchestra (EUGENE GOOSSENS)*

a CR374–3 BORIS GODUNOV Act 4 (Mussorgsky)
   Death of Boris – The bell! The passing bell

b CR374–4 DB934 As above
   CR377–1 BORIS GODUNOV Prologue (Mussorgsky)
   Coronation scene (pt 1), chorus & orchestra only

c	CR377-2		As above
	CR378-1		BORIS GODUNOV Prologue (Mussorgsky)
			Coronation scene (pt 2): I am oppressed
d	CR378-2		As above
e	CR378-3		As above

46. *31st May, 1926. Royal Opera House, Covent Garden, London. 12" red label Gramophone*

Recordings made during the public performance of Mefistofele (Boito). Sung in Italian.

Mefistofele	F I CHALIAPIN	Wagner	LUIGI CILLA
Faust	FRANCESCO MERLI	Elena	BIANCA SCACCIATI
Margherita	BIANCA SCACCIATI	Pantalis	JANE BOURGUIGNON
Marta	JANE BOURGUIGNON	Nereo	LUIGI CILLA

ROYAL OPERA CHORUS & ORCHESTRA conducted by VINCENZO BELLEZZA

	CR382-1			Prologue (pt 1), chorus & orchestra only
	CR383-1	(DB940)		Prologue (pt 2), chorus & orchestra only
	CR384-1	(DB940)		Prologue (pt 3): Ave Signor
a	CR385-1A	D1109		Prologue (pt 4): Salve Regina chorus & orchestra only
b	CR386-1A	D1109		Prologue (pt 5): chorus & orchestra only (Chaliapin whistles)
	CR387-1			Act 1: Ju-hè! Ju-hè! chorus & orchestra only
c	CR388-1	DB942	15-1042	Act 1: Mefistofeles' ballad – Son lo spirito che nega
d	CR389-1			Act 2: Mefistofeles' ballad – Ecco il mondo
e	CR390-1A	DB942		Act 2: Ridda e fuga infernale – Sabba, Sabba, Sabboè

[Note: D1109 is a black label record also issued in Italy as AW4074, in Spain as AB189 and in Australia as ED1]

47. *15th March, 1927. Church Building, Camden, NJ. 10" (BVE) & 12" (CVE) red label Victor. With orchestra (ROSARIO BOURDON)*

a   CVE26102–3   IL BARBIERE DI SIVIGLIA Act I (Rossini)
Don Basilio's aria – La calunnia è un venticello (in Italian)

b   CVE26102–4   As above

c   BVE27089–5   MEFISTOFELE Prologue (Boito)
Ave Signor (in Italian)

d   BVE27089–6   As above

e   BVE29248–2   Pilgrim's song Op 47 No 5 (Tchaikovsky)
(Blest be these forests)

f   CVE37851–1   6783   The song of the flea (Mussorgsky)
(Once upon a time there was a King)

48. *16th March, 1927. Church Building, Camden, New Jersey. 10" red label Victor. With orchestra (ROSARIO BOURDON)*

a   BVE26100–4   DA891   1237   BORIS GODUNOV Act I (Mussorgsky)
Varlaam's song – In the town of Kazan

b   BVE26100–5   As above

c   BVE27088–3   LA SONNAMBULA Act I (Bellini)
Count Rodolfo's recitative & cavatina – Il mulino, il fonte . . . Vi ravviso (in Italian)

d   BVE27089–7   DA962   1269   MEFISTOFELE Prologue (Boito)
Ave Signor (in Italian)

e   BVE27091–2   DA891   1237   PRINCE IGOR Act I (Borodin)
Galitsky's song – I can't conceal that I dislike boredom

49. *18th March, 1927. Church Building, Camden, NJ. 10" (BVE) & 12" (CVE) red label Victor. With orchestra (ROSARIO BOURDON)*

a   CVE26102–5   IL BARBIERE DI SIVIGLIA Act 1 (Rossini)
                 Don Basilio's recitative & aria – Dunque la calunnia cos'è . . . La calunnia (in Italian)

b   CVE26102–6   6783   As above

c   BVE27088–4   LA SONNAMBULA Act 1 (Bellini)
                 Count Rodolfo's recitative & cavatina – Il mulino, il fonte . . . Vi ravviso (in Italian)

d   BVE27088–5   DA962   As above

e   BVE37854–1   DA993   The blind ploughman (Clarke) (in English)

50. *7th April, 1927. Liederkranz Hall, New York. 12" red label Victor. With orchestra (ROSARIO BOURDON)*

a   CVE26102–7   IL BARBIERE DI SIVIGLIA Act 1 (Rossini)
                 Don Basilio's aria – La calunnia è un venticello (in Italian)

b   CVE38334–1   DB1096   DON QUICHOTTE Act 5 (Massenet)
                 Death scene (pt 1): Oh, mon maître (in French)

c   CVE38335–1   DB1096   DON QUICHOTTE Act 5 (Massenet)
                 Death scene (pt 2): Oui! Je fus le chef (in French), with soprano OLIVE KLINE

51. *13th June, 1927. Small Queen's ball, London. 12" red label Gramophone. With orchestra (LAWRANCE A COLLINGWOOD)*

a   Cc10938–1   BORIS GODUNOV Act 4 (Mussorgsky)
                 Death of Boris – The bell! The passing bell

b   Cc10938–2   6724   As above

c   Cc10938–3   DB934   6813   As above

52. *15th June, 1927. Small Queen's Hall, London. 12" red label Gramophone. With orchestra (LAWRANCE A COLLINGWOOD)*

a	Cc10957–1	7199	The prophet Op 49 No 2 (Rimsky-Korsakov) (Parched with spiritual thirst)
b	Cc10958–1	7199	When the King went to war Op 7 No 6 (Koenemann)
c	Cc10958–2		As above
d	Cc10958–3		As above
e	Cc10959–1		SADKO Scene 4 (Rimsky-Korsakov) The Varangian Merchant's song – On fearful crags

53. *17th June, 1927. Small Queen's Hall, London. 12" red label Gramophone. With orchestra (LAWRANCE A COLLINGWOOD)*

a	Cc10961–1	DB1068	In questa tomba oscura (Beethoven) (in Italian)
b	Cc10961–2		As above
c	Cc10961–3		As above

54. *27th September, 1927. Paris. 12" red label Gramphone. With the D I ARISTOV CHOIR & balalaika orchestra (A A SCRIABIN)*

a	CTR3079–1		Ah, thou red sun Op 10 No 1 (Slonov)
b	CTR3079–2		As above
c	CTR3080–1	15236	Black eyes (gipsy folksong)
		DB3463	
		DB4540	
d	OEA5647–1		As above, 10" transfer from CTR3080–1, 27 August, 1937, master damaged
e	OEA5647–2		As above, 27 August, 1937
f	OEA5647–3		As above, 16th September, 1937

55. *September, 1927. Paris. 12" red label Gramophone. Accompaniment not specified*

a   CTR3106–1   Open the Gates of Repentance (Wedel)

b   CTR3106–2   As above

56. *11th October, 1927. Royal Albert Hall, London. 12" red albel Gramophone*

   Recordings made during the public concert performance of MOZART & SALIERI (Rimsky-Korsakov)

       Salieri   F I CHALIAPIN

       Mozart   THEODORE RITCH

       Blind Violinist   NICOLAS LAVRETSKY

       LONDON SYMPHONY ORCHESTRA (ALBERT COATES)

a   CR1525–1   Scene 1 (pt 1): They all say there is no truth on earth

b   CR1526–1   Scene 1 (pt 2): With earnest, strenuous constancy I've achieved at last

c   CR1527–1   Scene 1 (pt 3): Like a certain cherub he has brought us heavenly songs

d   CR1528–1   Scene 2: You will sleep for ever, Mozart

e   CR1529–1   BORIS GODUNOV Act 1 (Mussorgsky)

                 The Inn scene (pt 1): (pp 65–71)

f   CR1530–1   BORIS GODUNOV Act 1 (Mussorgsky)

                 The Inn scene (pt 2): Varlaam's song – In the town of Kazan

57. *17th October, 1927. Small Queen's Hall, London. 12" red label Gramophone. With orchestra (LAWRANCE A COLLINGWOOD)*

a   Cc11705–1   SADKO Scene 4 (Rimsky-Korsakov)

                 The Varangian Merchant's song – On fearful crags

58. *20th October, 1927. Small Queen's Hall, London. 12" red label Gramophone. With orchestra (ALBERT COATES)*

a	Cc10957–2	DB1103	The prophet Op 49 No 2 (Rimsky-Korsakov) (Parched with spiritual thirst)
b	Cc10961–4	DB1068	In questa tomba oscura (Beethoven) (in Italian)
c	Cc11705–2	DB1104	SADKO Scene 4 (Rimsky-Korsakov) The Varangian Merchant's song – On fearful crags
d	Cc11709–1	DB1103	Ei ukhnem! (folksong arr Chaliapin & Koenemann) (The song of the Volga boatmen)
e	Cc11709–2		As above
f	2EA277–4	DB2455	As above, transfer of part of Cc11709–1, May, 1935, 'Cavalcade of Famous Artistes'
g	Cc11710–1		PRINCE IGOR Act 2 (Borodin) Khan Konchak's aria – Are you well, Prince?
h	Cc11710–2	DB1104	As above

59. *19th June, 1928. Small Queen's Hall, London. 10" red label Gramophone. With orchestra (JOHN BARBIROLLI)*

a	Bb13832–1A	DA994	DON GIOVANNI Act 1 (Mozart) Leporello's catalogue aria (pt 1) – Madamina (in Italian)
b	Bb13833–1	DA994	DON GIOVANNI Act 1 (Mozart) Leporello's catalogue aria (pt 2) – Nella bionda (in Italian)
c	Bb13834–1		Oh, could I in song tell my sorrow (Malashkin) (in English)
d	Bb13834–2		As above

60. *22nd June, 1928. Royal Opera House, Covent Garden, London. 10" (BR) & 12" (CR) red label Gramophone*

Recordings made during the public performance of FAUST (Gounod). Sung in French

Mephistopheles	F I CHALIAPIN	Faust	JOSEPH HISLOP
Marguerite	MARISE BEAUJON	Valentin	JOHN CHARLES THOMAS
Siebel	JANE LAUGIER	Wagner	FRANCLYN KELSEY
Martha	JANE BOURGUIGNON		

ROYAL OPERA CHORUS & ORCHESTRA conducted by EUGENE GOOSSENS

	CR2097–1		Act 1, Faust: Rien! En vain j'interroge
	CR2098–1		Act 1, Faust: Paresseuse fille, with chorus
a	CR2099–1		Act 1, Duet Faust-Mephistopheles (pt 1): Mais ce Dieu, que peut-il pour moi?
b	CR2100–1		Act 1, Duet Faust-Mephistopheles (pt 2): Et que peut-tu pour moi?
c	CR2101–1		Act 1, Duet Faust-Mephistopheles (pt 3): Et bien, que t'en semble?
d	CR2103–1		Act 2, Scene Wagner-Mephistopheles & couplets: Allons amis . . . Le veau d'or, with chorus
e	CR2104–1	DB1189	Act 2, Scene Faust-Mephistopheles: Nous nous retrouverons, with Siebel & chorus
	CR2105–1	DB1189	Act 3, Siebel's air: Faites-lui mes aveux
f	CR2106–1		Act 3, Faust's cavatine: Salut, demeure chaste et pure
	BR2107–1		Act 3, Mephistopheles' invocation: Il était temps
	BR2108–1		Act 4, Soldiers' chorus: Déposons les armes
g	CR2109–1		Act 4, Scene Faust-Mephistopheles & serenade: Qu'attendez-vous . . . Vous qui faites l'endormie

61. *30th June, 1928. Small Queen's Hall, London. 10" (Bb) & 12" (Cc) red label Gramophone. With orchestra (EUGENE GOOSSENS)*

a	Cc13897–1A	DB1184	7116	Der Doppelganger D957 (Schubert) (Schwanengesang No 13)
b	Cc13897–2			As above
c	Cc13898–1	DB1184	7116	Der Tod und das Mädchen D531 (Schubert)
d	Cc13898–2			As above
e	Cc13898–3			As above
f	Bb13899–1			Oh, could I in song tell my sorrow (Malashkin) (in English)
g	Bb13899–2	DA993	1365	As above

62. *4th July, 1928. Royal Opera House, Covent Garden, London. 12" red label Gramophone*

Recordings made during the public performance of BORIS GODUNOV (Mussorgsky). Sung in Russian and Italian

Boris Godunov	F I CHALIAPIN
Policeman	MICHELE SAMPIERE
Tshelkalov	ARISTIDE BARACCHI
Prince Shuisky	ANGELO BADA
Pimen	LUIGI MANFRINI
Wet-nurse	JANE BOURGUIGNON
Feodor	MARGHERITA CAROSIO
Xenia	THERESA AMBRAUSE
Marina Mnishek	IRENE MINGHINI CATTANEO
Inn Hostess	OLGA DE FRANCO
Grigori/Dmitri	DINO BORGIOLI
Varlaam	SALVATORE BACCALONI
Misail	GIUSEPPE NESSI
God's Fool	OCTAVE DUA

ROYAL OPERA CHORUS & ORCHESTRA conducted by VINCENZO BELLEZZA

	Matrix			Description
	CR2124–1			Prologue Scene 1 (pt 1): Introduction (Policeman & chorus)
	CR2125–1			Prologue Scene 1 (pt 2): Continued (Policeman, Tshelkanov & chorus)
	CR2126–1			Prologue Scene 1 (pt 3): Chorus of pilgrims (chorus)
	CR2127–1			Prologue Scene 2 (pt 1): Coronation scene – Gloria allo Zar Boris! (Shuisky & chorus)
a	CR2128–1			Prologue Scene 2 (pt 2): Coronation scene – I am oppressed (Boris)
b	CR2129–1			Act 1: Clapping game and entry of Boris (Boris, Feodor, Xenia & Wet-nurse)
c	CR2130–1A	DB1181		Act 2: Scene Boris-Feodor & monologue (pt 1) – And you, my son . . . I have attained the highest power
d	CR2130–2A	DB1181	15–1043	As above, transfer from CR2130–1A, 27 October, 1938, master damaged
e	CR2131–1A	DB1181	15–1043	Act 2: Boris' monologue (pt 2) – Heavy is the hand of retribution
f	CR2132–1			Act 2: Boris-Shuisky duet (pt 1)
g	CR2133–1			Act 2: Boris-Shuisky duet (pt 2)
h	CR2134–1A	DB1182	15–1044	Act 2: Clock scene – My heart is heavy (Boris)
	CR2135–1			Act 3: Polonaise (Marina Mnishek & chorus)
	CR2136–1			Act 4: Riot scene at Kromy (pt 1) (chorus)
	CR2137–1			Act 4: Riot scene at Kromy (pt 2) (chorus)
	CR2138–1	DB1182		Act 4: Scene in the Duma (pt 1) – Su, boiardi, incominciamo (chorus)
	CR2138–1T1	DB1182		As above, transfer from CR 2138–1
i	CR2139–1A	DB1183		Act 4: Scene in the Duma (pt 2) – Ma qui non è Shuisky (Boris, Shuisky & chorus)
j	CR2140–1			Act 4: Scene in the Duma (pt 3) – I have called you, Boyards (Boris, Shuisky, Pimen & chorus)
k	CR2141–1A	DB1183	15–1044	Act 4: Boris' farewell – Leave us . . . Farewell, my son
l	CR2142–1	DB3464	15177	Act 4: Boris' prayer – Lord God, look down
m	CR2143–1	DB3464	15177	Act 4: Death of Boris – Weep, weep, people (Boris, Feodor & chorus)

63. *13th June, 1929, Small Queen's Hall, London. 10" (Bb) & 12" (Cc) red label Gramophone*

a	Bb16990–1		Down the Petersky (folksong arr Chaliapin), with the 'Petersky' balalaika orchestra
b	Bb16990–2		As above
c	Bb16990–3		As above
d	Bb16990–4	DA1061	As above
e	Bb16991–1	1557	Mashenka (folksong) (They won't let Masha walk by the brook), unaccompanied
f	Bb16991–2		As above
g	Bb16991–2T1	DA1061	As above
h	Cc16992–1	1557	Siberian prisoner's song (folksong arr Karatygin) (Farewell to thee, my joy), with piano by IVOR NEWTON
i	Cc16992–2	DB1352	As above
		7601	

64. *14th June, 1929, Small Queen's Hall, London. 12" red label Gramophone. With orchestra (GEORGE W BYNG)*

a	Cc17102–1		Le cor (Flégier) (in French)
b	Cc17102–2A		As above
c	Cc17102–2AT1	DB1342	As above, transfer from Cc17102–2A
		7422	
d	Cc17102–1		The old corporal (Dargomyzhsky)
e	Cc17103–2		As above
f	Cc17103–2T1	DB1342	As above, transfer from Cc17103–2
g	Cc17104–1	7422	Persian song Op 34 No 9 (Rubinstein) (The turbulent waters of Kur)
h	Cc17104–2		As above

65. *19th June, 1929. Small Queen's Hall, London. 12" red label Gramophone. With piano (IVOR NEWTON)*

a   Cc17114–1   Nochen'ka (folksong arr Chaliapin) (Night), with cello by CEDRIC SHARPE and piano

b   Cc17115–1   She laughed (Lishin)

c   Cc17115–2   DB1352   7601   As above

d   Cc17115–3   As above

66. *21st June, 1929. Small Queen's Hall, London. White label private Gramophone. Unaccompanied*

a   Test 792–1   Meeting with SASHA GUITRY and YVONNE PRINTEMPS. Sketch of a telephone conversation

b   OEA249–1   As above, transfer from Test 792–1, 17 December, 1934

67. *7th November, 1929. Small Queen's Hall, London. 10" (Bb) & 12" (Cc) red label Gramophone. With piano (MAX RABINOWITSCH)*

a   Bb18142–1   The prisoner Op 78 No 6 (Rubinstein) (I sit behind cold prison bars) (10" master)

b   Cc18142–2   As above (12" master)

c   Cc18142–3   As above

d   Cc18142–4   As above

e   Cc18143–1   Doubt (Glinka) (Be stilled, you gusts of passion), with viola by WILLIAM PRIMROSE & piano

f   Cc18144–1   Nochen'ka (folksong arr Chaliapin) (Night)

68. *11th November, 1929. Small Queen's Hall, London. 12" red label Gramophone. With orchestra (LAWRANCE A COLLINGWOOD)*

a	Cc18156–1	DB2145	ALEKO Act 1 (Rachmaninov) Aleko's cavatina – All the gipsy camp is sleeping
b	Cc18157–1	DB1511	Songs and Dances of Death (Mussorgsky) No 1: Trepak – Still is the forest

69. *27th February, 1930. Salle Pleyel, Paris. 12" red label Gramophone*
With the CHORUS & ORCHESTRA of the THEATRE DE L'OPERA (HENRI BUSSER)

a	CF3000–1		FAUST Act 2 (Gounod) Scene Wagner-Mephistopheles & couplets: Un rat . . . Le veau d'or, with MICHAEL COZETTE (in French)
b	CF3000–2	DB1437 IRX80	7600	As above
c	CF3001–1		FAUST Act 4 (Gounod) Mephistopheles' serenade – Vous qui faites l'endormie (in French), without chorus
d	CF3001–2	DB1437 IRX80	As above
e	CF3001–3	DB1437	As above
f	CF3002–1		7600	DON QUICHOTTE Act 4 (Massenet) Sancho Panza's air – Ça vous commettez tous un acte épouvantable (in French)
g	CF3002–2		As above

574

70. 12th June, 1930. Salle Chopin, Paris. 10" (BF) & 12" (CF & 2EA) red label Gramophone. With piano (JEAN BAZILEVSKY)

a	CF3357–1			Sten'ka Razin (folksong)
b	CF3357–2			As above
c	CF3357–3	DB1469	7679	As above
d	CF3358–1			Doubt (Glinka)
				(Be stilled, you gusts of passion), with violin by LUCIEN SCHWARTZ & piano
e	CF3358–2	DB1469	15422	As above
f	BF3359–1			The prisoner Op 78 No 6 (Rubinstein)
				(I sit behind cold prison bars)
g	BF3359–2			As above
h	2EA5705–1			As above, transfer from BF3359–2, 10" to 12", 1 February, 1938
i	2EA5705–2	DB3463	15236	As above, 8 April, 1938
j	2EA5705–3			As above, 8 April, 1938
k	CF3360–1			Nochen'ka (folksong arr Chaliapin)
				(Night)
l	CF3360–2	DB2145	15422	As above

71. 21st January, 1931. Salle Pleyel, Paris. 12" red label Gramophone. With chorus only

a	2G111–1		Open the gates of repentance (Wedel)
b	2G111–2	DB1510	As above
c	2G112–1		Now let Thy servant depart in peace, Prayer (Strokin)

575

72. *22nd January, 1931. Salle Pleyel, Paris. 12" red label Gramophone*
With the Paris Russian Opera Chorus (D ARISTOV) and balalaika orchestra (O TCHERNOYAROV)

a	2G112–1	DB1510	Now let Thy servant depart in peace, Prayer (Strokin), with chorus only
b	2G113–1		THE POWER OF EVIL Act 2 (Serov)
			Eremka's song – I'll amuse my hostess . . . Merry Shrovetide
c	2G113–2	DB1511	As above

73. *23rd January, 1931. Salle Pleyel, Paris. 12" red label Gramophone.*
With the Paris Russian Opera Company Chorus & Orchestra (MAX STEIMANN)

a	2G114–1		BORIS GODUNOV Prologue (Mussorgsky)
			Coronation scene (pt 2): I am oppressed
b	2G114–2		As above
c	2G115–1		BORIS GODUNOV Act 4 (Mussorgsky)
			Death of Boris
d	2G115–2		As above

74. *13th May, 1931. Small Queen's Hall, London. 12" red label Gramophone*

a	2B883–1		Doubt (Glinka)
			(Be stilled, you gusts of passion), with cello by CEDRIC SHARPE & piano by IVOR NEWTON
b	2B883–2	DB1469	As above
c	2B884–1	7679	Persian song Op 34 No 9 (Rubinstein)
			(The turbulent waters of Kur), with orchestra LAWRANCE A COLLINGWOOD
d	2B884–2		As above
e	2B884–3	DB1525	As above
f	2B885–1	DB1525 (7575)	Elégie (Massenet)
		DB4540 14902	(Oh, where are they, days of love?), with cello by CEDRIC SHARPE & piano by IVOR NEWTON

g	2B885–2			As above
h	2B885–3			As above

75. *6th June, 1931. Kingsway Hall, London. 12" red label Gramophone*
With the LONDON SYMPHONY ORCHESTRA (MAX STEIMANN)

a	2B577–1A			BORIS GODUNOV Act 2 (Mussorgsky) Boris' monologue – I have attained the highest power
b	2B577–2	DB1532		As above
c	2B577–3	DB1532		As above
d	2B578–1		14517	BORIS GODUNOV Act 2 (Mussorgsky) Clock scene: My heart is heavy
e	2B578–2	DB1532	14517	As above

76. *8th June, 1931. Kingsway Hall, London. 12" red label Gramophone*
With the LONDON SYMPHONY ORCHESTRA (MAX STEIMANN)

a	2B579–1			RUSALKA Act 1 (Dargomyzhsky) The Miller's aria – You young lasses are all alike
b	2B579–2A	DB1530	7704	As above
c	2B580–1	DB1531	11–8695	RUSALKA Act 3 (Dargomyzhsky) Mad scene (pt 1): Good morrow, son-in-law, with tenor GEORGI POZEMKOVSKY
d	2B581–1	DB1531	11–8695	RUSALKA Act 3 (Dargomyzhsky) Mad scene (pt 2): Why do I suffer so? with tenor GEORGI POZEMKOVSKY
e	2B582–1			RUSLAN AND LUDMILLA Act 2 (Glinka) Farlaf's rondo – Oh joy . . . The hour of my triumph is near
f	2B582–2	DB1530	7704	As above
g	2B582–2A	DB1530		As above, different master from same performance as 2B582–2

77. *29th January, 1932. Salle Chopin, Paris. 12" red label Gramophone*
With the Choir of the Russian Metropolitan Church (N P AFONSKY)

a	2W1227–1			Liturgica Domestica Op 79 (Grechaninov) The Creed
b	2W1227–2			As above
c	2W1228–1			Now let Thy servant depart in peace, Prayer (Strokin)

78. *30th January, 1932. Salle Chopin, Paris. 12" red label Gramophone. With male chorus (N P AFONSKY)*

a	2W1229–1			The legend of the twelve brigands (folksong arr S Zharov)
b	2W1229–2			As above
c	2W1229–3			As above

79. *26th February, 1932. Salle Pleyel, Paris. 12" red label Gramophone*
With the Choir of the Russian Metropolitan Church (N P AFONSKY)

a	2W1227–3			Liturgica Domestica Op 79 (Grechaninov) The Creed
b	2W1227–4			As above
c	2W1227–5			As above
d	2W1228–2			Now let Thy servant depart in peace, Prayer (Strokin)
e	2W1228–3	DB1699	7716	As above
f	2W1229–4	DB1700	7717	The legend of the twelve brigands (folksong arr S Zharov), with male chorus only
g	2W1229–5			As above
h	2W1327–1	DB1699	7716	Open the gates of repentance (Wedel)
i	2W1328–1			Down Mother Volga (folksong arr A V Alexandrov)
j	2W1328–2	DB1700	7717	As above
k	2W1328–3			As above

80.   *1st March, 1932. Salle Pleyel, Paris. 12" red label Gramophone*
With the Choir of the Russian Metropolitan Church (N P AFONSKY)

a	2W1328–4		Down Mother Volga (folksong arr A V Alexandrov)
b	2W1337–1		Liturgica Domestica Op 79 (Grechaninov)
			Twofold Litany – Glory to Thee, O Lord, with organ
c	2W1337–2		As above, without organ
d	2W1337–3	DB1701	As above, with organ
e	2W1338–1		The Creed (Arkhangelsky)
f	2W1338–2	DB1701	As above

81.   *9th January, 1933. Salle Chopin, Paris. 10" red label Gramophone*
Music for the film 'Don Quichotte' with orchestra conducted by the composer, JACQUES IBERT

a	OPG425–1		Chanson à Dulcinée (in English)
b	OPG426–1		Chanson du départ
			This castle new (in English), with instrumental quartet
c	OPG427–1		Chanson du duc (in English)
d	OPG427–2		As above
e	OPG428–1		Chanson du duc
			Je veux chanter ici la Dame de mes songes (in French)
f	OPG428–2		As above
g	OPG429–1		Chanson du départ
			Ce château neuf, ce nouvel édifice (in French)
h	OPG429–2		As above
i	OPG430–1	DA1311 VA26	Chanson à Dulcinée
			Un an, me dure la journée (in French)
j	OPG431–1	HMA46	Bolero (Dargomyzhsky)
			(The Sierra Nevada is hidden in mist), with piano by PIERO COPPOLA
			(in Russian)

579

82. *13th March, 1933, Salle Chopin, Paris. 10" red label Gramophone*
Music for the film 'Don Quichotte' with orchestra conducted by the composer JACQUES IBERT

	Matrix	Catalogue	Title
a	OPG428–3		Chanson du duc / Je veux chanter ici la Dame de mes songes (in French)
b	OPG428–4	DA1310 VA25	As above
c	OPG429–3	DA1310 VA25	Chanson du départ / Ce château neuf, ce nouvel édifice (in French)
d	OPG430–2		Chanson à Dulcinée / Un an, me dure la journée (in French)
e	OPG430–3		As above
f	OPG635–1		Chanson de la mort de Don Quichotte / Don't cry, Sancho (in English)
g	OPG636–1		Chanson de la mort de Don Quichotte / Ne pleure pas, Sancho (in French)
h	OPG637–1	DA1311 VA26	As above
i	OPG637–2		As above

83. *19th March, 1934. Salle Chopin, Paris. 10" red label Gramophone. With the AFONSKY CHOIR & balalaika orchestra*

	Matrix	Catalogue		Title
a	OPG1422–1	DA1371	1983	The song of the needy pilgrim (Manykin-Nevstruev) (I walk through meadows)
b	OPG1423–1			Arise, red sun (folksong)
c	OPG1423–2			As above, transfer from OPG1423–1, 12 April, 1934, to increase volume
d	OPG1423–3	DA1371	1983	As above

84. *6th February, 1936. Tokyo. 12" red label Victor. With piano (G. GODZINSKY)*

a   8112–1   The song of the flea (Mussorgsky)
                (Once upon a time there was a King)
b   8112–2   As above
v   8112–3   As above
d   8112–4   14901   As above
e   8113–1   Ei ukhnem! (folksong arr Chaliapin & Koenemann)
                (The song of the Volga boatmen)
f   8113–2   As above
g   8113–3   As above
h   8113–4   14901   As above

Alphabetical Index to the Recordings

(The numbers refer to Recording Sessions in the Discography)

CHALIAPIN

INDEX TO RECORDINGS

CHALIAPIN

Appendix I – Numerical List of Japanese Victor Issues

The following records are Japanese domestic double-sided issues:

D 8002	84d	JD1277	47f	JF 62	83a	NF4090	48a	
	84h		58d		83d		48e	
						NF4167	34b	
HL 11	63d	JD1278	68b	ND 2	84d		34c	
			74e		84h			
JD 10	68b	JD1279	51c	ND 277	70c	RL 7	84d	
	72c		75c		79f		84h	
JD 32	74e	JD1518	62d	ND 559	68b			
	74f		62e		74e	VD8026	70c	
JD 80	79e	JD1519	62h	ND569	76b		79f	
	79h	62-CR2138-1T1			76f	VD8027	70l	
JD 149	76c	JD1520	62i	ND601	72c		79j	
	76d		62k		79j	VD8400	76b	
JD 226	75c	JD2001	51c				76f	
	75e		75e	NF4053	83a			
JD 328	80d				83d	VF2001	63d	
	80f	JE 164	63d	NF4070	63d		83d	
JD 502	68a		63g		63g			
	70l	JF 22	82b	NF4081	82b			
JD 723	68b		82c		82c			
	72c	JF 23	81i	NF4082	81i			
JD 862	44c		82h		82h			
	51c							

Appendix II – Deutsche Grammophon & Opera Disc Issues

In 1914 the British owned assets of the Gramophone Company (HMV) in Germany were seized and sold as enemy property, the new independent German company being known as Deutsche Grammophon Gesellschaft (DGG). After the war, both HMV and DGG pressed records from identical pre-war masters and, until the question of copyright was finally settled, DGG exported many of these to America. To avoid using the Dog Trade Mark, which was the exclusive property of HMV in Europe and of the Victor Talking Machine Company in America, DGG devised new labels for use in Europe and for export. The export label carried the title 'Opera Disc'.

10" records

	Opera Disc (single)	Domestic Coupling
17h	74609	
17d	74610	80070
17f	74611	80070
17j	74612	80072
17l	74613	80072

12" records

4d	76012	85106	8c	76433	85237
4e	76013	85017	8e	76434	85235
4b	76216	85230	8i	76435	85236
6d	76217	85108	10d	76436	85107
15b	76218	85114	10f	76437	85242
15a	76221	85110	10g	76438	85241
15f	76222	85110	11d	76439	85244
16a	76223	85112	11f	76440	85245
16b	76224	85108	12b	76441	85246
16c	76225	85114	12c	76442	85246
10e	76370	85241	12d	76443	85248
4f	76371	85106	12e	76444	85249
8f	76397	– – –	12f	76445	85245
15c	76416	85112	14a	76446	85244
6c	76427	85231	13b	76447	85230
9b	76428	85231	13c	76448	85248/85249
7f	76429	85233	13f	– – –	85109
7a	76430	85233	16e	– – –	85109
7c	76431	85235	8b	– – –	85237
7d	76432	85236	16d	– – –	85242

SOURCE NOTES

Prologue

1 Chekhov, A. F.: Letter to V. M. Sobolevski, April 20th, 1904. Complete works, Moscow 1983, vol. 12, p. 93
2 Gorky, Maxim: Letter to Chaliapin March 1st (14th old style) 1913, in *Fedor Ivanovich Chaliapin*, vol. 1: Literary works, letters. Moscow 1976, p. 349
3 Kuznetsov, Mikhail: *This was a great school*. Iskuvsstvo kino, no. 10. Moscow 1983, p. 110
4 In Nikolai Gorchakov: *Stanislavsky's lessons in stagecraft*. Moscow 1950, p. 115
5 Christy, G.: *Stanislavsky's work in operatic theatre*. Moscow 1952, p. 59
6 Gorky, Maxim: Collected works in 30 volumes. Moscow 1949–1956, vol. 29, pp. 298–299
7 Swan, Alfred J. and Katherine: 'Rachmaninoff – Personal Memories', part 2. *The Musical Quarterly*, New York, April, 1944, p. 186
8 Korovin, Konstantin: *Chaliapin – encounters and life together*. La Renaissance, Paris 1939, p. 57
9 Andreev, Leonid: 'About Chaliapin', in *Fedor Ivanovich Chaliapin (biography and stage creations)*. Rampa i zhizn', Moscow 1915, pp. 33–34
10 Dal Monte, Toti: 'Grande Barbiere' in *Fedor Ivanovich Chaliapin*, vol. 2: Memories of Chaliapin. Moscow 1977, p. 492
11 Farrar, Geraldine: *Such sweet compulsion*. The Greystone Press, New York 1938, p. 71
12 Ponselle, Rosa: *A singer's life*. Doubleday & Co., New York 1982, p. 92
13 'Dame Nellie Melba and Chaliapin', *Evening Standard*, May 26th, 1926.
14 *Titta Ruffo: an anthology*. Edited by Andrew Farkas. Greenwood Press, Westport, Connecticut; London, England 1984
15 Ibidem, p. 112
16 Archive F. I. Chaliapin – Bibliothèque de l'Arsenal, Paris. R. Supplement 199
17 Craig, Gordon: *The Measure of Irving*. J. M. Dent and Sons Ltd., London 1930, p. 50
18 Monfried, Walter: 'Chaliapin, greatest singing actor in history, handy with fists', series of articles from *The Journal*. Archive of the Museum of Performing Arts, Lincoln Center, New York
19 Schipa, Tito: 'Memories of Chaliapin' in *F. I. Chaliapin*, vol. 2, p. 492
20 Gavazzeni, Gianandrea: 'About Chaliapin' in *Fedor Ivanovich Chaliapin*, vol. 3: Articles, comments, additions. Moscow 1979, p. 225
21 Hotter, Hans: Interview on BBC Radio 4 'Kaleidoscope', November 29th, 1983
22 Hotter, Hans: Letter to the author, December 18th, 1983.
23 Stanislavsky, K.S.: Collected works in 8 volumes, vol. 6. Moscow 1954–1961, pp. 215–216
24 Finck, Henry: 'Chaliapin, the Russian Mephistopheles'. *The Century Magazine*, New York, November 1910, p. 235

25 E. B.: 'Chaliapin in *Mefistofele*'. *Manchester Guardian*, May 26th, 1926
26 von Karajan, Herbert: Letter to author, December 9th, 1983
27 Daniels, Robin: *Conversations with Cardus*. Gollancz, London, 1976, p. 103
28 Benois, Alexander: *Alexander Benois reminisces* ... Moscow 1968, p. 492
29 Repin, Ilya: Letters. Moscow 1949, vol. 2, p. 249
30 New material about Repin. Leningrad 1969, p. 25
31 Feschotte, Jacques: *Ce Géant: Féodor Chaliapine*, La Table Ronde, Paris 1968, p. 173
32 Chaliapin, F. I.: *Mask and Soul – my forty years in the theatre*. Contemporary notes. Paris 1932, p. 179
33 Nemenova-Lunz, M. C.: 'My encounters with Chaliapin' in *F. I. Chaliapin*, vol. 2, p. 271
34 Fokine, Mikhail: *Against the stream – memories of a choreographer*. Leningrad 1981, p. 177
35 Evans, Edwin: Chaliapin's BBC obituary broadcast April 12th, 1938. BBC archive, Caversham
36 From Chaliapin's Memoirs. 'The Press and I', *Sinii zhurnal*, St. Petersburg, 1912, no. 50, p. 2
37 Gorky, Maxim: Collected works in 30 volumes. Moscow 1949–1956, vol. 29, p. 95
38 Letter to Irina Chaliapina, April 14th, 1916, in *F. I. Chaliapin*, vol. 1, p. 489
39 Letter from Gorky to Timiryazef, August 2nd, 1916. Ibidem
40 Chaliapin, F.: Letter to M. Gorky, September 7th 1926. Sydney. Ibidem, p. 357
41 Gorky, A. M.: letter to F. I. Chaliapin, June 29th, 1927, Sorrento. *Novyi mir*, Moscow 1986, no. 1, January, p. 190
42 Chaliapin, F. to M. Gorky, July 19th 1927, in *F. I. Chaliapin*, vol. 1, p. 358
43 Gorky, A. M.: Letter to F. I. Chaliapin, October 16th, 1926. *Novyi mir*, no. 1, Moscow, January 1986, p. 189
44 Gorky, Maxim: Letter to the newspapers *Pravda* and *Izvestia* in M. Gorky complete works, vol. 12, Moscow 1971, p. 607
45 *F. I. Chaliapin*, vol. 1, p. 665
46 Gorky, Maxim: Letter to F. Chaliapin, August 9th, 1930 in *F. I. Chaliapin*, vol. 1, p. 362
47 Gorky readings. Moscow 1954, pp. 60–61
48 Crankshaw, Edward: 'Gorky's greatest character', *Observer*, London, December 3rd, 1967
49 Chaliapin, F. I.: *Mask and Soul*, p. 338
50 Ibidem, p. 290
51 Gorky, Maxim: 'Nesvoyovremenye mysli' (Untimely thoughts), articles from the years 1917–1918. Compiled, prefaced and annotated by T. Ermolaev. Paris 1971, p. 103
52 Ibidem, p. 132
53 Ibidem, p. 166
54 Chaliapin-Schouvalova, Dasya: 'My father, Chaliapin'. *Strelets*, September 1984, no. 9, p. 30
55 *F. I. Chaliapin*, vol. 1, p. 622
56 Chaliapin, F. I.: *Mask and Soul*, p. 9
57 Chaliapin, F. I.: *Pages from my life*. vol. 1, p. 75
58 Strakhova-Ermans, Varvara: 'Memories of Chaliapin', *Novyi zhurnal*, New York 1953, vol. xxxiv, p. 251
59 Skitalets, Stepan: F. I. Chaliapin, vol. 2, p. 169

60 Feschotte, Jacques: *Ce Géant: Féodor Chaliapine*, pp. 212–213
61 Chaliapina, Lydia: 'As I remember him', *F. I. Chaliapin*, vol. 2, p. 92
62 Chaliapin, F. I.: *Mask and Soul*, p. 20
63 Pokhitonov, Daniil: *From the past of Russian Opera*, *F. I. Chaliapin*, vol. 2, p. 242
64 'The Week in Music', *Jewish Guardian*, London July 5th, 1928
65 Telyakovsky, Vladimir: 'My Colleague Chaliapin'. *Akademia*, Leningrad 1927, p. 159–160
66 Gaisberg, Fred: 'Recording Chaliapin in Moscow', May 14th, 1913. Typescript. EMI archive, Hayes, Middlesex
67 Gaisberg, Fred: 'Chaliapin' typescript. Quoted from Jerrold Northrop Moore: *A voice in time: the gramophone of Fred Gaisberg 1873–1951*. Hamish Hamilton, London 1976, p. 119
68 Chaliapin, F. I.: *Pages from my life*, vol. 1, p. 68
69 Davydov, Alexander: 'Memories of Chaliapin', *F. I. Chaliapin*, vol. 2, p. 97
70 Chaliapina, Irina: 'Memories of my Father', *F. I. Chaliapin*, vol. 2, p. 20
71 Chaliapin, F. I.: *Mask and Soul*, p. 96

Chapter 1

1 Chaliapin, F. I.: *Pages from my life* in *Fedor Ivanovich Chaliapin*, vol. 1: Literary works, letters. Moscow 1976, p. 47
2 Rachmaninov, S.: Literary works. Moscow 1978, vol. 1, pp. 278–279
3 Chaliapin, F. I.: *Pages from my life* in *F. I. Chaliapin*, vol. 1, p. 58
4 *Fedor Ivanovich Chaliapin (biography and stage creations)*. Rampa i zhizn, Moscow 1915, p. 2
5 Chaliapin, F. I.: *Pages from my life* in *F. I. Chaliapin*, vol. 1, p. 49
6 Ibidem, p. 61
7 *The Sun*, U.S.A. April 14th 1938
8 Lipaev, Ivan: *Fedor Ivanovich Chaliapin, singer and artist*, St. Petersburg 1914, p. 3
9 Chaliapin, F. I.: *Pages from my life* in *F. I. Chaliapin*, vol. 1, p. 62
10 Chaliapin, F. I.: Ibidem, p. 70
11 *Chronicle of the life and career of F. I. Chaliapin*, compiled by Yu. Kotlyarov and V. Garmash. Leningrad 1984, vol. 1, p. 26
12 Chaliapin, F. I.: *Pages from my life* in *F. I. Chaliapin*, vol. 1, p. 71
13 Ibidem, p. 47
14 Ibidem, p. 46
15 Ibidem, p. 75
16 Beecham, Sir Thomas: *A Mingled Chime*. Hutchinson & Co. Ltd., London 1944, pp. 120–121
17 Chaliapin, F. I.: *Pages from my life* in *F. I. Chaliapin*, vol. 1, p. 192
18 Korovin, Konstantin: *Chaliapin – encounters and life together*. La Renaissance, Paris 1939, pp. 100–101
19 Chaliapin, F. I.: *Mask and Soul – my forty years in the theatre*. Contemporary notes. Paris 1932, p. 38
20 Chaliapin, F. I.: *Pages from my life* in *F. I. Chaliapin*, vol. 1, p. 77
21 Chaliapin, F. I.: *Mask and Soul*, p. 31
22 Chaliapin, F. I.: *Pages from my life* in *F. I. Chaliapin*, vol. 1, p. 65
23 Chaliapin, F. I.: 'Soul, not technique, makes stars ...' New York Public Library, Music Division

24 Chaliapin, F. I.: *Pages from my life* in *F. I. Chaliapin*, vol. 1, p. 65
25 Ibidem, p. 67
26 Ibidem, p. 67
27 Chaliapin, F. I.: 'Fame and famous men'. *Evening News*, London October 8th 1931
28 Chaliapin, F. I.: *Pages from my life* in *F. I. Chaliapin*, vol. 1, p. 67
29 Bogolyubov, Nikolai: *Sixty years in the theatre*. Moscow 1967, p. 17
30 Chaliapin, F. I.: *Pages from my life* in *F. I. Chaliapin*, vol. 1, pp. 80–81
31 Ibidem, p. 81
32 Karsavina, Tamara: *Theatre Street – the reminiscences of Tamara Karsavina*. Dance Books Ltd., London 1981, p. 268
33 Bogolyubov, Nikolai: *Sixty years in the theatre*, p. 16
34 Chaliapin's beginnings (in an interview with Semyonov-Samarsky), *Peterburgskaya gazeta* 1910, no. 255, September 17th, p. 3
35 Chaliapin, F. I.: *Mask and Soul*, pp. 44–45
36 Solovyova, Inna: *Nemirovich-Danchenko*, Moscow 1979, p. 85
37 *Pages from my life* – an autobiography by Fedor Ivanovich Chaliapin (authorised translation by H. M. Buck). Revised enlarged and edited by Katharine Wright. New York and London. Harper & Brothers 1927, p. 325
38 Chaliapin, F. I.: *Mask and Soul*, p. 145
39 *Chronicle of the life and career of F. I. Chaliapin*, vol. 1, p. 47
40 Chaliapin, F. I.: *Pages from my life* in *F. I. Chaliapin*, vol. 1, p. 106
41 Chaliapin, F. I.: Ibidem, p. 106
42 Michel, Georges: *Candide*. Paris, April 21st, 1938
43 Chaliapin, F. I.: *Pages from my life* in F. I. Chaliapin, vol. 1, p. 108
44 Finck, Henry: *The Century Magazine*, New York, December 1910
45 Chaliapin, F. I.: 'Help', *Izvestia*, No. 172, Moscow August 6th, 1921
46 Chaliapin, F. I.: *Pages from my life* in *F. I. Chaliapin*, vol. 1, p. 109
47 Gaisberg, F. W.: *Music on record*, Robert Hale Ltd., London, 1948, p. 220
48 Chaliapin, F. I.: *Pages from my life* in *F. I. Chaliapin*, vol. 1, p. 111
49 Chaliapin, F. I.: Ibidem, p. 111
50 *Fedor Ivanovich Chaliapin (biography and stage creations)*, p. 18
51 Strakhova-Ermans, Varvara: 'Memories of Chaliapin', *Novyi zhurnal*. New York 1953, vol. XXXIV, pp. 242–243
52 Bessel, Vassily: *Muzikal'nyi listok* 1873, no. 28, p. 454
53 Collections of articles, 'Tchaikovsky and the theatre', Moscow 1941, p. 379
54 Chaliapin, F. I.: 'The old man who taught me to act', *Evening News*, London, October 14th, 1931
55 Strakhova-Ermans, Varvara: *Memories of Chaliapin*, p. 243
56 Beecham, Sir Thomas: *A Mingled Chime*, p. 60
57 'Faust', *Nizhni-Novgorod listok*, July 1st, 1896
58 Feodor Chaliapin: 'The singer's art', conversation with R. N. Wollstein. *Etude Music Magazine*, New York January 1936, p. 7
59 Levik, Sergei: *Memoirs of an opera singer*, Moscow 1962, p. 483
60 'Chaliapin's debt to the Eccentric Teacher of Tiflis', by a *Times* correspondent. *The Times*, London September 12th, 1957
61 Chaliapin, F. I.: *Mask and Soul*, p. 49
62 Chaliapin, F. I.: Ibidem, p. 50
63 Page, Philip: 'Chaliapin – the man of Paradox'. *Sunday Express*, May 26th, 1926
64 Levik, Sergei. *Memoirs of an opera singer*, p. 490
65 Chaliapin, F. I.: *Mask and Soul*, p. 51

66 Chaliapin, F. I.: 'A singer on the operatic stage' in *F. I. Chaliapin*, vol. 1, p. 308
67 Chaliapin, F. I.: *Mask and Soul*, p. 51
68 Chaliapin, F. I.: *Pages from my life* in *F. I. Chaliapin*, vol. 1, p. 118
69 Chaliapin, F. I.: *Mask and Soul*, p. 51
70 V. A.: 'Chaliapin's concert', *Orlovskii vestnik*, November 24th, 1901
71 Chaliapin, F. I.: *Mask and Soul*, p. 60
72 Frankenstein, Alfred: 'Chaliapin great in song recital', *San Francisco Chronicle*, April 2nd, 1935
73 Ippolitov-Ivanov, Mikhail: *Fifty years of Russian music in my memories*, Moscow 1934, pp. 77–78
74 'Theatre and Music', *Tiflisski listok*, No. 207, September 10th, 1893, p. 4.
75 Chaliapin, F. I.: *Pages from my life* in *F. I. Chaliapin*, vol. 1, p. 116
76 Kotlyarov, Yuri.: *Chronicle of the life and career of F. Chaliapin* in *F. I. Chaliapin*, vol. 3: Articles, comments, additions. Moscow 1979, pp. 253–254
77 *Chronicle of the life and career of F. I. Chaliapin*, vol. 1, p. 79
78 'Theatre and Music' – *Moscovskaya Teatral'naya gazeta*, November 21st 1893
79 Chaliapin, F. I.: *Pages from my life* in *F. I. Chaliapin*, vol. 1, p. 118
80 Theatre and Music – *Kavkaz*, no. 20, November 1893
81 Korganov, Vassily: Our Opera – *Kavkaz*, February 25th, 1894
82 Chaliapin, F. I.: *Pages from my life* in *F. I. Chaliapin*, vol. 1, p. 118
83 Chaliapin, F. I.: *Pages from my life* in *F. I. Chaliapin*, vol. 1, p. 75
84 Komissarzhevsky, Fedor: Aida, *Novoye Obozrenie* October 5th, 1893
85 Chaliapin, F. I.: *Mask and Soul*, p. 52
86 Chaliapin, F. I.: Ibidem, pp. 119–120
87 Chaliapin, F. I.: *Mask and Soul*, p. 52
88 Chaliapin, F. I.: *Pages from my life* in *F. I. Chaliapin*, vol. 1, p. 123
89 Musical News – *Artist*, August 1894, p. 203
90 Chaliapin, F. I.: *Pages from my life* in *F. I. Chaliapin*, vol. 1, p. 124
91 Theatre and Music – *Novoe vremya*, no. 6667, September 20th, 1894, p. 4
92 Chaliapin, F. I.: *Pages from my life* in *F. I. Chaliapin*, vol. 1, p. 125
93 Yurev, Yuri: *Memoirs*. Leningrad/Moscow 1963, vol. 2, p. 549
94 Levik, Sergei: *Memoirs of an opera singer*, pp. 470 & 512–513
95 *Impresario*: a memoir by Sol Hurok, in collaboration with Ruth Goode. Macdonald & Co. Ltd., London 1947, p. 55
96 Chaliapin, F. I.: *Pages from my life* in *F. I. Chaliapin*, vol. 1, p. 129
97 Bunin, Ivan: Chaliapin, in *Memories*, Paris LEV 1950, pp. 105–106
98 Perestiani, Ivan: *Seventy-five years of life in the arts*, Moscow 1962, p. 94
99 Chaliapin, F. I.: *Mask and Soul*, p. 53
100 Chaliapin, F. I.: Ibidem, p. 54
101 Chaliapin, F. I.: *Pages from my life* in *F. I. Chaliapin*, vol. 1, p. 125
102 *Theatre* – 'Chaliapin's contract'. Moscow 1973, No. 3, March, pp. 101–102
103 V. B.: 'Faust', *Peterburgskaya gazeta*, April 7th, 1895
104 Theatre and Music, *Novoe vremya*, September 6th, 1895
105 Quoted from the book by M. Yankovsky, *Chaliapin*, Leningrad 1972, p. 80
106 Chaliapin, F. I.: *Mask and Soul*, p. 58
107 Chaliapin, F. I.: Ibidem, p. 57
108 Chaliapina, Lydia: *As I remember him* in *F. I. Chaliapin*, vol. 2, p. 93
109 Levik, S. Y: *Memoirs of an opera singer*, p. 473
110 Chaliapin, F. I.: *Mask and Soul*, p. 55
111 Pazovsky, A. M: *Memoirs of a conductor*, Moscow 1966, p. 434
112 Theatre and Music: *Faust*, Volgar May 20th, 1896, no. 137

113 Pokhitonov, Daniil: *From the past of Russian Opera*, Leningrad 1949, p. 122
114 Chaliapin, F. I.: *Pages from my life* in *F. I. Chaliapin*, vol. 1, p. 128
115 Chaliapin, F. I.: *Mask and Soul*, p. 63
116 Chaliapin, F. I.: Ibidem, p. 67
117 Chaliapin, F. I.: *Pages from my life* in *F. I. Chaliapin*, vol. 1, p. 129
118 Gozenpud, Abram: *Russian opera theatre and Chaliapin*, Leningrad 1974, p. 95
119 Gozenpud, Abram: Ibidem, pp. 93–94
120 Pokhitonov, Daniil: *From the past of Russian opera*, p. 211
121 'Ruslan and Ludmilla'. *Peterburgskaya gazeta*, April 19th, 1895
122 Chronicle of the life and career of Chaliapin. Vol. 1, p. 93
123 V. B.: 'Ruslan and Ludmilla'. *Peterburgskaya gazeta*, November 25th, 1895, no. 324
124 Telyakovsky, Vladimir: *My colleague Chaliapin*, Leningrad–Moscow 1965, pp. 365–366
125 Korovin, Konstantin: *Chaliapin, encounters and life together*, p. 214
126 N. K.: *Moskovskie vedomosti*, February 4th, 1905
127 Chaliapin, F. I.: *Mask and Soul*, pp. 65–66
128 Makovsky, Sergei: *Portraits of Contemporaries*, The Chekhov Press, New York 1955, pp. 172–173
129 Theatre and Music – *Novoe vremya*, September 19th, 1895
130 *Carmen – Novoe vremya*, November 12th, 1895
131 Yurev, Yuri: *Memoirs*. Leningrad-Moscow 1963, vol. 1, p. 558
132 Makovsky, Sergei: *Portraits of Contemporaries*, p. 173
133 Chaliapin, F. I.: *Mask and Soul*, p. 67
134 Chaliapin, F. I.: *Pages from my life* in *F. I. Chaliapin*, vol. 1, p. 139
135 Chaliapin, F. I.: *Mask and Soul*, p. 67
136 Chaliapin, F. I.: Ibidem, p. 66
137 Chaliapin, F. I.: Ibidem, p. 70
138 Chaliapin, F. I.: Ibidem, p. 79
139 Chaliapin, F. I.: *Mask and Soul*, p. 70
140 Pokhitonov, Daniil: *From the past of Russian opera*, p. 211
141 Yurev, Yuri: *Memoirs*, vol. 2, p. 239
142 Chaliapin, F. I.: *Mask and Soul*, p. 72
143 Khodotov, Nikolai: *Near and Far*. Moscow–Leningrad 1962, p. 67
144 Drankov, V.: *The Nature of Chaliapin's talent*. Leningrad 1973, p. 86
145 Chaliapin, F. I.: *Mask and Soul*, pp. 69–70
146 'Chaliapin as Boris Godunov', *Wiener Zeitung*, May 20th, 1927
147 An Englishman: 'The greatest actor of our time', July 25th, 1914. Press Cuttings, Theatre Museum, London.
148 Stark, Edward: *Chaliapin*. Petersburg 1915, pp. 30–31
149 Chaliapin, F. I.: *Mask and Soul*, p. 72
150 Chaliapin, F. I.: Ibidem, p. 73
151 Chaliapin, F. I.: *Pages from my life* in *F. I. Chaliapin*, vol. 1, p. 133
152 Chaliapina, Irina: *Tales of my mother* in *F. I. Chaliapin*, vol. 2, p. 11
153 Chaliapina, Irina: Ibidem, p. 10
154 Korovin, Konstantin: *Chaliapin*, Paris 1939, p. 22
155 Chaliapin, F. I.: *Mask and Soul*, p. 76
156 Korovin, Konstantin: *Chaliapin*, pp. 17–18
157 Mamontov, Vsevolod: *Memoirs of Russian Artists*. Moscow 1950, pp. 60–61
158 Chaliapin, F. I.: *Mask and Soul*, p. 79
159 Yurev, Yuri: *Memoirs*, p. 559

Chapter II

1 Chaliapin, F. I.: *Mask and Soul – my forty years in the theatre*. Contemporary notes. Paris 1932, pp. 77–78

2 Shkafer, V. P.: *Forty years on the Russian operatic stage*. Leningrad 1936, pp. 142–143

3 Chaliapin, F. I. *Mask and Soul*, p. 84

4 Correspondence of S. I. Mamontov. Theatre Museum named after Bakhrushin. Manuscript section no. 63717, Moscow

5 Mamontov, V. S.: *Reminiscences about Russian painters*. Moscow 1950, p. 63

6 Draft of letter from K. S. Stanislavsky to S. I. Mamontov, TSGALI SSSR Moskva (Central State Archive of Literature and Art of the USSR Moscow). Mamontov archive no. 799, entry 1, book 505/9, folio 4

7 Stanislavsky, K. S.: Collected works in 8 volumes, vol. 6. Moscow 1954–1959, pp. 96–97

8 Ibidem, vol. 1, p. 83

9 Salina, N. V.: *Life and Stage*. Moscow-Leningrad 1941, p. 62

10 Quoted from the book by M. Yankovsky: *Chaliapin and Russian operatic culture*. Leningrad-Moscow 1947, p. 61

11 Salina, N. V.: *Life and Stage*, pp. 61–62

12 Nelidov, V. A.: *Theatrical Moscow*. Berlin-Riga 1931, pp. 108–109

13 Chaliapin, F. I.: *Mask and Soul*, p. 84

14 Ibidem, p. 140

15 From Chaliapin archive. 'Teatr', Moscow, March 1973, p. 104

16 'Mr. Chaliapin greatest operatic artist'. Obituary, *The Times*, London, April 13th 1938

17 Shkafer, V. P.: *Forty years on the Russian operatic stage*, pp. 132–133

18 Salina, N. V.: *Life and Stage*, p. 68

19 Stanislavsky, K. S.: *My Life in Art*. Moscow-Leningrad 1941, p. 33

20 Mamontov, P. I.: 'Savva Ivanovich Mamontov'. Typescript TSGALI SSSR, Moscow Archive No. 799: entry 1, book 4, folio 107

21 Cui, César: 'Farewell performances of the Moscow Private Russian Opera'. *Novaya birzhevaya gazeta*, April 22nd 1898

22 Rimsky-Korsakov, N. A.: Complete Works, vol. 1. Moscow 1955, p. 212

23 Rimsky-Korsakov, N. A.: *Chronicles of my musical life*. Moscow 1955, p. 209

24 Ippolitov-Ivanov, M. M.: *Fifty years of Russian music in my recollections*. Moscow 1934, p. 95

25 'The Snow Maiden'. *Novosti dnya*, September 9th, 1896

26 Kruglikov, Semyon: 'The Snow Maiden', *Novosti dnya*, September 10th, 1896

27 Kochetov, N.: 'History of Private Opera in Russia', TSGALI SSSR, Moscow. Archive S. I. Zimin: no. 764, book 1, item 213

28 Ibidem

29 Mamontov, P. N.: 'Savva Ivanovich Mamontov'. Typescript TSGALI SSSR, Moscow. Archive no. 799, book 1, item 367; book 2, item 4

30 Lossky, V. A.: *Memoirs, articles and speeches*. Moscow 1959, p. 151

31 Chaliapin, F. I.: *Mask and Soul*, p. 76

32 Ibidem, pp. 79–80

33 'Chaliapin alive and well'. *Musical America*, New York, February 14th 1920

34 Stark, Edward: *Chaliapin*. Petersburg 1915, pp. 275–276

35 Weer, Richard: 'Wenn Chaliapin zu singen begann …' *New Yorker Staats Zeitung*, April 17th 1938

36 Makovsky, Sergei: *Portraits of contemporaries*. The Chekhov Press, New York 1955, p. 189
37 Rumyantsev, P. I.: *Stanislavsky and Opera*. Moscow 1969, p. 187
38 Chaliapin, F. I.: *Pages from my life* in *Fedor Ivanovich Chaliapin*, vol. 1: Literary works, letters. Moscow 1976, pp. 137–138
39 Ibidem, p. 142
40 Stasov, V. V.: 'Boundless Joy', in *Fedor Ivanovich Chaliapin*, vol. 3: Articles, comments, additions. Moscow 1979, pp. 10–11
41 'Chaliapin's benefit performance'. *Novosti dnya*, February 26th 1899
42 Strakhova-Ermans, Varvara: 'Singing' Paris 1945, in *F. I. Chaliapin*, vol. 1, p. 633
43 Plotnikov, B. E.: 'Chaliapin in America', in *F. I. Chaliapin*, vol. 2, Moscow 1977, p. 506
44 Nikulin, L.: *Fedor Chaliapin*. Moscow 1954, pp. 137–9
45 *Peterburgskaya gazeta* 1911, no. 309
46 Hurok, Sol: *Impresario*. Macdonald & Co., London 1947, p. 51
47 Vertinsky, Alexandr: *Memoirs of a Russian Pierrot*. New York 1982, p. 82
48 *Fedor Ivanovich Chaliapin*: articles, comments, memoirs about Chaliapin, vol. 2. Moscow 1958, p. 421
49 Buchkin, P. C.: *What I remember*. Leningrad 1962, p. 134
50 Chaliapin, F. I.: *Mask and Soul*, pp. 84–85
51 TSGALI SSSR Moscow. Archive 964, book 1, item 24, folios 22–23
52 Stark, Edward: *Chaliapin*, p. 139
53 Engel, Yuri: *Through the eyes of a contemporary*. Collected articles. Moscow 1971, p. 37
54 'Judith'. *Russkoe slovo*. November 25th, 1898, no. 329
55 Nikulin, L.: *Fedor Chaliapin*, p. 50
56 *Fedor Ivanovich Chaliapin* (*biography and stage creations*). Moscow 1915, p. 61
57 Buchkin, P. D.: *What I remember*, p. 136
58 Chaliapin, F. I.: *Mask and Soul*, p. 86
59 *Fedor Ivanovich Chaliapin* (*biography and stage creations*), p. 61
60 Ibidem, p. 60
61 Timofeev, G.: '*Judith* with F. I. Chaliapin'. Petersburg *Rech'* November 12th, 1908. Quoted from the book by Yu. Kotlyarov and V. Garmash: *Chronicle of the life and career of F. I. Chaliapin*, vol. 1, p. 288
62 Newmarch, Rosa: *The Russian Opera*. Herbert Jenkins Ltd., London 1914, pp. 390–391
63 Orlovskaya, A.: 'Chaliapin and young singers' in *F. I. Chaliapin*, vol. 2. Moscow 1958, pp. 520–521
64 Pokhitonov, Daniil: *From the past of Russian opera*. In *F. I Chaliapin*, vol. 2, p. 240
65 Kashkin, Nikolai: 'A Life for the Tsar'. *Russkie vedomosti*, September 29th, 1896
66 Kruglikov, Semyon: 'A Life for the Tsar'. *Sem'ya*, 1896, no. 29
67 Stark, Edward: *Chaliapin*, pp. 170–174
68 Chaliapin, F. I.: *Mask and Soul*, p. 81
69 Doroshevich, Vlas: in *Fedor Ivanovich Chaliapin* (*biography and stage creations*), p. 72
70 Belyaev, Yuri: Ibidem, p. 73
71 Makovsky, Sergei: *Portraits of contemporaries*. New York 1955, p. 174
72 Kollar, V. A.: '187 days of Chaliapin's life'. *Volgo-Vyatskoe izdatelstvo* 1967, p. 31

73 Chaliapin, F. I.: *Pages from my life* in *F. I Chaliapin*, vol. 1, p. 136
74 Ibidem
75 'Behind the scenes at Covent Garden'. *Weekly Despatch*, June 24th, 1928
76 Interview with Chaliapin. *Narodni listy*, Prague, December 25th, 1929
77 Quoted in book by A. Gozenpud: *Russian opera theatre and Chaliapin, 1890–1904*. Leningrad 1974, p. 132
78 Kashkin, Nikolai: 'Theatre and music'. *Russkie vedomosti*, October 5th, 1897
79 Gozenpud, A.: *Russian opera theatre and Chaliapin 1890–1904*, p. 139
80 Wittenham: Letter to the editor of *The Times*, 'Impressions of the season'. *The Times*, London July 4th 1928
81 'Rusalka'. *Russkie vedomosti*, October 3rd, 1896
82 Stark, Edward: in *Fedor Ivanovich Chaliapin (biography and stage creations)*, p. 59
83 Belyaev, Yuri: Ibidem, p. 59
84 Kruglikov, Semyon: 'Rusalka'. *Moskovskie vedomosti* 1896, no. 272
85 *Fedor Ivanovich Chaliapin (biography and stage creations)*, p. 66
86 Balliman, Raymond: 'Ami du peuple du soir'. Paris, May 29th, 1932
87 Rosenfeld, Semyon: *Story about Chaliapin*. Leningrad 1966, p. 149
88 Kruglikov, Semyon: 'Prince Igor', *Novosti dnya* 1896, no. 4851
89 Feschotte, Jacques: *Ce Géant: Féodor Chaliapine*. La Table Ronde, Paris 1968, pp. 121–122
90 Van Vechten, Carl: *Interpreters and Interpretations*. Alfred Knopf, New York 1917, p. 112
91 Nesterov, Mikhail: *Far away days*. Moscow 1959, p. 248
92 'The Art of Chaliapin. Action and Song. The secret of his Appeal'. *The Times*. London June 6th, 1914
93 Chaliapin, F. I.: *Pages from my life* in *F. I. Chaliapin*, vol. 1, p. 138
94 Ibidem
95 Ibidem
96 See Gozenpud, A.: *Russian opera theatre and Chaliapin 1890–1904*, p. 141
97 Kliuchevsky, Vasili: Works in 8 volumes. Moscow 1957, vol. 2, pp. 186–187
98 Chaliapin, F. I.: *Mask and Soul*, pp. 17–18
99 Ivanov, Mikhail: *Novoe vremya* 1898, no. 7934
100 Chaliapin, F. I. *Mask and Soul*, pp. 17–18
101 See Kovalevsky, P. I.: *Ivan the Terrible and his mental state*. St. Petersburg 1893
102 Stasov, V. V.: 'Kurinaya slepota' (Night blindness) in *F. I. Chaliapin (biography and stage creations)*, p. 68
103 Chaliapin, F. I.: *Mask and Soul*, p. 118
104 Quoted by Drankov, V. in his book, *The nature of Chaliapin's talent*. Leningrad 1973, p. 166
105 Ibidem
106 Turgenev, Ivan Sergeievich: Complete Works. Moscow 1967, vol. 14, p. 247
107 Chaliapin, F. I.: *Pages from my life* in *F. I Chaliapin*, vol. 1, p. 138
108 Rimsky-Korsakov, N. A.: *Chronicle of my musical life*. Moscow 1955, p. 276
109 Quoted from the book by Gozenpud, A.: *Russian opera theatre of the 19th century*. Leningrad 1973, pp. 51–52
110 Quoted from the book by Gozenpud, A.: *Russian opera theatre and Chaliapin*. Leningrad 1974, p. 144
111 Chaliapin, F. I.: *Pages from my life* in *F. I. Chaliapin*, vol. 1, p. 138
112 Chaliapin, F. I. *Mask and Soul*, pp. 87–89

113 Feschotte, Jacques: *Ce Géant, Féodor Chaliapine*, p. 130
114 Nesterov, Mikhail: *Far away days*, p. 219
115 Stark, Edward: *Chaliapin*, p. 121
116 Chaliapin, F. I.: *Mask and Soul*, pp. 117–118
117 Lipaev, Ivan: *Teatral* 1897, no. 101. p. 106
118 An Englishman: 'The Greatest Actor of our Time'. July 25th 1914. Press cuttings, Theatre Museum, London
119 Stasov, Vladimir: 'Chaliapin in Petersburg'. *Novosti*, October 30th, 1903, no. 306
120 Mamontov, Pavel: 'Memories of Chaliapin' in *F. I Chaliapin*, vol. 2, p. 120
121 Nesterov, Mikhail: *Far away days*, p. 249
122 Cui, César: Selected articles Moscow 1954, p. 33
123 Ibidem
124 Mussorgsky, M.: Literary works. Moscow 1971, vol. 1, p. 227
125 Rimsky-Korsakov, N. A.: Literary works and correspondence. Collected works. Moscow 1963, vol. 2, p. 15
126 Engel, Yuri: 'Russian Opera and Chaliapin', in *F. I. Chaliapin*, vol. 3, p. 22
127 Findeizen, Nikolai: *Russkaya musikal'naya gazeta* 1897, no. 2, p. 296
128 K.-O. *Nizhegorodski listok*, March 8th, 1897
129 Chaliapin, F. I.: *Pages from my life* in *F. I. Chaliapin*, vol. 1, p. 146
130 *Ibidem*, pp. 146–147
131 *Ibidem*
132 Chaliapin, F. I.: *Mask and Soul*, pp. 168–169
133 Chaliapin, F. I.: *Pages from my life* in *F. I. Chaliapin*, vol. 1, p. 149
134 Filatova, Yulya: *Memories of Rachmaninov*. Collected materials. New York 1946, p. 106
135 Somova, Elena: Ibidem, p. 83
136 Chaliapin, F. I.: *Mask and Soul*, p. 155
137 Pribytkova, I.: *Memories of Rachmaninov*, Moscow, vol. 2, p. 97
138 Korganov, V. D.: Articles, memoirs, travel notes. Erevan 1968, pp. 242–243
139 Nemenova-Lunz, M. S.: 'My encounters with Chaliapin' in *F. I. Chaliapin*, vol. 2, p. 271
140 Teleshev, Nikolai: 'From a writer's notes'. Collection *Memories of Rachmaninov*, Moscow, vol. 2, p. 44
141 Chaliapin, F. I.: *Pages from my life* in *F. I. Chaliapin*, vol. 1, p. 139
142 Rozhanskaya-Vinter, E. R.: *Memories of Rachmaninov*, vol. 2, p. 23
143 Chaliapin, F. I.: *Pages from my life* in *F. I. Chaliapin*, vol. 1, p. 141
144 Ibidem, p. 154
145 Chaliapin, F. I.: *Mask and Soul*, pp. 49–50
146 Ibidem, p. 61
147 Ibidem, p. 52
148 Chaliapin, F. I.: Letter to Stasov, January 7th, 1899, in *F. I. Chaliapin*, vol. 1, p. 373
149 Chaliapin, F. I.: *Mask and Soul*, p. 14
150 Ibidem, pp. 15–16–17
151 Ibidem, p. 165
152 Ibidem, p. 67
153 Chaliapin, F. I.: 'The singer on the operatic stage', in *F. I. Chaliapin*, vol. 1, p. 307
154 *Quoted from the book by Yankovsky, M. O.: Chaliapin and Russian operatic culture*. Leningrad-Moscow 1947, p. 78

155 Archives of A. N. Rimsky-Korsakov. XXII, no. 79. Leningrad, Institute of Theatre, Music and Cinema: Manuscripts section
156 Ibidem
157 Shkafer, Vasili: *Forty years on the Russian operatic stage*, pp. 153–154
158 *Nature and significance of schism in Russia*. St. Petersburg 1881, p. 10
159 Chaliapin, F. I.: *Pages from my life* in *F. I. Chaliapin*, vol. 1, p. 141
160 Kashkin, N.: 'Khovanshchina'. *Russkie vedomosti* 1897, no. 329
161 Plevako, S.: 'Khovanshchina'. *Novosti sezona* 1897, no. 384
162 Van Vechten, Carl: *Interpreters and Interpretations*, p. 111
163 Findeizen, Nikolai: *Russkie vedomosti* 1897, no. 329
164 Cui, César: *Novosti*, 1898, no. 54
165 'Pskovitanka' *Sankt Peterburgskie vedomosti*, February 26th, 1898
166 Rimsky-Korsakov, V. N.: 'Fedor Ivanovich Chaliapin at the Rimsky-Korsakov's', in *F. I. Chaliapin*, vol. 2, p. 167
167 Shkafer, V. P.: *Forty years on the Russian operatic stage*, p. 158
168 Quoted from the book by Raskin, A.: *Chaliapin and Russian painters*, Leningrad-Moscow 1963, p. 45
169 Levik, Sergei: *Notebooks of an opera singer*. Moscow 1962, p. 528
170 Chaliapin, F. I.: *Pages from my life* in *F. I. Chaliapin*, vol. 1, p. 142
171 Pokhitonov, Daniil. *From the past of Russian opera* in *F. I. Chaliapin*, vol. 2, p. 246
172 Chaliapin, F. I.: *Pages from my life*, p. 142
173 Mamontov, S. I. to Rimsky-Korsakov, N. A.: 25th November 1898. Leningrad public library named after Saltykov-Shchedrin: Archive N. Rimsky-Korsakov. Published in the book by Gozenpud, A.: *Russian opera theatre and Chaliapin 1890–1904*, p. 194
174 Engel, Yuri.: 'Mozart and Salieri'. *Russkie vedomosti*, November 27th, 1898
175 *Chronicle of the life and career of F. I. Chaliapin*, compiled by Yu. Kotlyarov and V. Garmash, Leningrad 1985, vol. 2, p. 40
176 Nelidova-Fiveiskaya, A.: 'Ten encounters with Chaliapin in America'. *Novaya Sibyr*, Irkutsk 1957, book 36, p. 198
177 Chaliapin, F. I.: *Pages from my life* in *F. I. Chaliapin*, vol. 1, p. 143
178 Chaliapin, F. I.: *Mask and Soul*, p. 23
179 Kaplan, E.: 'Chaliapin and our generation' in *F. I. Chaliapin*, vol. 2, pp. 344–345
180 Ibidem, p. 349
181 Ibidem, p. 350
182 Ibidem, p. 350
183 Ibidem, p. 352
184 Ossovsky, A.: *Articles of musical criticism*, Leningrad 1971, p. 126
185 Kaplan, E.: 'Chaliapin and our generation', in *F. I. Chaliapin*, vol. 2, p. 353
186 Ossovsky, A. V.: 'The Mariinsky Theatre. F. I. Chaliapin', in *Articles of musical criticism*. Leningrad 1971, p. 127
187 Feschotte, Jacques: *Ce Géant: Féodor Chaliapine*, p. 147
188 Ossovsky, A. V.: 'The Mariinsky Theatre, F. I. Chaliapin', in *Articles of musical criticism*, p. 356
189 Siegfried (Edward Stark): 'Chaliapin-Salieri', *Sankt-Peterburgskie vedomosti*, 13th January, 1906
190 MacCarthy, Sir Desmond: *Drama*, London 1940, p. 377
191 Old Gentleman (Amphitheatrov): review of 'Mozart i Salieri', in *Teatral'nyi album*, *Rossiya*, August 12th, 1901, no. 824
192 Ibidem

193 Ossovsky, A. V.: *Articles of musical criticism*, p. 350

194 Kashkin, Nikolai: 'Triad of operas on the stage of the new theatre'. *Moskovskie vedomosti*, November 14th, 1901

195 Dialogue between Lord Harewood and David Lloyd-Jones, *Boris Godunov* programme notes, ENO London 1980

196 Stasov, V. V.: Letters to relatives, Moscow 1954, vol. 1, part 2, p. 98

197 ENO programme, London 1980

198 Glazunov, A. K.: 'Letter to M. M. Ippolitov-Ivanov', September 4th, 1926. In Pazovski, A. M.: *Memoirs of a conductor*. Moscow 1966, p. 118

199 Abbado, Claudio: Conversation with the author on the occasion of Royal Opera House Covent Garden production of *Boris Godunov*, October 10th, 1983

200 Stanislavsky, K. S.: 'Letter to Hengood', March 22nd, 1928. In the collection 'Stanislavsky – reformer of operatic art'. Moscow 1983, p. 159

201 Chaliapin, F. I.: 'On Boris', *New York Times*, May 18th, 1932

202 Stasov, Vladimir: 'Boris Godunov', *Novosti i birzhevaya gazeta* 1896, no. 332

203 *Sovietskaya musika* 1959, no. 3, pp. 54–55

204 Chaliapin, F. I.: *Pages from my life* in *F. I. Chaliapin*, vol. 2 p. 139

205 Shkafer, Vasili: *Forty years on the Russian operatic stage*, p. 166

206 Chaliapin, F. I.: *Mask and Soul*, pp. 100–101

207 Vasilenko, Sergei: *Pages of memories*. Moscow 1949, p. 158

208 Chaliapin, F. I.: *Pages from my life* in *F. I. Chaliapin*, vol. 2, p. 140

209 Ibidem

210 Kliuchevski, V. O.: Works in 8 volumes, Moscow 1957, vol. 2, p. 23

211 Chaliapin, F. I.: *Pages from my life* in *F. I. Chaliapin*, vol. 2, p. 140

212 'Gor'kovskie chteniya' (Gorky readings), Moscow 1954, p. 74

213 *Moskovski listok* 1898, no. 342

214 Buchkin, P. D.: *What I remember*. Leningrad 1963, p. 137

215 Chaliapin, F. I.: 'The Singer's Art'. *Etude Music Magazine*, New York. January 1936, p. 8

216 Quoted from the book by Gozenpud, A.: *Russian opera theatre and Chaliapin 1890–1904*, p. 208

217 Leningrad public library named after Saltykov-Shchedrin: Archive Rimsky-Korsakov, folio 640, p. 10

218 Engel, Yuri: *Russkie vedomosti* 1898, no. 280

219 Ossovsky, A. V.: *Articles of musical criticism*, p. 104

220 Rozanov, Edward: *Novosti dnya* 1898, no. 5579

221 Russian musical newspaper. St. Petersburg 1899, no. 1, pp. 352–353

222 Yankovski, M. O.: 'Boris Godunov', *Kievlyanin* 1902, no. 75

223 Chaliapin, F. I.: *Pages from my life* in *F. I. Chaliapin*, vol. 1, p. 142

224 Ibidem, p. 140

225 Chaliapin, F. I.: *Mask and Soul*, p. 356

226 Theatre and Music. *Novoe vremya*, January 30th, 1899

227 Chaliapin, F. I.: *Pages from my life* in *F. I. Chaliapin*, vol. 1, p. 146

228 Strakhova-Ermans, Varvara: 'Memories of Chaliapin'. *The New Review*, New York 1953, p. 247

229 Chaliapin, F. I.: *Pages from my life* in *F. I. Chaliapin*, vol. 1, p. 146

230 Telyakovsky, Vladimir: *My colleague Chaliapin*, Leningrad-Moscow 1965, pp. 354–355

231 Chaliapin, F. I.: *Mask and Soul*, p. 55

232 Chaliapin, F. I.: Letter to Stasov on April 7th, 1899, in *F. I. Chaliapin*, vol. 1, p. 372

233 Rimsky-Korsakov, N. A.: *Chronicles of my musical life*, p. 212
234 Quoted from the book by Koller, V. A.: *Chaliapin on the Volga*, Gorki 1982, p. 80
235 Quoted from the book by Yankovsky, M.: *Chaliapin*, p. 170

Chapter III

1 Stuart, N.: 'Chaliapin on the public stage'. *Moskovskie vedomosti* October 8th, 1899, no. 277
2 Telyakovsky, V. A.: *Memoirs*. Leningrad-Moscow 1965, p. 356
3 'Faust'. *Russkie vedomosti*, September 25th, 1899
4 V. B.: 'Chaliapin's début'. *Peterburgskaya gazeta*, December 21st, 1899
5 Telyakovsky, V. A.: *Memoirs*, p. 136
6 Ibidem, p. 356
7 Chaliapin, F. I.: *Pages from my life* in *Fedor Ivanovich Chaliapin*, vol. 1: Literary works, letters. Moscow 1976, p. 146
8 Telyakovsky, V. A.: *Memoirs*, pp. 352–353
9 Quoted from *Chronicle of the life and career of F. I. Chaliapin*, compiled by Yu. Kotlyarov and V. Garmash. Leningrad 1984, book 1, p. 130
10 Sobinov, Leonid Vital'evich: Letters. Moscow 1970, vol. 1, p. 72
11 *Russkie vedomosti*, October 1st, 1899, no. 271
12 Chaliapin, F. I.: *Pages from my life*, p. 146
13 *Pages from my life* – an autobiography by Fedor Ivanovich Chaliapin (authorised translation by H. M. Buck). Revised, enlarged and edited by Katharine Wright. New York and London 1927, pp. 210–211
14 Salina, N. V.: *Life and Stage*. Leningrad-Moscow 1941, pp. 111–112
15 Ibidem, p. 153
16 *Chronicle of the life and career of Chaliapin*, p. 156
17 Kashkin, N.: 'Moscow Musical Year'. *Moskovskie vedomosti*, January 7th, 1900
18 Stuart, N.: 'Chaliapin on the public stage'. *Moskovskie vedomosti*, October 8th, 1899
19 Kashkin, N.: 'Moscow Musical Year'. *Moskovskie vedomosti*, January 14th, 1900
20 Engel, Yuri: 'Russian Opera and Chaliapin'. *Russkie vedomosti*, September 28th, 1899
21 Chaliapin, F. I.: *Mask and Soul – my forty years in the theatre*. Contemporary notes, Paris 1932, pp. 351–352
22 Hammond, A.: Interview, London April 13th 1983
23 Engel, Yuri: *Russian opera and Chaliapin*
24 *The Russian Opera*, by Rosa Newmarch. Herbert Jenkins Ltd., London 1914
25 Chaliapin, F. I.: *Mask and Soul*, p. 94
26 Kashkin, N.: *Moskovskie vedomosti*, January 7th and 14th, 1900
27 Belyaev, Yuri: *Fedor Ivanovich Chaliapin* (*biography and stage creations*). Rampa i zhizn 1915, p. 78
28 'Famous interpreters of the best roles of their repertoire'. *Musica*, Paris July 1912, no. 118, reprinted in the periodical 'Teatr', Moscow June 1983, no. 6
29 Stark, Edward: 'Mephistopheles-Chaliapin'. *Rossiya*, August 5th, 1901, no. 817
30 Kashkin, N.: 'Theatre and Music'. *Russkie vedomosti*, October 5th, 1897
31 Baskin, V. S.: 'Chaliapin-Mephistopheles', in *Fedor Ivanovich Chaliapin* (*biography and stage creations*), p. 74

32 *Musica*, Paris, June 1912
33 Quoted from the book by A. Gozenpud: *Russian opera theatre between two revolutions*. Leningrad 1975, p. 34
34 *Musica*, Paris June 1912
35 Chaliapin, F. I.: *Mask and Soul*, pp. 81–82
36 Stuart, N.: 'Chaliapin on the public stage'. *Moskovskie vedomosti*, October 1899, no. 277
37 *Fedor Ivanovich Chaliapin (biography and stage creations)*, p. 73
38 Stark, Edward: *Chaliapin*. Petrograd 1915, p. 82
39 Chaliapin, F. I.: 'A singer on the operatic stage' in *F. I. Chaliapin*, vol. 1, p. 306.
40 Ibidem
41 Quoted from the book by A. Gozenpud: *Russian opera theatre between two revolutions*, p. 35
42 *Musica*, Paris, July 1912, no. 118
43 Siegfried: *Rossiya*, August 5th, 1901, no. 817; *Faust* translation by Louis Mac-Neice, Faber & Faber Ltd, London
44 *Fedor Ivanovich Chaliapin (biography and stage creations)*, p. 74
45 *Nizhegorodskii listok*, August 26th, 1901, no. 245
46 Stark, E.: *Chaliapin*, pp. 81–82
47 Gozenpud, A.: *Russian opera theatre between two revolutions*, p. 39
48 Ossovsky, A. V.: *Articles of musical criticism (1894–1912)*. Leningrad 1971, p. 102
49 Gozenpud, A.: *Russian opera theatre between two revolutions*, p. 39
50 'Faust': *Observer*, June 24th, 1928
51 Belyaev, Yuri: 'Chaliapin in *Faust*', in *F. I. Chaliapin (biography and stage creations)*, p. 53
52 Stark, Edward: *Chaliapin*, p. 88
53 Levik, S.: *Memoirs of an opera singer*, p. 510
54 E. N.: 'The Devil of the Week'. *Sunday Times*, June 24th, 1928
55 Levik, S.: *Memoirs of an opera singer*, p. 495
56 *Fedor Ivanovich Chaliapin (biography and stage creations)*, pp. 74–75
57 Lauri-Volpi, Giacomo: *Voci parallele*. Garzanti, Milan 1955, p. 188
58 'Faust'. *Kievskoe slovo* 1902, no. 1, p. 17
59 *Russkaya musikal'naya gazeta* 1900, no. 1, p. 17. Quoted from the book by A. Gozenpud: *Russian opera theatre between two revolutions*, p. 42
60 Stark, Edward: *Chaliapin*, p. 90
61 Lehman, Lotte: 'Twelve singers and a conductor – Chaliapin' in *Opera 66*, edited by Charles Osborne. Alan Ross, London, p. 70
62 *Musica*, Paris, July 1912, no. 118
63 *Nizhegorodskii listok* 1902, no. 232
64 Ibidem
65 'Faust': *Gazzeta dei teatri*, Milan, March 10th, 1904
66 Stark, Edward: *Chaliapin*, p. 91
67 Levinson, André: *Comoedia*, December 23rd, 1932
68 B.-N. N.: 'A great Mephisto'. *Daily Telegraph*, June 23rd, 1928
69 Chaliapin, F. I.: *Pages from my life*, p. 154
70 Gatti-Casazza, Giulio: *Memories of the opera*. John Calder, London 1977, p. 115; © 1941 Leon Schaefler, and ancillary executor; copyright renewed © 1969 estate of Gatti-Cassazza. Reprinted with the permission of Charles Scribner's Sons.
71 Doroshevich, V. M.: 'Chaliapin at La Scala'. *Rossiya*, St Petersburg, March 27th, 1901, no. 676
72 Gatti-Casazza, G.: *Memories of the opera*, pp. 115–116

73 Letter of June 14th (27th), 1900, in the book *Vasili Kalinnikov* – letters, documents, material. Moscow 1959, vol. 2, p. 251

74 Chaliapin, F. I.: *Pages from my life*, p. 155

75 Chaliapin, F. I.: Interview with the periodical *Musica*, Paris July 1912, no. 118

76 M.: 'Great singer thrilled by Covent Garden'. *Daily Chronicle*, May 27th, 1926

77 Chaliapin, F. I.: *Pages from my life*, p. 155

78 Ibidem

79 Ibidem

80 Ibidem

81 Ibidem, p. 156

82 Ibidem, p. 160

83 Gatti-Casazza, G.: *Memories of the opera*, p. 118

84 M. K.: 'Essay on the life and career of Fedor Ivanovich Chaliapin'. Moscow 1903, pp. 60–61

85 Gatti-Casazza, G.: *Memories of the opera*, p. 118

86 Chaliapin, F. I.: *Pages from my life*, pp. 157–158

87 Ibidem, p. 158

88 M. K.: 'Essay on the life and career of Fedor Ivanovich Chaliapin', pp. 61–63

89 Doroshevich, V. M.: 'Chaliapin at La Scala'. *Rossiya*, St Petersburg, March 27th, 1901, no. 676

90 Masini, Angelo: Letter to the newspaper *Novoe vremya*, St Petersburg March 15th (28th), 1901, no. 996

91 *Gazetta musicale di Milano*, March 21st, 1901, no. 12

92 *Il Trovatore*. Milan March 23rd, 1901, no. 13

93 Gigli, Beniamino: *Memoirs*. Cassell and Company Ltd., London 1957, p. 131

94 N. F.: 'Music of the Week – Chaliapin'. *The Observer*, May 30th, 1926

95 Letter to V. A. Tikhonov, March 19th, 1901 in *F. I. Chaliapin*, vol. 1, p. 403

96 M. K.: 'Essay on the life and career of Fedor Ivanovich Chaliapin', p. 59

97 Chaliapin, F. I.: *Pages from my life*, p. 166

98 M. K.: 'Essay on the life and career of F. I. Chaliapin', p. 63

99 'Mefistofele, Boito'. *Gazetta musicale di Milano*, March 28th, 1901, no. 14

100 Chaliapin, F. I.: *Pages from my life*, p. 166

101 Ibidem

102 Ibidem, p. 169

103 Ibidem, p. 180

104 Telyakovsky, V. A.: *Memoirs*, pp. 360–361

105 Kashkin, N.: 'Private opera stages'. *Ruskoe slovo*, April 9th, 1907

106 Stark, Edward: *Chaliapin*, p. 72

107 *Fedor Ivanovich Chaliapin* (*biography and stage creations*), p. 78

108 Chaliapin, F. I.: *Pages from my life*, p. 179

109 Ibidem

110 Ibidem, p. 178

111 Telyakovsky, V. A: *Memoirs*, p. 360

112 'At Chaliapin's'. *Peterburgskaya gazeta*, April 1st, 1911, no. 288

113 K. I.: Bolshoi Teatr. 'Boris Godunov'. *Ruskoe slovo*, January 19th, 1902, no. 18

114 Kruglikov, Semyon: 'Boris Godunov'. *Novosti dnya*, April 15th, 1901, no. 6499

115 Chaliapin, F. I.: *Pages from my life*, pp. 207–208

116 Old Gentleman (Amphiteatrov, A.), *Teatral'nyi album*. *Rossiya*, June 7th, 1901

117 Bunin, I. A.: *Memoirs*, chapter entitled 'Chaliapin'. La Renaissance, Paris 1950, pp. 112–114

118 Conversations with Cardus by Robin Daniels. Gollancz, London 1976, p. 106

119 Chaliapin, F. I.: *Mask and Soul*, p. 352
120 Malkov, N.: 'Guest artist per natura'. *Teatr i iskusstvo* 1915, no. 40, p. 732
121 Strakhova-Ermans, V.: 'Memories of Chaliapin', *Novyi Zhurnal* – The New Review. New York 1953, vol. xxxiv, p. 248
122 Conversations with Cardus, p. 103
123 Frankenstein: 'Chaliapin Great in Song Recital'. *San Francisco Chronicle*, April 2nd, 1935
124 'The week's music', *Jewish Guardian*, London June 4th, 1926
125 Engel, Yuri: 'The Power of Evil' (Bolshoi Teatr) *Russkie vedomosti*, October 2nd, 1902
126 Ossovsky, A.: 'Memoirs, essays'. Moscow 1971, p. 42
127 Stravinksy, I. F.: 'Dialogues'. Leningrad 1971, p. 61
128 Yastrebstev, V. V.: *Memoirs* – Rimsky-Korsakov, N. A. Leningrad 1960, vol. 2, p. 223
129 Rimsky-Korsakov, N. A.: *Chronicle of my musical life*. Moscow 1955, p. 209
130 Telyakovsky, V. A.: *Memoirs*, pp. 392–393
131 'Boris Godunov', *Nizhegorodskii listok*, September 2nd, 1901
132 Yankovskii, K.: 'Boris Godunov'. *Kievlyanin* April 1st, 1902, no. 75
133 'Boris Godunov'. *Novoe vremya*, August 22nd, 1904, no. 10228
134 Thompson, Oscar: *Musical American*, New York 1921, no. 8, vol. XXXV, p. 13
135 Newman, Ernest: 'Music of the day', *Glasgow Herald*, June 28th, 1928
136 Kaplan, E.: *Life in the music theatre*, Leningrad 1961, p. 38
137 Chaliapin, F. I.: *Mask and Soul*, pp. 166–167
138 Sheean, Vincent: 'Chaliapin remembers'. *New York Herald Tribune*, December 25th, 1932
139 Chaliapin, F. I.: *Mask and Soul*, p. 140
140 Kashkin, N.: 'Boris Godunov'. *Moskovskie vedomosti*, April 15th, 1901, no. 102
141 Kashkin, N.: 'Boris Godunov'. *Moskovskiye vedomosti*, January 20th, 1902, no. 20
142 Chaliapin, F. I.: *Mask and Soul*, p. 18
143 Levik, S. Y.: *Memoirs of an opera singer*. Moscow 1962, p. 505
144 Capell, Richard: 'Chaliapin, the greatest opera actor'. *Daily Mail*, London July 2nd, 1914
145 Levik, S. Y.: *Memoirs of an opera singer*, p. 505
146 Stark, Edward (Siegfried): *Chaliapin*, p. 28
147 Toye, Francis: 'Chaliapin in Boris Godunov'. *The Graphic*, July 14th, 1928
148 David Bicknell's personal recollection of conversations with Sacha Guitry and Yvonne Printemps in London (1927), as quoted in letter to author of July 10th, 1985
149 Ossovsky, A.: 'Boris Godunov'. *Slovo*, August 20th, 1905, no. 230
150 Ozerov, N. V.: 'The lessons of Chaliapin' in *F. I. Chaliapin*, vol. 2, p. 531
151 Marcato: 'Chaliapin in his greatest part'. *Evening News*, June 29th, 1928
152 Stark, Edward (Siegfried): *Chaliapin*, p. 99
153 Steimann, M. O.: 'F. I. Chaliapin – My work with him', Moscow 1947. *Vserossiskoe teatral'noe obshchestvo*: Section of music theatres, manuscript
154 'Chaliapin as Boris Godunov'. *Neue freie Press*, Vienna May 19th, 1927
155 Nesterov, I.: *Teatr i iskusstvo* 1904, no. 35, p. 637
156 Schneider, Louis: *Le Theatre*. Paris 1908, no. 230, p. 8
157 Chaliapin, F. I.: *Mask and Soul*, p. 102
158 Stark, Edward (Siegfried): *Chaliapin*, p. 106

159 Cherkasov, N. K.: *Memories of Chaliapin* in *F. I. Chaliapin*, vol. 2, Moscow 1977, p. 409
160 Chaliapin, F. I.: *Mask and Soul*, p. 109
161 *Alexander Benois reflects . . .* Moscow 1968, pp. 495–496
162 Chaliapin, F. I.: *Mask and Soul*, p. 110
163 Cherkasov, N. K.: *Memories of Chaliapin*, vol. 2, p. 410
164 Stark, Edward (Siegfried): *Chaliapin*, p. 109
165 Cook, Ida (alias Mary Burchell): *We followed our stars*. Harlequin, Mills and Boon Ltd., Canada 1976, pp. 41–42
166 'The week's music', *Sunday Times*, June 16th, 1929
167 Stark, Edward (Siegfried): *Chaliapin*, p. 110
168 Cherkasov, N. K.: *Memories of Chaliapin*, vol. 2, p. 411
169 Asafev, B.: *Chaliapin* in *F. I. Chaliapin*, vol. 3, p. 117
170 Cherkasov, N. K.: *Memories of Chaliapin*, vol. 2, p. 411
171 Pinza, Ezio: *An autobiography*. Rinehart and Company, New York – Toronto 1958, p. 176
172 Cherkasov, N. K.: *Memories of Chaliapin*, vol. 2, p. 412
173 Ibidem, p. 413
174 Capell, Richard: 'Chaliapin at his best'. *Daily Mail*, June 29th, 1928
175 Belyaev, Yuri: 'Boris Godunov'. *Novoe vremya*, January 8th, 1911, no. 12509
176 Nikulin: *Fedore Chaliapin*. Moscow 1954, pp. 180–181
177 Gavoty, B.: Preface to *Ce Géant: Féodor Chaliapine* by Jacques Feschotte, pp. 14–15
178 Deems Taylor: 'Chaliapin as Boris'. *New York World*, December 10th, 1921
179 Capell, Richard: 'Chaliapin the superb'. *Daily Mail*, June 13th, 1929
180 *Conversations with Cardus* by Robin Daniels, p. 104
181 Glebov, Igor (B. V. Asafev): 'Boris Godunov'. *Russkaya volya*, October 5th, 1917
182 Gatti-Casazza, G.: *Memories of the opera*, p. 207
183 Toye, Francis: 'Chaliapin in *Boris Godunov*'. *The Graphic*, July 14th, 1928
184 Telyakovsky, V. A.: *My colleague Chaliapin*. Leningrad 1927, p. 64
185 Telyakovsky, V. A.: *My colleague Chaliapin*. Leningrad-Moscow 1965, p. 373
186 Telyakovsky, V. A.: *Memoirs*, pp. 386–387
187 Ibidem, p. 385
188 Chaliapin, F. I.: *Mask and Soul*, p. 309
189 Telyakovksy, V. A.: *Memoirs*, p. 203
190 Ibidem, p. 202
191 Leonidov, A. D.: *Memories and Encounters*. Rampa i zhizn', Paris 1955, p. 291
192 Korovin, Konstantin: *Chaliapin*. La Renaissance, Paris 1939
193 Bunin, I. A.: *Memoirs*. La Renaissance Paris 1950, p. 110
194 *Chronicle of the life and career of F. I. Chaliapin* compiled by Yu. Kotlyarov and V. Garmash. Leningrad 1984, vol. 1; 1985, vol. 2
195 Ibidem, p. 186
196 Ibidem, p. 208
197 Ibidem, p. 157
198 Chaliapina, Irina: *Memories of my father* in *F. I. Chaliapin*, vol. 2, p. 38
199 Walz, K. F.: *Sixty-five years in the theatre*. Leningrad 1928, p. 206
200 Strakhova-Ermans, V.: 'Memories of Chaliapin', *Novyi zhurnal* – The New Review. New York 1953, book xxxiv, pp. 251–252
201 Letter to Gorky April 19th, 1913, *F. I. Chaliapin*, vol. 1, p. 352
202 Ibidem, p. 520

203 Gaisberg, F. W.: *Music on record*. Robert Hale Ltd, London 1948, p. 228
204 Chaliapin, F. I.: *Mask and Soul*, p. 321
205 Telyakovsky, V. A.: *Memoirs*, p. 398
206 Chaliapin, F. I.: *Mask and Soul*, pp. 323–324
207 Telyakovsky, V. A.: *Memoirs*, p. 402
208 Chaliapin, F. I.: Letter to Telyakovsky March 25th (April 7th), 1911, in *F. I. Chaliapin*, vol. 1, p. 435
209 'Hostile demonstration against Chaliapin'. *Kievskaya pochta*, June 12th, 1911, no. 718. (In Yu. Kotlyarov and V. Garmash, vol. 2, p. 22)
210 Chaliapin's explanation. *Kievskaya pochta*, June 21st, 1911, no. 727 (quoting French newspaper *L'Intransigeant*)
211 Telyakovsky, V. A: *Memoirs*, p. 406
212 Chaliapin, F. I.: *Mask and Soul*, p. 328
213 Gorky, M.: Letter to Chaliapin of July 1st (14th), 1911 (date established by Yu. Kotlyarov). In *F. I. Chaliapin*, vol. 1, p. 333
214 Andreeva, M. F.: Correspondence, memoirs, articles, documents. Moscow 1963, p. 171
215 Chaliapin, F. I.: *Mask and Soul*, pp. 328–329
216 Doroshevich, Vlas: 'Demon' in *Staraya teatral'naya Moskva*: selected articles. Petersburg-Moscow 1923, p. 31
217 *Fedor Ivanovich Chaliapin (biography and stage creations)* p. 62
218 Gerken, E.: 'Chaliapin's jubilee celebrations'. *Zhizn' iskusstva*, April 26th, 1919, no. 122, p. 1
219 Kruglikov, Semyon: 'Demon', *Novosti dnya*, January 18th, 1904, no. 7405
220 Belyaev, Yuri: 'Chaliapin Demon'. *Novoe vremya*, January 1st 1906, no. 10706
221 Stasov, V. V.: 'Exhibitions'. *Novosti i birzhevaya gazeta*, January 27th, 1898, no. 27
222 Benois, Alexander: *Vrubel*. Mir Iskusstva, Petersburg 1903, vol. X, pp. 177–178
223 Benois, Alexander: *Rech'*, April 3rd, 1910, no. 91
224 *Fedor Ivanovich Chaliapin (biography and stage creations)*, p. 62
225 'The Demon at the Bolshoi Theatre', *Golosa Moskvy*, January 18th, 1904, no. 19. Quoted from the book by A. Gozenpud: *Russian opera theatre between two revolutions*, Leningrad 1975, p. 47
226 Kruglikov, Semyon: 'Demon'. *Novosti dnya*, January 18th, 1904, no. 740
227 Gozenpud, A.: *Russian opera theatre between two revolutions*, p. 49
228 Zbrueva, E. I.: *Memoirs*, Musical heritage (collection of articles). Moscow 1962, vol. 1, p. 392
229 Ossovsky, A. V.: *Articles of musical criticism (1894–1912)*. Leningrad 1971, p. 132
230 Serebrov, Alexandr: *Fedor Ivanovich Chaliapin* – memories of Chaliapin. Moscow 1977, vol. 2, p. 255
231 Ossovsky, A. V.: *Articles of musical criticism*, pp. 132–133
232 Pokhitonov, D. I.: *Memories of Chaliapin*, vol. 2, p. 234
233 Ossovsky, A. V.: *Articles of musical criticism*, p. 132
234 Kolomiitsov, V. P.: 'Chaliapin-Demon'. *Molva*, Moscow January 1st, 1906 (Quoted in Yu. Kotlyarov and V. Garmash: *Chronicle of the life and career of F. I. Chaliapin*, vol. 1, p. 251)
235 Zbrueva, E. I.: *Memoirs*, p. 392
236 Salina, N. V.: *Life and stage*, pp. 117–118
237 Engel, Yuri: 'Demon' (Chaliapin's benefit performance). *Russkie vedomosti*, January 20th, 1904, no. 20

238 'Chaliapin's benefit performance', *Peterburgskii listok*, January 28th, 1907, no. 26

239 Ossovsky, A. V.: *Articles of musical criticism*, p. 133

240 Serebrov, A.: 'Demon' in *F. I. Chaliapin*, vol. 2, p. 259

241 Telyakovsky, V. A.: *Memoirs*, p. 272

242 Kolomiitsov, V.: 'Chaliapin-Demon', *Molva* January 1st, 1906

243 A. K.: AYA 'After the concert'. *Kharkovskii listok*, February 27th, 1903, no. 1005

244 Myasoedov, V.: *Kharkovskii listok*, April 30th, 1905, no. 1757

245 Chekhov's funeral. *Russkoe slovo*, July 10th, 1904

246 Archive A. M. *Gorky*. Moscow 1954–1976, vol. 5, pp. 119–120

247 Chaliapin, F. I.: *Pages from my life*, vol. 1, p. 173

248 Sobinov, L. V.: Letters. Moscow 1970, vol. 1, p. 403

249 Chaliapin, F. I.: *Pages from my life*, vol. 1, p. 174

250 Benois, Alexander: About Diaghilev. In the book *Sergei Diaghilev and Russian art:* open letters, interviews, correspondence, contemporaries on Diaghilev. Moscow 1982, vol. 2, p. 235

251 Ibidem

252 Ibidem

253 Yakovlev, I.: 'Historical Russian concerts at the Grand Opera'. *Novoe vremya*, May 9th, 1907

254 Benois, Alexander: 'Russian concerts in Paris'. *Slovo*, May 31st, 1907, no. 162

255 *Alexander Benois reflects* ..., compiled, introduced and annotated by I. S. Silberstein and A. N. Savinov. Moscow 1968, p. 501

256 *Peterburgskaya gazeta*, July 4th, 1907, no. 180

257 Rimsky-Korsakov, N. A.: *Chronicle of my musical life*. Moscow 1955, pp. 297–298

258 *Teatr i iskusstvo*, 1908, no. 16, p. 286

259 Chaliapin, F. I.: *Pages from my life* vol. 1, p. 181

260 Meltzer, Charles Henry: *Musical America*. New York June 9th, 1907

261 'A new Russian Mephisto', *Musical America*. New York October 16th, 1906

262 'Chaliapin's method of singing', *Musical America*. New York November 6th, 1907

263 Krehbiel, Henry: *New York Tribune*, November 22nd, 1907

264 New York Public Library, Music Division, F. I. Chaliapin file

265 *Vogue*, New York May 23rd, 1907

266 *Musical America*, New York February 16th, 1907

267 New York Public Library, Music Division, F. I. Chaliapin file

268 See *Chronicle of life and career of F. I. Chaliapin*, p. 271

269 Chaliapin, F. I.: Letter to Gorky November 2nd (15th), 1907, New York, in *F. I. Chaliapin*, vol. 1, p. 238

270 *Vogue*, New York, May 23rd, 1907

271 New York Public Library, Music Division, F. I. Chaliapin file

272 Chaliapin, F. I.: Letter to Telyakovsky March 27th (April 9th), 1908. Archive V. A. Telyakovsky, State Central Theatre Museum named after A. A. Bakhrushin (Moscow). Archive 280, item 823, no. 227764. Quoted in *Chronicle of life and career of F. I. Chaliapin*, p. 280

273 By Fédor Chaliapin, as told to Sulamith-Ish-Kishor: 'America's future in the Arts'. *Musical America*, April 24th, 1929

274 Chaliapin, F. I.: *Pages from my life*, vol. 1, pp. 182–183

275 Ibidem, p. 183

276 'Pages from my life' – an autobiography by Feodor Ivanovich Chaliapin. New York 1927, p. 255

277 Van Vechten, Carl: *Interpreters and interpretations*. Alfred Knopf, New York 1917, p. 100

278 Quoted from the book by Robert Tuggle: *The golden age of opera*. Holt, Rinehart and Winston, New York 1984, p. 171

279 Gatti-Casazza, G.: *Memories of the opera*, p. 107

280 *Impresario*. A memoir by Sol Hurok. 'A comet named Feodor. First round to the critics'. Macdonald & Co. (Publishers) Ltd., London 1946, p. 27

281 *Musical Courier*, New York, January 22nd, 1908

282 *New York Tribune*, January 26th, 1908

283 W. J. Henderson: 'Devils, polite and rude'. New York *Sun*, November 24th, 1907

284 Van Vechten, Carl: *Interpreters and interpretations* pp. 99–100

285 'Opera at the Metropolitan'. *Musical Courier*, November 27th, 1907

286 'Brilliantly sung'. *Pilgrim*, New York, December 13th, 1907

287 Rawling, Sylvester: 'Chaliapin makes hit as Basilio'. *Evening World*, December 13th, 1907

288 Chaliapin, F. I.: *Pages from my life*, vol. 1, p. 184

289 Van Vechten, Carl: *Interpreters and interpretations*, p. 101

290 Ibidem

291 Ibidem

292 Ibidem, pp. 98–99

293 Chaliapin, F. I.: *Mask and Soul* p. 119

294 Fedor Ivanovich Chaliapin: Literary works, letters. I. Chaliapin: *Memories of my father*, Moscow 1957, vol. 1, p. 137

295 Kessel, K.: 'Le Sorcier'. *Gringoire*, Paris May 29th, 1929

296 See Calvocoressi, M.: *Modest Mussorgsky*, London 1946, p. 222–223

297 Chaliapin, F. I.: *Pages from my life*, p. 175

298 Ibidem

299 Benois, Alexander: *Memories of Diaghilev*. In collection *Sergei Diaghilev and Russian art*. Moscow 1982, vol. 2, p. 243

300 Fourque, J.: 'Boris Godunov'. *Le Gaulois*, Paris May 20th, 1908

301 Quoted from A. A. Gozenpud: *Boris Godunov by M.P. Mussorgsky in France 1876–1908*. Collection 'Perception of Russian Culture in the West'. Leningrad 1975, p. 244

302 Brioussel, R.: 'Boris Godunov'. *Le Figaro*, Paris May 20th, 1908

303 Benois, Alexander: *Memories of Diaghilev*, vol. 2, pp. 240–241

304 Makovsky, Sergei: *Portraits of contemporaries*, New York 1955, pp. 177–178

305 Letter to P. I. Postnikov, June 27th, 1908, Rio de Janeiro in *F. I. Chaliapin*, vol. 1, p. 424

306 Chaliapin, F. I.: *Pages from my life*, vol. 1, p. 185

307 Chaliapin, F. I.: Letter to V. A. Telyakovsky, August 12th, 1908. State Theatre Museum. A. A. Bakhrushin Archive 280, Folio 822, no. 227763. See also V. A. Telyakovsky: *Memoirs*, p. 389

308 Chaliapin, F. I.: *Pages from my life*, vol. 1, pp. 191, 193

309 *Pages from my life* – an autobiography by Feodor Ivanovich Chaliapin. New York 1927

310 Newmarch, Rosa: *The Russian Opera*. Herbert Jenkins Ltd., London 1914, pp. 387–388

311 Chaliapin, F. I.: *Pages from my life*, p. 146

312 An Englishman: 'The greatest actor of our time'. London July 25th, 1914. Archive Theatre Museum London
313 'The Art of Chaliapin: the secret of his appeal'. *The Times*, London June 6th, 1914
314 Capell, Richard: 'Chaliapin, the greatest opera actor'. *Daily Mail*, London July 2nd, 1914
315 McN: 'Chaliapin'. *The Musical Times*, May 1938, p. 381
316 Chaliapin, F. I.: *Pages from my life*, p. 191
317 Chaliapin, F. I.: Letter to Irina Chaliapina June 29th (July 12th), 1913, in *F. I. Chaliapin*, vol. 1, p. 481
318 Chaliapin, F. I.: *Pages from my life*, p. 209

Chapter IV

1 Chaliapin, F. I.: *Mask and Soul*. Paris 1932, p. 217
2 Ibidem, p. 220
3 *Pages from my life* – Autobiography by Feodor Ivanovich Chaliapin. Harper & Brothers. New York 1927, p. 300
4 Chaliapin, F. I.: *Mask and Soul*, p. 217
5 Ibidem, pp. 351–352
6 Ibidem, p. 154
7 Levik, S. Y.: *Memoirs of an opera singer*. Moscow 1962, p. 507
8 Chaliapin, F. I.: Letter to A. M. Gorky, Vichy July 18th, 1911 in *F. I. Chaliapin* vol. 1: Literary works, letters. Moscow 1976, p. 335
9 Capell, Richard: 'Chaliapin's many gifts'. *Daily Telegraph*, London April 13th, 1938
10 Korganov, V.: *Memories of Chaliapin*. In the collection 'From the history of Russo-Armenian musical links'. Memoirs, letters. (1827–1917). Yerevan 1971, p. 50
11 *Peterburgskaya gazeta*, October 28th, 1911. Quoted from *F. I. Chaliapin*, vol. 1, p. 649
12 Chaliapin, F. I.: *Pages from my life*, vol. 1, p. 179
13 Pokhitonov, D. I.: *From the past of Russian opera*, Leningrad 1941, p. 86
14 Ibidem
15 *F. I. Chaliapin*, vol. 1, p. 649
16 Chaliapin, F. I.: Interview with the Petersburg newspaper *Birzhevye vedomosti*, 1913. In the book by Gozenpud, A. A.: *Russian opera theatre between two revolutions*. Leningrad 1975, p. 331
17 Chaliapin, F. I.: *Mask and Soul*, p. 115
18 Ibidem, p. 117
19 Zbrueva, E. M.: '*Memoirs*' in *Musical heritage*. Moscow 1962, vol. 1, p. 403
20 Ibidem
21 Engel, Yuri: 'Mussorgsky's *Khovanshchina*'. *Russkie vedomosti*, Moscow December 14th, 1912
22 Sakhnovskii, Yuri: 'The first night of *Khovanshchina* at the Mariinsky Theatre'. *Russkoe slovo*, Petersburg November 9th, 1911
23 Belyaev, Yuri: *Novoe vremya*, Petersburg November 11th, 1911, in *F. I. Chaliapin*, vol. 1, p. 650
24 Newman, Ernest: 'Music of the Day'. *Glasgow Herald*, June 3rd, 1926
25 F. I. Chaliapin to A. M. Gorky, November 15th, 1911, in *F. I. Chaliapin*, vol. 1, p. 340

26 Quoted from Rudnitsky, K.: *Meyerhold*, Moscow 1981, pp. 139–140

27 *Politiken*: 'Chaliapin after the break: "It is not Gounod's *Faust* that is being performed at the Royal Theatre says Fedor Chaliapin" '. Copenhagen December 8th, 1935

28 Aftenavis, December 7th, 1935. *Socialdemokraten*, Børzen, Copenhagen December 8th and 9th, 1935

29 Newton, Ivor: *At the piano*. Hamish Hamilton, London 1966, p. 88

30 Chaliapin, F. I.: *Mask and Soul*, p. 145

31 B. P.: 'Chaliapin's greatness.' *The Referee*, May 30th, 1926

32 'Fedor Chaliapin guest singer at the National Theatre'. *Narodni listy*, Prague June 6th, 1934

33 By Fedor Chaliapin, as told to Sulamith Ish-Kishor: 'America's future in the arts'. *Musical America*, April 24th, 1929

34 Chaliapina, Irina: *Memories of my father*. In *Fedor Ivanovich Chaliapin*, vol. 2: Memories of Chaliapin, Moscow 1977, p. 42

35 Asafev, B. V.: *Chaliapin*, in *Fedor Ivanovich Chaliapin*, vol. 3: Articles and comments, Moscow 1979, p. 121

36 Quoted from the book by M. Yankovsky: *Chaliapin*, Leningrad 1972, p. 264

37 Siegfried (Edward Stark): 'Theatre and Music'. *Rossiya*, Petersburg August 22nd, 1901

38 Gorky, A. M.: From a letter to I. I. Brodsky, November 19th, 1911, Capri. In *F. I. Chaliapin*, vol. 1, p. 369

39 Chaliapin, F. I.: *Pages from my life*, vol. 1, p. 196

40 From a correspondent: 'Chaliapin on his art'. *Morning Post*, June 25th, 1923

41 Levik, S. Y.: *Memoirs of an opera singer*. Moscow 1962, p. 503

42 Chaliapin, F. I.: *Mask and Soul*, p. 347

43 Asafev, B. V.: *Chaliapin*, in *F. I. Chaliapin*, vol. 3, p. 117

44 Chaliapin, F. I.: *Mask and Soul*, p. 348

45 Kolomiitsov, V.: 'A. Ziloti's Concert'. *Molva*, St. Petersburg, December 7th, 1905

46 Van Vechten, Carl: 'The prodigious Russian'. *Boston Evening Transcript*, November 5th, 1921

47 Levik, S. Y.: *Memoirs of an opera singer*. Moscow 1962, p. 169

48 Enesco, Georges: *Memoirs*. Moscow 1966, pp. 131–132

49 'The Return of Chaliapin'. *Truth*, London June 2nd, 1926

50 Kahskin, N. D.: *Moskovskie vedomosti*, December 17th, 1902

51 Engel, Yuri: *Russkie vedomosti*, December 17th, 1902

52 Gorky, A. M.: Letter to K. P. Pyatnitsky, December 16th, 1902, in *F. I. Chaliapin*, vol. 1, p. 364

53 Vivien, L. S.: 'Chaliapin in *The Singers*'. *Teatr*, Moscow 1873, no. 3, p. 106

54 Yurev, Y. M.: *Memoirs*. Leningrad-Moscow 1963, vol. 2, pp. 280–281

55 Ibidem, pp. 283–284

56 'Roles by Fedor Chaliapin'. *The Ladies Home Journal*. New York May 1925, p. 31

57 Gladkov, Alexander: *Theatre*, memoirs and reflections. Moscow 1980, p. 317

58 'The Art of Chaliapin – Action and Song'. *The Times*, London June 6th, 1914

59 Pazovsky, A.: *Memoirs of a conductor*. Moscow 1966, p. 56

60 Levik, S. Y.: *Memoirs of an opera singer*, p. 476

61 Markov, P. A.: *Book of memories*. Moscow 1983, p. 335

62 Chaliapin, F. I.: 'Letter to the public'. Paris May 22nd, 1929. Archive EMI Hayes no. 94005

63 Levik, S. Y.: *Memoirs of an opera singer*, p. 481
64 G. B.: 'Chaliapin the Actor'. *Daily Express*, June 13th, 1929
65 A. K.: AYA: 'After the concert'. *Kharkovskii listok*, February 27th, 1903, no. 1005
66 Old Music lover: 'Chaliapin's concert'. *Kavkazskie mineral'nye vody*. Pyatigorsk, July 22nd, 1904
67 *Novoe obozrenie*, Tiflis, July 9th 1893. Quoted from *Annals of the Life and Career of F. I. Chaliapin*, vol. 1, compiled by Yu. Kotlyarov and V. Garmash. Leningrad 1984, p. 69
68 Korganov, V. D.: *Articles. Memoirs*. Yerevan 1968, p. 191
69 'With Battistini', *Odeskii listok*, February 27th, 1903, no. 54, p. 3
70 Prince Igor. Mamontov's opera. *Moskovskie vedomosti*, November 4th, 1897
71 Levik, S. Y.: *Memoirs of an opera singer*, p. 478
72 Klein, Herman: 'The Art of Chaliapin', *The Musical Times*, London November 1st, 1921, p. 786
73 *The Listener*, London April 20th, 1938
74 Levik, S. Y.: *Memoirs of an opera singer*, p. 479
75 Capell, Richard: 'Chaliapin's many gifts'. *Daily Telegraph*, April 13th, 1938
76 Quoted from Hurok, Sol: Press releases. New York Public Library, Music Division
77 Gigli, Beniamino: *Memoirs*. Cassell & Co. Ltd. London 1957, p. 112
78 Rubinstein, Arthur: *My young years*. Alfred A. Knopf Inc., New York 1973, p. 153
79 St. John, Christopher: 'Boito and Verdi at Covent Garden'. *Time and Tide*, June 11th, 1926, p. 526
80 Levik, S. Y.: *Memoirs of an opera singer*, pp. 479–480
81 Klein, Herman: 'The Art of Chaliapin'. *The Musical Times*, London November 1st, 1921, p. 786
82 Capell, Richard: 'Chaliapin the greatest opera actor.' *Daily Mail*, London July 2nd, 1914
83 'Chaliapin in Prague', *Narodni listy*, October 11th, 1925
84 Pitts, Sanborn: 'Boris Godunov'. *Globe*, New York January 13th, 1922
85 Newmarch, Rosa: *The Russian Opera*, Herbert Jenkins Ltd., London 1914, pp. 391–393
86 Newman, Ernest: 'Music of the Day'. *Glasgow Herald*, June 3rd, 1926
87 Article by Ernest Newman in the *Manchester Guardian* of 1921. Quoted from Hurok, Sol: Press Releases. New York Public Library, Music Division.
88 C. B.: 'Chaliapin – Magician: haunting sounds'. *Daily Express*, November 28th, 1929
89 de Paulowski, G.: *Journal*, Paris June 5th, 1932
90 Levik, S. Y.: *Memoirs of an opera singer*, pp. 482, 483, 489
91 Makovsky, Sergei: *Portraits of contemporaries*. Chekhov Press, New York 1955, pp. 179–180
92 Kaplan, E. M.: *Life in the music theatre*, Leningrad 1969, p. 39
93 Ibidem, pp. 168–169
94 Wollstein, R. H.: 'The singer's art'. *Etude Music Magazine*, New York January 1936, p. 8
95 Capell, Richard: 'Chaliapin's many gifts'. *Daily Telegraph*, April 13th, 1938
96 Interview with *Etude Music Magazine*, p. 7
97 Ibidem
98 Page, Philip: 'The Daddy of the Lot', *Evening Standard*, London June 26th, 1928

99 Evans, Edwin: 'Opera and Chaliapin'. *Time and Tide*, London April 30th, 1938, p. 608

100 Gunst, Evgenii: 'Chaliapin's stage creations' in *Fedor Ivanovich Chaliapin (biography and stage creations)*. Rampa i zhizn', Moscow 1915, p. 55

101 E. B.: 'Chaliapin's Great Part'. *The Manchester Guardian*, June 30th, 1928

102 Deems Taylor: 'Chaliapin as Boris'. *New York World*, December 10th, 1921

103 'Death of Chaliapin'. New York Public Library, Press Cuttings, Music Division

104 De Curzon, Henri: Obituary. *Débats*. Paris April 13th, 1938

105 'Greatest Operatic Artist'. Obituary, *The Times*, April 13th, 1938

106 Maurice Leonard: *Slobodskaya*. Gollancz, London 1979, p. 57

107 Levik, S. Y.: *Memoirs of an opera singer*, p. 494

108 Sobinov, L. V.: Letters. Moscow 1970, vol. 1, p. 64

109 Ossovsky, A. V.: *Articles of music criticism*. Leningrad 1971, p. 124

110 Moore, Gerald: *Am I too loud? – the memoirs of a piano accompanist*. Hamish Hamilton, London 1962, p. 70

111 Chaliapin, F. I.: *Pages from my life* in *F. I. Chaliapin*, vol. 1, p. 141

112 Haughton, John Alan: 'Let not tradition become paramount'. *Musical America* January 2nd, 1926, p. 24

113 Kruglikov, Semyon: 'Boris Godunov at the Bolshoi Theatre'. *Novosti dnya*, April 15th, 1901

114 Stanislavsky, K. S.: Collected works in 8 volumes. Moscow 1960, vol. 2, p. 29

115 Chaliapin, F. I.: *Mask and Soul*, pp. 97–98

116 Ibidem, p. 119

117 Ibidem

118 Chaliapina, Irina: *Memories of my father*, in *F. I. Chaliapin*, vol. 2, p. 68

119 Toporkov, V.: *K. S. Stanislavsky in rehearsal*. Moscow 1949, p. 149

120 Stanislavsky, K. S.: Complete works in 8 volumes, vol. 5, p. 530

121 Chaliapin, F. I.: *Mask and Soul*, p. 114

122 *Musical America*, December 10th, 1914

123 Chaliapin, F. I.: *Mask and Soul*, pp. 120–121

124 Haughton, John Alan: "Let not tradition become paramount'. *Musical America*, January 2nd, 1926, p. 24

125 Chaliapin, F. I.: *Mask and Soul*, p. 121

126 *F. I. Chaliapin*, vol. 2, p. 68

127 Chaliapin, F. I.: *Mask and Soul*, pp. 122, 123

128 Orlovskaya, A.: 'Chaliapin and young singers'. In the collection Fedor Ivanovich Chaliapin. Articles, comments, recollections about F. I. Chaliapin. Moscow 1958, vol. 2, p. 521

129 Thompson, Oscar: 'Feodor Chaliapin'. Obituary, *Sun*, New York April 16th, 1938

130 'I on Me' by Chaliapin. London June 29th, 1923. Press cuttings, Theatre Museum London

131 Chaliapina, Irina: *Memories of my father* in *F. I. Chaliapin*, vol. 2, p. 42

132 Plotnikov, B. E.: 'Chaliapin in America' in *F. I. Chaliapin*, vol. 2, pp. 505–506

133 Pokhitonov, D. I.: *From the past of Russian opera*. Quoted in *F. I. Chaliapin*, vol. 2, p. 237

134 Makovsky, Sergei: *Portraits of contemporaries*. New York 1955, pp. 182, 183, 184

135 Golovanov, N. S.: 'F. I. Chaliapin'. In the collection literary heritage, correspondence, contemporary memoirs. Moscow 1982, pp. 42–3

136 Chaliapin, Feodor: Newspaper cuttings. Music Research File, New York Public Library, Music Division

137 Goury, Jean: 'Fédor Chaliapin'. Paris, Société de Diffusion d'Art Lyrique 1969 (Monstres Sacrés), p. 48

138 Fokine, M.: *Against the stream – memories of a choreographer*. Leningrad 1981, pp. 126, 127

139 Aldrich, Richard: 'Don Carlos at the Metropolitan'. *The Times*, December 3rd, 1922

140 Chaliapin, F. I.: *Mask and Soul*, p. 103

141 Ibidem

142 Ibidem, p. 100

143 Zon, B. V.: 'Encounters with Stanislavsky'. 'Theatrical heritage'. Moscow 1955, vol. 1, p. 474

144 Chaliapin, F. I.: *Mask and Soul*, p. 108

145 Ibidem, p. 108

146 Ibidem, p. 110

147 Stanislavsky, K. S.: Complete works, vol. 2, p. 53

148 Quoted from Drankov, V. L.: *The nature of Chaliapin's talent*. Leningrad 1973, p. 156

149 Chaliapin, F. I.: *Mask and Soul*, p. 107

150 Skitalets, S.: *Tales and stories*. Moscow 1960, p. 486

151 Chaliapin, F. I.: *Mask and Soul*, p. 111

152 Rozhdestvensky, V.: 'Chaliapin at Gorky's'. Leningrad *Neva* 1956, no. 8, p. 161

153 St. John, Christopher: 'Boito and Verdi at Covent Garden'. *Time and Tide*, London June 11th, 1926, p. 526

154 'The Art of Chaliapin: the secret of his appeal'. *The Times*, London June 6th, 1914

155 Chaliapin, F. I.: *Mask and Soul*, p. 107

156 'The week's music', *Jewish Guardian*, London June 4th, 1926

157 Quoted from the article by Andronnikov, Irakil: 'Chaliapin's talent'. *Teatr*, Moscow March 1973, p. 94

158 Stanislavsky, K. S.: Complete works, vol. 7, p. 148

159 Pazovsky, A. M.: *Memoirs of a conductor*. Moscow 1966, pp. 57–58

160 Stanislavsky, K. S.: Complete works, vol. 3, p. 85

161 'Chaliapin in comic vein: droll and sinister'. *Evening News*, London May 29th, 1926

162 Capell, Richard: 'Chaliapin as music master'. *Daily Mail*, London May 29th, 1926

163 Page, Philip: 'Chaliapin's comic genius in *Barber of Seville*'. *Evening Standard*, London May 29th, 1926

164 dal Monte, Toti: *Grande Barbiere* in *F. I. Chaliapin*, vol. 2, p. 493

165 Stark, Edward: *Chaliapin*. Petrograd 1915, p. 160

166 dal Monte, Toti: *Grande Barbiere* in *F. I. Chaliapin*, vol. 2, p. 494

167 Capell, Richard: 'Chaliapin as Music Master'. *Daily Mail*, London May 29th, 1926

168 Feschotte, Jacques: *Ce géant: Féodor Chaliapine*. La Table Ronde, Paris, 1968, pp. 104–106

169 Chaliapin, F. I.: *Mask and Soul*, p. 105

170 Chaliapina, Irina: *Memories of my father*, vol. 2, p. 76

171 Stark, Edward: *Chaliapin*, pp. 164–165

172 Newman, Ernest: 'Music of the day'. *Glasgow Herald*, June 3rd, 1926

173 N. A. S.: 'New triumph in *Il Barbiere* – mournful part made jovial'. *Westminster Gazette*, London May 29th, 1926

174 'Il Barbiere di Siviglia'. *Corriere della Sera*, April 22nd, 1933
175 Finck, Henry T.: 'Chaliapin the Russian Mephistopheles'. *The Century Magazine*, New York December 1910, pp. 232–233
176 Bernstein, Hillel: 'The white hope of 102nd street'. *The New Yorker*, October 14th, 1950, p. 61
177 'Grand Opera Grock', *Evening Standard*, May 26th, 1926
178 Newman, Ernest: 'Music of the day'. *Glasgow Herald*, June 3rd, 1926
179 Toye, Francis: 'Chaliapin out of place as Don Basilio'. *Morning Post*, May 26th, 1926
180 Toye, Francis: 'Star gazing'. *Morning Post*, London June 2nd, 1926
181 Sakhnovsky, Yu.: 'The Barber of Seville at the Bolshoi Theatre'. Moscow, November 16th, 1913
182 Daniels, Robin: *Conversations with Cardus*. Gollancz, London 1976, p. 104
183 Evans, Edwin: 'Opera and Chaliapin'. *Time and Tide*, April 30th, 1938, p. 608
184 Chaliapin, F. I.: *Mask and Soul*, p. 106
185 Sakhnovsky, Yu: 'Don Carlos'. *Russkoe slovo*, Moscow, February 11th, 1917
186 Quoted from Kotlyarov, Yu. and Garmash, V.: *Chronicle of the life and career of F. I. Chaliapin*. Leningrad 1985, vol. 1, p. 118
187 Quoted from Tuggle, Robert: *The Golden Age of Opera*. Holt, Rinehart and Winston, New York 1983, pp. 184–185.
188 Chaliapina, Irina: *Memories of my father* in *F. I. Chaliapin*, vol. 2, p. 36
189 Levik, S. Y.: *Memoirs of an opera singer*, p. 506
190 Levik, S. Y.: *A quarter of a century in opera*. Moscow 1970, p. 405
191 Chaliapina, Irina: *Memories of my father*, p. 36
192 Vinogradov-Mamont, N.: 'Don Carlos'. *Moskovskie vedomosti*, February 11th, 1917
193 Levik, S. Y.: *A quarter of a century in opera*. Moscow 1970, p. 401
194 Pazovsky, A. I.: *Memoirs of a conductor*, pp. 522–523
195 Quoted from Tuggle, Robert: *The Golden Age of Opera*, p. 185
196 Gilman, Lawrence: 'Don Quichotte'. *New York Herald Tribune*, April 5th, 1926
197 *Pages from my life*, an autobiography by Feodor Ivanovich Chaliapin (authorised translation by H. M. Buck). Harper and Brothers, New York and London 1927, pp. 286–287
198 Chaliapin, F. I.: Letter to Gorky, Paris June 22nd, 1909, *F. I. Chaliapin*, vol. 1, p. 331
199 Makovsky, Sergei: *Portraits of contemporaries*, pp. 181–182
200 Karatygin, V. T.: Selected articles. Leningrad 1965, pp. 294–295
201 Chaliapin, F. I.: *Mask and Soul*, p. 105
202 Quoted from *The Century Magazine*, 'Chaliapin, F. I., the Russian Mephistopheles', by Henry T. Finck, New York, December 1910
203 Gorky, A. M.: Preface to Romain Rolland's novel *Jean Christophe*. Leningrad 1933, p. 5
204 Turgenev, I. S.: *Hamlet and Don Quixote*, Complete works in 12 volumes. Moscow 1956, vol. 11, pp. 170–171
205 Feodor Chaliapin. 'Guest singer at the National Theatre'. *Narodny listy*, Prague June 6th, 1934
206 Feschotte, J.: *Ce Géant Féodor Chaliapine*, p. 142
207 Markov, P. A.: *Book of memories*. Moscow 1983, p. 332
208 Newton, Ivor: *At the Piano*. Hamish Hamilton, London 1966, p. 90
209 Levik, S.: *Memoirs of an opera singer*, p. 505

210 Slobodskaya, Olga: *Memoirs*. Gollancz, London 1979, p. 135
211 'With . . . Virginia Boren at the famed basso's concert', *Seattle Times*, April 9th, 1935
212 Newton, Ivor: *At the Piano*, p. 92
213 Lemeshev, S.: *The Road to Art*. Moscow 1968, p. 46
214 A. G.: 'Un grande artista: "Scialiapin"'. *La Tribuna*, Rome, March 29th, 1933
215 W. F.: 'He delights the Albert Hall audience – and himself'. Royal Opera House Covent Garden archive, Chaliapin cuttings.
216 'Vocal spells at the Albert Hall.' *The Times*, London November 4th, 1925
217 Moore, Gerald: *Am I too loud?*, pp. 69–70
218 *The diaries of Sofia Tolstoya*, eds. D. A. Golinenko, S. A. Rozanova, etc.; translated by Cathy Porter. Jonathan Cape, London 1985. Entry dated January 18th, 1904, p. 475
219 Gorky, A. M.: Letter to V. A. Posse, October 14th, 1901, in *F. I. Chaliapin*, vol. 1, p. 363
220 Frankenstein, Alfred: 'Chaliapin Great in Song Recital'. *San Francisco Chronicle*, April 2nd, 1935
221 'Chaliapin at Queen's Hall'. *The Times*, London June 29th, 1924
222 Lemeshev, S. *The Road to Art*, p. 46.
223 Ibidem, pp. 47–48
224. McN.: 'Chaliapin', *The Musical Times*, London May 1938, p. 381
225 'Chaliapin birthday recital'. *New York Evening Post*, February 16th, 1928
226 'Chaliapin', *Daily Telegraph*, London October 18th, 1922
227 'The escape from the Red Terror' by Feodor Ivanovich Chaliapin. *The Evening News*, London October 15th, 1931
228 'Chaliapin as I knew him'. Typescript, archive of the Gaisberg Family
229 Gaisberg, F. W.: *Music on Record*. Robert Hale Ltd., London 1943, pp. 220–221
230 Klein, Herman: 'The Art of Chaliapin'. *The Musical Times*, London November 1st, 1921
231 'The Escape from the Red Terror' by Feodor Ivanovich Chaliapin, *The Evening News*, October 15th, 1931

Epilogue

1 Page, Philip: 'Chaliapin, the man of paradox'. *Sunday Express*, London May 30th, 1926
2 *Pages from my life* – an autobiography by Fedor Ivanovich Chaliapin (authorised translation by H. M. Buck). Harper and Brothers, New York and London, 1927, p. 312
3 'The Volga boatmen is not a song, but a confession', by Fedor Chaliapin (in an interview). *The Refereee*, London June 17th, 1928
4 Sedykh, Andrei: 'Far, near.' *Novoe russkoe slovo*, New York 1979, p. 130
5 'Ein Gespraech mit Schalyapin', *Wiener Zeitung*, October 26th, 1927
6 Chaliapin, F. I.: *Mask and Soul*, Sovremyennye Zapiski. Paris 1932, p. 329
7 Ibidem, p. 334
8 Freddi-Chaliapina, Marina: 'Nel mio salotto è passata la storia'. *Europeo*, Rome March 1986, p. 109
9 Quoted from *Chronicle of Life and Career of F. I. Chaliapin* compiled by Yu. Kotlyarov and V. Garmash. Leningrad 1985, vol. 2, p. 211
10 Chaliapin, F. I.: *Mask and Soul*, pp. 332–333

11 Reizen, Mark: 'Chaliapin's death'. *Izvestia*, Moscow April 14th, 1938
12 Sedykh, Andrei: 'Far, near', p. 131
13 Yankovsky, I.: *Chaliapin*, Leningrad 1972, p. 346
14 Kozlovsky, I.: 'Love and suffering'. *Ogonyok*, Moscow February 1973, p. 19
15 Chaliapina-Shuvalova, Dasya: 'My father, Chaliapin', *Strelets*. Paris September 1984, no. 9, p. 37
16 Freddi-Chaliapina, Marina: 'Nel mio salotto è passata la storia', *Europeo*. Rome March 1986, p. 109
17 Paklin, I.: 'Bequeathed by the great singer'. *Izvestia*, Moscow October 30th 1984
18 Chertok, Shimon: 'Encounter with Chaliapin's son'. *Novoe russkoe slovo*, New York June 23rd, 1985
19 Chaliapin, F. I.: *Mask and Soul*, p. 247
20 Ibidem, p. 181
21 Ibidem, p. 20
22 Ibidem, p. 222
23 Ibidem, p. 224
24 Ibidem, p. 224
25 Gul', Roman: *I took Russia away with me.* Vol. 1, *Russia in Germany*. Most, New York 1984, p. 23
26 Bunin, I. A.: *The accursed days.* Zarya, London–Canada 1973, p. 203
27 Chaliapin, F. I.: *Mask and Soul*, p. 225
28 *From Bunin's lips*, diaries of Ivan Alexeevich and Vera Nikolaevna, and other archives. Edited by Militsa Green, in 3 volumes. Vol. II. Posev. Frankfurt am Main 1981, p. 296
29 Chaliapin, F. I.: *Mask and Soul*, pp. 185–187
30 *From Bunin's lips*, vol. 2, p. 319
31 Chaliapin, F. I.: *Mask and Soul*, p. 284
32 Ibidem, p. 283, 266
33 Ibidem, p. 257
34 Ibidem, p. 240
35 Ibidem, p. 341
36 Chaliapina-Shuvalova, Dasya: 'My father, Chaliapin'. *Strelets*, September, no. 9, p. 37
37 Chaliapin, F. I.: *Mask and Soul*, p. 335
38 *Fedor Ivanovich Chaliapin*, vol. 1: Literary works, letters. Moscow 1976, p. 550
39 Hurok, Sol: *Impresario*. Macdonald & Co. Ltd., London, p. 56
40 Gaisberg, F. W.: Handwritten note. Family archive.
41 Gaisberg, F. W.: *Music on Record*. Robert Hale, London 1943, p. 230
42 Hurok, Sol: *Impresario*, pp. 56–57
43 Leonidov, L. D.: *Memories and encounters.* Rampa i zhizn', Paris 1955, p. 296
44 Gaisberg, F. W.: *Music on Record*, p. 230
45 Sedykh, Andrei: 'Far, near', p. 131
46 'Reminiscences of Chaliapin by his daughter Marfa Gardner'. Transmission: Saturday March 4th, 1950. Script BBC Archive, Caversham, Reading, pp. 2, 7
47 Hudson-Davies, Marfa: Programme for Radio 4, written and compiled by Peggy Brandford, produced by Alan Haydock. Script BBC Archive, Caversham, Reading, p. 3. Transmission February 11th, 1973
48 EMI Archive F. I. Chaliapin. Hayes, London, no. 76880
49 *F. I. Chaliapin*, vol. 1, p. 553–554
50 Chaliapin, F. I.: *Memories of my father*, vol. 2, p. 81

51 Rachmaninov, S.: Literary heritage in 3 volumes. Letters. Moscow 1980, vol. 3, p. 125

52 Lifar, Serge: *Le Figaro*. Paris April 13th 1938

53 Obituary, 'Greatest Operatic Artist'. *The Times*, London April 13th, 1938

54 Newton, Ivor: 'At the Piano'. Hamish Hamilton. London 1966, p. 98

55 Chaliapin, F. I.: *Mask and Soul*, p. 356

INDEX

Numerals in *italics* refer to captions and illustrations, and Fedor Ivanovich Chaliapin is generally abbreviated to C.